*The Romantic Foundations of*
*the American Renaissance*

# The Romantic Foundations of
# the American Renaissance

## LEON CHAI

## CORNELL UNIVERSITY PRESS

### ITHACA AND LONDON

Cornell University Press gratefully acknowledges
a grant from the Andrew W. Mellon Foundation
that aided in bringing this book to publication.

First published 1987 by Cornell University Press.
First published, Cornell Paperbacks, 1990.

International Standard Book Number 0-8014-1929-8 (cloth)
International Standard Book Number 0-8014-9715-9 (paper)
Library of Congress Catalog Card Number 87-5428
Printed in the United States of America
*Librarians: Library of Congress cataloging information
appears on the last page of the book.*

♾ The paper used in the text of this publication meets the minimum
requirements of American National Standard for Information Sciences—
Permanence of Paper for Printed Library Materials, ANSI Z39.48-1984.

In memoriam
Samuel Geremia
1953–1971
*Vir nobilis*

# Contents

# Preface

My subject is a history of the assimilation and transformation of the
cultural legacy of European Romanticism from roughly 1780 to 1830 by
a group of great American authors of the mid-nineteenth century—
above all, Poe, Emerson, Hawthorne, and Melville. I explore this process
by tracing the development of certain governing concepts or tendencies
from their rise in the Romantic period itself to their subsequent appropriation by the American Renaissance authors. Among such concepts
and tendencies I include the shift from allegory to symbolism, that is,
from a mode of writing based upon a theory of correspondences between fictional signs and their objects to one that attempts to reveal
through Nature an immanent divine presence; forms of science in the
Romantic Age, including biological classification, vitalism, and the theory of probability; the secularization of religion; the gradual emergence
of a historical consciousness and a philosophy of history; pantheism; the
theory of subjectivity and objectivity in Romantic philosophy, that is, the
relation between mind or self and external Nature; and, finally, Romantic poetics or theory of literature, with its emphasis upon the role of the
creative and perceiving consciousness.

My book explores material from a variety of nineteenth-century fields
or disciplines: literature of course primarily, but also philosophy, theology, the natural sciences, and to a lesser extent historiography and the
visual arts. Of course I do not pretend to assume that the material
amassed from these various sources is fundamentally the same: the form
in which thought is expressed necessarily affects, to some extent, the
nature of that thought itself. What I have sought to establish, however,
are not simply the intellectual affinities between, for example, Emerson
and Schleiermacher, or Poe and Laplace, but rather the tendencies or
forces that manifest themselves in the development of such thought and
its expression. Such tendencies I do not see as rational in themselves:

hence this history is not a teleology or a form of *Geistesgeschichte*. Instead, I conceive of them as purely formative: such tendencies conduce to the formation of thought and achieve consciousness in expression. My concern is with the different forms Romantic thought assumes in the course of its development, the nature and process of its transmission, the alterations it experiences—in short, the whole course of its growth and transformation.

In some respects, the relation between literary criticism and literary history in this work is a special one; hence a few remarks concerning it will perhaps seem appropriate. It would have been possible to survey the material treated here from a different perspective, by allowing the form of a comparison between two authors, or, on a broader scale, between European Romanticism and the American Renaissance, to dictate both form and content of my presentation. The result might then have been the exhibition of more affinities, both formal and thematic, between authors or movements. What would have been lost is some deeper sense of historical development, of the rise and transmission of different forms of thought and of the tendencies that underlie and produce these forms. By focusing upon concepts rather than authors, I hope to make possible the tracing of this development. Insofar as the interpretations proposed proceed from the elucidation of particular Romantic concepts, they both presuppose and form a part of that literary history which consists of the expression of such concepts. Conversely, that literary history is itself inseparable from the interpretations upon which it is based.

At various points, I speculate about the nature of specific aspects of American and European Romanticism, as well as about their relation to each other. Here I venture some more general remarks about these movements as a whole. Despite obvious discontinuities, it seems possible in at least some respects to regard the American Renaissance as the final phase of a movement that begins with European Romanticism. This would mean placing it in a relation to European Romanticism comparable to that, say, of the High Renaissance to the Quattrocento, or of Mannerism to the High Renaissance. All the strains and tensions incident to the late phase of a great historical and creative epoch might then become discernible in the complex and problematic relationship between Romanticism and the American Renaissance. After certain aesthetic or conceptual norms attain the level of conscious expression, as with the High Renaissance or neoclassicism, they become fraught with extraordinary tensions that prevent the possibility of their perpetuation. What so often results might be described as a subjectivization of those norms, that is, their externalization into the medium of expression itself, and a simultaneous inner transformation of their content and significance. Mannerist distortion of forms is one example of such a phenomenon; the rise of formal self-consciousness in the novel or the emergence of increasingly subjective concerns in later eighteenth-century literature might be another. In short, if we pursue the American Renaissance itself to its culmination, what we find is (in such works as *Billy Budd*, Hawthorne's late romances, and Emerson's later essays) no longer a literature of prophecy and promise, but one filled with its own sense of an imminent ending. From this perspective, there is both finality and originality in the developments imparted by the American Renaissance to the formation of Romanticism.

In writing this book, I have received assistance from various sources. I would like, first of all, to thank Jonathan Arac, whose constant help and kindnesses over the years and whose unwavering faith in this work have done so much to make it possible. I also take this opportunity to thank Sacvan Bercovitch for his friendly help and encouragement. My sister, Jean, performed an indispensable service by procuring for me many of the sources on which this study is based. I am also happy to record the similar aid I have received from Ceil Friedman. In both form and substance, some parts of this work in its earlier stages have benefited from the comments and suggestions of David Levin and Raymond Nelson.

For help with the French translations in the text, I am grateful to Jacqueline Gallard.

Some of the material on Melville and Shelley appeared in *ESQ* (1st Quarter, 1983). I wish to thank Walker Cowen for permission to use material from his dissertation, "Melville's Marginalia" (Harvard, 1965). Quotations from Shelley are reprinted, where applicable, from *Shelley's Poetry and Prose*, selected and edited by Donald H. Reiman and Sharon B. Powers, A Norton Critical Edition, by permission of W. W. Norton & Company, Inc., copyright © 1977 by Donald H. Reiman and Sharon B. Powers. I wish to acknowledge the University of Illinois Research Board for its support, as well as the various libraries from which I have received assistance: the University of Maine at Orono, the Jesup Library in Bar Harbor, the College of the Atlantic, Harvard University, and the University of Illinois.

Finally, I wish to thank Cary Nelson, who in innumerable ways has helped to bring this work to its final realization.

LEON CHAI

*Bar Harbor, Maine*

# A Note on the Sources

Primary sources, listed in full at the back of the book, are cited in the text and notes in abbreviated forms. I use the following general abbreviations to cite editions by various authors:

| | |
|---|---|
| *Coll. W.* | *Collected Works* |
| *C.W.* | *Complete Works* |
| *G.W.* | *Gesammelte Werke* |
| *O.C.* | *Oeuvres complètes* |
| *P.W.* | *Poetical Works* |
| *S.W.* | *Sämtliche Werke* (or *Sämmtliche Werke*) |

In addition, I use these specific abbreviations:

| | |
|---|---|
| Centenary | *The Centenary Edition of the Works of Nathaniel Hawthorne* |
| *EL* | *The Early Lectures of Ralph Waldo Emerson* |
| *JMN* | *The Journals and Miscellaneous Notebooks of Ralph Waldo Emerson* |
| Myerson | Margaret Fuller, *Essays on American Life and Letters,* ed. Joel Myerson |
| Reiman and Powers | *Shelley's Poetry and Prose,* ed. Donald H. Reiman and Sharon B. Powers |

Other primary sources are cited by short titles.

Secondary sources, which are not listed in a separate bibliography, are cited in full at the first reference in each chapter and by short titles thereafter.

All translations in both text and notes are my own, unless otherwise acknowledged. Regrettably, it has not proved possible to print the foreign-language originals, but the list of primary sources should enable interested readers to consult these for themselves.

*The Romantic Foundations of*
*the American Renaissance*

# Introduction

For the form of his great work *The Civilization of the Renaissance in Italy,* Jacob Burckhardt adopted a scheme often characterized as "spatial," to the extent that it does not treat the Renaissance from a chronological perspective but instead surveys each of its aspects from a nondevelopmental point of view. As a result, Burckhardt's work has been faulted for its lack of attention to development and change. These charges, it seems to me, rest upon a fundamental misapprehension of its purposes. To appreciate the rationale behind his presentation, we must, I believe, consider not only the content of the period he treats, but also its relation to the nature of historical representation itself. What Burckhardt sought, in the spatial arrangement of his oeuvre, was to express above all the sense of pictorial composition which he felt to constitute the ordering principle of the Italian Renaissance. To express that principle, however, it had been necessary for him to incorporate it into the very form of his work: such are the requisite claims of relation between a period and its representation.

I have felt the force of a similar principle, but one that has taken, for the different nature of the period I discuss, a different form. Instead of striving for the spatial effect of composition, I have sought to represent the process of a development that would correspond in some sense to what I perceive as the fundamental formative principle of Romanticism itself. For this reason I begin with the shift from allegory to symbolism, both in European Romanticism and its later American phase. With this shift it becomes possible to express the transition from Classicism to Romanticism, a transition that is not, by the way, fully or unambiguously resolved within the Romantic period. One might even go so far as to say that Romanticism encompasses the transition within itself, a fact particularly evident in the case of Poe, which is why it is so important to begin with Poe and end with Melville. With Poe, on account of his simul-

taneous neoclassical and Romantic preoccupations, allegory is both preserved and transformed. For Melville, on the other hand, the return to
allegory in *The Confidence-Man* possesses a crucial significance only because he begins with Romantic symbolism.

Allegory is formal, as is the concept of the foundations of a particular
discipline. This concept, and the sense of its significance, may be traced
back to Kant and the later eighteenth century. Hence it is no accident
that the two American authors possessing the deepest affinities with
neoclassicism, Poe and Emerson, should also be those most explicitly
concerned with the dream of a universal science based upon general
theoretical principles. But the desire for universal science assumes for
Romanticism a very different form from that which it displays in the
eighteenth century. As a result of the Romantic expansion of self-consciousness, such a desire now becomes a concern with the very nature of
theory itself.

If there is a single theme common to the four chapters on secularization of religion, the historical consciousness, pantheism, and subjectivity
and objectivity, it must be that of consciousness. Pre-Romantic sensibility
had explored the nature of consciousness and experience (for example,
Rousseau's *Reveries du promeneur solitaire*), but it was left to Romanticism
proper to establish the significance of consciousness for the content,
as well as the form, of thought. With Romanticism, consciousness or
the apprehension of the object (whether the I or the external world)
becomes itself the content of thought. Nowhere is this more apparent
than in Schleiermacher, from the early exhortations of *Über die Religion*
and the *Monologen* to the mature speculations of *Der christliche Glaube*.
The importance of the identification of subjective and objective in post-
Kantian transcendental idealism is not properly appreciated if one fails
to recognize its effect in redefining the nature of thought. Even for
Rousseau, consciousness is in many respects merely the antithesis of rationalism. For Romanticism, on the other hand, the identification of
subjective and objective signifies the possibility not only of apprehension, the connection or relation of things, but of creation, the formation
of the external world through the formation of thought and consciousness. Here, thought does not simply create the external world within
itself. Instead, the process of the formation of thought is also that of the
world, and there is no realm of thought separate from that of the simultaneous formation of both. This redefinition of the nature of thought
makes possible the relation of Romanticism to itself. Such self-relation,
which had not been possible to earlier periods as part of their proper
thought content, is now brought to objective form in Hegel's doctrine of
Essence as the self-reflection of Being. This self-relation of Romanticism
is more, however, than simply a consequence of the emphasis on consciousness. It also makes possible a new approach to the whole question

of form and content. The dissolution of form *in* content, the assertion of the immanent form of content itself—these phenomena we witness both in Hegel's reflections on philosophical systems and in Friedrich Schlegel's announcement of a new poetics, that of the "essentially modern" (*wesentlich-Moderne*).

For Romanticism, significantly, poetics constitutes the fruit of prior reflection in other disciplines: aesthetics, of course, but also the new psychology of consciousness and the self, the formulations of Schiller's "Über naive und sentimentalische Dichtung" (On Naive and Sentimental Poetry). Poetics can also comprise reflection on the nature of the Romantic and its opposition to the Classic, as in Goethe and Emerson, an opposition that is itself part of Romanticism. That same opposition, however, can also redefine itself in other terms, as in the relation between the individual author or poet and tradition. This relation, with Keats, for example, becomes part of the content of consciousness, and that same consciousness can also impart a form to the romance.

Finally, I close with what I would like to think of as a coda: the different transformations of an image, that of Beatrice Cenci, in successive Romantic writers, which offers a glimpse of the progressive development of Romanticism itself in a more traditional historical sense. It seems especially appropriate that we should receive this glimpse through the representations of a visual image: unlike a narrative, which exhibits internal as well as external change, the image presents external change only—that of the viewers who observe and reproduce it. Hence the change is one proper to the movement of Romanticism itself, as captured by its relation to the stasis of a visual work of art.

The Romantic or nineteenth-century concept of tradition, as well as the controversy over Classicism versus Romanticism, constitutes aspects of the process of Romantic canon formation. Keats's evocation of his illustrious poetic predecessors and Goethe's encomiums to the "noble spiritual company" can in turn raise the question whether the present work should also concern itself with the problem of a canon in the American Renaissance. Before resolving such an issue, we must consider the concept of the canon itself from a historical perspective. As the researches of Ernst Robert Curtius in *European Literature and the Latin Middle Ages* make clear, the notion of a canon in literature implies some form of Classicism. This need not be as narrowly restrictive as, say, that of Augustan England or French neoclassicism (Boileau), but it does embody the aspiration toward an aesthetic ideal which is expressed in, yet transcends, the authors whose works compose the canon. The nineteenth century, it seems to me, beginning with the Romantic period, pushes the concept of a canon to an extreme that verges upon self-contradiction and hence meaninglessness. By emphasizing authors rather than their works (one has only to think of Keats's or Wordsworth's relation to Milton), such a canon loses sight of form, which, after all, had been the governing aesthetic principle or ideal. In so doing, however, it also sacrifices the canon's essential purpose, since, if there is nothing transcending the authors (that is to say, an aesthetic ideal), neither can there be any principle of selection or exclusion to express the idea behind the canon—exemplariness.

From various indications we may surmise that the Romantic canon emerges as a result of the primacy accorded to consciousness. The increasing significance of mind or self dictates a new relation to the literature of the past, one defined not so much by norms embodied in the works as by authorial relation to the mind or spirit expressed in them. In addition, with the Romantic rejection of the distinction between form and content, the notion of a formal ideal disappears. What Romanticism had sought to achieve with its radical transformation of the traditional concept of the canon was, in effect, a means of representing its relation to the literature of the past which could be contained within the work itself: Keats's struggle to supersede his predecessors, which becomes the subject of the two *Hyperion*s, or Goethe's representation of the conflict between Romantic excess and Classical restraint in *Torquato Tasso*. Because of the primacy of consciousness, the relation of Romanticism to the past can no longer consist simply of pursuit of a formal ideal. Instead, each individual subjectivity must now confront the consciousness of the past, as expressed in the minds of one's predecessors.

The attempt by Modernism to construct a new canon (Pound in "Hugh Selwyn Mauberley," T. S. Eliot in "Tradition and the Individual Talent" as well as *The Waste Land*) is significant, if for no other reason, because it reveals the limits inherent in the concept of the canon itself, limits reached already in the late nineteenth century. Fundamentally, the concept of a canon espoused by Modernism is a formal one, corresponding to its attempt at a revolution in poetic style. Thus, in "Tradition and the Individual Talent," what Eliot describes is a relation not between authors but between works, the totality of which are said to form an expanding constellation.

But if we no longer need to espouse the ideals of Modernism, the concept of a canon in the sense proposed by that movement becomes equally meaningless—as well as, perhaps, a canon in any other sense. Such a notion is at best significant only for the relation of a literature to itself, forming, as we have seen, that literature's definition of the nature of literature. In literary history, however, the formation of a canon can have no place. What we are now attempting to formulate is not the relation of a past literature to itself but its relation to the present. The creation of a canon solely from within that period is therefore meaningless: it serves neither the period nor ourselves. In short: the purposes of a literary history and of canon formation are antithetical.

What I have sought to achieve is a representation of the literary history of the American Renaissance from one perspective, its relation to European Romanticism. For this reason, it was not possible to offer inclusive treatment of the American Renaissance. Thus I discuss some figures normally considered minor (Theodore Parker, Margaret Fuller, Bronson Alcott), without attempting to incorporate others (Jones Very, Ellery Channing, Holmes, Longfellow, Lowell, the American historians). The principle of inclusion or exclusion has had to be quite narrow: not only the presence of a visible relation to European Romanticism but a relation that conforms to the Romantic concepts I had chosen to discuss. This focus also meant the exclusion of certain significant European figures of influence, above all, Byron. Apart from the Shelleyan passages of canto III of *Childe Harold's Pilgrimage,* Byron's themes fall largely outside the scope of my investigations. Hence his well-known influence on Melville (especially in *Moby-Dick* and *Pierre*) must be more or less passed over, as well as his effect upon the early Poe. To concentrate, on the other hand, solely upon major figures would also be to give a misleading impression. To some extent, literary-historical considerations impose certain choices of authors and works. But I have also indulged some personal preferences: Margaret Fuller's literary criticism (too little appreciated, it seems to me) and Theodore Parker's theological speculations.

One major figure, however, looms over the work as a numinous presence: Wordsworth. Wordsworth's relation to American Romanticism can be expressed, I think, only by confronting the totality of his oeuvre with that of Melville or Emerson. Much might be said about his sense of Nature as rival power to that of the human intellect, the revelation of the Romantic sublime and the apocalypse of the mind compared with similar elements in Melville, or about his exploration of the nature of consciousness and the experience of divine presence compared to Emerson's. Such subjects could be treated at some length, were it possible to develop the nature of the Wordsworthian consciousness in relation to that which informs *Moby-Dick* or Emerson's *Nature.* To do so, however, would require juxtaposing a comprehensive interpretation of *The Prelude* and other poems with that of *Moby-Dick* or *Nature* (rather than treating merely concepts or *topoi* from these works), a procedure quite different from mine.

It remains for me to say something about the overall view of the American Renaissance proposed here, especially its relation to British and European Romanticism. By my title I do not wish to suggest that the American Renaissance derives exclusively from Romanticism; as a result of certain recent studies (particularly Sacvan Bercovitch's *Puritan Origins of the American Self* and *The American Jeremiad*), its connections with American Puritan literature and thought are now well known. The concept of foundations itself, however, reflects a Romantic notion or perspective, embodied in such works as Kant's *Foundations of the Metaphysics of Morals* or Fichte's *Foundations of the Entire Doctrine of Science* (*Grundlagen der gesammten Wissenschaftslehre*). Hence it seems appropriate to speak specifically about the Romantic foundations of the American Renaissance.

If we compare the relation between the American Renaissance and Romanticism with that between the former and American Puritanism, certain significant differences emerge. Because of the long hiatus represented by the eighteenth century (neoclassicism), the Gothic and pre-Romantic (exemplified in America by Charles Brockden Brown), and Romanticism itself, the American Renaissance manifests more a recovery or renewal than a continuation of Puritan modes of thought and expression. With Romanticism, on the other hand, the American Renaissance is historically and intellectually continuous: nothing typifies such continuity better than Emerson's visit (full of hope and, unfortunately, disappointed expectations) to Wordsworth and Coleridge in the summer of 1833. With Carlyle he could speak as to a contemporary, and if one considers Carlyle's complex and problematic relation to Romanticism, the suggestion of Emerson's similar situation is bound to arise. Melville's relation to Romanticism is, of course, somewhat different. For him the Romantics represent, in the words of Charles du Bos, "the great dead" (*les grands morts*). His situation toward them is symbolized by his visit in the winter of 1857 to the graves of Keats and Shelley in the Protestant Cemetery in Rome. One might summarize by saying that the American Renaissance is in one sense the final phase of Romanticism, embodying all the tensions and pressures incident to the culmination of a movement, as the High Renaissance, for instance, had had to bear these in relation to the Quattrocento, or Mannerism vis-à-vis the High Renaissance.

One might also speak about the nature of the relation between the American Renaissance and European Romanticism, the differences that emerge and develop from their continuity. In particular, one might point out the increasing subjectivization of thought and consciousness (witness Poe's allegories of the mind, Hawthorne's *Blithedale Romance*, and Melville's *Pierre*) or the deepening opposition between materialism and spiritualism, which rejects the efforts of eighteenth-century panpsychism (Diderot, La Mettrie) and Romantic *Naturphilosophie* to reconcile matter with mind in one progressive continuum. Here we encounter one of the distinctions between Poe, with his theory of the ether ("Mesmeric Revelation," the letter to James Russell Lowell, *Eureka*), and Melville's late spiritualism (his affinity in *Billy Budd* with the Balzacian theory of the will).

In the present study I focus essentially upon Poe, Emerson, Hawthorne, and Melville. The inclusion of Poe in the American Renaissance canon raises the question of my exclusion of Thoreau and Whitman. To be sure, these figures display manifest affinities with some of the above, especially with Emerson. But it seems to me that the inclusion of Poe necessarily alters somewhat the shape of the American Renaissance. Poe exhibits a continuity not only with Romanticism but also with the eighteenth century: his inclusion permits the resolution of certain problematic questions concerning American Romanticism and, by the perspective it introduces, makes it possible to view Thoreau and Whitman as representative of a later phase of the American Renaissance, one in which the relationship with Romanticism is mediated through the vision of Emerson.

Having said something concerning the relation of American Renaissance authors to their American and European predecessors, I now wish to say something about their relation to each other. In so doing, I hope to clarify somewhat the overall "form" of the American Renaissance in terms of literary history.

The shift from allegory to symbolism as a doctrine of poetics which occurs with Romanticism discloses certain new possibilities for literary representation. If we consider both allegory and symbolism as differing modes of representation, the one expressive through signs, the other through immediate revelation (apocalypse), it becomes apparent that the abandonment of allegory in its traditional form need not imply the adoption of a Romantic symbolism. It would also be possible to envision other, more radical forms of allegory, in which the subjectivizing tendencies of Romanticism are expressed so as to create an experience of pure transparence, of immediate symbolic correspondence, without having to rely upon natural objects. In short, the external world need not necessarily reveal the awesome sense of a divine presence; it can also serve as medium for the transparent moment in which the self beholds the reality of its own mind. Romantic nature symbolism affords a glimpse of higher, transcendental realities that are external or objective; a more radical form of allegory could reveal the internal or subjective reality of the self. This second possibility becomes the aim of Poe's tales and poems. What makes such a project both difficult and problematic is the tendency of the mind to resist that moment of pure transparence in which it is revealed to itself. As a result, it enters into a conflicting play of desire and repulsion with the allegory itself, which it seeks to objectify as allegory to avoid the disclosure.

The longing to surmount the kind of impasse or blockage created by the mind's relationship to its own allegory leads to the somewhat different experience of transparence we encounter in Emerson. Here, transparence occurs as the dissolution of the external world through the process of perception itself. What Emerson refers to is the experience of pure seeing, devoid of all phenomenal content received through external impressions. In such experience, the mind necessarily confronts the process of its own consciousness, or the reality of consciousness itself. This sublime moment Emerson also characterizes as an apprehension of the divine essence. For him in his early phase, that essence is nothing other than consciousness's apprehension of itself. At such moments, all trace of individuality or self disappears. What remains is the overwhelming experience of divine consciousness.

For Emerson, then, the subjectivization of allegory brings about ultimately a fusion of internal and external, subjective and objective. For Hawthorne, on the other hand, pure subjectivity or self-consciousness, the exclusion of the whole phenomenological richness of existence, is bound to lead to sterile solipsism. From the perspective of his later years, such indeed might be described as the problem of the early tales. Another theme however runs through them as well: the apprehension of the beautiful. From "The Artist of the Beautiful" to *The House of the Seven Gables,* the experience of beauty is arrested and fixed within the literary work so as to yield a higher, symbolic significance: for Hawthorne the apprehension of beauty could never be in itself the essence of the divine, but only a symbolic revelation of it. Nowhere does this appear more clearly than in his last finished novel, *The Marble Faun,* in which the whole history of human life, the passage from innocence to experience, becomes symbolic of the progress of art, from its naive or pagan form to its endowment with a higher Christian consciousness.

Like Hawthorne, Melville might also be said to begin with the problem raised by Emerson through his identification of subjective and objective, self and divinity. But if so, he differs ultimately in pursuing the implications of Emersonian symbolism to an opposite extreme: what if the dissolving of self and external world in the medium of consciousness should lead, not to an apprehension of consciousness itself, but rather to that of an unknown and unknowable Other? An aura of the sacred surrounds its mysterious presence, but its impenetrability leads Melville finally to a rejection of the Romantic symbolic perspective in *The Confidence-Man.* Henceforth, in the works of Melville's later phase, there will be a return to "Nature" in humanity, but never again to the problematic natural symbolism of *Moby-Dick.* In its place Melville sets a spiritualism akin to what E. R. Curtius has called the "All-Unity theory" of Balzac, one that regards matter and spirit as part of one vast continuum.

For the Romantic period the foundations of science embrace much more than the natural or experimental sciences. As envisioned by post-Kantian transcendental idealism, its objective could be nothing less than a theoretical apprehension of the whole of existence. This dream of a universal science, cherished earlier by Leibniz and others in the seventeenth and eighteenth centuries, comes to Poe in the form of rationalism. Reason as apprehension of the formal relations between things—thus Poe might have defined rationalism. What distinguishes him from the Enlightenment is his desire to see the theoretical structure of science as something more than human or subjective rationalization, the mind's effort to bring the external world into conformity with its own nature. Instead, the deep subjectivizing tendency of Romanticism operates in him upon rationalism itself, transforming rational thought into spiritual perception of the true essences of things. For Poe, one might say, the universe consists of the sum of its ideational relations. Where Emerson and others affirm the primacy of consciousness as an experience of the divine, Poe can assert that the perfection and symmetry of the laws of the universe constitute the expression of a divine force immanent in matter itself. For him, then, the universe is more than evidence of providential design, the justification of a theodicy: in its workings he discovers the activity of the divine energeia itself, one whose form becomes manifest above all in rationalism.

Like Poe, Emerson could also feel the attraction of theory in the sciences. Unlike Poe, however, he regards the will to theory simply as an innate tendency of the human mind. The result: a "humanization" of science, but only if we qualify this by recalling simultaneously his identification of pure consciousness with the divine. Because of this equation of the divine with consciousness rather than reason (in Poe's sense), his conception of the nature of theory in the sciences was also bound to differ. For him scientific thought is not so much recognition of certain ideal laws governing all of existence (though he affirms these too) but rather of an ideational element into which the mind translates its perceptions concerning material substances. His later essays and lectures demonstrate an increasing preoccupation with what he termed the "natural history of intellect." It seems appropriate to offer this as a designation of Emerson's own enterprise, since his ultimate concern is not so much with the results of speculation but rather with its tendencies.

Both Poe and Emerson assert the primacy of theory in the sciences, which we can interpret as expressing either an inclination toward rationalism or toward the "humanity of science." In both cases, the essence of science is seen to consist of thought itself. For Hawthorne, on the other hand, the increasingly speculative and theoretical character of the sciences threatens to disrupt human existence. He himself, in all likelihood, was not aware of the renewal of vitalism (Van Helmont, Bichat, among others), nor of the recent emergence of biology as an independent discipline (the term *biology* had just been coined by Lamarck at the beginning of the nineteenth century). But, through the mediation of Balzac, he participates in the growing reaction against the abstract tendencies fostered by the immense prestige of the physical sciences (Newtonian mechanics in particular) in all realms of scientific endeavor. Against the claims of thought he sets those of life. The recognition of life itself as a source of immanent values, which begins with Goethe and Nietzsche, is often opposed to rationalism, especially throughout the nineteenth century. Hawthorne himself does not reject rationalism categorically, but he shares the increasing tendency of the later nineteenth century to seek the source of its values elsewhere.

The phenomenon I refer to as the secularization of religion, which begins with Romanticism, marks a major aspect of the nineteenth-century "transvaluation of all values." The primacy of consciousness which we have seen to form one of Romanticism's principal characteristics plays a crucial role here too: Schleiermacher's radical approach to religion, which manifests itself already in *Über die Religion* and the *Monologen,* emerges from an atmosphere of deep skepticism engendered by Hume and the Enlightenment attacks upon the bases of religious belief. Against these, it was necessary to find the source of religion within consciousness itself, as the one undeniable Cartesian datum: to create out of the epiphanic experience of consciousness a sense of the sublime and the infinite, a new content of religious awareness.

But the grounding of religion upon the nature of consciousness leads to pantheism, and with the reaction against the latter which sets in during Romanticism's later phase, Schleiermacher embraces the opposite extreme: a founding of religion upon the feeling of absolute dependence, the failure of consciousness to find the presence of the divine within itself and its consequent positing of God as external Other. Theodore Parker sensed the dilemma of this position but did not solve it. In his works we encounter the conflicting play of opposing tendencies: attraction toward a pantheism that celebrates the beauty of the cosmos and its mirroring in consciousness, and a simultaneous and equally powerful desire to transcend the material sphere through moral action and a faith that discovers its strength in the nature of its own impulse. It remains for Emerson to seek to combine these two deeply opposed tendencies. His radical Christology in the Divinity School Address posits the attainment of an epiphanic consciousness as a result of moral insight into the nature of our existence. Such epiphanic moments unite the subjective apprehension of religion which begins with Romanticism to the sense of a divine presence acting upon the external universe.

With Schleiermacher, Parker, and Emerson, the deep subjectivizing tendency of Romantic religion leads to isolation of the self from others: whether in the form of epiphanic consciousness or its opposite, the feeling of absolute dependence, the experience of the sacred invariably excludes relation to another self. For Hawthorne, on the other hand, our relation to others is all we know of the sacred. It consists of the moment in which one individual surrenders his self or her self to another. This moment, which retains a hallowed aura, need not, however, embrace the consciousness of a divine presence. With that exclusion, the process of religious secularization enters a new phase. Previously, association of the religious with the subjective had presupposed a divinization of consciousness—in effect, the transformation of human to God-like consciousness. Such had been the burden of Hölderlin's *Der Tod des Empedokles*. By endowing the purely human element of the subjective with the attributes of the sacred, Hawthorne alters the meaning of this concept. Whereas earlier the sacred had implied similarity or identification with the divine nature, it now suffices to have merely the experience of the divine, an experience that is possible in the realm of human affections.'

In a sense, such a shift is only the last step in the subjectivization of religion. But it can also lead, as with Melville, to a questioning of the very meaning and place of the sacred itself. These concerns we find explored largely in *Moby-Dick* and *Pierre*, as well as *The Confidence-Man*. But if Melville had already exposed in these works the problematic status of the sacred, it is only much later, in *Billy Budd*, that he is able to accept and affirm a more secularized religion. Here, by means of his assimilation of the Balzacian theory of the will and the spiritualism of *Séraphîta*, a new conception of religion emerges, one that no longer associates it with belief or even with feeling, but simply with a primordial will or desire that transcends the limits of material existence. In this fashion, religion remains internalized within the self but, in contrast to earlier developments, no longer associated with the subjective realm of consciousness. Instead, Melville equates it with the element of will, the vital force of life itself—which is to say, with a spiritualism that no longer opposes life but elevates and transforms it.

As a result of the Romantic emphasis upon mind and consciousness, Romantic theories of history differ from their predecessors in presenting the significance of history as internalized within history itself. Even Herder (*Ideen zur Philosophie der Geschichte der Menschheit*) and Lessing (*Erziehung des Menschengeschlechts*) had defined the meaning of history from an external or objective perspective. Emerson, in treating similar material and with a somewhat similar approach, will nevertheless attempt in his early *Philosophy of History* lectures to express the subjective unity of history by regarding its various epochs and aspects as the manifestations of one mind. In his later essay "History" (*Essays: First Series*), of course, this point of view is expanded and developed: not only are all parts of history related to each other, but those relations are themselves given a higher reality by subsisting within a universal element of mind or consciousness.

If the philosophy of history represents one form of historical consciousness, the historical novel, beginning with Scott, may be said to constitute another. It was Scott's insight to have perceived the necessity of creating the historical consciousness of an era out of the partial perspectives and lived experiences of its protagonists. By equating that consciousness with what Goethe might have called the "life-relations" of the participants, Scott makes possible a new apprehension of the nature and reality of that consciousness. In Hawthorne, the significance of Scott's insight is fully appreciated and renewed in another context, from his early tales to *The Scarlet Letter*. With the unfinished late manuscripts, however, Hawthorne carries Scott's methods even one step further, to an apprehension not only of a given historical moment but of the very nature of history itself.

Of pantheism something has already been said. It remains to point out the relational nature of the divine energeia in Poe. This energy consists of the repulsive force between particles of matter. Thus its existence becomes manifest only through those particles it separates from each other. Poe does not ascribe a specific nature to such energy. Its element is spiritual and, as such, something transcending human comprehension. In this sense he retains the influence of the Enlightenment: however significant the nature or substance of that spiritual energy, it remains a noumenon of which we perceive only the phenomenal appearance. The desire for identification of the divine with substance remains, as it were, in suspension. With Emerson, on the other hand, the nature of that divine substance becomes one with consciousness. But Emerson, too, begins with a formalistic point of departure: Hedge's misprision of Fichte's *Wissenschaftslehre*, especially its transition from the purely logical $A = A$ to the epistemological $I = I$, produces for Emerson the rich yield of a self-grounding for consciousness. What had been for Fichte the formal relation of the self to itself now discloses for Emerson the infinite nature of the perceiving consciousness. Even that consciousness, however, was to prove but a transitional phase in the development of Romantic pantheism. For Melville, as for Coleridge before him, the "one Life within us and abroad" supersedes consciousness as an identification of the pantheistic principle, insofar as it reveals the presence of an energy within consciousness itself. That energy, in turn, is one and the same with that which animates external Nature. But the destructive force of Nature leads ultimately to the question whether even this universal energy is to be equated with God, or whether the nature of the latter subsists in some higher principle than that of life itself.

Of subjectivity, too, some mention has already been made. Perhaps what is most significant about the subjective tendency of American Romanticism is not so much its exploration of the nature of the subjective consciousness (Emerson is the exception)—that had already been depicted by the European Romantics—but rather its probing of the psychological and moral consequences of such "self-anatomy." Here we might cite first of all Margaret Fuller's great insight into the creative and dialectical interplay between masculine and feminine natures in both men and women, and the possibilities in that interplay toward the development of higher forms and relations of social existence. In particular, the dialectic of masculine and feminine participates in the formation of aesthetic appreciation and the creation of works of art. Both Emerson and Margaret Fuller had seen consciousness as essentially passive and receptive. In *The Blithedale Romance,* however, Hawthorne exposes the desire for psychological possession which colors and determines the nature of perception itself. To be sure, European Romanticism had already attested to the suffusion of perception and consciousness by feeling. What Hawthorne reveals, nevertheless, is a different form of the subjective element: the will to power as desire for knowledge of the inner self of another. Almost simultaneously, Melville in *Pierre* could demonstrate the potentially destructive character of the subliminal impulses and the problematic moral issues raised by their passing into consciousness. Ultimately, his concern is theological: at what point does responsibility for the arising of such impulses revert to their original cause? In his examination of the unsounded depths of consciousness, Melville also opposes quite sharply Emerson's identification of epiphanic consciousness with the divine essence.

The earlier poetics of the American Renaissance owes its origins to late eighteenth-century and even neoclassical concerns. In his adoption of Cousin's schema of the faculties (moral, intellectual, aesthetic) Poe affirms a perspective that may be traced back, in America, to Charles Brockden Brown (*Wieland* especially) and, in Europe, to Kant and Schiller, among others. The subsequent development of his aesthetic views sets him somewhat apart from his great contemporaries: from the late eighteenth-century or pre-Romantic style of his earlier speculations, he then passes, through his defense of Keats and Shelley as poets of beauty, to a poetics that anticipates virtually all the features of the Symbolist movement and the Pre-Raphaelite circle.

Apart from Poe, American Renaissance poetics shares a central concern with that of European Romanticism: the relation of "modernity" to tradition. For both Emerson and Margaret Fuller, modernity consists above all of a specific mode of consciousness: subjective as opposed to objective, a literature of feeling and mind as against the literal rendering of an external world. It was Hawthorne's role to promote a reconciliation of these opposing tendencies, above all in *The House of the Seven Gables.* For him, a theory of romance is also a theory of consciousness— but not of that pure consciousness envisioned by Emerson: what he evokes is rather that mixture of actual and ideal, feeling and external appearance, which together create the reality of fiction. In Melville, finally, we encounter once more what had appeared earlier as the opposition of Classic to Romantic, but raised now to a more universal level where it becomes simply the relation of each author to the past or tradition. Like Shelley, he can sympathize with the concept of "that great poem, which all poets, like the co-operating thoughts of one great mind, have built up since the beginning of the world," although more aware perhaps than Shelley of the precarious nature of the subjective consciousness in which that poem must have its existence. Yet what distinguishes his view most of all from Shelley's—as well as from that of European Romanticism as a whole—lies in its affirmation of another "world" even larger and more significant than that of literature: the realm of the self. In his efforts to capture the reality of this world, the author becomes significant not for his accomplishment but for the Faustian nature of his striving, in a quest that can never be complete.

# PART I

# From Allegory to Symbolism

# 1  *Poe*

## Allegory of the Mind

On the eve of his marriage to Maggie Verver in Henry James's *Golden Bowl*, the Prince decides to call upon his friend Fanny Assingham. En route in a cab to her house in Cadogan Place, he reflects upon his present situation. A recollection emerges: "He remembered to have read as a boy a wonderful tale by Allan Poe . . . the story of the ship-wrecked Gordon Pym, who, drifting in a small boat further toward the North Pole—or was it the South?—than any one had ever done, found at a given moment before him a thickness of white air that was like a dazzling curtain of light, concealing as darkness conceals, yet of the colour of milk or snow. There were moments when he felt his own boat move upon some such mystery. The state of mind of his new friends, including Mrs. Assingham herself, had resemblances to a great white curtain" (*Novels and Tales*, XXIII, 22). This state of mind is, of course, a curtain only from the point of view of the Prince. But it is characteristic of James that even the images within his works should comprise reflections of his characters' perceptions.

From various indications, one may surmise that James himself had been engaged in reading Poe at the time of composing *The Golden Bowl*.[1] Nevertheless, it must be said that, by James's period, we no longer find any trace of the original significance of Poe's conclusion to *Arthur Gordon Pym*. This fact is itself symptomatic. It indicates to what extent allegory had gone out of fashion in *fin de siècle* nineteenth-century literature—for the significance of Poe's image of the dazzling curtain of whiteness is

---

[1] James A. Harrison's edition of Poe's *Complete Works* had just appeared in 1902. The celebrated "pagoda" image that opens vol. II of *The Golden Bowl* derives, if I am not mistaken, from a passage in Poe's criticism. Even the motif of the golden bowl itself (Eccles. 12:6) is alluded to twice by Poe, in "The Premature Burial" (*Coll. W.*, III, 955) and "Lenore" (*Coll. W.*, I, 336).

allegorical. We may trace the image to Tertullian's *Apology:* "So, when the limit and boundary line which gapes widely in the midst is at hand, so that even the temporal aspect of this world is changed, which is stretched out like a curtain against the disposition of eternity, then shall the entire human race be restored to settle the account for the good or the evil it has merited in this world, from then on to be requited for a limitless and unending eternity."[2] What assurances do we have, however, of Poe's knowledge of Tertullian? A paradox from *De Carne Christi* is quoted in both "Berenice" and the "Marginalia": "Mortuus est Dei filius; credibile est quia ineptum est; et sepultus resurrexit; certum est quia impossibile est" (*Coll. W.*, II, 213; *C.W.*, XVI, 90–91). The first version of "Lionizing" incorporates an allusion to Minucius Felix, the model for Tertullian's *Apology* (*Coll. W.*, II, 173). Elsewhere, in "The Man of the Crowd," Poe cites Jean-Louis Guez de Balzac's remark on the style of Tertullian (*Coll. W.*, II, 511; see note, 517).

It need not surprise us to find a motif from one of the most celebrated of the early Church Fathers embedded in *Arthur Gordon Pym,* for the pattern of Poe's reading is consciously and explicitly one of diversification. In an early review he defines "true erudition" simply as "much diversified reading" (*C.W.*, X, 47). In addition Poe exhibits, even in his early years, a definite interest in Christian theology and apologetics.[3] One may also observe the numerous scriptural references scattered throughout his tales and poems. His theology is, to be sure, hardly orthodox: at times he was much attracted to the doctrine of pantheism. It influences his conception of a cyclical process in which birth (or creation) represents a diffusion from the divine Spirit, death, the reabsorption or return into that Spirit. The fate of Arthur Gordon Pym presents a fictionalized account of such notions. Just as the white curtain of mist (also described, significantly enough, as a "veil") has been seen to exemplify the boundary between life and death, time and eternity, it becomes possible in a similar fashion to see in what follows an allegorical illustration of the soul's reabsorption into the Spirit in death: "And now we rushed into the embraces of the cataract, where a chasm threw itself open to receive us. But there arose in our pathway a shrouded human figure, very far larger in its proportions than any dweller among men. And the hue of the skin of the figure was of the perfect whiteness of the snow." This figure may be taken to signify either the Angel of Death (whom Poe elsewhere designates as "Azrael") or perhaps even God him-

[2]*Tertullian: Apologetical Works,* The Fathers of the Church, vol. x (New York: Catholic Univ. of America Press, 1950), p. 120.

[3]See for instance his remark apropos of Stephens's *Arabia Petraea:* "We look upon the *literalness* of the understanding of the Bible predictions as an *essential* feature in prophecy—conceiving minuteness of detail to have been but a portion of the providential plan of the Deity for bringing more visibly to light, in after-ages, the *evidence* of the fulfilment of his word" (*C.W.*, X, 9).

self, although Poe later remarks that "the bestowing upon Deity a human form, is at best a low and most unideal conception" (*C.W.*, xi, 21).[4]

But Poe's interest in the early Christian Fathers reveals something more than merely a source of his allegorical imagery. It also affects, in part, his conception of allegory itself. Early Christian biblical exegesis had sought to distinguish between differing figural senses of Scripture: allegoresis or allegorical interpretation concerned itself with the moral *exempla* educible from the Old and New Testaments, while typology was seen as the study of those persons and events in the Bible which "prepare and prefigure the mystery which is one day to be fulfilled in Christ." But, as the late Church historian Jean Daniélou has pointed out, "It would be an entire abuse of language to include moral allegory with typology under the one heading of the spiritual sense, as opposed to the literal sense: typology is a legitimate extension of the literal sense, while moral allegory is something entirely alien: the former is in truth exegesis, the latter is not."[5] The moral allegoresis of Scripture originates with Philo and exercises a decisive influence upon the Alexandrian Fathers Origen and Clement of Alexandria. There are traces of this influence in Ambrose as well. Typological interpretations, on the other hand, predominate in Irenaeus and Tertullian.[6]

It is necessary to insist upon the distinction between these two forms of biblical "exegesis" because of its effect upon Poe's conception of allegory. He does not, to be sure, employ typology in either his tales or his poems, nor will one find it discussed anywhere in his critical reviews or essays. For Poe, as for Emerson and Hawthorne, the word *type* itself must be understood in its Romantic sense, as a concrete yet universal representation of essential attributes.[7] Thus in "The Man of the Crowd" the

---

[4]See Patrick F. Quinn, *The French Face of Edgar Poe* (Carbondale: Southern Illinois Univ. Press, 1957), p. 213, who, however, attributes no specific significance to the image. More recently, Poe, *Collected Writings*, i, 355–59 (nn. 24.14B–D), which refers to Benjamin Morrell's *Narrative of Four Voyages* (New York, 1832) with regard to the whiteness and offers various conjectures on the figure confronting Pym; most persuasive, in my view, are the biblical parallels, esp. in light of the white curtain symbolism.

[5]*From Shadows to Reality*, trans. Wulstan Hibberd (Westminster, Md.: Newman Press, 1960), pp. 11, 64.

[6]On Philonic allegoresis and symbolism, E. R. Goodenough, *By Light, Light: The Mystic Gospel of Hellenistic Judaism* (New Haven: Yale Univ. Press, 1935), pp. 83–84, 242–44, and C. H. Dodd, *The Interpretation of the Fourth Gospel* (Cambridge: Cambridge Univ. Press, 1953), esp. pp. 55–57. On Irenaeus, Daniélou, pp. 33–37. See also Erich Auerbach, "Figura," in his *Scenes from the Drama of European Literature* (New York: Meridian Books, 1959).

[7]See, e.g., in Emerson, "The soul of man must be the type of our scheme [i.e., philosophy], just as the body of man is the type after which a dwelling-house is built" (*C.W.*, iv, 160–61); "All great natures are lovers of stability and permanence, as the type of the Eternal" (*C.W.*, viii, 333–34). In Hawthorne: "His visionary edifice was Hollingsworth's one castle in the air; it was the material type, in which his philanthropic dream strove to embody itself" (Centenary, iii, 56).

narrator can assert that the man he has been following is "the type and genius of deep crime" (*Coll. W.*, II, 515). Only in early Melville do we see traces of a typology in the scriptural sense. On the other hand, it seems clear that the relegation of allegoresis in early Christian tradition to an eliciting of moral *exempla* from the Scriptures is in some measure responsible for the moralistic conception of allegory which appears in Poe's early criticism. In a review of Thomas Moore's *Alciphron* he observes:

> The truth is that the just distinction between the fancy and the imagination (and which is still but a distinction of *degree*) is involved in the consideration of the mystic. We give this as an idea of our own, altogether. We have no authority for our opinion—but do not the less firmly hold it. The term mystic is here employed in the sense of Augustus William Schlegel, and of most other German critics. It is applied by them to that class of composition in which there lies beneath the transparent upper current of meaning an under or *suggestive* one. What we vaguely term the *moral* of any sentiment is its mystic or secondary expression. It has the vast force of an accompaniment in music. This vivifies the air; that spiritualizes the *fanciful* conception, and lifts it into the ideal. (*C.W.*, x, 65)

This passage represents the first sustained theoretical discussion of allegory in Poe's criticism (it is anticipated, as far as I am aware, only by his review of De la Motte Fouqué's *Undine* of September, 1839). Remarkably, the term *allegory* does not enter into the discussion here at all. Nor does Poe attempt to distinguish between allegory and symbolism—although such a distinction is clearly present in August Wilhelm Schlegel (*Krit. Schriften*, v, 81). But, in addition, only the symbolic can be said to have a "mystical" sense in Schlegel. In his posthumously published *Vorlesungen über schöne Literatur und Kunst* he declares that "The Beautiful is a symbolic representation of the Infinite" (*Krit. Schriften*, II, 81).[8] In Poe, by contrast, the allegorical and symbolic are merged into one. As a result, allegory escapes the wholesale condemnation Poe was to direct at it in later years.[9] Such condemnation could come only when he had

---

[8]For Poe and A. W. Schlegel, see G. R. Thompson, *Poe's Fiction: Romantic Irony in the Gothic Tales* (Madison: Univ. of Wisconsin Press, 1973), pp. 26–34, which discusses mainly Romantic irony. For earlier treatments, A. J. Lubell, "Poe and A. W. Schlegel," *Journal of English and Germanic Philology*, 52 (1953), 1–12; Margaret Alterton, *Origins of Poe's Critical Theory* (Iowa City: Univ. of Iowa, 1925), pp. 30–32, 68–72, 75–77; and Henry A. Pochmann, *German Culture in America* (Madison: Univ. of Wisconsin Press, 1957), pp. 406–8.

[9]Even in 1841 Poe already declares: "Pure allegory is at all times an abomination—a remnant of antique barbarism—appealing only to our faculties of comparison, without even a remote interest for our reason, or for our fancy. Metaphor, its softened image, has indisputable force when sparingly and skilfully employed" (*C.W.*, x, 130). Poe's most famous comment, from the 1847 review of Hawthorne, must be quoted for its specific argument: "In defence of allegory, (however, or for whatever object, employed,) there is scarcely one respectable word to be said. Its best appeals are made to the fancy—that is to say, to our sense of adaptation, not of matters proper, but of matters improper for the

worked out for himself his own highly personal theory of symbolism. To be sure, there is in his review of *Undine* an implicit objection to allegory in general. But the sense of a higher meaning in things themselves (which was to find expression in his doctrine of symbolic correspondences) makes him reluctant to dismiss allegory altogether, for it would have been possible to interpret it, like symbolism, simply as a reflection of that higher meaning within the things themselves.

The absence of a distinction between allegory and symbolism in the passage from Poe I have just quoted is scarcely more significant than the comparison he draws between an undercurrent of meaning (allegory) and an accompaniment in music. René Wellek has rightfully pointed out that the English Romantics took little interest in music.[10] Only in French and German Romanticism is the parallel drawn between music and literature. By means of this parallel, literature is defined as one of the affective arts. A new perspective in thus disclosed: through this comparison, we seem at once to look back to eighteenth-century aesthetics and forward to the Aestheticism of late nineteenth-century England and France. Romanticism—with its concepts of symbolism, myth, and organic form—is bypassed in the process—or perhaps, more accurately: transmuted into a different but analogous form.

For Poe, situated between these two epochs, the problematic aspect of allegory inheres in its arbitrary attempt to create an objective correspondence between allegorical figure and significance. Such arbitrariness results from the individual or subjective nature of all perception. Here Poe's emphasis is not so much upon the relativism of each individual perspective but rather upon the nature of mind itself and its predetermination of the very conditions under which we receive external impressions. From this standpoint the only valid subject for allegory must

---

purpose, of the real with the unreal; having never more of intelligible connection than has something with nothing, never half so much of effective affinity as has the substance for the shadow. . . . One thing is clear, that if allegory ever establishes a fact, it is by dint of overturning a fiction. Where the suggested meaning runs through the obvious one in a *very* profound under-current so as never to interfere with the upper one without our volition, so as never to show itself unless *called* to the surface, there only, for the proper uses of fictitious narrative, is it available at all" (*C.W.*, XIII, 148). Here Poe clearly echoes Coleridge in *The Statesman's Manual* (see below), but more significant is the provision for something like what Tennyson would later term "allegory in the distance" (apropos of his *Idylls of the King*). The need for a replacement for traditional allegory leads not only to Romantic symbolism but to what I would like to call "transformed" versions of allegory. The attractions of such "transformed" or modified allegory are felt in particular by those with tendencies toward Aestheticism. Thus not only Poe but—among the Romantics—Keats especially (*Eve of St. Agnes*), and, among Poe's contemporaries, Tennyson (esp. the early poems) and Baudelaire (cf. his "Allégorie" in *Les Fleurs du mal*). Such "transformed" versions of allegory preserve and emphasize the archaic aspect of allegory as an aesthetic feature: the creation of a form of mediation between the object and its significance—the *deferral* of that significance, so to speak—becomes the means of its intensification.

[10]*Confrontations* (Princeton: Princeton Univ. Press, 1965), pp. 24–27.

therefore be the mind itself.[11] In Poe's mature tales the mind emerges as both subject and object of its own allegory. In such tales the allegorical process consists of the mind's reflection upon itself, that is to say, upon its own nature. Such allegory is clearly self-conscious: the mind within the tale, in "representing" itself, neither can nor wants to lose sight of the effect of this representation upon itself.[12]

In fact, if we examine the progressive development of Poe's allegory, what emerges is an increasing awareness of the subjective limits of allegory, the limits the mind imposes upon its own self-representation. Such limits arise not only from its anxiety over possible disclosures but equally from its fascination with the allegorical medium itself. From these simultaneous but diametrically opposed feelings arises in turn the dialectic of repulsion and desire which engages the mind in its own allegory. In an early tale such as "William Wilson" it had been possible to assert the "objective" significance of the allegory as a revelation of the nature of the mind itself: William Wilson's "double" *is*, within the tale's allegorical mode, the protagonist's conscience. In later tales such as "The Black Cat" or "The Tell-Tale Heart," the mind's complicity in shaping its own allegory precludes any such "objective" presentation.

At this stage Poe exhibits an increasing awareness of possibilities of a more complex treatment of his subject, one that encompasses the mind's reaction to its own allegorical creation and its attempts both to "possess" and repress it. At the moment at which it feels these conflicting desires, the mind has become fully conscious of the representational purpose of its own allegory: what it now seeks is a means of identifying with that allegory in order to assume for itself the power of representation. Hence the sympathetic identification in a tale such as "The Cask of Amontillado" between murderer and victim: as in earlier tales (for example, "The Fall of the House of Usher"), the entombed or walled-in victim invariably signifies what the mind seeks to repress, but the cry or scream that divulges this is one in which the mind itself participates. Through its participation, the mind seeks to dominate and hence to possess the act of disclosure. By allegorically divulging its own secret, so to speak, it attempts to control the means of self-representation, wresting these away from deeper, unconscious forces.

In the nascent stages of Romanticism which we now call pre-Roman-

[11]An insight clearly expressed by Richard Wilbur in his pioneering essay "The House of Poe," rpt. in Eric W. Carlson, ed., *The Recognition of Edgar Allan Poe* (Ann Arbor: Univ. of Michigan Press, 1966), p. 260: "What I am saying is that the scenes and situations of Poe's tales are always concrete representations of states of mind."

[12]Some recent theoretical discussions of allegory that bear upon the topics developed here: Angus Fletcher, *Allegory: The Theory of a Symbolic Mode* (Ithaca, N.Y.: Cornell Univ. Press, 1964); Paul de Man, *Allegories of Reading* (New Haven: Yale Univ. Press, 1979); Stephen Greenblatt, ed., *Allegory and Representation* (Baltimore: Johns Hopkins Univ. Press, 1981).

ticism, the possibilities for the imagination as self-gratifying and allegory as self-reflexive becoming increasingly apparent (Rousseau's reflections on the imagination in his *Confessions;* the climactic apocalypse of Blake's *Jerusalem*). By contrast, with its theory of symbolism, Romanticism introduces a fundamentally different perspective: instead of the limits of solipsism, creation of the objective *within* the subjective, and vice versa. Poe's theory of allegory (if we may call it such) does not participate in this process. Nevertheless, in its gradual unfolding and development, it presents an analogue to it: in a unique fashion, Poe's allegory realizes the Romantic dream of an immediate relation between the subjective and an absolute. Instead of postulating that absolute as an external "objective," however, Poe's allegory discovers it within itself. It remains now to trace in detail the stages by which allegory arrives at its "subjective" objectivity.

## "Ligeia"

The opening to "Ligeia" evokes a Romantic mood of soulful introspection. The narrator conjures up the image of "some large, old, decaying city near the Rhine" where he first met Ligeia. Other details fade into the dim twilight of forgotten memory. An aesthetic mood is created in which color and nostalgia mingle together. It is the atmosphere of Romance which, with its lights and shadows, recalls the novels of Sir Walter Scott. By drawing upon its characteristic features, Poe achieves a similar effect. Everything appears in harmony with the exception of a few touches that, together, sound a discordant note. The narrator begins by confessing, "I cannot, for my soul, remember how, when, or even precisely where, I first became acquainted with the lady Ligeia." Isn't there something odd about this? Doesn't one tend to remember virtually everything, down to the smallest minutiae, connected with a person one loves? If we compare this memory lapse with similar phenomena in other Poe tales, a significant pattern emerges. In "The Black Cat," the narrator suffers a perceptual failure: how did he fail to notice, in the "den of more than infamy" to which he repairs after the death of the first cat, the second cat perched upon "one of the immense hogsheads of Gin, or of Rum"? As in "The Black Cat," a psychological explanation suggests itself in the case of "Ligeia." Indeed, the narrator himself observes: "Or, perhaps, I cannot *now* bring these points to mind, because, in truth, the character of my beloved, her rare learning, her singular yet placid cast of beauty, and the thrilling and enthralling eloquence of her low musical language, made their way into my heart by paces so steadily and stealthily progressive that they have been unnoticed and unknown" (*Coll. W.,* II, 310). A tradition that reaches back to Boethius's *Consolation of Philosophy* had identified wisdom or knowledge (scientia) with a beautiful lady (Lady Philosophy in Boethius's work). In his pursuit of "erudition," Poe might have encountered it. If so, "Ligeia" then represents his adaptation of it to his own purposes.

Hence when the narrator remarks on how Ligeia's features "made their way into my heart by paces so steadily and stealthily progressive that they have been unnoticed and unknown," such a process may be seen as mirroring the growth of his own passionate desire for knowledge, what the Middle Ages had termed the *libido sciendi,* now embodied, in a fashion characteristic of Poe, in an external figure as the woman one loves. Similarly, Hawthorne had depicted the rise in individuals of an obsessive passion. Not infrequently, it assumes the same form of a boundless quest for knowledge. Almost contemporaneously we witness a similar representation in Balzac's *La Recherche de l'absolu.* What distinguishes Poe's treatment of the subject from the others is his use of allegory. But—and this is what separates his use of an allegorical persona from that of the Middle Ages—Poe's "Lady Philosophy" signifies not only wisdom or knowledge but the desire for that knowledge as well. Thus Ligeia embodies, not only the knowledge the narrator craves, but his passion for it as well. For this reason, he can speak of her increasing possession of his soul: what possesses him is not the knowledge he acquires, but the passion that intensifies with each acquisition.

By portraying such passion allegorically, Poe can depict the mind's relationship to its own desire. Desire generates desire: the thirst for knowledge becomes itself the source of yet another passion, one that seeks to possess the first. The literal embodiment of the *libido sciendi* in the beloved makes possible a delineation of this "desire for desire." The narrator affectionately recalls the features of his love:

> In stature she was tall, somewhat slender, and, in her latter days, even emaciated. I would in vain attempt to portray the majesty, the quiet ease, of her demeanor, or the incomprehensible lightness and elasticity of her footfall. She came and departed as a shadow. I was never made aware of her entrance into my closed study save by the dear music of her low sweet voice, as she placed her marble hand upon my shoulder. In beauty of face no maiden ever equalled her. It was the radiance of an opium dream—an airy and spirit-lifting vision more wildly divine than the phantasies which hovered about the slumbering souls of the daughters of Delos. (*Coll. W.,* II, 311)

Here, as elsewhere in the tale, the figure of Ligeia is evoked primarily through the narrator's impressions. The "incomparable lightness and elasticity of her footfall" suggests a spiritual rather than material presence—one that becomes even stronger after her death. The narrator dwells upon "the dear music of her low sweet voice"—as if to imply her communicating through some medium transcending words. Music, of course, corresponds to a faculty of the soul, hence the possibility of a spiritual communion that dispenses with language. Above all, the ethereal quality of Ligeia's presence points to her subjective rather than objective reality.[13] When, later in the tale, the narrator informs us of his resorting to opium, the hint of the hallucinatory nature of his perception of Ligeia is developed. But the visionary atmosphere surrounding even her earlier appearance permits us to infer that what is important here is not the question of the illusory versus the actual but rather the mental or subjective nature of these appearances. Whatever allegorical significance such a figure possesses must accordingly be understood in terms of the mind's relation to itself. What Ligeia represents cannot, in other words, be defined as part of an objective treatment of the subjective.

From the beginning, then, Poe's allegory is radically subjective: not only does the figure of Ligeia signify something subjective, the mind's passion for knowledge; even the existence of the allegory itself originates in a subjective cause, the mind's wish to embody in visible form its own desire. At this stage Poe does not yet conceive of a dialectical engagement between the mind and its allegory. Instead, the relationship remains one between mind and that which its allegory represents, the passion for knowledge. Only indirectly is the pleasure of allegory itself (the pleasure in representation) hinted at. In his recollections, the narrator speaks of the beauty of Ligeia as "the radiance of an opium dream." Such dreams create pleasure not merely through their content but from the dream-state itself. The inducement to dream derives from its "spirit-lifting vision," which the narrator apostrophizes as "more wildly divine than the phantasies which hovered about the slumbering souls of the daughters of Delos."

By means of the visionary consciousness inspired by Ligeia then, the mind approaches a Godlike state. How precisely are we to account, though, for Ligeia's influence? The mind's depiction of its desire for knowledge in an allegorical figure creates the image of beauty. This image captures the essence not only of knowledge but also of the passion for it as well. The beauty of Ligeia is thus the beauty experienced in the dream of an absolute possession of knowledge, in which desire becomes one with its object. Such a condition does not spell the disappearance of that desire but rather its intensification: since knowledge is limitless, desire can only increase with possession. The "wildly divine" aspect of

[13]The following interpretation shares some affinities with G. R. Thompson's account (*Poe's Fiction*, pp. 77–84), but I differ from him in regarding the allegorical element of "Ligeia" not simply as an explanation (of the narrator's delusive madness) but as an independent active force in the relationship between the mind and its desire. For other interpretations of "Ligeia," see Roy P. Basler, "The Interpretation of 'Ligeia,'" *College English*, 5 (1944), 363–72; Clark Griffith, "Poe's 'Ligeia' and the English Romantics," *Univ. of Toronto Quarterly*, 24 (1954), 8–25; and James Schroeter, "A Misreading of Poe's 'Ligeia,'" *PMLA*, 76 (1961), 397–406.

the visionary consciousness inspired by Ligeia thus expresses an infinitude of desire. God is nothing more than infinite consciousness, and the desire for knowledge, carried to its extreme, becomes one form of that consciousness.

Beauty arises from the contemplation of an object; to Ligeia the narrator ascribes simultaneously the "radiance" of an opium dream. If beauty occurs through the perception of something external, radiance (specifically: the radiance of a dream) can only signify the fusion of the mind with that which inspires it, the aura of consciousness produced by possession of that which the mind strives for. In this sense, radiance originates from a source within the mind itself. It describes the feeling of bliss instilled not by the external object but by its representation (such as Ligeia), which remains, all along, within the individual. From this figural expression of its own desire, the mind attains the pleasure, the intoxication of actual possession. By transforming its desire into fantasy, it achieves imaginative fulfillment. As allegory, Ligeia offers both adumbration and realization of the joys of such fulfillment.

We have seen that Poe is not, at this stage, able to conceive of allegory itself as an object of passion or desire. That possibility, and others, were to be explored later. At present what chiefly preoccupies him is the wish to express, through allegory, something like pure beauty. In its sensuousness, such beauty (as in Ligeia) approaches that of external things, or Nature; in other words, allegory here verges upon symbolism. In "Ligeia" Poe offers an elaborate description of the physical appearance of the heroine. It constitutes, in effect, an expression of his aesthetic. What prevents this description from being symbolic in the Romantic sense is that it is not so much the apprehension of something objective but rather, quite self-consciously, the expressive formulation of a subjective ideal. For this reason, it can possess a unique aesthetic appeal, as the objectification of a desire or aspiration (an ideal) rather than the "subjectivization" of an external object or Nature. In the latter case, desire does not and cannot exert a significant role; as already recognized in the late eighteenth century, especially by Rousseau, the actual object elicits an emotion far different from that inspired by one's dreams. If *phantasy* emerges as the name most appropriate for the latter, even the term *imagination* can also, in this pre-Romantic phase, suggest something radically different from the mind's re-creation of external Nature within itself. Specifically, the object conceived by the imagination, the image, carries the quality of something illusory and unreal, not because it errs in reproducing the actual but because it deliberately conforms to the pressures of desire, which seeks its individual "phantasy" rather than the objective or actual. The essence of allegory in pre-Romanticism, then, is desire, but a desire that tends toward the formation of an image in which it mirrors itself.

In "Ligeia" the sensuousness evoked by the image results from its embodiment of that desire. Nevertheless, if subjective in its origin, the allegorical figure aspires to an objective role in its expression of beauty. One must not equate "objective" here with "universal." Poe clearly distinguishes between the claims of a "universal" aesthetic, which imply a definite formal ideal of beauty (such as we find in all classicizing tendencies) and his own aesthetic, which fuses the feeling elicited by a form with that form itself. Thus in the case of Ligeia, her beauty is as much a creation of the narrator's perceptions as of the figure itself. But the two are in fact inseparable: feeling influences form, and the presentation of Ligeia which emerges from Poe's tale is one in which the very form of the beloved expresses aesthetic fulfillment of the mind's desire. Here a certain subjective distance from the object becomes as significant as the identification with it through immediate sensuousness. Thus the narrator speaks of his beloved's "majesty," the "incomprehensible lightness and elasticity of her footfall," her ability to "come and depart as a shadow." Set against the detailed physical description that follows, this evocation of the immateriality or intangibility of Ligeia creates a distinctly double impression (possession and the impossibility of possession) that conforms to the nature of the representation itself.

But the feeling of beauty inspired by Ligeia is not confined to her alone. In his desire to establish its resemblance to the impressions produced by other external objects, the narrator manifests the "universalizing" tendency of Poe's aesthetic, one based not upon the classical appreciation of a particular form but upon the apprehension of an idea or theme within the whole range of natural phenomena. Speaking of the expression of Ligeia's eyes, the narrator can liken its effect to that of other perceptions and impressions:

> And (strange, oh strangest mystery of all!) I found, in the commonest objects of the universe, a circle of analogies to that expression. I mean to say that, subsequently to the period when Ligeia's beauty passed into my spirit, there dwelling as in a shrine, I derived, from many existences in the material world, a sentiment such as I felt always aroused within me by her large and luminous orbs. Yet not the more could I define that sentiment, or analyze, or even steadily view it. I recognized it . . . sometimes in the survey of a rapidly-growing vine—in the contemplation of a moth, a butterfly, a chrysalis, a stream of running water. I have felt it in the ocean; in the falling of a meteor. (*Coll. W.*, II, 314)

By tracing the analogy that pervades both individual subjectivity and the universalism of external Nature, the narrator approaches the Romantic concept of symbolism from another perspective. For Poe, the revelation vouchsafed by these natural phenomena is not—as for Coleridge—unmediated experience of the divine essence, but rather an idea, whose association with the traditional theme of mutability has been rightly identified by Mabbott (Poe, *Coll. W.*, II, 332, n. 12). At the same time, these phenomena also suggest something more—the presence of a will that seeks to overcome the natural cycle. In the ocean and the falling of a meteor, we find its energy projected onto a cosmic scale.

What is significant above all, however, is Poe's attempt to capture and render the beauty of his idea or theme. It accounts for the special quality of his prose in this passage, which seeks to adumbrate what it cannot precisely define. Do we not find an anticipation here of Pater's celebrated account of Leonardo's *Mona Lisa* from *The Renaissance*, with its "presence that rose thus so strangely beside the waters," "expressive of what in the ways of a thousand years men had come to desire"? But if it looks forward to Pater, Poe's reverie also recalls, quite clearly, that of Wordsworth:

> And I have felt
> A presence that disturbs me with the joy
> Of elevated thoughts; a sense sublime
> Of something far more deeply interfused,
> Whose dwelling is the light of setting suns,
> And the round ocean and the living air,
> And the blue sky, and in the mind of man:
> A motion and a spirit, that impels
> All thinking things, all objects of all thought,
> And rolls through all things. (*P.W.*, II, 261–62)

To which Poe himself, under the guise of Glanvill, can add: "Who knoweth the mysteries of the will, with its vigor? For God is but a great will pervading all things by nature of its intentness" (*Coll. W.*, II, 314).

Here, however, Poe's concern is not with the relation of spirit to matter, which he formulates elsewhere, but with the aesthetic possibilities contained in the expression of a theme. We have seen how, in "Ligeia," will assumes the specific form of the *libido sciendi*, the passion for knowledge. By embodying this passion in Ligeia, Poe manages to depict its life cycle or biology. From this perspective, the narrator's efforts after Ligeia's death to find solace in renovating an ancient English abbey are to be understood not with reference to magic but as an attempt to relinquish the quest for knowledge in favor of the pleasures of aestheticism (hence the long descriptions of the abbey décor, in which Poe seizes the opportunity to set forth his views on interior decoration). The reawakening of the intellectual or "scientific" passion in the narrator, dramatized by the revival of Ligeia under the guise of Rowena, is significant above all not for what it asserts about the will but for what it implies concerning the nature of allegory and its relation to the mind that creates it. For this reason Poe's letter to Philip Pendleton Cooke (Sept. 21, 1839) is of the highest importance. In it, touching "Ligeia," he writes: "The *gradual* perception of the fact that Ligeia lives again in the person of Rowena is a far loftier and more thrilling idea than the one I have embodied. It offers, in my opinion, the widest possible scope to the imagination—it might be rendered even sublime" (*Letters*, I, 118). If the life and death of Ligeia may be taken to represent, so to speak, the life and death of allegory within the mind, Poe's emphasis upon the narrator's perception of the allegory reveals his preoccupation with its aesthetic expressiveness. The cyclical pattern of revivification and collapse, with its progressively increasing vitalism, was to have accompanied, apparently, an increasing consciousness of the allegory and its significance. Even here, nevertheless, as appears from Poe's letter, the mind is not permitted to attain awareness of its own psychological relationship to its allegory. Such awareness becomes apparent only with the later development of Poe's own highly personal allegorical mode, a development that brings him in turn closer to Romantic symbolism.

## "The Black Cat"

In the tales of his later years we witness a change in Poe's allegorical manner—one that appears to correspond with a renewed and deeper exploration of the nature of allegory itself. Gone are both the purely sensuous or aesthetic lure of allegory—as in "Ligeia"—and the intellectual attractions of a strict formal schema of correspondences, as in "William Wilson." Here, to be sure, appreciation of the ingenuity manifested in the schema itself had counted for much in the aesthetic evaluation of the composition. In his later tales, by contrast, Poe seems willing to allow the allegory to unfold itself more naturally, exploring its own nature in the very process of unfolding. This more "natural" development reflects the increasingly pervasive psychologizing tendency of Poe's mature thought, one that leads him to view allegory less as a formal literary schema than as a mode of expression whose bases inhere in the faculties of the mind itself. In some respects, historically speaking, such a development could easily assume the appearance of a backward step, from the Romantic passions of Poe's youth to a neoclassical preoccupation with faculty psychology and the aesthetics of effect rather than the Romantic poetics of symbolism. From a higher perspective, however, this shift becomes comprehensible as part of Poe's deepening exploration of the nature of the self, on the one hand, and of the relation between matter and spirit, which is also that of subjective to objective.

Hence Poe's later allegory, in spite of its psychological coloring, does not so much anticipate Freudian notions of dream-condensation, symbolism, or repression; what it offers instead is a depiction of the mind engaged in a process of self-discovery in which the medium of allegory becomes itself an object of conflicting desires as it mirrors and then absorbs the self's diverse passions. Thus in this later phase allegory is no longer "innocent": by assimilating desire, allegory becomes charged with its energy, whence its efficacy as both instrument and obstacle for a mind that seeks simultaneously to expose and conceal the deeper recesses of its nature.

These contradictory motives may serve to explain in part the various reversals that govern the plot of "The Black Cat." The allegorical significance of the cat is explained by an earlier prose piece of Poe's: "Instinct Versus Reason—A Black Cat." Speaking of the differences between man and the lower creatures, Poe observes: "The line which demarcates the instinct of the brute creation from the boasted reason of man, is, beyond doubt, of the most shadowy and unsatisfactory character—a boundary line far more difficult to settle than even the North-Eastern or the Oregon. The question whether the lower animals do or do not reason, will possibly never be decided—certainly never in our present condition of knowledge. While the self-love and arrogance of man will persist in denying the reflective power to beasts, because the granting it seems to derogate from his own vaunted supremacy, he yet perpetually finds himself involved in the paradox of decrying instinct as an inferior faculty, while he is forced to admit its infinite superiority, in a thousand cases, over the very reason which he claims exclusively as his own" (*Coll. W.*, II, 478).

As in the later *Eureka*, the term *shadowy* possesses a special resonance here. For Poe it invariably connotes a relationship between the material and spiritual spheres, and the progressive continuum or scale through which we pass, by imperceptible degrees, from one to the other. Hence the merely quantitative, rather than absolute, boundary between instinct and reason, which also explains how the one can allegorically represent the other. The superiority of instinct to reason, Poe goes on to say, results from the direct or immediate influence of the divine power upon the former. With reason, on the other hand, some inner resistance appears to render such influence impossible. At a later stage, the complex feelings that govern its response to divine influence will also be seen to determine the mind's attitude toward the imaginative medium in which it embodies its own self-knowledge: allegory.

The prologue to "The Black Cat" begins by portraying the very relationship between the protagonist and what he sees as problematic: "For the most wild, yet most homely narrative which I am about to pen, I neither expect nor solicit belief. Mad indeed would I be to expect it, in a case where my very senses reject their own evidence" (*Coll. W.*, III, 849). To be sure, the claim that the senses "reject their own evidence" is hardly ingenuous. In actuality, the mind that rejects such evidence attempts to impute the unreliability of this evidence to some intrinsic property. The will to disbelieve, which is operative here, thus establishes from the outset a tension between the mind and what it purports to represent. But repression of knowledge forces that knowledge to assume an indirect form—such as allegory. A second attempt to repress occurs when the narrative "I" seeks to raise the question of illusion versus reality: "Yet, mad am I not—and very surely do I not dream." For Hawthorne (as in *The Blithedale Romance*) the essence of dreams consists of anxiety and wish-fulfillment (desire). By contrast, Poe employs dreams primarily to suggest poetic illusion (with the possibility of visionary realization) or a conflict between natural and supernatural where the supernatural element brings into question the nature and limits of our knowledge of the world and of self. His repeated quotation of Novalis's aphorism "When we dream that we dream, we are close to waking" (from the *Blüthenstaub*) bears upon this theme, as does Shelley's notion of a spectral self in *Epipsychidion* and *The Triumph of Life*. Perhaps one might also add Nerval's dictum: "The dream is a second life" (from *Aurélia*, in *Oeuvres*, I, 359).

In effect, however, the introduction of dreams and madness is misplaced—deliberately so, since it enables the mind or I to obscure the true matter at issue. Thus we may say: no, he is not mad, neither is he dreaming (taking dreams to refer to the illusion-reality opposition). But such admissions are not really to the point. They fail to touch upon what the questions themselves suppress: the self-knowledge embodied in the events about to be described by the "I." Nevertheless, the presence of such self-knowledge does not engender an ironic perspective (irony in terms of Friedrich Schlegel's Romantic conception: "clear consciousness of the eternal Agility, of the infinitely abundant chaos"). Since the "I" or self creates the allegory by which it is to be understood, it possesses a certain complicity in its own self-delusion. The narrator's next utterance manifests it: "Hereafter, perhaps, some intellect may be found which will reduce my phantasm to the common-place—some intellect more calm, more logical, and far less excitable than my own, which will perceive, in the circumstances I detail with awe, nothing more than an ordinary succession of very natural causes and effects" (*Coll. W.*, III, 850). To reduce a series of events to a succession of causes and effects—for Poe, this is to affirm the triumph of reason over chance (responding, perhaps, to Hume's attack on the analysis of causation). Causation, Hume would have maintained, does not really inhere in the events themselves—all the more justification, then, according to Poe, for celebrating a faculty that imposes order upon randomness, creating a rational structure out of the chaos of mere existence.

Here, however, what actually transpires is not the subjection of chance to reason but a tale of the mind's attempt to resist and ultimately destroy that reason. Its appeal to "some intellect more calm, more logical" than its own accordingly possesses something of the force of Baudelaire's peroration: "Hypocrite lecteur, —mon semblable, —mon frère!" In its allegory it embodies the reason to which it now appeals. By asking another to find rational order within its allegory, it asks that other in effect to find reason in its own attempt to destroy reason—an attempt that, the "I" implies, is not merely individual and subjective but based upon a universal human impulse.

The narrator's desire for an animal or pet during his childhood poses an apparent contradiction, since it is allegedly his "tenderness of heart" that inspires such a wish. The conflict between head and heart, reason and feeling, is thus alluded to at the outset, but in such a fashion as to suggest that feeling or sensibility actually fosters the passion for reason. Moreover, the allegorical figure for reason is not a superior human being—as in "Ligeia"—but an animal, a creature supposedly devoid of reason.

These difficulties for the allegorical scheme merely intensify the mind's desire to express its meaning allegorically: the author insists that his favorite pet, a cat, was "a remarkably large and beautiful animal, entirely black, and sagacious to an astonishing degree" (*Coll. W.*, III, 850). We may recall the description of Ligeia, of whom, as allegorical figure, the cat represents the equivalent. By transforming the traditional allegorical figure for wisdom into a cat, the narrator distances himself, as it were, from the significance of his own allegory. As the allegorical figure for wisdom or knowledge par excellence, like Boethius's Lady Philosophy, Ligeia's immediate sensuous appeal for the narrator is but an allegorization of his own *libido sciendi*. But if Ligeia's beauty virtually compels the narrator's admiration and his absorption in her (such that he wishes even the death of the later Rowena), absorption in the allegorical dream of possession, what the substitution of the cat permits is a fundamental ambivalence toward the object of desire: as creature, the cat is at once something more, and something less, than man. In this regard, the otherwise inexplicable remark of the narrator's wife, comparing the cat to a witch, a remark the narrator dwells upon with some emphasis, may be seen as an allusion to the animal's relation to the supernatural—hence to a power higher than man.

As a result of his descent into alcoholism (that is, loss of self-control or reason), the narrator's attitude toward the cat progressively deteriorates to the point of violence:

One night, returning home, much intoxicated, from one of my haunts about town, I fancied that the cat avoided my presence. I seized him; when, in his fright at my violence, he inflicted a slight wound upon my hand with his teeth. The fury of a demon instantly possessed me. I knew myself no longer. My original soul seemed, at once, to take its flight from my body; and a more than fiendish malevolence, gin-nurtured, thrilled every fibre of my frame. I took from my waistcoat-pocket a pen-knife, opened it, grasped the poor beast by the throat, and deliberately cut one of its eyes from the socket! I blush, I burn, I shudder, while I pen the damnable atrocity. (*Coll. W.*, III, 851)

In the cat's avoidance of the narrator's presence Poe depicts reason's flight from uncontrollable frenzy or obsession. Significantly, the "I" refuses to accept this departure. Instead, it impulsively attempts to possess reason even as, by its own actions, it repels it. This desire for "possession" of reason constitutes but another form of the libidinal impulse. Such possession could only signify the dissolution of reason in irrational passion, whose nature demands transformation of the object of desire into the element of desire itself. At this point the allegory becomes self-reflexive: not only the opposition of reason to irrational passion (may we read the "wound" which the cat inflicts as one of conscience? hence the "fury" of the "I" which, oblivious to all else, still retains a trace of moral sensibility) but also the internal resistance of the allegory to banishment by the mind. "Internal," insofar as the source of this resistance lies within the mind's own fascination with the allegorical image it creates and, ultimately, the possibilities of self-representation.

For these reasons, the allegorical figure (the cat) cannot be simply eliminated. Its presence, on the other hand, imposes a check upon the irrational passions. On these reason sheds the clear light of self-consciousness. By cutting out one of the cat's eyes, the narrator seeks ineffectively to deprive reason of its insight into the mind's inner nature. In this context, it is revealing that the narrator should remove but one eye: to cut out both would be to impose mental blindness. Such blindness is equivalent to elimination of the allegorical figure. And that is precisely what the narrator (the mind) cannot bring itself to accomplish.

Its violence remains, then, on the allegorical level: it gouges out one of the eyes of a creature that is itself but an allegorical presence. Yet on another level this violence is real. For if the cat represents the mind's rational faculty, to seek to harm it is to practice violence upon oneself. And this is what the mind desires. "A more than fiendish malevolence," the narrator confesses, "thrilled every fibre of my frame": "more than fiendish" because of its self-destructive, masochistic impulse. To lose one's sanity completely, to unleash the subliminal passions from the controlling constraints of reason, exerts the same fascination as the temptation of falling into an abyss. But the mind can express its self-destructive impulse only if its object is embodied in some tangible form. The fascination of allegory derives from the possibility it offers of satisfying such impulses. This fascination compels the mind not only to want to "possess" but in some sense also to destroy its allegory of itself, when it becomes conscious of the allegorical figure (the black cat) *as* allegory. At that moment, the mind realizes that what it seeks to destroy exists in reality only within itself.

In impelling the mind into a self-reflexive stance through the medium of allegory, Poe departs from the Romantic attitude toward the latter, but in such a way as to manifest, simultaneously, similar underlying tendencies. We have seen how his attitude toward allegory had been shaped by neoclassical preconceptions. By formulating the mind's relation to itself, or self-consciousness, in terms of allegory, Poe ultimately strives for an end similar to that of Romanticism: the dream of an unmediated knowledge of self. At first glance, allegory, by its very nature, could not but seem ill suited for such a purpose. In essence, it depends upon an objective view of the world in which the arbitrariness of specific correspondences is redeemed in advance by a prevailing harmony informing the collective world-view. In "The Black Cat" Poe reverses these conditions: an intensely subjective or individual perspective pervades the allegory, but simultaneously the correspondences between allegorical figure and significance are no longer arbitrary but instead highly charged with meanings other than those designed to be conveyed by the correspondences themselves. What Poe appears to recognize at this stage is that only by turning allegory back upon its source in the mind itself can it be made to yield genuine knowledge. Such knowledge proceeds not so much from what the allegory signifies (the black cat as representing reason) but rather from the mind's emotional engagement with allegory itself.

Already in his earlier years, with "William Wilson" and "Ligeia," Poe had demonstrated his insight into allegory not merely as formal device but as the expression of a certain frame of mind. In both tales, but in "William Wilson" especially, the impenetrability or opacity of the allegory to the mind within the tale (for instance, the knowledge that William Wilson's "double" represents his conscience) allows for significant self-revelation. Only with the later tales does the allegory become transparent to the mind or "I" within the tale. This increased consciousness permits in turn a formal awareness of the allegorical object itself not possible in the earlier stories. Such consciousness also exposes more clearly the difficulty of attaining an unmediated relation to the self. By giving sensuous embodiment to the faculty of reason through the image of the black cat, the mind achieves greater clarity with regard to its own emotions and desires. In recognizing the cat as an allegory of its own reason, it perceives such emotions as only ostensibly directed toward an external creature. Its acceptance of these (fascination and the self-destructive wish) enables it to achieve a catharsis in which it "loses" itself and hence the burden of self-consciousness. But, inasmuch as the allegory disappears only to be renewed (that is, in the appearance of the second cat), Poe's purpose can ultimately be seen to consist of self-revelation. As such, his motive corresponds, on the subjective level, with the Romantic desire for what Coleridge terms an apprehension of "the Eternal in and through the Temporal." Instead of turning to Nature, however, the mind's gaze is focused inward, upon itself. The similarity that binds the two tendencies together occurs in their common apocalyptic moment, with its experience of an intensified or heightened consciousness resulting from revelation.

Through the illumination that ensues, the narrator can observe:

> Yet I am not more sure that my soul lives, than I am that perverseness is one of the primitive impulses of the human heart—one of the indivisible primary faculties, or sentiments, which give direction to the character of Man. . . . Have we not a perpetual inclination, in the teeth of our best judgment, to violate that which is *Law,* merely because we understand it to be such? This spirit of perverseness, I say, came to my final overthrow. It was this unfathomable longing of the soul *to vex itself*—to offer violence to its own nature—to do wrong for wrong's sake only—that urged me to continue and finally to consummate the injury I had inflicted upon the unoffending brute (*Coll. W.*, III, 852)

The "Law" that perverseness attempts to violate is not that which defines human justice; it approximates rather the eighteenth-century concept of natural law. In *The Friend* Coleridge had characterized Law as that which "in its absolute perfection, is conceivable only of the Supreme Being, whose creative IDEA not only appoints to each thing its *position,* but in that position, and in consequence of that position, gives it its qualities, yea, it gives it its very existence, as *that particular* thing. . . . As such, therefore, and as the sufficient cause of the reality correspondent thereto, we contemplate it as exclusively an attribute of the Supreme Being, inseparable from the idea of God . . . " (*Coll. W.*, IV:1, 458–59).

To seek to "violate that which is *Law*" amounts, then, to defiance of God. Perhaps for this reason the narrator can admit that in killing the cat he knew "that in so doing I was committing a sin—a deadly sin that would so jeopardize my immortal soul as to place it—if such a thing were possible—even beyond the reach of the infinite mercy of the Most Merciful and Most Terrible God" (*Coll. W.*, III, 852). His sin consists not merely of attempting to destroy himself (in other words, his faculty of reason, that which endows him with his place and existence within the scale of being), but, through such self-destruction, to obliterate the "IDEA" that had given it existence, an Idea whose life inheres in God himself. But, precisely because its disappearance would imply the mind's own, the cat does not and cannot really disappear. Its persistence reflects that of the rational impulse within the mind; hence the sudden and mysterious appearance of the second cat after the death of the first.

As perduring as the allegorical impulse itself, on the other hand, is that which the narrator terms "the unfathomable longing of the soul *to vex itself.*" To speak of an "unfathomable longing" here evokes the feeling of the Romantic aspiration for the infinite, the absolute. Perhaps, in some sense, the soul's desire can be seen as precisely that: an urge to destroy itself, to pass beyond the limits of its proper being, hence to achieve some form of negative transcendence. Moreover, in vexing itself the soul specifically opposes its innate rational tendencies. Its rebellion against the rational signifies the mind's desire to break free of limits imposed from within by reason itself.

The killing of the first cat fulfills, at least temporarily, this aim. But crime engenders guilt. In the allegorical logic of Poe's tale, the feeling of guilt results in a psychological magnification of the cat's image, which, through a somewhat fortuitous train of circumstances, appears in enlarged form upon a plaster wall of the narrator's house after a fire. Correspondingly, the embedding of the image in the wall connotes the "impression" of the crime upon the mind. As in "The Haunted Palace" or "The Fall of the House of Usher," the house itself typifies the mind. Its burning may accordingly be equated with the consuming of the mind by irrational passions after the loss of reason (the death of the cat). The appearance of a second cat now fills the lacuna formed by the death of the first. "Fully as large as Pluto, and closely resembling him in every respect but one," it carries upon its breast a mysterious white spot, the significance of which is subsequently made clear:

> The reader will remember that this mark, although large, had been originally very indefinite; but, by slow degrees—degrees nearly imperceptible, and which for a long time my Reason struggled to reject as fanciful—it had, at length, assumed a rigorous distinctness of outline. It was now the representation of an object that I shudder to name—and for this, above all, I loathed, and dreaded, and would have rid myself of the monster *had I dared*—it was now, I say, the image of a hideous—of a ghastly thing—of the GALLOWS!—oh, mournful and terrible engine of Horror and of Crime—of Agony and of Death! (*Coll. W.*, III, 855)

Ironically, it is reason that "for a long time . . . struggled to reject as fanciful" what the narrator perceives. In allegorical terms: reason refuses to accept the existence of those irrational impulses that seek to destroy it. At the same time, there is a fascination in contemplating what one refuses to acknowledge. Only by such continuous contemplation could the indefinite white spot be made to resolve itself into the clarity of a specific image. This fascination is accompanied by fear of naming the object. Instead, the mind remains absorbed in representation. Such absorption can explain the impulse that compels it to create an allegory of itself. In so doing it experiences the allure of that self-knowledge it both shuns and attempts to obscure. Its fascination with allegory proceeds from this simultaneous attraction and repulsion when confronted by the allegorical expression of its own self-knowledge. Representation, as the power that both reveals and suspends revelation by transposing it into another form, thus absorbs and assimilates the mind's psychic energies. In so doing, it becomes itself a medium for those energies.

Here we might pause to consider Poe's insight into the self-reflexive possibilities of allegory from a historical perspective. The problem posed for allegory by the Romantic desire for fusion between subjective and objective occurs only when allegory is seen as failing to achieve such fusion, which would necessitate identification of the figure with its significance, in order to make possible the immediate apprehension of that significance. But what if the objective were to be created within the subjective? To be sure, the motives that impel Poe to such a course have little or nothing to do with the idealism of Berkeley. As little, perhaps, as with the transcendental idealism of a Fichte or Schelling. The objective arises in Poe through the intuition that whatever the mind erects as an obstacle to its own self-reflection becomes an object, something opaque that resists the desire to penetrate it, hence a focus of psychic energies. But since this object (that is to say, the allegory) arises within the mind itself, its essence is necessarily the same as the mind's own. "Identification" thus takes place, but of a sort differing from that envisaged by Coleridge or Schelling. In "The Black Cat" the identification between the "I" and the second cat is one not of knowledge but desire: the appearance of the cat manifests the mind's desire to affirm its crime (its attempt to destroy its faculty of reason) while simultaneously deferring that desire into representation. From this standpoint we perceive how charged "representation" is for Poe. It constitutes an objectification of desire, but one that does not preclude the possibility of identification—what it creates is, rather, a medium through which the mind both expresses and obscures its own volition.

For the later Poe, then, allegory no longer functions as either an objective representation of the world nor (as in his earlier phase) an objective representation of the mind. Now the objectifying process itself becomes the essence of allegory, whose significance must be understood not only in terms of its content but also of the interaction between allegory and the mind that confers an objective quality upon it.

Nowhere perhaps are the tensions aroused by such a relationship more apparent than in the conflict between reason and feeling, head and heart, to which the allegory gives rise:

> And now was I indeed wretched beyond the wretchedness of mere Humanity. And *a brute beast*—whose fellow I had contemptuously destroyed—*a brute beast* to work out for *me*—for me a man, fashioned in the image of the High God—so much of insufferable wo! Alas! neither by day nor by

night knew I the blessing of Rest any more! During the former the creature
left me no moment alone; and, in the latter, I started, hourly, from dreams
of unutterable fear, to find the hot breath of *the thing* upon my face, and its
vast weight—an incarnate Night-Mare that I had no power to shake off—
incumbent eternally upon my *heart!* (*Coll. W.*, III, 856)

Here, by transposing the terms of his opposition into allegory, Poe imparts an ironic twist to his narrative. A Christian tradition extending
back to the Church Fathers had defined man's likeness to God as one of
mind: through the faculty of reason, man is enabled to rise over all other
material creatures. In the present instance, however, it is the cat, rather
than the "I," that represents the rational faculty. The roles are reversed:
instead of being tormented, the cat (the reason) now torments the "I,"
which assumes the role of "the heart" or feeling. As a result, reason,
instead of calming the mind, now drives it to the brink of madness.

But if the cat is merely an allegorical projection, its tormenting of the
mind only embodies the latter's own self-destructive wish. That wish
attains new proportions as the "I" magnifies the menace of the cat,
transforming it from an individual creature into "*the thing.*" The mind
now feels its helplessness in the face of that which it can no longer keep
at a distance through allegory: "an incarnate Night-Mare that I had no
power to shake off." What it fears above all is loss of self, that is, loss of
self-control to the daemonic force it has unleashed. As a last attempt to
resist the latter's encroachment, the narrator walls up the cat, along with
his murdered wife. But the cry of the entombed cat, "at first muffled
and broken, like the sobbing of a child, and then quickly swelling into
one long, loud, and continuous scream, utterly anomalous and inhu-
man—a howl—a wailing shriek, half of horror and half of triumph," is
in fact that of the "I" itself. Its note of sadness—the sobbing or wailing
quality—is its mourning over its loss of self. It begins by returning to
childhood through memory, to the experience of pain (hence the sobbing) as its first awakening to consciousness, then progressively becomes
dehumanized as the "I" ceases to be the true self—as it succumbs to the
reason it has sought to destroy.

In a curious fashion, the narrator's final confession—"I had walled
the monster up within the tomb!"—links this tale to earlier compositions
such as "The Fall of the House of Usher," with its motif of entombment
of a living creature (Roderick's sister Madeline) and its suggestion of
psychological repression. Here the entombment of the cat depicts reason
as the repressed force of the psyche: its irruption at the end signifies a
reversal, with the narrative "I" now marked out for destruction. The
reversal illuminates, as well as anything else, the psychological essence of
Poe's later allegory: in the soul's subjective drama, the figural ceases to
connote external reality, but assumes a life of its own within the confines
of the mind.

# 2 *Hawthorne*

## The Imaginary and the Real

In his preface to *The Snow-Image, and Other Twice-told Tales* Hawthorne remarks: "In youth, men are apt to write more wisely than they really know or feel; and the remainder of life may be not idly spent in realizing and convincing themselves of the wisdom which they uttered long ago. The truth that was only in the fancy then may have since become a substance in the mind and heart" (Centenary, xi, 6). This remark might be applied to an aspect of Hawthorne's own development, the shift in his works from allegory to a certain form of symbolism. This shift is, to be sure, only a gradual one, nor does Hawthorne ever distinguish in a conscious and explicit fashion between allegory and symbolism. His renunciation of the one and adoption of the other is in fact characterized by numerous regressions and hesitations. But beneath all the surface uncertainties, like one of those voices of the mind issuing forth to silent light which Wordsworth had described in the concluding book of *The Prelude,* an intuition that is at first only dim and faint comes to manifest itself with increasing clearness until, in Hawthorne's final works, it achieves at last a definitive clarity. We may perhaps best describe this intuition as a consciousness or recognition of the spiritual and even magical quality of the actual. It would be a mistake to associate it with the symbolism of a Goethe, or a Schelling or Coleridge, no less than with that of an Emerson. In Hawthorne the actual does not merely serve as a form of the Temporal through which the Eternal can shine forth in infinite splendor. Instead, the realm of the actual, of the here and now, possesses itself a kind of spiritual iridescence.[1] That is why all the attempts to establish a connection between Hawthorne's symbolism and that of Transcendentalism must ultimately break down.[2] In "The Hall of Fantasy," contemplating the prospect of a final holocaust that would consume the world, the narrator says: "What I should chiefly regret in her destruction would be that very earthliness, which no other sphere or state of existence can renew or compensate. The fragrance of flowers, and of new-mown hay; the genial warmth of sunshine, and the beauty of

---

[1] Cf. Nina Baym, *The Shape of Hawthorne's Career* (Ithaca, N.Y.: Cornell Univ. Press, 1976), pp. 49–50.

[2] Cf. Baym, p. 10, and Hyatt H. Waggoner, *Hawthorne: A Critical Study,* rev. ed. (Cambridge: Harvard Univ. Press, 1963), pp. 15–16, 30–31.

39

a sunset among clouds; the comfort and cheerful glow of the fireside; the deliciousness of fruits, and of all good cheer; the magnificence of mountains, and seas, and cataracts, and the softer charm of rural scenery; even the fast-falling snow, and the gray atmosphere through which it descends—all these, and innumerable other enjoyable things of earth, must perish with her" (Centenary, x, 183–84).

Hawthorne did not immediately arrive, however, at a perception of how such an intuition might be translated into literature. This was a process that would in fact require several decades. Only in his final works—*The Marble Faun* and his unfinished romances—does it at last achieve its consummation. We witness the image of this process in that development through which he passes from allegorical constructions to a more symbolic form of expression.[3]

These differing forms are, to be sure, never clearly distinguished in Hawthorne; the difference between them resolves itself into one of degree rather than of essence. To some extent, all the diverse phenomena of life are capable of being converted into allegorical significance. But this phenomenal surface also possesses a symbolic radiance. Thus both allegory and symbolism in Hawthorne can be seen to draw upon a common source. But in allegory all the splendor of phenomena must in some measure cease to shine forth as a thing in itself—such phenomena exist merely to signify the truths of a higher reality.

From the first, literature represents for Hawthorne a medium through which such higher truths can be expressed. It is significant that both he and Poe should have reserved their highest admiration for Shelley, but for entirely different reasons. Witnessing the conflagration that consumes all the productions of the human imagination—a conflagration that is at the same time a trial-by-fire of the world's literature—the narrator of "Earth's Holocaust" observes: "methought Shelley's poetry emitted a purer light than almost any other productions of his day; contrasting beautifully with the fitful and lurid gleams, and gushes of black vapor, that flashed and eddied from the volumes of Lord Byron" (Centenary, x, 397). This "purer light" symbolizes a quality that we may designate ideality. For Poe, Shelley is the poet of a "supernal Loveliness," a beauty of which it is possible on earth to obtain only brief and fleeting glimpses. For Hawthorne, Shelley meant something else: the celebrator of an ideal realm, in which all the dross of earthly things has

---

[3]In this light Hawthorne's own later remarks on *Mosses* must be judged significant: "Upon my honor, I am not quite sure that I entirely comprehend my own meaning, in some of those blasted allegories; but I remember that I always had a meaning, or at least thought I had. I am a good deal changed since those times; and, to tell you the truth, my past self is not very much to my taste, as I see myself in this book. Yet certainly there is more in it than the public generally gave me credit for at the time it was written" (letter to Fields, April 13, 1854, from James T. Fields, *Yesterdays with Authors* [Boston: Osgood, 1872], p. 75).

been purged away in order for this higher reality to manifest itself in a luminous and dazzling clearness. Here we find the spiritual or ideal contrasted and opposed to the actual. This opposition is characteristic of the early Hawthorne: the ideal manifests itself at the expense of the real, and conversely. From such a standpoint he could profess an admiration for Southey and, among his own American contemporaries, Jones Very. We know that he was attracted to the resplendent realm of celestial palaces that forms the poetic world of *The Curse of Kehama*. A similar affinity appears to draw him toward the transfiguring mysticism of Jones Very. In sum: a visionary Romanticism, in which the ideal is exalted over the real, a pattern that could not but correspond in Hawthorne to a highly conscious form of allegorical expression. Such allegory had always consisted, for Hawthorne, of something more than bloodless abstractions or illusory appearances. Almost invariably, the source of this allegory is in fact the world of actual phenomena and occurrences. It becomes the purpose of literature to represent these in such a fashion as to elicit from them a higher, allegorical significance.

At a later stage, this visionary or ideal Romanticism is in turn replaced by a form of symbolism that associates itself most closely with the concept of a coloration imposed upon the external world by the subjective self, a concept Hawthorne was to derive in part from Mme de Staël, and which appears in Benjamin Constant as well. Only as a result of a new psychological understanding of symbolism (exemplified in *The Scarlet Letter*) does it become possible for Hawthorne to embrace such a concept. Yet even it must yield to another: the intuition of a spiritual radiance in the phenomenal surface of the real world, one that comes to it not on account of the presence of the divine essence within it (pantheism) but simply in virtue of what it is in itself.

Through this natural symbolism, what had initially manifested itself only in an allegorical dress is now represented as concrete and living reality. The "truth that was only in the fancy" indeed becomes "a substance in the mind and heart." It would be a mistake, nevertheless, to see in this reality merely an expression of that tendency which later finds fulfillment in "realism."[4] For the reality of *The Marble Faun* and the unfinished romances is something both natural and supernatural at the same time. It represents, in effect, the consummation of a development that begins with European Romanticism: a vision of fusion between the ideal and the actual, the spiritual and the real. This vision represents something different from anything Romanticism had to offer, just as it would have been impossible without Romanticism. But the final development of Hawthorne's symbolism differs not only from that of Roman-

[4]Cf. Richard Brodhead, *Hawthorne, Melville, and the Novel* (Chicago: Univ. of Chicago Press, 1976), p. 4.

ticism, but equally from that of an Emerson or a Melville. It constitutes part of his contribution to what the French critic Charles du Bos liked to call "spirituality" in literature.

## "Rappaccini's Daughter"

We know that both Hawthorne and his wife were familiar with Mme de Staël's *Corinne* from their youth. It is possible to surmise something of what this novel must have meant to them from the fact, recorded in Hawthorne's French and Italian Notebooks, that one of their first visits on arriving in the Eternal City was to the Trevi Fountain, in order to find out whether it was actually possible for Corinne to see Lord Nelvil's reflection in its waters.[5] Later in the course of the same novel, it becomes necessary at one point for the heroine and Lord Nelvil to leave Rome in order to avoid the pestilential air that habitually infects the city during summer. Of the effects of this atmosphere upon the city itself, the author observes: "The foul air is the scourge of the inhabitants of Rome, and menaces the city with entire depopulation, but it adds perhaps more to the effect produced by the superb gardens that one sees in the precinct of Rome. The malign influence does not make itself felt by any exterior sign; you breathe an air which seems pure and which is quite agreeable; the earth is smiling and fertile; a delicious freshness reposes you during the night from the burning heats of the day; and all this is death!" (*O.C.*, VIII, 179–80).

In this passage it is possible to discern one of the buds that unfolds in "Rappaccini's Daughter." The garden of Rappaccini is said to represent "an Eden of poisonous flowers" (Centenary, X, 115). Displaying a brilliant array of colors, these flowers exhale an ethereal and deadly fragrance whose first impression on the senses is nevertheless one of almost imperceptible sweetness. Such a setting, charged as it is with symbolic overtones, remains firmly grounded in the realm of the actual. The impulse toward a greater realism even in allegory begins to manifest itself at this stage of Hawthorne's development. Nor is it the only impulse.

Equally apparent is the existence of what we may describe as illusory allegorical appearances. Perhaps the most striking of these is Rappaccini's garden, which the young Giovanni at first takes for an "Eden of the present world," but which turns out in actuality to contain the most deadly and poisonous flowers. No less illusory is the figure of Beatrice herself, who in spite of her lethal influence on the forms of life around

---

[5]Centenary, XIV, 180. On Hawthorne and Mme de Staël, see Jane Lundblad, *Nathaniel Hawthorne and European Literary Tradition* (Upsala: Lundequistska, 1947), pp. 150–65.

her retains the moral purity of a virgin soul. Her status is further complicated by her possible relationship to Keats's Lamia. The deceptive
nature of allegorical or symbolic appearances is made possible by the
necessity of their filtration through the perceiving consciousness. The
ambiguities inherent in perception itself thus become one of the themes
of the story. In gazing down from his window upon Beatrice as she
embraces one of the garden's flowering bushes, Giovanni rubs his eyes in
uncertainty as he begins to doubt "whether it were a girl tending her
favorite flower, or one sister performing the duties of affection to another" (Centenary, x, 98). And Beatrice herself can only add to this
ambiguity when she tells him: "Believe nothing of me save what you see
with your own eyes."[6]

To the misapprehensions that arise through confused and erroneous
perceptions we must add the "interpretation" necessarily imposed upon
all symbolic appearances by the subjective consciousness through which
they pass. Hawthorne here touches upon an insight that receives its
fullest development only with *The Scarlet Letter*—the realization that all
symbolic appearances can only possess a relative rather than absolute
significance, insofar as this significance consists of an interpretation of
the external world by an individual consciousness. In *The Scarlet Letter,* as
we shall see later, this "relativity" of symbolism becomes itself the only
absolute. All higher significances must be engendered within the subjective consciousness, rising from its depths in moments of insight or intuition. As Kierkegaard, in his *Concluding Unscientific Postscript,* asserts,
"Truth is Subjectivity."

In "Rappaccini's Daughter" the whole problem of subjectivity as a
barrier to the apprehension of higher symbolic truths is surmounted
from a higher perspective. Speaking from this standpoint, Hawthorne
can say: "There is something truer and more real, than what we can see
with the eyes, and touch with the finger. On such better evidence, had
Giovanni founded his confidence in Beatrice, though rather by the necessary force of her high attributes, than by any deep and generous faith,
on his part" (Centenary, x, 120).

But what could be "truer and more real, than what we can see with the
eyes, and touch with the finger"? A realm of the spirit, in which all

---

[6]Perhaps the general problem of interpretive ambiguities experienced by commentators
on "Rappaccini's Daughter" derives from Hawthorne's own uncertainties in composition.
Julian Hawthorne preserves the following anecdote of Hawthorne and Sophia: "he read to
her the unfinished tale of 'Rappaccini's Daughter,' and when she asked him whether he
were going to make the girl an angel or a devil, he replied, with some emotion, that he did
not know" (*Hawthorne Reading: An Essay* [Cleveland: The Rowfant Club, 1902; rpt.
Folcroft, 1969], pp. 122–3). See also the relevant remarks in Richard Harter Fogle,
*Hawthorne's Fiction: The Light and the Dark,* rev. ed. (Norman: Univ. of Oklahoma Press,
1964), pp. 91–92.

earthly illusions necessarily disappear. Plato had conceived of it as a realm of ideal forms, calling it "the really real reality."[7] There is something neoplatonic in Hawthorne's own vision (despite the attempts of his commentators to wish this away), which also invokes the theme of the illusoriness of earthly appearances, and the notion of the body as a prison of the soul. In dying, Beatrice tells her father: "But now it matters not; I am going, father, where the evil, which thou hast striven to mingle with my being, will pass away like a dream—like the fragrance of these poisonous flowers, which will no longer taint my breath among the flowers of Eden" (Centenary, x, 127). Here we find the true Eden contrasted with the false: the spiritual against the material.

On earth, this spiritual world manifests itself through the influence that passes from one soul to another—a motif that recurs in Hawthorne's later works. Such influence cannot be belied, for it constitutes an involuntary and unconscious expression of the very essence of the soul. This essence is revealed through the affections. Hawthorne here approaches Keats's passionate affirmation of "the holiness of the heart's affections." Only their relation to such affections can elevate Beatrice's utterances above the ironic perspective. What the soul cannot disclose through any effort of its own will passes forth independently of all volition. By this means is the true nature of Beatrice communicated to Giovanni: "But, with her actual presence, there came influences which had too real an existence to be at once shaken off; recollections of the delicate and benign power of her feminine nature, which had so often enveloped him in a religious calm; recollections of many a holy and passionate outgush of her heart, when the pure fountain had been unsealed from its depths, and made visible in its transparency to his mental eye; recollections which, had Giovanni known how to estimate them, would have assured him that all this ugly mystery was but an earthly illusion, and that, whatever mist of evil might seem to have gathered over her, the real Beatrice was a heavenly angel" (Centenary, x, 122).

We have already seen the form allegory, and later, symbolism, assumes for Hawthorne. Beginning as an unconscious opposition between the ideal and the actual, it subsequently becomes explicit and, at a still later stage, is "resolved" in what amounts to an entirely new form. As a stage in this development, "Rappaccini's Daughter" offers not only a greater allegorical realism but also insight into the effect of subjective consciousness upon the perception of higher truths. Above all, it expresses a new relation between the spiritual and the material, in which the latter becomes mere "earthly illusion," a mask that conceals the true nature of higher reality. That reality must now be approached through a

[7]For a discussion of which, see Gregory Vlastos, "A Metaphysical Paradox," in his *Platonic Studies* (Princeton: Princeton Univ. Press, 1973), pp. 43–57.

species of intuition in which the mind apprehends the spiritual essence that incarnates itself in a material form, the soul within the body. How does this essence manifest itself? Keats had said:

"Beauty is truth, truth beauty,"—that is all
Ye know on earth, and all ye need to know.

For Hawthorne too, beauty becomes inseparable from spiritual reality, as one form under which the latter expresses itself: a theme whose fullest ramifications were only to become clear to him at a much later stage. We recall his dictum: "The truth that was only in the fancy then may have since become a substance in the mind and heart." Already in fancy it was possible for him at this time to give exemplary expression to that idea. The result: "The Artist of the Beautiful."

## "The Artist of the Beautiful"

Among the effusions of his early years, Friedrich Schlegel had written in praise of idleness. Keats, too, had extolled its virtues in poetry. Several decades later, speaking of what he calls the "all" feeling in a letter to Hawthorne, Melville writes: "You must often have felt it, lying on the grass on a warm summer's day. Your legs seem to send out shoots into the earth. Your hair feels like leaves upon your head. This is the *all* feeling." Still later we find an echo of the same theme in an anecdote from the last years of William Morris. As he began visibly aging, his friends would often worry about his health. On occasion, while walking through the fields, Morris would pause and sit down on the grass for a while. To his friends he would explain: "I like to soak up the energy of the Earth."

From all these somewhat disparate accounts, a common theme emerges: the recognition of idleness, not as a state of morally culpable inactivity, but rather as a gathering up of creative energies, an amassing of the soul's spiritual resources. By means of this passive process, the wellsprings of the spirit silently accumulate until the moment when they finally overflow in the abundance of artistic creation.

Hawthorne is also aware of this process, which he embodies in his "Artist of the Beautiful." Here idleness assumes the form of wanderings through the woods and fields, and along the banks of streams. But the artist, Owen Warland, has one passion in particular—the pursuit of butterflies, a pursuit that carries with it certain symbolic overtones: "There was something truly mysterious in the intentness with which he contemplated these living playthings, as they sported on the breeze; or examined the structure of an imperial insect whom he had imprisoned.

The chase of butterflies was an apt emblem of the ideal pursuit in which he had spent so many golden hours. . . . Sweet, doubtless, were these days, and congenial to the artist's soul. They were full of bright conceptions, which gleamed through his intellectual world, as the butterflies gleamed through the outward atmosphere, and were real to him for the instant, without the toil, and perplexity, and many disappointments, of attempting to make them visible to the sensual eye" (Centenary, x, 457–58).

Transmuted within the medium of the creative imagination, the butterfly ceases to be merely a natural object and becomes a symbol of the soul itself. As Hawthorne undoubtedly well knew, the same Greek word had served to designate both—*psyche*. In "The Artist of the Beautiful" their equation is hinted at in various places. Elsewhere—as in his story "The New Adam and Eve," for example—Hawthorne expresses it more explicitly. Encountering a cemetery at the end of a day's peregrinations, the progenitors of a new human race begin to form a conception of death. "But were they to choose a symbol for him, it would be the Butterfly soaring upward, or the bright Angel beckoning them aloft, or the Child asleep, with soft dreams visible through her transparent purity" (Centenary, x, 267). Here the butterfly soaring upward must be interpreted as the soul after death, as it wings its way up to heaven. In "The Journal of a Solitary Man" the narrator observes: "Scarcely had I thus fixed the term of my mortal pilgrimage, than the thought grew into a presentiment that, when the space should be completed, the world would have one butterfly the less, by my far flight" (Centenary, xi, 317). The appearance of the butterfly becomes for the artist the summons to a higher calling, a spiritual mission. Like a leitmotif, it recurs throughout his life, a symbol of the quest he must take up again after each temporary setback, each discouragement, each consequent lapse into idleness, this period in which the creative soul recovers its energies before launching itself anew. Thus it is that, after one of the numerous periods of depression brought about by the destruction of his mechanical contrivance, a depression he seeks to quell in riotous drinking, the artist finds himself summoned again to his mission by the apparition of a splendid butterfly entering through an open window and hovering about him: "It might be fancied that the bright butterfly, which had come so spiritlike into the window, as Owen sat with the rude revellers, was indeed a spirit, commissioned to recall him to the pure, ideal life that had so etherealized him among men. It might be fancied, that he went forth to seek this spirit, in its sunny haunts; for still, as in the summer-time gone by, he was seen to steal gently up, wherever a butterfly had alighted, and lose himself in contemplation of it. When it took flight, his eyes followed the winged vision, as if its airy track would show the path to heaven" (Centenary, x, 462).

Earlier, we are told, it had been one of the dreams of the artist's youth to effect a "spiritualization of matter." During a period of depression (signalized by his succumbing to a form of materialism), Owen Warland looks back upon it retrospectively: "In his idle and dreamy days, he had considered it possible, in a certain sense, to spiritualize machinery; and to combine with the new species of life and motion, thus produced, a beauty that should attain to the ideal which Nature has proposed to herself, in all her creatures, but has never taken pains to realize" (Centenary, x, 465–66). The spiritualization of machinery is nothing less than a metaphor for the artistic process. It symbolizes the attempt to endow the literary work with a semblance of life—to create, from the arsenal of effects that make up the artist's technique (his "machinery," so to speak), the illusion of life. But art seeks more than merely the "illusion" of life. From the standpoint of the relation established earlier between the butterfly and the soul ("psyche"), one may say that, for Hawthorne, art consists of the attempt to *create* a soul. Owen Warland's efforts to produce a mechanical butterfly with the appearance of life symbolize his attempt to fashion a work that shall be instinct with spiritual life. That it should only be mechanical cannot be grounds for negative criticism—art itself is, after all, only "mechanical," or artificial. Nor can the diminutive size of Owen's creation to held against him.[8] For "The Beautiful Idea has no relation to size, and may be as perfectly developed in a space too minute for any but microscopic investigation, as within the ample verge that is measured by the arc of the rainbow" (Centenary, x, 450).

Whereas neoclassical aesthetics (Burke, for example) had sought to associate properties of size with the respective ideas of the sublime and the beautiful, Hawthorne envisages beauty not as an effect of our perception of things, but rather as a spiritual quality belonging to a higher and more ideal realm. As a result, the artist's apprehension of the beautiful becomes, in quasi-platonic fashion, participation in the "Beautiful Idea." But if such is the source from which all artistic inspiration springs, it remains for the artist to give some embodiment, some tangible realiza-

[8]*Pace* Nina Baym's claim (pp. 110–11), "In a literal sense, the miniature that he produces represents the belittling of imagination." To be sure, this also seems to be the view of Millicent Bell in what remains the most considered treatment of Hawthorne on art to date, *Hawthorne's View of the Artist* (New York: State Univ. of New York Press, 1962) esp. pp. 95–96. One suspects that the diminutive and artificial nature of Owen Warland's creation has been made to tell against him with the critics. But is not Hawthorne himself conscious of both qualities in his own published works to date? Cf. "M. de l'Aubépine," author of "'Le Voyage Celeste à Chemin de Fer,' 3 tom. 1838," and other voluminous productions (Centenary, x, 92). Even in his last works, Hawthorne continues to speak of the artist's isolation, but as a necessary condition for the life of the imagination. In studying the appearance and motions of the butterfly, Owen Warland attempts in effect to capture the "soul" of life or human existence, that which transcends its phenomenology. That art should fail to represent adequately the inner vision is a commonplace of neoplatonic aesthetics popularized by Vasari's life of Michelangelo in his *Lives*.

tion, to his vision. At this point it may be objected that such a formulation of the artistic process is too vague, too "ethereal" (to use a characteristic Hawthornesque term). But Hawthorne's concern is not with a
practical poetics. What he seeks to express is the spiritual and aesthetic
ideal of all higher art, specifically his own.

From the above, it is possible to trace two distinct stages in the process
of artistic creation. In the first stage, the artist apprehends and possesses
the beautiful in its inmost essence, as idea. Through this apprehension,
platonic in character, the mind becomes one in substance with the Beautiful, being elevated to the level of the ideal, which it recognizes as its
own true element. From this single source derive all the forms of artistic
expression. All are infused by a single spirit, that of the soul itself. Hence
"the deeds of earth, however etherealized by piety or genius, are without
value, except as exercises and manifestations of the spirit" (Centenary, x,
467).

In its second stage, spirit infuses matter, through which it expresses
itself, as through a symbol. We are not to see in this, nevertheless, a
Transcendentalist aesthetics, despite the apparent similarity on account
of a common affinity with platonism. For Emerson the symbol constitutes an immediate revelation of the divine, a medium through which
we communicate with God himself. For Hawthorne, the symbol is merely a means through which the mind is drawn upward to a higher, more
spiritual level. It preserves the essence of a spiritual substance that is
clearly distinguished from that of the divinity.

An emblem of this process appears on the cover of the little box from
which Owen Warland removes his mechanical invention: "It was carved
richly out of ebony by his own hand, and inlaid with a fanciful tracery of
pearl, representing a boy in pursuit of a butterfly, which, elsewhere, had
become a winged spirit, and was flying heavenward; while the boy, or
youth, had found such efficacy in his strong desire, that he ascended
from earth to cloud, and from cloud to celestial atmosphere, to win the
Beautiful" (Centenary, x, 469–70).

As for the invention, we are not to see in it, as some critics have done,
an example of Hawthorne's interest in the possibilities and limits of
mechanical contrivances. For Hawthorne, there remains always an essential difference between vital and mechanical processes, one that Poe
had pointed out in his analysis of Maelzel's chess-player and that
Hawthorne himself had touched upon in "The Birth-mark" and to
which he would return in his Elixir of Life manuscripts. The mechanical
butterfly that Owen Warland produces must accordingly be seen, not as
mechanism but, in the purest sense, as symbol. It is instinct with life
itself. To Annie, Owen says: "it absorbed my own being into itself; and in
the secret of that butterfly, and in its beauty—which is not merely outward, but deep as its whole system—is represented the intellect, the

imagination, the sensibility, the soul, of an Artist of the Beautiful!" (Centenary, x, 471). In a literal sense it reproduces the equation, pointed out earlier, between the butterfly and the soul. But it does so only through the artist's ability to "spiritualize" matter.

This spiritualization is itself, however, merely the means by which the inward apprehension of the beautiful is to be conveyed to others. In its pure form, such beauty remains beyond the material sphere. It is not contained within the symbol, but simply represented by it. Thus the destruction of that symbol (the mechanical butterfly) cannot affect beauty itself, which constitutes, like the Platonic Idea, an imperishable spiritual substance. From this perspective, the artist can thus calmly look on as the infant child of the Danforths crushes the butterfly in its grasp. For Owen Warland himself "had caught a far other butterfly than this. When the artist rose high enough to achieve the Beautiful, the symbol by which he made it perceptible to mortal senses became of little value in his eyes, while his spirit possessed itself in the enjoyment of the Reality" (Centenary, x, 475).

## The Scarlet Letter

Shortly after his arrival in the Bay colony, the physician Roger Chillingworth selects the Reverend Arthur Dimmesdale for his spiritual guide. "The young divine," the author reports, "was considered by his more fervent admirers as little less than a heaven-ordained apostle, destined, should he live and labor for the ordinary term of life, to do as great deeds for the now feeble New England Church, as the early Fathers had achieved for the infancy of the Christian faith" (Centenary, I, 120). Subsequently, a description of the minister's library depicts it as "rich with parchment-bound folios of the Fathers, and the lore of Rabbis, and monkish erudition, of which the Protestant divines, even while they vilified and decried that class of writers, were yet constrained often to avail themselves" (Centenary, I, 126). We know that, in actual fact, Puritan ministers often modeled their discourses after patterns drawn from Patristic literature. In order to recover the true Christian doctrine, it had been necessary to go back to these early sources. Among the concepts that appear there, one in particular possesses a special significance for the theme of Hawthorne's novel—that of the letter and the spirit.

St. Paul had taught that according to a strict application of divine law, all were necessarily condemned; only through the grace that proceeds from divine mercy was it possible to be saved: "The letter killeth, but the spirit giveth life" (2 Cor. 3:6). In the course of development of early Christian theology, however, it had also become possible to view this pronouncement in another light, as justification for the allegorical interpretation of Scripture. St. Augustine himself had formulated this argument in a brief early treatise, *On the Advantage of Believing*. A later work, *On the Spirit and the Letter*, returns to the original Pauline sense. In his *Retractions* he states that the latter had brought out the signficance of the scriptural passage "in a more appropriate way." Nevertheless, speaking of his earlier interpretation, he then says: "the aforementioned meaning is not to be rejected." Medieval exegesis preserved both. Hawthorne, in turn, combines them in unique fashion in *The Scarlet Letter*.

In the sketch that precedes the body of the novel, the narrator recalls how he had first discovered the scarlet letter among a collection of private papers in the second story of the Custom-House. At the moment of examining it he had felt, he says, the sense of "some deep meaning in it, most worthy of interpretation, and which, as it were, streamed forth from the mystic symbol, subtly communicating itself to my sensibilities, but evading the analysis of my mind" (Centenary, 1, 31). The incident intimates the role the scarlet letter will play in the novel itself. Here the symbol becomes, not revelation, but something that obscures a meaning at the same time it suggests it—hence, an object of interpretation.

This phenomenon is nevertheless but the manifestation of a deeper process, one I would like to call the *psychologization of symbolism*. In Hawthorne's early stories a material object is occasionally portrayed as expressing a higher or spiritual significance (the Reverend Hooper's black veil, for example). Hawthorne himself refers to the object as a symbol or type. It embodies a relation between the material and the spiritual. This relation possesses a validity independent of the spectator's perception of it. In *The Scarlet Letter,* by contrast, the "reality" of such a relation is called into question. Hence the scarlet letter Hester wears upon her breast gives rise to not one but many interpretations, none of which claim more than a subjective validity. As a result, the idea of a suprapersonal symbolism conveying eternal truths disappears. All symbolic disclosures must now pass through the medium of individual consciousness.

Thus when Dimmesdale ascends the scaffold one night in early May and witnesses an apparition in the sky, the significance he associates with it is ascribed to his own state of mind: "We impute it, therefore, solely to the disease in his own eye and heart, that the minister, looking upward to the zenith, beheld there the appearance of an immense letter, —the letter A, —marked out in lines of dull red light. Not but the meteor may have shown itself at that point, burning duskily through a veil of cloud; but with no such shape as his guilty imagination gave it; or, at least, with so little definiteness, that another's guilt might have seen another symbol in it" (Centenary, 1, 155). This apparition, the minister later learns, is also seen by a number of the townspeople, who attribute to it a wholly different meaning, interpreting it as a portent of the passage of Governor Winthrop's soul to heaven and consequent transformation into an angel (whence the letter A).

Nowhere, however, is the psychologization of symbolism more manifest than in the case of the scarlet letter itself. At first the visible emblem of Hester Prynne's shame, it acquires, over a space of years, a different meaning to the sick, the dying, and those in distress, to whom she brings aid and consolation: "There glimmered the embroidered letter, with comfort in its unearthly ray. Elsewhere the token of sin, it was the taper of the sick-chamber. It had even thrown its gleam, in the sufferer's hard extremity, across the verge of time. It had shown him where to set his foot, while the light of earth was fast becoming dim, and ere the light of futurity could reach him. . . . The letter was the symbol of her calling. Such helpfulness was found in her, —so much power to do, and power to sympathize, —that many people refused to interpret the scarlet A by its original signification. They said that it meant Able; so strong was Hester Prynne, with a woman's strength" (Centenary, I, 161). Through her efforts, the symbol once more acquires a mediating function, as a bridge between the temporal and the eternal. But whereas in Hawthorne's earlier works this relation had been presented as an objective one, through which a genuine knowledge of higher reality is vouchsafed, it now appears in a different light: not as objective revelation, but as subjective presentment or feeling. Thus for the dying, Hester's badge signifies above all the offices of love, which is the true bridge between life and death, time and eternity.

In this fashion symbolism becomes not so much a disclosure as the expression of a state of mind. It represents the subjective orientation of the minister as he reveals his guilt to the assembled colony, thereby becoming himself a symbol: "The sun, but little past its meridian, shone down upon the clergyman, and gave a distinctness to his figure, as he stood out from all the earth to put in his plea of guilty at the bar of Eternal Justice" (Centenary, I, 254).

The scene suggests a correspondence between inner and external world that is borne out elsewhere in the novel. It forms, in effect, another aspect of the symbolism of *The Scarlet Letter*, embodying the mind's projection upon external reality, which becomes the picture or image of an inner feeling. After the crisis in which they resolve to leave the Puritan colony together, Hester and Dimmesdale behold a change in the landscape around them: "All at once, as with a sudden smile of heaven, forth burst the sunshine, pouring a very flood into the obscure forest, gladdening each green leaf, transmuting the yellow fallen ones to gold, and gleaming adown the gray trunks of the solemn trees. The objects that had made a shadow hitherto, embodied the brightness now. The course of the little brook might be traced by its merry gleam afar into the wood's heart of mystery, which had become a mystery of joy" (Centenary, I, 202–203). Of this transformation the author comments: "Such was the sympathy of Nature—that wild, heathen Nature of the forest, never subjugated by human law, nor illumined by higher truth—with the bliss of these two spirits! Love, whether newly born, or aroused from a deathlike slumber, must always create a sunshine, filling the heart so full of radiance, that it overflows upon the outward world. Had the forest still kept its gloom, it would have been bright in Hester's eyes, and bright in Arthur Dimmesdale's!" (Centenary, I, 203).

We are not to see here, as Ruskin would have it, an instance of the affective fallacy. The scene Hawthorne depicts is not merely an appearance suffused by a particular mood or feeling, but one fraught with symbolism. In the sunlight that penetrates the forest we find, as it were, an image of the life force itself. This force brings about change (the "transmuting" of the fallen leaves to gold, revivification of what had fallen into decay). A complete reversal of the psychological situation of Hester and the minister is then indicated: "The objects that had made a shadow hitherto, embodied the brightness now." That brightness is in turn associated with the element of mystery that pervades all the deepest and most intimate relations of the heart ("the wood's heart of mystery, which had become a mystery of joy").

It would be a mistake, nevertheless, to identify Hawthorne's symbolism with that of Coleridge or Goethe, Schelling or Emerson. The Nature Hawthorne depicts is never "illumined by higher truth," hence incapable of revealing or manifesting the divine essence. It corresponds to the human sphere alone, a symbolic image of the thought that fills the individual consciousness. If we search for the sources of this form of symbolism, we encounter them in the early flowering of French Romanticism, the period of Mme de Staël, Benjamin Constant, and Chateaubriand. In Mme de Staël's *Corinne* the heroine, at one point late in the novel, decides to follow her lover to England but neglects to inform him. Arriving in London, she finds him in the company of a young girl (in fact her half-sister) without being noticed by him. When she finally musters enough courage to call at his London address, she learns that he has just departed for his estate in the northern part of England. En route to it, she suffers a dangerous illness, from which she emerges physically much altered. On finally reaching Lord Nelvil's estate, she finds him at a ball; she approaches the mansion closely enough to see and hear him talking to someone on a balcony, but, by a fatality of constraint, does not go into the house or seek him out. She then wanders down to a nearby stream, where she sees the following: "There were many trees on one of the banks, but the other displayed nothing but barren masses of rock covered with mist. In walking, Corinne found herself close to the stream; there she heard at the same time the music of the ball and the murmur of the waters. The gleam of the ballroom lights was reflected down to the middle of the stream, while the pale shimmer of the moon illuminated only the deserted expanses of the other side" (*O.C.*, IX, 329).

The scene symbolically contrasts the differing fortunes of Corinne and her younger sister: the one prosperous and happy (signified by the abundance of trees on one bank), the other consumed by sorrow and despair (the bank that exhibits only "barren masses of rock covered with mist"). Transposed onto another level, the scene opposes the social universe of the one (the bank illuminated by ballroom lights) to the other's solitude (the deserted expanses lighted only by the moon). These contrasts are not so much objective as subjective, expressing as they do the perceptions of an individual consciousness.

A similar form of symbolism manifests itself in Benjamin Constant's *Adolphe*. Shortly before her death, in one of the last stages of her illness, Ellénore asks her lover Adolphe to accompany her on a walk in the countryside. "It was one of those winter days," he recalls, "where the sun seems to illuminate the gray countryside cheerlessly, as if it looked with pity upon an earth it had ceased to warm." The following scene spreads itself out before them: "The sky was serene; but the trees were without leaves; no breath of wind stirred the air, no bird crossed it: everything was motionless, and the only sound to be heard was that of the frozen grass which broke under our steps" (*Oeuvres*, p. 75). As in Hawthorne, there is the image of the sun as a symbol of the life force, a life force that no longer touches the soul ("as if it looked with pity upon an earth it had ceased to warm"). A crystalline stillness portends the narrator's state of mind following the death of his beloved, which occurs shortly after this scene.

Like Poe, Hawthorne's affinities at this stage are more with French than German or English Romanticism, which also implies a certain distance or difference from Transcendentalism. Through the motif of the scarlet letter Hawthorne had managed to express the opacity of the symbol, its openness to interpretation. That is one of its aspects. But it also possesses another. Through it we encounter the theme of moral law and grace, one that Hawthorne treats (as he does symbolism) in a psychological sense. In his novel we find the Pauline dictum that "the letter killeth" invested with psychological reality. It appears in the change wrought by the letter not only upon Hester's nature but even her physical appearance. Characteristically, the psychological is portrayed through material things endowed with symbolic overtones. Through the "light and graceful foliage" of Hester's former character, Hawthorne conjures up reminiscences of Milton's Eve, whose hair the poet had associated with an imagery of tendrils and vines that constitutes the symbolic expression of her womanliness. Similarly, the "rich and luxuriant hair" of Hester also expresses her nature.

In the magical scene in which Hester and the minister resolve to flee the colony together, Hawthorne resumes the thread of this symbolism. For one blessed moment, the casting-off of the scarlet letter, symbolic of the destructive effects of the law, makes possible a blossoming of Hester's nature. Connotations of abundance describe her transformation. They serve to characterize the biology of the soul, whose life is revitalized through an influx of the affections which forms the psychological equivalent of grace. Just as the lethal nature of moral condemnation is exhibited in psychological terms, so the grace that redeems the soul receives its psychological counterpart as well.

By casting off the scarlet letter, Hester experiences freedom and fulfillment in her affections. Clearly, her action represents a necessary step or phase in her development. But at the same time, for various reasons, it cannot mark the final phase. Rejection of the letter had been necessary insofar as the wearing of it had signified tacit acceptance of its symbolism, the stigma, both social and moral, associated with adultery. In assuming this "badge of shame," Hester yields to the viewpoint of the collective consciousness. Applied to the individual, such a viewpoint can only produce harmful constraints, resulting in a loss of self.

At a later stage, however, the letter becomes necessary once more, for the same reasons as those which compel Hester to return to Boston. "Here had been her sin; here, her sorrow; and here was yet to be her penitence." The Romantic concept of the life cycle as a return to one's beginnings finds expression here, as does the notion of an inner entelechy of the self. Hester's resumption of her badge is made possible by her feeling of the necessity of transforming its significance. "In the lapse of the toilsome, thoughtful, and self-devoted years that made up Hester's life," Hawthorne writes, "the scarlet letter ceased to be a stigma which attracted the world's scorn and bitterness, and became a type of something to be sorrowed over, and looked upon with awe, yet with reverence too" (Centenary, I, 263). A deeply human and fundamentally conservative impulse demands preservation of the literal, the material. As Hölderlin observes in his poem "Patmos," "Most of all, the solid letter should be cared for, and the existing well interpreted" (S.W., II:1, 172). Among other things, the literal and material become the resource of the preserving memory. By envisioning the possibility of transforming the significance of the letter, moreover, Hawthorne takes the psychologization of symbolism one step further. Earlier, he had indicated the conflict between differing interpretations of the same symbol. Now he traces the replacement of one interpretation by another, adding a historical dimension to symbolism. The process by which the transformation of meaning occurs is not an abstract or formal but a vital one. It encompasses the whole of Hester Prynne's life, her work, her suffering, her reflections. The resultant transformation of a symbol's significance is not merely one of change but also a deepening of meaning. It indicates how Hawthorne himself had passed from a quasi-allegorical view of symbolism to the perception of it as reproducing and assimilating, in some fashion, the nature of the life process itself.

## The Marble Faun

In an entry in his French and Italian Notebooks (March 14, 1858) Hawthorne records attending a dinner in Rome at the house of Thomas Buchanan Read, an artist and poet, at which he met a number of painters and sculptors. Apart from the conversation of an Englishman, John Gibson, he had heard, he writes, "nothing worth remembering or repeating, from anybody's lips, except the following, which is attributed to Thorwaldsen—"The Clay is the Life; the Plaster is the Death; and the Marble is the Resurrection" (Centenary, xiv, 133)—a remark that contains the germ for the theme of the novel he was about to write: *The Marble Faun*. Earlier, in his story "The Artist of the Beautiful," Hawthorne had defined art as "the spiritualization of matter." The artist apprehends in visionary intuition a higher Reality, the "Beautiful Idea," which he then attempts to express through material forms that will elevate the mind to this more spiritual level. A dichotomy is thus erected between the ideal and the material, over which art attempts to mediate. It can do so, however, only because it possesses within itself a direct apprehension of the Beautiful, an ideal platonic essence high above all material forms.

In *The Marble Faun*, by contrast, Hawthorne introduces a new concept of art, one that abolishes the platonic or neoplatonic notion of the apprehension of an ideal and its expression, and substitutes for it the Romantic concept of a spiritual quest. This quest in turn assumes the structure of the "Fortunate Fall," a process consisting of three stages: an Edenic state, followed by the development of self-consciousness as a result of sin and suffering, leading subsequently to a higher (because more intellectual) spiritualization than that which had previously been possessed even in the Edenic phase. This schema is then applied to the history of art, which is seen to consist of an idyllic pagan stage, serene through its possession of a primitive happiness reflected in its art, followed by a Christian stage in which the awareness of sin and suffering is mixed with the intuition of a higher, more spiritual existence, which it becomes the function of Christian art to symbolize.[9]

To be sure, some features of this conception had already appeared before, in the interpretation of Greek art which begins in Germany with Winckelmann and continues through Goethe and Hegel, in the opposition of "naive" to "sentimental" poetry propounded by Schiller, and in the contrast of pagan to Christian art which we find in Mme de Staël's *De l'Allemagne*. Only in Hawthorne, however, does the opposition between Classic and Christian art pass from irreconcilable conflict to a process of necessary spiritual development, of which the two forms represent the stages. Seen from this standpoint, the history of art becomes suffused with a religious significance, symbolizing in itself the aspirations of the soul toward a higher consciousness.

As a system of symbolism, art no longer represents an ideal perceived in the mind of the artist. Now the artistic imagination is itself depicted as participant in an endless quest. Its object is the expression of a spiritual perfection that cannot be apprehended until humanity itself has attained it. In the process of striving toward this goal, art recapitulates and mirrors those stages that humanity passes through in its progress toward a more spiritual level. In this fashion the whole relation of art to life, which Hawthorne had touched upon already in *The House of the Seven Gables*, is now redefined. No longer a sterile opposition, it becomes a symbolic correspondence, in which the stages toward a higher Christian form of art reflect the history of humanity's own progressive spiritualization.

Among the legendary beings of the Golden Age, Greek mythology had postulated the existence of certain creatures bearing the attributes of both animals and man. For Hawthorne, even the very consciousness of such creatures becomes itself an expression of the mixture of these two kinds of attributes: "Perhaps it is the very lack of moral severity, of any high and heroic ingredient in the character of the Faun, that makes it so delightful an object to the human eye and to the frailty of the human heart. The being, here represented, is endowed with no principle of virtue, and would be incapable of comprehending such. But he

[9]In his study *Hawthorne's Tragic Vision* (Austin: Univ. of Texas Press, 1957), pp. 163–65, Roy R. Male points out the parallelism between art and life in *The Marble Faun*, but seems to me to spoil his interpretation by a too literal application of Thorwaldsen's analogy. Shortly after Hawthorne's finishing the novel, Sophia wrote to her parents (Sept., 1859): "As usual, he thinks the book good for nothing, and based upon a very foolish idea which nobody will like or accept" (quoted from Rose Hawthorne Lathrop, *Memories of Hawthorne* [Boston and New York: Houghton, Mifflin, 1898], p. 347). Might not this "very foolish idea" involve the art-life analogy itself? In any case, the novel seems to call for a somewhat metaphorical, rather than literalistic, interpretation—as evidenced in Hawthorne's letter to John Lothrop Motley (George Parsons Lathrop, *A Study of Hawthorne* [Boston, 1876: rpt. New York: AMS Press, 1969], pp. 262–63).

would be true and honest, by dint of his simplicity. . . . It is possible, too, that the Faun might be educated through the medium of his emotions; so that the coarser, animal portion of his nature might eventually be thrown into the back-ground, though never utterly expelled" (Centenary, IV, 9).

In the statue of Praxiteles, the Edenic consciousness achieves embodiment in a material form, a mediation between man and Nature, almost indescribable in words, but endowed with a permanent reality through the art of classical antiquity, whose agency allows us to contemplate their almost miraculous mixture. Hence, "if the spectator broods long over the statue, he will be conscious of its spell; all the pleasantness of sylvan life, all the genial and happy characteristics of creatures that dwell in woods and fields, will seem to be mingled and kneaded into one substance, along with the kindred qualities in the human soul. Trees, grass, flowers, woodland streamlets, cattle, deer, and unsophisticated man! The essence of all these was compressed long ago, and still exists, within that discoloured marble surface of the Faun of Praxiteles" (Centenary, IV, 10).

From both *The Marble Faun* and other sources, it seems clear that for Hawthorne the essence of history consists not so much of events but rather of stages of consciousness through which humanity passes. From this standpoint, it becomes possible to imagine an analogy between the history of the race in general and that of an individual. Within the novel itself the history of humanity's spiritual development is summed up or recapitulated in that of Donatello, the Italian nobleman whose features and temperament are noticed at the beginning to bear a remarkable resemblance to those of Praxiteles' Faun.

Like the Faun, too, he brings with him the spirit of an earlier time, a time of innocence, in which life consumes itself in the enjoyment of play or sport amid the woodlands' pageantry of sylvan scenes and animal life. Frolicking with Miriam in the woods, twining garlands about her head, he recalls the aura of humanity's Edenic phase: "It was a glimpse far backward into Arcadian life, or, farther still, into the Golden Age, before mankind was burthened with sin and sorrow, and before pleasure had been darkened with those shadows that bring it into high relief, and make it Happiness" (Centenary, IV, 84).

But this blissful state comes abruptly to an end with the murder of the Capuchin, which Donatello commits at Miriam's voiceless instigation. The crime brings about the beginning of his inner transformation: "It had kindled him into a man; it had developed within him an intelligence which was no native characteristic of the Donatello whom we have heretofore known. But that simple and joyous creature was gone forever" (Centenary, IV, 172). With this first sin of the Faun's, there comes not only the consciousness of guilt but an awakening into knowledge. And,

once "awakened," he cannot return to former innocence. As in Melville's
*Billy Budd,* that innocence is itself equated with a certain spiritual defi-
ciency: the absence of a moral consciousness.

It is precisely this absence of the moral consciousness that had made
possible the immediate relation or sympathy of man with Nature. As in
*The Scarlet Letter,* Nature remains outside the moral sphere. We are not
to see in Hawthorne's version of Nature, as in Wordsworth's, a power
that participates in man's moral education. Intuitive or instinctive harmony with Nature becomes, on the contrary, one of the things humanity
must abandon in the process of its spiritual development. It belongs to
its first phase alone, the phase of innocence. "We all of us," Kenyon tells
Donatello, "as we grow older, lose somewhat of our proximity to Nature.
It is the price we pay for experience" (Centenary, IV, 250).

In this process of growth, nevertheless, what is lost on one level need
not be irrecoverable but perhaps is renewed on a higher level, which is to
say: at the level of moral consciousness. This renewal, brought visibly
before Kenyon's eyes during a walk in the twilight hours at Monte Beni,
in which he sees his friend reassume his resemblance to the Faun of
Praxiteles, could not but be at the same time a renewal with a difference:
"Yet his face brightened beneath the stars; and, looking at it through the
twilight, the sculptor's remembrance went back to that scene in the Cap-
itol, where, both in features and expression, Donatello had seemed identical with the Faun. And still there was a resemblance; for now, when
first the idea was suggested of living for the welfare of his fellow-crea-
tures, the original beauty, which sorrow had partly effaced, came back
elevated and spiritualized." This appearance is itself the reflection of
Donatello's advancement to a new spiritual stage: "In the black depths,
the Faun had found a soul, and was struggling with it towards the light
of Heaven" (Centenary, IV, 268).

At this point in the novel Hawthorne takes up once more the symbolic
correspondence of art to life. Just as Donatello's earlier spiritual state
had found its expression in art in the marble Faun of Praxiteles, so with
his inner transformation there emerges the possibility of a new representation. In his attempt to achieve it, certain difficulties emerge. But
Kenyon "was chiefly perplexed how to make this genial and kindly type
of countenance the index of the mind within." The source of this difficulty is not technical but spiritual: "His acuteness and his sympathies,
indeed, were both somewhat at fault in their efforts to enlighten him as
to the moral phase through which the Count was now passing" (Centenary, IV, 270).

In desperation, the artist turns to intuition alone: "Hopeless of a good
result, Kenyon gave up all pre-conceptions about the character of his
subject, and let his hands work, uncontrolled, with the clay, somewhat as
a spiritual medium, while holding a pen, yields it to an unseen guidance

other than that of her own will. Now and then, he fancied that this plan was destined to be the successful one. A skill and insight, beyond his consciousness, seemed occasionally to take up the task. The mystery, the miracle, of imbuing an inanimate substance with thought, feeling, and all the intangible attributes of the soul, appeared on the verge of being wrought. And now, as he flattered himself, the true image of his friend was about to emerge from the facile material, bringing with it more of Donatello's character than the keenest observer could detect, at any one moment, in the face of the original. Vain expectation! Some touch, whereby the artist thought to improve or hasten the result, interfered with the design of his unseen spiritual assistant, and spoilt the whole. There was still the moist, brown clay, indeed, and the features of Donatello, but without any semblance of intelligent life" (Centenary, IV, 271).

Here it becomes apparent that art, too, like the life that forms its subject, must undergo an organic process of development. Only thus, and not otherwise, can it attain its result. Attempting to hasten the process, Kenyon inevitably spoils the whole. Through this description, what emerges is not merely the law of all artistic creation (organicism) but also, with equal clarity, the nature of such creation, itself defined as a spiritual quest whose object is nothing less than the life of the soul. The system of symbolism through which art represents life is hereby extended to the process of art, which requires, like life itself, various stages of maturation. Corresponding to those of life, these stages exhibit a movement of progressive spiritualization. As a result, it was necessary that, in his attempt to capture the new and higher expression of Donatello's countenance, Kenyon should in his own efforts reproduce the earlier stages of the life of his subject as well: "By some accidental handling of the clay, entirely independent of his own will, Kenyon had given the countenance a distorted and violent look, combining animal fierceness with intelligent hatred. Had Hilda, or had Miriam, seen the bust, with the expression which it had now assumed, they might have recognized Donatello's face as they beheld it at that terrible moment, when he held his victim over the edge of the precipice" (Centenary, IV, 272). In the detail of an "accidental handling of the clay" Hawthorne offers yet another indication of the organic nature of the process. Here what the artist himself has never seen (Donatello at the moment of his crime) he nevertheless manages to recreate. The law that governs his recreation: symbolic correspondence between the stages of art and those of life.

We witness its operation in the next phase as well, in which (again through accidental touches) he now gives to the bust "a higher and sweeter expression than it had hitherto worn" (Centenary, IV, 273). As in the case of the Faun himself, Kenyon's new effort represents renewal with a difference, "for here were still the features of the antique Faun, but now illuminated with a higher meaning, such as the old marble never bore" (IV, 274).

In this fashion, Hawthorne is able to depict the triumph of Christian over classical art, a triumph that issues not from conflict with, and overcoming of, the old forms, but rather their elevation to a higher level. Such continuity is itself based upon that of pagan and Christian modes of consciousness, the necessary development from a state of innocence to one of higher knowledge, the awareness of good and evil. For Hawthorne it is precisely such knowledge that makes possible the spiritual development of humanity, or the growth of the soul. The higher or Christian art thus signifies both a preserving of classical form and its investiture with a new significance—hence, an art like that of the Italian Renaissance, for which Hawthorne had had the profoundest admiration. In Michelangelo in particular (whom he esteemed above all others), he could have found the manifestation of that process he had sought to describe in his novel, the conservation of classical form and its endowment with Christian significance.

He could also have found in Michelangelo the aesthetic of the "non finito" (a creation of Michelangelo's commentators rather than of the artist himself, who is known to have once criticized Donatello for the lack of finish in his statues), an aesthetic embodied in *The Marble Faun*. In an entry in his French and Italian Notebooks, written after seeing Michelangelo's unfinished *St. Matthew,* Hawthorne observes: "The conceptions of this great sculptor were so godlike, that he appears to have been discontented at not likewise possessing the godlike attribute of creating and embodying them with an instantaneous thought; and therefore we often find sculptures from his hand, left at the critical point of their struggle to get out of the marble. This statue of Saint Matthew looks like the antediluvian fossil of a human being, of an epoch when humanity was mightier and more majestic than now, long ago imprisoned in stone, and half-uncovered again" (Centenary, XIV, 372–73). In his discussion of Kenyon's process of modeling the clay, Hawthorne returns to this theme: the idea of forming matter through an impulse of thought. Elsewhere, speaking of the *Lorenzo de' Medici* in the Medici Chapel, he says: "It is all a miracle; the deep repose, and the deep life within it; it is as much a miracle to have achieved this, as to make a statue that would rise up and walk. . . . How wonderful! To take a block of marble and convert it wholly into thought . . . " (Centenary, XIV, 327–28). To convert a material form wholly into thought—that would be the apotheosis of art. And, in a similar sense, must not the final degree in the process of humanity's spiritualization consist of that stage in which one becomes, as it were, pure thought or pure soul? But the existence of the soul at this stage must be associated, as in art, not with abandonment of the corporeal form, but rather with its transfiguration, through which the spiritual expresses itself.

For this reason, Kenyon's final attempt at a bust of Donatello remains—and must remain—incomplete. In it he had sought to portray
the spiritualization of the Italian count, a process that can never be
finished. "And, accordingly, Donatello's bust (like that rude, rough mass
of the head of Brutus, by Michel Angelo, at Florence) has ever since
remained in an unfinished state. Most spectators mistake it for an unsuc-
cessful attempt towards copying the features of the Faun of Praxiteles.
One observer in a thousand is conscious of something more, and lingers
long over this mysterious face, departing from it, relunctantly, and with
many a glance thrown backward. What perplexes him is the riddle that
he sees propounded there; the riddle of the Soul's growth, taking its first
impulse amid remorse and pain, and struggling through the incrusta-
tions of the senses" (Centenary, iv, 381).

In her book *De l'Allemagne* Mme de Staël had sought to promote a
Romantic art that would vouchsafe to the spectator a glimpse of the
infinite. In gazing at the spectacle of the heavens, she writes, "our
thought loses itself in the infinite, our heart beats for the unknown, for
the immense, and we sense that it is only above the realm of earthly
experiences that our true life should begin" (*O.C.*, xi, 403). That is the
Romantic concept of the infinite, an infinite that manifests itself in art
through a symbolism that conveys an immediate revelation of the divine.
We have seen that this symbolism (which is also that of Emerson) could
not be Hawthorne's. But it was possible for him to approach the idea of
the infinite from another aspect, as the quest to portray in art a spiritual
perfection that would climax the progress of humanity. For this conjunction in Hawthorne of the spiritual and the artistic, two impulses which by
the nature of their objects remain perpetual, there is perhaps no more
appropriate image than that of the city of Camelot in Tennyson's *Idylls of
the King*, this "city of the soul" (but in how different a sense from Byron's) which, as the Seer tells Gareth,

> like enow
> They are building still, seeing the city is built
> To music, therefore never built at all,
> And therefore built for ever. (*Poems*, 1491)

Nor is it less significant that, like Tennyson, Hawthorne had found
himself compelled to reject Aestheticism, the "religion of art," as insufficient. In *The Marble Faun*, as in his last unfinished romances, what we
find instead is, as we have seen, a new form of symbolism—not, to be
sure, like Hawthorne's earlier neoplatonic one, but one in which the
ideal or higher reality symbolized by art has now become nothing other
than the essence of life itself.

# 3 Emerson

## Correspondences

In a letter first published several decades after his death during Voltaire's controversy with Maupertuis, Leibniz, speaking of the concept of the *scala natura* or "great chain of being," says: "All the different classes of beings which taken together make up the universe are, in the ideas of God who knows distinctly their essential gradations, only so many ordinates of a single curve so closely united that it would be impossible to place others between any two of them, since that would imply disorder and imperfection. . . . And, since the law of continuity requires that when the essential attributes of one being approximate those of another all the properties of the one must likewise gradually approximate those of the other, it is necessary that all the orders of natural beings form but a single chain, in which the various classes, like so many rings, are so closely linked one to another that it is impossible for the senses or the imagination to determine precisely the point at which one ends and the next begins."[1] Leibniz's formulation of the idea of the *scala natura* is itself, of course, but one portion of a long tradition tracing its origins back to classical antiquity and whose expression reaches to Romanticism and its aftermath.[2] Emerson invokes this concept on numerous occasions. One of its corollaries, the theory of correspondences between aspects of the different classes or species of being, possesses for him a particular importance. Seen in its proper context, it forms part of his doctrine of symbolism.

As a result of the Romantic transformation of the concept of the *scala natura* itself, Emerson's theory of its correspondences could not but differ from that of a Leibniz. For the eighteenth century, the *scala natura* enshrined a principle of order and harmony which in turn buttressed the edifice of natural religion. In the *scala natura* this principle expresses itself by a stability (of classes or species, hence of the relations or correspondences between them) that is fundamentally incompatible with the idea of either change or "temporalization." This need not imply the existence of any inherent contradiction between the two principles, since

---

[1] Quoted from Arthur O. Lovejoy, *The Great Chain of Being: A Study of the History of an Idea* (Cambridge: Harvard Univ. Press, 1936), pp. 144–45.
[2] Ibid., passim.

by a continuous transformation of the species the correspondences between them could conceivably be preserved. What it suggests, rather, is the neoclassical identification of stability with *immutability of forms* (here the attributes of the species or classes)—hence the suggestion, in Leibniz and others, of the forms of these species being contained as ideas in the mind of God, which precludes their undergoing change. Even the idea of a temporalization of the chain of being, by which various lacunae are progressively filled by new species in the course of time, could not fundamentally alter this idea, insofar as they did not affect the forms of existing species. That is because the significance of the notion of stability of forms inheres above all in the belief that in such forms and their relations to each other one might find a reflection of the mind of their Creator and source, God. This belief, enshrined at the core of classical physics by Newton, to whom space was "as it were, the sensorium or organ of God," and of which we find traces even in the nineteenth century (for example, in Agassiz), presupposes an overflowing of the divine essence into the nature of its creation, rendering that creation not only an expression but also an externalization of its source.[3] In this respect, both philosophy and science could perceive the significance of Nature in its forms, as something that imparted a form to the divine essence itself. Hence, the fixation of the order of Nature, which is elevated to the status of a theological concept.

But if thus regarded, the idea of the *scala natura* could be modified only by altering the very concept of God and his relation to the world. This, accordingly, was one of the tasks Romanticism set itself. Of the fundamental changes it introduced, two may be mentioned here. First, in the nature of the conception of God as infinite: whereas previous speculation had sought to express such infinity in quantitative terms, as the superseding of all finite limits (or even in spatial/geometric terms, as in Nicolas Cusanus), what now appears in its place is a qualitative separation or disjuncture between the very natures of finite and infinite,[4] a separation that manifests itself in the abolishing of all spatial localization, as in Hölderlin's "Patmos": "Nah ist / Und schwer zu fassen der Gott" [Near is / And difficult to grasp, the God] (*S.W.*, II:1, 165). In her *De l'Allemagne*, Mme de Staël asserts: "One asks if it is possible to conceive

[3]Cf. Agassiz, *Essay on Classification*, p. 10: "If it can be proved that man has not invented, but only traced this systematic arrangement in nature, that these relations and proportions which exist throughout the animal and vegetable world have an intellectual, and ideal connection in the mind of the Creator . . . —if, in short, we can prove premeditation prior to the act of creation, we have done once and for ever with the desolate theory which refers us to the laws of matter as accounting for all the wonders of the universe and leaves us with no God but the monotonous, unvarying action of physical forces, binding all things to their inevitable destiny."

[4]See, e.g., the discussion in Hegel's *Wissenschaft der Logik* [Science of Logic], in *G.W.* XXI, 124–37, esp. 130–37.

the infinite; nevertheless, doesn't one conceive it, at least in a negative manner, when, in mathematics, one cannot posit a limit to duration nor to extension? This infinite consists in the absence of limits; but the feeling of the infinite, such as the imagination and the heart experience it, is positive and creative" *(O.C.,* XI, 402). This positive and creative feeling of the infinite is nothing other than a consciousness of the divine presence. It is effected by the second of the two changes wrought by Romanticism that I wish to mention here: the internalization of the divine essence within the mind or self. Whereas traditional theology had professed to see the nature of God in the external world, Romanticism now asserts its presence within the soul. To be sure, on account of a renewal of pantheism brought about by the revival of interest in Spinoza, even the external world continues to possess a sacrality of its own. This sacrality, however, belongs not to its forms but to its substance, which is now pervaded by the divine presence. As a result, all matter becomes sentient with spirit.

In the relation between matter and spirit (or mind) we encounter the determining element of Emerson's doctrine of correspondences.[5] For him, every material aspect of Nature reflects its spiritual counterpart. As he declares in *Nature,* "Every natural fact is a symbol of some spiritual fact" *(Coll. W.,* I, 18). In one important respect, such a correspondence differs from the kind postulated by Leibniz, inasmuch as it is projected over a fundamental opposition in nature between the two elements. For spirit and matter do not correspond as do two attributes of differing species of the *scala natura,* but only symbolically—which is to say: through the mediation of mind, which translates the meaning of a material fact into its spiritual equivalent.

In this sense, matter and spirit are not equal, but opposing, forces: "To the rude it seems as if Matter had absolute existence, existed from an intrinsic necessity. The first effect of thought is to make us sensible that Spirit exists from an intrinsic necessity, that Matter has a merely phenomenal or accidental being, ⟨ex⟩ being created from Spirit, or being the manifestation of Spirit" *(JMN,* V, 125). And elsewhere: "There seems to be a necessity in spirit to manifest itself in material forms; and day and night, river and storm, beast and bird, acid and alkali, preëxist in necessary Ideas in the mind of God, and are what they are by virtue of preceding affections, in the world of spirit. A Fact is the end or last issue

---

[5]See especially the discussion of Emerson's doctrine of correspondences in B. L. Packer, *Emerson's Fall* (New York: Continuum Press, 1982), pp. 39–40, 64, 73–75, 78–82, describing the necessity and precariousness of "coincidence" of vision as mediation between self and world, and Sherman Paul, *Emerson's Angle of Vision* (Cambridge: Harvard Univ. Press, 1952), pp. 2–4, 32–34, 66–70, 130–31, 134, which aptly remarks (pp. 130–31): "Correspondence as a doctrine of expression was not, as Emerson used it, the assigning of symbolic value to an object. It was, instead, the *perception* of the symbolic import of an object: a way to apprehend reality."

of spirit. The visible creation is the terminus or the circumference of the invisible world" (*Coll. W.*, 1, 22). Here Emerson reflects a trace of the Leibnizian and traditional conception that associates material forms with preexistent and necessary ideas in the mind of God. Fundamentally, nevertheless, Emerson's doctrine of correspondences differs from his predecessors' in envisioning a world in which matter is not only conjoined with, but actually pervaded and impelled by, spirit. This spiritual realm is not a mere colorless, substanceless All, but rather a concentration of energies that express the affections. Medieval scholasticism had held that God was above the sphere of feelings and emotions. By attributing phenomena such as day and night, rivers and storms, beasts and birds to "preceding affections, in the world of spirit," Emerson alters the traditional formula, which represents these solely as ideas in the mind of God.

Traditionally, the idea or concept of a thing had been equated with its form. Form represents the essence of the object; through it, we define the latter. Here the form of which we speak is, of course, the pure rather than empirical form of an object. In positing the creation of a thing from its idea in the mind of God, scholasticism had sought to represent God as the very source of the being of a thing—hence to certify a creation that would be *ex nihilo* in the true sense.

For Emerson, by contrast, form becomes merely an expression of the spiritual element or divine energy. Form is now distinguished from content, which is identified with the spiritual element. In the Emersonian version of Romantic pantheism, spirit pervades matter or form as an immanent presence. In his *Ethics* Spinoza had associated God with the being of things—a fundamental revision of medieval ontology, for which God represents the source of this being. Form thus ceases to be of consequence, and what develops as a result is a theory of divine immanence which characterizes thought (as being) as that which permeates substance.

To the extent that it professes a fundamental opposition between matter and mind, or spirit, Romanticism, in its renewal of Spinozism, could hardly avoid engendering a separation of form from content— and this in spite of its explicit desire for their fusion in art (cf. Friedrich Schlegel). For Emerson at least, a new understanding of form becomes possible as a result. No longer the defining attribute of a thing, it represents for him the means by which we are allowed to trace the flow of spiritual energy in matter,a process he likens to a constant succession of waves, each overlapping its predecessor and leaving its stamp upon some new class of beings. Thus forms become fluid, endlessly dissolving and being transformed into new appearances. Correspondingly, Emerson's metaphor of circles delineates the pattern of an irradiation of force.

The necessity for spirit "to manifest itself in material forms" is above all the impulse for creative expression. It represents certain inclinations or tendencies belonging to a world above that of human passions which yet retain some likeness. In the famous concluding lines of "Die Freund-schaft," Schiller ascribes such an emotion to God:

> Friendless was the great master of worlds,
> Felt the *lack*—therefore he created spirits,
> Blessed mirrors of *his* blessedness!
> The highest essence surely found no equal,
> Out of the chalice of the whole kingdom of souls
> Foams forth *for him*—the infinite. (*Werke*, I, 111)

The power that binds matter and spirit together in correspondence can only reside in spirit. Spirit attracts matter to itself, employs it to express its own affections. In *Adonais,* his elegy on Keats, Shelley observes how

> the one Spirit's plastic stress
> Sweeps through the dull dense world, compelling there,
> All new successions to the forms they wear;
> Torturing th'unwilling dross that checks its flight
> To its own likeness, as each mass may bear;
> And bursting in its beauty and its might
> From trees and beasts and men into the Heaven's light. (Reiman and Powers, p. 402)

For Emerson, as for Shelley, a fact is merely "the end or last issue of spirit." But in Emerson's vision—more ecstatic, less Platonic in this re-spect than Shelley's—matter ceases when viewed from the proper per-spective to be the prison-house of spirit, becoming instead a transparent glass through which we catch gleams of a higher radiance. Simul-taneously, spirit appears as a pervading and infusing force, imparting to matter its own divine energy: "A fact is only a fulcrum of the spirit. It is the terminus of a past thought but only a means now to new sallies of the imagination & new progress of wisdom. . . . A man, I, am the remote circumference, the skirt, the thin suburb or frontier post of God but go inward & I find the ocean; I lose my individuality in its waves. God is Unity, but always works in variety. I go inward until I find Unity univer-sal, that Is before the World was; I come outward to this body a point of variety" (*JMN*, v, 177).

But if a fact is only "a fulcrum of the spirit" by which the latter expresses itself, the ultimate end or aim of all symbolic correspondences must be the progressive revelation of spirit to itself. In the process of self-revelation, Emerson's system of correspondences—this last vestige of the traditional scheme of the *scala natura*—both retains its religious significance and at the same time transforms it. Whereas the earlier theology had posited creation as an externalization of God, Emerson depicts it as a means by which the self shall finally realize its own divine nature, through the symbolic revelations of the external world. Pervaded by the divine energy, Emerson's world, like the *scala natura,* possesses a sacred aura, but unlike the latter, its divine energy is not something foreign to the self but rather, as we have seen, the revelation of an inner infinitude. Emanating from a divine source, the creation, in moments of high vision, assures the soul of its oneness with that source. Emerson's neoplatonism differs in this respect from its traditional predecessors, insofar as it embodies the Romantic pattern of a return to one's beginnings with an awakened and higher consciousness. To be sure, Renaissance neoplatonism had already projected similar cyclical patterns (as in Ficino's commentary on Plato's *Symposium*). What is original in Emerson's conception is the subjective turn introduced by Romanticism: an identification of the return to the source with a return to one's self, the attainment of self-consciousness. In such moments the soul realizes its own divinity. It is to this purpose that Nature ministers. Hence Emerson's dictum: "Nature is thoroughly mediate. It is made to serve" (*Coll. W.,* I, 25).

But the correspondences in which Nature participates are perceptible, according to Emerson, only at given moments, the moments of vision or spiritual perception. In this respect their validity differs from that of the correspondences in the traditional *scala natura.* They have a subjective rather than objective character—a reflection of the influence of Romantic nature-speculation.[6] But Romantic influences are operative in another fashion as well. We have seen that "a fact is only a fulcrum of the spirit," an assertion that implies, among other things, the possibility of various or multiple significances in a single symbol: hence the dependence of the precise significance of a symbol at any given moment upon the nature of the individual observer. In this sense, the system of correspondences of which Emerson speaks is not a rigid and immutable set of hierarchical relations governing the structure of the visible universe, but a kaleidoscope of endless possibilities, responding to the inspiration and receptivity of the individual psyche.[7] Despite its shift from an objective to subjective perspective, however, the doctrine of correspondences does

[6]On which, cf. Packer, pp. 78–82.

[7]Hence Emerson's criticism of Swedenborg in *Representative Men* for the rigidity of his system of correspondences. For "in nature, each individual symbol plays innumerable parts, as each particle of matter circulates in turn through every system. The central identity enables any one symbol to express successively all the qualities and shades of real being" (*C.W.,* IV, 121). On Emerson and Swedenborg, see Paul, pp. 62–65, and on Emerson's theory of symbolism, René Wellek, *A History of Modern Criticism: 1750–1950* (New Haven: Yale Univ. Press, 1955–), III, 167–70.

not suffer any loss of validity. In place of its earlier external manifestation, we now find it confirmed by the subjective experience of the individual self.

## The Language of Nature

In his famous poem "Correspondances" Baudelaire, speaking of a certain mysterious symbolic significance in Nature, says:

> Nature is a temple where from living pillars
> Are sometimes breathed forth confused words;
> Man there passes through forests of symbols
> Which observe him with familiar glances. (*O.C.*, I, 11)

In *Die Lehrlinge zu Sais* Novalis, in a similar vein, declares: "Various are the roads men take. He who follows and compares them, will see wonderful figures emerge; figures, which seem to belong to that great cipher, which man everywhere, in wings, eggshells, in clouds, in snow, in crystals and in stone formations, on ice-covered waters, on the inside and outside of mountains . . . and in strange conjectures of chance, glimpses" (*Schriften*, I, 79). Of the significance of this sign-language (*Chiffernschrift*), man catches glimpses only at moments; nevertheless, all appears bound together in secret harmony, forming a magical Whole. This Whole, moreover, is in some indescribable and as-yet-unknown sense intimately related to man: hence the "forests of symbols / Which observe him with familiar glances."

In Emerson, too, the world appears as a "forest of symbols." A celebrated passage from his essay "The Poet" proclaims: "We are symbols, and inhabit symbols; workmen, work, and tools, words and things, birth and death, all are emblems; but we sympathize with the symbols, and, being infatuated with the economical uses of things, we do not know that they are thoughts." Of the faculty of poetic inspiration, by which the mind sees through such symbols to their significances, Emerson then says:

> The poet, by an ulterior intellectual perception, gives them a power which makes their old use forgotten, and puts eyes, and a tongue, into every dumb and inanimate object. He perceives the thought's independence of the symbol, the stability of the thought, the accidency and fugacity of the symbol. As the eyes of Lyncaeus were said to see through the earth, so the poet turns the world to glass, and shows us all things in their right series and procession. For, through that better perception, he stands one step nearer to things, and sees the flowing or metamorphosis; perceives that thought is multiform; that within the form of every creature is a force impelling it to

ascend into a higher form; and, following with his eyes the life, uses the forms which express that life, and so his speech flows with the flowing of nature. . . . He uses forms according to the life, and not according to the form. This is true science. (*Coll. W.*, III, 12–13)

Here the symbolic character of Nature is ascribed, ultimately, to an inner movement or tendency by which all things aspire to a higher, more spiritual level. Nature is thus not static but progressive. Elsewhere in the same essay Emerson observes: "But nature has a higher end, in the production of new individuals, than security, namely, *ascension*, or, the passage of the soul into higher forms" (*Coll. W.*, III, 14). Only its material form prevents Nature from expressing itself as thought, or, more precisely, purely as thought. Through its striving to express itself as thought, it produces symbolism, which we may define as the product of Nature's aspiration to express thought through matter or things. It is this striving that creates the "correspondences" between mind and matter, nature and spirit. Such correspondences represent not merely the result of a preestablished harmony (Leibniz) but the incarnation of thought in matter, an immanence of the spiritual within the material, which seeks to turn all into its own likeness as thought. In this sense, thought does not merely correspond to matter but actually pervades it, and the immanence of God in the world is for Emerson the immanence of thought in Nature: "In the divine order, intellect is primary: nature, secondary: it is the memory of the mind. That which once existed in intellect as pure law, has now taken body as Nature. It existed already in the mind in solution: now, it has been precipitated, and the bright sediment is the world" (*Coll. W.*, I, 123).

But if Nature constitutes the impure material expression of eternal laws, it is also, as memory, that which seeks to recapture its original pristine essence, which it preserves within itself. This process does not originate with Nature, but with mind or spirit, that which by an outward manifestation of itself creates Nature but in such a fashion as to remain immanent within it. Embodied in Nature, it assumes the form of spiritual energy. As such it volatilizes, dissolves, and transforms matter, producing a constant succession of forms through which we perceive, with ever-increasing clearness, the presence of a governing or dominating thought. In this respect, the different classes or species of being represent merely different stages in the progression from matter to spirit.

The fluidity of Nature or things—and hence of their symbolic correspondences—is not to be confused with the character of the relation between words and things, which Emerson defines quite differently. In a passage from his journals he writes: "As Boscovich taught that two particles of matter never touch, so it seems true that nothing can be described as it is. The most accurate picture is only symbols & suggestions of ⟨i⟩ the thing but from the nature of language all remote[.]" And elsewhere: "There is every degree of remoteness from the line of things in the line of words. By & by comes a word true & closely embracing the thing. That is not Latin nor English nor any language, but *thought*. The aim of the author is not to tell truth—that he cannot do, but to suggest it" (*JMN*, v, 353, 51; see also 246). At best, then, language achieves merely an approximation to the description or naming of a thing; an ideal language would consist of fixed and exact relations between words and things. But there is, so to speak, a "language beyond language," the language of thought, an idea which Emerson perhaps borrows from Augustine (*De Trinitate*, bk. xv, chs. 10, 11), indicating the end toward which all language strives, which remains, by its very nature, forever beyond the reach of the empirical word. For Emerson, language can have no part in the continuum that binds matter to spirit, but stands outside this sphere, seeking only by signs to make it intelligible to the spirit. Thus the poet who creates a symbolic discourse out of language does so not by employing the symbols themselves (which are objects of nature) but by making use of the signs that indicate these symbols. As a result, symbolism appears as something independent of language and, consequently, of literature. For that reason, it is important to distinguish the symbol from allegory. In his Vienna *Vorlesungen über dramatische Kunst und Literatur* August Wilhelm Schlegel writes: "Allegory is the personification of a concept, a fiction proposed solely for this purpose; symbolic however is that which the imagination indeed from other causes imagines, or what otherwise possesses an actuality independent of the concept, but which nevertheless willingly lends itself to a symbolic interpretation and even offers one itself" (*Krit. Schriften*, v, 81). The symbol itself is not the "symbolic interpretation" (*sinnbildlichen Auslegung*) but merely that which gives rise to it. Hence the possibility of multiple significances or interpretations, which I have spoken of earlier (cf. Emerson's dictum that "every hose fits every hydrant"). These significances are not arbitrary and unrelated but form, rather, partial elucidations of a single Whole.

Concerning the content of such elucidations Emerson declares: "The moral law lies at the centre of nature and radiates to the circumference. It is the pith and marrow of every substance, every relation, and every process" (*Coll. W.*, 1, 26). In her *De l'Allemagne* Mme de Staël had already remarked: "It is a beautiful conception which tends toward finding a resemblance between the laws of human understanding and those of nature, and which considers the physical world as the relief-image of the moral one." To join these two worlds, the physical and the moral, forms the function of the poet: "The poet knows how to reestablish the unity of the physical world with the moral one; his imagination forms a link between the one and the other" (*O.C.*, xi, 294; x, 305). For Emerson too, this sacred office belongs by right to the poet. In moments of poetic inspiration—which are, above all, moments of visionary insight—the world of Nature becomes transparent to him, revealing the radiance of eternal laws. But the realm of Nature is, as we have seen, more than an analogy to the realm of spirit: through its unceasing striving to reach a higher sphere it reveals the spiritual element within it as the force impelling it to expression. In their form, then, natural laws mirror spiritual laws not on account of a preordained design, but because of the presence of the same force in both. That this force should seek to express itself represents, according to Emerson, a necessity of its nature: spiritual energy is by definition creative, hence must manifest itself in a never-ending succession of new forms, just as energy seeks always to discharge itself.

But since forms themselves are constantly dissolving into new forms, mind or spirit seeks a higher level on which to eternalize its self-expression. This it finds in law. For Emerson law represents the constant or unchanging patterns that the spirit follows in its acts. Such patterns fulfill the role of necessity or fate in the Emersonian vision of the world. As such, they are not the result of external forces but proceed from the nature of the spiritual element in the self. In this sense, law cannot be imposed on the self from without but must issue from its own inner tendencies, or what we may call its entelechy. To the extent that it acts from the fullness of its own nature, the self in conforming to its law also experiences an inner freedom. This freedom represents above all the fulfillment of its own nature. Only when it fails to live up to its own higher law does the individual soul find itself in opposition to Nature. At that point it ceases to be one with its ideal self. In its unity with this self, on the other hand, Nature no longer appears as something external to it but rather as part of itself, what we might describe as its external self.

Expressed in their purest form, the laws of Nature are none other than those of Reason. In a passage from his journals, Emerson had identified Reason in its uncompounded, unalloyed essence as God (*JMN*, v, 270). But Reason can express itself only through laws. Here we must distinguish Emerson's concept of symbolism from that of a Coleridge or a Goethe. What Nature reveals in symbolic form is finally, according to Emerson, neither an eternal reality nor the immutable and ineffable divine essence, but the principles of moral nature. As the highest form of Reason, such principles contain the divine element. To this extent, Emerson adheres to the Romantic view that sees in symbolism the transient and momentary revelation of the divine. But the identification of God with Reason (interpreted in a neo-Kantian rather than Enlightenment sense) strikes a chord more reminiscent of late eighteenth-century thought than of anything in the Romantic Age. Similarly, by its expression of moral laws, Nature in Emerson's conception also bears a resemblance to the traditional *scala natura,* which with its hierarchical order finds its parallel in the monarchical form of government, with its carefully graduated series of ranks and social classes. But if the content of Nature's symbolic revelation is a disclosure of higher laws rather than the pure essence of the divine, we must take this not in the sense of a mere inculcation of precepts but as glimpses afforded initiates of a mystery rite, the privileged possession of secrets which, in their full splendor, would constitute a ravishment of both senses and spirit. As a character in Novalis's *Heinrich von Ofterdingen* says to the protagonist: "You speak entirely truly, and now it will be easily comprehensible to you, that the whole of Nature exists only through the spirit of virtue and should ever more constantly. It [the spirit] is the all-kindling, all-animating Light within the earthly enclosure" (*Schriften,* i, 333). In Emerson too there occurs a description of the moment of revelation: "for the universe becomes transparent, and the light of higher laws than its own, shines through it" (*Coll. W.,* i, 22).

Like a tutelary goddess, Nature thus assumes the role of educator to the soul. In Wordsworth's "Tintern Abbey," the narrator confesses:

> For I have learned
> To look on nature, not as in the hour
> Of thoughtless youth; but hearing oftentimes
> The still, sad music of humanity,
> Nor harsh nor grating, though of ample power
> To chasten and subdue. And I have felt
> A presence that disturbs me with the joy
> Of elevated thoughts; a sense sublime
> Of something far more deeply interfused,
> Whose dwelling is the light of setting suns,
> And the round ocean and the living air,
> And the blue sky, and in the mind of man:
> A motion and a spirit, that impels
> All thinking things, all objects of all thought,
> And rolls through all things. (*P.W.,* ii, 261–62)

For Wordsworth, as for Emerson, it is the presence of the self in Nature which makes possible the latter's overseeing and guiding function, by which it reveals to the self the innermost depths of the latter's own nature. This awful presence of the self in Nature, consecrated by Wordsworth with an almost religious reverence, "disturbs" the poet, but with "the joy of elevated thoughts" rather than fear, the "sense sublime of something far more deeply interfused": the fusion of self with world, a process in which it experiences the loss of selfhood while simultaneously assuming the consciousness of Nature as its own, this "sense sublime" in which it confronts an infinite Power only to merge with it as the pure form of its own nature. But this Power is "far more deeply interfused" in yet another sense, insofar as the poet feels it as something within himself. Thus its residence is not only "the light of setting suns" but "in the mind of man." In his effort to isolate this Power he is not only brought outside himself, toward the external world, but, to an equal degree, within himself. In this sense there is, in reality, no such thing as an external world but only that which the mind traverses on its inner quest for its true self. Hence Emerson's assertion, that "nature is a discipline" (*Coll. W.*, I, 23).

We have seen how for him spirit both pervades and impels matter, a view I have attempted to trace in its Romantic context to Shelley. The same view appears in Wordsworth, as the bridge between subjective and objective ("All thinking things, all objects of all thought"), an *Urphänomen*, to use Goethe's expression, that points to the fundamental unity underlying spirit and matter. As in Emerson, moreover, this unity is one of spirit, but of a spirit that can also be conceived of as motion—hence, spiritual energy or force.

In *The Prelude* Nature fulfills its tutelary role by revealing to the poet the transcendent power and infinitude of the mind, which carries with it both its obligation and its privilege. In "Tintern Abbey" a similar pattern emerges—Nature disciplining the self by revealing to it the limits and responsibilities of its own nature. For the Emerson of *Nature*, such discipline assumes the form of a two-stage process: "Every property of matter is a school for the understanding, —its solidity or resistance, its inertia, its extension, its figure, its divisibility. The understanding adds, divides, combines, measures, and finds everlasting nutriment and room for its activity in this worthy scene. Meantime, Reason transfers all these lessons into its own world of thought, by perceiving the analogy that marries Matter and Mind" (*Coll. W.*, I, 23).

If we attempt to summarize the nature of these two stages, we arrive at (1) immersion of the mind in nature, and (2) elevation of natural science to spiritual science. By means of the understanding, mind re-creates Nature within itself. Such re-creation differs from its original inasmuch as it assumes a rational form—the form of mind, rather than of the material chaos. In its attempt to penetrate matter, mind assimilates only its properties and not its substance: solidity or resistance, inertia, extension, figure, divisibility. Through the assimilation of properties, mind is enabled to perceive the presence in matter of spirit. That is because these attributes possess a symbolic as well as descriptive significance. When isolated from their material context, their higher meaning emerges. The process of science is thus a process of fragmentation, but one that leads ultimately not to dissolution but rather to spiritual re-creation.

# 4  Melville

## Moby-Dick and Symbolism

In November of 1849 Melville was in London. During his stay he spent much time simply wandering about the various streets of the metropolis and the surrounding environs. An entry for Friday, November 9, in his journal records the following impressions: "While on one of the Bridges, the thought struck me again that a fine thing might be written about a Blue Monday in November London—a city of Dis (Dante's)—clouds of smoke—the damned &c.—its marks are left upon you" (*Journal*, ed. Metcalf, p. 25).

It was the nineteenth century that first elevated Dante to a position among the three greatest writers of world literature (along with Homer and Shakespeare). Prior to that, Petrarch's *Canzoniere* had been preferred over the *Commedia*. Even as late as 1850 Sainte-Beuve still found himself unable to admit Dante into the Temple of Taste ("le Temple du Goût"), which he announces must be rebuilt as the "Panthéon de tous les nobles humains."[1] His judgment, however, reflects the opinion of a waning "official" Classicism rather than the living reality of literary history (had not the same critic praised Voltaire and Mme du Deffand as "the two great classics" of the eighteenth century?). Already the Romantic Age had witnessed the beginnings of Dante's ascendency. Along with Petrarch, he figures among the principal influences on Shelley's unfinished poem "The Triumph of Life." Even more extraordinary is his role in Keats's *Fall of Hyperion*. In this poem, Keats, who had read *The Divine Comedy* in H. F. Cary's translation (the same used by Melville thirty years later), undertakes a symbolic ascent to the shrine of Moneta, goddess of poetry, who then initiates him into a higher knowledge, as Beatrice had done for Dante.[2]

But the discovery of the great Italian poet was not limited to the poets alone. In 1847, speaking of the *Commedia* as an epic, Balzac could say that it was "the only one which the moderns can set against that of

[1]On Dante as a classic, see E. R. Curtius, *European Literature and the Latin Middle Ages*, trans. Willard Trask (New York: Bollingen, 1953), pp. 348–50, and on the problem of modern canon formation in general, ibid., pp. 264–72.

[2]See Walter Jackson Bate, *John Keats* (Cambridge: Harvard Univ. Press, 1963), pp. 212–13, 588–89.

74

Homer . . . THE DIVINE COMEDY seems to me an immense enigma, of which the solution has not yet been found by anyone, least of all by the commentators. To thus understand Dante is to become great like him . . . " (*La Comédie humaine*, VII, 53). In one of his early reviews for the *Southern Literary Messenger* Poe had even thought it worthwhile to call his readers' attention to Niebuhr's interpretation of the first canto of the *Inferno* (*C.W.*, VIII, 164).

What was it that attracted the Romantics to Dante? In the *Commedia* a relation is established between the material and the spiritual, the temporal and the eternal. In Beatrice this relation acquires concrete embodiment. At once both an earthly figure and celestial guide, she incarnates the splendor of divine grace in a human form, the immanence of the supernatural within the natural. Seen from such a perspective, it was possible for Romanticism to find in her the expression of its doctrine of symbolism. By means of this and other connections, a new appreciation of Dante is engendered. In an early discussion of the *Divine Comedy* (1791) August Wilhelm Schlegel had sought to point out the peculiar nature of Dante's allegory, in which he perceived something more than a mere concept of the understanding. A Romantic aesthetics of symbolism is here established for allegory, which must immerse itself in the sensuous shape, and shine through it as a soul shines through its body. Dante's personnel are praised for meeting this requirement; they are said to embody something more than what can be resolved into concepts. "We everywhere tread solid ground, surrounded by a world of reality and individual existence."[3]

For Goethe this world of reality associates itself with the pictorial quality of Giotto: "With regard to recognition of the great spiritual and emotional properties of Dante, we are much advanced in the appreciation of his works when we see that exactly during his time, when *Giotto* also lived, the pictorial art in all its natural force emerged again" (*Werke*, XII, 339), an association that makes it possible to speak in turn of the "sinnbildlich bedeutend wirkende Genius" (symbolically significant affective genius) of Dante (ibid.). It is equally significant that August Wilhelm Schlegel should later have come to employ precisely the same word—*sinnbildlich*—for symbolism.

But if the example of Dante had served to inspire Romantic speculation on symbolism, it is no less the case that through its formulation of a doctrine of symbolism (as opposed to allegory) Romanticism had itself paved the way for a new appreciation of Dante. By opposing symbolism

---

[3]For discussion of Dante's role in A. W. Schlegel's formation of a Romantic concept of symbolism, René Wellek, *A History of Modern Criticism: 1750–1950* (New Haven: Yale Univ. Press, 1955–), 41–42. Quotation from Schlegel cited from p. 42.

to allegory in terms of their respective relation of the particular to the general, Goethe had become "apparently the first to draw the distinction between symbol and allegory in the modern way."[4] This occurs in his essay "Über die Gegenstände der bildenden Kunst," which appeared in the journal *Die Propyläen* in 1797. Many years later, as a result of editing his correspondence with Schiller, he recurs to this distinction. In his *Maximen und Reflexionen* it receives the following form: "There is a great difference, whether the poet seeks the particular for the general or sees the general in the particular. From the first procedure arises allegory, where the particular serves only as an example of the general; the second procedure, however, is really the nature of poetry: it expresses something particular, without thinking of the general or pointing to it. Whoever vitally grasps this particular, obtains the general simultaneously, without being aware of it, or only later" (*Werke*, XII, 471).

The "nature of poetry" is thus associated with the symbolic. A subsequent maxim defines it further: "True symbolism is where the particular represents the more general, not as a dream or a shadow, but as a living momentary revelation of the Inscrutable" (*Werke*, XII, 471, trans. from Wellek).

In allegory, according to Goethe, the particular is without concrete substance; it embodies nothing in itself but merely serves to exemplify. The symbol cannot be considered as an exemplification in the same sense. In symbolism the general (*das Allgemeine*) no longer means the same thing as in allegory. As something literally revealed by the symbol, it is not an abstract quantity but an eternal essence. Symbolism is thus a relation of phenomena to noumena rather than of examples to abstract truth. For this reason the symbol can offer only a "living momentary revelation" of the Inscrutable. In its material existence, as the particular, it belongs to the world of phenomena, a world subject to flux and change. Only at certain given moments does it reveal the eternal essence contained within it.

It is necessary at this point to stress the peculiar nature of Goethe's concept of the symbol. He calls it "a living momentary revelation of the Inscrutable"—as if to emphasize, not merely its precariousness, but also its apocalyptic and sacral quality. For the "Inscrutable" is, in effect, nothing else than the divine essence, or God himself. Through the symbol, therefore, we receive a glimpse of the nature of God—an assertion that will later have significant consequences for Melville's theory of symbolism. In *Moby-Dick* especially, the apocalyptic overtones of Goethe's insight are both preserved and elevated to a new, problematic level.

[4]Wellek, *History*, I, 211; for Goethe's concept of symbolism, pp. 210–12. Also Karl Viëtor, *Goethe the Thinker*, trans. Bayard Quincy Morgan (Cambridge: Harvard Univ. Press, 1950), pp. 174–9.

Another aphorism from the *Maximen und Reflexionen* elaborates further upon the nature of symbolism: "Symbolism changes the phenomenon into the idea, the idea into the image, in such a way that the idea remains always infinitely active and unapproachable in the image, and will remain inexpressible even though expressed in all languages" (*Werke*, xii, 470, trans. from Wellek). A two-stage process is thus outlined, in which the final result is the creation of an image that does not cancel out the idea but acts in some sense as its complement. This image is at the same time distinguished from the appearance, possessing a kind of eternal existence that elevates it above the change and flux of the phenomenal world.

There is, to be sure, something curious in the idea's being simultaneously "infinitely active" and "unapproachable" in the image. It presupposes a genuine immanence of the idea in the image. What is "expressed in all languages" is the image rather than the idea, which Goethe calls "unapproachable" insofar as its own nature is not conveyed by the image. The idea is at the same time "infinitely active" by expressing itself through the image, which conveys the "experience" of that idea. We may distinguish the symbol from the allegorical figure by saying that the former has both a concrete content and actual substance independent of literature. Behind the surface of its phenomenal appearance stands its noumenal essence. Circumstances combine to create a "revelation" of that essence as the experience of a transcendence of the realm of phenomena. In both concrete and psychological terms, then, the symbol is more "real" than allegory: first, because it constitutes an actual object in the natural world, or Nature itself; second, because the experience of something that transcends phenomena which symbolism affords is not merely intellectual or cognitive but one that approaches the character of a religious revelation. Goethe suggests the latter aspect when he says "True symbolism is where the particular represents the more general, not as a dream or a shadow. . . ." Such language carries a specific resonance. We have seen in our discussion of Poe how medieval allegoresis had sought through figures of the Old Testament to establish prophetic anticipations of events in the New, as well as of the person of Christ. During the Renaissance such figures begin to be called "types." Since it was also customary to refer to them as "shadows," Goethe, by pointing to the illusory nature of the shadow, underscores the unreality of allegory as opposed to the symbol.

From the standpoint of criticism, recent years have witnessed a renewed interest in allegoresis. Along with it has come a tendency to regard symbolism simply as another form of allegory; the Romantic distinction between them is dismissed as obscuring their fundamental identity. Like the allegorical figure, the symbol has come to be considered merely as a sign.[5] Historically speaking, such a notion is, as we have seen, based upon a serious misconception, since the Romantic symbol is a concrete thing rather than a sign. As something having an actual existence in Nature, it possesses a reality to which allegory cannot aspire. A passage from Coleridge's *Statesman's Manual* comments upon their difference: "Now an Allegory is but a translation of abstract notions into a picture-language which is itself nothing but an abstraction from objects of the senses; the principal being more worthless even than its phantom proxy, both alike unsubstantial, and the former shapeless to boot. On the other hand a Symbol (ὅ ἐστιν ἀεὶ ταυτηγόρικον) is characterized by a translucence of the Special in the Individual or of the General in the Especial or of the Universal in the General. Above all by the translucence of the Eternal through and in the Temporal. It always partakes of the Reality which it renders intelligible; and while it enunciates the whole, abides itself as a living part in that Unity, of which it is the representative" (*Coll. W.*, VI, 30).

Goethe and August Wilhelm Schlegel had already advanced a similar charge against allegory. In offering his critique, Coleridge presents the notion of different "levels" of symbolism, each manifesting itself through the one below it and in turn revealing a yet higher level. A Plotinian hierarchy of Being is constructed, in which the One or the Universal proceeds by ontological descent through the various degrees of being down to the particular concrete existence. But at each level, there remains the translucent projection of a higher one, so that the movement of descent becomes one of ascent as well. These levels are not merely the result of an artificial schema of thought but correspond to the actual conformation of things, whereby the One or Universal emerges as the most real of all.[6]

For Coleridge the revelation of symbolism is assured by an organic unity that signifies a continuity of the material and the spiritual. Such continuity elevates the material to the level of the spiritual and simultaneously permits the latter to express itself through the material. The concept of organic unity also opens up for Romanticism the possibility of

[5]Cf., e.g., Angus Fletcher, *Allegory: The Theory of a Symbolic Mode*, (Ithaca, N.Y.: Cornell Univ. Press, 1964), pp. 13–19. The effect of such discussions has been precisely to obscure the true nature of Romantic symbolism, which, on account of its crucial significance for the literary history of Romanticism itself, must now be recovered. With some of Coleridge's remarks, as well as modern discussions, we encounter a psychologization of symbolism which, while germane to Coleridge's particular interest in psychology, colors somewhat our perspective upon what is essentially a religious notion, with its specific place in the Romantic secularization of religion. See further, Thomas McFarland, *Originality & Imagination* (Baltimore: Johns Hopkins Univ. Press, 1985), pp. 186–87.

[6]For Coleridge's concept of symbolism, see J. Robert Barth, *The Symbolic Imagination: Coleridge and the Romantic Tradition* (Princeton: Princeton Univ. Press, 1977), esp. pp. 7–10, 13–15, 111, 116–19. Speaking of symbolism in the Coleridgean sense, Barth states: "The sacred is no longer awesomely apart; it is awesomely present" (p. 136).

unconscious symbolic expression. In a passage from one of his essays Coleridge addresses himself to this issue: "Of most importance to our present subject is this point, that the latter (allegory) cannot be other than spoken consciously;—whereas in the former (the symbol) it is very possible that the general truth may be unconsciously in the writer's mind during the construction of the symbol . . . " (*Miscellaneous Criticism*, p. 29).

This passage enables us to place Melville's own remarks on the composition of *Moby-Dick* in a new light. In his well-known letter of January 8, 1852, to Sophia Hawthorne he writes: "But, then, since you, with your spiritualizing nature, see more things than other people, and by the same process, refine all you see, so that they are not the same things that other people see, but things which while you think you but humbly discover them, you do in fact create them for yourself—Therefore, upon the whole, I do not so much marvel at your expressions concerning Moby Dick. At any rate, your allusion for example to the 'Spirit Spout' first showed to me that there was a subtile significance in that thing—but I did not, in that case, *mean* it. I had some vague idea while writing it, that the whole book was susceptible of an allegoric construction, & also that *parts* of it were—but the speciality of many of the particular subordinate allegories, were first revealed to me, after reading M$^r$ Hawthorne's letter, which, without citing any particular examples, yet intimated the part-&-parcel allegoricalness of the whole.—" (*Letters*, p. 146). Some may wish to discern an ironic tone here. To do so, however, is to neglect, first of all, Melville's awareness of Sophia's closeness to her husband, which would make writing to her tantamount in this case to addressing Hawthorne himself. But it also neglects the reality of literary history at that time. Hadn't Poe, for instance, only a few years earlier, attacked allegory as that "of which there is not one respectable word to be said"? The problem is that we do not sufficiently distinguish between allegory and symbolism: for Melville to profess not having an allegorical significance in mind does not imply the absence of any significant intention whatsoever.

Moreover, there is the content of the letter itself to consider. In it, Melville remarks of Sophia's penchant for seeing allegorical significances that "while you think you but humbly discover them, you do in fact create them for yourself." Had she but inferred his own intentions, wouldn't it have been simpler to say so? What is remarkable is that, even while observing that she in fact creates these significances, he does not disavow them. In so doing, he allows for the possibility of latent meaning. Here, the "vague idea" or intuition of which Melville speaks presents an analogue to Coleridge's notion of unconscious symbolic expression. This possibility, as we have seen, is itself inseparably joined to the Romantic concept of the organic unity of the creative process.

Through such unity, the distinction between avowed and submerged content disappears; both are subsumed under the creative assertion of the imagination, as the expression of its will. In this respect, it suffices for the author to evoke the object in order to conjure up the resources of its symbolism.

Among the concepts that make up Goethe's theory of literature, one in particular may be said to occupy a central position: the equation of the growth process of a work of art with that of organic life. On account of his biological studies this association must have possessed a special meaning for him. The vision of the organic unity of art, its similitude in form to the world of Nature, runs through all of Romantic criticism. In his reading of Coleridge's *Biographia Literaria* Melville would have encountered it. He could also have found it in another source: Emerson. The concept of the organicism of a work of art, expressed in a passage of Emerson's *Essays: Second Series,* represents but one of the many grounds from which it would be possible to trace a spiritual affinity. Speaking of the situation of the poet, Emerson says: "Nature offers all her creatures to him as a picture-language" (*Coll. W.,* iii, 8). This picture-language is not that of allegory (which Coleridge had criticized in his *Statesman's Manual*) but rather of the image as Goethe describes it in his *Maximen und Reflexionen,* one that itself forms part of the natural order of things. We recall also Goethe's assertion that "the idea remains infinitely active and unapproachable in the image." To this Emerson now adds the testimony of the Neoplatonist Iamblichus: "Things more excellent than every image are expressed through images," a saying that induces the following conclusion: "Things admit of being used as symbols, because nature is a symbol, in the whole, and in every part" (both citations from *Coll. W.,* iii, 8).

We have seen earlier how Emerson himself had drawn upon some of the same Romantic writers with whom Melville was later to experience a similar affinity. The sharing of common tendencies imparts a special significance to the crossing of the paths of these two American authors. In the winter of 1849 Melville attended one of Emerson's lectures in Boston. A well-known passage from a letter to Evert Duyckinck registers his reaction: "Now, there is a something about every man elevated above mediocrity, which is, for the most part, instinctuly perceptible. This I see in M$^r$ Emerson. And, frankly, for the sake of the argument, let us call him a fool;—then had I rather be a fool than a wise man. —I love all men who *dive.* Any fish can swim near the surface, but it takes a great whale to go down stairs five miles or more; & if he dont attain the bottom, why, all the lead in Galena can't fashion the plumet that will. I'm not talking of M$^r$ Emerson now—but of the whole corps of thought-divers, that have been diving and coming up again with bloodshot eyes since the world began" (*Letters,* p. 79).

Of Emerson's numerous remarks on natural symbolism, it suffices to cite one to reveal his affinity with Melville. A passage from "The Poet," quoted earlier, reads: "As the eyes of Lyncaeus were said to see through the earth, so the poet turns the world to glass, and shows us all things in their right series and procession." Here, as in Coleridge, symbolism is defined as a "translucence of the Eternal through and in the Temporal." At the same time, Emerson can also assert that "within the form of every creature is a force impelling it to ascend into a higher form." The force of which he speaks is in fact nothing other than life in its purest form. As such it contains within itself the divine essence, which aspires to the highest state of spiritual reality, that represented by Unity or the One.[7]

This essence is at the same time visibly revealed through the natural world. In Ishmael's description in *Moby-Dick* of his impressions on seeing an albatross for the first time, we obtain a glimpse of it:

> It was during a prolonged gale, in waters hard upon the Antarctic seas. From my forenoon watch below, I ascended to the overclouded deck; and there, dashed upon the main hatches, I saw a regal, feathery thing of unspotted whiteness, and with a hooked, Roman bill sublime. At intervals, it arched forth its vast archangel wings, as if to embrace some holy ark. Wondrous flutterings and throbbings shook it. Though bodily unharmed, it uttered cries, as some king's ghost in supernatural distress. Through its inexpressible, strange eyes, methought I peeped to secrets which took hold of God. As Abraham before the angels, I bowed myself; the white thing was so white, its wings so wide, and in those for ever exiled waters, I had lost the miserable warping memories of traditions and of towns. Long I gazed at that prodigy of plumage. I cannot tell, can only hint, the things that darted through me then. (*Moby-Dick,* p. 165)

Melville here confers upon the albatross the vestiture of sacrality: "it arched forth its vast archangel wings, as if to embrace some holy ark." The "holy ark" recalls, of course, the Ark of the Covenant, visible sign of God's presence. This Ark is a symbol in the Romantic sense: it expresses the divine presence and is, simultaneously, consecrated by that presence.

---

[7]For Melville's relation to Emerson, see Merton M. Sealts, Jr., "Melville and Emerson's Rainbow," in his *Pursuing Melville, 1940–1980* (Madison: Univ. of Wisconsin Press, 1982), pp. 251–77, and for Melville's reading of Emerson specifically, pp. 266, 268–70. Sealts also observes: "However much or little of Emerson Melville had read by 1850 and 1851, he obviously knew other Transcendental scripture, and it seems safe to say that his reading of one book in particular—Carlyle's *Sartor Resartus,* with its central idea of 'all visible things' as 'emblems' of the invisible, and of Nature itself as '*the living visible Garment of God*'—had at least as much to do with the symbolism of *Moby-Dick* as anything in the 'Language' chapter of Emerson's *Nature*" (p. 268).

A concrete object having actual existence, it participates at the same time in the suprasensual. By metaphoric association, the symbolic properties of the Ark are bestowed upon the albatross. Ishmael then compares it to the ghost of Hamlet's father: "Though bodily unharmed, it uttered cries, as some king's ghost in supernatural distress." Why the allusion? The ghost of Hamlet's father must communicate a secret to the prince. Melville here introduces another aspect of the theme of revelation, its problematic nature. For there is something morally unfathomable in the secret communicated to Hamlet by his father.[8]

Earlier we encountered Goethe's description of the symbol as "a living and momentary revelation of the Inscrutable." In Ishmael's account of the albatross Melville employs a similar notion: "Through its inexpressible, strange eyes, methought I peeped to secrets which took hold of God." On account of the transient nature of the revelation, Ishmael receives but a glimpse of the Eternal. His bowing to the albatross in acknowledgment of its sacrality touches upon yet another aspect of the symbol. Participation in a higher Reality confers sacrality upon Nature.[9] Among the Romantics the theme appears in both Hölderlin and Wordsworth. Hölderlin's poem "Bread and Wine" is a vision of natural things endowed with sacrality by means of grace. But the notion of transubstantiation does not appear in it. The divine grace that blesses Nature does not transform it into something else. There is an innate sacrality in the things of nature themselves, which creates the aura of grace. Wordsworth, too, can affirm the sacrality of Nature. It pervades the poetry of both his early and middle years, the simple pieces like "Nutting" as well as the great poems like "Tintern Abbey" and the Immortality Ode.

From his experience of the sacrality of Nature, Ishmael unconsciously passes to thinking of the albatross as a literal incarnation of the divine. He likens himself to Abraham receiving the apparition at Mamre (Gen. 18). In this story, three angels disguised as men visit the patriarch. Only gradually does awareness of their true nature dawn upon him. God appears to Abraham in the form of the three men (the text is not wholly clear as to whether he assumes the form of one or of all three at the same time). These men do not merely signify the divine presence to Abraham: in a radical sense, they incarnate it. Incarnation thus comes to represent symbolism at its most extreme. When Ishmael worships the albatross, he pays homage to it as an incarnation of the divine presence itself. He confesses: "the white thing was so white, its wings so wide, and in those

---

[8] Melville returns, of course, to the relationship of Hamlet and his father in *Pierre*, in which Pierre's confrontation and dialogue with the portrait in bk. IV manifests echoes of Hamlet's colloquy with the ghost of his father.

[9] In his generally fine analysis of Melvillean symbolism, F. O. Matthiessen seems to me to miss this particular aspect of it. See his *American Renaissance* (London: Oxford Univ. Press, 1941), pp. 246–52.

forever exiled waters, I had lost the miserable warping memories of traditions and of towns." These "warping memories" make up the orthodox Christian doctrine he has renounced. In place of it, he gives himself over to a Romantic symbolism that associates a symbol with the divine presence. Finally he intimates: "I cannot tell, can only hint, the things that darted through me then." We recall Melville's praise of Shakespeare in the essay "Hawthorne and His Mosses": "But it is those deep far-away things in him; those short, quick probings at the very axis of reality;—these are the things that make Shakspeare, Shakspeare" (*Representative Selections*, p. 334).[10] In like fashion, the things that dart through Ishmael constitute "probings at the very axis of reality," sudden and momentary apprehensions of the true nature of the divine. That nature reveals itself in the form of the albatross, whose appearance offers, in effect, a genuine theophanic apparition.

In concluding his own description of the albatross, Ishmael informs the reader of his ignorance of Coleridge's "Rime of the Ancient Mariner" at the time of his first sighting the bird. The disavowal of direct influence is then transformed into encomium: "Yet, in saying this, I do but indirectly burnish a little brighter the noble merit of the poem and the poet" (*Moby-Dick*, p. 165). A similar symbolism pervades both works. Inasmuch as Coleridge had likened the albatross of his poem to a "Christian soul," the Mariner's shooting of it constitutes a fundamental violation of natural piety, a charge that is later applied to Ahab's quest for the White Whale. Such natural piety assumes in both works an added importance on account of the symbolic aspect of Nature, which both contains and reveals the divine presence.[11]

[10]For the Shakespearean influence upon *Moby-Dick*, see Matthiessen, pp. 412–17, 423–31, 431–35, 449–51, and Charles Olson, *Call Me Ishmael* (New York: Reynall & Hitchcock, 1947), pp. 39–73.

[11]On the symbolism of Coleridge's "Rime of the Ancient Mariner," see, *inter alia*, Humphrey House, *Coleridge: The Clark Lectures 1951–52* (London: Rupert Hart-Davis, 1962), pp. 88–104, esp. 88, 92, 104; George Watson, *Coleridge the Poet* (New York: Barnes & Noble, 1966), pp. 94–104; and Walter Jackson Bate, *Coleridge* (New York: Macmillan, 1968), pp. 57–65. One might well agree with Bate about the insufficiency of the poem's concluding moral—which is not to say that such a conclusion is irrelevant. But perhaps it would be more plausible to argue that the killing of the albatross—involuntary as it seems—represents an internal act of the psyche, the symbolic expression of a subliminal impulse, which then requires an inward *metanoia*, or fundamental change of attitude on the Mariner's part. This occurs with the blessing of the water snakes, which opens up the Mariner's soul to the possibility of receiving a blessing—i.e., grace. Like the killing of the albatross, it, too, is involuntary; the Mariner confesses: "A spring of love gushed from my heart, / And I blessed them unaware." The whole poem may be seen to concern the need and longing for grace (which Coleridge defines in psychological terms), the necessity for redemption from the subconscious impulses of the psyche. The various tortures the Mariner undergoes represent in effect self-tortures: the mind externalizes itself in Nature (natural appearances) as a means of symbolizing its state to itself. Under these circumstances the grace or redemption the Mariner longs for is equated with the possibility of expressing love. To be able to do so brings about a form of psychological release. Hence the special import of

From Goethe, Emerson, and Coleridge, among others, Melville could have obtained his concept of symbolism. Another source suggests itself as well: Carlyle.[12] In *Heroes and Hero-Worship* (which he read in the summer of 1850), he would have found the Romantic concept of symbolism embodied in Carlyle's idea of Man:

> But now if all things whatsoever that we look upon are emblems to us of the Highest God, I add that more so than any of them is man such an emblem . . . . The essence of our being, the mystery in us that calls itself 'I,'—ah, what words have we for such things? —is a breath of Heaven; the Highest Being reveals himself in man. This body, these faculties, this life of ours, is it not all as a vesture for that Unnamed? 'There is but one Temple in the Universe,' says the devout Novalis, 'and that is the Body of Man. Nothing is holier than that high form. Bending before men is a reverence done to this Revelation in the Flesh. We touch Heaven when we lay our hand on a human body!' (*Works*, v, 10)

To preclude the possibility of misunderstanding, Carlyle hastily adds: "This sounds much like a mere flourish of rhetoric; but it is not so. If

---

the conclusion: "He prayeth best, who loveth best / All things both great and small; / For the dear God who loveth us, / He made and loveth all." This is to say that prayer (the longing for redemption from one's sinful nature) achieves its ends only through the capacity for love (which effects the mind's psychological release from its own self-destructive tendencies). Love here appears (as elsewhere in Coleridge) as the means of achieving sacramental communion with the other: as such it brings about deliverance from the dangers of solipsistic self-consciousness and subjectivity. In this particular context, God is addressed as the source of the expressive, externalizing (creative) activity of love. By surrendering itself to such love, the mind becomes capable of experiencing Nature not as hostile other but as an expression of the self.

In *Moby-Dick* Ishmael experiences a similar self-destructive impulse (the desire to destroy the White Whale, a desire which exacts its own retributive response), which Melville relates in a more problematic fashion to the incapacity to love ("the visible spheres of the world were formed in love, but the invisible spheres were formed in fright"). Here Melville implies that this incapacity is itself the result—rather than cause—of a hostility in Nature, which is not simply the projection or externalizing of the self but a positive force in its own right (cf. "The Mast-head"). But were it possible to love, this might produce a catharsis or spiritual release comparable to that which Ishmael experiences at the end of the novel, where the destruction of the ship and of Ahab seems to bring about simultaneously the consummation of the internal destructive energy in Ishmael himself, which, by being expressed through Ahab, can then disappear with him. But the sacramental closure of "The Rime of the Ancient Mariner" is lacking here, if only because the activity of love does *not* lead (in contrast to Coleridge's poem) to communion with the other, with Nature, and hence ultimately with the creative impulses of the psyche. Rather, Nature remains in this work something distinctly other, so that the experience of the sacred becomes one of the *difference* of an other from the self (cf. the albatross in "The Whiteness of the Whale"). The experience of difference becomes one of sacredness through feeling a loss of the human (the self) *in* that other, its assimilation by that other, which indicates the other's power.

[12]For Melville and Carlyle in terms of Carlylean heroism and related perspectives, see Jonathan Arac, *Commissioned Spirits: The Shaping of Social Motion in Dickens, Carlyle, Melville, and Hawthorne* (New Brunswick, N.J.: Rutgers Univ. Press, 1979), pp. 139–63.

well meditated, it will turn out to be a scientific fact; the expression, in such words as can be had, of the actual truth of the thing. *We* are the miracle of miracles, —the great inscrutable mystery of God."

Man is the supreme emblem of God because "the essence of our being, the mystery in us that calls itself 'I,' . . . is a breath of Heaven." There is something inexpressible about this essence ("what words have we for such things?"). It derives from the fact that the element of such an essence is the suprasensual; Carlyle calls it the "breath of Heaven." Here we may understand *breath*—as Carlyle himself probably did—in the Biblical sense, which equates it with *life.* Thus the essence of man is the essence or life of Heaven. Man contains the element of the divine or suprasensual within himself. In this sense it becomes possible to speak of the body as a "vesture" for the Unnamed; hence the definition of man as a symbol who reveals in his soul the higher or suprasensual Reality. Here the reason for the difficulty of describing the human essence is also touched upon: its participation in the element of the Unnamed, God. Carlyle says explicitly: "the Highest Being reveals himself in man"—an idea to which the passage from Novalis offers additional emphasis. The more common Romantic identification of Nature as the temple of God is refuted; instead, the place of Nature is assigned to man himself. Such symbolism confers sacrality upon man as one who both partakes of and reveals the divine.

At this point, a distinction must be made between the symbolism of Carlyle and Novalis and the kind of Romantic pantheism that takes Spinoza as its starting point. In Carlyle and Novalis the assertion that man possesses the element of the divine need not necessarily lead to the assumption of his oneness with God: equally possible is a descent of the element of divinity from a supreme Being into lesser beings, in whom it assumes the form of a love through which the world will in turn be sanctified. In the *Hymnen an die Nacht* the poet recalls his mission: "the Mother sent me with my brothers and sisters to dwell in your world, to sanctify it with love, so that it will become an eternally visible monument—to plant it with unfading flowers" (*Schriften,* 1, 139). The transmission of the element of the divine represents something more than what is contained in the traditional concept of grace. Even in its human form, this element retains (through love) the power to consecrate. Sacrality thus comes to mean: possession of the divine element by that which is not intrinsically divine. Hence Novalis's assertion concerning man: "Nothing is holier than that high form." On that condition alone, "bending before men is a reverence done to this Revelation in the Flesh." Before the albatross, Ishmael bows himself in similar homage. Like man, the bird, too, is in the fullest sense a symbol, which is to say: a revelation of the nature of the divine.

Through the symbolism of the albatross in *Moby-Dick*, it becomes possible, then, to associate Melville with a theory of the symbol that originates in Goethe and subsequently comes to pervade all of Romanticism. But Melville does not merely assimilate this theory; he also transforms it. If the symbol is supposed to reveal the divine essence, its failure to do so (in other words, its opacity) makes it possible to doubt the existence of God himself. It is this doubt which Melville ascribes to Ahab, to whom the adjective "ungodly" is applied. Such atheism owes its origin to the opacity of the symbol, its failure to reveal the divine. To Starbuck Ahab says: "All visible objects, man, are but as pasteboard masks" (*Moby-Dick*, p. 144).

The sacrality that originally belongs to Nature by virtue of its participation in the divine now qualifies it as the only possible object of worship in a world where God has apparently ceased to exist. In this sense the pantheism of *Moby-Dick* differs fundamentally from that of a Wordsworth or a Schelling: the sacrality of Nature is all that remains after the disappearance of God. In a letter to Hawthorne, Melville had written: "I feel that the Godhead is broken up like the bread at the Supper, and that we are the pieces" (*Letters*, p. 142).

What Ishmael worships in the albatross, then, is not the Christian God but what he sees as the sacred or divine essence of Nature. In his description of the bird he singles out its whiteness. Subsequently, he gives this as his reason for worshiping it. But, as Ishmael comes to realize, simply to worship will not suffice. He feels impelled by a desire to know what constitutes the nature of that whiteness itself:

But not yet have we solved the incantation of this whiteness, and learned why it appeals with such power to the soul; and more strange and far more portentous—why, as we have seen, it is at once the most meaning symbol of spiritual things, nay, the very veil of the Christian's Deity; and yet should be as it is, the intensifying agent in things the most appalling to mankind. Is it that by its indefiniteness it shadows forth the heartless voids and immensities of the universe, and thus stabs us from behind with the thought of annihilation, when beholding the white depths of the milky way? Or is it, that as in essence whiteness is not so much a color as the visible absence of color, and at the same time the concrete of all colors; is it for these reasons that there is such a dumb blankness, full of meaning, in a wide landscape of snows—a colorless, all-color of atheism from which we shrink? And when we consider that other theory of the natural philosophers, that all other earthly hues—every stately or lovely emblazoning—the sweet tinges of sunset skies and woods; yea, and the gilded velvets of butterflies, and the butterfly cheeks of young girls; all these are but subtle deceits, not actually inherent in substances, but only laid on from without; so that all deified Nature absolutely paints like the harlot, whose allurements cover nothing but the charnel-house within; and when we proceed further, and consider that the mystical cosmetic which produces every one of her hues, the great principle of light, for ever remains white or colorless in itself, and if operating without medium upon matter, would touch all objects, even tulips and roses, with its own blank tinge—pondering all this, the palsied universe lies before us a leper; and like wilful travellers in Lapland, who refuse to wear colored and coloring glasses upon their eyes, so the wretched infidel gazes himself blind at the monumental white shroud that wraps all the prospect around him. And of all these things the Albino Whale was the symbol. Wonder ye then at the fiery hunt? (*Moby-Dick*, pp. 169–70)

The whiteness of which Ishmael speaks is initially termed "the most meaning of spiritual things." Almost immediately, however, he hints that it conceals rather than revealing: it is the "veil of the Christian's Deity." For the ending of his *Narrative of Arthur Gordon Pym* Poe had used the image of a veil of whiteness (was Melville familiar with it?). But the whiteness of *Moby-Dick* presents an ambiguous symbol.[13] One cannot be certain what it reveals. Even the individual possibilities can be self-contradictory ("a dumb blankness, full of meaning"). The possibility is also raised of its not having any meaning at all. A question comes to mind at this point: what is the "colorless, all-color of atheism" to which Ishmael refers? Whiteness is both "the visible absence of color" and the "concrete of all colors." Ishmael seeks to imply that the essence of color is precisely ths absence of color. By analogy the essence of Nature might therefore be pure void, pure nothingness. But, as we have seen, the essence of Nature is also the divine essence itself, which thus equals that same nothingness. Hence the "colorless, all-color of atheism."

From these considerations, it is but a logical step to the formation of a "theory of color." Color is independent of substance: in themselves, substances have no color at all. The intrinsic absence of color from substance suggests that the whiteness Ishmael regards as a symbol and which he believes to reveal the nature of things does not in fact participate in that nature at all, but represents merely one of the conditions of perception that the mind itself creates.

Light produces color. If color is a symbol, the divine essence must be the source that both literally and figuratively illuminates symbolism. Melville calls light "the mystical cosmetic." The Middle Ages had developed a tradition that professed to see a literal truth in the metaphor of

---

[13]On the image of whiteness from a phenomenological perspective, Paul Brodtkorb, *Ishmael's White World: A Phenomenological Reading of Moby-Dick* (New Haven: Yale Univ. Press, 1965). With regard to the ambiguities of symbolism in the work, Walter Bezanson aptly remarks: "The symbolism in *Moby-Dick* is not static but is in motion; it is in process of creation for both narrator and reader. Value works back and forth: being extracted from objects, it descends into the consciousness; spiraling up from the consciousness, it envelops objects" ("Moby-Dick: Work of Art," in Tyrus Hillway and Luther Mansfield, eds., *Moby-Dick Centennial Essays* [Dallas, Tex.: Southern Methodist Univ. Press, 1953], p. 47).

God as light. Its scriptural text was 1 John 1:5: "For God is light." In the passage we are now considering illumination assumes an ironic significance. Light produces the effect not of "enlightening" but of obscurity: "the great principle of light . . . if operating without medium upon matter, would touch all objects, even tulips and roses, with its own blank tinge." In a similar fashion, symbolism is produced by a "medium" that creates the conditions of perception: the human mind. Thus the symbol does not actually partake of the divine, and could not reveal it. "Revelation" through symbolism becomes an illusion: in the divine itself there would be no revelation at all. By its nature, it can neither reveal itself nor make it possible to apprehend anything else. It produces exactly the opposite effect: it annuls the possibility of sight.

A result is the rejection of Romantic pantheism: "deified Nature absolutely paints like the harlot." We have seen how deified Nature had originally signified the presence of God in Nature, a presence that becomes apprehensible through the symbol. But symbolism has now been exposed as illusion—"deified Nature" itself, consequently, as self-deception by a mind that imposes the conditions of its own perception upon the external world.

The "colored and coloring glasses" to which Ishmael refers offer a material analogy to the conditions of such perception. The attempt to see without these, like the attempt to apprehend God without recourse to symbolism, necessarily ends in blindness. But blindness can result equally from either the fullness of the divine presence (a scriptural concept) or absolute nothingness. The former possibility is especially significant: as in "The Mast-head," Melville depicts a dazzling and hypnotic radiance whose effect proves ultimately destructive. If attributable to God, then it is God who deliberately causes such blindness. Ironically it results from the attempt to see him face to face.

Like others, this conclusion could be at best only a temporary one for Melville. As Hawthorne was later to observe of him, "He can neither believe, nor be comfortable in his unbelief." But if *Moby-Dick* typifies but one stage of a lifelong spiritual quest, it initiates, with regard to Melvillean symbolism, a development that culminates in the denial of symbolism altogether. For Melville, this denial could only imply the opposite of realism: a return to allegory.


*Theatrum mundi*

Toward the end of *The Confidence-Man* there occurs a brief interlude in which one of the characters pauses to reflect for a few moments upon the true identity of the Cosmopolitan. He remembers the familiar lines from Shakespeare:

> All the world's a stage
> And all the men and women merely players,
> Who have their exits and their entrances,
> And one man in his time plays many parts. (*As You Like It*, ii, vii)

During the Middle Ages and the Renaissance this metaphor had received a particular designation: *theatrum mundi*, the theater of the world. It also characterizes the world of Melville's novel. Within the novel itself Melville explicitly compares the world of his fiction to that of a play: "In this way of thinking, the people in a fiction, like the people in a play, must dress as nobody exactly dresses, talk as nobody exactly talks, act as nobody exactly acts" (*Writings*, x, 183). Here the pageant-like nature of drama is emphasized. It is designed to satisfy "the implied wish of the more indulgent lovers of entertainment, before whom harlequin can never appear in a coat too parti-colored, or cut capers too fantastic" (p. 183).

We know that at a later point in his life Melville was to discover for himself the dramas of Calderón. In them he might have found what he had sought to embody years earlier in this novel: an allegorical depiction of the world in which individuals are transformed into representative figures, through whose history or experiences higher truths are revealed. Shelley, too, had discovered and been fascinated by Calderón during his last years. In the works of the Spanish playwright he could have perceived certain dramatic anticipations of what he was himself to seek to transpose onto the poetic plane in his "Triumph of Life": an allegorical-symbolic representation of life as a kind of endless pageant, which through the illumination vouchsafed by death assumes a spiritual significance. But if "The Triumph of Life" attempts to fuse the symbolic with the allegorical, the allegory of *The Confidence-Man*, by contrast, develops out of conscious opposition to the tenets of Romantic symbolism.

Such symbolism necessarily implies pantheism, the revelation of the nature of the divine essence through the symbol presupposing the presence of the divine in Nature, as the Being of things. It is this Being that the symbol renders visible or expresses. As a result of his turning away from pantheism (indicated already to some extent in *Moby-Dick*) Melville would have been led to a renunciation of symbolism as well—one that results in a return to allegory.[14]

---

[14]Among studies of Melville's allegory in *The Confidence-Man*, pride of place must still be accorded Elizabeth Foster's introduction to the Hendricks House edition (*The Confidence-Man* (New York: Hendricks House, 1954). For a summary of the reception and criticism of the novel, see the "Historical Note" to the Northwestern-Newberry edition. In the following interpretation I make particular use also of Hershel Parker, "The Metaphysics of Indian-hating," *Nineteenth-Century Fiction*, 18 (Sept. 1963), 165–73. Thus far, to my knowledge, the motives for Melville's shift specifically from symbolism to allegory (as opposed to the reasons for his use of allegory per se) seem not to have received sufficient consideration.

By a law of reaction analogous to that governing the physical sphere, Melville's allegory constitutes in effect a diametrical opposite to the symbolism he had affirmed before. What emerges in *The Confidence-Man* is, then, not the allegorical realism of a Dante—which could inspire the Romantics to their theory of symbolism—but a form whose closest affinities are with Bunyan and Hawthorne's "Celestial Railroad."

Symbolism posits the personal uniqueness of the individual. Each character possesses a particular consciousness of the world. The individual is both individual and representative figure at the same time. We recall Coleridge's definition of the symbol: "It always partakes of the Reality which it renders intelligible; and while it enunciates the whole, abides itself as a living part in that Unity, of which it is the representative." Even in representing a higher Reality, the individual is not annulled but preserves individuality.

In the sphere of allegory, by contrast, everything appears as transient, shifting, illusory. It was upon precisely these grounds that Romanticism had based its criticism of allegory. In the context of Melville's novel, however, these defects now assume a positive value, reflecting the insubstantiality of life itself. What had previously been perceived as a weakness becomes thematically significant, as an illumination of the fundamental nature of life. Through its constantly shifting kaleidoscope of scenes, nevertheless, certain themes emerge, modified, to be sure, by variations in expression, yet preserving, like themes in music, a basic identity that assures the unity of the work.

In the opening chapter Melville introduces a symbolism of light and darkness which undergoes development in some of the final scenes of the novel. By means of such symbolism a spiritual contrast is effected between, on the one hand, the lamblike stranger who boards the *Fidèle* at the beginning of the book and China Aster, both—in different senses— "givers of light," and, on the other, the Cosmopolitan, who extinguishes the lights of Scripture at the end. The opening scene announces a second theme as well: the conflict of spiritual and material values. Embodied initially in the contrasting signs of the lamblike stranger and the barber, it resurfaces in different ways in "The Metaphysics of Indian-hating" and the story of China Aster. Its expression defines the essence of Melville's allegorical *theatrum mundi*, a world in which appearances belie their true spiritual significances.

Nowhere is this more evident than in "The Metaphysics of Indian-hating." The story of Colonel John Moredock, the Indian-hater, also introduces Melville's polemic against "nature," portrayed allegorically in the guise of the Indians. The theme reappears in somewhat different form in the tale of China Aster, where it becomes associated with the candlemaker's friend Orchis, who joins the sect of the "Come-Outers"— in Melville's allegorical language, those who seek the "free development of their inmost nature." Like lights directed upon a stage from different angles, each of these themes illuminates some aspect of the *theatrum mundi* of Melville's novel. Through their interrelations, it becomes possible to discern the structure of this world.

From the opening scene its two fundamental planes, the earthly and the divine, are juxtaposed against each other. The scene begins with the appearance of "a man in cream-colors" who boards the steamer *Fidèle* at St. Louis. His appearance is likened to that of Manco Capac at lake Titicaca, a comparison that turns out to be "an allusion to the mysterious advent of the founder of the Inca empire, sent to earth by his father, the sun." The allusion reflects the influence, from the late eighteenth century onward, of a new discipline in the field of biblical studies: comparative mythology. Research into Oriental religions had made possible attempts at a formal or morphological comparison between the stories of the Bible and the myths of other ancient religions. The poetry of Blake exhibits the impact of these researches. One discerns the existence of an original myth, an *Ur*-myth, that manifests itself in different forms among the ancient religions. All have captured something of the original truths and, to a corresponding extent, constitute valid expressions of it.

Thus, by way of comparative mythology, a mythic parallel is established with Christ. For he, too, is sent to earth by a divine father, in order to found a kingdom. Like the appearance of the Indian god, moreover, his advent is shrouded in obscurity. Finally, as the founder of the Inca empire had been the offspring of the sun, so Christ too is associated with light. The prologue to the gospel of John declares: "That was the true Light, which lighteth every man that cometh into the world" (John 1:9).

The individual who seeks to bring the presence of the divine into the world must renounce all the things of the world. He exists in the world but is not part of it. He is a pilgrim, which means: a traveler. In his *Génie du christianisme* (a book we may surmise Melville to have read sometime before the composition of *Clarel*), Chateaubriand had remarked that whereas Odysseus in Homer's *Odyssey* identifies himself with Ithaca, his homeland, Jacob the patriarch, when questioned by the Pharoah about himself, answers simply that he is a traveler on the pilgrimage of life. The lamblike figure, too, is a traveler who has abandoned the things of the world: "He had neither trunk, valise, carpet-bag, nor parcel. No porter followed him" (Melville, *Writings*, x, 3). We may compare his condition to that of Christian in Bunyan's *Pilgrim's Progress*, who abandons his baggage at the beginning of his pilgrimage to the Celestial City, a gesture by which he renounces material concerns for those of the spirit. In one of his early letters to Hawthorne, Melville had written: "For all men who say *yes*, lie; and all men who say *no*,—why, they are in the happy condition of judicious, unincumbered travellers in Europe; they cross the frontiers into Eternity with nothing but a carpet-bag [we know from Hawthorne's English Notebooks that when Melville visited Europe and the Near East in 1856–57 he carried with him only a tooth-brush and a carpet-bag],—that is to say, the Ego. Whereas those *yes-gentry*, they travel with heaps of baggage, and, damn them! they will never get through the Custom House" (*Letters*, p. 125).

The spiritual isolation of the pilgrim in the world is now elaborated upon more explicitly: "He was unaccompanied by friends. From the shrugged shoulders, titters, whispers, wonderings of the crowd, it was plain that he was, in the extremest sense of the word, a stranger" (*Writings*, x, 3), a situation that again corresponds to that of the Redeemer in the gospel of John: "He was in the world, and the world was made by him, and the world knew him not. He came unto his own, and his own received him not" (John 1:10–11). His spiritual isolation places the lamblike figure in diametrical opposition to the Cosmopolitan, the prin-cipal disguise of the Confidence-Man. Cosmopolitan signifies one who is "at home" in the world. He is "of the world," hence in contrast to the pilgrim, who undertakes to introduce the divine (here symbolized by light) into the world without becoming part of it himself.

This divine light constitutes an allegorical investiture for charity. Charity is the theme of the lamblike figure's silent exhortations (they are written upon a slate), which are opposed by the sign of the boat's barber: "NO TRUST." The barber's inscription accords with the attitude of the passengers. Its message is one that "though in a sense not less intrusive than the contrasted ones of the stranger, did not, as it seemed, provoke any corresponding derision or surprise, much less indignation; and still less, to all appearances, did it gain for the inscriber the repute of being a simpleton" (*Writings*, x, 5). It is the "wisdom of the world." By contrast we are told that both the lamblike figure and his message are regarded as "somehow inappropriate to the time and place" (p. 4). Here the theme of the "Chronometricals and Horologicals" discourse in *Pierre* is repeat-ed; divine and earthly wisdom are seen to belong to two wholly different spheres. As a result divine wisdom must remain incomprehensible to the world. A spiritual abyss separates the heavenly from the earthly.

Rebuffed by the crowd, the Christ-figure withdraws to a quiet corner of the forecastle and falls asleep beside a ladder, up and down which some of the boatmen occasionally pass in discharging their duties. This detail, too, has its parallel in the Gospels. To a scribe who wishes to follow him Jesus says: "The foxes have holes, and the birds of the air have nests; but the Son of man hath not where to lay his head" (Matt. 8:20). Falling asleep, the lamblike figure regains an inner tranquility: "Gradually overtaken by slumber, his flaxen head drooped, his whole lamb-like figure relaxed, and, half reclining against the ladder's foot, lay motionless, as some sugar-snow in March, which, softly stealing down over night, with its white placidity startles the brown farmer peering out from his threshold at daybreak" (*Writings,* x, 6). This beautiful image signifies a kind of benediction, the bestowal of a divine grace from above. It is a grace that descends upon the receiver unawares, achieving thereby a silent consecration of the soul. The consecration itself, moreover, attests to the fact that the relation between heaven and earth still exists and is being preserved.

It is only appropriate, then, that the sleeping Christ-figure should be likened to Jacob dreaming at Luz. Jacob's dream is the vision of a tie that unites earth to heaven: "And he dreamed, and behold a ladder set up on the earth, and the top of it reached to heaven: and behold the angels of God ascending and descending on it" (Gen. 28:12). A restoration of the original communion between the divine and the terrestrial is here envisaged. At present impossible, it remains a spiritual possibility. As such, it is suspended over the remainder of the novel. It explains why the conclusion ends with the words "Something further may follow of this Masquerade."

The work possesses, nevertheless, a kind of formal unity: all the events take place within the span of a single day. It begins with the appearance of the Christlike figure at sunrise and ends at midnight with the Cosmopolitan extinguishing the allegorical lamps of Scripture and leading an old man away into the darkness. We know, however, that the inner dialogue which Melville carried on with himself and which prompted him to the writing of his novel was not resolved at the time he finished it. It was the observation of this fact which had prompted Hawthorne to say, "He can neither believe, nor be comfortable in his unbelief."

Earlier, in *Moby-Dick,* Melville had questioned the capacity of Nature to reveal the divine, a capacity that forms the basis of Romantic symbolism. A subsequent passage from *Pierre* asserts: "Say what some poets will, Nature is not so much her own ever-sweet interpreter, as the mere supplier of that cunning alphabet, whereby selecting and combining as he pleases, each man reads his own peculiar lesson according to his own peculiar mind and mood" (*Writings,* vii, 342). In *The Confidence-Man* this skeptical tendency achieves its culmination. The twenty-third chapter carries the title: "In which the powerful effect of natural scenery is evinced in the case of the Missourian, who, in view of the region roundabout Cairo, has a return of his chilly fit." With a touch of macabre humor, Melville presents Nature not in its majesty and sublimity but in all its ugliness. Instead of life, it engenders only sickness and death: "At Cairo, the old established firm of Fever & Ague is still settling up its unfinished business; that Creole grave-digger, Yellow Jack—his hand at the mattock and spade has not lost its cunning; while Don Saturninus Typhus taking his constitutional with Death, Calvin Edson and three undertakers, in the morass, snuffs up the mephitic breeze with zest. In the dank twilight, fanned with mosquitoes, and sparkling with fire-flies, the boat now lies before Cairo. . . . Leaning over the rail on the inshore side, the Missourian eyes through the dubious medium that swampy and squalid domain; and over it audibly mumbles his cynical mind to himself, as Apemantus' dog may have mumbled his bone" (*Writings*, x, 129). Ironically, the subject of his meditations is in fact not God but the Confidence-Man, who appears to him earlier on board the steamboat and whose identity he now vaguely surmises to be that of the Devil. Thus Nature becomes indirectly the means of revealing, not the divine, but the satanic.

In this manner Melville introduces a polemic against Nature that is subsequently taken up again in the chapter on "The Metaphysics of Indian-hating." Here the word *metaphysics* must be understood in a special sense, as a higher truth that systematically negates appearances. In other words—as a denial of symbolism. The chapter attributes the "metaphysics of Indian-hating" to the views of "one evidently not so prepossessed as Rousseau in favor of savages." For Rousseau, the savages had represented the pristine state of uncorrupted nature, humanity before the advent of civilization. A similar view informs Chateaubriand's *Atala*. In pre-Romantic as well as Romantic thought, the savage embodies an existence in harmony with nature, and thus also with God. Imbued with natural piety, the savage beholds in the beauty and order of Nature a manifestation of the splendor and majesty of the divine. From its natural religion Romanticism creates a theory of symbolism. In Wordsworth and Coleridge the Eternal shines through the forms of Nature. As a result, it becomes possible to associate the Rousseauistic view of savages not only with natural religion, but also with symbolism. If Nature reveals the divine, then the natural state of humanity is also its most spiritual state. In that state it enters into harmony with Nature and, through Nature, God.

Against the Romantic and pre-Romantic notion, Melville now advances another view, according to which Nature becomes associated with the doctrine of an innate human depravity. Pitch, the Missourian—who bears a resemblance in many respects to Colonel Moredock, the Indian hater—informs the Confidence-Man that his favorite text is "St. Augustine on Original Sin" (*Writings*, x, 125). It was at a relatively late stage of his life that Augustine became involved in the Pelagian controversy from which were to issue the majority of his pronouncements on the doctrine of Original Sin. His opponents, Pelagius and later Julian of Eclanum, had maintained a belief in the perfectibility of man, the possibility of attaining a state of absolute grace. Their view was based upon a doctrine of natural goodness: the fundamental goodness of the basic instincts, the essential innocence and purity of human nature. Against these notions, Augustine draws a contrasting picture of the subconscious sense of guilt in all men, which in turn springs from an awareness of the innate depravity of human nature. These two conflicting views of the soul are not merely the fruit of fifth-century religious speculation but present attitudes that find recurrent expression throughout history. In Melville's time the conflict takes the form in England of the opposition between the Pre-Raphaelites and the later Tennyson; in America, between Emerson and the Melville of *The Confidence-Man* and *Pierre*. In his early essay on "Coleridge's Writings" (1866), Pater had rightly perceived that the time was drawing near when it would become necessary to choose between the vision of a "world of fairer and fairer forms" and the "vision of St. Augustine."

We know that Melville himself had felt even at an earlier stage an inner affinity with the vision of the world embodied in the doctrine of innate depravity. In his essay on "Hawthorne and His Mosses" he had associated it with the "power of blackness" in Hawthorne, which, he observes, "derives its force from its appeals to that Calvinistic sense of Innate Depravity and Original Sin, from whose visitations, in some shape or other, no deeply thinking mind is always and wholly free." "For," he continues, "in certain moods, no man can weigh this world without throwing in something, somehow like Original Sin, to strike the uneven balance" (*Representative Selections*, p. 333).

In "The Metaphysics of Indian-hating" the natural state becomes one of sin. Transformed into allegorical personifications of evil, the Indians are likened to Adam after the Fall—natural man after commission of the first sin, which results from innate tendencies of his nature. They flee from Colonel Moredock, "for Moredock's retributive spirit in the wilderness spoke ever to their trepidations now, like the voice calling through the garden" (*Writings*, x, 153). The Cosmopolitan, too, reveals himself as one of these allegorical Indians. Before the beginning of the discourse on "The Metaphysics of Indian-hating" he professes an admiration for Indians. Later he interrupts in order to "refill his calumet." In the depiction of the "friendly Indian" Melville offers perhaps a characterization of the Confidence-Man himself.

By contrast, the Indian-hater is portrayed as the antithesis of the Indian, an opposition that juxtaposes the overcoming of nature against that same nature. Nature describes the sinful state. It is the state from which humanity must be redeemed. Its overcoming assumes the form of a religious asceticism: "With the solemnity of a Spaniard turned monk, he takes leave of his kin; or rather, these leave-takings have something of the still more impressive finality of death-bed adieus" (*Writings*, x, 149). Among the notes to his *Génie du Christianisme*, Chateaubriand had thought it appropriate to preserve the letters of a French aristocrat who, finding himself in Spain at the time of the French Revolution, decides to enter a Spanish monastic order rather than return to his homeland. In his letters from the monastery, he lays the details of daily life before the eyes of the spectator: fasting, prayer, penance, and mortification. The newly converted monk knows he will never see his family again, that the remainder of his life will be passed within the walls of the monastery. All earthly ties must be severed. The same holds true for the Indian-hater: "In the settlements he will not be seen again; in eyes of old companions tears may start at some chance thing that speaks of him; but they never look for him, nor call; they know he will not come. Suns and seasons fleet; the tiger-lily blows and falls; babes are born and leap in their mothers' arms; but, the Indian-hater is good as gone to his long home" (*Writings*, x, 150). This "long home" is, of course, death, for the Indian-hater, like the monk, has "died to the world." He obeys the scriptural injunction: "For whosoever will save his life shall lose it; but whosoever shall lose his life for my sake and the gospel's, the same shall save it" (Mark 8:36).

The overcoming of nature that defines the object of monastic life is also that of the Indian-hater. It explains the emphasis upon his solitude. Enforced upon him by the nature of his life, it requires that he sever all bonds of affection. To do so involves an overcoming of nature, for "nearly all Indian-haters have at bottom loving hearts" (*Writings*, x, 154). The consequences, on the other hand, of failure to achieve restraint are made clear by the citing of instances where, "after some months' lonely scoutings, the Indian-hater is suddenly seized with a sort of calenture; hurries openly towards the first smoke, though he knows it is an Indian's, announces himself as a lost hunter, gives the savage his rifle, throws himself upon his charity, embraces him with much affection, imploring the priviledge of living a while in his sweet companionship. What is too often the sequel of so distempered a procedure may be best known by those who best know the Indian" (*Writings*, x, 150).

Solitude is also the sign of the spiritual life. Asceticism is preached throughout the early Christian centuries. It was not necessary, however, to understand the "flight from the world" in a material sense. In *De fuga saeculi*, St. Ambrose had undertaken to give it a spiritual meaning. Almost invariably, it appears linked to another theme: the wandering in the wilderness. That too could assume a spiritual as well as material significance. It becomes particularly appropriate in an American context, where the two meanings are fused into one. Thus American Puritan literature could describe the vocation of New England as a sacred one: colonization of the new land represents an "errand into the wilderness."

To be sure, the mission of the Indian-hater is also an "errand into the wilderness." In Melville's novel the errand is elevated to a purely spiritual level, for the Indians are, as we have seen, not real Indians but allegorical personifications of evil. They represent the Satanic forces. That they are to be encountered in the wilderness is also significant.

From the New Testament on, the wilderness is singled out as the site of temptation. Before beginning his ministry, Christ must undergo the trial of temptation in the wilderness: "Then was Jesus led up of the Spirit into the wilderness to be tempted of the devil." The wilderness becomes the field of spiritual conflict. As a result of his mission, the Indian-hater appears as a "captain in the vanguard of conquering civilization" (*Writings*, x, 145). This too possesses an allegorical meaning. In one of his letters to Hawthorne, Melville had written: "This most persuasive season has now for weeks recalled me from certain crochetty and over doleful chimearas, the like of which men like you and me and some others, forming a chain of God's posts round the world, must be content to encounter now and then, and fight them the best way we can. But come they will,—for, in the boundless, trackless, but still glorious wild wilderness through which these outposts run, the Indians do sorely abound" (*Letters*, p. 132).

Melville does not wish to sound here the theme of the corruption of natural innocence by civilization. He had indeed treated it, to be sure, on numerous occasions in his earlier novels. Now, on the contrary, civilization is endowed with a positive value. Julius Caesar and Moses contribute equally to its lustre. The Indian-hater is a "Pathfinder . . . worthy to be compared with Moses in the Exodus, or the Emperor Julian in Gaul, who on foot, and bare-browed, at the head of covered or mounted legions, marched so through the elements, day after day" (*Writings*, x, 145). The progress of civilization is understood as a spiritual march through the wilderness. Nature (allegorically embodied in the barbarians of Gaul) is overcome. The significance of the whole process: a spiritualization of the soul.

Through the myths associated with Manco Capac, the opening chapter had imparted to the theme of light-giving a spiritual significance. In the story of China Aster this theme is taken up once more, forming a thematic contrast to the extinguishing of the lamps of Scripture with which the novel concludes. The allegorical significance of the candlemaker's occupation is intimated within the text itself: "a kind of subordinate branch of that parent craft and mystery of the hosts of heaven, to be the means, effectively or otherwise, of shedding some light through the darkness of a planet benighted" (*Writings*, x, 208).

Inheriting his father's candlery, the candlemaker borrows a thousand dollars from his friend Orchis in order to shift from the manufacture of tallow to spermaceti candles (an allusion, perhaps, to Melville's abandonment of the autobiographical travelogue—*Typee* and *Omoo*—for the romance—*Moby-Dick* and *Pierre*). Significantly, he does so only at the insistent urging of Orchis. Later we learn that this friend undergoes an inner transformation, subsequently joining the sect of "Come-Outers," a sect whose creed is "free development of one's inmost nature." A theme from "The Metaphysics of Indian-hating," the polemic against the "natural" self, reappears, transposed now from the allegorical onto the moral plane. Commenting upon the beliefs of the "Come-Outers" through China Aster's friend Old Plain Talk, the author remarks: "if some men knew what was their inmost natures, instead of coming out with it, they would try their best to keep it in, which, indeed, was the way with the prudent sort" (*Writings*, x, 217).

As a result of indoctrination in the beliefs of his new sect, Orchis feels no hesitation in demanding repayment from the candlemaker, who in the meantime fails financially in his venture of manufacturing spermaceti candles. Attempting to repay his friend, China Aster finds himself driven to mortgage all his property, plunging thereby into further debt. His business worsening, he finally collapses from the strain of his efforts, dying soon after of brain fever. On his tombstone, at the request of one of his father's old friends, the following epitaph is placed: "The root of all was a friendly loan." Its form recalls the medieval formula, which Melville could have found in Chaucer (whom he in fact mentions earlier in the novel): "radix malorum est cupiditas." The root of all evil is cupidity. In its attenuated form, Orchis manifests this impulse: after apparently giving money to China Aster, he then seeks repayment. Associated with his joining the sect of "Come-Outers," it can only signify expression of the natural instincts.

In spite of the failure of China Aster's life in worldly terms, it remains a triumph of the soul over material adversity, for the making of candles is an allegory for the creation of those works of art which constitute the inexhaustible sources of spiritual illumination. Melville here develops a theme enunciated at the very beginning of the novel: the giving of light to the world. It is only appropriate that the encouragement to begin the manufacture of spermaceti candles should come to the candlemaker from the vision in his dream of an angel, who pours out from her cornucopia a shower of gold upon him. He mistakes this vision for a presentiment of worldly prosperity. But its true significance is to be found on the spiritual plane: "Lay not up for yourselves treasures upon earth, where moth and rust doth corrupt, and where thieves break through and steal: but lay up for yourselves treasures in heaven . . . for where your treasure is, there will your heart be also" (Matt. 6:19–21). On each of the subsequent occasions when he is about to relinquish his business in despair, the candlemaker receives another visitation from the angel. He dies still a lightgiver to the world.

Through our study of Melville's symbolism, it should be apparent that his development follows a different course from that of either Poe or Hawthorne—one whose governing law is not that of organic growth but rather of a dialectical process of opposition and resolution on a higher level. Significantly, after his renunciation of symbolism in *The Confidence-Man,* Melville does not in his later works return to the Romantic notion of it. Instead he moves toward an affirmation of Nature itself, and, at a yet later stage, the organic transformation of nature into spirit (*Billy Budd*). As we shall see later, that final stage involves a return to the idea of a divine revelation, but one from which the concept of symbolism has been excluded. On account of a new conception on Melville's part of the relation between the material and the spiritual, it becomes possible to approach symbolism at another level of "transcendence."

# PART II

# The Foundations of Science

# 5  *Poe*

The Mathematization of Non-formal Concepts

In 1811, as the fruit of courses conducted at the Ecole Normale in 1796 and 1797, Laplace was able to bring out his *Théorie analytique des probabilités*. Two years later he added, by way of a preface, an exposition of the principles upon which the larger work had been based—to which he accordingly gave the title *Essai philosophique sur les probabilités*. At the beginning of his preliminary essay he says: "I shall present here, without the help of analysis, the principles and general results of the theory of probability outlined in this work, in applying them to the most important questions of life, which are only, for the most part, problems in probability" (*O.C.*, VII, v). Is it possible that his views had already attracted attention elsewhere than in purely mathematical circles? In her *De l'Allemagne* Mme de Staël remarks: "One wishes to demonstrate everything, ever since the taste for the exact sciences became the fashion among intellects; and because the calculus of probabilities makes it possible to submit the uncertain itself to rules, one flatters oneself with having resolved mathematically all the difficulties presented by the most delicate questions, and with having thus made the spirit of algebra reign over the universe" (*O.C.*, XI, 351). But it is significant to know that in her earlier *De la littérature* she could also say: "If one could discover one day in the calculus of probabilities a method which would be suitable for purely moral questions, this would be to make an immense step in the progress of reason" (*O.C.*, IV, 496–97).

Nevertheless, she continues, such a step is necessarily beset with difficulties: "Doubtless it will be difficult to submit to a calculus, even that of probabilities, that which relates to moral arrangements. In the exact sciences, all the bases are invariable; with regard to moral ideas, everything depends on circumstances: one can only decide on something by means of a multitude of considerations, among which some are so fugitive as to escape even words, and hence all the more, a calculus" (*O.C.*, IV, 497). To be sure, Laplace himself was also aware of these difficulties. They could be met in part by increasing the number of causal factors or variables to be introduced into the framework of the equation used to represent the problem in question. Quantitatively, in cases in which the calculation of a combination of probabilities (through multiplication) becomes necessary, the method of calculation itself becomes susceptible to refinement through mathematical analysis, which leads to the use of what Laplace himself designates as "fonctions génératrices" (discriminant functions) (see *O.C.*, VII, xx, 450; xxix, 7). Furthermore, the differing probabilities of the causes themselves are taken into account. In the *Essai philosophique* Laplace observes: "Each of the causes to which an observed event may be attributed is indicated with just as much likelihood as it is probable that, supposing this cause to exist, the event will take place; the probability of the existence of any one of these causes is then a fraction, of which the numerator is the probability of the event's resulting from this cause, and of which the denominator is the sum of the corresponding probabilities relative to all the causes. If these various causes, considered *a priori*, are unequally probable, it is necessary, in place of the probability of the event resulting from each cause, to employ the product of this probability by that of the cause itself" (*O.C.*, VII, xiv–xv).

But even after the introduction of all these refinements, a basic issue remains unresolved—namely, how moral questions are to be translated into purely formal terms. The basis of the theory of probability developed by Laplace and his predecessors is above all an epistemology: which is to say, a philosophical orientation toward the world defined through and in terms of the process of knowing or cognition. As such, the theory of probability seeks to establish through formal means what may be determined about the unknown on the basis of what is known. Characteristically, it had experienced its rise in the seventeenth century, the century of Descartes, through the work of Pascal and Fermat, subsequently developed during the course of the eighteenth century. For this and other reasons, Laplace's treatment exhibits the influence of the Enlightenment.[1] That aspect of his work should not be allowed to obscure the extent to which he affirms the spirit of Romanticism as well.[2]

---

[1] One might compare his work, for instance, with Francis Hutcheson's *An Inquiry into the Original of Our Ideas of Beauty and Virtue* (1725), with its quantitative analysis of morality and the virtues. For background, see Georges Canguilhem, *La Mathématisation des doctrines informes* (Paris: Hermann, 1972).

[2] In *The Edge of Objectivity* (Princeton: Princeton Univ. Press, 1960), pp. 176–78, Charles C. Gillispie characterizes Lagrange, Laplace, Cuvier, Lamarck, and Monge as inheritors of the Enlightenment. But the global perspective claimed by Laplace for his theory of probability, plus the relationship it poses between an abstract principle or idea and material

In Romantic science we encounter the desire to achieve a total or comprehensive and unifying theoretical explanation of material phenomena. For Dalton it assumes the form of the atomic theory of matter, in Davy the idea of the existence of a single primal substance (a theory to which Balzac gives magnificent expression in his novel *La Recherche de l'absolu*), in Geoffroy Saint-Hilaire the vision of all species as constituting merely the differing forms of a single animal. By means of this definition of Romantic science (as the attempt at a total or unifying theoretical explanation) it becomes possible to embrace within its boundaries not only a Goethe or an Oken but equally a Dalton or a Cuvier, a Galois or a Carnot. Insofar as he had sought to confer upon the theory of probability the role of a theoretical model sufficient to resolve all the fundamental problems of life, Laplace, too, may be allowed to take his place as part of this tradition. If in its philosophical orientation, constructed upon epistemological foundations, it displays its affinities with the Enlightenment, in its attempt to attain an abstract or theoretical universality the Laplacean theory of probability expresses equally the fundamental impulse of Romantic science. Through the twofold nature of its tendencies, it can help to clarify the unique character of Poe's own Romanticism, with its special mixture of neoclassicism and (in the sphere of science) intuitive apprehension of some of the preoccupations of our own century.

We have seen how, in Laplace's theory of probability, a theoretical orientation is inseparably bound up with the representation of nonformal aspects of life in formal terms, or—to borrow a phrase from the Belgian historian of science Georges Canguilhem—the "mathematiza-

---

phenomena, where the former really contains or embodies the essence of the latter, seems to me expressive of a Romantic rather than an Enlightenment tendency. One sees a similar attempt to define material phenomena by means of a global abstract principle in the famous formula of Malthus's work on population: "Population, when unchecked, increases in a geometrical ratio. A slight acquaintance with numbers will shew the immensity of the first power in comparison of the second. . . . This implies a strong and constantly operating check on population from the difficulty of subsistence. This difficulty must fall some where and must necessarily be severely felt by a large portion of mankind" (Malthus, *An Essay on the Principle of Population*, p. 20). But Malthus can also say, with an air strikingly anticipative of Emerson or Poe: "It is an idea that will be found consistent equally with the natural phenomena around us, with the various events of human life, and with the successive Revelations of God to man, to suppose that the world is a mighty process for the creation and formation of mind" (p. 86). For Kant, on the other hand, (who in this respect may be said to characterize Enlightenment science), the idea always remains external to the thing itself; concepts merely serve to connect one thing with another (*Prolegomena* sec. 14, *Gesammelte Schriften*, IV, 294). The criterion of Romantic science is aptly expressed by a dictum from Novalis's *Blüthenstaub:* "Shouldn't the distance of a particular science from the universal, and thus the rank of the sciences in relation to each other, be determined according to the number of their fundamental principles? The fewer principles, the higher the science" (*Schriften*, II, 451).

tion of non-formal doctrines." The idea of formal representation or mathematization is in turn taken up by Poe, who incorporates aspects or elements of the theory of probability into his tales of ratiocination. That he should do so is itself highly revealing, expressive as it is of certain essential features of his thought.

By means of mathematization, qualitative elements or substances are in effect transformed into quantitative expressions. Such a transformation necessarily overlooks qualitative differences between causes or things, or (in some instances) translates these into quantitative differences. One could describe the implied opposition between qualitative and quantitative as one between physics and biology, each striving to establish itself as the paradigm for science in the Romantic age.[3] But it would be incorrect to identify Romantic science with biology alone. Many of the principal figures of the Romantic movement possess affinities with other sciences—Coleridge and Schelling with chemistry, Novalis with geology, Poe and Shelley with astronomy, Friedrich Schlegel and others with geometry.

From a more comprehensive standpoint, then, Poe's relation to science is neither more nor less Romantic than Goethe's. To the extent that quantitative science—in this case, the theory of probability—contains the possibility of a mathematization of nonformal elements or concepts, it attains a theoretical elegance compared with which the life sciences could have nothing to offer. And is this not perhaps at bottom the source of Poe's attraction to the quantitative sciences, to mathematics, physics, astronomy? Various indications from *Eureka* and elsewhere attest to his belief in the identity of the beautiful and the true—which must be taken not merely as the expression of a neoplatonic tendency but equally as an affirmation of the unity of theoretical elegance and truth in science. With regard to probability, such elegance consists principally in the capacity of mathematization to establish order over a large and seemingly heterogeneous mass of data. Such order must not be seen merely as a superimposition of theory upon experience. Throughout his writings Poe repeatedly asserts the primacy or essentiality of logical relations over material appearances. Already in 1839, speaking of music, he concludes: "The sentiments deducible from the conception of sweet sound simply are out of the reach of analysis—although referable, possibly, in their last result, to that merely mathematical recognition of *equality* which seems to be *the root of all beauty*" (*C.W.*, x, 41).[4] And are we not justified in seeing in "The Purloined Letter" Poe's own remarkable illustration of

[3]See Gillispie, p. 199.
[4]For Poe's knowledge of mathematics and of music, see Killis Campbell, *The Mind of Poe and Other Studies* (Cambridge: Harvard Univ. Press, 1933), pp. 11, 16.

this assertion, where Dupin, by reproducing in his mind the thought process of the Minister D——, discovers the hiding place of the letter?[5]

As for the equality that Poe speaks of, it represents a logical rather than quantitative relation. Nevertheless, the science of numbers constitutes one of the avenues by which one may approach those logical relations that form the ground of all appearances. The capacity of mathematics to do so furnishes Poe's justification for the mathematization of the nonformal in the theory of probability: by means of such representation, the eternal laws of logic are stripped of unnecessary encumbrances and allowed to stand in their purest and most revealing form. In that form they appear completely identical with the true. As the writer of the letter in "Mellonta Tauta"—in a passage reproduced by Poe in *Eureka*—exclaims: "Does it not seem singular how they should have failed to deduce from the works of God the vital fact that a perfect consistency *must be* an absolute truth!" (*Coll. W.*, III, 1298; cf. *Poetry and Tales*, 1269). Laplace, too, had envisaged the theory of probability in relation to the expression of larger or more general laws. As a consequence of one of the theorems of the theory he observes: "It follows moreover from this theorem that, in a series of events indefinitely prolonged, the action of regular and constant causes should prevail in the long run over that of irregular causes" (*O.C.*, VII, xlviii).[6] And elsewhere, remarking on the relation between probability and the concept of analogy: "Analogy is founded on the probability that similar things have causes of the same type and produce the same effects. The more perfect the similitude, the more this probability increases" (p. cxli).

For Poe, obviously, the use of numbers could only represent a means to an end. In a highly revealing passage from his criticism he says: "A book without action cannot be; but a book is only such, to the extent of its thought, independently of its deed. Thus of Algebra; which is, or should be, defined as 'a mode of computing with symbols by means of signs.' With numbers, as Algebra, it has nothing to do; and although no algebraic computation can proceed without numbers, yet Algebra is only such to the extent of its analysis, independently of its Arithmetic" (*C.W.*, XI, 11–12). Such a passage might easily be said to capture the essence of the theory of algebraic groups, developed in Poe's time through the work of Lagrange, Abel, Cauchy, and others. With regard to Poe him-

---

[5]In this respect is it fair to claim, with Campbell, that "Poe attached too much importance, relatively, to facts and too little to ideas" (p. 30)?

[6]Cf. Malthus, *An Essay on the Principle of Population*, p. 61: "The constancy of the laws of nature and of effects and causes is the foundation of all human knowledge, though far be it from me to say that the same power which framed and executes the laws of nature, may not change them all 'in a moment, in the twinkling of an eye.' Such a change may undoubtedly happen. All that I mean to say is that it is impossible to infer it from reasoning."

self, it indicates that mathematization could never represent an actual transformation of the qualitative into the quantitative, but rather a means by which the essential abstract or logical relations are brought to the surface. It constitutes an intellectual construction, with a heuristic rather than absolute value.[7] Poe does not subscribe, in other words, to any form of Pythagoreanism. On the contrary, he remains very much conscious of the gulf between the quantitative nature of the theory of probability and that of the subjects to which it might be applied. In "The Mystery of Marie Roget" the narrator comments: "Now this Calculus is, in its essence, purely mathematical; and thus we have the anomaly of the most rigidly exact in science applied to the shadow and spirituality of the most intangible in speculation" (*Coll. W.*, III, 724).

The application of the theory of probability accomplishes the first stage of a two-stage process. By means of its mathematization of the nonformal, it creates order out of the heterogeneous and confused nature of appearances. At the second stage the mathematical is elevated to the level of the ideal, the abstractly logical. By so doing, Poe subordinates the mathematical to what he considers a higher form of thought. In his discussion of mathematics in "The Purloined Letter" Dupin declares: "I dispute the availability, and thus the value, of that reason which is cultivated in any especial form other than the abstractly logical. I dispute, in particular, the reason educed by mathematical study. The mathematics are the science of form and quantity; mathematical reasoning is merely logic applied to observation upon form and quantity. The great error lies in supposing that even the truths of what is called *pure* algebra, are abstract or general truths." In other spheres, purely mathematical truths fail to apply: "What is true of *relation*—of form and quantity—is often grossly false in regard to morals, for example. In this latter science it is very usually *un*true that the aggregated parts are equal to the whole. In chemistry also the axiom fails. In the consideration of motive it fails; for two motives, each of a given value, have not, necessarily, a value when united, equal to the sum of their values apart" (*Coll. W.*, III, 987).

The tendency to see mathematics as no more than a partial science was one that had only gradually developed in Poe. Even in 1842 he could still maintain: "The highest order of the imaginative intellect is always preëminently mathematical; and the converse" (*C.W.*, XI, 148). Only with "The Purloined Letter" does he begin to distinguish between the mathematical and the imaginative. Speaking of the Minister D——, Dupin

---

[7]On this point, cf. Poe's attitude with Einstein's critique of Hume and Bertrand Russell: "As a matter of fact, I am convinced that even much more is to be asserted: the concepts which arise in our thought and in our linguistic expressions are all—when viewed logically—the free creations of thought which cannot inductively be gained from sense experiences" (Albert Einstein, *Ideas and Opinions* [New York: Crown, 1954], p. 22).

remarks: "As poet *and* mathematician, he would reason well; as mere mathematician, he could not have reasoned at all, and thus would have been at the mercy of the Prefect" (*Coll. W.*, III, 986). The abstract or general truths Poe speaks of in the passages above are not to be encompassed even within the confines of formal logic. It, too, fails to attain a sufficiently universal level. Later, in *Eureka*, Poe denies the existence of all "self-evident" truths, in other words, all those deducible by logic alone. In retrospect, it becomes possible to see the pattern of cosmic expansion and contraction in *Eureka* as perhaps the one sufficiently universal expression of truth—one that is "synthetic" rather than a priori or "self-evident." It attains the level of universality inasmuch as all things are originally motivated by the force of divine expansion and, upon its withdrawal, by that of gravitation. Such a theory receives its ultimate confirmation not on the basis of factual evidence, but because of its beauty as theory—a criterion Poe might have wished to ascribe to the theory of probability as well. Through this criterion of "intellectual beauty" (Shelley), art and science are surveyed from a unified perspective. What Poe's aestheticism offers is not a principle of exclusion (as with the Pre-Raphaelites) but of inclusion and universal comprehension. Its basis is that intellectual essence, immanent in all the highest spheres of human activity yet perceived only by fleeting glimpses, for which rational thought has no single name, an essence Poe elsewhere describes simultaneously under its twin aspects of the beautiful and the true.

## The Nature of Ratiocination

In his "Autobiographical Notes" Einstein relates the circumstances leading to his formulation of the theory of special relativity. Beginning by working from experimental data, he found himself obliged after a time to abanon his attempts. "By and by," he continues, "I despaired of the possibility of discovering the true laws by means of constructive efforts based on known facts. The longer and the more despairingly I tried, the more I came to the conviction that only the discovery of a universal formal principle could lead us to assured results" ("Autobiographical Notes," p. 49). His experience only confirms the assertion that, throughout the history of science, theory does not issue from facts. In the words of the historian Georges Canguilhem: "If we transpose this finding, which is of an epistemological order, onto the plane of the philosophy of knowing, we should assert, contrary to the empiricist commonplace frequently adopted without criticism by the *savants* when they elevate themselves to the philosophy of their experimental knowledge, that *theories never proceed from facts*. They only proceed from preceding—

and frequently quite old—theories. Facts are only the road, rarely direct, by which theories proceed from one another."[8]

Poe, too, senses the separation between theory and facts. In his universe theory leads an ideal existence, one that is altered by the intrusion of empirical events. "The Mystery of Marie Roget" opens with an epigraph from Novalis: "There are ideal series of events which run parallel with the real ones. They rarely coincide. Men and circumstances generally modify the ideal train of events, so that it seems imperfect, and its consequences are equally imperfect" (*Coll. W.*, III, 723). The same applies to the theoretical models of classical mechanics, which do not take into account the action of friction and other empirical forces. Similarly, Poe can point out that "the theory of chance, or as the mathematicians term it, the Calculus of Probabilities, has this remarkable peculiarity, that its truth in general is in direct proportion with its fallacy in particular" (*C.W.*, XIV, 186).

Thus it becomes apparent that the process leading to the formation of a theory need not possess more than an incidental connection with the facts. For these, as Einstein remarks in his "Autobiographical Notes," can be accommodated to the theory—once it has been constructed—through a series of "artificial additional assumptions."[9] Such assumptions are allowed in part because it is impossible to determine in advance which facts are crucial to the confirmation or refutation of a theory. Only in retrospect, from the vantage point of a new theoretical perspective, does it become possible to assess the importance of particular facts, either in rejection of a former theory or confirmation of a new one. In the process of its formation, such a theory is thrown primarily upon its own resources. At that moment empirical criteria yield to the purely theoretical. The resultant viewpoint, Einstein observes, "is not concerned with the relation to the material of observation but with the premises of the theory itself, with what may briefly but vaguely be characterized as the 'naturalness' or 'logical simplicity' of the premises (of the basic concepts and of the relations between these which are taken as a basis)" ("Autobiographical Notes," p. 23).

Such is the point of view from which we are asked to regard the Minister D——'s choice of a hiding-place for the letter. "I saw, in fine," says Dupin, "that he would be driven, as a matter of course, to *simplicity*, if not deliberately induced to it as a matter of choice" (*Coll. W.*, III, 989). Here, internal and external aspects of the Minister's situation correspond to the two criteria from which a theory is to be surveyed: conformation to external facts and "naturalness" or "logical simplicity." But

---

[8]*La Connaissance de la vie*, rev. ed. (Paris: Vrin, 1965), p. 50. See also Paul Feyerabend, *Against Nature* (London: NLB, 1975), p. 168.

[9]"Autobiographical Notes," pp. 21, 23. An early article on Poe and Einstein: George Norstedt, "Poe and Einstein," *Open Court*, 44 (March, 1930), 173–80.

logical simplicity alone would have sufficed to determine the Minister's choice. And in a sense that choice is made prior to considering external circumstances. Significantly, moreover, neither simplicity nor external circumstances in fact suffice to define the exact hiding-place for the letter. When Dupin pays his first visit to the Minister, he possesses only a knowledge of the theoretical description to which the hiding-place must answer. Hence his initial examination of the large writing table heaped with letters and papers, and the one or two musical instruments. Only after the failure of his efforts here is his eye caught by the sight of the "trumpery fillagree card-rack of pasteboard" containing the letter. The Minister begins his own process of selecting a hiding-place in the same fashion that Dupin commences his search for it—with a purely theoretical description.

At this point the reader will perhaps ask: in what sense does the necessity for conforming to external circumstances (the assumption of the efforts to be made by the Parisian police to recover the letter) conduce to simplicity in the choice of a hiding-place? Here it becomes apparent that even the external circumstances are themselves susceptible of analysis by the Minister. He begins with a theoretical understanding of the methodology they will employ to recover the letter. The imaginative structure behind "The Purloined Letter" thus consists not only of Dupin's attempt to identify his mode of thinking with the Minister's, but also of the Minister's effort to comprehend at a theoretical level the methodology of the Parisian police so as to devise a means of frustrating their efforts. Upon their tendency to search out the most obscure and inaccessible hiding-places, he bases his own corresponding quest for absolute simplicity.[10]

Such simplicity can be achieved only by avoiding concealment altogether. Even the appearance of the letter itself is significant. In his survey of the filagree pasteboard rack, Dupin notices that it contains "five or six visiting cards and a solitary letter." "This last," he continues, "was much soiled and crumpled. It was torn nearly in two, across the middle—as if a design, in the first instance, to tear it entirely up as worthless, had been altered, or stayed, in the second. It had a large black seal, bearing the D—— cipher *very* conspicuously, and was addressed, in a diminutive female hand, to D——, the minister, himself. It was thrust carelessly, and even, as it seemed, contemptuously, into one of the upper divisions of the rack" (*Coll. W.*, III, 991). The description of the letter

---

[10]In this context it is interesting to note J. M. Daniel's account of Poe's conversational habits: "In his animated moods he talked with an abstracted earnestness as if he were dictating to an amanuensis, and, if he spoke of individuals, his ideas ran upon their moral and intellectual qualities rather than upon the idiosyncrasies of their active visible phenomena, or the peculiarities of their manner" (quoted from Sarah Helen Whitman, *Edgar Poe and His Critics* [1860; rpt. New York, AMS Press, 1966], p. 43).

appears to contain an implicit contradiction. If the letter bears the cipher of the Minister, it should not be addressed to him, but rather by him, since it is the sender who impresses his or her seal upon a letter. Such an oversight (perhaps on Poe's part as well as the Minister's) is highly revealing. It indicates to what degree the course of the story is governed by the abstract assumptions of each party and the interaction of these assumptions with each other.

In his account of the letter Dupin appears not to notice the contradiction in its appearance. Instead he focuses his thoughts upon the contrast between it and the supposed appearance of the document he himself is in search of. He suspects the soiled and crumpled letter to be the object of his search because of its *exact* antithesis to the true appearance of his object. "No sooner had I glanced at this letter," he informs the narrator, "than I concluded it to be that of which I was in search. To be sure, it was, to all appearance, radically different from the one of which the Prefect had read us so minute a description. Here the seal was large and black, with the D—— cipher; there it was small and red, with the ducal arms of the S—— family. Here, the address, to the Minister, was diminutive and feminine; there the superscription, to a certain royal personage, was markedly bold and decided; the size alone formed a point of correspondence. But, then, the *radicalness* of these differences, which was excessive; the dirt; the soiled and torn condition of the paper, so inconsistent with the *true* methodical habits of D——, and so suggestive of a design to delude the beholder into an idea of the worthlessness of the document; these things, together with the hyperobtrusive situation of this document, full in the view of every visiter, and thus exactly in accordance with the conclusions to which I had previously arrived; these things, I say, were strongly corroborative of suspicion, in one who came with the intention to suspect" (*Coll. W.*, III, 991).

In "The Murders in the Rue Morgue" and "The Mystery of Marie Roget," Dupin had already expressed his view that "it is by prominences above the plane of the ordinary, that reason feels her way, if at all, in her search for the true" (*Coll. W.*, III, 736–37). The present instance confirms his assertion. It reveals the nature of Poe's conception of the relation between theory and external facts (hence science) in general. Instead of seeking to explain the extraordinary or *outré* (to use one of his own favorite terms) by means of ad hoc adjustments to a theory based upon the majority of instances, Poe argues for the need of a theory that will account for all the extraordinary facts or occurrences. To be sure, such a theory must also explain the "normal" as well. Poe's implicit assumption however is that these "normal" circumstances will in fact permit a much greater range of possible explanations—hence the concentration upon the extraordinary or *outré*. In retrospect, it was precisely such emphasis upon the exceptional which had made possible the revolution of twentieth-century physics, with its twin branches of quantum mechanics and relativity theory.

In the nineteenth century this attitude is anticipated by various developments. One may mention, for instance, Augustin Fresnel's theory of wave mechanics for light. Fresnel had held that even the slightest experimental deviation from the predictions of his theory would be sufficient to invalidate it.[11] The same period had also witnessed Carnot's formulation of the general principles of thermodynamics, which Einstein would later describe as "the only physical theory of universal content concerning which I am convinced that, within the framework of the applicability of its basic concepts, it will never be overthrown" ("Autobiographical Notes," p. 33). Such theories did not, so far as one can tell, make much impression outside the purely scientific circles. Neither Fresnel nor Carnot is mentioned by Poe, nor by Emerson (who could rely upon his brother-in-law, Charles T. Jackson, for scientific information). Nevertheless, if it is possible to speak of an intellectual affinity between figures in widely different spheres with no knowledge of each other, we may perhaps claim a kinship between Poe and these French physicists. Had he not asserted from intuition, as a purely general principle, that which they had borne out in particular instances? Through all these figures, a common insight emerges. It is the conviction that only a theory possessing an "inner perfection" (Einstein's phrase) will finally be able to account for all the facts within its domain. From this standpoint, Poe could feel himself justified in arguing, in his *Eureka,* that the beauty of a theory forms a proof of its truth.

We have seen the importance Poe attaches to the capacity of a theory to explain the extraordinary or the *outré*. That is one aspect of his concept of the nature of ratiocination—that only by taking into account such phenomena can reason "feel its way" toward the true. His description of the power of analysis exemplifies a second aspect of the rational, one that must be clearly distinguished from other faculties. In "The Murders in the Rue Morgue" Dupin observes: "The analytical power should not be confounded with simple ingenuity; for while the analyst is necessarily ingenious, the ingenious man is often remarkably incapable of analysis. The constructive or combining power, by which ingenuity is usually manifested . . . has been so frequently seen in those whose intellect bordered otherwise upon idiocy, as to have attracted general observation among writers on morals. Between ingenuity and the analytic ability there exists a difference far greater, indeed, than that between

[11]Gillispie, p. 432.

the fancy and the imagination, but of a character very strictly analogous. It will be found, in fact, that the ingenious are always fanciful, and the *truly* imaginative never otherwise than analytic" (*Coll. W.*, ii, 530–31).

A comparison of this passage with earlier utterances makes apparent some of the changes and developments in Poe's thought. Two years before, speaking of the distinction between fancy and imagination, he had averred, "'The fancy,' says the author of the 'Ancient Mariner,' in his *Biographia Literaria*, 'the fancy combines, the imagination creates.' And this was intended, and has been received, as a distinction. If so at all, it is one without a difference; without even a difference of *degree*. The fancy as nearly creates as the imagination; and neither creates in any respect. All novel conceptions are merely unusual combinations. The mind of man can *imagine* nothing which has not really existed. . . . Thus with all which seems to be *new*—which appears to be a *creation* of intellect. It is resoluble into the old. The wildest and most vigorous effort of mind cannot stand the test of this analysis" (*C.W.*, x, 61–62).

Although Poe later in the same piece concedes at least a difference of degree between fancy and imagination (p. 65), the overall impression conveyed remains somewhat unclear. No doubt it reflects his own uncertainty at this stage about the proper definition of imagination. To assert the absence of any distinction whatsoever between the two is felt—despite its polemical effect—as somehow unsatisfactory. To be sure, Poe will consistently maintain throughout his later criticism that imagination does not actually create but merely combines. Nevertheless, by 1842 the need for a reformulation of the distinction becomes clear to him. Imagination is now associated with the power of analysis. Insofar as it consists of the capacity to break down or dissolve a subject into its constituent elements, it represents the converse of the combining power. Consequently, the faculties of art and science become one and the same; in "The Murders in the Rue Morgue" Dupin can say: "The faculty of resolution is possibly much invigorated by mathematical study, and especially by that highest branch of it which, unjustly, and merely on account of its retrograde operations, has been called, as if *par excellence*, analysis" (*Coll. W.*, ii, 528).

This association of imagination and analysis also derives from Coleridge's *Biographia Literaria*, in which the secondary Imagination is defined as that which "dissolves, diffuses, dissipates, in order to re-create" (*C.W.*, vii:i, 304). Through the notion of dissolution (or "re-solution," as Poe would have it, employing a metaphor from chemistry), Poe seeks in effect to indicate a comprehension that penetrates, as it were, into the very essence of its subject, breaking it down into its component parts, achieving an understanding of its constitution and innermost structure. Such an operation is beyond the fancy, which merely combines without a deeper knowledge of those elements it brings together. That deeper knowledge belongs to art and science. As a result, the two disciplines are now perceived from a higher perspective as differing means toward a single end: a universal vision that encompasses both the beautiful and the true. In one of his later essays Poe makes use of the chemical process of combination to typify the activity of the imagination: "But, as often analogously happens in physical chemistry, so not unfrequently does it occur in this chemistry of the intellect, that the admixture of two elements will result in a something that shall have nothing of the quality of one of them—or even nothing of the qualities of either" (*C.W.*, xii, 38–39).

The use of a chemical metaphor should not obscure the fact that for Poe, at this late stage, the unity of art and science must now be sought on different grounds. Even the truths of pure algebra, as we have seen, are no longer permitted to claim for themselves the validity of abstract or general truths. In speaking of mathematical analysis Dupin remarks: "The French are the originators of this particular deception; but if a term is of any importance—if words derive any value from applicability—then 'analysis' conveys 'algebra' about as much as, in Latin, 'ambitus' implies 'ambition,' 'religio' 'religion,' or 'homines honesti,' a set of *honorable* men" (*Coll. W.*, iii, 987). The reaction against mathematics as the paradigm of rationality can be explained in terms of an increasing tendency toward aestheticism which manifests itself in Poe's late poetry and criticism. It results also in a redefinition of imagination, which is now distinguished from fancy and the other faculties on the grounds that "from novel arrangements of old forms which present themselves to it, it selects only such as are harmonious." "The result, of course," Poe continues, "is *beauty* itself—using the term in its most extended sense, and as inclusive of the sublime" (*C.W.*, xii, 38).

In science such a distinction could only imply an increasing emphasis upon the "inner perfection" of a theory. In *Eureka* Poe asserts that the beauty of his argument is what constitutes it true. Theory is now conceived of not merely as an analysis of appearances, but rather as an attempt to express the essential structure or nature of things. As a result, it becomes possible to perceive its fundamental unity with poetry, and in particular with that "ideal poetry" Poe had praised earlier in Lamartine. In this form of Romanticism, then, poetry and science are not viewed as disparate and conflicting disciplines, but rather as differing means toward a common objective. Like Shelley's Laon in *The Revolt of Islam*, Poe himself might say:

> Our toil from thought all glorious forms shall cull,
> To make this Earth, our home, more beautiful,
> And Science, and her sister Poesy,
> Shall clothe in light the fields and cities of the free! (*P.W.*, p. 92)

## The Theory of Probability

On various occasions Poe devoted much praise to the theory of probability. "The Murders in the Rue Morgue" records Dupin's tribute to it as "that theory to which the most glorious objects of human research are indebted for the most glorious of illustration" (*Coll. W.*, II, 556). Even during the "Longfellow War," while discussing the question of plagiarism, Poe finds an opportunity of introducing it: "The affair is one of *probabilities* altogether, and can be satisfactorily settled only by reference to their Calculus" (*C.W.*, XII, 66). In "The Mystery of Marie Roget" he attempts to apply this theory to the process of ratiocination by which Dupin elucidates the mystery of the grisette's murder. These applications are significant insofar as they reveal something not only about his concept of ratiocination and science, but also about his intellectual orientation in general.[12]

We have seen earlier the extent to which the theory of probability depends upon a mathematization of the nonformal. In the course of his analysis Dupin observes: "It is no longer philosophical to base, upon what has been, a vision of what is to be. *Accident* is admitted as a portion of the substructure. We make chance a matter of absolute calculation. We subject the unlooked for and unimagined, to the mathematical *formulae* of the schools" (*Coll. W.*, III, 752). Laplace's more formal exposition (in the *Essai philosophique*) states: "The theory of accidents consists of reducing all events of the same type to a certain number of equally possible cases, which is to say, such that we are equally undecided about their existence, and of determining the number of cases favorable to the event of which one seeks the probability. The relation between this number and that of all the possible cases is the measure of this probability, which is thus nothing more than a fraction of which the numerator is the number of favorable cases, and of which the denominator is the number of all the possible cases" (*O.C.*, VII, viii–ix).

By means of such formulae, it becomes possible to impose a certain structure upon the world of appearances. Beginning with a given number of known facts and ascribing formal or quantitative representation to all the relevant possibilities, the theory of probability enables its

---

[12]For Poe's actual attempt to solve the mystery of Mary Rogers's murder, see John Walsh, *Poe The Detective* (New Brunswick, N. J.: Rutgers Univ. Press, 1968), esp. pp. 43, 44–46, 66, 68–73. Walsh shows how Poe modifies New York newspaper accounts of the Mary Rogers case in the process of incorporating them into his tale, as well as the effect of the Weehawken incident with Mrs. Loss upon his revisions for the 1845 Wiley and Putnam edition of his *Tales*, but does not discuss the application of the theory of probability to the case. For a treatment that includes some mention of the latter, see William K. Wimsatt, "Poe and the Mystery of Mary Rogers," *PMLA*, 41 (March, 1941), 230–48.

user to arrive at a form of truth which possesses nearly absolute certainty regarding the outcome of a large number of events or occurrences, and a heuristic or predictive value for the nature of each particular instance in question.

It is this predictive value that Dupin attributes to the hypothesis of the "L'Etoile" concerning the fate of the drowned body of Marie Roget. That hypothesis, based upon the rule that drowned bodies or bodies thrown into the water immediately after death from violent causes require from six to ten days in order to resurface, has been accepted, Dupin notes, by all the newspapers of Paris with the exception of "Le Moniteur," which "endeavors to combat that portion of the paragraph which has reference to 'drowned bodies' only, by citing some five or six instances in which the bodies of individuals known to be drowned were found floating after the lapse of less time than is insisted upon by L'Etoile." "But," he continues, there is something "excessively unphilosophical" in this attempt to rebut the general assertions of L'Etoile by citing a few exceptions: as long as the argument proposed by the latter refers only to probabilities, that probability will remain in its favor "until the instances so childishly adduced shall be sufficient in number to establish an antagonistical rule" (*Coll. W.*, III, 740).

The probability of the girl's body rising to the surface in less than three days, consisting of a fraction in which the numerator represents all the occurrences of such a phenomenon, and the denominator, all the cases in which such occurrences were possible, will necessarily remain small unless (as Dupin observes) the number of these occurrences comes to constitute a large proportion (over one-half) of the total number of cases. To be sure, the probability ratio is by no means equivalent to actual truth in any particular instance. Nevertheless (and this is Dupin's assumption) its predictive value in those situations in which the ratio is either overwhelmingly close to 1 (signifying certainty) or infinitesimally small permits the individual to base further conjectures upon an assumption derived from this probability, without significantly diminishing the possibility of arriving at a correct solution of the mystery. Insofar as the likelihood of attaining a solution through the ratiocinative process is itself a matter of probability, there can be no qualitative difference between the original assumption and the remainder of the steps involved.

Such a process can, however, in certain instances, approach certainty. This occurs when a specific combination of events, each independent of the other, is seen to take place. Here the probability of such a specific combination coming to pass is so small that its occurrence cannot easily be ascribed to chance alone. Thus, in his refutation of "L'Etoile"'s argument that the body of the murdered girl is not that of Marie Roget, Dupin has only to observe how the probability of M. Beauvais being correct in his identification of Marie's body increases in a geometrical ratio with the addition of each identifying mark or feature.[13]

In so doing, Dupin does no more than apply a principle laid down by Laplace in his *Essai philosophique sur les probabilités:* "If the events are independent of one another, the probability of the existence of their ensemble is the product of their particular probabilities. Thus the probability of obtaining an ace with one die being a sixth, that of obtaining two aces in throwing two dice at the same time is a thirty-sixth. In effect, each of the faces of the one being capable of combining with the six faces of the other, there are thirty-six equally possible cases, among which only one will give the two aces. Generally, the probability that a simple event, in the same circumstances, will occur a number of times in a row is equal to the probability of this simple event, raised to a power indicated by that number" (*O.C.*, VII, xii). Concerning this principle Laplace comments that it is "one of the most important points of the Theory of Probabilities, and that which lends itself the most to illusions" (p. xii)—a remark Poe will reiterate at the conclusion of his tale.

With regard to the arguments advanced by "L'Etoile" against the identification of the girl's corpse with Marie Roget, Dupin's refutation thus clearly proceeds from the principle enunciated by Laplace. Here the extremely small probability of achieving, in any given case, an accidental coincidence between the features of the corpse and those of Marie Roget creates a correspondingly large probability that this corpse is in fact that of Marie herself. In other words, by a gradual decrease in the probability of an accidental coincidence between the features of the corpse and Marie's, we in effect progressively eliminate all the possibilities (the quantitative elements of a probability ratio for such a coincidence) *other than* that of an identity between Marie and the body of the girl.

Later on in the story Dupin applies the same principle in even more straightforward fashion. On account of the perpetration of several similar crimes by gangs during the same period, some of the newspapers had proposed the possibility of a gang-murder of the girl. "But," Dupin points out, "in fact, the one atrocity, known to be so committed, is, if anything, evidence that the other, committed at a time nearly coincident, was *not* so committed. It would have been a miracle indeed, if, while a gang of ruffians were perpetrating, at a given locality, a most unheard-of wrong, there should have been another similar gang, in a similar locality, in the same city, under the same circumstances, with the same means and appliances, engaged in a wrong of precisely the same aspect, at precisely the same period of time!" (*Coll. W.*, III, 757). With regard to

[13]One might see in Poe's assertion that the increase in probability will not be "in a ratio merely arithmetical, but in one highly geometrical" a reflection of Malthus (see above), whose work had achieved a *succès de scandale* in the early decades of the nineteenth century.

these remarks W. K. Wimsatt has commented: "Poe has asserted the contrary of one of the principles of *a priori* probability. A seven thrown once has no effect on the *chance* that seven will be thrown again. One girl seized by a gang has no effect on the *chance* that another will be seized. In the case of crimes (as in the case of dice if seven is thrown too often) some causality is operating. The second girl is either less likely or more likely to be seized—accordingly as a temporary caution in a single gang, for example, or the boldness of many gangs may be the deciding cause."[14]

To infer such a specific relation of cause to effect, however, is beyond the limits of the theory of probability. Concerning the tracing of events to causes by means of probability Laplace states only that "Each of the causes to which an observed event may be attributed is indicated with just as much likelihood as it is probable that, supposing this cause to exist, the event will take place; the probability of the existence of any one of these causes is then a fraction, of which the numerator is the probability of the event's resulting from this cause, and of which the denominator is the sum of the corresponding probabilities relative to all the causes. If these various causes, considered *a priori,* are unequally probable, it is necessary, in place of the probability of the event resulting from each cause, to employ the product of this probability by that of the cause itself" (*O.C.,* VII, xiv–xv).

Inasmuch as the calculation of the probability of an event or occurrence resulting from a specific cause must take into account all occurrences of that type (as well as all possible causes), there can be no more reason to suppose—from a probabilistic point of view—that the murder of Marie Roget should constitute the work of a gang rather than of an individual. For of the sum total of all murders of this type committed at that time, presumably at least half were the result of action by a single individual rather than a group, hence the probability of any given murder being ascribable to either cause could not exceed one-half. Even here, however, we have taken into account—as Dupin does not—the prevalance of gang murders in New York at the period of Mary Rogers' death. From the standpoint he assumes (that is, a more general one, in which all murders of this type are taken into account rather than simply those committed in New York during a specific period), the probability of a gang murder must be somewhat smaller. Thus the probability of a coincidence in time of two gang murders could only be, correspondingly, much smaller even than that of a single gang murder—if we calculate upon the basis of the principle stated by Laplace earlier (see above).

It is this principle that Poe specifically refers to at the conclusion of his tale. Speaking of the parallel between the case of the fictional Marie

[14]Wimsatt, p. 236.

Roget and that of Mary Rogers, he warns, "we must not fail to hold in view that the very Calculus of Probabilities to which I have referred, forbids all idea of the extension of the parallel: —forbids it with a positiveness strong and decided just in proportion as this parallel has already been long-drawn and exact" (*Coll. W.*, iii, 773). In support of his warning he then offers the same illustration of the dice employed by Laplace. Commenting on the common beliefs regarding that illustration, he concludes: "The error here involved—a gross error redolent of mischief—I cannot pretend to expose within the limits assigned me at present; and with the philosophical it needs no exposure. It may be sufficient here to say that it forms one of an infinite series of mistakes which arise in the path of Reason through her propensity for seeking truth *in detail*" (*Coll. W.*, iii, 773–74). We must discount Wimsatt's jeering remark: "It is hardly necessary to say that Poe stands almost alone among the 'philosophical.'"[15] It should be clear by now that Poe's assertion is no more than a simple repetition of Laplace's third principle. His caution against the "propensity for seeking truth in detail" is, moreover, significant, demonstrating as it does the primacy he accords to theory over isolated individual facts. As such, his tendency constitutes a step on the road that will finally lead him to the cosmogony of *Eureka*.

## Mechanism and Vitalism

In the history of early nineteenth-century biology one phenomenon stands out: the controversy between mechanism and vitalism. It has become customary to identify Romantic biology (for example, Lorenz Oken) with the doctrine of vitalism.[16] From this perspective, a biologist such as Cuvier would be excluded from the Romantic circle, despite the tangible affinity that binds him to Agassiz, and hence to Emerson, insofar as Cuvier had sought to define life not as an independent principle, but rather as the sum of certain physical, quasi-mechanical processes. In his *Leçons d'anatomie comparée* he asserts: "Thus, as living bodies do not grow indefinitely, but rather have limits which they cannot surpass assigned to each of them by nature, they must lose on one side at least a great part of what they receive on the other; and in effect attentive

15Ibid.
16See Canguilhem, *La Connaissance de la vie*, pp. 58–59. Of the vitalists Canguilhem writes: "They considered the universe as an organism, which is to say, as a harmonious system regulated simultaneously by laws and aims (ends). They conceived of themselves as an organic (organized) part of the universe, a sort of cell of the organic (organismic) universe; all the cells were unified by an internal sympathy, such that the destiny of an individual organ seemed to them to be naturally related to the movements of the heavens" (p. 88). On vitalism and mechanism, see esp. the chapters "La Théorie cellulaire," "Aspects du vitalisme," and "Machine et organisme."

observation teaches that transpiration and a multitude of other means take away continually from their substance. This should modify the idea which we formed initially of the principal phenomenon of life: in place of a constant union among the molecules, we should see there a continuous circulation from without to within, and from within to without, constantly maintained and yet fixed within certain limits. Thus living bodies should be considered as species of foyers, in which inanimate substances are brought successively to be combined amongst themselves in various ways, to occupy a place there and to exert an action determined by the nature of the combinations into which they have entered, and to escape one day in order to return to the laws of inanimate nature" (I, 4–5). And later, describing animals in general: "Each of them may be considered as a partial machine, coordinated with all the other machines of which the ensemble forms this world; the organs of movement are the wheels, the levers, in a word all the passive parts: but the active principle, the spring which gives the impulse to all the other parts, resides uniquely in the sensitive faculty, without which the animal, immersed in a continual sleep, would be really reduced to a purely vegetative state" (I, 18).[17]

With this passage, new perspectives open up. If animals in their passive state may be described as machines, by what means is their "active principle," residing in the sensitive faculty, to be distinguished or defined? Furthermore, in what sense can such a distinction contribute toward the establishment of a new model for the biological sciences? In his book *The Edge of Objectivity* Charles Gillispie has aptly pointed out that "the real question in criticizing . . . the whole tradition of biological romanticism, is not whether an animal is more than a classical machine. Obviously it is. So too, since relativity, is the solar system, and this is a circumstance which makes physics neither more nor less humane, neither more nor less accessible to theology. The serious question is what model of order biology will contemplate, and what instruments it will employ."[18]

In light of such a question it becomes possible to see the significance of the description proposed by Cuvier. The division of animals into passive (physico-chemical or mechanical) and active (sensitive) parts opens the doors to physical and chemical analysis of living phenomena in a way that could hardly have been possible in terms of vitalism. At the same time, biology could reserve to itself the right to distinguish between the essence of living and nonliving things—a distinction that would now, as

---

[17]But even Bichat, almost invariably classed as a vitalist, says: "All animals are an assemblage of divers organs which, executing each a function, concur, each in its manner, to the conservation of the whole. These are so many particularized machines in the general machine which constitutes the individual" (*Anatomie générale*, I, lxxix).

[18]Gillispie, p. 262.

a result of physical and chemical investigations, be redefined on a higher or more theoretical plane. Such a distinction is possible, however, only insofar as biology does not attempt to fence off the phenomenon of life (the life force) as something wholly separate from chemical and physical processes. It could avoid such artificial isolation of its subject if it were prepared to regard the concept of the machine itself in a new light.

It is here that Poe's contribution to our topic fits in. To be sure, it could hardly have had any effect on the course of science at that time. Nevertheless, in the retrospective judgment furnished by the history of science, it has been awarded high praise.[19] Poe's reflections on the concept of the machine occur in the course of his analysis of "Maelzel's Chess Player"— a supposed automaton capable of engaging in games of chess, gaining through its exhibitions in Poe's time much celebrity both in the United States and Europe. After a detailed analysis of the mechanism of the Chess-Player (in which he advances his reasons for supposing it to conceal a human agent), Poe then observes:

> Arithmetical or algebraical calculations are, from their very nature, fixed and determinate. Certain *data* being given, certain results necessarily and inevitably follow. These results have dependence upon nothing, and are influenced by nothing but the *data* originally given. And the question to be solved proceeds, or should proceed, to its final determination, by a succession of unerring steps liable to no change, and subject to no modification. This being the case, we can without difficulty conceive the *possibility* of so arranging a piece of mechanism, that upon starting it in accordance with the *data* of the question to be solved, it should continue its movements regularly, progressively, and undeviatingly towards the required solution, since these movements, however complex, are never imagined to be otherwise than finite and determinate. But the case is widely different with the Chess-Player. With him there is no determinate progression. No one move in chess necessarily follows upon any one other. . . . in proportion to the progress made in a game of chess, is the *uncertainty* of each ensuing move. A few moves having been made, *no* step is certain. Different spectators of the game would advise different moves. All is then dependent upon the variable judgment of the players. (*C.W.*, XIV, 9–11)

If one were asked to single out the most striking feature of this passage, one might well wish to point to the absence of any mention of the mechanical mode of operation peculiar to what one would normally call "machines." Instead, Poe classifies even algebraic and arithmetical calculations under the mechanistic rubric.[20] In this respect, he does not distinguish between material and immaterial processes. Above all, the machine is now described simply as the agent of a process. This process

---

[19]See Canguilhem, *La Connaissance de la vie*, p. 111.
[20]In this respect, one might consider the analysis of Turing machines.

must conform to a certain type, in which each step is necessarily predetermined. It is the process, however, and not any inherent physical or mechanical features, that characterizes a machine. Thus, even human beings at times become machines (as, for instance, when they perform arithmetical calculations).

To the type of process in which all steps are predetermined, Poe opposes the notion of an indeterminate process, in which choices are required. But choice also means: occurrence of arbitrary variations. Such variations (not counting those manifesting themselves in machines on account merely of physical forces such as friction, and the like) are necessarily brought about through the intervention of an immaterial principle—mind or intellect. A "machine" acted upon by mind in such a way as to produce arbitrary or voluntary acts ceases to be a machine and becomes something else. As a result, the sharp distinction heretofore prevailing between organisms and machines disappears: a "machine," acted upon by mind, becomes an "organ" or extension of that mind—hence something indistinguishable in theory from a so-called living organ, or the parts of a living being.

Thus the distinction between organisms and machines ceases, in effect, to be one between different classes of things, becoming instead one between different states of things. In fulfilling the necessary vital functions, the living organs are—as Cuvier had already observed—no more than machines. Only by virtue of their relation to the sentient faculty—and in higher species, to the mind or intellect—can they be described as organismic. Intellect, insofar as it chooses and acts in a manner not predetermined (so as to allow for different actions in similar circumstances), serves to distinguish living from nonliving things. Put in more general terms, living may be contrasted with nonliving things through the possibility of variation in actions not caused merely by external physical forces. By means of the principle of variability, Poe's distinction reaches to the lowest spheres of life. Even these, to the extent that they possess such variability, illustrate a process to which Poe recurs elsewhere: the effect of immaterial impulses on material forms. Only in *Eureka,* however, does the relation finally receive a definitive formulation.

## The Nebular Hypothesis

The history of science celebrates Buffon (1707–1788) for his comprehensive description of natural history, the *Histoire naturelle, générale et particulière.* In this monumental work (forty-four quarto volumes, published in Paris from 1749 to 1804), the first modern attempt to encompass all the domains of scientific knowledge, he had sought to offer, among other things, a new cosmogony, differing from virtually all previous theories by its attempt to explain the formation of the solar system by natural laws alone. He attributes the origin of the system not to divine intervention but to a collision between a comet and the sun: "The comet, by falling obliquely on the sun . . . must have forced off from his surface a quantity of matter equal to a 650th part of his body. This matter being in a liquid state, would at first form a torrent, of which the largest and rarest parts would fly to the greatest distances; the smaller and more dense, having received only an equal impulse, would remain nearer the sun; his power of attraction would operate upon all the parts detached from his body, and make them circulate round him; and, at the same time, the mutual attraction of the particles of matter would cause all the detached parts to take on the form of globes, at different distances from the sun, the nearer moving with greater rapidity in their orbits than the more remote."[21]

Buffon's account of the origin of the planets failed to win general acceptance—in part for religious reasons. In his recent book *Creation by Natural Law*, Ronald Numbers says of it nevertheless that "it remained, despite its scientific inadequacies, the most serious challenge to the Mosaic account of creation through the last half of the eighteenth century."[22] In 1796 it was superseded by a new theory, Laplace's nebular hypothesis, which then came to dominate nineteenth-century cosmogonic speculation.[23] As the basis for his theory, which he first published as an appendix to his popular exposition of astronomy, the *Système du monde*, Laplace conjectured the existence of a vast gaseous nebula, extending beyond the orbit of the most distant planet in the solar system. This nebula determines the features of that system.

The nebula's pattern of progressive contraction comes about through the interaction of two forces, the centrifugal impulse and gravity, each operating upon the nebulous matter or atmosphere in its rotation about a central point. But, according to Laplace, "The atmosphere of the sun cannot extend itself indefinitely; its limit is the point where the centrifugal force due to its movement of rotation balances gravity; thus, to the degree that cooling contracts the atmosphere and condenses at the surface of the star the neighboring molecules, the movement of rotation increases; for, by virtue of the principle of surfaces, the sum of the surfaces described by the radius vector of each molecule of the sun and of its atmosphere and projected onto the plane of its equator being

---

[21]Quoted from Ronald L. Numbers, *Creation by Natural Law: Laplace's Nebular Hypothesis in American Thought* (Seattle: Univ. of Washington Press, 1977), p. 7.

[22]Ibid., p. 8.

[23]See ibid., passim, for an account. Interestingly enough, one of the most violent opponents of the nebular hypothesis in America was Poe's correspondent George W. Eveleth (on whom, see ibid., p. 68). By a curious coincidence, shortly after the publication of *Eureka*, the nebular hypothesis received significant confirmation through the so-called Kirkwood analogy.

always the same, the rotation should be faster when these molecules are closer to the center of the sun. The centrifugal force due to this movement thus becoming greater, the point where gravity is equal to it is closer to the center. Supposing then, what it would be natural to allow, that the atmosphere was extended until a given period up to its limit, it would have had, in cooling, to abandon the molecules situated at that limit and at the limits successively produced by the increase in the rotation of the sun. These abandoned molecules would have continued to circulate around the star, since their centrifugal force was balanced by their gravity. But, this equality having no existence in relation to the atmospheric molecules placed on the parallels to the solar equator, these would have, by their gravity, come closer to the atmosphere to the degree that they condensed, and they would only have ceased to belong to to the extent that by this movement they would have drawn closer to the equator" (*O.C.*, VI, 501).

Perhaps on account of Laplace's argument concerning a progressive contraction of the nebular atmosphere, arrived at on the basis of the equality of the sums of the areas described by the radius vector of each molecule of the sun or its atmosphere, Poe had been led to describe the nebular hypothesis in *Eureka* as having both a mathematical and dynamical demonstration. In his *Système du monde* Laplace represents the nebular atmosphere as giving off "zones of vapors." These zones, once given off, assume the form of rings: "These zones should have in all likelihood formed, by their condensation and the mutual attraction of their molecules, various concentric rings of vapors, circulating around the sun. The mutual friction of the molecules of each ring should have accelerated some and retarded others, until all had acquired the same angular movement" (*O.C.*, VI, 501).

The angular movement into which the molecules of the nebular rings subside describes a series of concentric orbits on the same plane. But the difficulty of preserving an equilibrium in the process of condensation forces the nebular atmosphere to undergo yet another change:

If all the molecules of a ring of vapors continue to condense themselves without separating, they will eventually form a liquid or solid ring. But the regularity that this formation requires in all parts of the ring and in their cooling would render the phenomenon extremely rare. Moreover the solar system offers only one example, that of the rings of Saturn. Almost always each ring of vapors would have broken off into numerous masses which, moving at nearly the same speeds, would have continued to circulate at the same distance about the sun. The masses would have assumed a spheroid form, with a movement of rotation tending in the direction of their revolution, since their inferior molecules have less real velocity than their superior ones; they would then have formed so many planets in the vaporous state. But if one of them had been powerful enough to reunite successively through its attraction all the others around its center, the ring of vapors would thus have been transformed into a single spheroid mass of vapors, circulating around the sun, with a rotation tending in the direction of its revolution. (*O.C.*, VI, 502)

Here the process of condensation that had led to the formation of the planetary vapors repeats itself once more, producing a new succession of nebular rings around each planetary sphere. From these rings emerge the moons that circle about the planets—except in the case of Saturn, whose concentric rings Laplace accounts for through the preservation of an equilibrium in the process of their condensation. Thus, by means of the nebular hypothesis, Laplace could offer a theory of the origin of the solar system that takes into account not only the formation of the various planets and their satellites but also the movements of rotation and revolution described by each of these bodies, as well as their occurrence on the same elliptical plane.

Despite its success among scientific circles in Europe, the nebular hypothesis appears to have remained almost unknown in America in the early nineteenth century. Of American astronomers, only Nathaniel Bowditch (mathematician and translator of Laplace's *Mécanique céleste*) may be credited with acquaintance with it. This situation was to change in the following years, in part through the publication in England (and subsequently in America) of the Bridgewater Treatises. Through the medium of these treatises, inaugurated by their founder to demonstrate "the Power, Wisdom, and Goodness of God, as manifested in the Creation," Laplace's hypothesis was able to receive discussion and hence to be brought to the awareness of a large public in America (Poe himself had even reviewed one of these treatises for the *Southern Literary Messenger*). William Whewell's *Astronomy and General Physics Considered with Reference to Natural Theology*, in particular, had devoted a whole chapter to Laplace.

Other causes also contributed to further its acceptance. In an astronomy course for the working classes in Paris, Auguste Comte had announced, on the basis of various numerical calculations, that, should the matter of the earth be extended to the distance of the moon, the resultant period of the earth's rotation would in fact almost exactly coincide with that of the moon's periodic time. Such an announcement (which Poe himself refers to in *Eureka*), along with its supporting calculations, was bound to reinforce the credibility of the hypothesis. As a result of all these developments, the Laplacean cosmogony had managed to achieve, by the early 1840s, acceptance in some American scientific circles, which led to its being taught at various colleges and universities.[24]

[24]Ibid., p. 25.

At this point it received yet further prominence as a result of the *succès de scandale* of Robert Chambers's *Vestiges of the Natural History of Creation*. In his book (subsequently to become famous in the history of science for its pre-Darwinian exposition of a theory of evolution), published anonymously in 1844, Chambers had sought to invoke the nebular hypothesis in support of his theory of evolution—a move that required some explanation of the hypothesis itself. His exposition is not, however, a literal recapitulation of Laplace, but differs in certain crucial points. Among these we must count Chambers's description of the nuclei of nebulae, depicted as solid masses detached from the rest of the atmosphere, which revolves around it: "Of nebulous matter in its original state we know too little to enable us to suggest how nuclei should be established in it. But, supposing that, from a peculiarity in its constitution, nuclei are formed, we know very well how, by virtue of the law of gravitation, the process of an aggregation of the neighboring matter to those nuclei should proceed, until masses more or less solid should become detached from the rest. It is a well-known law in physics that, when fluid matter collects or meets in a centre, it establishes a rotatory motion. . . . It thus becomes certain that when we arrive at the stage of a nebulous star, we have a rotation on an axis commenced" (*Vestiges*, pp. 12–13). By contrast, Laplace had supposed the whole of the nebular atmosphere (including its center) to be in rotation. In addition, the central portion remains in a gaseous (rather than solid) state. As a result of such differences, Chambers drew fire upon himself for what one critic described as the "crude sun-making" of *Vestiges*.[25]

His account also differs from Laplace's in its assumption of a process of incrustation, which he invokes to elucidate the formation of the nebular rings:

> If we suppose the agglomeration of a nebulous mass to be a process attended by refrigeration or cooling, which many facts render likely, we can easily understand why the outer parts, hardening under this process, might, by virtue of the greater solidity thence acquired, begin to present some resistance to the attractive force. As the solidification proceeded, this resistance would become greater, though there would still be a tendency to adhere. Meanwhile, the condensation of the central mass would be going on, tending to produce a separation from what may now be termed the *solidifying crust*. During the contention between the attractions of these two bodies, or parts of one body, there would probably be a ring of attenuation between the mass and its crust. At length, when the central mass had reached a certain stage in its advance towards solidification, a separation would take place, and the crust would become a detached ring. (*Vestiges*, pp. 14–15)

[25]See ibid., p. 34.

It was not necessary, of course, for Poe to incorporate any of the modifications introduced by Chambers into the nebular hypothesis (in fact, Poe's own account closely duplicates Laplace's).[26] On at least one level, nevertheless, it seems appropriate to compare the *Vestiges* with *Eureka*. Both exemplify efforts to generalize from a hypothesis applying only to the solar system to the formation of the universe as a whole.[27] Moreover, both works are infused with a consciousness of the ongoing nature of this process. In his *Vestiges* Chambers remarks: "The first idea which all this impresses upon us is, that the formation of bodies in space is *still and at present in progress*" (p. 21).

At this point the similarity between the two works disappears. Where Chambers interprets the continuing existence of nebulae as indicative of the coming into being of new celestial bodies, Poe asserts that the period of nebulae in the history of the universe has in fact passed, and that the only cosmic processes to occur henceforward must be those of convergence and attraction toward a common center. With regard to the resolution of nebulae into star clusters by the telescope of Lord Rosse, he declares: "If the propositions of this Discourse have been comprehended, it will be seen that, in my view, a failure to segregate the 'nebulae' would have tended to the refutation, rather than to the confirmation, of the Nebular Hypothesis" (*Poetry and Tales*, p. 1320).

According to Poe, the existence of the nebulae is explicable only in terms of a cosmic movement of expansion, which propagates the molecules or particles of matter outward from a common center: This movement derives from an original divine impulse; Poe describes the movement as unnatural, since it requires a positive force to propel the particles outward and thus contravenes the law of inertia. Since the nebulae owe their existence to a propelling diffusive force, its cessation at an arbitrary point in time (when the universe has achieved the limits originally designed for it by God) must result in a movement of reaction. That reaction causes the convergence of the previously diffused particles of the nebulae, a motion Poe ascribes to gravitation.

Although present during the universe's expansion, gravitation takes effect only when the original expansive force ceases to exert itself. Conversely, the presence of observable gravitational effects (for example, orbits of planets about a sun, or of satellites about a planet) makes it

[26]For Poe and Laplace, see ibid., p. 27.

[27]It seems appropriate at this point to consider the various attempts to correlate Poe's argument in *Eureka* with the traditional (esp. eighteenth-century) arguments from design. Cf. Barton Levi St. Armand, "'Seemingly Intuitive Leaps': Belief and Unbelief in *Eureka*," in *Poe as Literary Cosmologer*, ed. Richard P. Benton (Hartford: Transcendental Books, 1975), esp. pp. 8–9 (relating *Eureka* to Paley's *Natural Theology*) and p. 12 (Poe and Thomas Dick's *The Christian Philosopher*); Margaret Alterton, *Origins of Poe's Critical Theory*, pp. 112–31. But, as Ronald Numbers has shown (see esp. p. 14), Paley's *Natural Theology* belongs to a widely different intellectual context from the cosmogonic speculations of Laplace, Comte, Chambers, and others in the nineteenth century, with whom we must associate Poe.

possible to infer the cessation of the original expansive force. Such gravitational effects, which physics explains through the attraction between
bodies in space, embody a more elevated or universal law: the attraction
of all particles of matter to their original center. In conforming to the
rules of physics, these particles simultaneously reveal a higher conception or idea.

The tendency toward an idealization of physics, which would elevate it
to the level of metaphysics—according to Aristotle, the science of first
causes—constitutes the basic impulse of Poe's treatise. Such idealization
does not (as with Goethe or Schelling) object to the laws formulated by
classical mechanics, but seeks rather to discern in them a more avowedly
ideational content. For this reason Poe can completely and wholeheart-
edly affirm the nebular hypothesis, while regarding it merely as part of a
more comprehensive description of the cosmic entelechy. In so doing,
he represents a different but no less significant attitude toward science
than that of German *Naturphilosophie,* one that accords more closely with
the quantitative (physical and mathematical) than with the biological-
organic outlook of Romantic science.[28] Consequently, Poe begins by
accepting the Newtonian system of classical mechanics, then attempts to
substitute qualitative or substantive relations in place of its quantitative
formulae. Hence his translation of the Newtonian law that all bodies
attract each other with forces proportional to their quantities of matter
and inversely proportional to their distances into the proposition that
*"every atom, of every body, attracts every other atom, both of its own and of every*
*other body, with a force which varies inversely as the squares of the distances*
*between the attracting and attracted atom"* (*Poetry and Tales,* p. 1284).

Similarly, Laplace's hypothesis furnishes both the external form (progressive contraction of the nebulae through concentric rings) and elements (gravitational and centrifugal forces) of Poe's cosmology. But the
final product is neither wholly scientific (on account of the dominant
role conferred upon conjecture) nor antiscientific, inasmuch as it accepts
all the data of science; its unique mixture is perhaps best described in
terms of the utopian program laid down by Shelley almost half a century
earlier: the union of poetry and science.

## The "Inner Perfection" of Theory

In discussing Poe's concept of the nature of ratiocination, I have already alluded to Einstein's observation concerning the inner perfection
of a theory. This we have seen to consist of the naturalness or logical

---

[28]For comment on Poe's views from a scientific perspective, see Arthur Eddington's
remarks in Arthur Hobson Quinn, *Edgar Allan Poe: A Critical Biography* (New York :Ap-
pleton-Century, 1941), pp. 555–56.

simplicity of the basic concepts and their relations to each other. To the inner perfection of a theory Einstein had contrasted the standpoint of "external confirmation" as an equally necessary (although more flexible) criterion. In *Eureka,* however, the inner perfection of a theory becomes alone sufficient attestation to its truth. Accordingly the preface reads: "To the few who love me and whom I love—to those who feel rather than to those who think—to the dreamers and those who put faith in dreams as in the only realities—I offer this Book of Truths, not in its character of Truth-Teller, but for the Beauty that abounds in its Truth; constituting it true. To these I present the composition as an Art-Product alone: —let us say as a Romance; or, if I be not urging too lofty a claim, as a Poem" (*Poetry and Tales,* p. 1259). A similar validation accompanies Laplace's nebular hypothesis: "From whatever point we regard it, we shall find it *beautifully true.* It is by far too beautiful, indeed, *not* to possess Truth as its essentiality—and here I am very profoundly serious in what I say" (*Poetry and Tales,* p. 1312).

These utterances serve to define the final phase of Poe's aestheticism as well. By encompassing both science and art, such aestheticism differs from that of the Pre-Raphaelites and the early Tennyson, as well as Pater or Wilde. As in his late verse, Poe's position in *Eureka* recalls the stance of Keats. But whereas Keats had approached truth through beauty, Poe discerns beauty only in truth. This beauty is, as it were, the manifestation of Truth, "constituting it true" by revealing such truth to the intellectual sensibility. Henry Adams once remarked of Jefferson that his writings betrayed a concern for form, "a sure sign," Adams notes, "of intellectual sensuousness." A similar comment might be applied to Poe. Here the truth of which he speaks belongs neither to the phenomenology of existence nor an immediate higher Revelation. Instead, it issues from purely theoretical speculation. Thus the beauty that reveals or manifests truth becomes that of the theory itself, its "inner perfection." With regard to that perfection, it should now be clear why Poe dedicates his work "to those who feel rather than to those who think," to "the dreamers and those who put faith in dreams as in the only realities." For these intellectual aesthetes the "external confirmation" of a theory can have no significance. Its "inner perfection" alone suffices.[29]

To the concept of "inner perfection" some further clarification may be given. Aesthetically, we find it expressed in the criterion of symmetry, which in turn associates itself with consistency. The form of the universe reveals their identity: "And, in fact, the sense of the symmetrical is an instinct which may be depended on with an almost blindfold reliance. It

---

[29]One might apply this criterion to Poe's analysis of the ultimate origination of the universe, the creation of the first particle, which, he says, conforms to the necessity for absolute *"Simplicity."* Cf. Edward H. Davidson, *Poe: A Critical Study* (Cambridge: Harvard Univ. Press, 1957), p. 233.

is the poetical essence of the Universe—*of the Universe* which, in the supremeness of its symmetry, is but the most sublime of poems. Now symmetry and consistency are convertible terms:  —thus Poetry and Truth are one. A thing is consistent in the ratio of its truth—true in the ratio of its consistency. *A perfect consistency, I repeat, can be nothing but an absolute truth*" (*Poetry and Tales*, p. 1349).

Earlier, in another context, he had spoken of "the merely mathematical recognition of equality" as "the root of all beauty." Perhaps we may take both principles (equality and symmetry) as expressions of a more fundamental relation in Poe. This relation is in essence one of correspondence. It furnishes the basis for his equation of symmetry and consistency, and hence of poetry and truth. In making such assertions he might well have been thinking in particular of the pattern of universal expansion and contraction put forth in *Eureka*. Here the symmetry of the two movements (diametrically opposite in their nature, exactly equal in extent) gives substance to the claim of consistency advanced by that theory which embraces both, a theory for which each movement forms the necessary complement of the other. At the same time, the concept of consistency is redefined in the process. Like the concept of beauty, it comes to be regarded in formal terms. Correspondence between theoretical elements such as cause and effect, origin and end, becomes equivalent to the kind of purely formal correspondence (which we call symmetry) that appears in works of art. As a result, a new appreciation of theory on purely aesthetic grounds becomes possible. Its criterion: a theoretical symmetry, which Poe equates with the formal symmetry of the arts. On account of the identity of beauty and truth developed earlier, this theoretical symmetry—as the aesthetic quality of thought— must also be what certifies it as true. Their equivalence allows Poe to claim that "a perfect consistency . . . can be nothing but an absolute truth." The consistent is adduced as true, not on the grounds of its rationality (which implies attention to the content of its terms) but because of its theoretical symmetry, its beauty as thought or (to return to Einstein's phrase) its "inner perfection" as theory.

We have seen the extent to which inner perfection remains independent of external confirmation. For Poe, the two are complementary rather than conflicting spheres (hence his attempt to incorporate the accounts of Lord Rosse's telescopic resolutions of nebulae as actual confirmation of his theory). At the same time, any determination of the nature of the origin of the universe must be developed on the basis of theoretical considerations alone. The origin of the universe is really the origin of its idea, which Poe traces to the origin of thought itself: "It will now be readily understood that no axiomatic idea—no idea founded in the fluctuating principle, obviousness of relation—can possibly be so secure—so reliable a basis for any structure erected by the Reason, as *that* idea—(whatever it is, wherever we can find it, or *if* it be practicable to find it anywhere)—which is *ir*relative altogether—which not only presents to the understanding *no obviousness* of relation, either greater or less, to be considered, but subjects the intellect, not in the slightest degree, to the necessity of even looking at *any relation at all*" (*Poetry and Tales*, p. 1303).

The notion of an "irrelative thought" helps us to connect Poe with Romantic philosophical speculation. Almost half a century earlier, the necessity of an unmediated beginning in philosophy had impressed itself upon Fichte, Schelling, and Hegel with almost equal force (see, for example, Hegel, *G.W.*, xxi, 62). This beginning (in Fichte the principle $A = A$ or its corollary, self-consciousness; in Schelling the identity of subject and object; in the later Hegel, pure being) must justify itself on purely theoretical grounds: one begins with what is absolutely immediate, that whose existence does not depend on its relation to anything else, since that alone can form an *absolute* beginning.

But if the notion of an irrelative thought manifests an affinity with Romantic philosophy, other aspects of Poe's thinking reveal still other tendencies. His opposition to axiomatic reasoning, for instance, anticipates in a general fashion the impulse toward mathematical intuitionism, with its denial of the validity of certain axioms of logical entailment or implication. But although we find some references to mathematical axioms (for example, that the whole is equal to the sum of its parts) in *Eureka* and elsewhere, it is obvious that the main thrust of Poe's critique is directed at philosophical speculation, as that which most closely approximates the nature of thought in general. Hence the satirical letter (which also appears in "Mellonta Tauta"), with its caricatures of the Aristotelian and Baconian systems. In his synoptic "history" of thought, Poe notes how "Aries Tottle flourished supreme, until the advent of one Hog, surnamed 'the Ettrick shepherd,' who preached an entirely different system, which he called the *à posteriori* or *inductive*" (*Poetry and Tales*, pp. 1263–64). This "historical" account is then followed up by a criticism of the paucity of both systems. Thus, with regard to Baconianism: "its most lamentable fount of error—lay in its tendency to throw power and consideration into the hands of merely perceptive men—of those inter-Tritonic minnows, the microscopical savans—the diggers and pedlers of minute *facts*, for the most part in physical science—facts all of which they retailed at the same price on the highway; their value depending, it was supposed, simply upon the *fact of their fact*, without reference to their applicability or inapplicability in the development of those ultimate and only legitimate facts, called Law" (*Poetry and Tales*, p. 1265). We have seen how "Law," for both Poe and Coleridge, defines the relation between one object or being and another. In criticizing Bacon, Poe enunciates a realization that emerges in the history of science with increasing clarity as one approaches our own century: that all facts assume meaning only insofar as they either support or contradict one theory or another.

But if empiricism is to be rejected for its failure to elevate itself to a sufficiently theoretical plane, the deficiencies of Aristotelianism are no less apparent. For "the simple truth is, that the Aristotelians erected their castles on a basis far less reliable than air; *for no such things as axioms ever existed or can possibly exist at all*" (*Poetry and Tales*, p. 1266). To this formal or axiomatic system Poe opposes a more "natural" type that takes into account not only the object of thought but the process by which thought apprehends that object. With regard to the existence of the infinite, the process of conceiving it assumes special importance:

> Nevertheless, as an individual, I may be permitted to say that I *cannot* conceive Infinity, and am convinced that no human being can. A mind not thoroughly self-conscious—not accustomed to the introspective analysis of its own operations—will, it is true, often deceive itself by supposing that it *has* entertained the conception of which we speak. In the effort to entertain it, we proceed step beyond step—we fancy point still beyond point; and so long as we *continue* the effort, it may be said, in fact, that we are *tending* to the formation of the idea designed; while the strength of the impression that we actually form or have formed it, is in the ratio of the period during which we keep up the mental endeavor. But it is in the act of discontinuing the endeavor—of fulfilling (as we think) the idea—of putting the finishing stroke (as we suppose) to the conception—that we overthrow at once the whole fabric of our fancy by resting upon some one ultimate and therefore definite point. This fact, however, we fail to perceive, on account of the absolute coincidence, in time, between the settling down upon the ultimate point and the act of cessation in thinking. (*Poetry and Tales*, p. 1274)

Almost three-quarters of a century later the German mathematician David Hilbert would advance a similar argument (in his essay "On the Infinite") against the postulation of a mathematical infinite: if the infinite is to have existence at all, it must have a numerical representation, and that representation will always result in a finite quantity. One need not claim that Poe anticipates Hilbert's concerns—clearly, his own are less with representation than the psychology of representation—but the comparison exemplifies shared underlying tendencies.

Perhaps no less remarkable is the attempt to take account of the role played by various processes of thought in the formation of a particular concept. To be sure, there are precedents for this, particularly in the English epistemological tradition that traces its history back to Locke. For Poe, however, the epistemological perspective forms but part of a larger enterprise. By becoming conscious of the nature of its own operations, the mind also comes to recognize the true nature of its objects as well. The reality of those objects, it now perceives, exists not in the external world but in itself. Even should the objects themselves actually have external existence, their reality can only consist of their presence within the mind. That presence is defined by their correspondence to the mind's nature. Hence the development and formation of concepts must be perfectly "natural": they must conform to the mind's innate tendencies and capacities, and not to what is believed to be the essence of the objects themselves. What is inaccessible to thought on account of the latter's very nature is excluded from the sphere of speculation. But this also implies: exclusion from the realm of truth. For Poe, the mind's natural tendency is toward the rational. That which cannot be expressed rationally can have no reality in itself. Here the rational is not to be equated with the logical. Its defining characteristic is, rather, intuitive perception of the ideal relation of one object to another. Because infinity does not possess the property of relation (that is, conceivability), Poe argues that it can have no existence in fact.

Thus the conditions of the mind's apprehension of things become, as it were, descriptive of the nature of truth as well. But the mind not only "receives," it also imagines. Consequently, the shape of the imagination dictates the shape of things. Its ability to conceive defines the concept of space: "It will now be understood that, in using the phrase, 'Infinity of Space,' I make no call upon the reader to entertain the impossible conception of an *absolute* infinity. I refer simply to the *'utmost conceivable expanse'* of space—a shadowy and fluctuating domain, now shrinking, now swelling, with the vacillating energies of the imagination" (*Poetry and Tales*, p. 1275).

Elsewhere in *Eureka* Poe elaborates upon the form of the mind's apprehension of truth. To the process of apprehension he assigns the name intuition, which is then defined as follows: "It is but *the conviction arising from those inductions or deductions of which the processes are so shadowy as to escape our consciousness, elude our reason, or defy our capacity of expression*" (*Poetry and Tales*, pp. 1276–77). Here it becomes necessary to qualify what was said earlier. Although those things which the mind cannot conceive of on account of its own nature remain necessarily null and void, Poe now postulates the existence of convictions whose truth rests upon subconscious inferences or deductions. Behind each of the mind's seemingly intuitive leaps emerges, on closer analysis, a series of steps or gradations by which it reaches its conclusions. In this respect, thought approaches what Poe elsewhere describes as the nature of things. In "Mesmeric Revelation" Vankirk observes: "But there are *gradations* of matter of which man knows nothing; the grosser impelling the finer, the finer pervading the grosser" (*Coll. W.*, III, 1033). The gradations or steps in the processes of thought correspond to gradations in matter or things. That would imply a shaping of mind by nature, hence what Poe refers to in *Eureka* as a "mutuality of adaptation." Such mutuality of adaptation is possible only because of the creation of the universe as a thought within the mind of God. In its attempt to reformulate the correspondence of mind to nature and nature to mind, Poe's cosmogony thus renews and revitalizes, within a wholly secular context, the aims of theology, as, literally, "divine science."

## Materialism and Spiritualism

In one of his essays C. D. Broad once characterized Leibniz as "the greatest intellect of which human history has any record." Poe, too, echoes this judgment on various occasions. In "The Man of the Crowd" he declares that "the intellect, electrified, surpasses as greatly its everyday condition, as does the vivid yet candid reason of Leibnitz, the mad and flimsy rhetoric of Gorgias" (*Coll. W.*, II, 507). And in *Eureka*, after observing the failure of Newton and Laplace to establish the metaphysical principle behind the law of gravity: "Nevertheless, we may well wonder that Leibnitz, who was a marked exception to the general rule in these respects, and whose mental temperament was a singular admixture of the mathematical with the physico-metaphysical, did not at once investigate and establish the point at issue" (*Poetry and Tales*, p. 1290). For, Poe continues, "it is almost impossible to fancy, of Leibnitz, that, having exhausted in his search the physical dominions, he would not have stepped at once, boldly and hopefully, amid his old familiar haunts in the kingdom of Metaphysics."

Various indications appear to point to an inner affinity between Poe and Leibniz. After all, could not the description of Leibniz's temperament as "a singular admixture of the mathematical with the physico-metaphysical" apply equally to Poe himself? We have seen already the attraction of Laplace's theory of probability for the latter. It would, no doubt, also be possible to describe *Eureka* itself as a meditation on a Leibnizian theme: the relation of matter to spirit (hence also, of mind to body), or the physical to the metaphysical. The "fellowship" of attraction and repulsion (which Poe equates with the material and spiritual principles) recalls Leibniz's concept of the preestablished harmony of mind and body, as does the description of particles (both in *Eureka* and elsewhere) the scheme of the "Monadology." Above all, the Leibnizian concept of substance embodies one of the central aspects of *Eureka:* the idea of matter (consisting of particles) as imbued with a divine force. To substance, Leibniz ascribes what he terms an "active force." It constitutes not merely a capacity for action (in the Aristotelian or Scholastic sense) but a positive quantity: "Active force, on the contrary, contains a sort of activity, an entelechy; it is intermediate between the faculty to act and the action itself, and involves an effort (conatus). Thus, it is brought into operation by itself alone, requiring for this purpose no help, but merely the suppression of impediments" (*Monadology*, p. 83).[30] The notion of an activity or entelechy of substance furnishes an analogue to what Poe will later describe as the divine force that imparts the original diffusive motion to matter, and, subsequently, the attractive or gravitational force that draws it once more to its point of origin.

But it would be misleading to infer from the apparent affinity between Poe and Leibniz (in part an unconscious one, since Poe—judging by his remarks in *Eureka*—does not appear to have been aware of the entire compass of Leibniz's metaphysics) that the essential cast of Poe's thought is neoclassical or derivative from that of eighteenth-century speculation. In fact, the Leibnizian system had itself undergone renewed appreciation in the light of German Romantic philosophy. In his *Science of Logic* Hegel accords it even higher praise than the system of Spinoza—although the revival of the latter is commonly considered one of the distinguishing features of Romantic thought. For, Hegel observes, "The lack *of reflection into itself* which the Spinozistic exposition of the absolute as well as the doctrine of emanation have in themselves, is supplied in the concept of the *Leibnizian monad*" (*G.W.*, XI, 378).

As a result of the principle of reflection-into-itself, Leibnizian substance becomes capable of assimilating the movement of thought, which is also that of becoming or development. This movement establishes the determination of the monad in both its specificity and universality (that is to say, in its substance and in its form). Only in terms of the nature of these determinations does the Leibnizian system ultimately fail to fulfill its promise: "But what appear in these determinations are only the usual conceptions, which are left without philosophical development and not raised to speculative Concepts. Thus the principle of individuation does not receive its deeper realization; the concepts concerning the differences between the various finite monads and their relation to their absolute do not spring out of this essence itself nor in an absolute fashion, but belong to rationalizing, dogmatic reflection and have therefore attained no inner coherence" (*G.W.*, XI, 379).

What the Leibnizian system fails to produce are the genuinely speculative concepts that would develop from the essence of the monads themselves and that would yield an original conceptual content. But in order for the determinations of the monads to produce something more than the notions established by previous philosophy, the nature of the concept itself (that is, of the content of the monad's determinations) must change.

---

[30]See also, on this point, Leibniz, in the *Nouveaux Essais*, *Sämtliche Schriften und Briefe*, VI:6, p. 65, 11. 19–23.

If we compare the above critique with the speculations of *Eureka,* what emerges is the possibility of a revision of the Leibnizian perspective that accords with the spirit of Romantic philosophy. Poe does not undertake, of course, to offer a new system, as do the Romantics themselves, nor does he present new concepts with a completely original content. Instead, if his treatise is seen as a Romantic transformation of Leibnizian substance (in the sense of developing a theme through variations), it becomes possible to arrive at a more accurate appreciation of its nature.

Poe begins with the elements of the Leibnizian system—spirit and matter, the relation of the physical to the metaphysical, corpuscular particles. In addition, Leibniz had postulated a spiritual-material continuum encompassing all of created being. Poe, too, conjectures the existence of gradations of matter which by progressive rarefaction arrive at the level of pure spirit. In "Mesmeric Revelation" Vankirk explains: "These gradations of matter increase in rarity or fineness, until we arrive at a matter *unparticled*—without particles—indivisible—*one;* and here the law of impulsion and permeation is modified. The ultimate, or unparticled matter, not only permeates all things but impels all things— and thus *is* all things within itself. This matter is God. What men attempt to embody in the word 'thought,' is this matter in motion" (*Coll. W.,* III, 1033). Mind, as substance, must be distinguished from its activity, which is thought. Motion can only be produced by a substance: "Motion is the action of *mind*—not of *thinking.* The unparticled matter, or God, in quiescence, is (as nearly as we can conceive it) what men call mind. And the power of self-movement (equivalent in effect to human volition) is, in the unparticled matter, the result of its unity and omniprevalence; *how* I know not, and now clearly see that I shall never know. But the unparticled matter, set in motion by a law, or quality, existing within itself, is thinking" (pp. 1033–34).

By supposing the existence of gradations of matter, Poe establishes the principle of a purely physical permeation of matter by spirit. As a result of such permeation, spirit can impart to matter impulses that adhere to the laws of physics. The source of all spiritual impulses is God; hence, God becomes equivalent to a divine energy, the universe the field of his energy. The former opposition between permeation and impulsion— the one an internal, the other an external principle—is abolished. Both are united in the divine energy, which not only permeates matter as its innermost essence, but also acts upon it externally by impelling it into motion. Hence Poe's claim that it is "all things within itself." By defining the unparticled matter as God, he annuls the opposition between matter and energy, and between matter and spirit. The universe now appears as a cosmic continuum of force, consisting of infinite gradations by which the tangible approaches the intangible, the concrete the ethereal.

By means of these relations, spiritual concepts are subjected to a physical interpretation. Consequently, it becomes necessary to distinguish between the action of mind and the action of thinking. The former represents a material principle (that is, the unparticled matter), the latter an independent immaterial force. The distinction between mind and thinking reduces itself to that of the two states of the unparticled matter, the quiescent (mind) and the active (thought). In its active state, such matter is inseparable from its activity. The fusion of substance and activity into one creates the power of self-movement, which Vankirk considers inexplicable because of the impossibility of comprehending an identification of two qualitatively different things (substance and activity). Through its power of self-movement, the unparticled matter recalls Aristotle's unmoved first mover, but with the difference that Poe's primordial first cause is envisioned in terms of an ultimately material, rather than immaterial, substance. Hence in his assertion (in "The Power of Words") that "true philosophy has long taught that the source of all motion is thought—and the source of all thought is—*God*," we are not to understand two principles (the material, or motion, and the immaterial, or thought) but rather a single principle of motion that assumes two forms: the immaterial, as the motion of the unparticled matter; the material, as the motion of tangible things (citation from *Coll. W.*, III, 1215). By postulating an energy that manifests itself in diverse ways, Poe avoids the dichotomy of an immaterial force acting upon material things.

With these preliminary indications, we may now approach the treatment of matter and spirit in *Eureka* itself. Here Poe attempts to construct a more precise description of the physical forces. Two in particular are singled out as representing the most elemental forms of force: electricity and gravitation. These may be reduced to yet more basic principles: "Discarding now the two equivocal terms, 'gravitation' and 'electricity,' let us adopt the more definite expressions, '*Attraction*' and '*Repulsion*.' The former is the body; the latter the soul: the one is the material; the other the spiritual, principle of the Universe. *No other principles exist. All phaenomena are referable to one, or to the other, or to both combined*" (*Poetry and Tales*, p. 1282).

Attraction signifies the material inasmuch as it brings about a coalescence of particles, and hence a loss of individuation. Repulsion, on the other hand, by insuring individuation, gives rise to consciousness: for Poe, consciousness results from recognition of the difference between oneself and another.[31] In associating consciousness with spirituality,

---

[31]In *Poe: A Critical Study* Davidson maintains: "Motion cannot therefore be called 'thought,' for the electrical force which is the energizing of thought is long antecedent to that thought and that action" (p. 229). Poe's own wording in *Eureka* is, however, significant:

moreover, Poe reflects the epistemological perspective of the preceding century. Diderot, La Mettrie, and others had all defined consciousness as a higher form of awareness, elevated above the mere sentience of the simple forms of life, yet connected with them by almost imperceptible gradations. Consciousness implies, however, possibilities of knowledge and reason which are denied to mere sentience. To the extent that these, too, depend upon the existence of differences between things (which allows the mind to establish relations between them), they, like consciousness, are possible only through individuation, which means, ultimately, the principle of repulsion.

The epistemological perspective of *Eureka* also affects the treatment of matter or substance. Contrary to the Romantic notion of substance, which ascribes to it a fundamental essence or being, Poe defines it strictly in terms of the principles it manifests: "So rigorously is this the case—so thoroughly demonstrable is it that Attraction and Repulsion are the *sole* properties through which we perceive the Universe—in other words, by which Matter is manifested to Mind—that, for all merely argumentative purposes, we are fully justified in assuming that Matter *exists* only as Attraction and Repulsion—that Attraction and Repulsion *are* matter" (*Poetry and Tales*, pp. 1282–83).

By defining matter solely in terms of its two contrasting forces, Poe reduces it to its relations. Matter, in other words, has no existence in itself: its only existence is through its action upon other substances or of other substances upon it. The mind, of course, cannot "know" substance in the sense of feeling or perceiving it—it can merely infer its existence. Hence Poe's dismissal of the notion of substance: if mind has no independent knowledge of its existence, to infer substance represents an "unnatural" effort. Following his inclination toward "intuitionism" outlined earlier, Poe now accepts only what the mind naturally formulates or represents to itself—in this case, the laws governing the actions of forces.

The existence of matter represents an equilibrium of forces. Such an equilibrium can be maintained only so long as the expansive force continues to exert itself. The natural tendency of the particles toward aggregation, on the other hand, results in their progressive movement

---

"To electricity . . . far less shall we be liable to err in attributing to this strictly spiritual principle the more important phaenomena of vitality, consciousness and *Thought*" (*Poetry and Tales*, p. 1282). To electricity, then, he attributes the *phaenomena* (phenomenon) of thought, but such phenomena (phenomenon) must necessarily differ from the essence of thought itself. In the earlier "Mesmeric Revelation," "P." remarks: "The metaphysicians maintain that all action is reducible to motion and thinking, and that the latter is the origin of the former"—to which Vankirk assents (*Coll. W.*, III, 1033). The manifestation of thought, its expression, so to speak, may occur through electricity, but, given Poe's earlier enunciated principle of gradations of matter, it is not likely for him to suggest that a more spiritual or ethereal force (thought) is to be produced by a less spiritual one (electricity).

toward a common center that is also their point of origin. But if matter consists simply of forces, it must upon their expenditure return to a state of nothingness: "when, I say, Matter, finally, expelling the Ether, shall have returned into absolute Unity, —it will then (to speak paradoxically for the moment) be Matter without Attraction and without Repulsion— in other words, Matter without Matter—in other words, again, *Matter no more*. In sinking into Unity, it will sink at once into that Nothingness which, to all finite perception, Unity must be—into that Material Nihility from which alone we can conceive it to have been evoked—to have been *created* by the Volition of God" (*Poetry and Tales*, p. 1355).

Upon the disappearance of matter, what remains can only be pure spirit, that is, unparticled matter. Since the unparticled matter originally occupies the space in which matter comes into existence, it necessarily enters into the substance of matter (since no displacement of the unparticled matter is possible). Its ability as a more ethereal element to penetrate matter forms the basis of the principle of permeation. As a result, matter encloses the unparticled matter or ether within itself. This ether is not merely in a quiescent state but impels itself by a form of self-movement. By remaining within matter, it also imparts its movement to matter. Consequently, both participate in the divine scheme: "With a perfectly legitimate reciprocity, we are now permitted to look at Matter, as created *solely for the sake of this influence*—solely to serve the objects of this spiritual Ether. Through the aid—by the means—through the agency of Matter, and by dint of its heterogeneity—is this Ether manifested—is *Spirit individualized*" (*Poetry and Tales*, p. 1354).

The individualization of spirit occurs through enclosure of the ether in individual material bodies. Such a phenomenon does not imply individualization of the substance of the ether, but simply its differentiation into discrete portions. As for the ether itself, it remains in substance exactly the same, unaffected by its apportionment. Its essential identity insures that all souls, or individualizations of the ether, must in fact be equal, since there can be no difference in their substance but merely in the external forms containing that substance. To this truth, the inner feelings bear witness:

> The utter impossibility of any one's soul feeling itself inferior to another; the intense, overwhelming dissatisfaction and rebellion at the thought; — these, with the omniprevalent aspirations at perfection, are but the spiritual, coincident with the material, struggles towards the original Unity— are, to my mind at least, a species of proof far surpassing what Man terms demonstration, that no one soul *is* inferior to another—that nothing is, or can be, superior to any one soul—that each soul is, in part, its own God—its own Creator: —in a word, that God—the material *and* spiritual God—*now* exists solely in the diffused Matter and Spirit of the Universe; and that the

regathering of this diffused Matter and Spirit will be but the re-constitution of the *purely Spiritual* and Individual God. (*Poetry and Tales*, p. 1357)

Later it will be necessary to consider the implications of this passage in terms of Poe's relation to pantheism. For now, it suffices that we here encounter his concept of the relation of matter to spirit in its final and most abstract form. On account of a teleological determination, matter itself is no longer defined in terms of physical forces, but simply as the apportionment of the ether. Paradoxically, in consequence of the creation of matter, humanity becomes capable of participation in divine life, or, more literally, partaking of God. But the interaction of matter and spirit, of the ether and its material enclosure, is itself grounded in Poe's earlier thought through the relation of thought to substance. Both, as we have seen, disclose an ideational essence. The intuition of the essence of matter as consisting of idea is a result of Poe's attraction to, and assimilation of, the results of the mathematical and empirical sciences. From these he could arrive at his affirmation of the theoretical structure of the world, of the ideational element as pervading matter. In this sense, the foundations of *Eureka* may be traced ultimately to Poe's relation to science.

# 6   *Emerson*

## Classification

Among the lectures he delivered for his series on *The Philosophy of History*, Emerson found it appropriate to give one on the theme of "Humanity of Science."[1] He begins it with the following assertion: "It is the perpetual effort of the mind to seek relations between the multitude of facts under its eye, by means of which it can reduce them to some order" (*EL*, II, 22). Later in the same lecture he declares: "Classification is one of the main actions of the intellect. A man of great sagacity divides, distributes, with every word he speaks. And we are always at the mercy of a better classifier than ourselves" (p. 25).[2]

[1]He must have thought reasonably well of this lecture, despite its remaining unpublished during his lifetime: in his 1847 English lecture tour he made use of it again (Ralph R. Rusk, *The Life of Ralph Waldo Emerson* [New York: Scribner's, 1949], p. 333).

[2]For Emerson's personal engagement in the practice of scientific classification and its results, David Robinson, *Apostle of Culture: Emerson as Preacher and Lecturer* (Philadelphia: Univ. of Pennsylvania Press, 1982), pp. 83–84, and for Emerson and science generally, pp. 74–85. On the latter topic, see also Harry Hayden Clark, "Emerson and Science," *Philological Quarterly*, 10 (July 1931), 225–60 (which, however, confuses Cuvier and Agassiz with evolutionism); Gay Wilson Allen, "A New Look at Emerson and Science," in *Literature*

For the reasons behind the preeminence of classification in Emerson's view of the sciences, we must turn not only to his own world-view but also to his historical situation, that is, the position of the natural sciences in his time. Inaugurated by Galileo's discoveries in kinematics and Newton's in dynamics, physics predominates in modern science from the seventeenth century onward.[3] With Lavoisier, the latter half of the eighteenth century witnesses the beginnings of chemistry. The first half of the nineteenth century, finally—a period that encompasses the Romantic epoch—ushers in the rise of geology and biology. With the development of biology in particular, classification receives a new importance. To be sure, the eighteenth century had already recorded the appearance of the Linnaean system. In its comprehensiveness, it breathes the Enlightenment spirit of "universal science," the same spirit that pervades the French *Encyclopedia*. And yet, without a complete and systematic exploration of the realms Linnaeus assimilated into his classification—the animal, vegetable, and mineral kingdoms—the standpoint for a proper appreciation and evaluation of his achievement remained lacking.

With the advent of the biological and geological sciences (the term *biology* was coined by Lamarck in 1802) that standpoint was attained. Cuvier's monumental work, *Le Règne animal* (1817), undertakes a systematic revision of one of the major portions of the Linnaean classification.[4] Through the investigations of Louis Agassiz, moreover—with whom Emerson had a personal acquaintance—the fundamental principles of Cuvier's system are sustained and developed.[5] Of the many tributes to Cuvier contained in Agassiz's own works, one is of particular importance for the light it sheds upon these principles. In his *Methods of Study in Natural History* (1864), reviewing the past history and development of biology, Agassiz writes: "But till Cuvier's time there was no great principle of classification. Facts were accumulated and more or less systematized, but they were not yet arranged according to law; the principle

and Ideas in America: Essays in Honor of Harry Hayden Clark, ed. Robert Falk (Athens: Ohio Univ. Press, 1975), pp. 58–78; Sherman Paul, Émerson's Angle of Vision (Cambridge: Harvard Univ. Press, 1952), pp. 206–220; Jonathan Bishop, Emerson on the Soul (Cambridge: Harvard Univ. Press, 1964), pp. 45–59; Stephen E. Whicher, Freedom and Fate: An Inner Life of Ralph Waldo Emerson (Philadelphia: Univ. of Pennsylvania Press, 1953), pp. 89–90. On Emerson's famous "experience" at the Jardin des Plantes (only briefly mentioned in Gay Wilson Allen, Waldo Emerson [New York: Viking, 1981]) see Rusk, pp. 187–88, and for Emerson and Charles Lyell, p. 345.

[3]See Georges Canguilhem, La Connaissance de la vie, rev. ed. (Paris: Vrin, 1965), pp. 53, 156.

[4]On Cuvier's system of classification, see Ernst Mayr, The Growth of Biological Thought (Cambridge: Harvard Univ. Press, 1982), pp. 182–84, and on the theory of classification in general, pp. 147–208, esp. 190–95, 198–201, 207–8.

[5]For Emerson and Agassiz, see Rusk, p. 450. For Emerson's holdings of Agassiz's works, see Walter Harding, Emerson's Library (Charlottesville: Univ. Press of Virginia, 1967), p. 6.

was still wanting by which to generalize them and give meaning and vitality to the whole. It was Cuvier who found the key. . . . He saw that animals were united in their most comprehensive groups, not on special characters, but on different *plans of structure*, —moulds, he called them, in which all animals had been cast" (pp. 7–8). These "plans of structure" are not autonomous creations, but arise through necessary relations between their component parts. In *Le Règne animal* Cuvier remarks: "The parts of a being presumably all having some mutual convenience, there are some traits of conformation or structure which exclude others; and there are some which, on the contrary, necessitate others; when one knows then such or such traits in a being, one can calculate those which will co-exist with these, or those which will be incompatible with them" (1, 10). Hence Cuvier's ability, noticed by Emerson on several occasions, to reconstruct the entire structure of a prehistoric animal from a single fossil relic.

But the necessary relations described by Cuvier are not restricted to those between the parts of an organism. They also include those between the organism and its environment. Through the necessity for considering what Cuvier terms an organism's "conditions of existence," natural history differs from the physical sciences: "Natural history has however a rational principle peculiar to it, and which it employs to advantage on many occasions; it is that *of the conditions of existence*, vulgarly termed *final causes*. Since nothing can exist if it does not unite the conditions which render its existence possible, the different parts of each being should be coordinated in such a manner as to render possible the complete being, not only in itself, but in its relations with those who surround it, and the analysis of these conditions frequently leads to general laws as clearly demonstrated as those which derive from calculation, or from experience" (1, 6).

In a sense, it is possible to define the organism itself as the sum of all these relations, internal and external. To the extent that such relations are based upon a concept of mutual interdependence, they manifest the presence of thought. Unlike the relation of cause and effect, the concept of mutual interdependence cannot be explained simply in terms of physical forces, that is to say, as a transmission of force from one object to another. Here relation assumes another aspect. If each organ or part of a living creature represents the concept of a particular function, the relation of different parts can then be expressed as one of different functions. Not all functions, however, are compatible with each other. Some necessitate others, some exclude others. Insofar as a function expresses an idea, the relation between such functions must be one of thought.

The totality of these functions, according to Cuvier, is life. As the embodiment of all the relations between these, life may be described as the result of thought, the force that determines the interdependence of the vital activities and brings them together. But if the relation between the parts of an organism is expressible only in terms of thought, the science that discovers such relations must also be more than mere observation. Classification is, then, that form of scientific thought which studies the relations between different vital functions, conceived of as biological concepts, their specification in concrete organs, and their harmonization in higher forms of organization, that is, living creatures. To the extent that these vital functions or biological concepts differ from other concepts, they define a sphere independent of the other sciences.

As the study of such concepts and their relations or interdependencies, classification could claim to represent a mode of thought distinct from that of both philosophy and physics (the paradigm at that time for the natural sciences). This mode of thought consists not merely of human rationalizations concerning the order of things, but attempts to reproduce, in effect, the thought process contained in Nature itself. Obviously, the validity of such a claim must depend in part upon sustained empirical confirmation of a particular system of classification. In his *Methods of Study in Natural History*, speaking of the success of Cuvier's arrangement, Agassiz comments: "This result is of greater importance than may at first appear. Upon it depends the question, whether all such classifications represent merely individual impressions and opinions of men, or whether there is really something in Nature that presses upon us certain divisions among animals, certain affinities, certain limitations, founded upon essential principles of organization. Are our systems the inventions of naturalists, or only their reading of the Book of Nature? and can that book have more than one reading? If these classifications are not mere inventions, if they are not an attempt to classify for our own convenience the objects we study, then they are thoughts which, whether we detect them or not, are expressed in Nature, —then Nature is the work of thought, the production of intelligence, carried out according to plan, therefore premeditated, —and in our study of natural objects we are approaching the thoughts of the Creator, reading his conceptions, interpreting a system that is his and not ours" (pp. 13–14). Similarly, in a passage from "The Naturalist," a lecture composed and delivered approximately one year before "Humanity of Science," Emerson had spoken of the attempts of Newton, Linnaeus, Davy, and Cuvier to ascend "from arbitrary to natural classes."

For Emerson, then, as for Agassiz, the attempt to define science through the concept of classification carries with it certain significant presuppositions as well as consequences. We have seen that classification (according to Agassiz and Cuvier) infers the existence of an innate order in things that expresses itself as thought. This thought possesses a specific content. It consists of relations between elements or parts embodying concepts. Classification presupposes the fixity and stability of these elements. Without such stability, relations become meaningless. And the thought content of classification inheres precisely in its description of such relations. This implies a certain view of the world and of physical nature. It suggests that the essence of such a world is to be grasped by defining the relations between its parts. For classification, the relation of parts to each other becomes the model of explanatory clarification. It also reveals why Emerson's evolutionism differs from that of Darwin, and accounts for the differences that separate him from Nietzsche, who recognized in him certain kindred aims and objectives.[6]

In Nietzsche thought (and "science") comes to signify: analysis and description of the fundamental processes occurring in individuals and things. The sum of these processes is "Nature." Such processes represent the transformations and expressions of a basic energy or force—in humanity, the "Will to Power." From these transformations or changes, a pattern emerges. Its formula is—the eternal recurrence. For Nietzsche, thought consists of defining the principles or laws behind the constant flux of change. In the "eternal recurrence" we find, so to speak, the "ideational form" of his thought. But if for Nietzsche thought represents the attempt to determine the constant pattern *in* change, for Emerson, in contrast, it is associated with what persists in spite of change—the essential relations between things. Only by means of these concrete and specific relations will it become possible to arrive finally at the most general and comprehensive relation—the connection between mind and matter, Nature and spirit.

## "Humanity of Science"

The question of the relation of science to humanistic concerns is one of the issues raised by Romanticism. In the wake of the emergence of mechanics as the model for physics and ultimately for its sister sciences throughout the seventeenth and eighteenth centuries, this development was perhaps bound to occur. Diderot already anticipates the increasing rift. Romantic *Naturphilosophie* attempts to bridge it by abolishing mathematics from the sciences.[7] But *Naturphilosophie* represents only one end of the spectrum of Romantic response to the issue. The investigations of Laplace and Lagrange, Dalton and Berthollet, and Cuvier parallel chronologically those of Oken and Goethe, and span the Romantic epoch. We know of the influence of physics and of quantitative methods

[6]On Emerson's shift from what he terms a subjective to objective idealism, cf. Stephen Whicher, p. 141.
[7]See Charles C. Gillispie, *The Edge of Objectivity* (Princeton: Princeton Univ. Press, 1960), pp. 156, 181–182, and, on Diderot, p. 188.

upon chemistry during this epoch, and of the influence of the "mechanistic" approach to biology, of which there are traces even in Cuvier. We also know of the interest of many Romantic authors in scientific researches that do not share the approach of Romantic *Naturphilosophie*— of Coleridge's interest, for instance, in the chemical investigations of Dalton and Humphry Davy, of Shelley in Laplace, and, in America, of Poe's assimilation of both the nebular hypothesis and the theory of probability. In some sense, all these interests are to be found in Emerson, with whom however biology possesses a particular importance.

Through their absorption in and concern with scientific pursuits, these Romantic authors usher in a new approach to the question of the relation between science and the humanistic disciplines. Their program: the unity of science and poetry, viewed as two aspects of a single, all-encompassing truth. From their standpoint, poetry, as beauty, becomes a neoplatonic revelation of the divine essence. Equally relevant is Kant's threefold distinction of the faculties corresponding to pure reason, practical reason, and judgment, and their objects: the Good, the Beautiful, and the True. Adopting the Kantian schema, Romantic authors are able to discern in poetry and science two aspects of a common endeavor, the attempt of the mind to assimilate all realms of experience, whether as aesthetic sensation or as cognitive apprehension. Hence Emerson's assertion in *Nature* that "Beauty, in its largest and profoundest sense, is one expression for the universe. God is the all-fair. Truth, and goodness, and beauty, are but different faces of the same All" (*Coll. W.*, 1, 17).

But the fundamental unity of science and humanistic pursuits reveals itself on other grounds as well. Through his lectures on science during the years 1835 and 1836, Emerson must have been induced to reflect upon this question. In his journal for June 4, 1836, he addresses the following note to himself: "Here are two or three facts respecting Science. 1. The tendency to order & classification in the mind. 2. The correspondent Order actually subsisting in Nature. 3. Hence the humanity of science or the naturalness of knowing; the perception that the world was made by mind like ours; the recognition of design like ours" (*JMN*, v, 168). And, in his lecture on "Humanity of Science" a few months later: "There is in nature a parallel unity, which corresponds to this unity in the mind, and makes it available. This methodizing mind meets no resistance in its attempts. The scattered blocks with which it strives to form a symmetrical structure, fit. . . . Not only man puts things in a row, but things belong in a row" (*EL*, II, 25). In his journal he added: "The showing of the true row is Science."

For Emerson, the "tendency to order & classification in the mind" is innate. It constitutes a tendency in an almost physical sense, like that of the law of inertia. Through such a tendency, mind projects or imposes itself upon the external world, organizing it according to a rational schema that reflects its own nature. That nature, however, is something it cannot know in itself, something it becomes conscious of only through its reflection in the world of things. Because of its lack of self-consciousness, mind has no direct access to itself. Like the phenomenon of vision, its tendency to order becomes apprehensible only through its action upon external objects. Only when mind becomes conscious of these as something external to itself can it perceive the order it imposes upon these things as one that corresponds to an inner rationality. Subjective consciousness appears only when the objective is recognized as objective, as something external to the self. Prior to that, subjective and objective share only the common undifferentiated experience of consciousness. It was one of Hegel's significant insights to have understood that these categories cannot exist as such until the mind perceives them by distinguishing the content of its consciousness from consciousness itself. For the mind, the idea of the subjective or objective is not something given, but one that arises only when its content (the experience of consciousness) is defined or recognized as content.

This is not to say that the concept of subjective and objective just developed is necessarily present in Emerson's passage, nor even to ascribe to him a conscious awareness of it. But in another sense, as the philosophical ground that makes possible his reflections, it remains implicit in such passages. The movement of mind or thought which he describes, projecting itself outward into the world, then turning back upon itself in self-conscious analysis, is one that derives in essence from German philosophy after Kant, the philosophy of Fichte, Schelling, and, finally, Hegel. By the innumerable indirect routes that would have led him back to these sources, Emerson could encounter and assimilate the form of their particular development. In his own thought, to be sure, the dialectic that makes possible such a development possesses at best only a minor importance. Emerson's concern is, rather, with the prospects or possibilities opened up for the soul by the realization of that correspondence between objective and subjective, mind and world. And yet it is necessary to elucidate this dialectic, if only in a cursory fashion, forming as it does a large part of absolute idealism and hence of that Romantic thought from which Emerson himself draws his inspiration.

Here it becomes necessary also to say something concerning the terms *humanity* and *science* in Emerson's usage. By a tradition bequeathed to rationalism in the centuries following the Renaissance by the scholasticism of the Middle Ages, the rational mind, *mens rationis,* had always stood for the defining characteristic of man, the specific quality that established his place in the scale of being.[8] Through the advent of Ro-

---

[8]See, *inter alia,* Arthur O. Lovejoy, *The Great Chain of Being: A Study of the History of an Idea* (Cambridge: Harvard Univ. Press, 1936), passim, and, for the Renaissance specifically, Pico della Mirandola's *Oration on the Dignity of Man.* For the Middle Ages, the notion would presumably have already been established through commentaries on Genesis by the Church Fathers, in particular by Augustine's *De Trinitate* (as well as his *De Genesi ad litteram*).

manticism, a new quality begins for some to take its place—feeling, or sensibility. We know of the excesses of feeling to which this could lead (as in the suicides of German youths after reading *The Sorrows of Young Werther*). Hence Hegel's admonition in the preface to the second edition of his *Science of Logic* that "Nowadays we cannot be too often reminded that it is *thinking* which distinguishes man from the beasts." For Emerson, feeling qualifies, but does not displace, rationality. As a result, a new perspective emerges: rationality not as a faculty of absolute knowing, but as the specific nature of the mind, forming a part of what Emerson calls its "natural history." The product of this faculty: ordering of things, apprehension of the relation between one object and another. For Emerson, as for others of his epoch, rationality is still the only form of thought—only in the generation of Nietzsche does the equivalence between the two break down. But if rationality is equated with thought, their identification implies that thought represents merely a special mode of the self's relation to the world. Consequently, if "humanity" is defined by the rational-human faculty, the *logos* must be seen as a human, rather than absolute, principle or tendency.

With regard to the term *science,* we may recall that Newton's magnum opus had borne the title *Principia mathematica naturalis philosophiae.* For several centuries after the Renaissance, "natural philosophy" continues to serve as a name for the sciences. Only around the beginning of the nineteenth century does a shift in nomenclature occur. Even at that point, however, the link with philosophy implicit in the earlier term survives. Fichte's major work is called *Die Wissenschaftslehre*—a title sometimes incorrectly rendered as "The Science of Knowledge" but whose true import is "The Doctrine of Science." Hegel's *Phenomenology of Spirit* (1807), according to its original title page, represents the "first part" of a "System of Science." These two works, which take up as their subject the dialectic of the self or of consciousness, possess a particular significance for the light they shed upon the term *science* in the Romantic epoch. Here science is seen to include, as one of its legitimate provinces, an analysis of the nature of mind (consciousness) from the perspective of pure thought rather than psychology. In his "Natural History of Intellect," several decades later, Emerson will undertake a similar enterprise, but under the aegis of "natural history" rather than of "science."[9] Thus the phrase "humanity of science" contains only an apparent paradox. In

---

[9]To be sure, the lectures that Emerson delivered for his Harvard courses consist in part of material collected or written years earlier. For further details, Rusk, pp. 442–3, 445–46, and Allen, *Waldo Emerson* pp. 640–43. The starting point for Emerson's deliberations may be situated in his "Intellect" essay from *Essays: First Series,* in which he discusses mental processes transcending the knowledge or awareness of the rational mind. Such processes follow their own inner entelechy. Taken collectively, they define the mind as a source of natural—rather than rational—forces or tendencies.

reality, for Emerson, there is no rift between them: "humanity" is defined by rational intellect, "science" comprises a form of thought, a thinking about Nature or things, but also about the nature of mind itself. As such, the two concepts may be said to form merely differing aspects of a fundamental and underlying unity.

We have seen that "there is in nature a parallel unity, which corresponds to this unity in the mind, and makes it available." Through its perception of the unity in nature, mind comes to know its own nature. By describing the turn toward self-awareness, Emerson appropriates the form of a dialectic of consciousness which I have sought to define earlier in Hegel. For Emerson, the externalization of mind, its outward projection into Nature, springs not only from an inner necessity but from the lure of the world itself: "Nature proceeds from a mind congenial with ours. Nature is overflowed and saturated with humanity. All things solicit us to know them by obscure attractions which we call the beauty of nature" (*EL*, II, 33).

By a process not unlike that of chemical or elective affinities, Nature and mind are thus brought together. Their interaction is possible insofar as they represent in essence two forms of a single all-pervading energy. Hence Emerson's assertion that "man may well be of the same mind as nature, for he too is a part of nature, and is inundated with the same genius or spirit. He lives by some pulsations of her life" (*EL*, II, 35). But if this assertion is in fact true, it implies that rational thought is itself merely a form of energy.[10]

Such an equation does not preclude the possibility of knowledge. According to Emerson, knowledge assumes the form of recognition: in external Nature, mind comes to recognize its own nature, fulfilling the so-called Socratic dictum that urges the individual to "know thyself." "For," he writes, "so much of nature as he is ignorant of, just so much of his own mind does he not yet possess" (*EL*, II, 34). Consequently it becomes possible to ascribe a teleology to science: to know Nature, not just for its own sake, but as a means to knowledge of the self (*EL*, I, 23). Such knowledge alone can enable the soul to fulfill the possibilities of its nature. As Coleridge had written, on the masthead of his journal *The*

[10]An assertion that might easily be borne out from "Circles." Significantly, the concept of mind as intellectual energy occurs often in William Ellery Channing the elder. See his *Works*, I: "It will be sufficient here to observe, that the greatness of the soul is especially seen in the intellectual energy which discerns absolute, universal truth" (p. vi); "We believe, that the human mind is akin to that intellectual energy which gave birth to nature, and consequently that it contains within itself the seminal and prolific principles from which nature sprung" (p. 190); "A beautiful literature springs from the depth and fulness of intellectual and moral life, from an energy of thought and feeling, to which nothing, as we believe, ministers so largely as enlightened religion" (p. 212). And elsewhere, "All men understand by reason the highest faculty or energy of the mind" (IV, 34). See also pp. 70–71, 124, 321–22.

*Watchman:* "That All may know the TRUTH; And that the TRUTH may make us FREE!!"

This nature of the mind, this object of self-knowledge, is Spirit. In recognizing itself as spirit, mind is transfigured. The means by which it arrives at such self-knowledge is—science. In exalted and rhapsodic prose, Emerson celebrates self-knowledge as one of science's highest functions: "A lesson which science teaches, unanimous in all her discoveries, is the omnipresence of spirit. Life, creation, and final causes meet us everywhere. The world is saturated with law. Beautifully shines a spirit through all the bruteness and toughness of matter. Alone omnipotent it converts all things to its own end" (*EL*, II, 29–30).

## On Theory and Method in the Sciences

Near the beginning of Balzac's *La Recherche de l'absolu*—one of the series of the *Études philosophiques*—a stranger spends a night at the house of Balthazar Claës, a Belgian nobleman. In their conversation after dinner, this stranger, in the course of elucidating his past, touches upon a subject that has for many years engaged his innermost thoughts: the theory of a single, all-unifying substance of matter, the Absolute. He explains to his host his personal views on the subject: "One substance common to all creations, modified by a single force, such is the distinct and clear statement of the problem posed by the Absolute, one which seems to me *resolvable*. There you will find the mysterious Ternary, before which Humanity has kneeled from the earliest times: the initial matter, the means, the result. You will find this terrible number Three in all human things, it dominates religions, the sciences, and the laws. . . . A SINGLE SUBSTANCE should be a principle common to the three gases and to carbon. The MEANS should be the principle common to negative and positive electricity. Proceed to the discovery of the proofs which establish these two truths, and you will then have the supreme cause of all the effects of nature" (*La Comédie humaine*, X, 717).

The theory of a single, unifying substance behind all forms of matter—a theory in which Balzac himself took the deepest interest—does not figure only in the realm of the novel during this epoch. In his *Elements of Chemical Philosophy* (1812) Sir Humphry Davy observes: "The term *element* is used as synonymous with *undecompounded* body; but in modern chemistry its application is limited to the results of experiments. The improvements taking place in the methods of examining bodies, are constantly changing the opinions of chemists with respect to their nature, and there is no reason to suppose that any real *indestructible principle* has been yet discovered. Matter may ultimately be found to be the same in essence, differing only in the arrangements of its particles; or two or three *simple* substances may produce all the varieties of compound bodies" (*Coll. W.*, IV, 132). And, later: "If that sublime idea of the ancient Philosophers which has been sanctioned by the approbation of Newton, should be true, namely, that there is only one species of matter, the different chemical, as well as mechanical forms of which are owing to the different arrangement of its particles, then a method of analysing those forms may probably be found in their relations to radiant matter" (p. 164).

From Davy and other sources, the idea is transmitted to Emerson himself. In his lecture on "Humanity of Science" he asserts: "Finally the sublime conjecture sanctioned by the minds of Newton, Hooke, Boscovich and now of Davy, that the forms of natural bodies depend upon different arrangements of the same particles of matter; that possibly the world shall be found to be composed of oxygen and hydrogen; and that even these two elements are but one matter in different states of electricity; —all these, whether they are premature generalizations or not, indicate the central unity, the common law that pervades nature from the deep centre to the unknown circumference" (*EL*, II, 29). And in "The Naturalist": "Nothing strikes me more in Nature than the effect of Composition, the contrast between the simplicity of the means and the gorgeousness of the result. . . . A few elements has Nature converted into the countless variety of substances that fill the earth" (*EL*, I, 73).

For Emerson, this "central unity" manifests itself not only on the physico-chemical but also on the biological plane. Like Balzac, he had encountered the theories of the French biologist Geoffroy Saint-Hilaire, whom he praises as a "poet in science," along with Goethe, Agassiz, Audubon, and Oken. In particular, he must have been struck by the concept that all animal species are but variations of a single basic plan, a concept first enunciated by Geoffroy Saint-Hilaire in a "mémoire" of 1796: "A constant truth for one who has observed a great number of the productions of the globe is that there exist, between all their parts, a grand harmony and necessary relations; that it seems Nature has enclosed itself within certain limits, and has formed all living beings upon a single plan, essentially the same in its principle, but which she has varied in a thousand ways in all its accessory parts." These variations arise through a modification in the organs of the different classes: "Thus the forms in each class of animals, however varied they may be, all result, at bottom, from organs common to all: Nature refuses to employ new ones. Thus, all the most essential differences which affect each family deriving from the same class originate solely from some alternative arrangement, some alternative complication, some modification, finally, of these same organs" ("Mémoire," pp. 20, 21). Like Cuvier, Geoffroy Saint-Hilaire envisages the various organs as modifications of a basic mold or pattern, while the animal's substance, like a plastic material, adapts itself to its specific variations. Formally, then, Geoffroy Saint-Hilaire's scheme differs from Cuvier's only in being more radical: instead of four plans, it postulates a single, unifying one.

The tendency toward theoretical simplicity expresses itself in other sciences as well. For historians of science, James Hutton's *Theory of the Earth* ushers in the modern study of geology. In this comprehensive work Hutton had proposed to regard all surface formations of the earth as resulting from the action of an intense heat, contained in the subsurface and erupting occasionally in the form of volcanoes. Because of the abnormally high temperatures produced, loose rock deposits become fused together, giving rise to igneous layers or masses. The heat of the earth is constant in its action. As a result, the history of the earth's geology forms a constant and unceasing process. In a remark preserved by Emerson, Hutton asserts: "We find no vestige of a beginning, —no prospect of an end" (*EL*, ii, 32). As a hypothesis of the earth's history, Hutton's theory (called Vulcanism) opposes catastrophist geology, which had postulated a single calamity, the Flood described in Genesis, as the unique and sufficient cause of the earth's present appearance. The "uniformitarianism" of Charles Lyell, friend and mentor of Darwin, assimilates and expands Hutton's theory. Taking as his point of departure the essential simplicity of Hutton's schema of the earth's development (for example, action of a single cause, no vestige of beginning or end), Lyell proposed in his *Principles of Geology* (1830–33) to regard the present visible causes of geological change as sufficient to account for all of the earth's past. From his perspective, development assumes a relatively simple form, uniform, unpunctuated by catastrophes, an indivisible continuum. Like Hutton's Vulcanism, "uniformitarianism" rejects the postulate of a dividing line in geological history. The "catastrophist" position, by contrast, had sought to affirm the immediate presence of God in his creation, a presence attested to by his direct intervention in the earth's history through geological catastrophes. Like the Christian schema of history, with its antitheses of fall and redemption, type and antitype, "catastrophist" geology seeks to impose a human and anthropocentric shape upon geological time. The form of history dictated by "catastrophist" geology itself presupposes and derives, however, from yet another concept: the relation of God to Nature.

For medieval theology, God announces himself in two ways, through the Book of Scripture and the "Book of Nature." Theology and science, the study of these two subjects, are therefore complementary endeavors. But by the end of the eighteenth century, in the forms of natural and revealed religion, they become contrasting approaches to sacred truth (in his 1795 lectures Coleridge had attempted to arbitrate between them). For natural religion, God reveals himself through the workings of Nature, the order and harmony of natural laws and processes. Fundamental to revealed religion, by contrast, is the assumption of divine intervention in human affairs (the concept of a Savior)—hence the introduction of the supernatural as its ground and basis. For revealed religion, God appears as a force that transcends Nature, leading ultimately to the antinomy of matter and spirit.

To the extent that it regards the Flood as an event transcending natural causes, "catastrophist" geology affirms through science the truth of revealed religion. For Vulcanism and "uniformitarianism," on the other hand, science could represent only a *via naturaliter negativa*, confirming the existence of a supreme Being through the order and harmony of the universe. For natural religion, the existence of God is attested not only by the order of nature, but also—and equally—by its simplicity. In his *Elements of Chemical Philosophy* Humphry Davy remarks: "It is contrary to the usual order of things, that events so harmonious as those of the system of the earth, should depend on such diversified agents, as are supposed to exist in our artificial arrangements; and there is reason to anticipate a great reduction in the number of the undecompounded bodies, and to expect that the analogies of nature will be found conformable to the refined operations of art. The more the phenomena of the universe are studied, the more distinct their connection appears, the more simple their causes, the more magnificent their design, and the more wonderful the wisdom and power of their Author" (*Coll. W.*, IV, 42). Geoffroy Saint-Hilaire too pays tribute in his *Philosophie anatomique* to "the a priori idea, the mother-idea and fundamental concept of the philosophy of Leibniz; the idea which this immense genius embodied in the expression, *diversity in unity*" (II, xxxiv).

But if Nature itself is simple, should this not imply the necessity for a corresponding simplicity in its theoretical description? Stressing the need for such simplicity, Cuvier could rightly remark that "the object of all sound method is to reduce the science to which one applies it to its minimal number of terms, in elevating the propositions it contains to the greatest generality of which they are capable" (*Leçons d'anatomie comparée*, p. 62). By striving for theoretical simplicity, science attains the ideal prescribed by Leibniz: variety *in* unity, the description of the maximum quantity of phenomena under the minimal number of general principles or propositions. Observing its procedure in practice, Emerson comments: "The most striking trait of modern science is its approximation towards central truths. On all sides it is simplifying its laws and finding one cause for many effects" (*EL*, II, 27). Elsewhere in the same lecture he ascribes this trait to an innate tendency of mind: "The mind is reluctant to make many classes or to suppose many causes. This reduction to a few laws, to one law, is not a choice of the individual. It is the tyrannical instinct of the mind" (p. 23).

We know from other passages in Emerson's writings of his belief in certain general characteristics of the mind, properties that, like those observed by a naturalist, serve to distinguish it from all other things in nature. The tendency toward simplification of theory has its historical dimension as well, one that permits him to associate it in particular with "modern science." For Emerson and for Romantic thought in general, such simplification is dictated not only by the simplicity of Nature but by a necessity inherent in the character of theory itself. For Emerson, theory is not merely a connection between observed phenomena (the position, later, of Mach and positivism) but an independent ideal structure. Through its idealism, Romantic science distinguishes itself not only from positivism but also from the twentieth century. Whereas for an Einstein theory constitutes an independent and autonomous creation of the human mind that seeks to describe the laws governing natural phenomena, Romantic science accords it an even greater role: not merely to describe such laws, but to comprehend in these the expression of an immanent idea. For Romantic science, then, phenomena are not something independent of thought but rather its manifestation in tangible form. Conversely, thought pervades phenomena, as their essence and core.

In recent years, historians of science such as Thomas Kuhn and Paul Feyerabend (among others) have disclosed the richness and complexity of the relation between theory and experimental research in the centuries following the Renaissance. What has not yet received sufficient attention, perhaps, is the gradual change in the nature of scientific theorizing itself—what one might call the "style" of scientific theory.[11] This is, obviously, not the place for extended discussion, but it seems at least appropriate to point out certain features that define the "form" of theory in Romantic science. Most significant of these is the extent to which metatheoretical objectives govern the form of the theories themselves. The desire for theoretical simplicity, for instance, which led Geoffroy Saint-Hilaire to posit the existence of "one animal" as the basis of all species of life, or Davy's postulation of a single elemental substance as the essence of all matter, constitutes one aspect of this tendency. Another feature is the belief in the presence of a thought element within Nature itself, so that the content of theory is really asserted to exist within the forms of matter as such rather than merely representing post facto human or rationalistic constructions. In the process, thought comes to be viewed as an activity (like that of pre-Darwinian evolution) of the material substance itself rather than of the rational intelligence seeking to establish relations between things.

[11]For some indications, see Thomas Kuhn, *The Essential Tension* (Chicago: Univ. of Chicago Press, 1977), pp. 21–30.

This belief in the inseparability of theory and fact permeates not only *Naturphilosophie* but Romantic science as a whole. Geoffroy Saint-Hilaire could with some justification claim, "What distinguishes . . . the works of our age is a clearly-marked tendency toward general propositions, and at the same time a reserve, an extreme circumspection in the use of means" (*Philosophie anatomique*, 1, xxx). Even Cuvier, in his *Leçons d'anatomie comparée*, had had to acknowledge the necessity for an independent development of theory, based only in a general sense upon empirical data (as opposed to attempting to theorize simply by connecting and relating observed facts and experiences). But it is Agassiz who furnishes the fullest rationale for the Romantic attitude:

> It is true that scientific results grow out of facts, but not till they have been fertilized by thought. The facts must be collected, but their mere accumulation will never advance the sum of human knowledge by one step; it is the comparison of facts and their transformation into ideas that lead to a deeper insight into the significance of Nature. Stringing words together in incoherent succession does not make an intelligible sentence; facts are the words of God, and we may heap them together endlessly, but they will teach us little or nothing till we place them in their true relations, and recognize the thought that binds them together as a consistent whole. (*Methods of Study*, p. 202)

Emerson, too, affirms the Romantic position. In his lecture "The Naturalist" he observes that "the later discoveries of naturalists seem to point more and more steadily at Method, at a Theory" (*EL*, 1, 82). Only by the proper formation of theory will it become possible for science to arrive at the true essence of Nature. A journal entry for 1836 states: "The physical sciences are only well studied when they are explored for ideas. The moment the law is attained i.e. the Idea, the memory disburthens herself of her Centuries of observation" (*JMN*, v, 123). And, a few weeks later: "Science to apprehend Nature in Ideas   The moment an idea is introduced among facts the God takes possession. Until then, facts conquer us. The Beast rules Man" (*JMN*, v, 146).

# 7   Bichat, Balzac, Hawthorne: Vitalism and Mechanism

In *La Messe de l'athée* Balzac introduces his readers to the young Horace Bianchon: "A physician to whom science owes a beautiful physiological theory and who, still young, attained a place among the celebrities of the École de Paris, center of luminaries to which the physicians of Europe all render homage . . ." (*La Comédie humaine*, III, 385). Balzac then describes Bianchon's apprenticeship to the illustrious surgeon Desplein at the Hôtel Dieu. Later, Bianchon succeeds his master as chief surgeon of the same hospital. Among the models for his fictitious physician, Balzac, it seems to me, must have had in mind the great anatomist Xavier Bichat (1771–1802).[1]

Like Bianchon, Bichat had begun his studies in surgery and anatomy—rather than medicine—with M. A. Petit (1766–1811), chief surgeon of the Hôtel Dieu at Lyons. In 1793 revolutionary disturbances drove him to Paris, where he became a pupil, then assistant, to the illustrious P. J. Desault. Before the age of twenty-eight, Bichat had already been appointed chief physician of the Hôtel Dieu in Paris. His fall from a staircase at the Hôtel Dieu brought about his early death, on July 22, 1802. His fame is based upon his pioneering study of human tissues, which helped to found histology, and upon his great works, especially the *Anatomie générale* (1801). From these, Balzac was able in part to develop his theory of the Will as the life force. In so doing, he must have recalled Bichat's famous formula: "Life is the ensemble of functions which struggle against death."[2]

It is both significant and revealing to see how Balzac transforms Bichat's concept of life in developing his own theory of the Will. The history of science numbers Bichat among the adherents of vitalism, the doctrine that ascribes the life of an organism to a vital principle distinct from chemical and other forces.[3] In his *Anatomie générale*, nevertheless, Bichat clearly distinguishes his own beliefs from the vitalism of a Stahl or a Van Helmont: "The general doctrine of this work does not precisely carry the stamp of any of those now reigning in medicine and in physiology. Opposed to that of Boerhaave, it differs also from that of Stahl and from those of the authors who, like him, have ascribed everything in the economy of life to a single principle, abstract, ideal and purely imagi-

---

[1]In his notes to *La Messe de l'athée* in the new Pléiade edition of *La Comédie humaine*, Guy Sagnes identifies Bianchon with Mardochée Marx (following Jacques Borel). But it seems to me Balzac would have had in mind a more illustrious model for the great physician of his *Comédie humaine*. His remark, when dying, to his own doctor is well known: "Bianchon would have cured me."

[2]Georges Canguilhem, *Études d'histoire et de philosophie des sciences* (Paris: Vrin, 1968), p. 158.

[3]See Canguilhem, *La Connaissance de la vie*, rev. ed. (Paris: Vrin, 1965), p. 85. Canguilhem's characterization of vitalism has a significant bearing upon Hawthorne's "Birthmark": "Thus vitalism and naturism [*naturisme*] are inseparable. Medical vitalism is, then, the expression of a distrust, which one must term instinctive, of the power of technics over life. There is an analogy here with the Aristotelian opposition between natural and violent movement. Vitalism is the expression of the confidence of the living in life, of the identity of life with itself in the living human being, conscious of being alive. We may then propose that vitalism represents a permanent necessity for life in the living, the identity with itself of immanent life in the living" (p. 86).

nary, whether one designate it by the name of *soul, vital principle, first principle,* or whatever" (i, vj–vij). And later, even more explicitly: "This principle which Barthez terms 'vital,' Van Helmont, 'primordial,' etc., is an abstraction which has no more reality than would a single physical principle which one might suppose to preside over all physical phenomena" (i, xxxix).[4]

For Bichat, only physical properties, rather than some intangible principle or essence, can actually define the true nature of life. These properties differ only qualitatively from other physical properties. The organic realm is thus continuous with the inorganic sphere of physical and chemical substances and forces. The concept of a property possesses for Bichat a special significance. It contains the basic tendency of a body or object, its disposition to act or react in a specific fashion when acted upon by external forces. This tendency is inseparable from the matter of the body, and as such must be considered almost as elemental as matter itself:

> These properties are so inherent to the one and the other, that one cannot conceive of these bodies without them. They constitute their essence and their attribute. To exist and to be in the enjoyment of these are inseparable things for them. Suppose that such properties were suddenly taken away from them; at that instant, all the phenomena of nature would cease, and only matter would exist. Chaos was only matter without properties; to create the universe, God endowed it with gravity, elasticity, affinity, etc., and in addition, one portion received for its part sensibility and contractility. (*Anatomie générale,* i, xxxvj–vij)

The properties of bodies contain the energy of those bodies: they are, so to speak, the energy immanent in matter. It is the nature of this energy to assert itself and distinguish itself from what is external to the body. Such energy possesses no medium other than matter. It cannot therefore be separated from matter (although matter could conceivably exist without it). It represents the self-defining tendency or property of matter, its striving to exist in a specific form determined by the composition of an individual body or object.

Among the bodies of the material universe, some possess special properties: sentience (*la sensibilité*) and contractility (*la contractilité*). These assume different forms in living bodies: organic sentience (*sensibilité organique*), the plant's ability to feel the fluids with which its fibers come in contact; organic unfelt contractility (*contractilité organique insensible*), the faculty of reacting upon these fluids; organic felt contractility (*la contractilité organique sensible*), which governs the movements of digestion

---

[4]On Bichat's vitalism, see, e.g., Canguilhem's "Claude Bernard et Bichat" in *Études,* pp. 156–62.

and circulation; animal sentience (*la sensibilité animale*), which results in the external sensations of sight, sound, etc.; and so on. By dividing the life force in this fashion into different "vital properties" (*propriétés vitales*), Bichat had sought to approach the real nature of life more closely, as an ensemble of faculties or physical properties, the tendency to perform certain specific actions or functions. Such functions, which permit of a physical description, make possible a definition of life itself in physicalistic terms. The definition of life establishes the nature of the causality that produces the different observable vital phenomena. By defining life as an ensemble or concurrence of different energies, Bichat was able to explain both the causal mechanism of the life processes and the manifold nature of vital effects: energy expresses or manifests itself in phenomena, and the ensemble of different specific energies accounts for the different effects. In contrast, by positing merely a generalized concept of the life force, vitalism had failed to offer a satisfactory analysis of either the causes behind the life processes or the appearance of varied effects from a single cause.

Bichat's theory is also innovative in another respect. Instead of a conscious representation of life, such as the idea of a vital principle, he had sought to express in the form of a concept the actual nature of its object. In rational apprehension, the form of the concept is determined by the mind or apprehending power. By reducing the concept of life to that of specific "vital properties," Bichat ascribes to that which had previously possessed an intelligible form (life = spirit) the form of elemental force or energy. His intuition is that the apprehension of the life force should not be mediated by its representation in an intelligible or rational form. Instead, form and content should be one and the same. His approach proceeds from a characteristic Romantic response to the whole problem of theoretical "representation." We find analogues to such an approach in Schelling's identification of subjective and objective, or Hegel's presentation of the Concept (*Begriff*) as pure content. Balzac, too, shares this mode of thought. His theory of the Will, as we shall see shortly, converts the idea of volition or choice into the notion of an elemental energy that conforms to laws analogous to those governing the physical sphere. From Balzac's theory of the Will, Hawthorne could develop his own intuition of life as an expression of the individual consciousness.

Bichat's influence upon Balzac manifests itself in other ways as well. A passage from the *Anatomie générale* describes the specific nature of the vital forces:

> It is the nature of the vital properties to exhaust themselves; time uses them up in the same body. Exalted during the first period of life, remaining stationary in adulthood, they weaken and become null during the last phases. It is said that Prometheus, having formed some statues of men,

robbed fire from heaven to animate them. That fire is the emblem of the vital properties; as long as it burns, life sustains itself; it disappears when the fire is extinguished. It is thus of the essence of these properties only to animate matter for a given time; hence the necessary limits upon life. By contrast, constantly inherent in matter, the physical properties never desert it: moreover the inert bodies have no limits to their existence, except those which chance assigns them. (I, lvij)

For Bichat, the presence of vital properties in a single medium or element is not sufficient to guarantee life: "I doubt that the purely inert fluids could, if put alone in vessels animated by life, circulate there like the vital fluids. Similarly, fluids animated by life could not move by themselves in vessels deprived of it. Life is thus equally necessary in the one and the other" (I, lxxij). To sustain life, it is necessary for the vital properties or forces to act upon each other. Their process of mutual action and reaction engages each of them while simultaneously preventing their premature dissipation. Along with the analogy of Promethean fire from the preceding passage, Bichat's reflections suggest the difference between vital and physical properties. The energy that characterizes the vital properties animates matter without being a property of the nature of matter. At the same time, unlike other forms of energy, the vital forces have no proper element or medium of their own: they cannot express themselves without matter. Hence they are neither spiritual nor, in the strictest sense, material. Thus life must be considered a distinctive form of being: it is energy that dissipates itself because it cannot be renewed, not having its source in the nature of matter.

In his novel *La Peau de chagrin,* one of the *Études philosophiques* that illuminate the spiritual and material universe of the *Comédie humaine,* Balzac draws upon the nonrenewable aspect of life in Bichat's theory, adapting it to his concept of the Will. Wandering into an antique shop, the protagonist, Raphaël de Valentin, is offered a mysterious talisman, a piece of shagreen leather that fulfills one's every wish, but only at the expense of diminishing one's vital energy. The properties of the talisman elucidate the nature of the Will itself. As the antiquary explains to Raphaël: "Man exhausts himself by two acts instinctively accomplished which dry up the springs of his existence. Two verbs express all the forms that these two causes of death assume: To Will and To be able to. Between these two terms of human action there is another formula which the sages use, and I owe it my happiness and my longevity. 'To Will' consumes us and 'To be able to' destroys us; but 'To know' leaves our frail organization in a perpetual state of calm" (*La Comédie humaine,* x, 85). Later in the novel Raphaël himself attempts to formulate a *théorie de la volonté* (theory of the will). Asked by Foedora about its contents, he explains to her that "the human will [is] a material force similar to vapor;

that, in the moral world, nothing [resists] this power when a man habituates himself to concentrating it, to handling the sum, to directing constantly upon souls the projection of this fluid mass; that this man can at will modify everything with respect to humanity, even the absolute laws of nature" (x, 149–50).

For Bichat, life possesses no relation to spirit. An involuntary energy informing certain material bodies, it follows an autonomous cycle of exaltation and dissipation. By equating the Will or life force with energy, Balzac preserves Bichat's intuition of life as a physical force. As energy, Will acts upon the material sphere, even while obeying its laws. At the same time, it also represents the power of aspiration or desire in man and other creatures. As such it necessarily enters into relation with the spiritual sphere. In his explanation of the shagreen skin's magic powers, the antiquary points out the affinity between Will and thought. Both are forms of the same elemental energy. Thought occupies a middle position between *vouloir* (to will) and *pouvoir* (to be capable of): it encompasses the desire of *vouloir* without having passed into the energy-consuming act that draws upon the force of *pouvoir*. Since thought is the means by which the soul discovers the possibility of a higher mode of existence, Will, through its connection with thought, participates in a similar relation to the spiritual sphere. As a result of this connection, the Will is transformed by a Romantic spiritualism. From the notion of merely physical force in Bichat, it now becomes, in Balzac, the element of a spiritual as well as material energy.

For Bichat, as we have seen, life assumes the form of an involuntary energy. Nothing in either the material or spiritual sphere can alter the essential nature of its course, although accidents or sickness may disrupt or arrest it prematurely. For Balzac, life in man and the animals manifests itself as Will. Like Bichat's life, the Balzacian Will is in some sense involuntary: expressing the vital force of a creature, it cannot be completely controlled by an effort of volition. The Will or *volonté* signifies in Balzac the desire for life that is simultaneously that vital force's self-assertion. But living things do not merely seek to preseve or perpetuate themselves. All of organic nature, from the lowest forms to the highest, is animated by the striving of being to transcend its own level, to raise itself to a higher state. A constant movement of spiritual ascension pervades the realm of Nature. This movement informs the Will and establishes its tendency. The Romantic "striving for the infinite" thus finds its place in Balzac, but as an innate vital impulse common to all creatures rather than an exclusively human ideal.[5]

<hr />

[5]On Balzac's theory of the Will, see esp. E. R. Curtius, *Balzac*, 2d ed. (Bern: A. Francke, 1951), pp. 64, 66–67, 68, 73. On Balzac's notion of desire, Curtius remarks: "Desire is the primary form and the natural aspect of striving. It is pure impulse (craving), yet below all spiritual values. It supplies the building-stone of the higher phenomena of passion. In this

Through its presence in all of animate Nature, that impulse acts as a spiritualizing influence upon the nature of the Will itself. By endowing it with a teleological aspect, this impulse raises the will above the level of purely physical force or energy. Such a transformation must, however, accentuate the opposition between the vital and nonvital, living creatures and inanimate matter. To some extent, Bichat had managed to avoid their opposition. In his system the vital properties, by being physical in nature, exist alongside of the physical and chemical forces. They are, as it were, superadded to these, bestowing animation upon a certain portion of matter. For Balzac, on the other hand, a radical abyss separates living from nonliving bodies. In many respects, this separation may be equated with that of spirit and matter. The presence of a spiritualistic tendency in the Will imparts to it a purposiveness absent from the purely physical forces. As a result, Balzac appears to revert to the vitalism of a Stahl or a Van Helmont. Such a reversion would in turn signalize a renewal of the old controversy between vitalism and mechanism, the belief in a unique vital principle and the view that life is but another expression of mechanical forces. But Balzac's vitalism must be distinguished from that of Bichat's predecessors, insofar as the Balzacian Will is not the soul of a creature but merely the force that animates it. Furthermore, the tendency informing the Will is not to be equated with an idea (a purpose): it proceeds, rather, from the nature of the vital energy itself.

This energy, for Balzac, assumes the qualities of an element or substance. In his speech to Foedora, Raphaël de Valentin had characterized it as "une force matérielle semblable à la vapeur" (a material force similar to steam), a "masse fluide" (fluid mass). By so describing it, he displays the unifying and reifying tendency of Romanticism: instead of Bichat's ensemble or concurrence of vital properties, a single force; and, in place of an energy that only animates matter without possessing a proper element or medium, the existence of an independent vital *fluidum*. Like the proponents of German *Naturphilosophie*, Balzac had sought to affirm the relation between the material and spiritual spheres. In his schema, the Will assumes a mediating position. Into it are absorbed both spiritual and material elements. These it contains by being itself a substance: hence its depiction as "cette masse fluide." The nature of such a *fluidum* establishes the possibility of a transition from the material to the spiritual: all forms of being are thus embraced and unified within a single harmonious continuum whose underlying element is energy.

Nevertheless, it remains necessary to distinguish between different

---

sense Balzac can define the passions as 'messes de désirs' (masses of desires)" (p. 92). And subsequently: "Desire, the primary form of human life, conveys its essence toward the infinite within itself. That is why the ultimate end of all passion for finite creatures constitutes a form of expression of the striving for the infinite" (pp. 106–7).

forms of energy, and especially between the vital and the mechanical. In *La Peau de chagrin,* the talisman given to Raphaël by the antiquary symbolizes the amount of his vital energy or Will. Each desire or wish he fulfills causes the piece of shagreen leather to diminish by an amount corresponding to the energy necessary to accomplish his desire.[6] When the shagreen reaches the point where no further shrinkage is possible, its possessor will die. The progressive diminution of the talisman expresses the gradual exhaustion of the life force or Will. The significance of the symbolism recalls Bichat's observation: "It is the nature of the vital properties to exhaust themselves; time uses them up in the same body." Raphaël begins by willing into existence the things he has longed for: a fortune, a mansion in Paris, and all the accompanying amenities. Curiously, his courtship and marriage with Pauline costs him little of his precious talisman—apparently relatively little energy is required, because of the concurrence of Pauline's love for him, leaving no resistance to be overcome. But various accidents happen: an argument involves him in a duel, and he is forced to will the death of his opponent, thereby sizably diminishing his talisman. In desperation, he consults the great men of science in Paris, hoping they will find some means of increasing the size of his talisman. His most remarkable encounter occurs with the engineer Spieghalter, who employs massive hydraulic presses in an attempt to stretch the magic skin. As he enters Spieghalter's establishment, Raphaël witnesses the following spectacle: "There was iron in the temperature, the men were covered with iron, everything reeked of iron, the iron possessed a life, it was organized, it fluidified itself, walked, thought in assuming all possible forms, in obeying all the caprices" (*La Comédie humaine,* x, 248). The iron symbolizes the colossal mechanical forces harnessed by Spieghalter. In his attempt to expand the skin with his hydraulic presses, however, the engineer fails completely. More than any of Raphaël's other efforts, the failure implies the uniquely vital nature of the Will and the difference between the life energy and mechanical forces. No amount of mechanical power can have any effect upon the dissipation of the vital *fluidum:* it is of another nature.

Finally, his energies fast decreasing as the precious talisman shrinks to almost nothing, Raphaël summons the greatest physicians of Paris to diagnose his case and attempt to save him. Among these illustrious savants, only the young Horace Bianchon arrives at the correct diagnosis: exhaustion of the Will, for which there can be no remedy.

Among the recurrent themes of Hawthorne's tales and romances, a similar concern with the quest of science to alter the fundamental nature

---

[6]On the relation of desire to "chagrin" in Balzac, Hans Aarsleff, *From Locke to Saussure* (Minneapolis: Univ. of Minnesota Press, 1982), pp. 38–41, esp. 40–41.

of things, especially in living beings, presents itself. "The Birth-mark," in particular, manifests an affinity with Balzac. Here I believe it is possible to speak not only of affinity but of an actual influence exerted by the great French author upon his American contemporary. A comment by Hawthorne himself attests the extent of his interest in the former: in 1836–37 he told Elizabeth Peabody he had read all of Balzac's works published up to that time.[7] Balzac's first great novel, *Les Chouans*, had appeared in 1829. By 1836–37, through almost superhuman efforts, he had produced more than half of the *Comédie humaine* and virtually all of the *Études philosophiques*. The magnitude of Hawthorne's reading of Balzac thus bears witness to his thorough immersion in the world of the *Comédie humaine*. Even among contemporaries, his affinity with the French author did not pass unnoticed.[8] Nowhere is it more clearly expressed than in "The Birth-mark," which, in addition to the vitalism of *La Peau de chagrin*, draws upon themes from another of the great *Études philosophiques: La Recherche de l'absolu*.[9]

Like *La Peau de chagrin*, "The Birth-mark" concerns itself with the nature of life, as distinguished from physical or mechanical forces. The birthmark that Georgiana bears upon her left cheek may be taken to symbolize the life energy contained in her emotions. It disappears in moments of warmth or passion when her cheek suffuses with a blush, only to reappear at times of shock or despair. Under varying circumstances it seems "now vaguely portrayed, now lost, now stealing forth again, and glimmering to-and-fro with every pulse of emotion that throbbed within her heart" (Centenary, x, 38). Its symbolic significance is aptly elucidated by Aylmer's dream: "He had fancied himself, with his servant Aminadab, attempting an operation for the removal of the birthmark. But the deeper went the knife, the deeper sank the Hand, until at length its tiny grasp appeared to have caught hold of Georgiana's heart; whence, however, her husband was inexorably resolved to cut or wrench it away" (Centenary, x, 40). The birthmark is inseparable from the very source of life. As Georgiana observes: "Or, it may be, the stain goes as deep as life itself" (p. 41).

Under the influence of transcendental idealism, German and, to a lesser extent, English Romanticism had identified human life with individual consciousness. A relation of subjective to objective, internal to

---

[7]George Parsons Lathrop, *A Study of Hawthorne* (Boston, 1876; rpt. New York: AMS Press, 1969), p. 164.

[8]See Mary R. Mitford's letter to Hawthorne, Aug. 6, 1852, in response to a presentation copy of *The Blithedale Romance*: "I forget, dear Mr. Hawthorne, whether I told you that the writer of whose works you remind me, not by imitation, but by resemblance, is the great French novelist, Balzac. Do you know his books?" (cited from Lathrop, *Study*, p. 230).

[9]For Hawthorne and Balzac, cf. Jane Lundblad, *Nathaniel Hawthorne and European Literary Tradition* (Upsala: Lundequistska, 1947), pp. 166–88, which discusses *La Peau de chagrin* and *La Recherche de l'absolu* in particular, but without mentioning Balzac's theory of the will.

external, informs the existence of man in Nature. "O Lady! we receive but what we give, / And in our life alone does Nature live," Coleridge had exclaimed. In contrast, Hawthorne equates life not with consciousness, the receiving and reflecting medium of thought, but with the affections. The living or vital relation between the birthmark and Georgiana's heart is entirely appropriate here, indicating as it does the life of the individual sensibility. The sensibility with which Hawthorne concerns himself is not to be confused with the late eighteenth-century concept of "sensibility" and its antithesis to reason. It signifies, rather, the whole sentient life of the individual subjective nature, in its relation to others. Consciousness, the receiving of external impressions, contains merely its passive sense. Its essential quality is to be found in the emotions that inform those acts by which we affect the life and consciousness of others, the feelings that express the affinity that brings one subjective nature into communion with another. In the sympathy by which each individual consciousness assimilates the passions and feelings of another, there is not only participation but mutual interaction, transforming the life of those same passions and feelings.

By comparison with the notions that precede it, such consciousness represents an elevation of the concept of life. For Bichat, life consists of a concurrence of physical forces similar to those of the mechanical and chemical spheres. Balzac endows it with a unique element and properties, transforming it into the vital *fluidum* of the Will. Even at that stage, however, life remains a form of energy analogous to physical force. By defining it in terms of individual sensibility or consciousness, Hawthorne appears to revert to the earlier vitalism that equates it with the soul, and hence to renew once more the conflict between vitalism and mechanism. Among his earlier researches, Aylmer is said to have "attempted to fathom the very process by which Nature assimilates all her precious influences from earth and air, and from the spiritual world, to create and foster Man, her masterpiece" (Centenary, x, 42). In other words, he had sought to comprehend the nature of life itself, through scientific investigations. Such efforts are doomed to failure, on account of the "influences . . . from the spiritual world," which are not susceptible to methods of scientific measurement and analysis. Failure leads to the realization that "our great creative Mother, while she amuses us with apparently working in the broadest sunshine, is yet severely careful to keep her own secrets, and, in spite of her pretended openness, shows us nothing but results" (p. 42).

Nevertheless, Aylmer's failure does not result from the attempt to reduce life to purely material elements. Unlike La Mettrie and the French materialists, he does not adhere to a belief in "l'homme machine." Elsewhere in "The Birth-mark," Hawthorne observes that Aylmer "handled physical details, as if there were nothing beyond them;

yet spiritualized them all, and redeemed himself from materialism, by his strong and eager aspiration towards the infinite. In his grasp, the veriest clod of earth assumed a soul" (Centenary, x, 49). Through spiritualization of the materialistic viewpoint, the vitalism-mechanism debate is raised to a higher plane. To assume the presence of a vital energy in living things does not suffice to explain the mystery of life. At the same time, the equation of life with individual sensibility or consciousness transcends the earlier vitalistic belief in the identity of life with the soul. By associating consciousness with the affections, Hawthorne endows it with a moral aspect. The essence of human life thus consists of those feelings that express the relation between one individual and another. Because such feelings are beyond the sphere of scientific investigation, the attempt to grasp or transform the nature of human life through science alone is doomed to failure.

Vitalism had postulated a soul or anima consisting of a quasi-material or spiritual substance. Mechanism or materialism had denied the existence of such a substance; hence the impasse. By locating the essence of human life in the affections, Hawthorne bypasses such considerations altogether. The essence of the affections inheres in the subjective *relation* between one individual and another: the life of feeling exists only in the consciousness of the indissoluble ties that bind us to each other, the sense that our lives must be carried out by acting upon other natures. In his later years, especially through his experiences at the English consulate, Hawthorne was to acquire a yet deeper knowledge of "all that warm mysteriousness that is between men, passing as they do from mystery to mystery in a little gleam of light"; but even in "The Birth-mark," he attains a clear glimpse of it. After administering the elixir that causes his wife to sleep, Aylmer "failed not to gaze often at the fatal Hand, and not without a shudder." Yet once, Hawthorne continues, "by a strange and unaccountable impulse, he pressed it to his lips" (Centenary, x, 54). In so doing, he yields to that spiritual attraction which brings each individual to share in the life of humanity.

Through a fuller participation in such life, it would have become possible to learn something of its true nature, to acquire the knowledge denied to science: "Yet, had Aylmer reached a profounder wisdom, he need not thus have flung away the happiness, which would have woven his mortal life of the self-same texture with the celestial. The momentary circumstance was too strong for him; he failed to look beyond the shadowy scope of Time, and living once for all in Eternity, to find the perfect Future in the present" (Centenary, x, 56).

For Hawthorne, transcendence of the limits of space and time occurs not through a science whose only knowledge derives from material means, but rather through what remains outside their sphere altogether: the realm of feeling and affection. In the final assessment, however, even the affections themselves are by their very nature human and finite. At the moment the birthmark disappears from her cheek, Georgiana is said to pass from the human to the celestial sphere. Because the birthmark had symbolized the life of the affections, its disappearance suggests that the source of their vitality differs from that of the soul. For Hawthorne, then, life itself does not assume the autonomous spiritual values it will subsequently embody for a Nietzsche or a Dostoyevsky. That phase belongs to a still later development of vitalism, one that no longer bears even a relation to science.

# PART III

# The Secularization of Religion

# 8 Emerson

## Schleiermacher

In the last years of the eighteenth century, after witnessing the early phase of the French Revolution, the city of Berlin found itself participating in the intellectual revolution then taking place in Germany. A circle of friends centered around Henrietta Herz, a talented patroness of the arts and fashions, ministered to the city's intellectual interests. Through his introduction to this circle in 1796, Friedrich Schleiermacher met and became friends with the young Friedrich Schlegel and the Romantic sophisticates who, saturated with the liberalism of the Enlightenment, affected to despise religion. To these intellectuals, the "cultured despisers" of religion ("die Gebildeten unter ihren Verächtern"), the youthful Schleiermacher addressed his first work, *Über die Religion* (1799). Forsaking traditional dogmatics and assuming a rhetorical posture, he attempted to establish a secular concept of religion, one that assumes only a relation between the self and its external world.[1] That relation becomes the basis of the new idea of religion: "Thus religion; the universe is in uninterrupted activity and reveals itself to us each instant. Each form, which it brings forth, each essence, to which it gives a separate existence from the fullness of life, each happening, which it spills out of its rich ever-fruitful lap, is an act of the same toward us; and so to accept each individual thing as a part of the Whole, everything finite as a representation of the Infinite, that is religion" (pp. 55–57). Such a universe must not be understood as something objectively independent of the self. Neither, on the other hand, is it simply a subjective idealization by the individual mind. It represents, rather, the mind's

---

[1] On Schleiermacher's rhetorical posture in *Über die Religion*, see Karl Barth, *The Theology of Schleiermacher*, ed. Dietrich Ritschl, trans. Geoffrey Bromiley (Grand Rapids, Mich.: Eerdmans, 1982), pp. 244–46.

perception (*Anschauung*) of an external world, where the seeing itself gives form to that world, pervades it as a subjective element, and imparts a life to it. Consciousness, according to Schleiermacher, is receptive: its existence implies the reception of impressions (a "world") that it perceives as external to itself. The sense of something external is thus part of the element of consciousness, which does not in fact apprehend anything other than the *impression* of something external. Hence the whole content of the apprehension is contained within the act of apprehension itself. This concept of consciousness, which betrays obvious affinities with ...ant's description of the apprehension of the noumena, differs nevertheless from Kant in assuming that the subjective nature must somehow pervade the external world formed through the mind's seeing, as an element of that world. The mind thereby perceives the subjective (its own nature) as something objective, as life, so that what is objective is both really objective (external to the self) and yet not different in nature from the subjective. The identification of subjective and objective is possible only because the seeing (*Anschauung*) is itself conditioned by an inner vital affirmation that is also the element assimilated into the external world.[2]

For Schleiermacher, revelation means witnessing the producing of life, the creation of new forms and essences by the life force. But the life force is nothing more than consciousness; out of pure consciousness emerge the individual and finite forms that express themselves through events of the external world. The essence of revelation consists of the finitization, so to speak, of consciousness, and its separation from its source in pure consciousness. As a result of the separation, it becomes possible for consciousness to perceive itself: the individual or finite mind, seeing the producing of new forms of life or consciousness in the universe, reexperiences its own coming into existence through apprehension of what it perceives as external to itself and yet simultaneously one with itself. Consciousness sees, in other words, how it becomes consciousness: the disclosure of the nature of consciousness yields the content of revelation.

The relation of consciousness to itself through the act of seeing also serves to explain Schleiermacher's definition, later in the same work, of revelation as "jede ursprüngliche und neue Anschauung des Universums" (*Über die Religion*, p. 116). If the universe consists of an externalization of consciousness (so that it becomes something genuinely ex-

---

[2]Karl Barth remarks: "One radically forgets that in these statements about such matters as revelation and miracle, or about the world, man, and the religions God is supposed to be the subject in some meaningful way. A human-natural something is put in his place. Or, conversely, we radically forget that in a meaningful statement about God, God can only be thought of as the *subject* and not the predicate. Instead, we operate here with a concept of God as the ineffable relationship of everything finite" (ibid., pp. 250–51).

ternal or objective to the original consciousness), the new and original seeing of this universe must consist of perceiving the nature of consciousness itself. Such a perception requires the actual experience of consciousness—which is to say: consciousness must experience itself. Here the individual or subjective nature of revelation for Schleiermacher becomes apparent. The mere passive witnessing of the spectacle of the universe cannot suffice to impart a true perception of the vital element in external things. For that, mind must experience itself as the external world. Only by passing into that world can the mind experience consciousness as something other than its own self. In so doing, it receives a "new and original" perception of itself—that is, a revelation. The "new and original" *Anschauung* of the universe thus justifies its description in subjective terms, as a new experience of the nature of the individual mind, seen now as objective rather than subjective.

Significantly, in his definition of revelation, Schleiermacher nowhere asserts the disclosure of any specific commandment or message. From the first revelations to Abraham, such utterances always presuppose their recipient as living in historical time, the consciousness of which these utterances develop or enhance. To conceive of revelation in a historical sense, however, presupposes acceptance on the individual's part of his role within a tradition. For the Old Testament, that tradition consists of the formation of the Chosen People through the shaping influence of the prophetic canon; for the New Testament, the eschatology of the Apostolic Age, with its belief in the imminent end of things and the *parousia* or second coming of Christ.[3] For a generation that refuses to accept itself as part of either of these traditions, nor as part of the later Christian concept of progressive spiritual development through the Church, Schleiermacher—like Emerson after him—has to appeal to a nontemporal and secular concept of revelation, in which the time element, losing its historical aspect, becomes both eternal and internalized within the individual. As a result of the new supratemporal perspective, the content of revelation also undergoes profound alteration, becoming a pure perception or consciousness (oneness in being) that excludes the possibility of specific utterance or disclosure.

For both Schleiermacher and Emerson, the ultimate effect of the eternization of revelation is not to abolish historical tradition altogether but rather to suggest the possibility of reappropriating it through a wholly different approach. This approach consists of its internalization as part

---

[3] For the Old Testament, Gerhard von Rad, *Old Testament Theology*, 2 vols., trans. D. M. G. Stalker (New York: Harper & Row, 1962, 1965), and for the New Testament sense of time, Oscar Cullmann, *Christ and Time*, trans. Floyd V. Filson, rev. ed. (Philadelphia: Westminster Press, 1964). See also the interesting remarks on the subject in Hans Conzelmann, *The Theology of St. Luke*, trans. Geoffrey Buswell (New York: Harper & Row, 1960), pp. 95–97, 131–32.

of the content of consciousness. Instead of situating the individual within the framework of a historical succession, secular religion assimilates that succession to individual consciousness. The individual now relates himself or herself to it through conscious choice and affective volition. The internalization of tradition was not to take place, however, in the early Schleiermacher, nor in the early Emerson of *Nature* and the Divinity School Address. Before attaining that stage, it had been necessary to establish the fundamentally secular character of revelation. It is the later Schleiermacher (the author of *Der christliche Glaube*) who effects the assimilation (and consequently the development of dogmatics). In America his work finds its reflection in Theodore Parker.

The secularization of revelation as an internal or subjective experience corresponds for Schleiermacher to the inner or subjective nature of religion itself, as a relation of mind to the external world within the sphere of consciousness. Like revelation, religion consists of a relation between subjective and objective, in which the objective contains the subjective element. Perceived as pure or universal consciousness, that element yields the feeling of the infinite. The infinite, or pure consciousness, is God. In relating the individual mind to such consciousness, Schleiermacher displays the profoundly secular aspect of the new Romantic concept of religion. Beginning with the Augustinian sense of religion as "religio," a binding tie or relation, he transforms it into an experience of the individual consciousness: "and so to accept each individual thing as a part of the Whole, everything finite as a representation of the Infinite, that is religion." Even God is contained within the individual consciousness as part of the perception of the relation between the individual or finite object (*alles Einzelne*) and the Whole (*Über die Religion*, pp. 132–33). The finite object offers a representation (*Darstellung*) or expression of the infinite, but only because of the nature of consciousness, which perceives its own life or element in both the object and the Whole. That element enters into God itself, which exists for consciousness only as the "fulfillment," so to speak, of what is expressed in the finite object. According to Schleiermacher, then, the relation to God which is religion is possible only through perception of an external world, whose finite objective nature becomes through consciousness the expression of an infinite objective nature, or God. Thus the essence of religion leads not toward exclusion of the external world; rather, "the religious feelings should like a holy music accompany all doings of man; he should do all *with* religion, not *from* religion" (*Über die Religion*, p. 71).

The relation of finite to infinite which defines religion consists not only of seeing but also—and equally—of feeling. Of these two elements Schleiermacher observes:

Seeing without feeling is nothing and can have neither the right source nor the right force, feeling without seeing is also nothing: both are only then and for that reason something, if and because they originally are one and inseparable. That first instant full of mystery, which comes with each sensuous apprehension, before seeing and feeling separate themselves, where sense and its object flow into one another and become one, as it were, before both return to their original places—I know how indescribable it is, and how quickly it passes over, but I wanted you to be able to grasp it and also in the higher and Godlike religious activity of feeling to know it again. (*Über die Religion,* pp. 76–77)

Seeing and feeling must be viewed as two aspects of a single fundamental impulse by which the self relates to its world. In that moment of sensuous apprehension in which the perceiving sense and its object stream together and fuse with each other, consciousness perceives an image and suffuses it with an emotion. Not, however, with the kind of emotional coloration that comes from pain or sorrow, joy or pleasure, but rather the pure sensibility that expresses the experience of perception. The fusion of feeling and perception is itself possible only because of the assimilation of individual consciousness into the world perception reveals to it. Within that world, which through assimilation becomes both objective and subjective, the perception of something carries with it a sensible awareness of that something as external to the self. In awareness, according to Schleiermacher, we encounter the element of feeling. Both the external world and the feeling that accompanies it are but elements of a single unifying consciousness. For such consciousness, each necessitates the other: the subjective assumes an objective sphere, the objective is experienced only through the subjective.

Through experience of the mutually exalting interaction of subjective and objective, Schleiermacher hopes his audience will recognize "the higher and Godlike religious activity of the soul." What appears then initially at the most fundamental level of consciousness also reappears at its highest stage: assimilation of different elements into a single soulful feeling by which the mind assumes an attitude toward its world and at the same time becomes that world. The passing of subjective consciousness into the world infuses it with a spiritual animation that dissolves the sense of the external, such that the world no longer appears as substance or only as the substance of perception. The simultaneous presence of feeling represents the specifically religious aspect of this process: through feeling, the mind becomes conscious of its immanence in the world and simultaneously of its realization of the objective as infinite or pure consciousness, in other words, as God. Reflecting upon the striving for clarity contained in that perspective, Schleiermacher could well assert that "Religion is the sense and taste for the Infinite" (*Über die Religion,* p. 49).

Such a formulation assumes its full significance, however, only when we recognize that the Infinite for which the mind yearns is in fact within itself. In his *Monologen,* published the year after *Über die Religion,*

Schleiermacher elaborates upon this theme: "My earthly activity flows into the stream of time, knowledge and feelings transform themselves, and I can hold nothing fast; the theater in which I playfully depict myself passes away, and from its steady source the stream constantly brings up something new to me: but so often as I turn my gaze upon my inner self, do I find myself in the realm of Eternity; I see the activity of the Spirit, that no world can change, and no time destroy, that activity which itself first creates world and time" (pp. 21–22).

What before had only been implied now appears explicitly and in such a fashion as to seem a new formulation altogether. Whereas the earlier *Über die Religion* had described, through the use of fluid metaphors, the assimilation of mind into the external world and the consequent appearance of subjective as objective, Schleiermacher now postulates explicitly the producing of the objective within the subjective, external world within the mind. Not, however, of the mind as individual and subjective but rather as pure consciousness: thus when I turn my gaze inward upon myself, I am "simultaneously in the kingdom of Eternity," the realm of pure Spirit or consciousness, which "itself first creates world and time."[4]

The realm of pure consciousness corresponds, in the earlier *Über die Religion,* to the Infinite of which each individual and finite object represents an expression; instead of situating the Infinite in the external world into which individual mind passes over, however, Schleiermacher now places it in the mind itself: it is the element of pure consciousness which the mind apprehends when it turns its gaze away from the stream of external sensations. "Through its mere being," Schleiermacher goes on to say, "Spirit contains the world within itself." For the nature of Spirit *(Geist)* is pure consciousness; simply by virtue of its existence, such consciousness implies the existence of its whole content, the sum-total of sensations and impressions that form the external world.

Through the assertion of this Spirit in its freedom, the world receives its life or animating force. The perception of the relation between finite and infinite that had characterized the religion of *Über die Religion* finds itself transformed into a purely introspective seeing, one in which all trace of individual subjectivity disappears, to leave only pure consciousness, the element of the Infinite. As with Emerson later, this Infinite is not to be conceived of as simply transcending the finite. Instead, it is infinite in and through its creation of the finite, the external world it produces in asserting itself as consciousness and as the source of all concrete perceptions. Accordingly, religion consists not of an apprehension of the relation of finite to infinite in which the mind or conscious-

[4]For a commentary on the *Monologen* in relation to its Romantic context, see the essay on Schleiermacher in Friedrich Gundolf's *Romantiker* (Berlin-Wilmersdorf: Heinrich Keller, 1930).

ness remains outside either, but rather of an assimilation of individual consciousness to that pure consciousness which is its element and which Schleiermacher defines as God. By the nature of this assimilation, the apprehension of God or pure consciousness becomes identical to being that consciousness. All trace of individuality disappears as the individual mind becomes, at the moment of apprehension, God itself. In that state, it would be incorrect to speak of the individual mind as God; instead, in becoming God, the individual mind ceases to be itself.

In the two stages of Schleiermacher's development I have traced thus far, we have seen how, in response to the worldly circles in which he moved during his early years in Berlin, he had been led to formulate a concept of God and of religion as something contained within the individual consciousness, hence something that does not need to confront the problem of the knowability of a God external to the mind. To be sure, this had also involved the exclusion of all dogmatic content from the concept of religion, which thus remains purely an apprehension of the nature of consciousness itself. His early phase thus exhibits Schleiermacher following a pattern similar to that of the early Emerson. In his later Berlin period, beginning with his return from Halle in 1807 and culminating in the two versions of *Der christliche Glaube* (1821–22 and 1830), he develops the system that will exercise a profound influence upon Theodore Parker. Schleiermacher's mature system differs from that of his early years not in its renunciation of the attempt to define religion in terms of the nature of consciousness, but in its analysis of that consciousness. For the later Schleiermacher—in contrast to the author of *Über die Religion* and especially the *Monologen*—the individual consciousness no longer contains God within itself. Instead, there is only the mind's awareness of its dependence upon something external to it.

For a more detailed comprehension of Schleiermacher's later views on religion, it is necessary to turn first of all to the famous formulae of *Der christliche Glaube* (secs. 3 and 4): "The piety that forms the basis of all ecclesiastical communions is, considered purely in itself, neither a Knowing nor a Doing, but a modification of Feeling, or of immediate self-consciousness," and "The common element in all expressions, however diverse, of piety, is this: the consciousness of being absolutely dependent, or, which is the same thing, of being in relation with God." Here it seems appropriate to consider the criticism advanced by the late Karl Barth, which helps to illuminate Schleiermacher's later concept of consciousness. In an afterword to a selection from Schleiermacher's writings, Barth poses the following question as crucial to any assessment of Schleiermacher: "In Schleiermacher's theology or philosophy, do persons feel, think, and speak (a) in relationship to an indispensable [*unaufhebbar*] Other, in accordance with an *object* which is superior to their own being, feeling, perceiving, willing, and acting, an object toward which adoration, gratitude, repentance, and supplication are concretely possible and even imperative? . . . Or, for Schleiermacher, do persons feel, think, and speak (b) in and from a sovereign consciousness that their own beings are conjoined, and are indeed essentially *united,* with everything which might possibly come into question as something or even someone distinct from them?"[5]

It would be relatively easy to point out passages from Schleiermacher's early writings matching the second description. Indeed, the essential task Schleiermacher sets himself in his early period is to establish a concept of religion that does not involve the problem of the knowability of God. With regard to his mature system, however, the answer must be: neither exclusively, or both in a qualified sense. Here it becomes necessary to turn to the discussion of absolute dependence:

> Thus in every self-consciousness there are two elements, which we might call respectively a self-caused element and a non-self-caused element; or a Being and a Having-by-some-means-come-to-be. The latter of these presupposes for every self-consciousness another factor besides the Ego, a factor which is the source of the particular determination, and without which the self-consciousness would not be precisely what it is. But this other is not objectively presented in the immediate self-consciousness with which alone we are here concerned. For though, of course, the double constitution of self-consciousness causes us always to look objectively for an other to which we can trace the origin of our particular state, yet this search is a separate act with which we are not at present concerned. In self-consciousness there are only two elements: the one expresses the existence of the subject for itself, the other its co-existence with an other. (*Der christliche Glaube,* trans. MacKintosh and Stewart, p. 24)

To these elements, according to Schleiermacher, there correspond in the subject the tendencies of "receptivity" and "spontaneous activity." In the self-assertion by which self-consciousness comes into existence, we find the expression of its spontaneous activity. Without a corresponding receptivity (that is, consciousness of an other), such self-assertion remains directionless, without an object. Consciousness of an other is that toward which the active impulse or assertion impels itself, the objective the mind conceives of to give form to what would otherwise be pure awareness without content, without anything of which it could be said to be aware. Consciousness, then, comes into existence through self-assertion, but without the apprehension of something external can have no content and hence no self-consciousness.

But—in contrast to Schleiermacher's earlier notion of consciousness—apprehension of an other in his later system does not imply that other's

---

[5]Barth, *Theology,* p. 275.

actual presence in the mind. Here, the content of consciousness is not to be equated with something external or objective. It consists only of the inference of such an object, deduced from the recognition that the individual mind is not the cause of its own being. For such an object to be "objectively presented" in self-consciousness would mean experiencing the external within consciousness itself. Such an experience would imply that the objective and subjective are the same. The "experience" of the external in consciousness means that consciousness experiences itself as something objective.

For the later Schleiermacher, these admissions cannot hold true. The inference that consciousness is produced by something external to it assumes no knowledge of the nature of its cause. The lack of such knowledge gives *Der christliche Glaube* its Kantian aspect—with the qualification that it postulates an affective tendency (active assertion of consciousness as the mode of its existence) foreign to the Critical philosophy. Returning now to the question posed by Barth, one can see how, for the later Schleiermacher, God appears neither as an object toward which adoration, gratitude, or supplication are possible, nor as something united with the individual consciousness. For God to become an object of consciousness (in other words, to be "objectively presented"), the objective would have to be formed within the subjective. And that is precisely what cannot be. It would amount to the subjective being represented to itself. But the nature of the cause of consciousness is not the same as that of consciousness itself. Neither can it be assimilated to consciousness, as self and external world are assimilated for the early Schleiermacher.

This fact about his later system—namely, its failure to correspond to either of the possibilities proposed by Barth—was to have important consequences for the theology of Theodore Parker. At present, it suffices to explore the reasons for Schleiermacher's turn toward Kantianism in *Der christliche Glaube*. The shift springs from the necessity of defining God as something truly external to the self. This condition could manifest itself to Schleiermacher through awareness of the need to redefine the true nature of religion and, in particular, of religious emotion. Such emotion is possible only when its object is conceived of as something higher than consciousness itself. The impossibility within the earlier framework of postulating the existence of anything higher than consciousness now leads to rejection of the self's assimilation to God through that consciousness. Instead, Schleiermacher asserts the mind's inability to apprehend God as an object of consciousness—that is, as something objective. To be genuine, the apprehension would have to originate as a producing of the objective within the subjective: "for just the same reason, this feeling [of absolute dependence] cannot in any manner arise from the influence of an object which has in some way to be *given* to us; for upon such an object there would always be a counter-influence, and even a voluntary renunciation of this would always involve a feeling of freedom" (*Der christliche Glaube*, sec. 4). And, subsequently: "If, however, word and idea are always originally one, and the term 'God' thus presupposes an idea, then we shall simply say that this idea . . . is nothing more than the expression of the feeling of absolute dependence" (sec. 4).

The expression of God as something objective within consciousness represents a finitization of the Infinite, which means here: of that whose nature lies beyond apprehension. At the same time, the influence of Schleiermacher's early thought still manifests itself. Once more, religion is defined in terms of feeling and consciousness. Within the framework of the mature system, however, the approach could only be problematic. Impelled on the one hand by the felt necessity of defining religion as a relation to something higher and genuinely external to consciousness, and on the other, of preserving religion as an experience of consciousness rather than a mere form of rationalism, Schleiermacher places the essence of religion within a structure of consciousness, the feeling of dependence, which cannot of itself possess actuality or permanence because it fails to impart a reality to its notion of God. To establish its validity, such a system would have had to formulate a concept of the Infinite or God. Only by so doing (neglecting for the moment the question of whether such a concept would actually *be* God—as in the early Schleiermacher—or merely a representation) could it actually receive a genuine apprehension of the divine. Since the medium of the mind is thought, the creation of a concept embodies the only possible "experience" of the reality of God. The formative process by which thought manifests its own creativeness mirrors the concept of the true Infinite and realizes that Infinite within the mind itself. Through its failure, then, to embody the object of its aspirations and thus to create a true "experience" of the divine, Schleiermacher's system passes on its complex and problematic legacy to its nineteenth-century Protestant successors, and—what is especially significant for us here—to Theodore Parker.


## Theodore Parker

In the letter to his congregation from Santa Cruz which forms his confession of faith, Theodore Parker recalls the beginning of his career as a minister: "I think I preached only what I had experienced in my own inward consciousness, which widened and grew richer as I came into practical contact with living men, turned time into life, and mere thought became character" (*Autobiography*, p. 306). At that time, he had just finished his studies in divinity school. During the preceding years, he had managed to read quite widely in the different branches of theology to which Germany was then making such significant and prolific contributions. In the resolution which he adopts for himself at the outset of his career, it is possible to trace the influence of the new Romantic religion professed by Schleiermacher and others. Nevertheless, the influence remains clearly subject to the very different conditions of American life in the first half of the nineteenth century. Through the "practical [moral] contact with living men," according to Parker, the confrontation with human passions, hopes, and desires, seen and felt within the terms of a social equality for which nothing comparable existed in the Germany of that time, consciousness ceases to remain isolated and assimilates the external world through the blending of thought with practice, aspiration with experience. In spite of these differences, an inner affinity manifests itself between the young Unitarian minister and his European counterpart in the sophisticated circles of cosmopolitan Berlin: the appeal to consciousness as the source of all religious doctrine, the development of religion as the progressive unfolding of the inner entelechy of that consciousness.

In his most famous sermon, more than a decade later, Theodore Parker appeals to the same principle as the criterion distinguishing the essence of religion from its transient forms:

> The form religion takes, the doctrines wherewith she is girded, can never be the same in any two centuries or two men; for since the sum of religious doctrines is both the result and the measure of a man's total growth in wisdom, virtue, and piety, and since men will always differ in these respects, so religious *doctrines* and *forms* will always differ, always be transient, as Christianity goes forth and scatters the seed she bears in her hand. But the *Christianity holy men feel in the heart,* the Christ that is born within us, is always the same thing to each soul that feels it. This differs only in degree, and not in kind, from age to age, and man to man. (*Transient and Permanent,* p. 31)[6]

Here the "Christ that is born within us" signifies above all a state of consciousness: oneness of the mind with God, a pure apprehension of the divine in which all trace of individual consciousness disappears. This radical Christology, made possible by the Unitarian interpretation of Christ as a human rather than divine figure, undergoes with Parker and his contemporary Emerson a transformation impossible to account for solely by the theology of Unitarianism itself, the sermons of William Ellery Channing or the professions of the Wares. By defining religion as

[6]For the circumstances of Parker's South Boston sermon, "The Transient and Permanent in Christianity," see Conrad Wright, introduction to *Three Prophets of Religious Liberalism: Channing, Emerson, Parker* (Boston: Beacon Press, 1961), pp. 36–43, and on Parker's role in the Unitarian controversy in general, Henry Steele Commager, *Theodore Parker* (Boston: Little, Brown, 1936), pp. 61–79.

a form of consciousness in a fashion similar to the early Schleiermacher, Parker can ascribe to Jesus a divinity based not upon his nature or essence but upon the mind's capacity for a clear and pure apprehension of the divine: "He felt that God's word was in him; that he was one with God" (*Transient and Permanent*, pp. 30–31).

Through this oneness with God, Parker affirms the divinity of Jesus as one possible for all men.[7] At the same time, it possesses a specific historical dimension, signalizing humanity's first realization of its innate spiritual potential. Because of the nature of the human mind, the process of divinization can never be complete. That limitation should not obscure the genuine form of divinity still possible to humanity: the experience of having passed, through the complete assimilation of volition to love, into consciousness of a divine presence within the mind, which is nothing other than the assertion of love as the mind's own expression of its creative potency and hence infinitude.[8] For Theodore Parker, this assimilation manifests itself as a transcendence of time. Nevertheless, through Jesus, it also occupies a specific and precise moment in history. By incorporating both historical and transcendental perspectives, Parker simultaneously preserves and transforms William Ellery Channing's interpretation of Jesus as distinguished from God by his human nature, hence someone to be regarded primarily as an inspiration for one's own moral development.

Parker's own Christology, however, expresses something more than the possibility of approaching God through perfection of one's moral nature. In actuality, it signifies nothing less than progressive identification with a God whose essence is indistinguishable from that of consciousness.[9] By equating God with a state of consciousness, Parker reaffirms Schleiermacher's concept of the Infinite and its relation to the finite. In his *Über die Religion*, Schleiermacher had depicted the finite as a representation (*Darstellung*) of the Infinite and, at the same time, as

[7]"For it is not so much by the Christ who lived so blameless and beautiful eighteen centuries ago that we are saved directly, but by the Christ we form in our hearts and live out in our daily life, that we save ourselves, God working with us both to will and to do" (*Transient and Permanent*, p. 33).

[8]Elsewhere Parker defines love in such a fashion as to reflect the influence of Coleridge and German *Naturphilosophie*, assimilating emotion to what Goethe might have called the "Urphänomene": "Self-love is the lesser cohesive attraction which keeps the man whole and a unit, which is necessary for his consistency and existence as an individual. It is a part of morality, and is to the man what impenetrability is to the atoms of matter. . . . Love is the greater gravitation which unites me to others; the expansive and centrifugal power that extends my personality, and makes me find my delight in others, and desire them to have theirs in me" (*Sermons of Religion*, pp. 81–82).

[9]In his letter to his congregation from Santa Cruz, Parker asserts: "To me the material world and the outward history of man do not supply a sufficient revelation of God, nor warrant me to speak of infinite perfection. It is only from the nature of man, from facts of intuition, that I can gather this greatest of all truths, as I find it in my consciousness reflected back from Deity itself" (*Autobiography*, pp. 337–38).

consisting of the element of the Infinite. This in turn had been possible because of the identification of that element with pure consciousness. But whereas Schleiermacher had represented the mind as external to the relation of finite to Infinite, Parker defines the relation as that of individual mind to God—of finite consciousness to infinite consciousness. Hence the description of Jesus as one to whom, "as the result of this virgin purity of soul and perfect obedience, the light of God shone down into the very depths of his soul, bringing all of the Godhead which flesh can receive" (*Transient and Permanent*, p. 30). Elsewhere, in his *Discourse of Matters Pertaining to Religion*, Parker portrays the condition of Jesus as one attainable by all: "In the high hour of religious visitation from the living God, there seems to be no separate thought; the tide of universal life sets through the soul. The thought of self is gone. It is a little accident to be a king or a clown, a parent or a child. Man is at one with God, and He is all in all" (p. 136). Here an Emersonian influence blends with that of the young Schleiermacher. Elsewhere in the *Discourse* Parker draws upon the mature Schleiermacher of *Der christliche Glaube*—as in his analysis of the religious element itself:

> and deeper down, beneath all the shifting phenomena of life, we discover the RELIGIOUS ELEMENT OF MAN. Looking carefully at this element; separating this as a cause from its actions, and these from their effects; stripping this faculty of all accidental circumstances peculiar to the age, nation, sect, or individual, and pursuing a sharp and final analysis till the subject and predicate can no longer be separated; we find as the ultimate fact, that the religious element first manifests itself in our consciousness by a feeling of need, of want; in one word by a SENSE OF DEPENDENCE. (*Discourse*, p. 7)

Of the nature of that element Parker goes on to say: "This primitive feeling does not, itself, disclose the character, and still less the nature and essence of the object on which it depends; no more than the senses disclose the nature of their objects; no more than the eye or ear discovers the essence of light or sound" (p. 7).

The moment at which "subject and predicate can no longer be separated" corresponds to what Schleiermacher had described as the passage of the self into immediate feeling (*Gefühl*) and perception (*Anschauung*). At that moment subjective and objective become one. What had previously seemed external now merges with the subjective element. Simultaneously the subjective sees itself as objective, containing not only the receptive element but a world in its concrete substance. As for Schleiermacher, however, that substance no longer belongs to something external. Instead, it becomes simply the element of perception. As such, it no longer possesses being in itself. But perception, too, lacks being in that sense: its whole existence is one of pure receptivity, consequently one dependent upon the existence of that which it perceives. Thus, through the fusion of subjective and objective, or subject with predicate, what had previously been an external world and an individual self is now transformed into a medium of passive receptivity.

This fusion of subjective and objective, according to Parker, leads ultimately to a feeling of want, or of what he calls (following Schleiermacher's terminology) a "sense of dependence." In coming into existence, consciousness experiences, as part of its immediate feeling, the sense of having been caused by something external to itself, an other. This sense of having been caused by an other—what Schleiermacher terms the "Irgendwiegewordensein" or the element of "Sichselbstnichtsogesetzthaben"—produces the feeling of want or dependence— the desire to apprehend the cause of one's existence, to achieve an objective presentation of such a cause within the consciousness. That desire, according to Parker, impels the mind to form the various faiths or creeds that constitute the history of religion, to whose analysis he subsequently devotes a large part of the Discourse of Religion.

Of equal significance in the passage we are now considering is the term feeling, which Parker equates with the sense of dependence. As with Schleiermacher, such feeling cannot be identified with the kind to which we ascribe an emotional coloration, the sensations of longing or desire, happiness or sadness. The feeling or which Parker speaks is, rather, the experience that accompanies the perceptions of consciousness. From such perceptions, it creates a subjective or self-related apprehension, the sense of self as that upon which the perception acts and which reacts to the perception, as the eye responds to light. Such a reaction cannot be divorced from the perception itself—in this case, the consciousness of something external as that which causes the self to be. Hence the necessity of the feeling of dependence upon an other. In this respect, religion (as the feeling of dependence) is both immediate—that is, something given with our very sense of being—and necessary (in contrast to free or arbitrary constructs of the mind).

By situating the religious element within the very nature of consciousness itself, Parker, like Schleiermacher before him, formulates an explicit response to the "cultured despisers," as well as the fanatics, of religion. In his letter to his congregation from Vera Cruz, speaking of his method, he observes: "Here, then, was the foundation of religion, laid in human nature itself, which neither the atheist nor the more pernicious bigot, with their sophisms of denial or affirmation, could move, or even shake" (Autobiography, p. 302). By thus locating the religious feeling within the innermost precincts of consciousness, one could address such a feeling or element as that beyond which mind or thought cannot go without denying its own existence, as the essential form of all its seeing. For the mind to deny the existence of an other as its cause would be to oppose the structure of consciousness itself, of that which gives us all our sense both of self and of everything external to us. That consciousness by which we perceive both ourselves and others must have a ground-form that makes all such perceptions possible and within which they occur. This ground-form, according to Schleiermacher, consists of the "double constitution of self-consciousness," the sense of self and of its external cause.

But the sense of that external cause offers no knowledge of its actual nature or essence. As with Schleiermacher, that cause cannot be anything capable of being "objectively presented" to consciousness. Whatever forms an object of consciousness becomes thereby something in relation to which the self can exercise a certain freedom, that is, in deciding what attitude to assume toward it, hence not something upon which it finds itself dependent. Of whatever is truly external to consciousness, on the other hand, it can form no conception whatsoever: in attempting to do so, consciousness ranges through the whole of its field or sphere, but apprehends such a cause only as that which lies beyond it, as something completely outside the field of consciousness.

Given the nature of its apprehension, which offers consciousness only the sense of something external as its cause, it is easy to perceive a resemblance to Kant's concept of the noumena, whose nature or essence remains beyond the grasp of the understanding. The Kantian aspect of Schleiermacher's analysis must in fact have been noticed by Parker himself—speaking of the absence of any knowledge of the character or essence of the object upon which religious feeling depends, he draws an analogy to the perception of physical phenomena by the senses, the same basis Kant had used for his discussion of the noumena. Independently of Schleiermacher, however, Theodore Parker was bound to encounter Kant in his quest for a theology based upon the fundamental nature of consciousness. In his autobiographical letter to his congregation from Vera Cruz he pays him the following tribute: "I found most help in the works of Immanuel Kant, one of the profoundest thinkers in the world, though one of the worst writers, even of Germany; if he did not always furnish conclusions I could rest in, he yet gave me the true method, and put me on the right road" (*Autobiography*, p. 301).

Yet, in spite of his admiration for Kant and the relevance of the Critical philosophy to Schleiermacher's and his own attempts to ground religious truth in the nature of self-consciousness, Parker appears to have felt—if only intuitively—the problematic aspect of the Kantian approach as well. In a footnote to his assertion of the sense of dependence as the essential religious element, he concedes: "Perhaps all will not agree with that analysis which makes a *sense of dependence* the ultimate fact of consciousness in the case. This is the statement of Schleiermacher, not to mention more ancient authorities." To which he adds: "I contend more for the *fact* of a religious element in man than for the above analysis of that element" (*Discourse*, p. 7), an admission that is followed up by an apparently laconic reference to Hegel's criticism of *Der christliche Glaube*. But Hegel's remarks, "the most violent and malicious attack" (Karl Barth) on Schleiermacher's system up to 1830, must have given Parker occasion for reflection. In a preface to Hinrichs' *Religionsphilosophie*, Hegel had written: "If religion in man were grounded only upon a feeling, this would rightly have no further determination beyond being the *feeling of his dependence*, and then the dog would be the best Christian, for he carries this feeling most strongly in himself and lives especially in it. He also experiences feelings of redemption when his hunger finds satisfaction through a bone" (*Berliner Schriften*, p. 74).

Perhaps partly as a response to this criticism, and to clarify for himself the exact nature of the sense of dependence which he, following Schleiermacher, had defined as the essential element of religion, Parker then explains:

> If the above statement [equating religion with the sense of dependence] be correct, then our belief in God's existence does not depend on the *a posteriori* argument, on considerations drawn from the order, fitness, and beauty discovered by observations made in the material world; nor yet on the *a priori* argument, on considerations drawn from the eternal nature of things, and observations made in the spiritual world. It depends primarily on no *argument* whatever; not on *reasoning* but *reason*. The fact is given outright, as it were, and comes to the man, as soon and as naturally, as the consciousness of his own existence, and is indeed logically inseparable from it, for we cannot be conscious of ourselves except as *dependent beings*. (*Discourse*, p. 11)

The perspective attained by situating the religious element or feeling in consciousness itself makes possible a rejection of the so-called argument from design of natural religion, as well as the traditional proofs of the existence of God found in medieval scholasticism. In their place, Parker advances the concept of an immediate apprehension of pure consciousness, one that "depends primarily on no *argument* whatever." Such an apprehension must consist not of "*reasoning* but *reason*"—which is to say: the immediate relation of oneself to something external, rather than the formation of any inductive or deductive inference thereupon. Such a relation implies that the essence of thought (or reason) consists of an apprehension, whose content will then be, as in Kant, a "relation between the determinations of things in their existence." Beginning with the experience of consciousness or self-consciousness, thought relates it to what is external to that consciousness. Whereas Schleiermacher had defined the relation as the sense of an external cause for the self (*Irgendwiegewordensein*), Parker merely postulates a sense of dependence. Perhaps his formulation may be summarized simply as the sense of something external to consciousness, produced by the experience of the latter's limits. But in his description of this sense as that which "comes to the man, as soon and as naturally, as the consciousness of his own existence," Parker has surely appropriated the concept of immediate feeling (*Gefühl*) and perception (*Anschauung*), whose presence forms the necessary accompaniment of consciousness for the author of *Der christliche Glaube*.

Even if we conceive of religion simply as the apprehension of something external to consciousness, however, the rebuke in Hegel's preface to Hinrichs' *Religionsphilosophie* retains its force. Quite apart from the malicious comparison between Christian and dog, the effect of situating religion in an apprehension of consciousness must be to exclude all possible development of religious doctrine (dogmatics). Henceforward, there is only feeling or consciousness and revelation. And this is, in effect, Hegel's objection to Schleiermacher's system—its exclusion of "speculative theology" from religion.

Beyond such a criticism, we may return once more to the considerations raised in discussing Schleiermacher: whether even the apprehension of a genuine relation between one thing and another is in fact possible without a concept of each, and whether the thought which forms such a concept is not already implicit in the very consciousness that apprehends that relation. Here the correctness of the concept is hardly of much consequence: what matters above all is the formulation of that concept, without which any genuine relation must remain impossible, because inexpressible. One can even go so far as to say—and I believe this would be consonant with the essential spirit and purposes of both Parker and Schleiermacher—that the relation of self or consciousness to the external something that is God is the only thing that matters. But one would then have to qualify that statement by adding: only through a concept of God can such a relation come into existence. The relation itself is realized in the formation of the concept. What appears in the concept is thus something more than its content. It offers to the mind, through the only medium in which immediacy is possible, the experience of the divine, which arises not so much through the content of the concept but through the mind's own feeling of creative potency in its inception.

## Emerson

On August 31, 1837, as part of the graduation exercises in the University Chapel, Emerson had delivered, before a formal assemblage of 215 gowned students and the faculty of Harvard College, his Phi Beta Kappa oration "The American Scholar." The pomp and dignity of the ceremonies, which included readings by both a poet and an orator, are reflected in his opening salutation as well as in the stately and solemn style of the whole discourse. In marked contrast are the circumstances of his address to the graduating class of the Harvard Divinity School, less than a year later. Here the faculty had had no part in the invitation and the exercises were strictly informal.[10] In accordance with such circumstances, a corresponding informality marks the opening of Emerson's address, which begins, not with a statement of his theme—the duties of the minister, the "crisis" confronting theology, or whatever—but an apparently casual observation on the beauty of the season: "In this refulgent summer it has been a luxury to draw the breath of life. The grass grows, the buds burst, the meadow is spotted with fire and gold in the tint of flowers. The air is full of birds, and sweet with the breath of the pine, the balm-of-Gilead, and the new hay. Night brings no gloom to the heart with its welcome shade. Through the transparent darkness the stars pour their almost spiritual rays."

In this resplendent display of Nature, Emerson seems to imply, we may well feel inclined to see the expression of a divine plenitude, an infinite grace that sheds its radiance on all things, vivifying all forms of life in Nature.[11] Such abundance suggests that a perception of the splendor of Nature is in fact part of the essence of religion. But if so, it is only a subordinate part. For "the moment the mind opens, and reveals the laws which traverse the universe, and make things what they are, then shrinks the great world at once into a mere illustration and fable of this mind" (*Coll. W.*, 1, 76). As in his earlier work *Nature*, Emerson appeals to the notion that the essence of Nature consists of those eternal laws that govern all phenomena; these laws, in turn, are said to correspond to the form thought assumes in the mind.[12] But, as in *Nature*, the mind of

[10]For the circumstances of Emerson's delivery of "The American Scholar," see Ralph R. Rusk, *The Life of Ralph Waldo Emerson* (New York: Scribner's, 1949), pp. 263, 265, 266, and for those of the Divinity School Address, pp. 267–69.

[11]On the strategy behind Emerson's opening for the Divinity School Address, Joel Porte, *Representative Man: Ralph Waldo Emerson in His Time* (New York: Oxford Univ. Press, 1979), pp. 118–20; and Jonathan Bishop, *Emerson on the Soul* (Cambridge: Harvard Univ. Press, 1964), pp. 87–91. On the immediate context of the address, Conrad Wright, "Emerson, Barzillai Frost, and the Divinity School Address," in his *The Liberal Christians: Essays on American Unitarian History* (Boston: Beacon Press, 1970). For the general eighteenth-century background to Unitarianism, see, in the same volume, "Rational Religion in Eighteenth-Century America."

[12]In his Divinity School Address, Emerson asserts: "The intuition of the moral sentiment is an insight of the perfection of the laws of the soul" (*Coll. W.* 1, 77). To my knowledge, certain elements of this passage are consistently overlooked in the Emerson scholarship. Here, significantly, Emerson begins by equating intuition with insight—a characteristically Emersonian gesture, but one that tends to distance him from his eighteenth-century predecessors. For Emerson, then, the moral sentiment is not so much a feeling (as it had been for the so-called Age of Sensibility) but rather a *perception*. Of the Unitarian definition of "sentiment," Daniel Howe observes: "Perhaps the most valuable

which Emerson now speaks is not the individual and subjective consciousness but rather the "one Mind" of which all such consciousnesses form a part. In his subsequent lecture "Religion" for the series *The Present Age,* Emerson develops in detail the law of universal consciousness:

> And this deep power in which we lie and whose beatitude is all accessible to us is not only self-sufficing and perfect in every hour but the act of seeing and the thing seen, the seer and the spectacle, the subject and object are one. An ignorant man thinks the divine wisdom is conspicuously shown in some fact or creature: a wise man sees that every fact contains the same. I should think water the best invention if I were not acquainted with fire and earth and air. But as we advance, every proposition, every action, every feeling runs out into the infinite. If we go to affirm anything we are checked in our speech by the need of recognizing all other things until speech presently becomes rambling, general, indefinite, and mere tautology. The only speech will at last be action. We see the world piece by piece, as the sun, the moon, the animal, the tree; but the Whole of which these are the shining parts is the Soul. (*EL,* iii, 284)

In his *Über die Religion* Schleiermacher had spoken of that "first instant full of mystery, which comes with each sensuous apprehension, before seeing and feeling separate themselves, where sense and its object flow into one another and become one, as it were, before both return to their original places," and of how one might experience the same consciousness in "the higher and Godlike religious activity of the soul." The concept of a merging or fusion of "seeing and the thing seen," of subject and object, is common of course not only to Schleiermacher and Emerson but to much of German Romantic philosophy as well. In its earliest form, it appears in Fichte and Schelling. Through his assimilation of the

---

emotions for aiding the conscience were the ones called 'sentiments.' A sentiment was an emotional regard for a rational principle. 'Sentiment is not mere feeling,' Dr. Channing explained; 'it is feeling penetrated with thought'" (*The Unitarian Conscience: Harvard Moral Philosophy 1805–1861* [Cambridge: Harvard Univ. Press, 1970], p. 62). By interpreting sentiment as perception, Emerson takes the process of redefinition one step further. The content of this perception consists of a realization of "the perfection of the laws of the soul." What does this mean? At this point, I believe, we must adduce something like the Emersonian doctrine of compensation: the laws of the soul are perfect inasmuch as every transgression necessarily produces a corresponding effect upon the soul. It is the *perception* of this perfection of the soul's laws which gives rise to the moral sentiment—which is to say: in perceiving the laws that govern its own soul, the mind recognizes not only the necessity of conforming to those laws but the beauty of purpose, which establishes the correspondence between its own nature and such laws. The perception of this beauty of harmony or correspondence inspires the mind with the *intuition* of the moral sentiment, the recognition that the beauty of the correspondence derives from its perception by the mind, which through its *experience* of that perception becomes one with the divine consciousness. On the "moral sentiment" see also Joel Porte, *Emerson and Thoreau: Transcendentalists in Conflict* (Middletown: Wesleyan Univ. Press, 1966), pp. 69–77, and Bishop, pp. 23, 66–72.

new currents of thought in Berlin, Schleiermacher was bound to encounter it. For Emerson, a similar influence manifests itself through
Coleridge's *Biographia Literaria* (with its plagiarism of Schelling's *System
des transscendentalen Idealismus*). But he would also have absorbed it
through his reading of his friend Frederic Henry Hedge's review of
Coleridge in *The Christian Examiner*, which, with its detailed exposition of
Fichte's system, afforded him the stimulus of new modes of thought at a
time when he found himself most eagerly in search of these.[13]

But if absolute idealism can lay claim to the notion of an identification
of subjective and objective, of "seeing and the thing seen," the religious
implications and consequences are developed above all by Schleiermacher and Emerson. For that purpose, in addition to the mediation of
Frederic Henry Hedge and his own reading, Emerson could also take
advantage of the influence of Schleiermacher himself.[14] Perhaps more
significant than any direct influence, however, is the existence of what is
best described as a "spiritual affinity" (Curtius) between them: the
youthful Emerson who had renounced his Unitarian ministry and beliefs, absorbed in the heady swirl of new currents of thought and feeling
known to its initiates as "the Newness" and later to receive the name of
Transcendentalism; the equally youthful Schleiermacher, severed from
his Moravian past and taken up in the gay and brilliant life of the
Romantic circles in Berlin. In these similar circumstances a similar objective presents itself to both thinkers: the necessity for a more "secular"
and personal form of religion, one that will possess the immediacy of
feeling and experience needed to persuade those disaffected with traditional forms of worship and belief.

Such immediacy could only be found in consciousness. Not only is it
the medium through which all external sensations and impressions must
pass in order to be perceived; in addition it represents, as it were, the
very element of the self, that without which the self could not be, and
which is simultaneously for the same reason something more than individual subjective nature. For Emerson—as for Schleiermacher before
him—such consciousness consists in essence of pure seeing in which all

---

[13]One might also mention James Marsh's American edition of Coleridge's *Aids to Reflec-
tion*, with its long introduction by Marsh himself. See also *Coleridge's American Disciples: The
Selected Correspondence of James Marsh*, ed. John J. Duffy (Amherst: Univ. of Massachusetts
Press, 1973).

[14]On Emerson and Schleiermacher, René Wellek, *Confrontations* (Princeton: Princeton
Univ. Press, 1965), pp. 196–97; Stanley Vogel, *German Literary Influences on the American
Transcendentalists* (New Haven: Yale Univ. Press, 1955), pp. 68, 86; and Henry Pochmann,
*German Culture in America* (Madison: Univ. of Wisconsin Press, 1957), p. 171 and n. 151. In
a letter to Hermann Grimm (Jan. 5, 1871) Emerson wrote of Schleiermacher: "his was
never one of my high names" (*Correspondence between Ralph Waldo Emerson and Herman
Grimm*, ed. Frederick William Hollis (Boston and New York: Houghton, Mifflin, 1903), p.
85. Such assertions, however, do not preclude the possibility of significant unconscious
affinities.

traces of individual feeling disappear, a seeing that in registering the external world simultaneously informs it, so that all we see contains the element of pure consciousness (the consciousness of being) that is Mind. This pure consciousness possesses self-awareness, which represents the element of being. Thus the external world perceived by the self has its being within that which imparts to the Mind its own self-consciousness. On account of its primacy in perception, Emerson can speak of Mind as the "deep power in which we lie and whose beatitude is all accessible to us": to the extent that it gives all things their being, Mind is not merely passive but a genuine power. At the same time it is one "whose beatitude is all accessible to us"—that is, one whose supreme blessedness, which consists of endowing things with their being, must be "accessible" since the element by which it does so is precisely that of consciousness.

Characteristically, Emerson refers to the mind's power or capacity as a "beatitude." Such a term signifies not only a state of blessedness but also, and equally, that of an exalted happiness. In Emerson's thought, the bestowal of being upon things is not only an act of power but one accompanied by a consciousness whose feeling in so acting can only be described as one of happiness. If such happiness must be interpreted in a divine rather than human sense, we may nevertheless be said to partici-pate in it. That is the basis of what Emerson elsewhere describes as his "optimism." It is not a mood or attitude of hopefulness toward the outcome of things, but a profound sense of all things as coming into existence through the element of consciousness, where the energy of Mind that impels their coming-into-existence is itself one of joy. Such energy must be self-sufficing insofar as it creates out of its own element, perfect inasmuch as it brings things into existence, an act that is itself a kind of perfection (termed by Leibniz the inner entelechy of things).

But since according to Emerson the act of seeing and the thing seen, the subject and the object become one in the moment of apprehension, the coming-into-existence of external things through consciousness be-longs in part to *our* consciousness as well. We also, in putting off all traces of individual feeling and thought, can experience this blessedness, this beatitude that proceeds from the creative energeia of the Mind. That element of self-awareness of which our consciousness consists and which assumes the form of being in things presents itself as one in all high moments of intuition: at such moments, the self-conscious element of mind externalizes itself as "representation" while remaining in nature one and the same with mind itself.

For Emerson, as for Schleiermacher, perception of the sameness of the I and the world defines the nature and essence of true religion. It signifies the consciousness not only of a higher mode of being, but of that higher mode as something within ourselves. Only in this fashion does a true religious exaltation become possible, of the sort described by

Mme de Staël in her *De l'Allemagne* as implied in the original meaning of "enthusiasm": God in us. To see the God within ourselves is, according to Emerson, to see the Infinite. Such a quality (for it is of a quality rather than a being that Emerson speaks) cannot be defined by any specific attributes. Thus "an ignorant man thinks the divine wisdom is conspicuously shown in some fact or creature: a wise man sees that every fact contains the same." Hence "as we advance, every proposition, every action, every feeling runs out into the infinite." As a result, language loses its capacity to name or describe things. That capacity depends upon the differences between one thing and another. In the infinite that Emerson envisions, however, all things ultimately converge. The result is not simply loss of all specific or distinguishing characteristics but a Oneness whose element is that of pure Mind.

In the Emersonian nomenclature, Mind is identified with Soul on account of its spiritualizing function, by which it penetrates the opaque denseness of matter to reveal those luminous higher laws governing its operation. In these laws, Mind perceives a reflection of itself. Soul, like Mind, is but another name for the Infinite. If all things receive their being from the element of Mind, it cannot suffice merely to perceive these things themselves: "We see the world piece by piece, as the sun, the moon, the animal, the tree; but the Whole of which these are the shining parts is the Soul." According to Emerson, then, it becomes necessary to see in the finite a manifestation of the Infinite. In his *Über die Religion* Schleiermacher had similarly declared: "and so to accept each individual thing as a part of the Whole, everything finite as a representation of the Infinite, that is religion." For Emerson too, one may say, the perception of the finite as participating in the Infinite defines the essence of religion.

The perception of the Infinite is not an intellectual apprehension but a phenomenon of consciousness. As such, it comes to the soul only in those high moments of religious exaltation in which it experiences, through a kind of pure seeing, the element of consciousness as something that pervades all things. For an analogue to this perception, one may turn to the Schleiermacher of the *Monologen,* who says: "but so often as I turn my gaze upon my inner self, do I find myself in the realm of Eternity; I see the activity of the Spirit, that no world can change, and no time destroy, that activity which itself first creates world and time." I have sought to show how Schleiermacher attempts to establish, first in an intuitive fashion in *Über die Religion* and the *Monologen* and later in the more formal analysis of *Der christliche Glaube,* the creation through perception of an external world in consciousness. Emerson's *Nature* exhibits a similar process. Common to both authors is the notion of an inward-turning or introspective gaze that yields a moment of pure transparence. For readers of Emerson this appears most memorably in the celebrated "transparent eyeball" passage when, as Emerson observes, "crossing a bare common, in snow puddles, at twilight, under a clouded sky, without having in my thoughts any occurrence of special good fortune, I have enjoyed a perfect exhilaration" (*Coll. W.*, 1, 14).

At such moments, mind or consciousness becomes a medium of pure seeing. Here the religious element consists of the apprehension of the Infinite, which results from the transparent quality of the seeing, the loss of individual self-consciousness in the perception. Whereas in normal perception we see all things with reference to ourselves, such that the very representation of these things is shaped by the human nature of consciousness, in the transparent seeing of which Emerson now speaks, the mind experiences a loss of that individual and finite self-consciousness. As a result, what is normally determined by our human relations and affections—our perception, for instance, of a close friend—undergoes a transformation or "distancing" effect so that the very humanness of our friend—that which forms the basis of our relation to him and hence of our perception of him—now appears as something strange or foreign to us, precisely because we ourselves have lost the humanness that had formed our image of him.

In this transparent seeing, perception ceases to regard anything as a subject, so to speak—as that which gives form to perception, transforming it into representation. Instead, perception now becomes conscious of itself as an act of pure seeing and assimilates the thing seen to the act of seeing. Through such assimilation of the thing seen to the act of seeing (rather than the converse), mind experiences the transparency of things (their capacity for such assimilation) and hence the unbounded nature of perception itself, the absence of any opaque objects obstructing its field of vision. This unboundedness of perception constitutes the Infinite. For Emerson, as for the early Schleiermacher, the Infinite thus consists not of Being but of seeing, the element of pure consciousness. As such, it is no longer something external to us (a God outside us) but rather within ourselves.

In pure perception, God or the Infinite presents itself not as an object but as a quality, one that belongs to our own consciousness and that we apprehend each time we attain to a perception of the element of consciousness itself. As with Schleiermacher, then, religion for Emerson becomes something immediate, innate. For Schleiermacher, establishment of the immediacy or innate character of religion had represented a response to the atheism or skepticism of its "cultured despisers" (a similar motive appears in Theodore Parker). In Emerson, "secularization" of religion has proceeded much further. With the perspective of hindsight, it is possible to see Schleiermacher's description of religion in *Über die Religion* as a somewhat special presentation, addressed specifically to the sophisticated Romantic circle in which he moved during his first

Berlin period. His objective consists of finding a basis for religion so immediate that it becomes impossible to deny its validity. But one may, I think, rightfully ask if Schleiermacher (even at this stage) did not in fact already envision a religion possessing a more specific doctrinal or theological content—in other words, religion with a dogmatics (in Coleridge's notebooks during the period after his conversion to Trinitarianism there appears the plan of a similar scheme, featuring the religious feeling or impulse as the portico or outer courtyard of the temple of religion and the specific doctrine of Christ's redemptive role as the inner sanctum or holy of holies).

For Emerson, on the other hand (fostered by liberal Unitarian influences as opposed to the austere pietistic tendencies of Schleiermacher's Moravian background), the redefinition of religion in terms of feeling and consciousness is not merely the outer courtyard but the inner sanctum of true religion as well.[15] From almost the very beginning his conception of religion had been of what Schleiermacher called "a holy music" that "should accompany all acts of man" so that he will "do everything *with* religion, and not *from* religion." In this respect, Emerson's conception of the essential office of religion is one of a calling: it is that which summons us to a higher way of life, a more exalted mode of existence in which we shall live always with the consciousness we now attain only in our highest and most spiritual moments. As a state of consciousness, the content of such a religion could only be secular: in the feeling that animates and inspires us at those moments when we perceive the element of the eternal in pure consciousness, Emerson finds the essence of true religion. A feeling, a consciousness that becomes self-consciousness without the restriction of any trace of a finite or individual

---

[15]In effect, Emerson's Christology becomes simply another expression of that consciousness. In Emerson's Christological conceptions, one encounters the influence of Channing: "He [Jesus] was alive to the worth and greatness of the human soul. He looked through what men were, looked through the thick shades of their idolatry, superstition, and vice, and saw in every human being a spirit of divine origin and godlike faculties, which might be recovered from all its evil, which might become an image and a temple of God. . . . His greatness consists in the greatness and sublimity of the action which he communicates to the human soul" (*Works*, IV, 212–13).

A remarkable anticipation of both Emerson's Christology and theology occurs in Clement of Alexandria: "And if by godliness we understand the habit of mind which preserves the fitting attitude towards God, then the godly alone is dear to God. And such would be he who knows what is fitting both in theory and in life, as to how one should live who will one day become god, aye and is even now being made like to God" (*Stromateis* VII, ch. I, 3). And, with regard to Clement's conception of Christ: "He is all reason, all eye, all light from the Father, seeing all things, hearing all things, knowing all things, with power searching the powers" (*Stromateis* VII, ch. II, 5; both quotations from *Alexandrian Christianity*, ed. J. E. L. Oulton and Henry Chadwick [Philadelphia: Westminster Press, 1954], pp. 95, 96).

For Emerson's relation to Unitarianism in general, see David Robinson, *Apostle of Culture: Emerson as Preacher and Lecturer* (Philadelphia: Univ. of Pennsylvania Press, 1982), and Lawrence Buell, *Literary Transcendentalism: Style and Vision in the American Renaissance* (Ithaca, N.Y.: Cornell Univ. Press, 1973).

perspective, a pure seeing that exults in its assimilation of all external things into the act of seeing—this feeling or consciousness will have no object outside itself; it is, as Emerson says, "self-sufficing and perfect in every hour," and the meaning it imparts to the concept of the secular is precisely this, that a secularization of religion need not imply a banishing of the sacred, but that the element of the sacred must now be sought not in something external but within ourselves.

It is Emerson's unique contribution that, having situated the divine within the human, he should then renounce (unlike Carlyle or Novalis) the temptation to objectify it once more within the human, as what we term our human nature. Instead, by defining it as pure consciousness, he transforms it into a possibility that by its very existence elevates whoever approaches it to a more spiritual level. To recognize the possibility of a higher existence—that should be, according to Emerson, the basis of our attitude to the way we live. Since this higher existence consists of a purer or more universal form of consciousness, we attain it only by first grounding ourselves in the proper attitude toward it. For Emerson the highest moments of consciousness come only to those who shape their lives with regard to its possibility. Like Schleiermacher, he affirms the Lucan theology of "The kingdom of God is within you" (Luke 17:20–21) but, unlike his German counterpart, he defines it not as a condition we can realize or actualize at will but one whose very possibility we must first create within ourselves.[16]

Another, equally significant aspect of the affinity between these two thinkers deserves mention here. We have seen how Emerson's refusal to objectify the concept of God as something external to the self had led to the redefinition of the divine essence not as a being but as a quality, the infinite nature of pure consciousness that assimilates all objects of perception into the act of seeing itself. For the early Schleiermacher as well, the Infinite discloses itself in the inward-directed gaze of self-consciousness, as the realm of the Eternal. As with Emerson, the Infinite is thus an aspect of consciousness. It characterizes the nature of perception when the mind sees only itself, the seeing of pure seeing. Religion then becomes the mind's apprehension of the relation of finite to Infinite—which means, for Schleiermacher: relation of each individual objectification of consciousness in a finite object to the infinite nature of the consciousness that produces it.

Considered from a historical perspective, what is remarkable in the resemblance between Emerson and Schleiermacher is that they alone, among all those affected by the intellectual revolution spawned by the new philosophy in Germany and, more broadly, by the all-pervasive

---

[16]Cf. Porte, *Representative Man*, pp. 76–78. Conzelmann in *The Theology of St. Luke* offers a different reading of the Lucan message (pp. 120–25).

Romantic concern with the nature of consciousness and subjectivity, should have been brought by such influences to a conception of God and of religion that differs in significant respects from that of any of their contemporaries. To be sure, this resemblance owes less to the effects of any individual influence than to their inspiration by common Romantic sources. Specifically it consists of their having chosen, in preference to the pantheism adopted by Coleridge, Wordsworth, Schelling, and others, an introspective and self-reflexive form of religious consciousness based upon equation of the divine essence with a state or modification of feeling rather than with a being. By refusing to objectify the experience of the divine (through formulation of a specific concept of God) they establish a significant precedent. In retrospect, one may interpret it as a response to the pressure of secularization itself: the unique form of the solutions proposed by Emerson and Schleiermacher derives not only from the Romantic emphases upon subjectivity and consciousness, but equally, for these two figures, from the new attitude toward dogmatics in theology that we—only vaguely—characterize by the term *secularization*, signifying by it the tendency toward elimination of all truth that does not proceed from an inner or subjective self.

# 9    *Hawthorne*

Among the plays composed during his period of flirtation with the theater, Charles Lamb's most serious effort is, by all counts, *John Woodvil* (1798–1802). In this tragedy the elder son of Sir Walter Woodvil associates himself with friends on the opposite side of his father and brother in one of the civil wars so frequently dividing medieval England. A moment of weakness brought on by too much wine and his own false pride leads him to betray the hiding place of these relatives, who had concealed themselves in a nearby refuge at the enemy's occupation of the family estate. His disclosure results in their capture and execution. Later, realizing the enormity of his action, he suffers the agony of guilt and repentance. In the conclusion to act IV he recalls the moment when, torn by such feelings, he had experienced on entering a church that accession of grief which represents the inward assurance of forgiveness and purification:

> So entering in, not without fear,
> I past into the family pew,
> And covering up my eyes for shame,
> And deep perception of unworthiness,

Upon the little hassock knelt me down,
Where I so oft had kneel'd,
A docile infant by Sir Walter's side;
And, thinking so, I wept a second flood
More poignant than the first;
But afterwards was greatly comforted.
It seem'd, the guilt of blood was passing from me
Even in the act and agony of tears,
And all my sins forgiven. (*Works*, v, 176)

With this we may compare the scene in "Roger Malvin's Burial" in which Reuben Bourne, having mistaken his son Cyrus for an animal in the woods, shoots and kills him. Upon the site of the unburied Roger Malvin's bones—a tangible reminder of the vow he failed to keep—he discovers the body of his dead son:

> At that moment, the withered topmost bough of the oak loosened itself, in the stilly air, and fell in soft, light fragments upon the rock, upon the leaves, upon Reuben, upon his wife and child, and upon Roger Malvin's bones. Then Reuben's heart was stricken, and the tears gushed out like water from a rock. The vow that the wounded youth had made, the blighted man had come to redeem. His sin was expiated, the curse was gone from him; and, in the hour, when he had shed blood dearer to him than his own; a prayer, the first for years, went up to Heaven from the lips of Reuben Bourne. (Centenary, x, 360)

Characteristic of both scenes is the accession of grief expressing release of the heart's long-restrained emotions. At the same time, such grief forms the act of psychological purification, enabling the soul to experience the feeling of forgiveness, the sense that through its suffering it has somehow atoned for its sin and that, simultaneously, the "curse" that had descended upon it as a result is now taken away. For both Lamb and Hawthorne it is, doubtless, significant that such forgiveness comes about, not through the mediation of another (for example, a priest or minister) but through an inward movement of the individual mind and conscience.[1] Such forgiveness is not one of absolute

---

[1]Recognition of the affinity between Hawthorne and Lamb begins with Hawthorne's contemporaries. See Arlin Turner, *Nathaniel Hawthorne, A Biography* (New York: Oxford Univ. Press, 1980), pp. 172, 180, 204–5. On Hawthorne's concept of sin, cf. Nina Baym, *The Shape of Hawthorne's Career* (Ithaca, N.Y.: Cornell Univ. Press, 1976), p. 68. With regard to this concept, it is precisely Hawthorne's unique and defining characteristic to have sought to establish a fusion of the psychological with the theological. When the narrator of *The Scarlet Letter* exclaims of Dimmesdale, in the chapter entitled "The Interior of a Heart," "All that guilty sorrow, hidden from the world, whose great heart would have pitied and forgiven," he refers not to the Puritan community but to something like the collective consciousness of humanity which expresses, in its feeling of compassion, the nature and presence of the divine. Here, as elsewhere, Hawthorne's assertion is that sacrality pertains

fiat, pronounced by a sanctified individual, but rather of a psychological or inner nature. Its evidence is the release of long-drawn-out tensions experienced by the sufferer, as if the grief itself were a form of blessing, an indication that the aridity of the soul which typifies the psychological reality of a curse has now been lifted. In the scene in the garden several days after his mother Monica's death, the Augustine of the *Confessions* had undergone a similar experience.[2] For all three writers, the purificatory nature of the water shed as tears is unquestionably significant. We know that for Augustine the rite of baptism had possessed a profound psychological significance, the immersion in water representing an almost tangible purification of the soul. Similarly, Lamb emphasizes the function of tears as water that "washes away" the sin and guilt of crime ("And, thinking so, I wept a second flood"; "It seem'd, the guilt of blood was passing from me / Even in the act and agony of tears"). For Hawthorne, the purificatory nature of such tears is endowed with a psychologically miraculous quality—hence the allusion to Moses and the issuance of water from the rocks during the Hebrews' passage through the Sinai desert.

The element of the psychologically miraculous also associates itself for Hawthorne with another quasi-magical element: the return to the past, the period of innocence (in Lamb it assumes the form of a return to childhood itself). Through the expiation of sin by suffering and the

---

to the realm of the affections: the impulse toward forgiveness, which subsumes the knowledge of sin into itself, and the subjective communion born of compassion, which identifies the self with the sinful other, reveal a moral disposition toward the world that, in its psychological quality, participates in what Hawthorne calls the infinite. For Hawthorne, if the Godlike or sacred manifests itself in human life not by material means but through the affections, it then becomes, as it were, internalized within those affections.

We know of Hawthorne's lifelong interest in the writings of De Quincey, who, like Lamb, exemplifies the Romantic psychologization of sacrality (for Hawthorne and De Quincey, see e.g., James T. Fields, *Yesterdays with Authors* [Boston: Osgood, 1872], p. 62, and Caroline Ticknor, *Hawthorne and His Publisher* [Boston and New York: Houghton Mifflin, 1913], pp. 83–84). In his *Autobiography* De Quincey relates how, at Lady Carbery's instance, he applied himself to the interpretation of John the Baptist's call for "repentance": "In my opinion, the Greek word *metanoia* concealed a most profound meaning—a meaning of prodigious compass—which bore no allusion to any ideas whatever of repentance. The *meta* carried with it an emphatic expression of its original idea—the idea of transfer, of translation, of transformation; or, if we prefer a Grecian to a Roman apparelling, the idea of a *metamorphosis*. And this idea, to what is it applied? Upon what object is this idea of spiritual transfiguration made to bear? Simply upon the *noetic* or intellectual faculty—the faculty of shaping and conceiving things under their true relations. The holy herald of Christ, and Christ himself the finisher of prophecy, made proclamation alike of the same mysterious summons, as a baptism or rite of initiation—viz., Μετανοεῖτε. Henceforth transfigure your theory of moral truth; the old theory is laid aside as infinitely insufficient; a new and spiritual relation is established. *Metanoeite*—contemplate moral truth as radiating from a new centre: apprehend it under transfigured relations" (*Coll. Writings*, 1, 369). On μετάνοια, see Rudolf Bultmann, *Theology of the New Testament*, trans. Kendrick Grobel, vol. 2 (New York: Scribner's, 1955), p. 76 and note.

[2] For the influence of Augustine's *Confessions* upon Romantic literature, M. H. Abrams, *Natural Supernaturalism* (New York: Norton, 1971), pp. 83–90, 166–67.

feeling of release that comes with grief and the act of weeping, the sufferer is enabled to cross the threshold of time, returning through living memory to the period of innocence. In the form of the archetypal Romantic return to one's beginnings (for Hawthorne it consists of a return to the youthful moment in which innocence was first lost) the past is experienced as a state of psychological purity. By cleansing away the consciousness of guilt, it enables the mind to enter into and relive it once more, albeit with a higher consciousness. In part that consciousness includes a realization of the necessity that has brought the individual back to his past, and of the role of the psychological "return to the beginning" in the process of inner redemption.[3]

But the moment of the return signifies more than recovery of a past innocence. Associated with it is a form of blessing, of benediction. Hawthorne expresses it symbolically in the dissolution of the withered bough upon which Reuben Bourne had fastened his handkerchief as a sign of his pledge to return for Roger Malvin. The debris is said to fall in "soft, light fragments upon the rock, upon the leaves, upon Reuben, upon his wife and child, and upon Roger Malvin's bones"—the visible image of a descent of grace. The withered bough, forming part of the "natural supernaturalism" of the world of Reuben Bourne, bears upon itself the sign of the curse that overtakes him: in its transformation into a symbol of divine grace it exemplifies (as in Coleridge's "Rime of the Ancient Mariner") the visible manifestation, in the realm of Nature, of inner spiritual change.

We have seen how the theme of grace undergoes for Hawthorne a transposition from the theological to the psychological plane. Specifically, it depends upon the possibility of a return in memory to an "object of the affections in the past" (Melville). Through its return, the self is able to appropriate, so to speak, its past. For Lamb, these affections embrace their object most fully and most consciously only when it has become a thing of their past, hence something whose essence is now contained in memory—for the self is always separated from another by the abyss of

---

[3]For the Romantic notion of a return to one's beginnings, see Abrams, esp. chs. 3–5. Of course, Hawthorne's story also involves a "return to one's beginnings" in another, historical sense. On this issue cf. Michael Colacurcio, *The Province of Piety* (Cambridge: Harvard Univ. Press, 1984), pp. 122–23. In light of the ending of Hawthorne's tale, however, one might well wish to ask whether "historical" time (the time of the tale, the memory of that time in Reuben Bourne's consciousness) is not subsumed into a larger, more fundamental or archetypal pattern. Specifically, does not historical time here undergo a process of psychologization, such that its assimilation into consciousness creates the possibility of its "transfiguration" or redemption through a posterior action (the killing of Cyrus) that enables the recovery or *"re-experiencing"* of that first moment, bringing back into conscious memory what had been excluded from it, and, in so doing, imparting to it a new significance, one of fulfillment by identification of the son with the friend? For another reading of this tale, see Frederick C. Crews, *The Sins of the Fathers: Hawthorne's Psychological Themes* (New York: Oxford Univ. Press, 1966), pp. 81–92.

subjectivity. As Hölderlin says: "Und die Liebsten / Nah wohnen, ermattend auf / Getrenntesten Bergen" (And the most loved / Live near, growing exhausted upon / most separate mountains) (*S.W.*, II:1, 165). Even in the actual past there could not have been an identification of the self with an other. John Woodvil's affection for Sir Walter, as an experience of that past, could only have been passive ("A docile infant by Sir Walter's side"). Only through memory does the identification of the self with the other become possible. The locus of that identification is not the subjective nature of the self or other, but rather the image of that other contained within the mind. As a result affection becomes in essence identification with the memory: for the self can identify only with the memory, not with the object itself.

For Hawthorne, however, this identification of the self with its memory is precisely what proves problematic. In "Roger Malvin's Burial" the self's avoidance of the memory transforms it into the locus of guilt: the life of Reuben Bourne, following his desertion of Roger Malvin, subconsciously expresses, not the recurrent memory of that desertion, but the desire to avoid its recollection. Hence the necessity for his return to the site of the original event: only thus can a confrontation with the memory actually take place. In effect, the accidental murder of his son Cyrus represents a reenactment of the desertion (hence involuntary murder) of Roger Malvin. The experience of the second event makes possible an identification with the first in the realm of "lived experience." To achieve that identification, it was also necessary that the site of the second event should coincide with that of the first. Through the experience of Reuben Bourne, this site has become essentially a locus of the mind rather than a physical place. As a result of the accidental murder of Cyrus, the original event (desertion of Roger Malvin), which has become problematic as memory, is now revived in the only fashion possible: not as direct remembrance but vicariously, through the experience of its elements in the repetition. Through such repetition and the ensuing access of grief, it becomes possible for Reuben Bourne to accept the memory of Roger Malvin. Only by so doing does he render himself capable of "grace," which is in effect nothing other than the capacity for expressing affection.

From the standpoint of the pattern of a return to one's beginnings, the tale affirms a quintessentially Romantic theme: identification with an object of the affections which is possible only in memory, since only in memory does the self achieve union with its object. For Hawthorne, however, even the accession of memory does not come simply through conscious will: like the affections themselves, it belongs to that "warm mysteriousness" of human feelings whose occurrence must finally be seen as an experience of "grace."

For Hawthorne, as for Lamb, it is significant that sacrality is conferred not by any external act but through an inner, psychological experience. This consecration belongs to all feelings possessing a moral element. In his letter to Benjamin Bailey (Nov. 22, 1817) Keats had spoken of "the holiness of the Heart's affections." Already in *Corinne* Mme de Staël had recognized the new turn imparted by Romanticism to religion. Speaking of the sojourn of Corinne and Lord Nelvil in Rome, she says: "They proceeded first of all to the Vatican Museum, this palace of statues, where one sees the human figure divinised by paganism as the feelings of the soul now are by Christianity" (*O.C.*, viii, 292). In the conclusion to his *Biographia Literaria,* moreover, Coleridge offers an apology for religion of which a high point is his claim that "The sense, the inward feeling, in the soul of each Believer of its exceeding *desirableness*—the experience, that he *needs* something, joined with the strong Foretokening, that the Redemption and the Graces propounded to us in Christ are *what* he needs—this I hold to be the true FOUNDATION of the spiritual Edifice" (*C.W.*, vii:ii, 243).

These are, to be sure, but a few indications of the complex transformation of religious attitudes then in the making. A century and a half earlier Pascal had insisted on a belief in the miracles as the principal criterion of true Christianity. Early in the eighteenth century there is the controversy over the nature of Transubstantiation which forms one of the central preoccupations of Leibniz's last years. With the advent of Romanticism, a new, subjective element enters into the definition of true religion. This subjective emphasis owes its origin in part to the rise of epistemology as the new norm of philosophy after Descartes and Locke. Through the epistemological revolution, the question of the certainty and limits of human knowledge assumes a new prominence. The skeptical mode of inquiry, with its radical questioning of the possibility of all knowledge, was bound to assert its relevance to religious concerns as well. In his *Dialogues Concerning Natural Religion* Hume had undertaken to examine natural religion in light of the criteria of the new epistemology. The legacy of Humean skepticism consists of works like Kant's *Religion within the Limits of Reason Alone.* The end of the eighteenth century witnesses the inauguration, in Germany, of the Higher Criticism— the application of historical methods of interpretation to the Scriptures. The impact of all these approaches, obviously, is one that necessarily brings the evidence of the miracles, and hence of Christianity, more and more into question.

As a result, it becomes imperative to search for a new ground or basis of religion. That basis Romanticism professes to find in the self: since whatever originates in the self possesses an undeniable certainty, there can be no doubt of its validity. But affirmation of the subjective self as the foundation of the new religion implies a reinterpretation of traditional religious concepts. Thus redemption, represented by an earlier theology as an act accomplished by Christ's death on the cross, now becomes an inner process to be reenacted in the life of each individual. On account of the subjective nature and limits of the self, the presence of the divine can no longer be known with objective certainty. But the effect of these limits is only to redefine the nature of the divine presence itself, as something that is felt in or by means of actions and things—like a "holy music" that accompanies our acts, as Schleiermacher had called it. In its most extreme form it becomes pantheism, which emerges in its Romantic interpretation as a response to the radical uncertainty regarding religious knowledge. The desire to feel "God in us" ("enthusiasm") finds its confirmation in human feeling and aspiration: the consciousness of something sacred, of a moral element in the feelings themselves now becomes their seal of sacrality, which as such possesses the quality of a perceived or felt experience.

In this respect, consecration assumes a new and subjective significance. Whereas traditional theology had defined the process of consecration as one in which the presence of Christ (God in the world) is transmitted to an object (such as the Eucharistic host) through persons who have themselves received this presence via the apostolic succession from Christ himself, thus establishing an objective sacrality by which Christ becomes physically present in the consecrated object, Romanticism seeks to impart a subjective aura to the process, locating it in the suffusion of an action or choice by a moral element or feeling. Unlike the objective sacrality of earlier religion, then, the subjective form can be known only through consciousness. But since feeling is itself subjective (and hence, as Friedrich Jacobi points out, capable of immediate apprehension), its perception by such consciousness is sufficient.

With the entrance of a subjective element into Christian belief, the mode of perceiving religious truth alters as well. The new Romantic perspective is manifest in one of the most moving passages of Hawthorne's American Notebooks, the account of the death of his mother:

> At about five o'clock, I went to my mother's chamber, and was shocked to see such an alteration since my last visit, the day before yesterday. I love my mother; but there has been, ever since my boyhood, a sort of coldness of intercourse between us, such as is apt to come between persons of strong feelings, if they are not managed rightly. I did not expect to be much moved at the time—that is to say, not to feel any overpowering emotion struggling, just then—though I knew that I should deeply remember and regret her. Mrs. Dike was in the chamber. Louisa pointed to a chair near the bed; but I was moved to kneel down close by my mother, and take her hand. She knew me, but could only murmur a few indistinct words—among which I understood an injunction to take care of my sisters. Mrs. Dike left

the chamber, and then I found the tears slowly gathering in my eyes. I tried to keep them down; but it would not be—I kept filling up, till, for a few moments, I shook with sobs. For a long time, I knelt there, holding her hand; and surely it is the darkest hour I ever lived. Afterwards, I stood by the open window, and looked through the crevice of the curtain. The shouts, laughter, and cries of the two children had come up into the chamber, from the open air, making a strange contrast with the death-bed scene. And now, through the crevice of the curtain, I saw my little Una of the golden locks, looking very beautiful; and so full of spirit and life, that she was life itself. And then I looked at my poor dying mother; and seemed to see the whole of human existence at once, standing in the dusty midst of it. Oh what a mockery, if what I saw were all, —let the interval between extreme youth and dying age be filled up with what happiness it might! But God would not have made the close so dark and wretched, if there were nothing beyond; for then it would have been a fiend that created us, and measured out our existence, and not God. It would be something beyond wrong—it would be insult—to be thrust out of life into annihilation in this miserable way. So, out of the very bitterness of death, I gather the sweet assurance of a better state of being. (Centenary, VIII, 428–29)

In reading this passage one cannot, I think, but be moved by the strangeness of human nature, the alien aspect it sometimes assumes. The perception of that strangeness, so characteristic of an Augustine (which helps to explain his attractiveness to the Romantics), beginning with "I did not expect to be much moved at the time," records how an involuntary will (if I may make use of a somewhat paradoxical expression) asserts itself as something separate from the conscious mind, leading Hawthorne to kneel by the bedside and take his mother's hand, and later moving him to tears and finally even to sobbing (we recall again the scene of Augustine in the garden after the death of Monica). All of which Hawthorne describes, not as something he himself wills or does, but rather as something that happens to him: his only assertion of will— an ineffective one—being the attempt to check his tears. There is of course a partial veiling of the experience, to the extent that he does not reveal his thoughts at the moment of his most intense suffering, saying only that "surely it is the darkest hour I ever lived." At the same time one is also conscious of the extent to which the whole account is presented as subjective experience: the apparition of Hawthorne's daughter Una, "so full of spirit and life," is equated unqualifiedly with life itself, an equation possible only within the realm of subjective perception.

But the rendering of the events described here as subjective is significant not only in itself but because it establishes the nature of the conclusion that follows, that "God would not have made the close so dark and wretched, if there were nothing beyond." This argument—common especially in eighteenth-century apologetics—is arrived at, not through abstract reasoning, but a kind of lived experience or *erlebnis* for which thought represents but one element of a more fundamental or essential movement of feeling that conduces to the final conclusion. Like the aspiration of the soul in Coleridge, such feeling seems to call for a response, some answering grace from a higher power, and the perception of a divine providence in things, the inward consciousness of immortality which Hawthorne will bring up in another context, suffices to assure its own truth.

For Hawthorne, the perception of this kind of moral truth, which concerns the existence of a divine providence, is and must necessarily be subjective. Such perception, however, can only be achieved through lived experience: it is the experience of death (the death of his mother) which gives Hawthorne the "assurance of a better state of being." What is felt thereby as morally impossible (that there should be no higher existence after death) is then rejected, but only after the individual, through experiencing life itself, as well as death, has come to know that life in its nature and fullness. Only then can he discern its proper measure and value, and infer the moral necessity for an existence hereafter. Between the beautiful child and the dying mother Hawthorne had "seemed to see the whole of human existence at once." That apprehension of life is not allegorical, but one that takes in all its phenomenological fullness, the shouts and laughter of the children (with its incongruous contrast to the quiet solemnity of the death-bed scene, an incongruity that typifies the essence of life itself), the radiant apparition of the child, unconscious of her father's thoughts at that moment. From its own lived experience the mind can then assess the value of life: "Oh what a mockery, if what I saw were all, —let the interval between extreme youth and dying age be filled up with what happiness it might!"— an assessment that in turn produces the inner or subjective and moral necessity of Hawthorne's conclusion.

But if consecration and the presence of a divine providence in things are now felt as aspects of subjective experience, the same is no less true of the redemptive process. As for Coleridge, redemption for Hawthorne consists not of an objective external act but a state of mind. "Metanoia," John the Baptist had preached, and it is only appropriate that De Quincey should point out that the word means literally not "repentance" but "change of mind"—which is to say: of the attitudes that determine the way we live. Of this new Romantic concept of redemption it suffices to give one illustration, an incident recorded by Hawthorne in his English Notebooks and later transferred to *Our Old Home*, the description of his encounter with a diseased child in an English almshouse who, putting itself directly before him, had "held forth its arms, mutely insisting on being taken up":

It said not a word, being perhaps underwitted and incapable of prattle. But it smiled up in his face—a sort of woeful gleam was that smile, through the sickly blotches that covered its features—and found means to express such a perfect confidence that it was going to be fondled and made much of, that there was no possibility in a human heart of baulking its expectation. It was as if God had promised the poor child this favor on behalf of that individual, and he was bound to fulfil the contract, or else no longer call himself a man among men. Nevertheless, it could be no easy thing for him to do, he being a person burthened with more than an Englishman's customary reserve, shy of actual contact with human beings, afflicted with a peculiar distaste for whatever was ugly, and, furthermore, accustomed to that habit of observation from an insulated stand-point which is said (but, I hope, erroneously) to have the tendency of putting ice into the blood.

So I watched the struggle in his mind with a good deal of interest, and am seriously of opinion that he did an heroic act, and effected more than he dreamed of towards his final salvation, when he took up the loathsome child and caressed it as tenderly as if he had been its father. To be sure, we all smiled at him, at the time, but doubtless would have acted pretty much the same in a similar stress of circumstances. The child, at any rate, appeared to be satisfied with his behavior; for when he had held it a considerable time, and set it down, it still favored him with its company, keeping fast hold of his forefinger till we reached the confines of the place. And on our return through the court-yard, after visiting another part of the establishment, here again was this same little Wretchedness waiting for its victim, with a smile of joyful, and yet dull recognition about its scabby mouth and in its rheumy eyes. No doubt, the child's mission in reference to our friend was to remind him that he was responsible, in his degree, for all the sufferings and misdemeanors of the world in which he lived, and was not entitled to look upon a particle of its dark calamity as if it were none of his concern; the offspring of a brother's iniquity being his own blood-relation, and the guilt, likewise, a burthen on him, unless he expiated it by better deeds. (Centenary, v, 300–301)

Like Dostoyevsky almost twenty years later in *The Brothers Karamazov,* Hawthorne presents here the notion of a collective guilt and responsibility for the sufferings and sins of each and every individual. This notion is itself based upon a new concept of humanity, one that differs from the eighteenth-century idea of the human and of *Humanität* but also from Victor Hugo's "ocean of humanity" on account of the abyss of subjectivity that divides each human consciousness from all others.

The idea of humanity as a secular concept, which begins to assume significance in the eighteenth century (*Menschengeschlechts* in Herder and Lessing, not *Humanität*—to which Herder and Kant, incidentally, ascribe very different meanings), had come for Herder to be associated with forces or energies (*organische Kräfte*), but not to the extent of seeing humanity as a concentration of such forces,—in other words, as a source of vital energy. Nor was this step achieved with the Romantic concept of "the people" (Michelet), the "ocean of humanity" described by Hugo (*O.C.*, III, 1002). The concept of Hugo and Michelet, which anticipates the notion of "the masses" and which through the loss of individuality sought by Romantic antiselfconsciousness had attempted to identify with the infinite, had, through its emphasis upon the contrast between the individual and the mass, overlooked in large part the earlier perception of "forces." By contrast, the later concept of humanity held by Hawthorne and Dostoyevsky translates the various human forces that had come through Romantic *Naturphilosophie* on the one hand and a French tradition (Balzac) on the other to be associated with physical forces (magnetism, electricity, and so forth) as psychological forces. These merge in a single basic essence of spiritual energy.

For Hawthorne the element that fuses individuals into a collective humanity subsists not in their common nature (with its postulation of a metaphysical oneness) but rather in the psychological agency of the affections. If affection signifies participation in the life of others, its relation of each individual to another ultimately results in the formation of a collective whole. He who severs all ties with others loses thereby all contact with "life" (the emotional life of humanity), ceasing in the highest sense to live. Through the medium of the affections (anticipated by the theory of "elective affinities") each individual is ultimately related to all others: in the collective whole represented by humanity, the suffering or injury that affects one individual makes itself felt, as through a conducting medium, by all the others. Guilt arises from the failure while participating in this nexus of affection to respond to the obligations of such a feeling, by alleviating the suffering that affects any other member of the whole. We only live truly in that affection if we respond to the needs of the life in which we participate. But since this "life" (the totality of human affections) encompasses all of humanity, we must dedicate ourselves to alleviating all suffering. To do otherwise, according to Hawthorne, is to renounce in some measure our participation in that affection, and hence in life itself.

By means of the element of affection, Hawthorne presents a divinization of humanity which replaces in effect the earlier form of consecration embodied in such concepts as Transubstantiation. But if humanity is now perceived as sacred on account of its participation in the life of the affections, that same participation can also represent, through the spiritual infinitude of such feelings, a fulfillment of the Romantic quest: the merging of the individual self with the infinite, the attainment of the absolute.

Equally significant in the above passage is the inward conflict described by Hawthorne, one that, as is clear from the English Notebooks, possesses an autobiographical relevance. Assuredly the external act that expresses its outcome is, in a sense, of only slight importance: a stranger, a visitor to an English alms-house, caresses a diseased and half-idiotic child in the children's ward. On the psychological plane, nevertheless, it necessitates for Hawthorne a kind of "metanoia," a change in mind, in his whole attitude toward things. "Accustomed to that habit of observation from an insulated stand-point which is said . . . to have the tendency of putting ice into the blood," he had had to learn the lesson of compassion and sympathy. Like Clifford in *The House of the Seven Gables,* who feels the impulse to plunge from the balcony of his house into the midst of the procession below, observing that, had he been able to do so, "it would have made me another man," Hawthorne himself finds in the shock of contact with humanity a saving grace, and in the feeling that impels him to take up the child, a force to overcome his instinctive weakness that advances the "metanoia" or change in mind that is the psychological reality behind his redemption. Thus he is "seriously of opinion that he did an heroic act, and effected more than he dreamed of towards his final salvation, when he took up the loathsome child and caressed it as tenderly as if he had been its father." If such salvation consists in bringing about a "metanoia," that change, in turn, can itself come about only through repeated fulfillment of a moral impulse, until what had once been done by conscious and anguished choice becomes, as it were, part of the individual's own nature.

From its earliest phase, Romanticism had affirmed the life of the emotions. Subsequently the affections in particular are endowed with an aura of sacredness. Similarly, in *The Scarlet Letter,* during their meeting in the forest, Hester can say to Dimmesdale: "What we did had a consecration of its own. We felt it so! We said so to each other! Hast thou forgotten it?" To which Dimmesdale, after attempting to demur, replies: "No; I have not forgotten!" (Centenary, I, 195). Even for Hester, significantly, the sacred quality that belongs to their union must not be confused with that possessed by others. Inseparably associated with it is the consciousness of sin, a concept that—like that of the sacredness of the affections—must here be understood in a psychological rather than theological sense. Its meaning is clarified through Dimmesdale's assertion that Chillingworth has "violated, in cold blood, the sanctity of a human heart." He is responsible for "the horrible ugliness of this exposure of a sick and guilty heart to the very eye that would gloat over it" (p. 194). In this respect, the relation between Dimmesdale and Chillingworth bears a resemblance to that between Falkland and the protagonist of Godwin's *Caleb Williams.* As a result of his attachment to Falkland as a secretary, Caleb Williams is able to observe the other's secret remorse. Through his efforts to trace it to its source, he discovers Falkland's secret murder of a neighboring squire who had insulted him during a brawl. At Falkland's trial, which finally takes place at the end of the novel, Caleb confesses his own sin: like Chillingworth (though innocently) he has "violated the sanctity of a human heart."

For both Hawthorne and Godwin, such sanctity proceeds from the fact that knowledge of another's innermost thoughts and feelings is tantamount to possession of that individual's very self, insofar as it endows the knower with power to produce in the mind of his subject feelings and impulses over which the latter has no control. The "violation of the sanctity of a human heart," immoral in itself since it occurs against the will of its object, becomes so in the extreme when the knower refuses to identify his own self with that of the other whom he now possesses: by taking away the other's relation to his inner self, yet refusing to assume that relation himself, he produces in effect a loss of self. Its visible expression is the loss of will in the other (a process we witness not only in Dimmesdale but also in the story of Alice Pyncheon in *The House of the Seven Gables*). Unlike the loss of self which occurs in positive forms of the Romantic desire for antiselfconsciousness, this loss does not proceed from conscious will but rather (in the case of Dimmesdale and Alice Pyncheon) against that will. Hence, where the willed loss of self (its submission to another) allows the life of that self (that is, the will) to continue in another, occurrence of this process without or against that will leads precisely to a loss of life or the self.

But if the nature of Chillingworth's crime against Dimmesdale is one of violating "the sanctity of a human heart," the same is no less true of the adulterous relation between the minister and Hester Prynne. In the interview between Hester and Chillingworth in the prison-house, Hawthorne makes use of their colloquy to place the Romantic theme of the "holiness of the Heart's affections" in a different and revealing perspective. Here Chillingworth discloses the motive that had induced him to marriage, which is not so much affection but rather the need for affection: "My heart was a habitation large enough for many guests, but lonely and chill, and without a household fire. I longed to kindle one!" The affection he seeks however is not one *from* another being but one which that other will engender *in* him as the object of his own feelings: "And so, Hester, I drew thee into my heart, into its innermost chamber, and sought to warm thee by the warmth which thy presence made there!" (Centenary, I, 74). That "presence" is not Hester herself but the heart's image of her, Hester as an object, rather than source, of the affections. Through her adultery, Hester violates—like Chillingworth himself—the "sanctity of a human heart" by her profanation of that heart's image, the object in the mind with which it associates its deepest affections. What Hester denies Chillingworth is thus not only her affections (a denial he seems willing enough to excuse) but the possibility of his own affection for her, the act of volition by which the self seeks to live in another by assimilating that other into itself, in the form of a psychological "presence."

Here we encounter once more the Romantic concept of the self as a creative and subjective nature, in terms of the affections. For Hawthorne, on account of his belief in the subjective abyss separating each individual from every other, it could not be literally possible to assimilate another's being or soul into oneself. What the mind assimilates is the image of that other (here, Chillingworth's image of Hester Prynne). As an object of the affections rather than perception, this image must be created by the mind (or heart) itself: its element is precisely the same as that of the mind that forms it. It is this image created by the mind which, Chillingworth hopes, the other will in turn perceive and respond to, realizing it has been created by the mind or heart out of its own affections (hence his locution "sought to warm *thee* by the warmth which *thy* presence made there!"). On account of its origin, the heart's image partakes of the sanctity of the heart itself. Chillingworth implies this when he says to Hester: "And so, Hester, I drew thee into my heart, into its innermost chamber." In her subsequent admission she in turn recognizes the nature and extent of her crime: "I have greatly wronged thee."

The perception of her sin (she perceives it as a sin against Chillingworth rather than society) remains with Hester throughout the novel (cf. "She knew that her deed had been evil," Centenary, 1, 89; "Here had been her sin," p. 263). But it does not affect the nature of her love for Dimmesdale, which retains from first to last its sacred and inviolable quality. That sacredness depends not upon any external circumstances but upon the inner and willed surrender of self to the being one loves, a surrender that, as the exposure of one's innermost feelings places the self voluntarily within the power of the other, allows one to be "possessed" by that other. Through the voluntary nature of the exposure, "possession" of the self by the beloved becomes in turn a pledge on his or her part of acceptance of the trust implied in such a surrender. Such trust allows both Dimmesdale and Hester to expect fulfillment of the weightiest and most solemn obligations from each other: witness Hester's desperate appeal at the Governor's mansion to Dimmesdale as one who "hadst charge of my soul" and who "knowest what is in my heart" as she pleads with the magistrates to retain custody of her child. It constitutes the one occasion in which, conscious of the sacred trust implied in their affection, she dares to demand something from him. But Dimmesdale also, in their meeting in the forest, on hearing that Chillingworth, his trusted physician and fellow inmate, is actually her husband and his deadliest enemy, can be moved to the most passionate anger only because of his consciousness of the trust he vouchsafed to Hester. That trust requires even that she break her oath of secrecy to Chillingworth, on account of the preciousness of her charge (the life of Dimmesdale's soul).

Its complex theme leads Hawthorne's novel to affirm simultaneously both the sinfulness of Hester's adulterous relationship and the sacredness of the affections from which it was engendered. Hawthorne here emerges as profoundly cognizant of the individual self's development in and through time. The irrevocable nature of an immoral act must not impede the soul's progressive spiritualization through the act's consequences. Conversely, the individual must always remain conscious of his or her past and the obligations that ensue from it. Concerning Dimmesdale's relationship with Hester, Hawthorne observes: "But this had been a sin of passion, not of principle, nor even purpose" (Centenary, 1, 200). Through Dimmesdale's fear, it remains concealed from the world, "whose great heart would have pitied and forgiven" (p. 139). In the world of *The Scarlet Letter* forgiveness must be understood as a development in the subjective relation between two beings. If sin consists of violating the sacred ties of humanity and affection, forgiveness is affection that assimilates that violation without surrendering either its possession of the sinner as an object of its affections nor the pledge by which it surrenders itself to that other. Thus Hester can bear the frown of the world (its refusal to forgive) and even of Heaven (which possesses for her only a remote and abstract existence) but not that of Dimmesdale— that would imply sundering the pledge by which she surrendered her self to him, hence violating or profaning her innermost nature, as well as his pledge to her, by which she retains him in her affections.

Through these affections arises the possibility of a development or transformation of her inner nature. The famous scene of her interview with Dimmesdale in the forest visibly depicts it:

> The stigma gone, Hester heaved a long, deep sigh, in which the burden of shame and anguish departed from her spirit. O exquisite relief! She had not known the weight, until she felt the freedom! By another impulse, she took off the formal cap that confined her hair; and down it fell upon her shoulders, dark and rich, with at once a shadow and a light in its abundance, and imparting the charm of softness to her features. There played around her mouth, and beamed out of her eyes, a radiant and tender smile, that seemed gushing from the very heart of womanhood. A crimson flush was glowing on her cheek, that had been long so pale. Her sex, her youth, and the whole richness of her beauty, came back from what men call the irrevocable past, and clustered themselves, with her maiden hope, and a happiness before unknown, within the magic circle of this hour. (Centenary, 1, 202)

Her transformation may be defined as one of successive accretions of consciousness. It begins with release from the "burden of shame and anguish" represented by the letter. Henceforth the perspective subtly modulates from external to internal. With the exclamation "O exquisite relief!" the narrative enters into Hester's own consciousness as it realizes the weight of the burden it has carried. The casting-off of the letter also allows Hester a deeper apprehension than any previously possible of its actual meaning. In what follows, she progresses to a realization of what the letter had attempted to deny: the sacredness of her affection for Dimmesdale, which must be distinguished from the sinfulness of her adultery and which she can now for the first time since their separation fully affirm to herself and to him. In realizing the sacredness of their affection, she can also affirm everything in her nature that had made it possible: her physical beauty, her sex, her emotional radiance, and the impulses it expresses. Through the introduction of a special narrative perspective that employs subjective emotional colorations (the "dark and rich" quality of her hair and its "abundance," the "charm of softness" in her features), comparison with the past from a standpoint of personal reflection (her cheek, "that had been long so pale"), and the experience of inner impulses (the smile "that seemed gushing from the very heart of womanhood"—a self-affirmation of her womanly nature), Hawthorne presents Hester, as it were, seeing herself as from an external perspective. The perspective is in effect that of Dimmesdale, within whom she situates herself through her affection. It is her affection, moreover, and not her innate rights or privileges as an individual being, that justifies the affirmation of her beauty. On this point Hawthorne differs from the Transcendentalist belief in developing one's natural capacities for their own sake. For Hawthorne, self-development is grounded in, and justified by, our relation to another (rather than to ourselves), finding its fulfillment in and for the sake of that other.

But there abides also in Hawthorne's idea of self-development a magical aura not found in Transcendentalism, one based upon the self's relation to its past and its perception of it through the medium of a higher consciousness. When the narrator says of Hester that "her sex, her youth, and the whole richness of her beauty, came back from what men call the irrevocable past," the statement signalizes a fundamental shift in perspective. Hester's recapturing of her past is effected not by the preserving memory but by a realization of the significance or meaning of that past. Her relationship with Dimmesdale can now be affirmed in a context other than the moralistic one. Its new interpretation is established by recognition of the sacredness of their affection. As a result of affirming her love for him, Hester renews her past through memory while at the same time seeing in it a higher possibility, "a happiness before unknown" which proceeds from experiencing once more the sanctity of her ties to Dimmesdale.

The Romantic theme of a return to the beginning with a higher consciousness receives in Hawthorne's novel one last permutation, which permits him to define his relation to Romantic tradition. At the very end of *The Scarlet Letter* Hester, after an absence of many years, returns to the Puritan colony. The narrator explains: "Here had been her sin; here, her sorrow; and here was yet to be her penitence" (Centenary, 1, 263). Whereas at an earlier stage it had been necessary for her to affirm her affection for Dimmesdale through a return to the past, she now does so to effect a reconciliation with its adulterous aspect through penance. For Hawthorne, then, the return to the beginning signifies something more than the Romantic recovery of an earlier spiritual radiance: it emerges rather as an affirmation of the whole process of the self's development, one that sees even in its immoral acts possibilities for the evolution of that higher consciousness that is for Hawthorne the essence of spiritualization.

# 10    *Melville*

## "Balzac visionnaire"

Near the beginning of Henry James's *The Ambassadors,* Lambert Strether, on arriving at his hotel in Chester, makes the acquaintance of Maria Gostrey. Taking the card he gives her, she pronounces his full name and observes that she likes it. "Particularly the Lewis Lambert. It's the name of a novel of Balzac's." "Oh I know that!" says Strether. "But the novel's an awfully bad one," she continues. To which Strether, smiling, replies: "I know that too."

With this judgment we may compare a comment from James's early book on Hawthorne. In speaking of *The Scarlet Letter,* James had presumed to criticize what he describes as Hawthorne's "extreme predilection for a small number of vague ideas which are represented by such terms as 'sphere' and 'sympathies.'" Of this failing he remarks: "Hawthorne makes too liberal a use of these two substantives; it is the solitary defect of his style; and it counts as a defect partly because the words in question are a sort of specialty with certain writers immeasurably inferior to himself" (*Hawthorne,* pp. 119–20). Yet such usages may also be found in Honoré de Balzac, whom James had elsewhere called "the father of us all" (*The Question of Our Speech,* p. 67). Pervading the whole of the *Comédie humaine* and especially the segment styled the *Études philosophiques* is a system that both assimilates and develops these concepts.

How, then, may we explain the contradiction between James's appreciation of Balzac and his dismissal of these confused and misguided tendencies? There have always been at least two widely divergent interpretations of Balzac. For some, including James, he is the founder and representative par excellence of Realism, an inexhaustible source of countless insights into the art of fiction. For others, he has seemed a very different figure, a visionary striving to express the transcendence of the spiritual over the material and, simultaneously, the encompassing of the two into a single, all-embracing Unity. Earlier we have seen instances of Balzac's affinity with Hawthorne, specifically on the theme of vitalism and (as I will try to show in more detail later) the quest for the absolute. But it is his relation to Melville which draws upon his most essential aspects. In exploring that relation, it becomes necessary to formulate an interpretation of his *oeuvre* as a whole, and specifically to examine the much-discussed question of his romanticism.

Speaking of Balzac in an essay on Gautier, Baudelaire observes: "I have more than once been surprised that the great glory of Balzac has been to have passed for an observer; it had always seemed to me that his principal merit was to be a seer [*visionnaire*], and a passionate one. All his characters are endowed with the vital ardor with which he himself was animated. All his fictions are as deeply colored as dreams. From the summit of the aristocracy to the depths of the masses, all the actors of his *Comédie* are more avid for life, more active and cunning in the struggle, more patient in misfortune, more greedy in pleasure, more angelic in devotion, than the comedy of the real world shows them to us. In brief, each one, in Balzac, even the porteresses, has genius. All the souls are firearms charged with will up to the muzzle. It is indeed Balzac himself. And since all the beings of the external world offered themselves to the eye of his mind in powerful relief and with an arresting grimace, he has made his figures convulse themselves; he has darkened their shadows and brightened their lights. His prodigious taste for detail, springing from an immoderate ambition to see everything, to make everything be seen, to divine everything, to make everything be divined, obliged him moreover to mark the principal lines with greater force, in order to save the perspective of the whole" (*O.C.*, II, 120).

Several decades later, a similar view of Balzac is expressed in the realm of art. For his statue of the French novelist, Rodin had immersed himself in Balzac's fictional world, his letters, his milieu, the portraits and daguerrotypes, the accounts handed down by contemporaries. Out of these emerged, finally, a Balzac remarkably different from the image enshrined by Zola and the reigning school of Naturalism. Rodin's Balzac joins the visionary depicted by Baudelaire and by Balzac's own friends and contemporaries. Of this statue, Rilke, who had worked during the period of its composition as Rodin's secretary, writes: "That was Balzac in the fertility of his abundance, the founder of generations, the squanderer of destinies. That was the man whose eye needed no objects; whose glance would have furnished the world had it been empty. That was the man who thought to become rich through legendary silver-mines and happy in a foreign love. That was Creation itself, assuming the figure of Balzac that it might appear in visible form; the presumption, the arrogance, the ecstasy, the intoxication of creation. The head, thrown back, crowned this figure like those spheres which dance upon the jets of fountains. All heaviness had become light and rose and fell."[1]

To an increasing extent, the interpretation of Balzac expressed by these intuitive perceptions has begun to prevail, I believe, in the Balzac criticism.[2] Such perceptions make it possible in turn to perceive Balzac's deep affinities with the spirit and thought of European Romanticism.[3] The classification of Balzac as a Romantic is incorrect if we think of French Romanticism strictly in terms of the beliefs and attitudes of a few figures like Mme de Staël, Benjamin Constant, Chateaubriand, and Lamartine. Like Stendhal, Balzac belongs to the Romanticism of a later

[1] Rainer Maria Rilke, *Selected Works*, vol. i, trans. G. Craig Houston (New York: New Directions, 1967), p. 133.

[2] See, e.g., E. R. Curtius, *Balzac*, 2d ed. (Bern: A. Francke, 1951); Albert Béguin, *Balzac lu et relu* (Paris: Seuil, 1965), containing his *Balzac visionnaire*—from which I draw the title for this section; and, more recently, P.-G. Castex's general introduction to the new Pléiade edition of *La Comédie humaine*. Significantly, many of the *Études philosophiques* have in recent years had individual studies devoted to them: see, in addition to those mentioned in following notes, Madeleine Fargeaud, *Balzac et "La Recherche de l'Absolu"* (Paris: Hachette, 1968).

[3] See on this subject René Wellek, "The Concept of Romanticism in Literary History," rpt. in Wellek, *Concepts of Criticism*, ed. Stephen G. Nichols, Jr. (New Haven: Yale Univ. Press, 1963), pp. 174–75. Also, Herbert J. Hunt, *Honoré de Balzac: A Biography* (London: Athlone Press, 1957), pp. 28–29. Wellek's essay constitutes a rejoinder to Arthur O. Lovejoy's well-known position piece, "On the Discrimination of Romanticisms," rpt. in *Essays in the History of Ideas* (Baltimore: Johns Hopkins Univ. Press, 1948), pp. 228–53. Of Balzac specifically, Wellek observes: "Balzac is not usually considered a romantic and he may not be one in many aspects of his stupendous work. But E. R. Curtius has rightly stressed an aspect which must have struck every reader of the *Human Comedy*—Balzac's interest in magic and the occult. . . . Though wide stretches of Balzac's work may not show it, he was inspired by a peculiar type of romantic metaphysics, physics, or energetics, with its supposed laws of compensations, polarities, fluids, etc." (pp. 174–75). With regard to the more general question of defining Romanticism, the issue is somewhat less clear; see, on this matter, Geoffrey Hartman, "Romanticism and Anti-Self-Consciousness" in *Beyond Formalism: Literary Essays 1958–1970* (New Haven: Yale Univ. Press, 1970), pp. 298–310. I cannot believe that it is of much significance merely to observe that certain features of Romanticism are to be found in the eighteenth century, or specifically, what we now call pre-Romanticism. That merely demonstrates the continuity of one epoch with another; continuity is not the same thing as identity. Perhaps in treatment of a given period, less emphasis should be placed upon certain concepts than upon their gradual transformation or development. With the Romantic concept of symbolism, for instance, the American Renaissance brings about crucial changes. We might say that what occurs is a psychologization of symbolism, whose result is to transform the symbol from a revelation of the divine essence to a revelation of the nature of the self. In the process, however, the self absorbs the sacrality of the divine. The internalization or absorption of such sacrality by the self defines the development as Romantic; in the later eighteenth century the formally similar process of the breakdown of allegory had led to a plurality of allegories or myths (e.g., in Blake). What distinguishes the Romantic development is its apparent desire to avoid the dispersion of symbolic significance into formal pluralism—hence the concentration into a new content, i.e., that of the self.

generation. As Stendhal himself demonstrates, such Romanticism is perfectly compatible with realism in fiction. The emergence of realism out of a later phase of Romanticism points to a development and transformation of certain fundamental Romantic impulses. For Romanticism, realism had signified a representation of the principle of life, of a vital or organic energy, as in Balzac's *Comédie humaine*. At that stage, it represents merely a concept within a larger system seeking to explain the relation of the spiritual to the material. Later, through autonomous development, Realism is transformed into a representation of the phenomenology of life, and ultimately—as in the later James—into a representation of life as subjective consciousness and its impressions.

Balzac's romanticism manifests itself above all in two recurrent themes that pervade the whole of the *Comédie humaine:* the relation of thought to Nature (the external world, the realm of phenomena), and the transcendence of spirit over matter. In a sense, these are but two aspects of a single subject. Yet they give rise in Balzac to two highly different but complementary modes of thought, exemplified respectively in *Louis Lambert* and *Séraphîta:* analysis (the mode of science) and intuitive or mystical apprehension (the mode of religion).

In terms of analysis, Balzac's *oeuvre* can be described as an attempt to master and, as it were, possess the world through theory or system. For Balzac, the world itself is but a system of energy, giving rise constantly to new manifestations and expressions.[4] To grasp the laws that govern that system from within is tantamount to possessing it. In the *Comédie humaine* Balzac confers the desire that animates him upon some of his characters: Vautrin the arch-criminal, who appears in various disguises to govern the lives of his "courtisanes" such as Lucien and Esther Gobseck, or, on the intellectual plane, Louis Lambert, whose *Traité de la volonté* embodies Balzac's own beliefs and inspirations. Through the desire to master the world by means of theory or system, through his belief in the sufficiency of theory to explain the conduct of all natural phenomena and, even more, to grasp the inner forces behind them, Balzac displays his affinity not only with Romantic science but with a Faustian aspiration to which Romantic literature had given enduring expression. Since thought itself in his view represents but a higher form of energy, its effort to comprehend the world signifies, in effect, a joining or identification of like with like. In addition, if thought participates in the same energy that animates natural forms, the laws of nature will themselves be revealed explicitly to the mind. For Balzac, a system is thus something more than merely a human representation of natural processes: since Nature itself is but a system of energy, such a theory expresses the very essence of Nature.

[4]On Balzac's system or theory of energy, see Curtius, *Balzac*, pp. 64, 66–67, 68.

Balzac's romantic aspect appears not only in his idea of the relation between theory or system and Nature but also, and equally, in a spiritualism that is something more, and something other, than orthodox religion. Like Emerson, Friedrich Schlegel, and others, he had felt the attractions of mysticism, of Swedenborg, Jakob Boehme, and Saint-Martin. In a letter to Mme Hanska he writes: "You know what my religions are. I am not at all orthodox and do not at all believe in the Roman [Catholic] Church. I think that, if there is a scheme worthy of it, it consists of the human transformations which make the individual or being proceed toward the unknown regions. That is the faith of superior creations. Swedenborgianism, which is only a repetition in the christian sense of ancient ideas, is my religion, with the addition I make of the incomprehensibility of God."[5] Such views comprise a secular religion. They permit a glimpse of the link between Balzac and Shelley, as well as with Keats, who professes a belief in the "grand march of Intellect," or Emerson. Through these figures, the nineteenth-century faith in the ideal of progress appears in its original, religious form: as a gradual spiritualization of humanity, an ascension to higher and higher modes of existence.

For the mature Balzac (of *Séraphîta* and the works from 1835 on), such spiritualization is to be achieved only through renunciation of the things of the world. Spirit is set over against matter as that which transcends it, a theme expressed not only in *Louis Lambert* and *Séraphîta* but also in *Le Lys dans la vallée* and, under a different guise, in works like *Le Médecin de campagne*. In affirming such beliefs, Balzac belongs to a later Romantic phase, like the mature Shelley or the Coleridge of the "Trinitarian" period. Like these figures, Balzac rejects the materialism of the preceding age, the "counting-house philosophy of Malthus and Paley." The affinities between his spiritualism and the Christianity of preceding centuries should not however obscure the essentially Romantic element of his religion, which gives it its significance for Melville, and especially for *Billy Budd*. In both its mystical and secular aspects, Balzac's religion is above all one of humanity. It sees in the development of the human faculties themselves the form of humanity's progressive spiritualization.

## The *Théorie de la volonté*

In his last years Melville appears to have "devoted much time to his collection of works by and about Balzac."[6] What attracted him to the

---

[5] Quoted from Henri Evans, *Louis Lambert et la philosophie de Balzac* (Paris: Corti, 1951), p. 209.

[6] Merton M. Sealts, Jr., *Melville's Reading: A Check-List of Books Owned and Borrowed* (Madison: Univ. of Wisconsin Press, 1966), p. 24. According to Sealts's catalogue, Melville

great French author? Assuredly not the depiction of French society that forms the ostensible subject of the *Comédie humaine* and that inspires the techniques of the realistic and naturalistic novel. From the social concerns that occupy most of the novels, one section of the work stands somewhat apart: the *Études philosophiques*. As E. R. Curtius remarks, it "looms over the massif of the *Études de Moeurs* like the interpretation over the realm of facts."[7] In it Balzac sets forth explicitly his theory of the relationship between thought and Nature, spirit and matter. Of particular significance for his relation to Melville is his theory of the Will. We find it expounded by two figures bearing marked resemblances to Balzac himself: Louis Lambert and Raphaël de Valentin. To each of these Balzac ascribes a treatise on the Will, whose contents furnish a suggestion of the work he himself once planned to write. In *La Peau de chagrin* Foedora asks Raphaël for an explanation of his theory. He tells her that "the human will [is] a material force similar to vapor; that, in the moral world, nothing [resists] this power when a man habituates himself to concentrating it, to handling the sum, to directing constantly upon souls the projection of this fluid mass; that this man can at will modify everything with respect to humanity, even the absolute laws of nature" (*La Comédie humaine,* x, 149–50). In *Louis Lambert,* similarly, the protagonist writes: "The Will is a fluid, an attribute of every being endowed with movement. Hence the innumerable forms which the ANIMAL affects, and which are the effects of its combination with SUBSTANCE" (xi, 685).[8]

With these utterances we may compare Melville's description of Claggart in *Billy Budd:* "With no power to annul the elemental evil in him, though readily enough he could hide it; apprehending the good, but powerless to be it; a nature like Claggart's, surcharged with energy as such natures almost invariably are, what recourse is left to it but to recoil upon itself and, like the scorpion for which the Creator alone is responsible, act out to the end the part allotted it" (p. 78). Like the Balzacian Will,

---

owned more than 20 of the 90-odd works of the *Comédie humaine* (for entries, see pp. 37–38), including *Séraphîta, Louis Lambert,* and *La Peau de chagrin.* Other works include a biography and a selection of Balzac's letters. In his *Herman Melville* (New York: Sloane, 1950), p. 227, Newton Arvin posits *Séraphîta* among the sources for *Pierre;* Sealts's catalogue lists nothing earlier than 1872 (*Eugénie Grandet*), and although that in itself is not conclusive, I am inclined in this case to doubt whether Melville would have read much—if any—Balzac earlier. The overwhelming majority of Sealts's entries date from Melville's last decade.

[7]Ernst Robert Curtius, *Essays on European Literature,* trans. Michael Kowal (Princeton: Princeton Univ. Press, 1973), p. 202. In his *Balzac visionnaire,* Albert Béguin remarks: "When one rereads the *Comédie humaine* as a single work and not as a series of autonomous works, the *Études philosophiques* appear more and more as the luminous foyer which illuminates the entire edifice from within, and innumerable connections spring up, which increase throughout this universe the circulation of the blood from which it draws its life" (*Balzac lu et relu,* p. 130).

[8]On the psychophysiology of *Louis Lambert,* see Evans, pp. 103–8.

this energy represents a purely natural force, the amount of which in each individual varies according to his or her nature. By representing that nature as a reservoir of energy, Melville introduces a new perspective upon his earlier analysis of free will and predestination. A nature "surcharged with energy" is bound to express it in acts, not because of any external compulsion, but simply from the need to discharge its energy. Thus God need not directly cause the individual actions of a creature: these arise from its very nature. Two centuries earlier Leibniz had pointed out that the freedom of the will rests upon its capacity or power to perform the acts it chooses. Since God's foreknowledge does not affect that capacity, the will remains free. By envisioning the will as a form of energy rather than conscious volition, Melville imparts a new character to necessity. Internal rather than external, since it proceeds from the nature of the will itself, the element of necessity in human affairs acquires the inevitability of laws of physics.

By linking the vital energy to an individual's moral nature, Melville's universe touches Balzac's in yet another respect. In *Illusions perdues*, Ève Sechard, anxious to know the fate of her brother Lucien in Paris, writes to his friend D'Arthez. He replies: "Rest assured, Lucien will never go as far as crime, he wouldn't have the force" (*La Comédie humaine*, v, 579). Later, during his colloquy with Lucien, Carlos Herrera asks: "Whence comes this power of vice? Is there a force proper to it, or does it come from human weakness?" (v, 693). For Balzac, the energy contained in beings is in some sense related to their moral nature. Like Balzac, Melville ascribes great potency to those possessed of evil impulses, which represent less the effect of conscious choice than a manifestation of the vital energy itself. Hence his commentary on Claggart: "With no power to annul the elemental evil in him, though readily enough he could hide it; apprehending the good, but powerless to be it." As a force proper to the individual himself, this "elemental evil" remains outside the sphere of thought. At the same time, it is what conditions or makes thought possible, the force or energy impelling the mind into activity. In his analysis of Claggart, Melville can therefore say:

> But the thing which in eminent instances signalizes so exceptional a nature is this: Though the man's even temper and discreet bearing would seem to intimate a mind peculiarly subject to the law of reason, not the less in heart he would seem to riot in complete exemption from that law, having apparently little to do with reason further than to employ it as an ambidexter implement for effecting the irrational. That is to say: Toward the accomplishment of an aim which in wantonness of atrocity would seem to partake of the insane, he will direct a cool judgment sagacious and sound. These men are madmen, and of the most dangerous sort, for their lunacy is not continuous but occasional, evoked by some special object; it is protectively secretive, which is as much as to say it is self-contained, so that when,

moreover, most active it is to the average mind not distinguishable from sanity, and for the reason above suggested: that whatever its aims may be—and the aim is never declared—the method and the outward proceeding are always perfectly rational. (*Billy Budd*, p. 76)

With this we may compare Balzac's description of the theory of the Will devised by Louis Lambert:

> The word WILL served to name the *milieu* where *thought* performs its evolutions; or, to use a less abstract expression, the mass of force by which man can reproduce, outside himself, the actions which compose his exterior life. VOLITION, a word which derives from the reflections of Locke, expressed the act by which man uses the Will. The word THOUGHT, for him the quintessential product of the will, also designated the *milieu* in which were born the IDEAS for which it [i.e., THOUGHT] serves as substance. The IDEA, a name common to all the creations of the brain, constituted the act by which man uses *Thought*. Thus Will and Thought were the two generative means [*moyens générateurs*]; Volition and Idea were the two products. Volition seemed to him to be idea which had passed from its abstract state to a concrete state, from its fluid generation to a quasi-solid expression, if these words may somehow formulate insights so difficult to distinguish. According to him, Thought and Ideas are the movement and the acts of our interior organism, just as Volitions and Will constitute those of the exterior life.
>
> He had made Will precede Thought. "To think, it is necessary to will," he would say. "Many beings live in a state of Will, without nevertheless arriving at the state of Thought." (*La Comédie humaine*, xi, 625–26)

Like Goethe and Nietzsche, Melville points to the existence of an immanent life force transcending reason and thought, which seeks at all costs to assert itself, employing even reason for its purposes. The possibility of using reason as an "implement" to achieve the will's desire presupposes that will is in some sense *anterior* to thought. In the system of Louis Lambert, for whom will represents a fluid dynamic force, the primacy or precedence of will receives a physicalistic explanation: will is the energy that makes all thinking possible. Melville's more radical relativization of reason deprives thought of even its quasi-independent status, making rationality no more than the form in which the will or life force asserts itself. In such instances, reason possesses no content or significance of its own. It becomes simply the mode by which the will achieves its purpose.

As with Balzac, the assertion of reason's subservience to the will depicts the latter as a life force that in effect vitalizes or energizes thought. To the extent that thought or reason forms the product of a mind impelled into activity by energy, the medium of thought can be none other than the vital *fluidum* of energy. But the life force obeys a principle of its own wholly separate from all rational activity. Speaking of the type of lunacy displayed by Claggart, Melville observes: "it is protectively secretive, which is as much as to say it is self-contained"—inasmuch as it possesses a life of its own. The condition ascribed to Claggart does not pertain to his type alone; in all its manifestations, the will is invariably a self-preserving force. By the relation each object bears toward the will, it would be possible to formulate a set of immanent values governing an individual's activity. Unlike Nietzsche, however, Melville does not attempt to construct an ethics based upon such values. Like Balzac, he adheres to a view that regards the theory of energy as a description of the human condition, without seeking to elicit from it moral and spiritual values.

Both Melville and Balzac may be said to belong to a period that witnesses the end of the reign of rationalism. In its place, Romanticism affirms its belief in an immanent organic principle, the life force. This force manifests itself in the later phase of the Romantic movement, in Goethe's late lyrics or Hawthorne's Elixir of Life manuscripts. In Balzac's system the vital energy is represented by a psychophysiology that draws upon the faculty psychology of Locke. Its "compartmentalized" form, with its division into two separate "moyens générateurs," reflects the legacy of the rationalism it seeks to replace. At the same time, by positing the *fluidum* of the life force as its source, the Balzacian psychophysiology both transcends and relativizes its rationalism. In Melville the theory of energy formulated by Balzac appears in a somewhat simpler form while retaining its essential content, the derivation of thought from a prior source in the soul's vital energy.

Differences in energy produce a difference in individual characteristics, or (to employ a term common to Melville and Balzac) *natures*. Balzac's Lucien de Rubempré exhibits one of the "weaker" natures: poetaster rather than poet, one who, as D'Arthez notes, craves the glory and rewards of poetry while unwilling to submit himself to the arduous toil necessary to arrive at them. In *Illusions perdues* this kind of nature is explained in terms of Balzac's system of energy. "There is no superiority without force, and Lucien is weak," says Ève to David Sechard (*La Comédie humaine*, v, 582). To Ève, Lucien himself confesses: "The struggle in Paris requires a constant force, and my will operates only by fits: my brain is intermittent" (p. 686). By contrast, there are natures like that of Balzac's Cousine Bette: "Virginity, like all monstrosities, has its special riches, its absorbing grandeurs. Life, whose forces are economized, has assumed in the virgin individual a quality of resistance and of incalculable duration" (VII, 152). Like Melville's Claggart, she is "surcharged with energy as such natures almost invariably are," and—also like Claggart— inclined toward evil of almost irrational malignity.

But there are other and nobler natures that, through the accidents of life, are occasionally brought together to participate in a form of communion that transcends the sphere of language. In Balzac's *L'Interdiction* we witness an instance of it. I do not know if Melville ever read this particular work of Balzac's. But since its climax shares certain similarities with the great scene in *Billy Budd* in which "two of great Nature's nobler order embrace," it seems appropriate to introduce it here, as exemplifying the possibilities inherent in a view of human nature whose similarity to Melville's I have attempted to point out. Popinot, the humble, compassionate, and discerning bourgeois judge, is assigned to administer judgment in a case of interdiction brought by the scheming Marquise d'Espard against her husband, one of Balzac's only examples of what he considers the true nobility. At the end of his investigation, in questioning the marquis, Popinot arrives at an understanding and resolution of his case which communicates itself without words to the defendant:

> These two natures, so abundant, so rich, the one bourgeois and divine, the other noble and sublime, had gently brought themselves into unison, without shock, without an outburst of passion, as if two pure lights had merged together. The father of an entire quarter or district felt himself worthy of pressing the hand of this man twice-noble, and the marquis experienced in the depths of his heart a movement which intimated to him that the hand of the judge was one of those from which escape incessantly the treasures of an inexhaustible beneficence. (*La Comédie humaine*, III, 491)

The mention of differences in nature implies the existence of some form of natural hierarchy, a gradation from lesser natures to those of "great Nature's nobler order."[9] Both Melville and Balzac adhere to the belief in a natural aristocracy separate from that of birth or wealth. At the beginning of his novel Melville attributes a "natural [the Genetic Text carries the even more telling adjective *innate*] regality" to the type of the Handsome Sailor. Such aristocracy is not one of intellect: in his marginalia Melville rejects this concept, which he encountered in Emerson. His own ideal equates itself with an individual's moral and spiritual nature. It represents a transformation and development of the Romantic concept of the self. But whereas Romanticism affirms its belief in the capacity of all individuals to arrive at the highest capacities of human nature, the late Melville relegates this possibility to a select few endowed by Nature with the requisite characteristics. Thus, for Melville, as for Balzac, the concept of "natures" replaces the Self of earlier Romantic thought, though not without transforming it. According to both authors, all natures experience an unfolding of their inner entelechy, by which they become what they are. Such development is no longer "free" in the

[9]For a commentary on *Billy Budd* from this perspective, see Warner Berthoff, *The Example of Melville* (Princeton: Princeton Univ. Press, 1962), pp. 183–203.

sense professed by the earlier Romantics. Instead, it conforms to strictly natural laws.

This view must not be confused with "naturalism" of any kind: both Melville and Balzac affirm the presence of higher spiritual values that possess an eternal and unchanging validity. The existence of such values is attested to by characters of all ranks and classes in the *Comédie humaine* and also by Claggart, as one "with no power to annul the elemental evil in him, though readily enough he could hide it; apprehending the good, but powerless to be it."[10]

Different natures are characterized in large part by differences in their passions. In Balzac each character is defined by a single, all-absorbing passion or desire: greed in misers like Grandet, thirst for a universal and all-encompassing knowledge in savants like Balthazar Claës and Louis Lambert, envy or jealousy in a Cousine Bette, love and devotion in angelic creatures such as Josephine Claës, Adeline Hulot, and Henriette (Madeline) de Mortsauf. These passions act in accordance with physical laws governing the soul's psychic energy. By means of such laws it becomes possible to determine the life course, duration, and intensity of each passion. Of the envy that possesses Cousine Bette, Balzac observes: "This girl [Cousine Bette] lost therefore all idea of rivalry and of comparison with her cousin [Adeline Hulot], after having felt the latter's divers superiorities; but envy remained concealed at the bottom of her heart, like the germ of a plague which could break out and ravage a city, if one opened the fatal bale of wool in which it was contained" (*La Comédie humaine*, VII, 82).

Here Balzac expresses the life of a passion by means of a biological metaphor. Elsewhere in the same work, speaking of the nature of hatred as opposed to love, he writes: "The pleasures of satisfied hatred are the most ardent, the strongest of the heart. Love is in some sense the gold, and hatred the iron, of this mine of sentiments lying within us" (VII, 200). And, a little later: "Love and hatred are feelings which feed themselves; but, of the two, hatred has the longer life. Love has for its limits finite forces, it draws its powers from life and from prodigality; hatred resembles death and avarice, it is in some sense an active abstraction, transcending beings and things" (p. 201).

With this we may compare Melville's analysis of Claggart's antipathy for Billy Budd. Of the source or cause of that antipathy, which does not spring from any tangible elements or motives, we are told:

> And yet the cause necessarily to be assumed as the sole one assignable is in its very realism as much charged with that prime element of Radcliffian

---

[10]Cf. Milton's Satan, to whom Melville explicitly likens Claggart in one of the canceled MS leaves (135f.): "Pale ire, envy, and despair." See also Henry Pommer, *Milton and Melville* (Pittsburgh: Univ. of Pittsburgh Press, 1950), pp. 83–85, 87–90.

romance, the mysterious, as any that the ingenuity of the author of *The Mysteries of Udolpho* could devise. For what can more partake of the mysterious than an antipathy spontaneous and profound such as is evoked in certain exceptional mortals by the mere aspect of some other mortal, however harmless he may be, if not called forth by this very harmlessness itself? (*Billy Budd*, p. 74)

Like the hatred of Cousine Bette for her cousin Adeline Hulot, Claggart's antipathy for Billy Budd is mixed with envy. Its sources the author then subjects to analysis:

> But Claggart's was no vulgar form of the passion. Nor, as directed toward Billy Budd, did it partake of that streak of apprehensive jealousy that marred Saul's visage perturbedly brooding on the comely young David. Claggart's envy struck deeper. If askance he eyed the good looks, cheery health, and frank enjoyment of young life in Billy Budd, it was because these went along with a nature that, as Claggart magnetically felt, had in its simplicity never willed malice or experienced the reactionary bite of that serpent. To him, the spirit lodged within Billy, and looking out from his welkin eyes as from windows, that ineffability it was which made the dimple in his dyed cheek, suppled his joints, and dancing in his yellow curls made him pre-eminently the Handsome Sailor. One person excepted, the master-at-arms was perhaps the only man in the ship intellectually capable of adequately appreciating the moral phenomenon presented in Billy Budd. And the insight but intensified his passion, which assuming various secret forms within him, at times assumed that of cynic disdain, disdain of innocence—to be nothing more than innocent! Yet in an aesthetic way he saw the charm of it, the courageous free-and-easy temper of it, and fain would have shared it, but he despaired of it. (*Billy Budd*, pp. 77–78)

As with the hatred described by Balzac, Claggart's antipathy for the Handsome Sailor constitutes an "active abstraction" transcending individuals and things. Like death and avarice, it does not touch its object personally or individually but only insofar as that object expresses or manifests the trait by which this passion distinguishes it. That "the mere aspect of some other mortal" should be sufficient to engender the feeling described is possible only if that aspect is itself representative of something antipathetic in nature to the being who experiences a hatred for it. Of the envy felt by Claggart, Melville remarks that it did not "partake of that streak of apprehensive jealousy that marred Saul's visage brooding on the comely young David." This envy possesses no personal or individual admixture, no element that brings the self into specific relations of interest or conflict with the object of its passion. Its only cause must lie in the relation between one nature and another, a relation that inspires the "antipathy spontaneous and profound" described earlier. Since each individual represents a *fluidum* of energy, the reaction of one on meeting another assumes the form of a "magnetic" apprehension: Claggart "magnetically felt" the difference between Billy Budd's nature and his own.

A higher form of psychic energy is thought. On the intellectual plane Claggart perceives the "moral phenomenon presented in Billy Budd," a perception that "but intensified his passion," which develops into "various secret forms within him."

Since the natures of beings are in effect only condensations of vital energies, feeling—or the reaction between two such natures—becomes subject to the same laws as physical phenomena. By depicting it in this fashion, Melville's final novel attests to an even more pervasive determinism than his earlier works. In *Pierre* he employs a chemical analogy, the concept of "elective affinities" by which an individual is said to have the "option" of associating himself to another. In *Billy Budd* this "elective" aspect of psychological affections disappears. Through his inner tendencies, each individual is now predestined to certain moral and spiritual relations with others. When Billy Budd, confronted by Claggart's false accusation, lashes out and kills his accuser, the reaction reflects Melville's new determinism. A discarded passage from the Genetic Text analyzes the foretopman's act: "Yes, the young mute's blow, an athlete's, a blow electrically [>con→<con→energised x→<x→ by] the inmost [<inmost] spasm of his heart, unintentionally had had upon its object the [*p add* all but] [>instantanious] operation of the divine judgement on Annannias" (*Billy Budd*, p. 376;[229a]). An observation from Balzac's *Louis Lambert* suffices to throw some light upon it: "Anger, like all our passionate expressions, is a current of the human force which acts electrically; its commotion, when released, acts upon the persons present even without their being the purpose or the cause" (*La Comédie humaine*, XI, 686).

The blow administered by Billy Budd, "a blow electrically energised," can thus be seen, according to Balzac's conception, as an involuntary expression of the Handsome Sailor's anger. Issuing as an electric current from the soul itself, the vital energy of the individual, through what Melville calls "the inmost spasm of his heart," it passes almost instantaneously through the arm of the athletic foretopman, producing the effect that results in the death of the master-at-arms. Like the magnetic spell cast by Isabel upon Pierre, it acts independently of, and dominates, all conscious thought or reflection. But whereas the earlier novel posits an element of consciousness separate from the spell, though ostensibly powerless to resist, Melville's final work shows consciousness annulled at the moment of the act. As with Balzac, will here precedes thought. If my conjecture concerning the discarded passage from the Genetic Text is correct, the blow from the foretopman's arm represents a concentration of the self's electrical energy—hence its sudden and violent discharge. From another perspective, the confrontation affords no possibility of conscious choice, since it is the vital nature itself which the master-at-arms attacks. Its instinct for self-preservation, most deeply grounded of the innate impulses, asserts itself in the form of energy because the vital nature itself is nothing but pure energy. The reaction explains Melville's declaration that the blow was energized by "the inmost spasm of his heart." It proceeds from the vital *fluidum* itself.

The Melvillean form of determinism that appears here must be distinguished from that of the Enlightenment. In Diderot, La Mettrie, and others, we encounter the concept of "l'homme machine" (as La Mettrie had called it).[11] The mechanical determinism that informs *Jaques le Fataliste* and other works draws ultimately upon the classical mechanics of Newton, with its description of interactions between solid bodies.[12] Melvillean determinism, by contrast, is one of energy or forces. Its model is the late eighteenth-century psychophysiology of Mesmer and others, which subsequently finds its way into the works of Balzac. Melville could also have absorbed it from Hawthorne, the Christian Science movement, and other American sources.

As a result of the shift from one concept of physical interaction to another (from that of solid bodies to forces or energy), the concept of causality itself changes. Unlike bodies, energies or forces act by their very nature upon other bodies or forces. These acts produce a transmission of energy from one force to another. The result forms a continuous process, rather than a series of discrete interactions. In asserting that the electric current of human force, once released, acts without being necessarily influenced by its immediate surroundings, Balzac conforms to such a conception.

For Melville the new concept of causality could provide the stimulus for revising his view of determinism and hence of the problem of free will and predestination. Earlier works such as *Moby-Dick* had opposed the self to external or physical Nature. In *Billy Budd* self and Nature are unified in a single, all-embracing field of energy which concentrates itself in individual beings. Its force is no longer the mechanical power defied by Ahab. Instead it assumes the nature of life, vital energy, a universal *fluidum* in which all things live and move. Through its agency, the self imposes its individual character upon things. By means of this new conception, the Romantic aspiration toward a fusion of self with Nature is both renewed and transformed. The idea of such a fusion, envisaged by Schelling and Coleridge as an identity of subjective and objective, precariously preserved by Wordsworth in intermittent moments of apocalyptic vision, now expresses itself in a universal life force whose highest forms of energy are spirit and intellect.

Like other forms of energy, the spiritual or intellectual element can

---

[11]At the end of *L'Homme machine*, La Mettrie proposes: "Let us, then, conclude boldly that Man is a machine; & that there is in the whole Universe only a single substance diversely modified" (p. 197).

[12]See *Jaques le Fataliste et son maitre*, pp. 349–50.

manifest itself through material aspects. Thus the physical appearance of an individual serves as an index to his intellectual disposition. For this idea, Balzac was able to draw upon the Swiss savant Lavater, whom he acknowledges in *Louis Lambert* (*La Comédie humaine*, XI, 623). Among the features of the physiognomy revealing the self's inner nature, the eyes are given especial significance. A passage from *Louis Lambert* recalls the protagonist's wonderful gaze: "But it was difficult to think of his face, otherwise very irregular, in seeing his eyes, whose look possessed a magnificent variety of expression and which seemed to contain a soul. Sometimes clear and penetrating to a dazzling degree, sometimes of a celestial sweetness, this look would become dull, without color, so to speak, in those moments in which he gave himself up to his contemplations. His eye then resembled a window-pane from which the sun had suddenly withdrawn after having illuminated it" (*La Comédie humaine*, XI, 605).

Windows upon the soul, the eyes allow one to observe its inner processes. We have seen how certain emotions like anger produce, according to Balzac, an electric current. Through the medium of the eyes, this current discharges itself, a phenomenon witnessed by the narrator in his friend Louis Lambert: "When he was violently drawn out of a meditation by the 'You aren't doing anything!' of the Master, it would often happen, at first without his being aware of it, that he would cast at this man a glance impregnated with an indescribable savage scorn, charged with thought as a Leyden jar is charged with electricity. This glance caused no doubt a disturbance in the Master who, wounded by this silent epigram, wanted the student to unlearn this lightning-like look. . . . Thus was revealed to him the oppressive power of his eye" (*La Comédie humaine*, XI, 612).

With this we may compare the effect upon the master-at-arms of a chance meeting with the foretopman: "But upon any abrupt unforeseen encounter a red light would flash forth from his eye like a spark from an anvil in a dusk smithy. That quick, fierce light was a strange one, darted from orbs which in repose were of a color nearest approaching a deeper violet, the softest of shades" (*Billy Budd*, p. 88).

The flash or spark of light discharged from the eyes of a Louis Lambert or a Claggart represents an involuntary act. But the Will can also produce a voluntary discharge of the electrifying force through the same medium. On account of its greater intensity such a discharge must, as Louis Lambert realizes, possess an even greater effect: "A logical and simple deduction from his principles had made him realize that the Will could, by a wholly contracting movement of the interior being, concentrate itself; then, by another movement, could be projected externally, and even confided to material objects. Thus the entire force of a man would have the property of acting upon others, and of penetrating them with an essence foreign to their own, if they did not defend themselves against this aggression" (*La Comédie humaine*, XI, 631).

Here we recall the "blow electrically energised by the inmost spasm of his heart" that Melville ascribes to Billy Budd, and that appears to result from a contracting or concentrating movement of the soul. To his protagonist at this moment Melville could apply a remark of Balzac's in *Le Colonel Chabert:* "In these moments, the heart, the fibers, the nerves, the physiognomy, the soul and the body, everything, even each pore, trembles. Life no longer seems to be in us; it departs from us and springs forth, it communicates itself like a contagion, transmits itself by a look, by the accent of the voice, by a gesture, in imposing our will upon others" (*La Comédie humaine,* III, 359).

Balzac himself believed in this power of the Will, not merely as a spiritual but as a physical force. In *L'Interdiction,* Popinot asks his nephew, the celebrated doctor Bianchon, whether he credits the "bêtises de Mesmer, à son baquet, à la vue au travers des murailles" (the nonsense of Mesmer, his tub, the seeing through walls). Bianchon replies: "Yes, uncle. . . . I can tell you that I have verified, in another sphere of action, several analogous cases, relative to the limitless empire which a man may acquire over another. I am, contrary to the opinion of my colleagues, entirely convinced of the power of the will, considered as a motivating force" (*La Comédie humaine,* III, 445).

But, of all the many instances throughout the *Comédie humaine* attesting to an individual's power to dominate others through an exertion of pure Will, perhaps the most remarkable is one Melville would have found in his reading of *Séraphîta:*

> One encounters in the unexplored nature of the Spiritual World certain beings armed with these unheard-of faculties, comparable to the terrible power possessed by gases in the physical world, and which combine with other beings, penetrate them as an active cause, produce in them spells against which these poor Helots [slaves] are defenseless: they enchant them, dominate them, reduce them to a horrible vassalage, and burden them with the magnificences and the scepter of a superior nature in acting now in the manner of the torpedo-fish which electrifies and numbs the fisherman; now like a dose of phosphorus which exalts life or accelerates its projection; now like opium which puts the corporeal nature to sleep, disengages the spirit from its bonds, allows it to soar over the world, shows the world to it in a prism, and extracts for it the aliment which pleases it most; now finally like a catalepsy which annuls all faculties for the benefit of a single vision.
> (*La Comédie humaine,* XI, 762)

With this and the preceding passages we may compare the scene in which Claggart, under the eye of Vere, confronts and accuses the foretopman:

> with the measured step and calm collected air of an asylum physician approaching in the public hall some patient beginning to show indications

of a coming paroxysm, Claggart deliberately advanced within short range of Billy and, mesmerically looking him in the eye, briefly recapitulated the accusation.

Not at first did Billy take it in. When he did, the rose-tan of his cheek looked struck as by white leprosy. He stood like one impaled and gagged. Meanwhile the accuser's eyes, removing not as yet from the blue dilated ones, underwent a phenomenal change, their wonted rich violet color blurring into a muddy purple. Those lights of human intelligence, losing human expression, were gelidly protruding like the alien eyes of certain uncatalogued creatures of the deep. The first mesmeristic glance was one of serpent fascination; the last was as the paralyzing lurch of the torpedo-fish. (*Billy Budd*, p. 98)[13]

Among his cancellations in the Genetic Text of this passage, Melville had used the phrase "mesmeric experts" (leaf 222, p. 373). And who were these? Who if not Mesmer himself, and the late eighteenth-century savants most often associated with him: Gall and Lavater. Gall, the pioneer in studies of brain physiology, proponent of the theory of cerebral localizations and the association of different mental functions with various areas of the brain; Lavater, creator of a theory of the significance of physiognomical features which enjoyed wide currency in the early nineteenth century. Records of his reading suggest Melville's familiarity with Lavater; of the others he could have obtained some knowledge from Balzac's *Louis Lambert,* which expounds and develops similar views.[14]

Through physiognomical studies and the theories of Mesmer, it becomes possible to explain the transformation in Claggart, whose eyes "underwent a phenomenal change, their wonted rich violet color blurring into a muddy purple." Like the eyes of Louis Lambert, which become "dull" or "terne" when their possessor is lost in thought, Claggart's eyes reveal through their change an intense concentration of energy in their subject. By this energy he seeks to subdue his opponent and victim. The exertion of such energy produces the phenomenon of mesmerism, a loss of will and hence of vital energy in the object.

At the moment of intense concentration Claggart's look changes from a "human expression" to that of "certain uncatalogued creatures of the deep." Here Melville evokes the assertion of the life force in its most primitive form. For the universe of *Billy Budd*, the ocean is, as Vere

---

[13]For another use of the torpedo-fish image, see Emerson's essay "Napoleon" in *Representative Men (C.W.,* IV, 257–58). In his *Pursuing Melville, 1940–1980* (Madison: Univ. of Wisconsin Press, 1982), p. 383, Merton M. Sealts, Jr., attempts to trace Melville's torpedo-fish image to Plato—an attribution that fails to take into account the association with mesmerism in both Melville and Balzac.

[14]*La Comédie humaine,* XI, 623. Here the canceled line from the Genetic Text containing the phrase "mesmeric experts" implies the need to ascribe to this passage a more specific meaning than that accorded it by F. O. Matthiessen, who saw in it only "a familiar strain of Melville's imagery" (*American Renaissance* [London: Oxford Univ. Press, 1941], p. 508).

observes, "inviolate Nature primeval," the "element where we move and have our being." The energy of the "uncatalogued creatures of the deep" expresses the essential life of both self and Nature. Through its immersion in Nature at its most primitive level, that of life without thought or pure animism, Melville's world touches Balzac's at yet another point.[15] In *La Peau de chagrin*, Raphaël de Valentin makes a final effort to conserve his vital energy by fleeing to the French countryside. Establishing himself in a peasant's cottage high in the mountains, he attempts to follow the life rhythms of the earth itself:

> He attempted to associate himself to the intimate movement of this nature, and to identify himself completely enough with its passive obedience so as to fall under the despotic and conservative law which governs the instinctive existences. He no longer wanted to be burdened with himself.... finally, he had so perfectly united himself to this animated earth, that he had in some sense seized its soul and penetrated its secrets. For him, the infinite forms of all the kingdoms were developments of the same substance, combinations of the same movement, the vast respiration of an immense being who acted, thought, walked, grew, and with which he wanted to grow, walk, think, act. (*La Comédie humaine*, x, 282)

The desire to immerse himself in the elemental life of Nature leads Raphaël to his simultaneous wish to be free of himself. With Claggart, the exertion of vital energy in its most primitive form implies a similar loss of self, of the specifically human and individual element of the soul.

Since his exertion of energy proceeds from the mind or intellectual nature, it is only appropriate that Billy Budd's answering blow should have taken effect "full upon the forehead, so shapely and intellectual-looking a feature in the master-at-arms." As the mesmeric force exercised by Claggart issues from his innermost nature, so Billy Budd's response proceeds from a similar source. All the action thus falls under the same necessity as that governing the interaction of physical forces. Apart from this realm of physical forces or nature, however, Balzac affirms the existence of another, higher sphere: the spiritual. By developing a similar conception, Melville in turn attempts to resolve his lifelong preoccupation with a related problem: the question of free will and predestination.

## "une seule et même Matière"

In *Louis Lambert* Balzac had addressed the question of the relation between soul and body, incorporating his reflections into a theory of the

[15]See, for Balzac, Curtius, *Balzac*, pp. 165–66.

Will. By visualizing the Will as a form of energy, a vital *fluidum*, he had shown how it expresses itself in various physical forms: the power of a mesmeristic glance or a sudden flash of light from the eye, the contraction of the heart which occurs in a concentration of vital energies. In *Séraphîta*, the novel he himself considered the crowning achievement of the *Études philosophiques*, he takes up a related question: the relation of spirit to matter, or, in its most comprehensive form, of the spiritual to the material universe. Questioned by the pastor Becker about the irreconcilability of these two realms, Séraphîta replies:

> Thus man presents a sufficient proof of these two modes, Matter and Spirit. In him a visible finite universe comes to an end; in him begins an invisible and infinite universe, two worlds which are alien to each other: the pebbles of the Fiord, are they aware of their combinations, are they conscious of the colors they present to the eyes of man, do they hear the music of the waves which caress them? Let us cross over, without sounding, the abyss which the union of a Material universe with a Spiritual universe offers to us, a visible, ponderable, tangible creation terminated by an intangible, invisible, imponderable one; the two completely dissimilar, separated by an abyss of nothingness, reunited by incontestable accords, brought together in a being participating in one and the other! Let us confound in a single world these two worlds irreconcilable for your philosophies and reconciled by fact. However abstract man imagines it, the relation which binds two things together carries a certain stamp. Where? upon what? We have not yet come to attempting to discover the degree attainable by the subtilization of Matter. If such were the question, I do not see why he who has sewn together by physical relations stars at incommensurable distances to form a veil could not create thinking substances, nor why you would deny him the faculty of imparting a body to thought? Thus your invisible moral universe and your visible physical universe constitute one and the same Matter. (*La Comédie humaine*, XI, 808)

Unlike Leibniz or Diderot, Balzac dismisses the panpsychism that ascribes to all things, animate or inanimate, some degree of consciousness and/or sentience. What his system shares nevertheless with these figures is the concept of a continuum of substances.[16] By progressive degrees such substances form an ascending hierarchy from pure matter to pure spirit, bridging over the opposition between the two elements in their

[16]For the history of this concept, Arthur O. Lovejoy, *The Great Chain of Being: A Study of the History of an Idea* (Cambridge: Harvard Univ. Press, 1936), esp. pp. 144–82 on Leibniz. For an analysis of the Balzacian All-Unity theory, or *All-Einheitslehre*, see Curtius, *Balzac*, pp. 35–38, and Henri Evans, p. 75. In Diderot's remarkable "Rêve de d'Alembert," Mlle de l'Espinasse reports d'Alembert as saying: "A living point. . . No, I'm mistaken. Nothing at first, then a living point. . . To this point another attaches itself, then another; and by these successive attachments there results a single unified being, for I am definitely one, I cannot doubt it . . . [. . .] But how was this unity achieved? [. . .] Hold, philosopher, I see clearly an aggregate, a tissue of little sensitive beings, but an animal! . . . a whole! a unified

pure state. Thus, although matter and spirit are by nature fundamentally opposed to each other, it remains possible to imagine forms of Spirit possessing material attributes. Such are, for instance, the "thinking substances" Balzac evokes, as an example of the degree attainable by the "subtilization of Matter." Here we encounter the characteristic distinguishing the Balzacian continuum from that of his predecessors. Whereas the Leibnizian monadology had postulated a single substance whose differing formations in various creatures or things produce the different species of the *scala natura,* Balzac, in contrast, envisions a continuum in which the species consist in effect of different substances. For Balzac, as for his contemporary Poe, the element of the spiritual may be defined as a more "subtilized" substance whose properties remain analogous to those of the material sphere. Seen in terms of the then-prevalent theory of matter, that element consists of a universe of atomic corpuscular bodies, so finely diffused as to form a kind of ethereal *fluidum.* In Balzac, the *fluidum* manifests itself as an element of vital or spiritual energy. It constitutes the medium of the Will.

Proceeding from common assumptions about the nature of substance, Balzac's concept of the material-spiritual continuum and his theory of the Will complement each other. Whereas two completely different substances cannot presumably touch or alter each other in any way (if one is nonspatial, for example, it cannot affect another with spatial properties, there being no medium for their interaction), the existence of similar properties makes it possible for one such element to affect another. That possibility, I believe, is what Balzac had in mind in his hypothesis about

---

system, possessing a consciousness of its unity! I don't see it, no, I don't see it . . ." (*Oeuvres,* p. 887).

Subsequently, in the same dream, he elaborates: "All beings circulate within [through?] each other, consequently all species . . . All is in perpetual flux . . . Every animal is more or less man; every mineral is more or less plant; every plant is more or less animal. There is nothing precise in nature" (p. 899). Together such beings or species form a continuum: "There is only a single grand individual, which is the whole. In this whole, as in a machine, as in any animal whatever, there is a part which you term such or such; but when you give the name of an individual to this part of the whole, it is by a concept as false as if, in a bird, you were to give the name of an individual to a wing, to a feather of the wing . . . " (pp. 899–900).

For La Mettrie, the Leibnizian definition of this continuum is objectionable on account of its spiritualism: "The Leibnizians, with their *Monads,* have constructed an unintelligible hypothesis. They have spiritualized Matter, rather than materializing the Soul. How can one define a Being whose nature is absolutely unknown to us?" (p. 149). With regard to the continuum of being itself, La Mettrie concludes: "From the Animals to Man, the transition is not violent; the true philosophers agree upon this" (p. 162). A remark of his on comparative anatomy ends with an observation significant for *Billy Budd:* "I will infer only what follows clearly from these incontestable Observations, 1[0]. that the more ferocious Animals are, the less brain they have; 2[0]. that this internal organ seems in some fashion to increase in size, in proportion to their docility; 3[0]. that there occurs here a singular condition invariably imposed by Nature, which is that, the more one gains on the side of Spirit [Mind], the more one loses on the side of instinct" (p. 158). On Balzacian spiritualism in general, see Jacques Borel, *Séraphîta et le mysticisme balzacien* (Paris: Corti, 1967).

"thinking substances." Through a conception of the spiritual realm as consisting not of a single and homogenous element but rather of substances representing different degrees of that same element, we arrive at a form of the spiritual so close to matter in its properties that matter impinges upon and virtually merges with it. This minimal form of the spiritual element, which Balzac situates in man along with a material element, might well be described as a form of thinking substance. Because of its quasi-material properties, it absorbs material effects and, what is equally significant, acts itself upon the material element as well.

To elucidate the nature of such action more fully, it becomes necessary to say something more about the concept of the continuum. Implicit in the concept, first of all, is the assumption that the differing elements which compose the continuum are but various forms of a single essence. Such an essence represents, as it were, the fundamental reality, transcending the differences between the substances into which these elements embody themselves. As a result, such substances become expressions of a quantitative, rather than qualitative, difference. This quantitative difference applies to the opposition between material and spiritual. Like colors from opposite extremes of the spectrum which share a fundamental sameness in the nature of color itself, such elements are said to form aspects of "one and the same Matter." The continuum that forms such Matter is traversed by different energies. Together, these establish a continuity of interaction between the different substances. Indeed, Matter itself seems imbued with many of the properties of energy, which perhaps accounts for the fundamentally conflicting relation between different elements in Balzac's universe.

The existence of a merely quantitative difference between different substances suggests that the acts of a creature of one species can resemble those of a higher species on account of similar characteristics in its substance. In Balzac's brief tale *Une passion dans le désert,* the passion of the panther for the soldier is endowed with virtually all the attributes of human passion, except thought, which belongs solely to the spiritual element.

By conceiving of the spiritual realm as a form of energy, Balzac is then able to explain the effect of spiritual upon material things. For the action of the soul upon the body, he employs the analogy of a physical energy or force affecting a material substance:

> The shock of these two powers, the Body and the Spirit, of which one partakes of the invisible action of the thunder, and of which the other shares with sensate nature this weak resistance which momentarily defies destruction; this combat, or rather this horrible coupling engenders unheard-of sufferings. The body has redemanded the flame which consumes it, and the flame has seized its prey again. But this fusion does not occur without boilings-over, without the explosions and the tortures of which the

visible signs are given to us by Chemistry when two hostile principles which she had been pleased to unite separate from each other. (*La Comédie humaine*, XI, 757)

With this we may compare Melville's description of Billy Budd after his court-martial and final interview with Captain Vere:

> Through the rose-tan of his complexion no pallor could have shown. It would have taken days of sequestration from the winds and the sun to have brought about the effacement of that. But the skeleton in the cheekbone at the point of its angle was just beginning delicately to be defined under the warm-tinted skin. In fervid hearts self-contained, some brief experiences devour our human tissue as secret fire in a ship's hold consumes cotton in the bale. (*Billy Budd*, p. 119)

Like the flame that consumes the body in Balzac's analogy, the passion of "fervid hearts self-contained" wears away the fleshly tissue. By ascribing to such passion a physical energy, Melville imparts to the descriptions from traditional romance a new significance. No longer does the material element merely symbolize the spiritual. Instead, it manifests its actual operation.

We have seen how, for Balzac, the concept of a material-spiritual continuum had furnished the necessary complement to his theory of the Will. For Melville's final novel the concept assumes an even greater importance. From almost the earliest phase of his development, continuing through the works of his maturity, the problem of free will and predestination runs like a leitmotif, assuming new forms in each of its successive appearances. In *Billy Budd* Melville returns to it once more, albeit from a perspective that differs significantly from that of his earlier romances. For this perspective, his absorption in, and affinity with, the Balzacian theory of the Will possesses a decisive significance. In "Bartleby" and *Pierre* Melville had placed the element of necessity in forces external to the self. His last brief narrative, in contrast, subsumes these forces into the self, where they form what Melville calls its "nature." In this conception his affinity with the Balzacian theory of the Will most clearly manifests itself: the tendency to see the will not as an aspect of the rational intellect, that decides between different possible acts, but as a vital energy whose nature already predisposes it to assert itself in certain specific ways. Nothing reveals its nonrational nature more clearly than the description of Claggart: "Though the man's even temper and discreet bearing would seem to intimate a mind peculiarly subject to the law of reason, not the less in heart he would seem to riot in complete exemption from that law, having apparently little to do with reason further than to employ it as an ambidexter implement for effecting the irrational" (*Billy Budd*, p. 76).

But if the individual's nature is already predisposed toward certain fundamental impulses, is it possible to speak of freedom at all? Here it becomes necessary to recall the Balzacian concept of a material-spiritual continuum. Corresponding to the progressive ascent from material to spiritual, one might say, there occurs a progressive development from necessity to free will. The greater the degree of spiritualization or dominance of the spiritual element, the greater the degree of freedom. Since humanity alone among living species possesses a spiritual element, only in its case can even the possibility of freedom exist. Because of the simultaneous presence of a material element in human nature, however, such freedom is only relative.

It is significant, moreover, that Balzac does not consider the mind or intellect as the highest form of the spiritual element in humanity. In Séraphîta's discussion mind is described as a "thinking substance," a form of the spiritual element retaining many material attributes. But if even the mind is only partially free, absolute freedom can pertain only to purely spiritual energy, a form of will transcending what we call Nature. Conversely, the individual in whom the material element predominates expresses the determinism of Nature. In his confrontation with Billy Budd, Claggart reveals the influence of this element upon the will. His eyes are said to undergo a "phenomenal change," "their wonted rich violet color blurring into a muddy purple. Those lights of human intelligence, losing human expression, were gelidly protruding like the alien eyes of certain uncatalogued creatures of the deep" (Billy Budd, p. 98).

As with Balzac, this shift from the human to the creature-like in Claggart's expression arises from the simultaneous presence of material and spiritual elements in human nature. Through the progressive aspect of the "phenomenal change," with its descent to more and more primitive forms of life, Melville suggests the existence of a continuum between the material and the spiritual. His depiction of the color change in Claggart's eyes beautifully reinforces this suggestion, for which he could also draw upon Hawthorne's portrayal of Chillingworth in the comet scene of The Scarlet Letter. Elsewhere in his novel, speaking of the dividing line between sanity and insanity, Melville writes: "Who in the rainbow can draw the line where the violet tint ends and the orange begins? Distinctly we see the difference of the colors, but where exactly does the one first blendingly enter into the other?" (Billy Budd, p. 102). Like the material-spiritual continuum to which they furnish an analogy, these colors form a continuous spectrum. Such a spectrum is also expressive of a material-spiritual continuum in yet another sense, insofar as the individual colors possess symbolic significance. Thus in the scene on the quarter-deck Melville can depict Vere's "gray eyes impatient and distrustful essaying to fathom to the bottom Claggart's calm violet ones," and later, the encounter between those same violet eyes and the "welkin eyes" of Billy Budd.

Earlier, Melville had ascribed to the master-at-arms the "mania of an evil nature, not engendered by vicious training or corrupting books or licentious living, but born with him and innate, in short 'a depravity according to nature'" (*Billy Budd*, p. 76). Now, by means of the association between Claggart and the more primitive forms of life, it becomes possible to place Melville's description in its true light. The resemblance between the "mania of an evil nature" and the impulse of the sea's primitive creatures implies that evil itself must be regarded not as a human phenomenon but rather as one pertaining to the natural or material sphere. Like the predatory character of certain sea creatures, it originates in the nature of certain individuals, from their subjection to the material element within themselves. Because of the dominance of the material element in such natures, no guilt or blame attaches to their acts. For them, there is no free self-assertion: they conform to the laws of Nature, necessitating (in their case) the acting out of evil impulses.

Such subjection to the material element applies not only to Claggart but also, in part, to Vere. Characterized by a "marked leaning toward everything intellectual" (*Billy Budd*, p. 62), he possesses only a partial freedom. Here we recall Balzac's classification of the intellect among the lower forms of the spiritual element. A "thinking substance," it partakes of various material properties and hence remains partly subject to the laws of matter. The limited freedom possible to a nature like Vere's, governed predominantly by its intellect, allows Melville to develop fully the rich ironic possibilities of his theme. Almost immediately after the foretopman fells Claggart, Vere exclaims: "Fated boy! what have you done." Yet the fatality surrounding Billy Budd's actions is largely one of Vere's own making: he both arranges the confrontation with Claggart and persuades the drum-head court to issue its condemnation. As if intensifying the irony, Vere will argue to his fellow officers that "in receiving our commissions we in the most important regards ceased to be natural free agents"—an assertion that leads to the even more casuistical question: "Would it be so much we ourselves that would condemn as it would be martial law operating through us?" (*Billy Budd*, p. 110).

The apparent necessity of such condemnation is virtually refuted by the extreme measures adopted to obtain it. By stressing also the possibility of Vere's temporary insanity, Melville reveals how subconscious forces act to bring about such a verdict. Nothing indicates their role more clearly than Vere's manner during the court's deliberations: "Turning, he to-and-fro paced the cabin athwart; in the returning ascent to windward climbing the slant deck in the ship's lee roll, without knowing it symbolizing thus in his action a mind resolute to surmount difficulties even if against primitive instincts strong as the wind and the seas" (*Billy Budd*, p. 109). Thus, the narrative implies, internal necessity creates external necessity. From Vere's innate tendencies issue the acts and initiatives leading to Billy Budd's condemnation.

At the same time, it would be a mistake to see in his course the same degree of necessity as that ascribed to Claggart. In the merging of thought and desire, unconscious impulse and conscious deliberation, there remains a precarious space between the conflict of opposing forces and its resolution, where the mind's consciousness of its own disposition expresses the degree of its responsibility for the outcome. Nor does the narrative itself fail to hint at the implied responsibility. In the immediate aftermath of Billy Budd's crime we are told: "The case indeed was such that fain would the *Bellipotent*'s captain have deferred taking any action whatever respecting it further than to keep the foretopman a close prisoner till the ship rejoined the squadron and then submitting the matter to the judgment of his admiral" (*Billy Budd,* p. 104). At this point, and even more in what follows, the narrative voice silently merges with the course of Vere's thoughts. But, as the outcome makes clear, that course is in fact opposed to his innermost tendencies. "Very far was he," continues the passage, "from embracing opportunities for monopolizing to himself the perils of moral responsibility, none at least that could properly be referred to an official superior or shared with him by his official equals or even subordinates." The ironic suggestion in the variance between this and the final outcome of Vere's acts represents the nature of the conflict between the opposing internal forces. The impulse that cannot verbalize or express itself—which for that reason does not fully enter into consciousness—eventually triumphs over the other.

If this outcome is in itself ironic, it also raises the question of the relation of such irony to the interpretation of the work as a whole. Specifically, one might well ask whether the ironic perspective that here manifests itself pervades the rest of the novel as well: is the thematic significance of *Billy Budd* ultimately an ironic one, insofar as it depends upon an implicit reversal of normal concepts of guilt and innocence? Can the question of Vere's guilt or innocence subvert even the "Christian" interpretation of Billy Budd's sacrifice, with its accompanying biblical symbolism? Is the final outcome ironic as an expression of the negative movement or thrust of the work, its tendency to deplete its content of meaning? And if so, is it possible to see this process of depletion itself as the ironic negation of value which refuses to become, *qua* negation, a positive value in any sense—a negation that negates even the possibility of such value? Such negation would be "ironic" only if it could maintain distance from its own negativity, if it refuses to press the absence of significance in the events of the novel as a polemical accusation against those involved. In short, to preserve its own irony, it can only present the absence of redemptive significance or moral justification for Billy Budd's acts or Vere's through the development of the narrative itself, without calling attention to its own ironic perspective.

Before taking up these issues, however, we must consider irony itself from a historical perspective. The Romantic conception of irony, especially with Friedrich Schlegel, had sought to locate the recognition of irony in consciousness. Whether we regard such irony as subjective or objective, it originates from a given appearance that the world presents to the individual self or mind, one we might call "dissimulative" in the sense that external phenomena fail to express what the mind affirms as higher realities. That appearance of the world, however, is itself the result of the informing presence of mind or consciousness. Kierkegaard, in a development we shall examine at greater length later, had altered this Romantic conception so as to free irony from its dependence upon consciousness. As a result, irony becomes a hermeneutic, rather than psychological, possibility (one sees this quite clearly in *Fear and Trembling*, with its differing accounts of Abraham's sacrafice of Isaac). In other words: irony as a mode of interpretation. A similar sense of the possibilities of irony informs Melville's *Moby-Dick*, which not only (like Kierkegaard's work) makes use of multiple perspectives but refuses to "resolve" these by recourse to higher authority.

In *Billy Budd*, composed almost forty years later, Melville may be seen to alter somewhat his concept of irony, in a fashion conforming to his late style. Instead of characterizing it in terms of a hermeneutic impasse—the absence of "resolution" among multiple thematic perspectives—what his final novel presents is the subsuming of the ironic perspective in a yet higher mystery: that of Billy Budd's "euthanasia." Not only does the failure to explain this phenomenon figure as something other than irony; it is precisely that which opposes our applying the ironic perspective to the whole of the novel, insofar as it establishes an internal source of value or meaning within the work, one that is inaccessible to the ironic interpretation. That which acts as motive or "cause" of Billy Budd's "euthanasia" is precisely what the irony of the work fails to account for: how account for what appears to proceed from a recognition of meaning or value within the protagonist himself, when the nature of that recognition is withheld from view, and when the negative thrust of the ironic mode depends upon external perception (by the reader) of the absence in the narrative of thematic significance? But if the irony of the narrative fails to subsume the phenomenon of "euthanasia," that phenomenon, conversely, will then subsume the ironic perspective. That perspective, as the absence of a "Christian" or other normative interpretation of the novel's events, must then yield to one that reveals only the "mystery" of those events. That mystery, however, if its nature (as the closeted interview between Vere and Billy Budd suggests) is one of plenitude rather than absence, can only point to a "resolution," though one whose fulfilment remains, within the confines of the work itself, only a promise.

If Vere is even partially aware of such a conflict, however, he possesses a certain amount of responsibility—and hence also of free will—for the outcome. His limited form of free will belongs to those natures in whom intellectual tendencies predominate. Here, as with Balzac, the will finds itself restricted by a material element that encompasses inner psychological forces. Complete freedom of will is thus possible only when the spiritual element alone expresses itself. This occurs in those higher affections in which the material element of instinct or desire disappears. Earlier, in *Pierre*, Melville had shown how the force of sexual attraction can adulterate apparently altruistic impulses. In their pure form, the higher affections express only a wish for communion in feeling and understanding that transcends the limits of human discourse. The final closeted interview between Vere and Billy Budd—about which the narrative permits itself only a conjecture—offers a glimpse of the nature of these affections:

> The austere devotee of military duty, letting himself melt back into what remains primeval in our formalized humanity, may in end have caught Billy to his heart, even as Abraham may have caught young Isaac on the brink of resolutely offering him up in obedience to the exacting behest. But there is no telling the sacrament, seldom if in any case revealed to the gadding world, wherever under circumstances at all akin to those here attempted to be set forth two of great Nature's nobler order embrace. There is privacy at the time, inviolable to the survivor; and holy oblivion, the sequel to each diviner magnanimity, providentially covers all at last. (*Billy Budd*, p. 115)

The affirmation of "what remains primeval in our formalized humanity" is Melville's equivalent to the spiritual element of Balzac's continuum.[17] In a narrative replete with references to Adamic innocence and the consequences of the Fall, it points to the prelapsarian or purely spiritual state of humanity, before its adulteration by the material element. As with Balzac, the contrast between "primeval" and "formalized" nature reveals itself in the relative amount of conscious volition or vital energy necessary to accomplish one's purpose. Whereas Vere's course in obtaining Billy Budd's condemnation had demanded an intense exertion of will, the movement of affection he is thought to express for the foretopman hardly requires any effort at all. One is reminded of a similar contrast in Balzac's *La Peau de chagrin*, in which the fulfillment of Raphaël de Valentin's wishes for wealth and the death or humiliation of enemies consumes large portions of his magic talisman (indicating the exertion of large amounts of will), while his love for and marriage with Pauline hardly affect the talisman at all. Similarly, Vere has only to "melt back" into what remains primeval in formalized humanity in order to disclose his profoundest feelings.

[17]For a reading of this passage from a Rousseauistic perspective, Lawrance Thompson, *Melville's Quarrel with God* (Princeton: Princeton Univ. Press, 1952), pp. 357, 366.

Insofar as such feelings represent the spiritual element in human nature, their expression is invested with an aura of sacredness. It allows Melville to speak of the "sacrament" wherever "two of great Nature's nobler order embrace." The form such affections assume is magnanimity. Its animating principle is a desire to give that proceeds from the innermost nature of the self. Such magnanimity contrasts diametrically with the fundamental impulse of a Claggart, which consists of the desire to absorb, to assimilate into oneself, the law of predatory and material nature as well as of the vital physical energies.

In an obscure fashion, Melville's narrative suggests that only those instances in which the self acts from a magnanimous impulse can truly manifest free will. In these alone does the self transcend the laws of material nature. All that tends to appropriate the external, whether individuals or things, to the self operates within the sphere of the material element. Only through loss of self does the spiritual element manage to free itself of its material admixture. As Séraphîta exclaims, shortly before her triumphant ascension, in a passage marked by Melville in his marginalia: "Take me so that I will no longer be myself" (*La Comédie humaine*, xi, 850; Cowen, ii, 176).

Here the whole problem of free will and predestination assumes a form radically different from that of Melville's earlier works. In "Bartleby," free will is juxtaposed against something like divine foreknowledge: can there be any possibility of free will if all our acts can be anticipated or known in advance? That is, of course, the classical statement of the problem. From a necessitarian perspective, foreknowledge presupposes knowledge of the causes behind a given act or occurrence. Once in possession of that knowledge, it becomes possible for one to predict the outcome. In his attempt to assert free will Bartleby represents the Romantic and Melvillean rebellion against the necessitarianism of an Edwards or a Priestley.[18] He seeks to prove that a knowledge of conditions and circumstances is not sufficient to predict the course an individual will pursue in any particular situation—in short, that free will exists. Asked by his employer why he refuses to perform a certain errand, he merely replies, "I would prefer not to." The absence of any justifiable cause or reason is precisely his reason for what he does.

Through a fundamental transformation of the very terms in which the problem of free will presents itself, Melville's final novel reverses the tragic outcome of a Bartleby. On account of a new concept of the self similar to that embodied in the Balzacian theory of the Will, Melville can speak of each individual as a fusion of material and spiritual energies. As a result, the problem of free will becomes one of freeing the self from the material element associated with it. At the same time, the element of

[18]On "Bartleby" see Allan Moore Emery, "The Alternatives of Melville's 'Bartleby,'" *Nineteenth-Century Fiction*, 31 (1976), 170–87.

necessity itself changes, from the relation between an act and its fore-knowledge to an attraction between different energies or forces. For both Balzac and Melville, a necessary or deterministic aspect manifests itself in everything governed by laws analogous to those of physical force. Since the self's assimilation into the spiritual element is one of degrees, the possibility of free will remains relative rather than abso-lute—as in Vere's role in the court-martial of Billy Budd.

This gradual assimilation of the self to its spiritual element appears most clearly in the foretopman himself. Near the beginning of the novel, by way of explaining Billy Budd's peculiar attitude toward his impress-ment, the narrator offers the following curious remark: "Like the ani-mals, though no philosopher, he was, without knowing it, practically a fatalist" (*Billy Budd,* p. 49). The comparison to animals recurs during the court-martial, when the foretopman is likened to a dog seeking from Vere as from its master some elucidation of what lies beyond its com-prehension. Such comparisons signify Billy Budd's subjection to the laws of the material element, the compulsion of instinct in the absence of any higher consciousness. The characteristic is evidenced early in the nar-rative: given a dig under the ribs by the Red Whiskers, "quick as light-ning Billy let fly his arm" (p. 47). The almost involuntary response—like that of an animal in self-defense—is repeated in the confrontation scene with Claggart: "The next instant, quick as the flame from a discharged cannon at night, his right arm shot out, and Claggart dropped to the deck" (p. 99). Later, describing the foretopman's imprisonment, Melville evokes the fatalistic nature of events even more explicitly: "But now lying between the two guns, as nipped in the vice of fate" (p. 119).

At the same time, the narrative can also describe a development of free will which is brought about by Billy Budd's progressive spiritualiza-tion. In this process the confrontation with Claggart represents his ex-posure to the true nature of evil, seen not as a human but rather material and predatory force. The experience of spiritual magnanimity in the closeted interview with Vere forms the second stage of the process. The possibility of transcending the laws of material necessity or fate through the spiritual element of the higher affections is glimpsed at here. The execution scene realizes the implied possibility. Here the spiritual ele-ment of the self is opposed to the ultimate law of material nature: death. Through the attitude with which it faces death, the self can either affirm its spiritual essence, asserting its free will, or surrender itself for the last time to the material nature within it. As Balzac's Séraphîta observes: "There are two ways of dying: for some, death is a victory; for others, it is a defeat" (*La Comédie humaine,* xi, 806). Victory consists of a transcen-dence of spirit over matter. In the death, which is simultaneously an apotheosis, of Séraphîta—the climax of the *Études philosophiques* and in a sense of the whole *Comédie humaine* in its extant form—Balzac ex-emplifies the possibility of such transcendence:

These last chants were expressed neither by word, nor by look, nor by gesture, nor by any of the signs men make use of to communicate their thoughts, but as the soul speaks to itself; for at the instant at which Séraphîta unveiled herself in her true nature, her ideas were no longer bound to human words. The violence of her last prayer had broken the bonds. Like a white dove, her soul rested poised for a moment upon this body of which the exhausted substances would soon annihilate themselves.

The aspiration of the soul toward heaven was so contagious, that Wilfrid and Minna did not even notice Death in regarding the radiant scintillations of Life.

They had fallen to their knees when *he* [Séraphîtüs-Séraphîta] commenced the journey to his orient, and they partook of his ecstasy.

. . . .

Though seized by the fear of God, as were some of those Seers called Prophets among men, they resisted it like them, finding themselves in the light which shone with the glory of the Spirit.

The veil of flesh which had hidden it from them hitherto evaporated imperceptibly, allowing them to see the divine substance.

They remained in the twilight of the Growing Dawn, whose feeble gleams prepared them for the seeing of the True Light, the hearing of the Living Word, without incurring death. (*La Comédie humaine,* XI, 850–51)

With the image of the soul as a white dove poised at the instant before flight, we may compare the passage in which Billy Budd speaks for the last time before his execution:

At the penultimate moment, his words, his only ones, words wholly unobstructed in the utterance, were these: "God bless Captain Vere!" Syllables so unanticipated coming from one with the ignominious hemp about his neck—a conventional felon's benediction directed aft towards the quarters of honor; syllables too delivered in the clear melody of a singing bird on the point of launching from the twig—had a phenomenal effect, not unenhanced by the rare personal beauty of the young sailor, spiritualized now through late experiences so poignantly profound. (*Billy Budd,* p. 123)

As with Balzac, the aspiration or feeling of the soul at the moment of spiritual exaltation communicates itself without words to the participants of the scene: "Without volition, as it were, as if indeed the ship's populace were but the vehicles of some vocal current electric, with one voice from alow and aloft came a resonant sympathetic echo: 'God bless Captain Vere!' And yet at that instant Billy alone must have been in their hearts, even as in their eyes" (p. 123). If the soul is, as in Balzac, the vital energy of the Will, the "vocal current electric" by which the foretopman's feeling communicates itself is then but a medium for the transmission of his will to others.

In the execution itself, the assimilation of self to the spiritual element assumes the appearance of an apotheosis. As in Balzac, this transfiguration occurs through the apparition of a visible radiance which is as a reflection of the spiritual one within: "The hull, deliberately recovering from the periodic roll to leeward, was just regaining an even keel when the last signal, a preconcerted dumb one, was given. At the same moment it chanced that the vapory fleece hanging low in the East was shot through with a soft glory as of the fleece of the Lamb of God seen in mystical vision, and simultaneously therewith, watched by the wedged mass of upturned faces, Billy ascended; and, ascending, took the full rose of the dawn" (*Billy Budd*, p. 124).

We have seen how for Balzac the death of Séraphîtüs-Séraphîta represents a "journey to his orient" (*quand il s'était dressé vers son orient*). For Melville, too, the East appears as a source of spiritual radiance, the "soft glory as of the fleece of the Lamb of God." The conclusion of Balzac's novel had depicted the soul's apotheosis as an assimilation into a realm of light. In Melville's naturalistic analogue, Billy Budd is said to take "the full rose of the dawn." For the final version's "the full rose of the dawn," Melville had written earlier: "the full shekinah of that grand dawn" (p. 412; leaf 320).[19] In penning this, he could have had in mind a passage he had read, years before, in Carlyle's *Heroes and Hero-Worship:*

> You have heard of St. Chrysostom's celebrated saying in reference to the Shekinah, or Ark of Testimony, visible Revelation of God, among the Hebrews: 'The true Shekinah is Man!' Yes, it is even so; this is no vain phrase; it is veritably so. The essence of our being, the mystery in us that calls itself 'I,'—ah, what words have we for such things?—is a breath of Heaven; the Highest Being reveals himself in man. . . . *We* are the miracle of miracles, —the great inscrutable mystery of God. (*Works*, v, 10)

Like the resemblances with Balzac, the echo of Carlyle reflects Melville's persistent tendency, in his last work, toward a secularization of the spiritual. Equally significant is the reference to the foretopman's death as an "ascension." Here Melville's usage parallels the fourth Gospel, which speaks of the Son of Man at his crucifixion as being "lifted up" (ὑψω-θῆναι) in the double sense of having his cross elevated and being exalted.[20] By speaking of Billy Budd's execution as an "ascension," Melville signifies simultaneously the hanging and the movement that liberates the spiritual element of the soul from the material.

Having said all this, one must observe the ironic perspective afforded by the narrative as well. Here it suffices to mention Melville's emphasis

[19]On Melville and the concept of the shekinah, Nathalia Wright, *Melville's Use of the Bible* (Durham: Duke Univ. Press, 1949), pp. 160–61.

[20]C. H. Dodd, *The Interpretation of the Fourth Gospel* (Cambridge: Cambridge Univ. Press, 1953), pp. 377–79. Also Rudolf Bultmann et al., *Kerygma and Myth: A Theological Debate*, ed. Hans Werner Bartsch (1953; rpt. New York: Harper & Row, 1961), pp. 38–39, and Bultmann, *Theology of the New Testament*, trans. Kendrick Grobel, vol. 2 (New York: Scribner's, 1955), p. 53.

upon the element of chance in the coincidence that produces the appearance of an apotheosis: "At the same moment it chanced that the vapory fleece . . . was shot through with a soft glory." For Melville, as for Hawthorne, the "natural supernaturalism" of his Romantic predecessors had always been problematic: both in *Billy Budd* and in the earlier works, Nature offers at best but an ambiguous revelation of the divine. In one of the chapters forming a kind of epilogue to the scene just described, the narrative records the dissolution of what had previously seemed a symbolic apparition: "And now it was full day. The fleece of low-hanging vapor had vanished, licked up by the sun that late had so glorified it. And the circumambient air in the clearness of its serenity was like smooth white marble in the polished block not yet removed from the marble-dealer's yard" (*Billy Budd*, p. 128). And so the cycle of natural processes continues, dawn giving way to day, radiant mist to serene clarity. Through its return to the natural cycle the narrative suspends judgment on the question of Billy Budd's "ascension": perhaps the "transfiguration" of the foretopman by the dawn's radiance represents merely a chance occurrence rather than spiritual reality. If so, the thematic significance of the tale must lie in its exploration of the moral sphere, and above all in the question of guilt and responsibility for Vere.

In either case, there remains the phenomenal fact disclosed fully only in the following chapter—the absence, namely, of any spasmodic movement in Billy Budd's body at the moment of hanging. Hence the justification for a discussion, in that chapter, of possible explanations for this phenomenon—a discussion that allows Melville to present his own view of the claims of science.

## Religion and Science

In the scene following the execution, a discussion ensues between the ship's purser and the surgeon as to the phenomenal nature of the foretopman's death. The purser attributes it to "will power," while the surgeon, denying the scientific validity of such a notion, finds himself unable to explain it. With their conversation we may compare the scene, mentioned earlier, from Balzac's *La Peau de chagrin* in which Raphaël de Valentin, much weakened and failing rapidly as his magic shagreen talisman shrinks to a smaller and smaller size, summons the most celebrated physicians of Paris to diagnose his case. Much perplexed, they arrive at differing conclusions; only one, the young Horace Bianchon, correctly attributes Raphaël's mysterious dissolution to a weakening of the will, which is to say: the life force. Bianchon arrives at his correct assessment not so much through scientific procedure as through what Balzac elsewhere describes as a kind of "second sight" (*une espèce de seconde vue,* or, to adopt Balzac's own terminology, *spécialité*). By means of such "second sight," Bianchon is able to penetrate the material surface of things and observe the spiritual element that operates within them. In *La Peau de chagrin* failure to recognize the spiritual element transcending matter forms the ground of Balzac's criticism of science.

A similar objection appears in *Séraphîta*. As the protagonist asserts in her discourse to the pastor Becker: "Nature consists only of bodies; your science combines only their appearances" (*La Comédie humaine,* XI, 822). Science, which even as it denies the spiritual element must acknowledge the existence of "several substances which traverse what you believe to be a void," removes the life from matter: "You obtain only lifeless substances from which you have excluded the unknown force which opposes the decomposition of things on earth, and of which attraction, vibration, cohesion and polarity are only the phenomena" (*La Comédie humaine,* XI, 823). This "unknown force" Balzac equates in its lower forms with the energy of the vital *fluidum,* the element of the Will; in its higher form, it becomes the spiritual element. The great anatomist Xavier Bichat had defined life as "the sum of all forces which struggle against death." Through his figure of Séraphîta, Balzac affirms a similar vitalism: "Life is the thought in bodies; they are only a means of concretizing, of containing it in its course; if bodies were themselves living beings, they would be *cause* and would not die" (*La Comédie humaine,* XI, 823). The definition of life as the "thought in bodies" permits a linking up of the Will with the next higher form of energy, and the lowest in the spiritual element: thought. In this fashion, Will and thought are distinguished from the material forces. Such a distinction may explain, in part, the feeling that inspired Melville to mark in his copy of *Séraphîta* the following passage: "there is, in effect, neither time nor place to the spirit. Space and duration are proportions created for matter, spirit and matter have nothing in common" (*La Comédie humaine,* XI, 848; cf. Cowen, II, 175).

But the existence of a spiritual element transcending the physical also suggests that the end and aim of human life cannot be simply the perfection of the sciences, since these concern themselves strictly with matter. On that point, Melville can concur with Balzac's Séraphîta that "If material science was supposed to be the aim of human efforts, confess, would societies, those great foyers in which men are brought together, would they always be providentially dispersed? If civilization were the aim of the Species, would intelligence perish? would it remain purely individual?" (*La Comédie humaine,* XI, 826; Cowen, II, 171). Ultimately, the question leads Wilfrid and Minna to the following perception, marked by Melville in his marginalia: "They recognized the puerility of human sciences, which they had been spoken to about" (*La Comédie humaine,* XI, 855; Cowen, II, 176). He must also have found a special significance in the passage from *La Peau de chagrin* describing Raphaël's visit to the savant Lavrille, whom he seeks out in hope of obtaining some information about the nature of his talisman as his life force ebbs away: "Raphaël saluted the savant naturalist, and rushed to Planchette's, leaving the good Lavrille in the midst of his study filled with jars and dried plants. He brought away from this visit, without knowing it, all of human science: a nomenclature!" (*La Comédie humaine*, x, 242; Cowen, ii, 155).

Similarly, in the dialogue between the purser and the surgeon some days after Billy Budd's execution, an argument arises over the validity of a nomenclature. Since the purser is "a rather ruddy, rotund person more accurate as an accountant than profound as a philosopher," their discussion appears to bear out the Pauline dictum about the foolish confounding the wise (1 Cor. 1:27). Because of his failure to consider the spiritual element in his account of things, the surgeon, as representative of science, is unable to explain one of the most remarkable phenomena of all. Nevertheless, even his attempt is revealing. It begins by assuming an extraordinary emotion in Billy Budd as the cause—a hypothesis that tacitly acknowledges the power of the spiritual element to transcend the laws of material nature. At this point the explanation halts; the surgeon refuses to elucidate what he scornfully terms the "imaginative and metaphysical." Yet that "imaginative and metaphysical" aspect is precisely what Melville had sought to depict. In transcending material forces the spiritual element permits the possibility of free will as an assertion of humanity's spiritual nature. Through its attempt to link this higher element with the material sphere, Melville's last novel represents something other than a reactionary response to the claims of science. Like Balzac, he belongs to a later phase of Romanticism whose tendency is to seek what Shelley described as the union of poetry and science. By identifying his thought with the Balzacian theory of the Will and the concept of a material-spiritual continuum, Melville could hope to show how material forces act and impinge upon higher realities. Through exploring the effects of such forces, he could then approach from a new perspective his lifelong concern with those problems of justification and ultimate moral responsibility that are for him inseparable from the question of free will and predestination.

# PART IV

# The Historical Consciousness

# 11  *Emerson: The Philosophy of History*

In his *Spirit of the Age* Hazlitt had sought to assimilate the German notion of the *Zeitgeist* as a new means of envisioning the content of history, and specifically, his own epoch. Significantly, however, one finds few references within the work itself to this notion. Nor does it play the role of an explanatory principle. Instead, the "spirit of the age" is something that itself requires characterization, elucidation, description. Such characterization it receives through the portrayal of individual figures, the significant and seminal minds of Hazlitt's time. The dependence of the general notion upon these specific instances is highly revealing.[1] It indicates, among other things, that for Hazlitt the spirit of the age is not yet conceived of as a force, a power that acts upon and through individuals in order to shape history as a means of self-expression. At this juncture, the spirit of the age has not yet become the immanent impulse behind nineteenth-century *Geistesgeschichte,* the history of the development of the spirit or consciousness. In part, the discrepancy can also indicate that—at least for Hazlitt—history is not yet identified with spirit or consciousness, as the "content" of that consciousness, embodied in the development of which such consciousness is the result.[2] The notion of history as the development of consciousness would have the effect, essentially, of transforming it not only from the notion of external occurrence (as opposed to the internal, the mind or self) but also of dis-

---

[1] To be sure, this translation of the general into the specific is also highly characteristic of Hazlitt in particular. Apropos of his politics, Leslie Stephen remarks: "He sees every abstract principle by the concrete instance . . . Tyranny with Hazlitt is named Pitt, party spite is Gifford, apostasy is Southey, and fidelity may be called Cobbett or Godwin" (quoted from Carl Woodring, *Politics in English Romantic Poetry* (Cambridge: Harvard Univ. Press, 1970), p. 244.

[2] As in, e.g., Hegel's *Phenomenology of Spirit,* where, as a result of such development, it becomes possible to present religion or art with a historical grounding, as the result of the successive transformations of consciousness, which yet embody in themselves forms of that consciousness.

tinguishing it from any idea of pattern, the concept of a historical happening (in this respect *Geistesgeschichte* could represent something more radical even than Vico or the later revival, as in Nietzsche, of notions such as "eternal recurrence" or "return"). In effect, equating history with the development of consciousness merges the activity of an impelling force with that force itself. The result—such activity no longer "passes away" but is preserved in the transformation of the impelling or causative force. Thus the "pastness" of history disappears, replaced by what amounts to an affirmation of the activity as content.

We may see in this—and I think rightly—an expression of the Romantic desire to avoid a dichotomy of subjective and objective, which becomes from the historical perspective a question of determining the effect of force upon an object, the whole issue of causation and necessary connection posed by Hume. What is both interesting and significant for our present purposes is how Emerson manages, in his early lecture series on "The Philosophy of History," to achieve an identification of the philosophy of history with spiritual expression and, at the same time, to bypass the whole problem of historical causation (causality) that such an identification had been meant to address. His unique situation may be explained in part by his highly personal theory of the relationship of the individual to what he calls the "Universal Mind." It also serves in some measure to explain that theory itself in its historical aspect, as proceeding from the absence of any notion of an immanent causative force within consciousness. In his "Introductory" to the "Philosophy of History" series Emerson asserts: "Of the Universal Mind which we have considered each individual man is one more incarnation. All its properties consist in him. To all its circle of perfections he has access. Though now only in the bud of his being; though now this great nature is opened to him under a single and necessarily partial and distorted view, yet is he the heir of it all, and in eternity, shall appropriate one after another, all its virtues and powers, until he lives with God, or the Individual is lost in the Universal Soul" (*EL,* II, 15; cf. *Coll. W.,* II, 4).

One might compare the relationship between individual man and Universal Mind to that of God the Father and Son, as suggested by the term *incarnation,* and Emerson is doubtless aware of the Alexandrian doctrine that defines God as νοῦς or "mind."[3] Such a comparison, how-

---

[3] An association aided in Emerson's case by the Alexandrian equation of Christ with the *Logos,* which, though capable of being read restrictively as "the Word" (F. C. Burkitt, *Church and Gnosis* [Cambridge: Cambridge Univ. Press, 1932], pp. 93–96, 98–99), in the prologue to the Fourth Gospel, would in all likelihood have meant "Reason" or "thought" for Emerson, esp. in light of his favorite opposition between "Reason" and "Understanding." On the Pauline or scriptural overtones of this opposition, see René Wellek, *Confrontations* (Princeton: Princeton Univ. Press, 1965), pp. 194–95. Emerson's association of Christ

ever, would only increase the complexity of the issue, since Emerson's own notion of the relationship of God to Jesus is in fact mediated by his theory of the relationship of individual to Universal Mind. The essence of Emerson's definition of this relationship is contained in the term *access:* the individual mind has "access" to the Universal Mind in the sense that this Universal Mind represents in effect a state of consciousness from which all individual distortions or idiosyncracies have been purged, a state of pure transparent *seeing* or receptiveness. Hence the individual mind passes over into the Universal simply by losing its finite or individual limitations; in actuality, there is no absolute difference between them. This is, of course, the same theory of Mind that Emerson expresses in *Nature* and to which he will recur, two years later, in the Divinity School Address. What is significant here is his application of this theory of Mind to history: the individual is said to live under the limits of the personal and subjective, "yet is he the heir of it all, and in eternity, shall appropriate one after another, all its virtues and powers, until he lives with God." Thus the historical essence of the doctrine is contained in the concept of the individual's progressive appropriation of the virtues and powers of the Whole. The progressive quality of that appropriation is subsumed under the metaphor of the "organic": "though now only in the bud of his being."

Through its use of an "organic" analogy, Emerson's view manifests its affinity with that espoused by Herder in his influential *Ideen zur Philosophie der Geschichte der Menschheit;* significantly, Herder envisions religion specifically as the fulfillment of this "organic" process of human development: "Religion is therefore, even when considered [merely] as the exercise of the understanding, the highest humanity, the noblest blossoming of the human soul" (*S.W.,* xiii, 163).[4] Earlier in the same work Herder had observed: "It is obvious that human life, insofar as it is vegetation [vegetative life], also has the destiny of the plants. . . . Our life-stages are the life-stages of plants; we come into existence, grow, bloom, fade, and die" (p. 52). Of especial importance is his emphasis upon religion as *Verstandesübung*—the exercise of the understanding. The role of religion in the development of the human faculties is here affirmed, but also—what is particularly important for Emerson—re-

---

with the Reason (if it be such) probably depends in large part upon the identification of Reason (*Vernunft*) with thought in Kant and post-Kantian speculation, as well as upon the legacy of eighteenth-century rationalism in general.

[4]For Emerson's reading of Herder and of the *Ideen* specifically, Kenneth Walter Cameron, *Ralph Waldo Emerson's Reading* (1941; rpt. New York: Haskell House, 1966), p. 78. Emerson borrowed two different editions, from the Harvard College Library and the Boston Athenaeum, respectively. He may also have been influenced in part by George Ripley's articles on Herder; Stanley Vogel, *German Literary Influences on the American Transcendentalists* (New Haven: Yale Univ. Press, 1955), p. 112.

ligion itself is implicitly defined in secular terms, its essence equated with the self's development. Specifically, Herder associates it with the use of the rational intellect, not solely for meditation upon religious subjects, but rather as part of a general or overall program of growth and self-fulfillment (in short: *Bildung*).

In the passage from the "Introductory" quoted above, Emerson speaks of how the individual shall, "in eternity," appropriate the virtues and powers of the Universal Mind. I have tried to show how such an assertion expresses an implicit progressivism; it remains now to explore the precise sense Emerson ascribes to eternity (and hence time) in this process of development. From other early writings of his, it should be apparent that the eternity he speaks of here is not the infinite extension of historical time but rather a state of mind or consciousness, that of the pure seeing which belongs to the Universal Mind. To say that in this eternity the individual mind shall appropriate the virtues and powers of the Universal Mind suggests that by elevating itself to the level of pure consciousness the mind transcends phenomenal or historical time, and in so doing simultaneously opens itself to the infinite awareness of the Godhead.

But since the process of the mind's elevation to the plane of Universal Mind is a progressive one, achieved through the development of its various faculties, we may describe its relation to eternity as being itself "progressive": the mind perceives eternity by degrees, as it enters partially into a state of higher consciousness. Thus the process of historical time is itself one of development, the increasing "realization" of the eternal *in* the temporal. More explicitly, historical time is strictly a content of consciousness: it defines a movement toward self-awareness on the part of that consciousness, hence a form of phenomenological, rather than merely phenomenal, time. In achieving such self-awareness, the mind is brought to reflect upon the nature of its own process of self-development. Its reflection, insofar as it occurs in time, becomes in part an assimilation of that time into thought, hence the conceiving of a process, which represents an activity in itself.

We have seen how Emerson's view asserts a reciprocal connection between the Individual and Universal Mind. In this respect, it is unique: instead of a purely expressive theory of history (history as the expression of spirit), it posits a conscious or apprehensive one as well. Not only does the individual embody the Universal Mind; it simultaneously possesses "an inlet to the same, and all of the same." Such reciprocity is in turn made possible by the nature of both individual and universal mind. Their essence Emerson defines as consciousness. For the individual to have "access" to the universal in this regard does not imply, then, its passing over to something external to itself: on the contrary, in assimilating itself to the Universal Mind it enters in actuality *into itself*. For Emerson, the Universal Mind may be said to represent the essence of the particular or individual one. It does so, however, in a specific and unique sense, by being the *activity* of that mind. The pure seeing or consciousness which Emerson calls the Universal Mind defines, then, the individual mind in its activity; in such activity, mind ceases to be an element and becomes energeia, the assertion of that element in its pure nature or essence. The individual mind entering into itself asserts its proper nature. But that assertion is itself what Emerson describes as the Universal Mind. For a purely expressive theory of history, the Universal Mind would necessarily be that element which the individual mind or thought consists of. Emerson's philosophy of history differs from the expressive form to the extent that it takes activity rather than an element to represent the essence of the individual. Correspondingly, it justifies its assumption by defining the individual in terms of consciousness, in other words, as one whose essence can only be activity, for which it represents the capacity.

Thus far I have attempted to distinguish Emerson's philosophy of history from an expressive one that assimilates such notions as that of the "spirit of the age" in its desire to represent historical forces. Yet Emerson's historical vision also possesses an expressive aspect, one that finds its clearest development in the summary he gives in the final lecture of that series, "The Individual":

> Cunningly does the world evermore with its thousandfold beauties and qualities tempt forth the spirit in man and challenge the faculties to unfold and play. . . . *Science* is the finding in the objects of nature the method of this one Mind. *Art* is the action of this mind upon nature through many individuals to ends of use or beauty. *Literature* is the record of this mind speaking to individual necessities. *Inspiration* is the reception of the pure influx of this Mind, which treating of the individual nature is *prophecy* and proclaiming the laws of the will is *Revelation* and of the Intellect is *Philosophy* and the laws of human life is *Ethics;* and *Religion* is the emotion of reverence which the conscious presence and activity of the Universal Mind inspires. (*EL,* II, 181)

In the earlier lecture "Literature" from the same series, Emerson had made the interesting distinction that "whilst Art delights in carrying a thought into action, Literature is the conversion of action into thought. The architect executes his dream in stone. The poet enchants you by thinking out your action. Art actualises an idea. Literature idealizes action" (*EL,* II, 55–56). The summary itself, similarly, observes the same reciprocity between inward and outward flux or movement: inspiration is the reception of the "pure influx of this Mind," but that same influx can also transform itself into outward expression, as prophecy and revelation. Such reciprocity, of course, conforms to the basic nature of the relationship between individual and Universal Mind, but it also indicates at the same time the essential quality of that relationship, one that Emerson designates by the word *reception*. To "receive" here implies an awareness of that which is being received, and that awareness in turn indicates the presence of consciousness.

In the same passage Emerson speaks of the "conscious presence" of the Universal Mind—a curious and suggestive locution, signifying as it does either the consciousness of the individual, or Universal, Mind. In the dialectic that defines their relation, each is therefore conscious, each expresses, each receives; the influx of the Universal into the individual mind is then transformed into expression as Art or Literature, thereupon reflecting the essence of that Universal Mind to itself. Moreover, even the act of expression is in a sense simultaneously reception—and conversely. When inspiration passes through influx into the mind it becomes, in treating of the individual nature, prophecy. Since the content of prophecy consists of what has been received from the Universal Mind, the enunciation or expression of that content is in essence the transmission of that reception. The very act of prophecy, furthermore, is itself valid only insofar as it constitutes inspired reception: the moment the individual mind departs from what it has received, it ceases to be prophetic.

Science Emerson here defines as "the finding in the objects of nature the method of this one Mind." As such, science epitomizes the interchangeability of expression and reception. In "finding," the mind both asserts itself in intellectual activity and at the same time receives. What it receives is a knowledge of "the method of this one Mind." But that mind is also its own in essence: hence what it receives is in effect the expression of its own mind, reflected back upon itself, even as the Universal Mind, in perceiving or experiencing its expression through individual minds, receives thereby a knowledge of itself. Such interchangeability of expression and reception reveals that, for Emerson, expression is always in some sense a "finding" or discovery of hidden laws, whether of Nature or of Art. Ultimately, both are the same, since with either the mind is led to a knowledge of itself.

Such knowledge differs, in at least one respect, from thought: it does not attain the finality or completeness of an *idea*. This is to say that Emerson's philosophy of history does not internalize its significance within itself. *Geistesgeschichte* possesses such self-sufficiency in the sense that within it, the activity of history achieves representation, as thought or idea; for Emerson, on the other hand, representation exists only for the mind that receives history. Nor could it be otherwise, since the nature of historical "representation" (and all other forms of representation) for Emerson is in essence self-representation, the reflection of the self's nature as Mind. Such self-representation implies an act or initiative

on the part of the self: without it, history remains on the purely phenomenal level, until elevated by mind to that of law or inner necessity. At
that level, the mind experiences self-recognition when it perceives that
the laws governing history are the same as those that regulate its inner
processes.

By refusing history the capacity to internalize or assimilate thought, by
asserting the significance of history only for the mind that receives it,
Emerson affirms the primacy of consciousness. For the early Emerson of
these lectures on the philosophy of history, thought itself must be subsumed or assimilated into consciousness. Hence "representation" in his
philosophy of history is equated with the individual mind's consciousness of the Universal Mind within itself, and conversely (the Universal
Mind's consciousness of the individual). Representation is thus nothing
more than the act or moment of consciousness in which the one perceives the other. As with Herder, such a philosophy of history affirms
the importance of religion. Here Emerson speaks of religion as "the
emotion of reverence which the conscious presence and activity of the
Universal Mind inspires." We have seen already how the "conscious
presence" of that Mind refers to an awareness within both individual
and Universal Mind. The activity of that same Mind appears under a
similar double perspective: if the Universal Mind is nothing more than a
state of consciousness, any activity must proceed from some individual
mind.

By engaging in the activity described here, however, that individual
mind *becomes* the Universal Mind; the state of consciousness Emerson
equates with such activity is itself the Universal Mind. Thus the activity
of the Universal Mind is at once both its own and the individual mind's,
but what the latter does in acting is, in effect, simply to *perceive* the
Universal Mind within itself. This is to say that it perceives *its own activity*.
In the form in which Emerson presents it, its perception *is* its activity,
and correspondingly its only activity must be that of perceiving itself.

The form such perception assumes is not intellectual or rational but
one of feeling, the "emotion of reverence." This emotion, as a state of
mind or consciousness, is that of the Universal Mind. Emerson's definition of religion asserts that the Universal Mind creates itself within the
individual mind. The "influx" by which it inspires the latter is the Universal Mind itself (since it consists of nothing more than a state of consciousness), but because the nature of that Mind is one of pure perceiving, its perception by the individual mind blends or merges with the
Mind itself, perceiving merging with perceiving, so that the creation of
the Universal Mind within individual consciousness is ultimately that
consciousness's perception of itself.

If the perception of the Universal Mind by the individual merges with
the perceptive nature of that Universal Mind, however, the question of

how the individual can be "representative" of the Universal Mind necessarily arises. Such representation assumes a certain opacity in the object that represents, something less than the complete or full transparence of pure seeing—or, at the very least, a certain amount of condensation that would (as in Freud's dream theory) produce the effect of opacity. The result would then be a form of "translucence" in the sense ascribed by Coleridge to the symbol: it allows the effulgence of the eternal to shine through it but is not the same as that effulgence itself. Emerson's theory of the relationship between individual and Universal Mind risks, to some extent, the danger of completely assimilating the one to the other. Consequently, it seems necessary to examine more closely his own theory of representativeness, as a means of clarifying or elucidating his theory of the Universal Mind and its relation to the self. For this purpose, two passages from his "Philosophy of History" seem especially appropriate. The first appears in the lecture on "Manners": "The character, the will, which is the ultimate object of history is ever invisible, inaccessible. It is only inferred from many signs as the language, laws, institutions, trade, customs, which he chooses or creates" (*EL*, II, 129). Herder, too, had spoken of the necessity for a "semiotics of the soul" (*Semiotik der Seele*) (*S.W.*, XIII, 187) in face of the impenetrability of individuals in history. In his *Ideen zur Philosophie der Geschichte der Menschheit* the problem is formulated in a fashion that recalls Hume:

> All our science reckons with departed individual external signs, which never touch the inner existence of a single thing, because for the feeling and expression of these we have absolutely no organ. We know no power in its essence, nor can we learn to know it: for even that which animates us, which thinks in us, we indeed enjoy and feel but we know it not. No connection between cause and effect can we understand, therefore, when we have no insight into either what causes or is caused, and when we have absolutely no concept of the being of a thing. Our poor reason is thus only a designating calculator, as its name in many languages signifies. (*S.W.*, XIII, 358–59)

In his *Enquiry concerning Human Understanding* Hume had asked how it was possible to have immediate experience of the power or force that gives rise to our notion of causality.[5] Even in the case of our bodies, he

---

[5]"Shall we then assert, that we are conscious of a power or energy in our own minds, when, by an act or command of our will, we raise up a new idea, fix the mind to the contemplation of it, turn it on all sides, and at last dismiss it for some other idea, when we think that we have surveyed it with sufficient accuracy? I believe the same arguments will prove, that even this command of the will gives us no real idea of force or energy.

"*First*, it must be allowed, that, when we know a power, we know that very circumstance in the cause, by which it is enabled to produce the effect: For these are supposed to be synonimous. We must, therefore, know both the cause and effect, and the relation between them. But do we pretend to be acquainted with the nature of the human soul and the nature of an idea, or the aptitude of the one to produce the other? This is a real creation; a

argues, we witness only the occurrence of motion following an impulse of will, without experiencing the causative connection itself. In our thoughts we know only that such events occur, but not the cause that produces or creates them. Herder considers the same problem in terms of history. What makes possible a genuine knowledge of the historical forces (*Kräfte*) that produce or cause events, if the nature of such forces must forever remain obscure to us? Hence his affirmation of the necessity of a "semiotics of the soul."

Emerson too can speak of such a semiotics, or symbolism; but for him this symbolism is to be found primarily in Nature, which constitutes a "hieroglyphics" for the mind. His notion of historical "representativeness" defines itself in other terms. In his lecture "The Present Age" he asserts: "Nay, I believe that representatives of every period may be found in any period and the image of each epoch in the successive states of one man's mind" (*EL*, II, 159). For Emerson, then, the problem of historical knowledge is resolved by equating that knowledge with states of consciousness. An epoch constitutes the equivalent of a state of mind or consciousness. To "know" an epoch is therefore to experience that state of mind. In this sense, historical knowledge does not consist of a concrete content (such as knowledge of the nature of certain specific historical forces) but rather of a mode of perceiving or experiencing. A given emotional coloration, a given mood or sense of what things signify in relation to the way we live—this is Emerson's notion of "historicity," of the various historical epochs and the passage from one to another.

Obviously, such a vision tends to preclude the cumulative nature of memory or reminiscence, the sense in which Hegel could speak of the child and the man pronouncing the same utterance but with a world of difference in meaning. In this respect, Emerson does not accept the notion of a burden of consciousness. His "mind" is consciousness solely in the sense of a mode of perceiving, such that each age will possess a fresh perception of the world. Hence his dictum that "each age must write its own books." Such a vision implies, among other things, the ultimate assimilation of knowledge to consciousness. For Emerson all "knowledge" is self-recognition, the perception of the nature of mind both in external Nature and in history. Precisely because of his reduction (of knowledge to self-knowledge), there can be for Emerson no fundamental problem of historicity and historical knowing such as that posed by Herder. If knowledge is equated with self-knowledge, knowledge

---

production of something out of nothing: Which implies a power so great, that it may seem, at first sight, beyond the reach of any being, less than infinite. At least it must be owned, that such a power is not felt, nor known, nor even conceivable by the mind. We only feel the event, namely, the existence of an idea, consequent to a command of the will: But the manner, in which this operation is performed, the power by which it is produced, is entirely beyond our comprehension" (*Enquiries*, pp. 67–68).

itself is then nothing more than consciousness. For the only form of self-knowledge is that which comes through experience of the mind in its activity—in other words, through consciousness.

The definition of history in terms of a series of epochs equivalent to states of mind or consciousness inevitably raises the question of historical progress. In what sense is it possible to speak, with regard to Emerson's philosophy of history, of what Keats called the "grand march of Intellect"? In his *Philosophie der Geschichte* Friedrich Schlegel had criticized Condorcet's notion of "perfectibility" and of history as the gradual perfection of the human race for what he describes as its failure to embody any genuine thought or idea: "And so it has no proper end or aim, for the mere projection into the infinite is no such end, no clearly determined objective and positive purpose" (*Krit. Ausgabe,* IX, 154). To some extent, Emerson shares a similar view of Enlightenment philosophies of history. In his own lectures on the subject, he makes it clear that his notion of "progress" applies only to the individual: "Truly speaking, all history exists for the Individual. Each of us stands absolutely alone in nature, and the great events of history only colossally represent the tendencies, the emotions, and the faculties of one man. I look therefore at the result of all the great agencies we have looked at in turn to be the education of the observer—of the private man. He takes them all up in his progress into himself" (*EL,* II, 173). And, a little later, even more emphatically: "All philosophy, all theory, all hope are defeated when applied to society. There is in it an incontrovertible brute force and it is not for the society of any actual present moment that is now or ever shall be, that we can hope or augur well. Progress is not for society. Progress belongs to the Individual" (*EL,* II, 176).

In rejecting the notion of any progress of humanity in general, and simultaneously affirming the need and possibility of individual culture, he could concur with Herder that "an inner spiritual man is developed within us, which is its own proper nature and which employs the body only as an instrument" (*S.W.,* XIII, 184). His vision of the final objective or goal of self-development also agrees with Herder's: "The clearer consciousness, this great privilege or advantage of the human soul, is itself in a spiritual fashion and indeed through humanity gradually first developed" (pp. 184–85). Surely in this notion of a "clearer consciousness" we find embodied and summarized everything Emerson had striven to express in his lectures on the philosophy of history. That it would be developed "in a spiritual fashion" constitutes a desideratum carried out in Emerson's description of the dialectical relation between individual and Universal Mind, the one engendering the other as its own activity within itself, the other transforming the consciousness of the former by raising it to a higher, purer level in which all traces of the finite self at last disappear. It remains only to give the peroration with which Emerson himself concluded his lectures on the philosophy of history, a conclusion that, like virtually everything else in his early phase, is both assertion and realization of a promise, of hitherto unfulfilled possibilities of the self:

> We see that nothing is without mind; that all things are steeped and bathed in mind; that it is like ourselves, yet overwhelms ourselves; that a power which we have not and are not, created the world, —yet is it so akin to man that the life we live, that thought we think, are the purlieus and precincts— yea, the first inspirations of that Absolute Mind. We feel within our imperfect private life the perfection of the universal. Into our little bay ebb and flow the tides of the great ocean. And when we look steadily into the deeps of our own being, into our sense of Justice, of Truth, of Benevolence, we see that we are not children of time: the body and the individual fortune is a circumstance and we hear with calm assent the primeval strains in which age chaunts to age the immortality of the soul. (*EL*, II, 187–88)

# 12    *Hawthorne*

Formally speaking, the story of Alice Pyncheon represents a discrete interlude in *The House of the Seven Gables*. Hawthorne deliberately contrasts it with the rest of his history by presenting it as a composition by Holgrave, the daguerreotypist. Yet, just as Holgrave's daguerreotypes have a way of bringing the essential or inner nature of their subjects into relief, so his story affords Hawthorne a means of illuminating the theme behind the Pyncheon history. Through a compact with Gervayse Pyncheon, who desires to obtain the lost deed for the Pyncheons' eastern territories, Matthew Maule is permitted to exercise his mesmerizing power over the beautiful Alice Pyncheon. In one of her trances she describes three figures as present "to her spiritualized perception":

> One of them, in truth—it was he with the blood-stain on his band—seemed, unless his gestures were misunderstood, to hold the parchment in his immediate keeping, but was prevented, by his two partners in the mystery, from disburthening himself of the trust. Finally, when he showed a purpose of shouting forth the secret, loudly enough to be heard from his own sphere into that of mortals, his companions struggled with him, and pressed their hands over his mouth; and forthwith—whether that he were choked by it, or that the secret itself was of a crimson hue—there was a fresh flow of blood upon his band. Upon this, the two meanly-dressed figures mocked and jeered at the much-abashed old dignitary, and pointed their fingers at the stain! (Centenary, II, 207)

The pantomime or visual allegory expresses the theme of the Pyncheon family history. It concerns a struggle for possession, in which one family (the Pyncheons) sacrifice their own souls or minds to obtain the wealth held by another. For the first Pyncheon, that wealth assumes the form of the land whose title he wrests from Matthew Maule; for his successors, it consists of the secret whereabouts of the Indian deed conveying to the Pyncheon family vast eastward territories. The struggle for possession leads to psychological obsession—such at least is one meaning of the original Maule's curse upon the Pyncheon house. Possession of the Maule's heritage at the price of violating another's rights leads to a secret guilt-consciousness emblemized in the gurgling within the throat hereditarily carried by the Pyncheon heirs, conforming to Maule's curse: "let them have blood to drink." The motions of the personages in the trance indicate the relation between the guilt obsession and the failure of the Pyncheon family to recover its fortunes: the efforts of the first Pyncheon to reveal the secret provoke repressive efforts by the Maules and—in consequence—the appearance of a fresh blood stain on the Pyncheon's ruff.

This stain symbolizes the guilt obsession that haunts the Pyncheon consciousness and prevents its members from reversing their gradual decline. It signifies in effect a crippling of the mind that acts upon the motive impulses and aspirations of the Pyncheons, frustrating their efforts with unseen inner constraints when objectives seem almost within their grasp. Hawthorne's mode of expressing himself is significant: "his companions struggled with him, and pressed their hands over his mouth; and forthwith—whether that he were choked by it, or that the secret itself was of a crimson hue—there was a fresh flow of blood upon his band." The "fresh flow of blood"—traditional indication of the presence of a murderer—refers symbolically to Pyncheon himself. Furthermore, the secret *is* figuratively "of a crimson hue," since the possession of the territories is, through the first Pyncheon, inseparably bound up with the guilt obsession derived from the Maules. The allegorical presence of the latter in Alice Pyncheon's trance signifies their psychological presence: Colonel Pyncheon's attempt to speak provokes a response from them that is as the guilt-prompting of an obsessed consciousness.

The guilt obsession that the Pyncheon successors carry with them is not, for Hawthorne, one of conscience, in the sense of moral awareness. It refers rather to a psychological force that those whose rights are violated have over their oppressors. In their struggle for possession of the lands, the Pyncheons expose themselves by revealing their secret desire; the Maules' knowledge of it guarantees their ascendancy over the Pyncheons. Symbolized in the story of Alice Pyncheon in terms of mesmerism, its true nature is simply knowledge of another's secret desire or motive—a knowledge that confers upon its possessor power to govern or destroy the subject of that desire.

The result of this struggle for possession—a dual conflict, since the Pyncheons' aspiration for territories is matched by the Maules' desire to possess their minds or souls—is, on the Pyncheons' side, a loss of self. Hawthorne expresses it in terms of the Romantic concept of self-consciousness. To lose one's self-consciousness (as in a mesmeristic trance) is to lose the power of choice and awareness of moral imperatives that comes with the sentience of individual identity, the sense of one's relation to others that determines the movements of feeling and desire in an individual. This consciousness of self is what Alice Pyncheon loses in her struggle with Matthew Maule. One may read her story as an allegory of seduction and sexual possession—which adds yet another dimension to the conflict between the two families, inextricably joined in a dialectic of desire and exploitation.

The consciousness of a striving for possession on one level or another is what is transmitted from generation to generation of both families. The transmission of this impulse ensures the continuity of history. That continuity is one of consciousness. For Hawthorne, historical development is neither a colorful pageantry of events nor the progress or decline of city-states, nations, or empires. It involves, rather, a progressive transformation of the individual consciousness from age to age, epoch to epoch. The history of the House of the Seven Gables thus exemplifies a gradual transformation of consciousness. The inner or psychological forces released by crime and its effects transform the consciousness of a family. Once released, these forces must be allowed to exhaust (expend) themselves—hence the narrative of suffering and guilt that accompanies successive generations as the effects of such forces manifest themselves in the tendency toward immoral desires and objectives that in turn produce their own consequences. For Hawthorne, historical consciousness is not knowledge of the past but rather transmission of the consciousness that had acted to form it: only by a knowledge of that past does it become possible to transform this consciousness.[1]

Such transcendence is possible only through an act of conscious volition which confronts and opposes the power of that consciousness. In *The House of the Seven Gables* Holgrave performs such an act when, imitat-

---

[1]Cf. Roy Harvey Pearce, "Romance and the Study of History," in *Hawthorne Centenary Essays*, ed. Roy Harvey Pearce (Columbus: Ohio State Univ. Press, 1964), pp. 225–30. With *The House of the Seven Gables*, however, one is tempted to ask: does the representation of the effects of the Pyncheon past upon the present (Clifford, Hepzibah) not exhibit in fact a certain form of historical determinism? To be sure, Holgrave exercises the possibility of choice ("Phoebe's Good Bye"), but one clearly tempered by the pressures of that determinism, as manifested in the internalization of the Maule impulse for psychological possession in Holgrave's consciousness. In this sense, history itself is internalized as the affirmation of a past impulse in the consciousness. Hawthorne's mode of historical explanation, then, translates the social into the psychological but within the latter realm adheres unswervingly to historical or causal explanation. One recalls his dictum that the romance (especially the historical romance, for which Scott furnishes his model) "sins unpardonably, so far as it may swerve aside from the truth of the human heart" (Centenary, II, 1).

ing the gestures of Matthew Maule as he reads the story of Alice Pyncheon, he produces on Phoebe the same mesmeric effect as that exercised by his ancestor. At that moment, "with but one wave of his hand and a corresponding effort of his will, he could complete his mastery over Phoebe's yet free and virgin spirit" (Centenary, II, 212). His refusal to do so is accompanied by full awareness of the power he thereby renounces. In so doing, he opposes and triumphs over the impulse toward spiritual possession which had obsessed his ancestor, the carpenter Matthew Maule.[2] This reenactment of the mesmeric seduction of Alice Pyncheon results in a different outcome because of the informing presence of another and higher consciousness than that possessed by Matthew Maule. "Let us," says Hawthorne, "concede to the Daguerreotypist the rare and high quality of reverence for another's individuality. Let us allow him integrity, also, forever after to be confided in; since he forbade himself to twine that one link more, which might have rendered his spell over Phoebe indissoluble" (Centenary, II, 212).

Such "integrity" consists of self-consciousness. It forms the necessary complement to the "reverence for another's individuality." Through self-consciousness, Holgrave becomes aware of the other *as* an other, a self different from himself. The force of self-consciousness acts as a repelling power, producing a distancing from the other in what we might describe as Hawthorne's dialectic of consciousness. In its form, that dialectic corresponds to the Romantic opposition between self and other in Wordsworth, Coleridge, or Shelley. At the same time Hawthorne differs from his Romantic predecessors inasmuch as his notion of self-consciousness is not a consciousness of consciousness but rather of feeling or sensibility, an awareness of the "I" as a suffering, sentient being moved by passions and impulses that transcend the rational intellect. The awareness of self as a subject of feeling becomes awareness of what opposes or confronts the self as a similar subject. Hence Hawthorne can speak of "reverence for another's individuality"—not for the other as an ideal self similar in essence to the "I," but as a being radically different in its humanness, the subject of other feelings and desires.

Holgrave's refusal to exert his power over Phoebe, to possess her spiritually, anticipates the moment of subjective communion at the end of the novel in which, according to Hawthorne, the historical consciousness is fully transcended:

And it was in this hour, so full of doubt and awe, that the one miracle was wrought, without which every human existence is a blank. The bliss, which

---

[2]This point nicely observed by Michael Davitt Bell, *Hawthorne and the Historical Romance of New England* (Princeton: Princeton Univ. Press, 1971), p. 216. For commentary on Hawthorne's general view of history as embodied in *The House of the Seven Gables*, see pp. 214–21.

makes all things true, beautiful, and holy, shone around this youth and maiden. They were conscious of nothing sad nor old. They transfigured the earth, and made it Eden again, and themselves the two first dwellers in it. The dead man, so close beside them, was forgotten. At such a crisis, there is no Death; for Immortality is revealed anew, and embraces everything in its hallowed atmosphere. (Centenary, II, 307)

Such magical moments do not come about without a precipitating cause—in this case Judge Pyncheon's death. Hawthorne's sense that the fatality of external circumstances can affect the life and development of consciousness—above all those of the affections—leads him to emphasize the human quality of these affections, their susceptibility to accidents of time and place, the pressure of events and impressions. The movement of feeling which leads Holgrave and Phoebe to confess their love to each other possesses what Hawthorne had elsewhere called the "warm mysteriousness that is between men," and it is significant that, as in that other instance (from *Septimius Felton*), the presence of death should be the cause of such reflections.

Unlike the moment of pantheistic communion described by Coleridge in his Notebooks or later by Melville in his famous response to Hawthorne's reception of *Moby-Dick,* the communion of Holgrave and Phoebe is not one in which each individual's consciousness of being merges with the other's. For Hawthorne, their communion is one of feelings alone. It is the knowledge they now share of being loved by the other. Such knowledge is itself a form of spiritually possessing the other. Only the fact of its being reciprocal enables it to transcend the desire for and abuse of possession that pervades the whole history of the two families. To expose one's inner feelings or affections creates a moment of vulnerability. In telling Phoebe he loves her, Holgrave voluntarily puts himself, spiritually speaking, in her possession. Significantly (and regardless of what these gestures may have to do with the conventions of nineteenth-century sensibility), Phoebe's first response is to refuse his affection, even though (as we learn almost immediately after) she loves him. Her refusal signifies a renunciation of the possibility of possession. An intense reverence for the other's individuality prompts her refusal, overcome only by Holgrave's insistence that she already possesses him, as it were, irrevocably, so that the only hope of restoring equilibrium in this dialectic of the affections is an answering affection. The acceptance by each of the other's love makes possible a transcendence of the inherited familial consciousness, with its dominant desire for possession. Holgrave and Phoebe must each renounce unilateral possession (which would become psychological or spiritual tyranny) before they can accept reciprocal possession.

Hawthorne's description of a transcendence of historical consciousness through the affections evokes the Romantic theme of a subjective transfiguration of the world which appears in both Shelley and Wordsworth. Such transcendence produces something like a new consciousness in which the sense of time, the element of temporality, disappears completely. This new consciousness is not merely one that subsumes the past. Rather, the nature of its perceptions causes the sense of time to disappear from our consciousness of things. Hawthorne employs the figure of an Edenic state, but his use of it suggests that this state is for him wholly subjective. By implication, historical time itself is also subjective: it represents a state of consciousness the mind transcends when it adopts another mode of perception. "At such a crisis," Hawthorne observes, "there is no Death, for Immortality is revealed anew, and embraces everything in its hallowed atmosphere." Such immortality does not refer to another life but rather to one that exists within the here and now.

The moments that bring about a communion of affections are, as we have seen, above time. For Hawthorne they are also sacred insofar as they express a pledge of the self. The consciousness of communion embraces more, however, than just its subjects. It extends to external things as well. The sacredness it confers upon these comes from the quality they possess in a moment of perception informed by feeling or affection. At such moments they become the content of that feeling, the image or reality that gives it color and life. Hawthorne thus moves toward a different conception of time, transcending historical or temporal consciousness. In his new mode of consciousness, which freely accepts its own subjective nature, all things assume a new significance by their role in moments of perception. The experience of their transfiguration accounts for Hawthorne's assertion that in such moments "Immortality is revealed anew."

In his celebrated description of the battle of Waterloo in *La Chartreuse de Parme* Stendhal presents the spectacle of the colossal and epoch-making conflict from a highly unusual perspective: no massed squares of infantry repelling frantic cavalry assaults, no storming of farmhouses or deafening artillery bombardments; instead, a series of isolated and confused movements by small groups of horsemen on a field removed from the general scene of the battle. Such is Fabrice's view of Waterloo. To appreciate its originality, one has only to contrast it with the scenes from the wars over the royal succession in Scotland which fill the pages of Scott's *Waverley* novels. There we receive accounts of the shock of encounter between large masses of troops, the dramatic charges and repulses of cavalry, and so on, described from an omniscient perspective that presents the whole sweep and grandeur of crucial historical moments. In contrast, what Stendhal's account emphasizes is in effect the irrationality and lack of apparent causality in events, which result from the absence of a pervading historical consciousness. This irrationality and incoherence of actions represents for Stendhal the reality of history. In its resemblance to Stendhal, Hawthorne's depiction of part of the battle of Concord in *Septimius Felton* reveals the differences that separate him not only from Scott but from his own earlier view of the historical process. As he ascends the hillside outside his house, Septimius witnesses the approach of the British troops:

> Listening eagerly, however, he at length fancied a mustering sound of the drum; then a march, as if it were coming towards him; while in advance rode another horseman, the same kind of headlong messenger, in appearance, who had passed the house with his ghastly cry of alarum, that morning; then appeared scattered countrymen with guns in their hands straggling across fields. Then he caught sight of the regular array of British soldiers, filling the road with their front, and marching on as firmly as ever; though at a quick pace, while he fancied that the officers looked watchfully around. While he looked, a shot rang sharp from the hillside, towards the village; the smoke curled up; and Septimius saw a man stagger and fall, in the midst of the troops. Septimius shuddered; it was so like murder that he really could not tell the difference; his knees trembled beneath him, his breath grew short, not with terror, but with some new sensation of awe. (Centenary, XIII, 24)

This example of Hawthorne's great late style, with all the purity and precision of his earlier compositions plus even more subtle harmonies and a more complex play of cross-lights, corresponds to an ever-deepening psychological awareness. The "objectivity" of the English and the French and Italian Notebooks achieves its full effect here, with the depiction of the approaching British troops and of the Yankee messenger who rides in advance to warn the Minutemen. All appearance of causality is carefully avoided in the account; one event succeeds another without the suggestion of any connection between them. The messenger is simply "another horseman," the frantic and uncertain mood of the moment indicated in his description as "the same kind of headlong messenger, in appearance, who had passed the house with his ghastly cry of alarum, that morning." The qualification "in appearance" is significant: Septimius himself is uncertain whether there is any relation. The "ghastly cry of alarum" suggests another mood than that of military ardor for the approaching conflict, a kind of terror as of enormous hidden forces or energies about to be unleashed. "Then appeared scattered countrymen with guns in their hands straggling across fields." Here the "then," denoting simply the passage of time, almost seems to imply the absence of any connection between their appearance and that of the messenger just before. Moreover, the narrative gives no hint of their objective; they are seen simply "straggling across fields." Only one touch is allowed to brighten the strangely objective perspective: the narrative refers to them as Septimius's "countrymen," indicating his unconscious identification with the rebel cause. The appearance of the British troops, finally, suggests yet further the uncertainty of the moment. Although presenting a "regular array," they march "at a quick pace," while Septimius fancies that the officers "looked watchfully around." Such suspicion implies awareness of an enemy as yet unseen. And, in the next instant, "While he looked, a shot rang sharp from the hillside, towards the village; the smoke curled up; and Septimius saw a man stagger and fall."

These visual and auditory impressions possess a crystalline clearness, which only serves to emphasize the isolation of each, the apparently unconnected sequence of the events Septimius witnesses. The measured cadence of the narrative imparts an almost surreal effect to the occurrence, and there is a palpable lingering, as if to appreciate the aesthetic aspect of the image, when after the sound of the shot Hawthorne describes how the smoke "curled up." With the observation that "Septimius saw a man stagger and fall, in the midst of the troops," Hawthorne subtly undercuts the protagonist's identification with the patriotic cause expressed earlier.[3] Of course the man who fell "in the midst of the troops" must have been an enemy soldier, yet the text remarks simply that Septimius "saw a man stagger and fall." The enemy soldier is nevertheless a human being, and at the moment of death Septimius feels the element of their common humanity. Yet the death itself seems strangely distant: Septimius only *sees* the man stagger and fall. There is no sound (which would make the impression more real) and no mention of the death itself. Despite the surrealism of the event, Septimius shudders. "It was so like murder that he really could not tell the difference." Behind the question he appears to put to himself, the narrative ironically asserts that there *is* no difference. With respect to Septimius himself there is, however, no irony: the fact that he "really could not tell the difference" indicates a moment of vertigo, in which the act appears denuded of all its ascribed value. The virtual equivalence of murder and patriotic defense cancels out both valuations, and the act then represents simply an event, without any associations at all. The realization of this denuding of the act produces a strange excitement in Septimius, and he reacts "not with terror, but with some new sensation of awe." Such awe could indicate reverence, and the suggestion would be in this case not inappropriate. What produces the feeling is Septimius's recognition of a similar impulse to kill within himself: "And, in a moment, the horse would leap; the officer would fall, and lie there in the dust of the road, bleeding, gasp-

[3]A strategy identified by Colacurcio with regard to Hawthorne's early tales; see Michael Colacurcio, *The Province of Piety* (Cambridge: Harvard Univ. Press, 1984), p. 463.

ing, breathing in gulps, breathing no more." At the last moment before death, life is reduced to the level of the purely physical, and it is especially significant that in a work concerned with the elixir of immortality the physical presence and quality of life should come to seem so important.

The impulse to kill which Septimius feels in himself produces awe because it seems to proceed from the life force itself, as an expression of its own vitality. At this moment the veil of historical consciousness which shrouds the events of the Revolutionary period is, as it were, rent asunder. What appears in its place is the energy of the life force as it asserts its own vitality with a violence that has nothing to do with the rational will. At the time of writing his narrative, Hawthorne himself is in fact almost a century removed from the events he describes; from that vantage point, they could already assume for him something of the same historical aspect they have for us. Yet, as frequently remarked, the presence of the Civil War as an immediate reality could also impart to his depiction of another, earlier war a very different perspective. On the other hand, a conflict such as the Civil War could not, needless to say, appear for Hawthorne through the medium of a historical consciousness. Such consciousness assumes and is based upon a sense of closure: the event or events in question must have already achieved completion in order for them to give a defining form to that consciousness, which is in essence the sense of a process or entelechy actualizing itself. The impression of temporality as a becoming, as the consciousness of a moment about to be, informing the whole with a teleology that makes the events themselves seem only an external expression of historical forces, the sense of time as the temporal element of consciousness itself, pervading its perceptions in an inescapable fashion—all this belongs to the historical consciousness as manifested in the romances of Sir Walter Scott, the Waverley novels with their re-creation of the most momentous and significant phase of Scotland's history.

Against such historical consciousness, Hawthorne in his Elixir of Life manuscripts (*Septimius Felton* and *Septimius Norton*) sets another, quite different mode of perception, one that presents the past moment as pure actuality, without awareness of a temporality of becoming which would lead that actuality into the next moment in time. What appears instead is an absence of causality: each individual moment not flowing into the next, every moment or act seeming suspended in isolation. Through and in pure actuality, the time consciousness so essential to history disappears.

In the Elixir of Life manuscripts, the Revolutionary War thus presents itself as something without precedent and without consequences, a timeless moment in which only the presence of life itself matters. In contrast to *The House of the Seven Gables*, there can never be a moment in which a higher consciousness confronts that of a past epoch and transcends it (as with Holgrave and Phoebe vis-à-vis the relation of their two families). Nor is the romance effect from the descent of a past atmosphere into the present achieved in the unfinished versions of either *Septimius Felton* or *Septimius Norton*. In fact, the pure actuality that gives to a moment of the Revolutionary War the nature of a timeless present exhibits hardly any consciousness at all—in the sense of a subjective medium through which external circumstances and events are brought into relation with each other. Septimius's perception of the skirmish preceding the battle of Concord displays the objectivity that comes of depriving events of their interrelatedness, this interrelatedness being, as it were, the subjective element of the perception. The moment of pure actuality defines Hawthorne's notion of the essence of historical time. For the later Hawthorne, the historical consciousness consists simply of the subjective element through which we perceive the past and by which we endow it with attributes it does not possess. Or perhaps it does possess them, but only because the consciousness of those who live through that specific moment later create for it a sense of historicity. Such historicity would then be the element of temporality inherent in consciousness itself. Consciousness, then, *creates* temporality, but only after the event itself is past, as if by so doing it could then recover that past for itself, form and assimilate it into memory. Hawthorne's notion of historical time in *The House of the Seven Gables*, a consciousness of the past descending down into the present, is not however completely negated here. Instead, Hawthorne turns to another question, the nature of the historical moment in itself rather than in the creative memory of subjective consciousness.

The same question is explored from a different perspective in the other unfinished project of Hawthorne's last years, the so-called American Claimant manuscripts. A young American, heir to an English estate as the only surviving descendent of the cadet branch of an aristocratic family whose elder branch has ceased to have direct descendents, returns to his ancestral homeland in hopes of piecing together his family history. In so doing, he encounters in one or another version of the manuscript some form of violent resistance and even an attempt at taking his life. After various experiences he decides to renounce his patrimony and return to America.

From the evidence of the manuscripts it appears that at least one of Hawthorne's intentions had been to depict the encounter of the new with the older, more archaic forms of consciousness. During his years as American consul in England, he was bound to have been struck by such phenomena on numerous occasions. In light of his other unfinished romance (the Elixir of Life manuscripts), with its attempts to expose the phenomenological essence of life itself, the exploration of the past here assumes a deeper form, as a quest for the true nature of the historical moment.

Because of the difference in modes of consciousness between one country and another, Middleton's journey to England assumes the appearance of a quest that confronts its own past as something present, that is, in its pure actuality. The result makes it clear that, for Hawthorne, the mere passage of time is not sufficient to ensure historical continuity or development, that such development belongs not so much to a "spirit of the age" but to the subjective nature of each individual. His choice of an Italianized nobleman as the current possessor of the English estate in the later versions of the manuscript reflects his awareness of the individual and emotional nature of a mode of consciousness. In Italy, even more than England, he would have found traces of the earlier strata of sensibility and feeling. Placed in direct and immediate confrontation with such forms of consciousness, one cannot "historicize" them. One either identifies with or renounces them. Middleton's sojourn in the pensioners' residence represents his initiation into the thought and feeling of a past epoch. His final decision to renounce the English heritage reflects an admission that the past as such (in its pure actuality) is not recoverable by the present, cannot be reconciled to the present. All that remains possible is the "historicizing" of it, which is the work of the subjective consciousness.

When all allowance has been made for the differences between Scott and Hawthorne, however, the true nature of Scott's legacy to his American successor becomes clearer. What distinguishes Scott's enterprise from that of its predecessors as the beginning of the modern historical novel is its attempt to portray what we might call the history of sensibility. From the very first Scott had been conscious in this respect of the originality of his purpose. In his preface to *Waverley* he states: "I must be understood to have [thrown] the force of my narrative upon the characters and passions of the actors;—those passions common to men in all stages of society, and which have alike agitated the human heart, whether it throbbed under the steel corslet of the fifteenth century, the brocaded coat of the eighteenth, or the blue frock and white dimity waistcoat of the present day" (p. 5). In according his novels this emphasis, he attempts to sustain the delicate balance between what we might term the eternism of the passions and the influence of historical forces and circumstances: "Upon these passions it is no doubt true that the state of manners and laws casts a necessary colouring; but the bearings, to use the language of heraldry, remain the same, though the tincture may be not only different, but opposed in strong contradistinction" (*Waverley*, p. 5).

In *Waverley* itself that balance appears as one between the emotion that ultimately draws Edward Waverley to Rose Bradwardine and that which attracts him to the cause of Fergus Mac-Ivor and the Scottish clans. Waverley's initial passion for Flora, Fergus's sister, exemplifies in its difficulties and ambivalences the ambivalent nature of Waverley's devotion to the Scottish cause. His sparing of Talbot's life, his relative absence of emotion over Fergus's execution (as well as his emotional distancing of himself from Fergus earlier) stand in irreconcilable conflict with his passionate adherence earlier to the Stuart succession and point to Scott's own juxtaposition between the historical element in human feelings and passions (the "tincture" or "colouring" they assume from the nature of their specific historical objects) and what I have referred to earlier as their "eternistic" aspect, their tendency toward certain recurrent modes of growth and development. It is hardly surprising that Scott should have found in *Romeo and Juliet* the model for his romance (see *Waverley*, p. 256), translating the Shakespearean fatalism of the "star-crossed lovers" into a more modern historical determinism that contrasts Waverley and Flora in terms of religious and social ideology.

A similar opposition between the historical and eternistic aspects of sensibility appears in *Old Mortality*, in which Henry Morton (like Edward Waverley) undergoes a shift of allegiance from one royal house to another. His transformation both parallels and counterpoints that of Claverhouse, who becomes, at the end, Viscount of Dundee, signalizing his change of allegiance. The historical nature of the passions in this novel appears perhaps most strikingly in Scott's portrayal of the fanaticism of Balfour of Burley. As Henry Morton observes: "Alas! what are we, that our best and most praiseworthy feelings can be thus debased and depraved. . . . But it is the same throughout; the liberal principles of one man sink into cold and unfeeling indifference, the religious zeal of another hurries him into frantic and savage enthusiasm. Our resolutions, our passions, are like the waves of the sea, and, without the aid of Him who formed the human breast, we cannot say to its tides, 'Thus far shall ye come, and no farther'" (*Waverley*, p. 198). The eternistic element of Morton's sensibility manifests itself most strongly in the sentiment that finally impels his return to Milnwood. This episode, which allows Scott to develop the Romantic motif of the return to one's beginnings with a higher consciousness, can also exemplify his own conception of the nature of the historical consciousness, as one involving transformation of the "colouring" of a feeling which—without altering that feeling itself—permits certain accretions of awareness in remembrance that are as the increment of historical comprehension of a past state of feeling or emotion.

With Hawthorne's *House of the Seven Gables*, similarly, we encounter the opposition (which is also interfusion) of historical and eternistic elements of sensibility. The Pyncheon desire for material possession, set against the Maules' passion for spiritual or psychological possession, reveals a similar mixture of feeling except that, in this case, Hawthorne emphasizes the sameness or eternism rather than historical difference. But the terms of the problem have also altered somewhat, since for

Hawthorne the opposition between eternistic and historical aspects of sensibility cannot be resolved simply by positing their simultaneous existence in some specific balance or relationship. For Hawthorne, the problem is rather that the historical must be in some sense overcome: the persistence of certain desires and tendencies signifies for him not only the historical element of consciousness but even the oppression of consciousness by its own historical awareness.

This relationship between consciousness and historical awareness is complicated further by the Romantic and subjective concept of time, one that permits the possibility of transcendence by transforming our perception of the temporal process. As a result of such temporal transcendence, the significance of the historical dimension is itself altered: instead of composing one of the inescapable and necessary conditions of our existence, it becomes merely one of the modes through which we perceive that existence. This radical subjectivization of history is in one respect merely the development of a process that begins with Scott's historicizing of emotion, but it also represents something more: a vision of the relation between subjectivity and the historical consciousness which sees that consciousness itself as subjective in the sense of containing internalized desires and impulses rather than simply an awareness of the past. The subjective, for Hawthorne, transcends that consciousness when it recognizes the historical as nothing more than the presence of past tendencies or desires in its own medium of awareness, while within itself, because of its possibility of dwelling in an eternal moment outside of time, it thereby sees the reality of history as having only a subjective, rather than objective, existence.

Another of Scott's notable innovations had been the introduction of a new historical perspective. The portrayal of historical events through the eyes of a representative of the "middle way" rather than one of the great historical personages places such events in a new light.[4] To witness the wars over the Hanoverian succession or the religious wars of the seventeenth century through the eyes of a Waverley or a Henry Morton is to see the interpretation of those conflicts become in itself an object of struggle and oscillation. Waverley's shift of allegiance colors subsequent events with a different significance, and Henry Morton's return from the Continent after years of exile coincides with the emergence of a new vision of English life and its possibilities. Hawthorne grasps the innovative character of Scott's treatment of historical perspective, but its effect is to move him to an even more radical or extreme approach. If the Waverley novels reveal a certain indeterminacy in the interpretation

---

[4]See on this point Georg Lukács's classic treatment of Scott in *The Historical Novel*, trans. Hannah Mitchell and Stanley Mitchell (London: Merlin Press, 1962), pp. 32–35, and, for a more recent study of Scott's historical fiction in general, Harry E. Shaw, *The Forms of Historical Fiction: Sir Walter Scott and His Successors* (Ithaca, N.Y.: Cornell Univ. Press, 1983).

of events and the determination of their value, Hawthorne's unfinished Elixir of Life romances, on the other hand, in their depiction of the early stages of the American Revolution, display a denudation of history so complete as to deprive events of all historical meaning whatsoever. When Septimius Felton witnesses the deaths of British soldiers on the retreat from Concord, what he sees is not the heroic defense of American freedom but rather simple murder. We may discern in this merely the intensification of a subjectivism already present in Scott. But what Hawthorne is progressing toward, ultimately, is perhaps best described as a transcendence of the historical perspective through one that has no "historical" element at all and whose only values are the immanent ones of life itself.

# PART V

## *Pantheism*

# 13  Poe: The Divine Energeia

Among the attacks on *Eureka*, one in particular seems to have aroused Poe's ire. Printed in the *Literary World*, then edited by Charles Fenno Hoffman, and signed " A Student of Theology," it prompted a response (September 20, 1848) from Poe to Hoffman. In his letter, after rebutting the charges of the "Student," Poe then observes that he "would have permitted their dishonesty to pass unnoticed," "were these 'misrepresentations' (*is* that the name for them?) made for any less serious purpose than that of branding my book as 'impious' and myself as a 'pantheist,' a 'polytheist,' a Pagan, or a God knows what (and indeed I care very little so it be not a 'Student of Theology,')" (*Letters*, II, 382).

This disclaimer of pantheism on Poe's part should not be disregarded. It points to the expression, in *Eureka*, of a theological cosmology much closer to the heretical systems surrounding and permeating primitive Christianity—Hermeticism, Gnosticism, the Logos-doctrine of Hellenistic Judaism—than to anything in Spinoza.[1] In his *Ethics* Spinoza had asserted that there is only one substance, God (Prop. xiv), and that "whatever is, is in God, and nothing can either be or be conceived without God" (Prop. xv). Substance does not create but simply *is*, so that, for Spinoza, it is more proper to say all things are in God (inherence) rather than that God is in all things (immanence). As the one substance, God contains all things by virtue of the act of being, but it would be impossi-

---

[1]*Pace* Vincent Buranelli, who claims: "His system is a kind of pantheism. His disclaimer to Charles Hoffman should not be allowed to go unchallenged; for, however much Poe may have disliked the term 'pantheist,' it applies to him because of the logic of his thought in 'Eureka'" (*Edgar Allan Poe*, 2d ed. [Boston: Twayne, 1977], p. 52). But if Poe associates a spiritual element in some sense with "Matter," it is significant that he equates this element with a principle that, if unopposed, would spell the collapse and ultimate disappearance of matter: "Discarding now the two equivocal terms, 'gravitation' and 'electricity,' let us adopt the more definite expressions, 'Attraction' and 'Repulsion.' The former is the body; the latter the soul: the one is the material; the other the spiritual, principle of the Universe" (*Poetry and Tales*, p. 1282).

ble for him to impart his essence to things in which it does not already inhere. This inference is based upon the intuition that the essences of things consist ultimately of an element like thought (Def. IV): hence the possibility of containing in one substance all the essences of things. The more attributes (or essences of things) something contains, the more real it is in itself (Prop. IX, argued from Def. IV).[2]

Against the Spinozistic system, so attractive to Coleridge, Wordsworth, and the German Romantics, one may set the traditions embodied in the Logos-doctrine of the fourth Gospel.[3] These traditions, which elaborate in their diverse ways a concept of emanationism, had held that the divine essence could impart itself to things and that it had created the cosmos (world) precisely for this purpose, as a means of releasing its superabundant plenitude.[4] Fundamental to such traditions and contrary to Spinozism is the belief that the infinity of God necessitates creation, an infinity based upon a constant expansion of the divine plenitude into new species or orders of things. To fulfill the need for expansion, it had been necessary to establish the difference between God and things: things are not inherent in God but must come into being *ex nihilo,* inasmuch as it would not be possible otherwise to define such a process as genuine creation, which implies an increase in substance that is not merely an actualization of the potential or the realization of an entelechy. In the Gnostic and Mandaean mythos, the divine essence must in some fashion create and descend into things. Its "descent" is not merely physical but spiritual, involving a mixture of the divine element with the earthly or material; subsequently the divine seeks to return to its source, bringing about a spiritualization of the earthly or mundane essence.

Poe affirms a similar pattern, but from a physicalistic-spiritualistic rather than mythical perspective. His schema involves the primordial or original creation by God of a single particle of matter and, subsequently, its division and diffusion until it assumes the form of a cosmos. This diffusion is not simply a physical process but one informed by teleological purposiveness. Its "ultimate design," according to Poe, is *"that of the utmost possible Relation"* (*Poetry and Tales,* p. 1280). But the purpose behind such relation would remain unfulfilled were it not for another force that prevents the diffused matter from recollapsing into the original unity or oneness. This force Poe describes as repulsion. Of it he writes:

[2]Def. IV: "By attribute, I understand that which the intellect perceives of substance, as if constituting its essence." Prop. IX: "The more reality or being a thing possesses, the more attributes belong to it."

[3]For which see C. H. Dodd, *The Interpretation of the Fourth Gospel* (Cambridge: Cambridge Univ. Press, 1953), pp. 263–85.

[4]Hence Proclus's assertion: "Every producing cause is productive of secondary existences because of its completeness and superfluity of potency" (prop. 27 from *The Elements of Theology,* 2d ed., ed. E. R. Dodds [Oxford: Clarendon Press, 1963], p. 31).

The *design* of the repulsion—the necessity for its existence—I have endeavored to show; but from all attempt at investigating its nature have religiously abstained; this on account of an intuitive conviction that the principle at issue is strictly spiritual—lies in a recess impervious to our present understanding—lies involved in a consideration of what now—in our human state—is *not* to be considered—in a consideration of *Spirit in itself.* (*Poetry and Tales*, p. 1281)

Thus the divine energy that had originally impelled the particles to diffuse themselves now acts as a deterrent to their reunion or recoalescence. Such energy is not to be conceived of as a divine being or presence immanent in the particles—if so, it could not depart from them at a given moment—but rather as a quasi-physical force that merely transmits its own energy to them for a determinate period of time, subsequently transforming itself into a force of repulsion. But if the divine essence is energy rather than being or substance, and if it does not always inhere in matter but only for a given interval, Poe's system cannot be termed pantheistic. It belongs, rather, to the classical tradition described earlier, in which the divine essence is viewed as a form of energeia, a creative and expansive energy that produces matter or things and then descends into them, filling them with its own irradiating force.

On account of its emanationism, then, we may compare the system of *Eureka* with that depicted by Shelley in poetic form in *Adonais,* in which

> the one Spirit's plastic stress
> Sweeps through the dull dense world, compelling there,
> All new successions to the forms they wear;
> Torturing th'unwilling dross that checks its flight
> To its own likeness, as each mass may bear;
> And bursting in its beauty and its might
> From trees and beasts and men into the Heaven's light.
> (Reiman and Powers, p. 402)

As with Poe, the energeia of the one Spirit does not identify itself with matter but merely impels it with its own energy ("compelling there, / All new successions to the forms they wear"). In its essence, this energy differs drastically from matter, whose physical nature is clearly emphasized: density is its characteristic property, here represented not only as inert mass but as substance that is of no account except for its resistance to energy ("th'unwilling dross"). That energy must proportion itself to the individual mass of each object ("as each mass may bear"). For Poe, similarly, each object or aggregate of matter is associated with an energy proportionate to its mass, and—as in Shelley—such energy is not that of the matter itself but one that merely imparts its own motion to it. Thus in *Eureka* the originally diffusive or expansive energy that creates the universe by impelling atoms outward from a center is replaced by a force of repulsion that prevents their collapse back upon that center: in either case, the energy must—as in Shelley—overcome the inertial tendency of matter itself.

In *Adonais* the process results in the conforming of matter to the "likeness" of the "one Spirit's plastic stress." Such likeness cannot be visual, since the resemblance is not to a visible object but to an impelling energy. As in Poe, it suggests the accordance of matter with the motion imparted to it by the "one Spirit." Given the classical framework of *Adonais*, the description of the Spirit's stress as "plastic" carries a special significance. Implicit here is the notion of an artistic shaping (consciously present, no doubt, to Shelley's mind, in view of his admiration for Greek sculpture), which in turn points toward a higher intention in the forming and transforming of matter. To be sure, Poe also exhibits consciousness of an aesthetic aspect in cosmic processes, although his analogy, as it turns out, will not be to sculpture but literature ("the plots of God are perfect. The universe is a plot of God"). As with Shelley, however, the aesthetic aspect of the cosmic process is inseparable from its very nature; hence its distinction from all human artistic productions.

Classical and Christian tradition had combined to associate the divine essence with circular motifs. Motion imparted from a divine source conforms to a circular pattern, consisting for Shelley of a descent of energy into the world and a return to its point of departure. Poe asserts the original diffusion of matter and its subsequent recoalescence in its source. Just as for Shelley the return to the source is endowed with a transfiguring radiance that assimilates all things "into the Heaven's light," so Poe affirms a corresponding inner transfiguration: the moment in which the individual soul attains awareness of its existence as God.

By elevating it to the level of human consciousness, Poe invests the neoplatonic motif of circularity with a Romantic significance. The circular movement that ultimately leads back to the source, and that appears in Ficino and others, becomes not merely an archetypal pattern embedded in the nature of things but an expression of teleological purposiveness. On its return, the spiritual energy brings with it the lower "successions" whose forms it impels, elevating them to a higher level. For Poe, it is the diffused matter that, on being reunited, is brought to a higher consciousness. For him and for the Romantics, the teleology behind such a pattern becomes expressive ultimately of a moral benevolence on the part of the divine essence which thereby imparts its own joy to the individual consciousnesses that fill the material sphere.

Thus far I have attempted to trace the affinities that relate the cosmology of *Eureka* to that of Shelley's *Adonais*. It remains now to consider their differences. For Shelley the motif of the return of things to their divine source had been associated with a biological concept—not, however, the Romantic notion of the organic, but the earlier Aristotelian scheme of "coming-to-be" and "passing away" (*De Generatione et Corruptione*), a concept that surfaces in Shelley's use of the term *successions*. Through his attraction to mathematics and the physical sciences, Poe had been led to conceive of the return to the source in different terms: in *Eureka* it assumes the aspect of mathematical symmetry. Characteristically, however, the symmetry that governs the movement of diffusion and recoalescence does not lead to a neoclassical affirmation of cosmic harmony but finds itself associated with the Romantic theme of the return as accession to a higher consciousness, in which the individual progressively becomes aware of his existence as God. Through this fusion of the mathematical or formal with the subjective nature of consciousness, Poe achieves a representation of process (diffusion-recoalescence) which is not inimical to quantitative description but assimilates it into its own nature while simultaneously transcending it. For Poe, as we have seen, mathematical formalism could never be self-sufficient but serves invariably as a cipher or symbolism for a higher, more essential mode of thought. For that mode of thought, contained in the cycle of diffusion and return, the motions of the celestial bodies themselves are in the end but a form of symbolism.

In spite of its emanationist form, it remains quite possible to misinterpret Poe's system in *Eureka* as a form of pantheism. Had not he himself, after all, asserted that "each soul is, in part, its own God—its own Creator: —in a word, that God—the material *and* spiritual God— *now* exists solely in the diffused Matter and Spirit of the Universe; and that the regathering of this diffused Matter and Spirit will be but the reconstitution of the *purely Spiritual* and Individual God" (*Poetry and Tales*, p. 1357). But, as Poe points out in his letter to Hoffman, the soul is only "in part" its own God (*Letters*, II, 381–82). Its divine quality comes from its association with the repulsive force that separates it from all other particles. Earlier this repulsive force, in the diffused state of matter, had represented the spiritual element, that is, God. But as the repulsive force it requires something to repel—in other words, matter. As repulsion, it remains inseparable from matter. With the disappearance of matter through its recoalescence into the one, the repulsive force as such disappears. Because it depends upon matter for its own existence, one must speak of a "material *and* spiritual (rather than purely spiritual) God," existing "in the diffused Matter and Spirit of the Universe." In that state, matter itself is not divine but merely establishes the necessary condition for the existence of the repulsive force.

With regard to the individual consciousness or self and its place in the cosmology of *Eureka*, we have seen that each individual soul is in part "its own God" and that, with the coalescence of all in the divine essence, individual consciousness will disappear. In the conclusion to *Eureka*, speaking of the role of individual souls in his cosmology, Poe writes:

> These creatures are all, too, more or less and more or less obviously, conscious Intelligences; conscious, first, of a proper identity; conscious, secondly and by faint indeterminate glimpses, of an identity with the Divine Being of whom we speak—of an identity with God. Of the two classes of consciousness, fancy that the former will grow weaker, the latter stronger, during the long succession of ages which must elapse before these myriads of individual Intelligences become blended—when the bright stars become blended—into One. Think that the sense of individual identity will be gradually merged in the general consciousness—that Man, for example, ceasing imperceptibly to feel himself Man, will at length attain that awfully triumphant epoch when he shall recognize his existence as that of Jehovah. In the meantime bear in mind that all is Life—Life—Life within Life—the less within the greater, and all within the *Spirit Divine*. (*Poetry and Tales*, pp. 1358–59)

Significantly, in his treatment of individual identity Poe refers to it not as the whole self but only as one aspect of it. If the self represents a part of the divine essence, its individual identity is but the consciousness of its separation from the whole. At the same time, it also possesses a consciousness of the divine element in which it participates, hence a consciousness of being God. Neither consciousness is, however, fixed, the one constantly diminishing as the other increases. In seeing consciousness in quantitative as well as qualitative terms, Poe is surely unique. For the system of *Eureka* it becomes apparent that there can be no such thing as an individual nature; according to Poe, the individual self represents not a nature but merely a state or condition—one in the process of constant alteration.

But if the sense of individual identity or consciousness is progressively decreasing, that decrease indicates in fact an increase in consciousness itself. On this point, a copy of *Eureka* found in Rufus Wilmot Griswold's library after his death contains the following handwritten note by Poe: "The Pain of the consideration that we shall lose our individual identity, ceases at once when we further reflect that the process, as above described, is neither more nor less than that of the absorption by each individual intelligence, of all other intelligences (that is of the Universe) into its own. That God may be all in all, *each* must become God."[5] To the extent that the self's disappearance increases consciousness (that is, of everything that all living things individually feel), Poe could concur with Shelley's reflection on Keats in *Adonais*:

---

[5]Quoted from Sarah Helen Whitman, *Edgar Poe and His Critics* (1860; rpt. New York: AMS Press, 1966), pp. 67–68.

He is made one with Nature; there is heard
His voice in all her music, from the moan
Of thunder, to the song of the night's sweet bird;
He is a presence to be felt and known
In darkness and in light, from herb and stone,
Spreading itself where'er that Power may move
Which has withdrawn his being to its own;
Which wields the world with never wearied love,
Sustains it from beneath, and kindles it above.

(Reiman and Powers, p. 402)

# 14   Emerson: The Divinity of the Self

When asked in later years about the precise meaning of his assertion in the Divinity School Address—"If a man is at heart just, then in so far is he God"—Emerson professed himself unable to recall whether he had meant, literally, that man *is* God or merely "is *as* God."[1] Like Newton's "tanquam" (as if) in his statement in the *Principia*, "space is the organ of God," this vacillation is highly significant.[2] It points to a shift, traceable through numerous utterances, from a pantheism that situates God in the inspired moments of the self to a more traditional affirmation of God as the creator of things, hence as something external to the self or consciousness.[3] But even from the beginning pantheism had been for Emerson highly problematic. To recover his early beliefs, we must turn to works such as *Nature* and the Divinity School Address, but above all to the journals of that period, in which these receive their fullest expression. An entry for May 26, 1837, states:

[1]See Lawrence Buell, *Literary Transcendentalism: Style and Vision in the American Renaissance* (Ithaca, N.Y.: Cornell Univ. Press, 1973), pp. 14–15.
[2]For a history of the differing copies of one edition of Newton's *Principia*, see Alexandre Koyré and I. Bernard Cohen, "The Case of the Missing *Tanquam*," *Isis*, 52 (1961), 555–66.
[3]Buell observes: "The central preoccupation of the movement was the relationship between self and God; compared to this, nature was of secondary importance" (p. 146). And, on the transient quality of moments of divine consciousness: "The theme of the growth of man's mind is alien to Transcendentalism; Transcendentalism recognizes, so to speak, no continuity between past and present; and once the experience of ecstasy is past there is no knowing whether it can be recovered" (p. 222). In *Freedom and Fate: An Inner Life of Ralph Waldo Emerson* (Philadelphia: Univ. of Pennsylvania Press, 1953), Stephen Whicher describes Emerson's pantheistic recognition: "Emerson's dawn came when his soul perceived God in the one place doubt could never reach—in itself" (p. 20). And subsequently: "The rock on which he thereafter based his life was the knowledge that the soul of man does not merely, as had long been taught, contain a spark or drop or breath or voice of God; it *is* God" (p. 21).

A certain wandering light comes to me which I instantly perceive to be the Cause of Causes. It transcends all proving. It is itself the ground of being; and I see that it is not one & I another, ⟨but⟩ but this is the life of my life. That is one fact, then; that in certain moments I have known that I existed directly from God, and am, as it were, his organ. And in my ultimate consciousness Am He. (*JMN*, v, 337)

And, on March 19, 1838: "To absolute mind, a person is but a fact, but consciousness is God" (*JMN*, v, 466). But if God is "the ground of being" (an intuition Emerson appears to borrow from Jakob Boehme's notion of the "Un-ground" that produces Being), the essence of being must be consciousness.[4] Which is to say: the medium of being is that of consciousness; being in its nature or element is nothing else than consciousness. Being asserts the existence of things. That assertion, however, must not be taken to belong to things; instead, it precedes them. In itself, the assertion is pure apprehension. As such it exists apart from all things.

If pure consciousness is God, the apprehension of pure consciousness must be the experience of God. In this experience, according to Emerson, all phenomena become as it were transparent to the self: what it perceives is only pure consciousness colored by phenomenal impressions.[5] In itself such consciousness can have no limits; it is infinite. But the apprehension of pure consciousness is in its nature no different from consciousness itself. Hence it merges with it, becomes one with it. Similarly, through its experience of God, the self *becomes* God. And in fact, for Emerson in his early phase, God *is* nothing else than the experience of pure consciousness.

On account of its preoccupation with the nature of consciousness, Emerson's subjective pantheism must be distinguished from traditional mystical experience. Unlike mysticism, it describes no image or revelation vouchsafed to the self in its moment of rapture.[6] In contrast to the former, it presupposes not a withdrawal from the world (which makes possible the formation of the inner image or the hearing of an "inner voice") but rather a mode of perception through which all external impressions are volatilized and dissolved into a single and radiant experience of pure *seeing* or consciousness. In this experience, finite objects

[4]On Boehme, see Alexandre Koyré, *La Philosophie de Jacob Boehme* (Paris: Vrin, 1929; 2d ed. 1971).

[5]For a view of this "transparency" as problematic, see Julie Ellison, *Emerson's Romantic Style* (Princeton: Princeton Univ. Press, 1984), p. 224; and, on the association between the religious or moral sentiment and the "illimitable" nature of consciousness (self-consciousness), see p. 106.

[6]In his essay on Emerson in *A History of Modern Criticism: 1750–1950* (New Haven: Yale Univ. Press, 1955–), René Wellek remarks: "Basically, Emerson's concept of the universe is Neoplatonic. It is an emanistic pantheism—modernized, however, by a certain fluidity and imaginative freedom opposed to literal mysticism and scholastic rigidity" (III, 165).

cease to appear as such: what the mind perceives is, instead, those impressions of light and form and color that coalesce to form its perception of an object, but seen now purely as phenomena of consciousness, aspects of the divine plenitude of its own experience of the infinite.

From such a perspective, the necessity in mystical experience for an arcane symbolism disappears. Now, all phenomenal impressions, properly perceived, can offer revelations of the nature of the infinite or divine essence. In this sense, Emerson's concept of Nature as the consecrated tabernacle of the divine manifests its affinity with the Romantic theory of symbolism.[7] For Emerson, however, the divine presence inheres not in the objects themselves but in the consciousness that perceives them. On that point he could concur with Coleridge: "O Lady! we receive but what we give, / And in our life alone does Nature live." An entry from Emerson's journals (Jan. 6, 1837) reflects the same thought: "It occurred to me at midnight with more clearness than I can now see it, that not in nature but in man was all the beauty & worth he sees; that the world is very empty & is indebted to this gilding & exalting soul for all its pride. . . . The vale of Tempe, Tivoli, & Rome are but earth & water, rocks & sky" (*JMN*, v, 279). But if the experience of divinity inheres in consciousness rather than Nature, it can occur anywhere, at any time, as for instance in walking across Boston Common, whose puddles on an overcast day reflect the sky, late one December afternoon (the experience that gives rise to the "transparent eye-ball" passage in *Nature*).[8]

At such moments, the self's experience is one of pure consciousness. The element of a thing's being (a finite object) is felt or experienced as that of its apprehension: the source of the impression of being which a thing conveys associates itself with the apprehension of that thing rather than with the thing itself. Thus consciousness assimilates all external impressions into itself. In so doing, it gives to such impressions and the "objects" they form the appearance of possessing being. What creates that being, however, is in fact not the objects themselves but the medium of apprehension or consciousness, which becomes conscious of itself as the "presence" of such things. For Emerson, there can be no such thing as being in an absolute sense, the property by which something exists in and through itself; rather, through pure consciousness, all finite objects are endowed for the mind with a quality of "presence."[9]

---

[7]On Emerson's theory of symbolism, ibid., pp. 163–64.

[8]On this celebrated metaphor in Emerson, see, in addition to Sherman Paul, *Emerson's Angle of Vision* (Cambridge: Harvard Univ. Press, 1952), pp. 72–102; James M. Cox, "R. W. Emerson: The Circles of the Eye," in *Emerson: Prophecy, Metamorphosis, and Influence*, ed. David Levin (New York: Columbia Univ. Press, 1975), pp. 57–81; and Jonathan Bishop, *Emerson on the Soul* (Cambridge: Harvard Univ. Press, 1964), pp. 37–40.

[9]In this notion of the mind's ability to apprehend the nature of its own consciousness, we discern Emerson's originality. Even Sampson Reed's *Observations on the Growth of the Mind* offers nothing really similar. In his work Reed observes: "Another object of the preceding

Hence the prevalence, throughout Emerson's works, of metaphors of flux, of ebbing and flowing. In *Nature:* "The currents of the Universal Being circulate through me; I am part or particle of God" (*Coll. W.,* 1, 10). Such metaphors describe the welling-up or eruption of pure consciousness within the self, the moment at which the mind becomes conscious of its perceptions *as* perceptions, as acts of an indwelling consciousness. It is the eruption of consciousness itself which conveys the impression of flux, the feeling of things dissolving or coalescing and hence of their essential transience. Because it is not merely a passive but assertive force, such consciousness is experienced as something deeper even than being. Considered in itself, pure seeing assumes the quality of a numinous presence. Its aura becomes for the later Emerson that of the divine creative force. Even as pure seeing, it not merely registers phenomenal impressions but transmutes them into dazzling reflections of its own radiance. In this sense, consciousness experiences itself as divine, through its power to spiritualize the material and external into expressions of a higher essence. Seeing thus represents a transforming power, one that transfigures the field of vision with its own inner splendor.

With the equation of seeing with being, however, a question arises: if mind in its highest state, that of pure consciousness or pure seeing, experiences and becomes one with the divine Essence, how does it then fall away from such a state? In a crucial passage from his journals (May 26, 1837) Emerson confronts this problem:

As a plant in the earth so I grow in God. I am only a form of him. He is the soul of Me. I can even with a mountainous aspiring say, *I am God,* by transferring my *Me* out of the flimsy & unclean precincts of my body, my fortunes, my private will, & meekly retiring upon the holy austerities of the Just & the Loving—upon the secret fountains of Nature. . . . Yet why not always so? How came the Individual thus ⟨accomplished⟩ ↑ armed & impassioned ↓ to parricide thus murderously inclined ever to traverse & kill the

---

remarks upon time, is that we may be impressed with the immediate presence and agency of God, without which a correct understanding of mind or matter can never be attained; that we may be able to read on every power of the mind, and on every particle of matter, the language of our Lord, 'My Father worketh hitherto, and I work'" (pp. 22–23). Which is to say: Nature and the self both manifest the existence of God, not by immediate apprehension or revelation, but by the traditional argument from analogy or design. Later Reed says of memory: "It is a consciousness of the will; a consciousness of character; a consciousness which is produced by the mind's preserving in effort, whatever it actually possesses" (p. 28). In other words, a consciousness of everything but the apprehensive condition of consciousness itself. And finally: "The mind will see itself in what it loves and is able to accomplish. Its own works will be its mirror; and when it is present in the natural world, feeling the same spirit which gives life to every object by which it is surrounded, in its very union with nature it will catch a glimpse of itself, like that of pristine beauty united with innocence, at her own native fountain" (p. 33). Thus the mind sees itself through the world, through Nature, but never directly or in itself.

divine life? Ah wicked Manichee! Into that dim problem I cannot enter. A believer in Unity, a seer of Unity, I yet behold two. (*JMN*, v, 336–37)

Like numerous other problems in the history of thought, the question raised by Emerson, if seen in its own terms, poses a certain insoluble dilemma. As with similar situations, it helps to inquire how such a dilemma could first arise. In his *Wissenschaftslehre* of 1794 (*Grundlage der gesammten Wissenschaftslehre*) Fichte had sought to establish the proper point of departure for all philosophy. It consists of finding "the most absolute, completely unconditioned fundamental principle of all human knowing" (*Gesamtausgabe,* 1:2, 255). Such a principle cannot be proved; it lies at the ground of all consciousness and is that which alone makes consciousness possible. This principle expresses the identity of each thing with itself. In formal terms, $A = A$. Such a principle is however purely formal; its equivalent in the realm of human consciousness is "I am I." Of the difference between the two assertions Fichte observes:

> But the proposition I am I has a wholly other meaning than the proposition A is A. —That is, the latter has a content only under a certain condition. *If* A is posited, it is, naturally, posited *as* A, with the predicate A. But it is not made clear through this proposition, *whether* it is actually posited, consequently, whether it is posited with any particular predicate. The proposition I am I, however, is valid unconditionally, and absolutely, for it is equivalent to the proposition X; it is valid not only in form but also in content. In it the I is posited, not conditionally, but absolutely, with the predicate of equivalence with itself; it *is* therefore posited; and the proposition may also be expressed as *I am*. (*Gesamtausgabe,* 1:2, 258)

By assuming the relational nature or essence of thought and the existence of logical form as immanent within thought itself, Fichte can postulate the principle of identity, $A = A$, as the absolute or unconditioned fundamental principle. But because of the separation between form and content in Fichtean thought, this assertion remains without content. On account of the absence of content, it can at most only be conditionally true: $A = A$ *if* A itself can be established. But there is nothing in the proposition $A = A$ to indicate that $A$ itself must exist, hence nothing to indicate that $A = A$ is necessarily true in the sense of belonging to the actual nature or state of things. For Fichte, nevertheless, this in no sense compromises the establishment of $A = A$ as the proper *form* of the point of departure for all true philosophy. From the preceding, in fact, it becomes apparent that such an assertion could give no more than a proper form to the point of departure. At the same time, on account of the relational nature of thought for Fichte, establishment of the proper form for thought must be seen as both necessary and independent of its content. It serves, in effect, as preliminary to establishing the first absolutely true principle: "I am I."

This principle is accorded the status of being absolutely true because it combines the proper form for a fundamental principle with the appropriate content. For the assertion "I am I" is unconditionally true inasmuch as, by simply asserting the "I," its existence is established, since only the "I" could possibly assert itself. Here assertion of the "I" unexpectedly affirms the Romantic belief in the fusion of form and content: the "I" that asserts itself attests to its own existence by the very form of its assertion, since the asserted "I" *is* nothing other than the "I" that exists expressing itself, an expression that confirms its own existence (in the case of $A = A$ there occurs, in contrast, merely a representation of the relation of $A$ to itself).

The content of this "I" is consciousness. Such consciousness must however be distinguished from the form it assumes in later thought; for Fichte, consciousness is not that which experiences specific thoughts, desires, wishes, volitions, but rather a consciousness of one's own being, of the being of the self. With the assertion of such consciousness (which at this stage is only implicitly self-consciousness—it does not become so explicitly until opposed to the "not-I") the nature of thought must also be redefined in part. For Kant, thought had been relational in its essential nature: it consists of the attempt to "connect the determination of things in their existence" (*Gesammelte Schriften*, IV, 294). By contrast, Fichte seeks to redefine its mode of existence. Whereas for Kant thought itself had been merely apprehension, to which external objects or determinations are given through the understanding (the sensuous manifold) and which it then connects by means of relations, Fichte ascribes to apprehension a constant indwelling object—the self. On account of its presence, thought need not connect external objects in order to assert its own existence. Instead, by its relation to the self, it already affirms its existence, and all its subsequent determinations can proceed from that affirmation as their ground or basis.

Through its apprehension of itself, consciousness for Fichte may be said to possess being. Indeed, in the Fichtean system, being is nothing other than the self-apprehension of consciousness. But if the nature of being consists of apprehending a thing (the self) in consciousness, it follows that the being of all other things (everything subsumed under the "not-I") must also lie in the apprehension of those things by consciousness. As that which confers being upon all other things, consciousness or the "I" assumes the role of the divine Essence, as the one thing that exists in and of itself.

It was this consequence of the Fichtean system that Friedrich Jacobi undertook to attack in an open letter to the author, which he published as *Jacobi an Fichte*. In his letter, written like Jacobi's other works not in the "systematic" style of Kant and his successors but a colorful and impassioned prose, Jacobi had sought to expose the pernicious religious

consequences of Fichtean idealism. His own position, based upon assertion of the validity of intuition or feeling, arrives through reason at an
awareness of an essence or being higher than the self: "So surely as I
possess reason, do I *not* possess with this my human reason the perfection of Life, the fullness of the Good and the True; and so surely as I do
*not* possess these with it, *and know this*, so surely *do* I know there is a *higher*
essence, in which I have my beginning. Thus is my and my reason's
answer not *I*, but rather, *more* than I!—one wholly *other*" (*Werke*, III, 35).
For Jacobi, one must choose between two alternatives: "God is, and is
*outside me*, a *living, self-subsisting Essence*, or *I* am God. There is no third
possibility" (p. 49). One may of course see in Jacobi's polemic merely a
variation upon the famous Cartesian proof of the existence of God set
forth in the *Discourse on Method*. What is new here is the emphasis upon
feeling as a mode of knowledge. For Jacobi the means by which the self
or "I" arrives at its knowledge of a higher being is not rational deduction
but rather the sense or consciousness of its failure to attain the "perfection of Life, the fullness of the Good and the True": this consciousness
or awareness, which comes to it only through intuition, leads the self to
*intuit* a higher being as the source of its own life and consciousness.

But if the "I" arrives at its conclusion through intuition, must this not
imply a subtle modulation or shift in the meaning of Reason (*Vernunft*)
itself? Earlier in the same work, Jacobi himself had pointed out that the
root of *Vernunft* was *Vernehmen* (to perceive, to become aware of) (*Werke*,
III, 19). What both Jacobi and Fichte (and later Emerson) witness is a
gradual transformation of the concept of Reason, the increasing tendency to see in it something other than a connecting of different determinations of existence, a tendency that finally leads to a merging of the
purely rational or relational with other modes of apprehension and
knowledge. Equally significant, for our present purposes, is the content
of reason's apprehension or intuition. For Jacobi this content is life.
Unlike being, life must be apprehended not as a fact but as a feeling. Its
source is animation, the sense of vital abundance, an emotion that floods
the consciousness. Like the "I"'s apprehension of itself in Fichte, such
feeling is immediate with consciousness itself but unlike self-consciousness does not assume the role of the divine Essence, of something
existing in and of itself. Having, like Fichte, begun with apprehension
(*Vernehmen*) or intuition as his point of departure, Jacobi's problem becomes one of explaining why such consciousness is not self-sufficient
and absolute in itself. Only by so doing will it be possible for him to avoid
the consequences toward which he perceives Fichtean idealism to tend,
namely: assertion of the self or consciousness as that which contains all
other things, hence that which endows them with being and thus fulfills
the role of the divine Essence.

Elsewhere Jacobi had perceptively observed that the only difference between Fichtean idealism and Spinozistic pantheism lay in the former's subjective nature: otherwise the two systems are equivalent, insofar as each postulates the existence of all things within a single medium (substance in Spinoza, consciousness in Fichte). By beginning with the subjective nature of the "I" and producing the "not-I" (the world) from it, Fichte in effect transforms the subjective into objective: "I" and "not-I" consist of one and the same element or substance. If the tendency of subjective idealism is thus toward pantheism (as, for instance, in Schelling), it was Jacobi's role to have first pointed out, with exemplary clarity, the problematic consequences.

In his own identification of God with a pantheistic consciousness and his subsequent disillusionment with this belief, Emerson adheres to a similar pattern. Like Fichte and Jacobi, he had begun with Kant's concept of the Reason (*Vernunft*) but—like Kant's successors—transformed it into one of consciousness or pure apprehension. In a special notebook on the Mind, dated 1835 but incorporating material from the three preceding years as well, he had written: "Our compound nature differences us from God, but our Reason is not to be distinguished from the divine Essence. We have yet devised no words to designate the attributes of God which can adequately stand for the Universality & perfection of our own intuitions. To call the Reason 'ours' or 'human', seems an impertinence, so absolute & unconfined it is. The best we can say of God, we mean of the mind as it is known to us" (*JMN*, v, 270–71). As with Jacobi, Reason is here equated with intuition. Nevertheless, Emerson can also speak of it as an element (like the divine Essence) and an absolute (hence its "Universality & perfection"). Moreover, since what we know of the mind comes from apprehension of our own consciousness, Emerson clearly also looks forward to his later identification of God with consciousness. Elsewhere he had depicted the mutual agreement between Nature and mind as consisting of the conformity of Nature to ideal laws that reflect those of the mind's own processes (*Nature*, "Humanity of Science"). Such laws by their very nature suggest connections between "the determination of things in their existence," which leads us back to the relational nature of thought in Kant.

In Emerson, then, all these differing elements and tendencies could be held together in a medium fraught with creative tensions. For such a situation to have come about, it was necessary to have had as a point of departure only a minimal knowledge of Kant—which could be obtained from various sources. In the foregoing, I have attempted to show how certain tendencies and perspectives could produce the transformation of Kant that appears in the *Wissenschaftslehre* and, by reaction, in Jacobi. To some degree, such tendencies develop naturally from the inner nature of Kantian thought itself. I have also sought to demonstrate how the relational nature of thought in Kant gives rise to the possibility of conceiving such relations in a pure or absolute form that transcends all concrete instances. For Emerson, the ideal laws to which Nature conforms transcend the realm of Nature. As a result, they no longer consist simply of connections between the determination of things in their concrete existence. The law of compensation, for instance, assumes in physics the form of the Newtonian principle of equality between action and reaction, but it possesses its equivalent in the moral sphere as well. As a law, however, compensation transcends both spheres. Its reality must be sought in the fact that it represents an innate tendency of thought: that thought in its definition of the relations between things must arrive at this particular determination.

But if mind consists on the one hand of innate tendencies of thought leading to the enunciation of certain transcendent laws or relations, it also represents, for Emerson, the element of apprehension in consciousness. As the element of Mind, such apprehension must be absolute not only because it contains within itself the ideal or transcendent laws of Nature and the moral realm, but also on account of the nature of apprehension itself, which is for Emerson a form of pure seeing, in which all external and material phenomena become transparent to reveal a divine Essence that is none other than Mind itself.

At this point the crucial question arises: if in pure consciousness the self becomes divine (becomes one with the divine Essence), how does it ever fall away from such a state? With some hindsight, one may now see that such a problem becomes irresolvable only because of the conflation of two different forms of consciousness: the Fichtean, which apprehends the being or existence of the self as a fact and which is hence universal or absolute, and that of Jacobi, consisting of intuition, which experiences the whole of life in its concrete fullness. By its very nature, the form of consciousness defined by Jacobi could not be universal and absolute, since its content consists solely of individual subjective experience. In equating pure consciousness with God, Emerson attempts in effect to force the subjective and individual nature of experience upon a consciousness conceived of as absolute (in other words, the Fichtean consciousness). For absolute consciousness, however, there can be neither the experience of the divine in the individual subjective sense postulated by Emerson nor the subsequent falling-away from such a state.

The conflation of the two forms of consciousness in Emerson is itself of the highest historical significance. What it indicates is—to use a Heideggerian phrase—an "end of philosophy," but one that is (unlike the end of Western metaphysics envisioned by Heidegger) only temporary. It expresses itself in the maintenance of disparate elements of thought within the confines of a single system. By *system* I do not mean necessarily a harmonious and unified theoretical structure but simply a body of concepts or thought-motifs which defines a certain attitude toward the world. Only in this larger sense can Emerson be said to have "system." The disparity between the different elements of thought that occurs when philosophy comes to an end results from an inability to apprehend the inner nature of such elements, to perceive the inner tendencies of development within these elements themselves. Thought becomes external to them, treats them as objects rather than as foci of its own vision. Eclecticism (as in Victor Cousin, but equally, for instance, in late antiquity) represents a manifestation of the end of philosophy. This is not to say that philosophy itself cannot be eclectic. But when eclecticism is espoused as an explicit program, it can only suggest that concepts or thought elements have become opaque. In a more complex fashion we find such opacity even in Nietzsche (which explains in part his affinity with Emerson), although forcefully offset by an extraordinary will to a *reinterpretation* of the whole history of Western thought. From this perspective, Emerson's early affirmation, and subsequent rejection, of the divine consciousness of the self must be seen not as part of philosophy but rather as an end to philosophy: as what occurs when thought ceases to think *within* the concepts it creates for itself and looks toward a purer and more immediate means of apprehension.

# 15    Alcott: Of "stages of the spiritual Being"

In the history of New England Transcendentalism one often encounters in descriptions of Alcott a certain element of the ridiculous, whether as a result of his "Orphic Sayings" or from other sources. In "Historic Notes of Life and Letters in New England" Emerson gives the following account of Alcott's famous "conversations": "One declared that 'It seemed to him like going to heaven in a swing;' another reported that, at a knotty point in the discourse, a sympathizing Englishman with a squeaking voice interrupted with the question, 'Mr. Alcott, a lady near me desires to inquire whether omnipotence abnegates attribute?'" (*C.W.*, x, 342).

Yet, in spite of this element of the ridiculous, which would make of Alcott a more benign version of William Godwin, Shelley's father-in-law, there remains much in him of rich interest and significance. Scattered throughout his voluminous journals are the sane, penetrating, and sympathetic portraits of Alcott's famous contemporaries, the faithful registration of five decades of lived experience and, perhaps most important, the record of an intellectual development that is not merely an echo of

Emerson's but that moves, especially in its later stages, through novel and colorful variations.

To approach the essence of that thinking it becomes necessary, however (as with much of Transcendentalism) to see through its utterances to the aspirations to which these give but imperfect expression. In a characteristic note to himself in his journals (Aug. 4, 1835) Alcott confesses: "I wish I could write as I feel and think—as I sometimes converse even. Not that I have ever, in any one instance, practically realized my conception of expression in any one of these forms, but approached more nearly in these than with my pen" (*Journals*, p. 60).

To the differing forms of pantheism manifested in his journals and other writings it will prove helpful to apply this remark. Summarizing briefly, we may say that Alcott's pantheism passes through several principal stages: a neoplatonic emanationism resembling that of Poe's *Eureka;* a vision of progressive "stages of the spiritual Being"; and finally, a concept of spiritual lineage that in yet another fashion attempts to incorporate history into the soul's development. Beyond all these stages, Alcott appears constantly searching for a more intuitive form of thought in which to embody his insights. As a result, it seems best not to take any of the foregoing as his definitive position. They represent, rather, in the Kierkegaardian formula, merely "stages on life's way."

Of his neoplatonic phase, the following journal entry (Feb. [undated], 1833) furnishes an indication: "The human soul has had a primordial experience in the infinite Spirit. The infinite is embodied in the finite, to be developed and returned again to the source of infinite energy from whence it sprang. This is spiritual and earthly experience, and all the phenomena of humanity arise from the union and evolution of these elements. The finite is but the return of the soul on the path of the infinite—the wheeling orb attracted toward, and yet preserved in the cycle of, the central sphere" (*Journals*, p. 35). Is it but one of the ironic coincidences of history that here, fifteen years before the publication of *Eureka*, we find Alcott invoking the very concept Poe will later develop as the basis of his cosmology? But if in Poe's depiction—perhaps as a result of neoclassical influences—the symmetry of correspondence between the diffusion of matter from its source and its subsequent return looms so large over his portrayal of the cosmic cycle, in Alcott, by contrast, what predominates is the spiritual aspiration for a reunion with the infinite, the sense of a progressive spiritual evolution in the soul's reascent to its divine source.[1] The Romantic topos underlying all narratives of a

---

[1]Traces of similar notions appear also in Alcott's later published writings. Cf. *Tablets,* p. 194: "Throughout the domain of spirit desire creates substance wherein all creatures seek conjunction, lodging and nurture. Nor is there anything in nature save desire holding substances together, all things being dissolvable and recombinable in this spiritual menstruum." And later: "Life is a current of spiritual forces" (p. 201). Elsewhere in the same

cyclical pattern that conclude with the protagonist's return home with a higher consciousness does not possess here the sense so much of a vouchsafing of higher revelation but rather a transformation of the individual self or being, an *evolution*, which becomes a hallmark in all of Alcott's subsequent professions.

In its next phase Alcott's doctrine of spiritual evolution achieves yet clearer expression:

> Every visible, conscious thing is a revelation of the invisible, spiritual Creator. Matter is a revelation of Mind, the flesh of the Spirit, the world of God. All growth, production, progress, are but stages of the spiritual Being. They denote the Spirit struggling to represent, reveal, shadow forth itself to the sense and reason of man. They are tests of his faith in the infinite, invisible, spiritual life that flows through and quickens all things and beings.
>
> The various kingdoms of matter, with all their array of forms and stages of growth, maturity, decay, are but so many modifications of the spiritual kingdom, whose laws they obey and by whose unseen yet ever-sustaining energy they are kept in their individual condition and attain to their absolute consummation and place. They are emblems and significant types of the Divine Spirit in whom alone is absolute Being and Life, Growth, and Vitality. They reveal the Latent One. (Sept. 21, 1835; *Journals*, p. 65)

Various sources reveal Alcott's affinities with, and interest in, the mystical thought of Jakob Boehme. In the concept of "the Latent One" there is a reflection of Boehme's notion of the Unground, which contains within itself the image of the real and which produces the real. The Unground is the divine source of reality, the origin of the being of all things. Its basic nature is will. Will in turn, according to Boehme, is the "driving of the essences."[2] These essences are the substances that make up the world; hence the world is created by will, which through its energy impels essences into being.[3] Like the system of *Eureka*, Boehme's theosophy is thus closer to emanationism than to the pantheism of a

---

work Alcott enunciates once more his personal doctrine of emanationism: "The new calculus is ours. An organon alike serviceable to metaphysician and naturalist—whereby things answer to thought, facts are resolved into truths, images into ideas, matter into mind, power into personality, man into God; the One soul in all souls revealed as the Creative Spirit pulsating in all breasts, immanent in all atoms, prompting all wills, and personally embosoming all persons in one unbroken synthesis of Being" (p. 164). See also Odell Shepard, *Pedlar's Progress: The Life of Bronson Alcott* (Boston: Little, Brown, 1938), pp. 239–46.

[2] Jacob Boehme, *Six Theosophic Points*, trans. John Rolleston Earle (Ann Arbor: Univ. of Michigan Press, 1958), p. 5. In the same chapter Boehme writes: "Thus life is the essences' son, and the will, wherein life's figure stands, is the essences' father; for no essence can arise without will. For in the will is originated desire, in which the essences take their rise" (p. 6).

[3] For more details see Alexandre Koyré, *La Philosophie de Jacob Boehme* (Paris: Vrin, 1929; 2d ed., 1971), pp. 320–27.

Spinoza. What it suggests is not that all things inhere in one substance, but rather that a primordial energy creates these things from nothing. For Alcott all visible things are "revelations" of their invisible divine source. As such they are expressions of a divine energy that "flows through and quickens all things and beings." Insofar as it posits the presence of a divine essence in all things, Alcott's system may be termed pantheistic. It accounts for his peculiar symbolism, with its notion of the special significance of the spinal column, the erectness of the human form, and so on. All these are expressions or manifestations of a divine energy assuming concrete or physical form.

In his *Über das Wesen der menschlichen Freiheit* Schelling had asserted that Being is Will.[4] Like Boehme (with whom he shares manifest affinities) he had sought to express the intuition: will *drives* the essences. The result: a more fluid form of thinking that abolishes rigid categories in favor of a constant unceasing movement, the passage from energeia to finite being, the apprehension of a force that moves through all things, so that thought becomes, not a reasoning with categories and distinctions, but an inner vision of the impelling energy as it creates and acts upon its creation. Characteristically Romantic is the concept of "stages of the spiritual Being," which are not stages in some unchanging *scala natura* or chain of being but rather stages of growth, of process, stages in the development of a single spiritual essence. Of this process Alcott goes on to observe that all forms of matter are but modifications of a spiritual kingdom, whose laws they obey and by whose energy they attain the perfection of their nature. One recalls the Leibnizian concept of an entelechy in things, but what is especially significant in the present context is the apprehension that all things conform to some inner law, an innate organic principle or idea that governs the growth and development of the spiritual essence and that comes to be contained in physical matter.

It was the quintessential intuition of Romantic *Naturphilosophie* to assert not only the presence of such an organic principle in things (appropriating the Leibnizian concept of the entelechy) but also the physical presence of a spiritual or ideational element in Nature, whether as being or energy (or, when Being is equated with will, as both). Energy not only drives the essences but also permeates them, striving within them to reach its utmost possible limits. By postulating the Spirit as "struggling to represent, reveal, shadow forth itself to the sense and reason of man" through Nature, Alcott displays his affinities not only with Romantic

---

[4]*Schellings Werke*, 4. Hauptband, 242 (*S.W.*, vii, 350): "There is in the last and highest instance no other Being than Will. Will is primordial Being, and to this alone apply all predicates of the latter: groundlessness, eternity, independence of time, self-affirmation. All philosophy strives only to find this highest expression."

*Naturphilosophie* but also with Shelley, Emerson, and Agassiz. It is important to mention the great naturalist here, for his adherence to this belief (albeit in a slightly different form from that of the earlier Romantics) attests to its pervasive presence in nineteenth-century science. The assertion of the possibility of a physical interaction, as it were, between spiritual energy and matter transcends the Spinozistic doctrine of the inherence of things in one substance, and creates the basis for the neoplatonic emanationism of a Poe as well as the Transcendentalism of an Alcott.

It also leads to a reformulation of the doctrine of symbolism. Earlier I attempted to trace, very briefly, the transformation of early Christian and medieval typology into the Romantic concept of symbolism. We have seen that the type, with its prolepsis or anticipation of future events and personages, is essentially historical in nature. God reveals his plan for the redemption of mankind proleptically, through the Old Testament, then brings it to fulfillment in Christ. Christ is the *parousia*, the appearance of the divine essence in the world. With the shift from traditional Christianity to a form of pantheism or emanationism in Romantic literature and thought, we witness simultaneously a shift in the definition and concept of the type. Briefly put, it passes from temporal to nontemporal. If the divine essence is immediately present in things, bringing them into being and infusing them with its own energies, such things must reveal that essence. This revelation occurs in a moment, but its nature transcends time, disclosing to the beholder the eternal reality behind things. Thus Alcott can say of them that they are "emblems and significant types of the Divine Spirit in whom alone is absolute Being and Life, Growth, and Vitality." It is both characteristic and significant that he should associate the two last-mentioned attributes with the divine essence. They indicate the affinity between the concept of divinity and that of organicism, the vital principle of life itself. Through that affinity, life, according to the Romantic attitude, becomes endowed with its own sacredness, participating by its nature in that of the divine.

In Alcott's later phase this concept of life is subjected to an important transformation. For Alcott (as for Margaret Fuller), life must be understood not as a physical principle but rather as the outward flow of the divine energy into things. In its expression, that energy assumes specific forms or types. Characteristic of Alcott's last years is the belief in a fixation of such types. "We are," he says, "with slight deviations, copies of our ancestors. . . . I am not yet persuaded of the truth claimed by certain theorists that types become intermingled and by circumstances blotted out. Rather it appears that, like ideas, their types are permanent and persistent, superior to outward accidents or physical conditions. Souls are typical, and mould bodies into forms corresponding. The types may vary, but never extinguish themselves" (*Journals*, p. 445).

The fixation into types must proceed from some inner necessity governing the expression of the divine energy. But if these types or forms are inseparably associated with such energy, they must themselves be in some sense divine, for they pertain to God not as concepts in the mind (which is free to conceive of other concepts) but as the expression of his very nature or essence. Here Alcott moves beyond even the views of Agassiz, who had seen in Nature an expression of the mode of divine thought. Insofar as they are created by pure energy, these types transcend the grasp of thought: their reason for being must be found not in reason but in the nature of the energy that forms them and that remains unknowable in its essence. If the energy that brings such forms into being is unknowable, however, the forms themselves may nevertheless be apprehended by the individual mind. Through its perception of these, mind becomes conscious not merely of the existence of God (natural religion) but is, as it were, assimilated to the nature of the divine energy itself. As a result, it becomes possible to ascribe a new meaning to the concept of revelation. For Alcott, the forms or types represent not merely the external appearance of God but, through their assimilation by the mind, his internal appearance within the self. Romantic subjectivity thus makes possible for Alcott a new form of pantheism, one that depends neither upon being (Spinoza) nor substance (Poe and Shelley) but upon the nature of the mind, which, through its representation of divinized forms, becomes itself a medium of the divine.

In the final phase of Alcott's thought, which also marks his involvement with the Concord School of Philosophy and the St. Louis Hegelians under William T. Harris, he becomes more conscious than ever (in part through his confrontation with the intricacies of the Hegelian dialectic as practiced by these American disciples) of the inadequacy of all formal modes of thinking. A passage from the autumnal and reminiscent *Concord Days* offers the clearest expression of this intuition, one that is the keynote or motif most characteristic of Alcott himself:

I look for a more flowing, inspiring type of thought, Teutonic as Greek, of a mystic coloring transcending Boehme, Swedenborg, and freed from the biblicisms of the schools of our time. Hegel's secret is that of pure thought akin with that of Parmenides, Plato, Aristotle, the ancient masters in philosophy. The One is One out of whose womb the Not One is born to perish perpetually at its birth. Whoso pronounces PERSON apprehensively, speaks the secret of all things, and holds the key to all mysteries in nature and spirit. (p. 145)

# 16 Melville

*"the one Life within us and abroad."*

During his voyage to London in the fall of 1849 Melville began a friendship with a German scholar, George Adler, which was to have fruitful consequences for his intellectual and spiritual development. Their conversations, as recorded in Melville's journal, touch frequently upon topics to which he would recur in his colloquies with Hawthorne and others. An entry for October 13 observes:

> Last evening was very pleasant. Walked the deck with the German, Mr. Adler, till a late hour, talking of "Fixed Fate, Free will, foreknowledge absolute" &c. His philosophy is Coleridgean: he accepts the Scriptures as divine, & yet leaves himself free to inquire into Nature. He does not take it that the Bible is absolutely infallible, & that anything opposed to it in Science must be wrong. He believes that there are things *out* of God and independent of him, —things that would have existed were there no God: —such as that two & two make four; for it is not that God so decrees mathematically, but that in the very nature of things, the fact is thus. (*Journal*, ed. Metcalf, p. 5)

From his identification of Adler's philosophy as Coleridgean one may infer Melville's acquaintance with the *Biographia Literaria.* In it Coleridge distinguishes between the truths of religion and those of pure Reason, which in themselves do not conduce to belief in the existence of a God but at the same time are in no way opposed to it.[1] Later, in *Moby-Dick,* the

---

[1] The passage Melville appears to have in mind is the following: "The question then concerning our faith in the existence of a God, not only as the *ground* of the universe by his essence, but as its maker and judge by his wisdom and holy will, appeared to stand thus. The sciential *reason*, whose objects are purely theoretical, remains neutral, as long as its name and semblance are not usurped by the opponents of the doctrine. But it *then* becomes an effective ally by exposing the false shew of demonstration, or by evincing the equal demonstrability of the contrary from premises equally logical. . . . having once fully admitted the existence of an infinite yet self-conscious Creator, we are not allowed to ground the irrationality of any other article of faith on arguments which would equally prove that to be irrational, which we had allowed to be *real*" (*C.W.*, VII: I, 203–4). For evidence of Melville's reading of Coleridge, see Merton M. Sealts, Jr., *Melville's Reading: A Check-List of Books Owned and Borrowed* (Madison: Univ. of Wisconsin Press, 1966), p. 52, which lists the *Biographia* and an edition of Coleridge's Shakespeare lectures. Unfortunately Melville's copy of the *Biographia* has not survived. There remains the possibility of his reading other works of Coleridge's through the influence of Evert Duyckinck, who (according to Leon Howard) "was a particular admirer of Coleridge" ("Melville's Struggle with the Angel,"

effects of the dichotomy between religion and reason will become apparent.

In the course of their voyage Melville and Adler discussed not only Adler's views but the prevailing systems of German philosophy as well. Melville's journal entry for October 22, 1849, remarks: "I forgot to mention, that *last night* about 9-1/2 P.M. Adler & Taylor came into my room, & it was proposed to have whiskey punches, which we *did* have, accordingly. . . . We had an extraordinary time & did not break up till after two in the morning. We talked metaphysics continually, & Hegel, Schlegel, Kant &c were discussed under the influence of the whiskey. I shall not forget Adler's look when he quoted La Place the French astronomer—'It is not necessary, gentlemen, to account for these worlds by the hypothesis' &c." (*Journal,* ed. Metcalf, p. 12). Apart from the convivial atmosphere engendered by "the influence of the whiskey," the anecdote about Laplace suggests that their talk was colored in part by a religious perspective.[2] Curiously, Melville mentions neither Spinoza (who for many at that time could still be associated with "the latest form of infidelity") nor the *Pantheismusstreit* (or pantheistic controversy) engendered by his system—surely one of the most prominent features of German idealism.[3] Yet he must at some point have encountered and assimilated the doctrine of pantheism. In a chapter of *Mardi* Taji alludes to it: "I began to bethink me of the Jew that rejected the Talmud, and his all-permeating principle, to which Goethe and others have subscribed" (*Writings,* III, 176). To this reference to Spinoza we may add a passage from a letter to Hawthorne (April? 16?, 1851) two years later: "We incline to think that God cannot explain His own secrets, and that He would like a little information upon certain points Himself. We mortals astonish Him as much as He us. But it is this *Being* of the matter; there lies the knot with which we choke ourselves. As soon as you say *Me,* a *God,* a *Nature,* so soon you jump off from your stool and hang from the beam. Yes, that word is the hangman. Take God out of the dictionary, and you would have Him in the street" (*Letters,* p. 125).

---

rpt. in *The Recognition of Herman Melville,* ed. Hershel Parker [Ann Arbor: Univ. of Michigan Press, 1967], p. 231). A footnote by Melville himself in "The Whiteness of the Whale" attests to his acquaintance with "The Rime of the Ancient Mariner." His praise for "the noble merit of the poem and the poet" allows one to infer his knowledge of other poems by Coleridge as well. Here the provisional status of Sealts's *Melville's Reading* must be pointed out—see, e.g., the recent discovery of Melville's copy of Wordsworth's *Poetical Works* (Thomas Heffernan, "Melville and Wordsworth," *American Literature,* 49 (1977), 338–51, and the addenda to *Melville's Reading* in Sealts's *Pursuing Melville, 1940–1980* (Madison: Univ. of Wisconsin Press, 1982).

[2] Asked by Napoleon about the place of God in his system of celestial mechanics, Laplace is alleged to have replied, "Sire, je n'ai pas eu besoin de cette hypothèse" (Sire, I had no need of that hypothesis) (Alexandre Koyré, *From the Closed World to the Infinite Universe* [Baltimore: Johns Hopkins Univ. Press, 1957], p. 276).

[3] Andrews Norton, *A Discourse on the Latest Form of Infidelity,* pp. 11–12.

Here—as elsewhere in the letters to Hawthorne—Melville's playful tone should not obscure an underlying seriousness. Like the Shakespeare of *Hamlet* and *King Lear*, whom he eulogizes in his "Hawthorne and His Mosses," he delights in a verbal play consisting of "those short, quick probings at the very axis of reality." In the present passages—despite ambiguities of phrasing and wording—the proper interpretation would seem to be the pantheistic one: there is an element common to all things, including the individual self, God, and Nature. To speak of any of these specifically is to isolate but one manifestation of the omnipresent element, which itself is God.[4]

The interest in pantheism suggests one of the principal causes behind Melville's attraction to Coleridge. To a large extent, his affinity with the British author corresponds to his absorption in, and subsequent rejection of, pantheism, a process that begins in *Mardi* and culminates in the "Mast-head" meditation of *Moby-Dick.*

The allusion to Spinoza in *Mardi* mentioned earlier points to at least some acquaintance on Melville's part with both Spinozistic pantheism and its Romantic successors. His own pantheistic beliefs differ nevertheless in certain significant respects. For Spinoza, the element of pure being is also that of thought: the One Substance contains all attributes (hence all things) within itself because to assert all things (to *be* all things, to sustain all things in their existence) is the same as the *thinking* of all things.[5] For Melville, on the other hand, thought represents an essentially human and psychological phenomenon: pure being precludes all trace of either thought or consciousness. Ahab's evocation in *Moby-Dick* of the blind, unconscious force that pervades the world and manifests itself in the White Whale is but another expression of the same belief.

---

[4]For another analysis of this passage, Sanford E. Marovitz, "Melville's Problematic 'Being,'" *ESQ,* 28 (1st Quarter 1982), 11–23.

[5]Thus Def. III of *Ethics,* pt. I: "By substance, I understand that which is in itself and is conceived through itself; in other words, that, the concept of which does not need the conception of another thing from which it must be formed" (White/Stirling trans.). Spinoza's Latin text reads: "Per substantiam intelligo id, quod in se est, & per se concipitur: hoc est id, cujus conceptus non indiget conceptu alterius rei, a quo formari debeat" (*Opera,* II, 45). To which we must add the definition of an attribute (Def. IV, pt. I): "By attribute, I understand that which the intellect perceives of substance, as if constituting its essence." In other words, the attributes are themselves apprehensions of thought. Hence their *element* must be thought itself. Since the one Substance, or God, contains all attributes, there must be an element of apprehension or thought within it. But this one Substance is "Being absolutely infinite, that is to say, substance consisting of infinite attributes." Being, then, contains infinite attributes: but if these are apprehensions of thought, it can contain them only if its element is also that of thought, i.e., if thought and being are one and the same. This sameness of being and thought implies that, for Spinoza, pure thought is essentially nonhuman in nature. Hence the Spinozistic God (unlike Melville's) possesses knowledge or "consciousness" of its attributes only through their being *thought* by the one Substance or God.

The God described by Melville in his letter is distinguished by another peculiar attribute: the impossibility of speaking about him as separate from anything else (even in Spinoza this had still been possible, insofar as all things through their attributes are contained in God). Here God is, strictly speaking, an action rather than an essence or substance—the assertion that sustains all things in their existence. Hence the awkward and somewhat ambiguous phrase Melville employs: "But it is this *Being* of the matter.*" Here the capitalized form must be taken to signify, not the traditional hypostatized entity, but the act of sustaining things in their existence, elevated by its fundamental quality to the divine plane. Thus we must interpret *Being* as a gerund form, a noun expressing the action of a verb ("to be") rather than a noun referring to a person or object.[6] Only on this supposition can we explain what follows, since it makes no sense to speak of a "*Being* of the matter" if by *Being* one means an individual person or thing. A further ambiguity remains: the term *matter* appears to refer not to concrete, physical matter, but rather to the subject about which one is speaking. The whole phrase might then be rendered: "but it is the act of assertion contained or involved in the subject about which we are speaking," which points to the aphoristic conclusion: "Take God out of the dictionary, and you would have Him in the street." Or: cease to hypostatize him as an individual entity, and he becomes the omnipresent element in all things.

It is, of course, also possible to see Melville as less concerned in this passage with the nature of God than with the inherent limits of language in describing its nature. Yet such a view does not account sufficiently, I think, for the strangeness of "this *Being* of the matter," and especially Melville's odd emphasis upon *being,* which if anything only calls more attention to the strangeness of the phrase. At the same time that he evokes the pantheistic notion of an element of pure being, Melville also depicts a pantheism based upon the presence of an all-pervasive life force, what Friedrich Schelling had called the "World-Soul" (*Die Welt-seele*). In another of his celebrated letters to Hawthorne, written after receiving the latter's response to *Moby-Dick,* Melville declares: "So now I can't write what I felt. But I felt pantheistic then—your heart beat in my ribs and mine in yours, and both in God's," an assertion that leads him to the rhetorical exclamation: "Whence come you, Hawthorne? By what right do you drink from my flagon of life? And when I put it to my lips—lo, they are yours and not mine. I feel that the Godhead is broken up like the bread at the Supper, and that we are the pieces. Hence this

---

[6]Here one recalls the Greek verb εἶναι, "to be," which is also the noun form corresponding to our *being*—a property of which Heidegger makes much in his *Introduction to Metaphysics.*

infinite fraternity of feeling" (*Letters*, p. 142). With this we may compare the following entry by Coleridge in his notebooks for 1810:

My love of ꓹ ꞇ ꓥy is not so much in my Soul, as my Soul in it. It is my whole Being wrapt up into one Desire, all the Hopes & Fears, Joys & Sorrows, all the Powers, Vigor & Faculties of my Spirit abridged into ⟨one⟩ perpetual Inclination. To bid me not love you were to bid me annihilate myself—for to love you is all I know of my Life, as far as my Life is an object of my Consciousness or my free Will. God is our Being, but thro' his works alone doth he reveal himself—and that for which all other Objects have a ⟨vital⟩ meaning, possess either force or attraction, are desired or avoided—that of which all other Objects are but a copious Language of epithets & synonymes—that is God appearing to me—in that he reveals himself—& in that I love & adore him. —I hold it therefore neither Impiety ⟨on the one hand⟩ nor Superstition on the other, that you are the God within me, even as the best & most religious men have called their Conscience the God within them. (*Notebooks*, III, 3996)

In this description of his relation to Sara Hutchinson, Coleridge evokes a mode of thought and feeling similar to that expressed by Melville. To be sure, Melville's self-conscious exaggerations differ in both commitment and tone from the impassioned introspection of Coleridge. That both should have been led to speak of their relationship to another within a pantheistic framework, however, attests to the pervasive influence of the pantheistic mode of thought. In these instances the specific form of pantheism expressed differs somewhat from that discussed earlier. Now, the presence of one subjective nature within another results from the indwelling of both in an omnipresent divine consciousness. Whereas to speak of God as pure being excludes all possibility of individual thought, consciousness, or feeling, the psychological *presence* of one self within another is possible only as a fusion of being and sentience (including thought and all other modes of feeling). In its presence within another, the individual consciousness both *is* and experiences self-awareness.

Such awareness if not only of self or other, but of that which contains both. It is the feeling of the presence of each in the other which expresses the nature of the divine essence. From his experience of this feeling, Coleridge can assert that his love of Sara Hutchinson "is not so much in my Soul, as my Soul in it." Similarly, Melville tells Hawthorne: "your heart beat in my ribs and mine in yours, and both in God's." And, a few lines later: "I feel that the Godhead is broken up like the bread at the Supper, and that we are the pieces." Here Melville's extraordinary expression of a pantheistic consciousness subsumes the symbolism of the Eucharistic transubstantiation of the bread into the body of Christ. In this sacrament, according to traditional Christian theology, Christ (as

God) becomes physically present in the bread. Similarly, for Melville, his consciousness becomes present in Hawthorne, and vice versa. The striking physical immediacy achieved in such presence of one self in another ("your heart beat in my ribs and mine in yours") expresses, in turn, the fundamentally human quality of this form of presence.

Through his use of a eucharistic symbolism Melville implies that such presence is not only human but divine. By being present in the other, each consciousness participates in a reality that is something more than either of them or even both together. The reality that reveals itself in the presence of each in the other is what Melville describes as the "Godhead." Although present in each individual, its reality is not that of the individual consciousness but of a communion of consciousness in which each subjective nature becomes that of another. Such a communion cannot be demonstrated but only felt. Hence the form of Melville's declaration: "I *feel* that the Godhead is broken up like the bread at the Supper."

The equating of being with consciousness leads to the permeation of the former by feeling. In the passage from Coleridge the "Being" of the poet is said to be "wrapt up into one Desire, all the Hopes & Fears, Joys & Sorrows, all the Powers, Vigor & Faculties of my Spirit abridged into ⟨one⟩ perpetual Inclination." Here being assumes the nature of a vital force, the involuntary assertion of life itself as it becomes manifest in a thinking and feeling consciousness. As the being of all living creatures, this vital force is God. Like the Godhead at the Supper, such Being can manifest itself only "in pieces." After the assertion that "God is our Being," Coleridge adds: "but thro' his works alone doth he reveal himself." For Coleridge, such revelation is tantamount to God's essence. Addressing Sara Hutchinson, he can then say: "I hold it neither Impiety ⟨on the one hand⟩ nor Superstition on the other, that you are the God within me."

The concept of the presence of one consciousness in another as the manifestation of God must be distinguished from the religion of Schleiermacher's *Über die Religion* or Emerson's *Nature*. For the young Schleiermacher the infinitude of human consciousness becomes a revelation of the divine essence. For Emerson the individual consciousness, in its highest moments, loses all trace of individual feeling, becoming that pure seeing or consciousness that is God. For Melville and Coleridge, on the other hand, the individual consciousness does not experience infinitude in itself but rather by entering another, equally finite consciousness. It is the feeling of indwelling in another who is still recognized as someone other that makes possible an awareness of the indwelling itself. The experience of this indwelling expresses the divine essence. By their emphasis upon a communion of consciousness, Melville and Coleridge depict a state of feeling remarkably close to that of the fourth

Gospel, with its description of the "indwelling" of the believer in Christ and of Christ in God the Father.[7]

Various instances attest to the special significance of love in Coleridge's system. This feeling is best seen not as a conscious affection for a specific object but as the assertion of an involuntary and fundamental impulse that sustains one's own life in and through that of another. In his other writings Coleridge had traced it from the lowest levels of creation, where it assumes a predominantly physical form as a quest for oneness by separate individual natures, to the highest, where it becomes interfused with feeling and consciousness. But the impulse itself, as a basic and creative *energeia*, transcends conscious feeling, imparting its energy to consciousness itself. The impulse may thus be equated in some sense with life itself, the desire for life which animates all living things.

In human nature, consciousness of the natural law by which each individual life is sustained in and through another leads to an awareness of the coalescence of all forms of the vital impulse into a single Whole. A letter to William Sotheby (Sept. 10, 1802) expresses this realization: "Nature has her proper interest; & he will know what it is, who believes & feels, that every Thing has a Life of its own, & that we are all *one Life*. A Poet's *Heart & Intellect* should be *combined, intimately* combined & *unified*, with the great appearances in Nature—& not merely held in solution & loose mixture with them, in the shape of formal Similies"[8] (*Collected Letters*, II, 864). We observe the progressive emphasis in the description of the poet's relation to Nature: from "*combined*" to "*intimately* combined" to "*unified*." For Coleridge, the relation of mind to Nature is not one of passive contemplation but rather of participation. Here the pantheism described earlier in terms of the presence of one subjective nature in another is expanded into participation in the "one Life" of all Nature. Such participation consists of awareness of the "great appearances of Nature" as expressions of the Life contained within the individual consciousness. Nature is thus but the life force of the mind when it expresses itself: instead of thoughts, the mind creates what we call the "realities" of external Nature.

In his letter to Sotheby, Coleridge had declared it was the poet's function to reveal the fundamental unity of mind with Nature. Through his own poetic explorations he assumes for Melville a special significance, disclosing the intimate association in pantheism between thought and feeling, image and intuition, external world and subjective consciousness. It is both characteristic and revealing that some of Coleridge's

[7]See C. H. Dodd, *The Interpretation of the Fourth Gospel* (Cambridge: Cambridge Univ. Press, 1953), pp. 187–200, esp. 194–96, 196–99.

[8]For a comprehensive account of Coleridge's pantheism, see Thomas McFarland, *Coleridge and the Pantheist Tradition* (Oxford: Clarendon, 1969).

earliest pantheistic affirmations should be expressed in poetic form. Thus in his "Religious Musings":

> There is one Mind, one omnipresent Mind,
> Omnific. His most holy name is Love.
> Truth of subliming import! with the which
> Who feeds and saturates his constant soul,
> He from his small particular orbit flies
> With blest outstarting! (*P.W.*, p. 113)

And, a few lines later:

>                         'Tis the sublime of man,
> Our noontide Majesty, to know ourselves
> Parts and proportions of one wondrous Whole!
> This fraternises man, this constitutes
> Our charities and bearings. But 'tis God
> Diffused through all, that doth make all one whole;
> This the worst superstition, him except
> Aught to desire, Supreme Reality! (*P.W.*, pp. 113–14)

With these utterances we may compare Ishmael's exclamation in chapter 26 of *Moby-Dick:*

But this august dignity I treat of, is not the dignity of kings and robes, but that abounding dignity which has no robed investiture. Thou shalt see it shining in the arm that wields a pick or drives a spike; that democratic dignity which, on all hands, radiates without end from God; Himself! The great God absolute! The centre and circumference of all democracy! His ominpresence, our divine equality! (p. 104)

The affirmation of the dignity of democratic man proceeds from the idea that each individual contains the "one Life" or God within himself.[9] Like Coleridge in the "Religious Musings," Ishmael equates "His omnipresence" with "our divine equality." This equality of one portion of God to another recalls Melville's declaration to Hawthorne, quoted earlier: "I feel that the Godhead is broken up like the bread at the Supper, and that we are the pieces." As in Coleridge, the knowledge that we are "ourselves / Parts and proportions of one wondrous Whole" "fraternises man, . . . constitutes / Our charities and bearings."

In his rhapsodic invocation Ishmael likewise employs a metaphor similar to that of the "Religious Musings": the notion of the soul as a celestial

[9]For another analysis of this passage (which does not mention Coleridge), see William Braswell, *Melville's Religious Thought* (Durham, N.C.: Duke Univ. Press, 1943), pp. 26–27.

body in orbit about a sun that symbolizes God, moving through a space that is also that of God. Where Coleridge had spoken of the soul who "from his small particular orbit flies / With blest outstarting," Melville, similarly, can celebrate the dignity that "radiates (like rays from a sun) without end from God," who is at once "the centre and circumference of all democracy."

In the present passage Melville's pantheistic symbolism serves to affirm the political doctrine of democratic equality. Earlier, in *Mardi,* he had imparted to the same symbolism an explicitly religious significance. Among the innumerable isles of the Mardian archipelago, the central one, Maramma, is crowned by a huge peak named Ofo. On his initial approach Taji is struck by its appearance: "Towering above all, and midmost, rose a mighty peak; one fleecy cloud sloping against its summit; a column wreathed. Beyond, like purple steeps in heaven at set of sun, stretched far away, what seemed lands on lands, in infinite perspective" (*Writings,* III, 160). The symbolic aspect of the image becomes clear when we consider the name given to God or the supreme Being in Mardi: Oro. This word, a slight modification of the Greek ὄρός (= mountain), assumes a special significance in the New Testament. In the gospel of Matthew, Jesus begins his ministry by laying down the New Law in his Sermon on the Mount, and ends it with an appearance on a mountain to his disciples after the Resurrection.[10] In the middle of this gospel, his Transfiguration occurs on a mountain: "And after six days Jesus taketh Peter, James, and John his brother, and bringeth them up into a high mountain apart, and was transfigured before them: and his face did shine as the sun, and his raiment was white as the light. And, behold, there appeared unto them Moses and Elijah talking with him" (17:1–3). The appearance of Moses in particular serves to link the New Dispensation with the Old, which had also been handed down on a mountain (Mount Sinai). The association of the Old Dispensation and its giver with a mountain is commemorated, moreover, by one of the names for God in the Old Testament: El Shaddai = the mountain-God.

In his description of the peak of Ofo, Taji observes the presence of "one fleecy cloud sloping against its summit." One may of course regard the motif as purely naturalistic. Nevertheless, an undercurrent of suggestion seems operative here. In the theophany on Mount Sinai the mountain is said to be obscured by a dense cloud (because Yahweh descends on it in the form of fire). As if to emphasize the parallel with the Old Testament, the first evangelist, in his account of the Transfiguration, notes that "while he [Peter] yet spake, behold, a bright cloud overshadowed them: and behold a voice out of the cloud, which said,

---

[10]Dodd, p. 333, n. The term ὄρος can refer to either a mountain or a hill (the actual setting of the Sermon on the Mount), according to Liddell / Scott's *Greek-English Lexicon,* 9th ed. (Oxford: Clarendon, 1940), p. 1255.

This is my beloved Son, in whom I am well pleased; hear ye him" (Matt. 17:5).

In the discussion that takes place between Melville's characters as they approach the isle of Maramma, much is made of the difficulties of ascending the peak of Ofo. The ascent is depicted in terms of a spiritual quest in which many will lose their lives. Part of the discussion appears to echo Yahweh's injunction to Moses: "Go down, charge the people, lest they break through unto the LORD to gaze [that is, warn the people not to pass beyond their bounds to come and look on Yahweh], and many of them perish" (Exod. 19:21). A remark of Mohi's explicitly recalls the end of the first gospel, mentioned earlier: "But Alma [= Christ] is also quoted by others, in vindication of the pilgrimages to Ofo. They declare that the prophet himself was the first pilgrim that thitherward journeyed: that from thence he departed to the skies" (*Writings*, III, 324).

To sum up: taken collectively, the elements of Melville's description of Ofo, with their biblical associations, evoke the idea of a divine presence visibly embodied at the very center of the Mardian archipelago. In both Old and New Testament contexts, the mountain (= ὄρός) signifies not merely a sacred place but one in which an actual revelation of the divine essence occurs, hence one endowed with the physical presence of the divine. In *Mardi* Melville attempts to suggest the mythological origins of this idea, while questioning its literal truthfulness. Simply to arrive at the concept of a visible embodiment of the divine presence, it would not have been necessary, obviously, to have recourse to Coleridge. Both Old and New Testaments contain suggestions of the concept. But the notion of that divine presence as a central point around which all other things revolve brings us much closer to Coleridge's "Religious Musings." The motif of divine centrality leads quite naturally to a planetary symbolism, especially to an association of the supreme being with the sun, not only because of the equation of God with light (1 John 1:5) but also because of the sun's life-giving role, as that which sustains all living things. For Coleridge and Romantic pantheism in general, the second aspect of the planetary symbolism is particularly significant; it emphasizes God not only as the source of life but, in effect, as a divine energy that is the life of all things. This divine energy radiates from its source and bestows an aura of supernatural splendor upon everything it touches:

> But lo! the bursting Sun!
> Touched by the enchantment of that sudden beam
> Straight the black vapour melteth, and in globes
> Of dewy glitter gems each plant and tree;
> On every leaf, on every blade it hangs!
> Dance glad the new-born intermingling rays,
> And wide around the landscape streams with glory!
>
> (*P.W.*, p. 113)

In Taji's initial approach to the Mardian archipelago, immediately after the description of the central isle Maramma and its dominant peak, the landscape appears wreathed in similar splendor: "The jeweled vapors, erewhile hovering over these violet shores, now seemed to be shedding their gems; and as the almost level rays of the sun, shooting through the air like a variegated prism, touched the verdant land, it trembled all over with dewy sparkles" (*Writings*, III, 160).

Taji himself, of course, is an emissary from the sun. Asked by the assembled chiefs of Mardi to identify himself, he informs them: "Men of Mardi, I come from the sun. When this morning it rose and touched the wave, I pushed my shallop from its golden beach, and hither sailed before its level rays. I am Taji" (*Writings*, III, 165–66). To be sure, his account is prompted by the necessity of ensuring a hospitable reception for himself and his companions. But it can easily assume a deeper significance. In the poem "Religious Musings" Coleridge asserts that he "who feeds and saturates his constant soul" from the oneness of the omnipresent Mind and Love "from his small particular orbit flies / With blest outstarting!" Similarly, the voyager proceeding from a sun symbolizing the divine life that infuses all things likewise departs from his source "with blest outstarting." Taji's recapitulation of an image from the earlier passage in *Mardi* describing the effect of sunlight on the landscape of the archipelago is surely also significant. When he tells the chiefs he "sailed before the level rays" of the sun (echoing the "almost level rays of the sun, shooting through the air like a variegated prism"), he symbolically implies that he proceeds from the divine energy infusing all things.

But the divine source of life is something more than pure energy. On the spiritual level it reveals itself as Truth. A chapter in which the narrator distances himself somewhat from the persona of Taji contains the significant admission: "God is my Lord; and though many satellites revolve around me, I and all mine revolve round the great central Truth, sun-like, fixed and luminous forever in the foundationless firmament" (*Writings*, III, 368). With this admission, the theme of revolving about a divine essence or being transcends the level of visible symbolism. Its meaning is now expressed within the individual consciousness. In a passage just before that quoted above, the narrator declares: "So, with all the past and present pouring in me, I roll down my billow from afar" (p. 368). But, qualifying his declaration, he adds: "Yet not I, but another." That other is God. If God is, then, both within the self and the center about which it revolves, he represents its essence. Reduced to its pure essence, the self thus loses all individuality, becoming one with the divine life that sustains all things.

Here Melville clearly anticipates the problematic apprehensions of self-consciousness in the "Mast-head" meditation of *Moby-Dick*. The notion that reducing the self to its pure essence signifies the loss of self is already present in *Mardi*, if only implicitly, as is that of the self as containing the whole of the external world within the medium of consciousness. As Babbalanja elsewhere affirms to Media: "But believe me, my lord, there is more to be thought of than to be seen. There is a world of wonders insphered within the spontaneous consciousness" (*Writings*, III, 352). His remark echoes the passage from Thomas Burnet prefixed by Coleridge to his "Rime of the Ancient Mariner": "Facile credo, plures esse Naturas invisibiles quam visibiles in rerum universitate" (*P.W.*, p. 186).

The illustration of the epigraph within Coleridge's poem, in which the slaying of the albatross and the confrontation with the phantom ship symbolize events within the individual consciousness, parallels Babbalanja's vision at the end of *Mardi*, which can likewise be seen as a revelation (apocalypse) of the nature of the self. At the climax of that vision, according to Babbalanja, "as poised, we hung in this rapt ether, a sudden trembling seized the four wings now folding me. And afar off, in zones still upward reaching, suns' orbits off, I, tranced, beheld an awful glory. Sphere in sphere, it burned:—the one Shekinah!" (*Writings*, III, 636). Here the motif of "sphere in sphere" possesses a Dantesque resonance (deriving most probably from the image of the Trinity in *Paradiso* XXXIII), but it also calls to mind Babbalanja's earlier claim: "there is a world of wonders insphered within the spontaneous consciousness." By juxtaposing these two passages, the meaning of the "insphering" or "sphere within sphere" motif becomes clear: God (Oro) is at the center of things, but this center subsists not in an external world but within the individual consciousness.

The suggestion that apparently external things are in fact contained within consciousness can also explain the similarities between Hautia and the lost Yillah which Taji discerns at the end of the romance. In a sense these personages are projections of his own consciousness.[11] Even as Yillah and Hautia anticipate the contrast of Lucy and Isabel in *Pierre*, so Melville's depiction of the world within consciousness in *Mardi* anticipates his treatment of the same theme in "The Mast-head" meditation of *Moby-Dick*. Even language and imagery in the earlier work point to the latter, as when Taji confesses: "But though he [Aleema] had sunk in the deep, his ghost sunk not in the deep waters of my soul" (*Writings*, III, 140). The difference is that whereas the earlier work had symbolically

[11]See *Mardi*, *Writings*, III, 158, and Merrell R. Davis, *Melville's* Mardi: *A Chartless Voyage* (New Haven: Yale Univ. Press, 1952), pp. 196–99.

asserted the presence of God within the individual consciousness, it remains for the latter to explore more deeply the actual nature of subjective pantheism.

In his later years, Coleridge returned once more to the poetic medium in order to express his concept of the relation of mind to Nature. The result appears in his celebrated 1817 addition to "The Eolian Harp":

> O! the one Life within us and abroad,
> Which meets all motion and becomes its soul,
> A light in sound, a sound-like power in light,
> Rhythm in all thought, and joyance every where—
> Methinks, it should have been impossible
> Not to love all things in a world so fill'd;
> Where the breeze warbles, and the mute still air
> Is Music slumbering on her instrument. (*P.W.*, p. 101)

Through the image of "A light in sound, a sound-like power in light," Coleridge suggests the presence of *Urphänomene* or elemental energies manifesting themselves in external Nature. Blending with physical forces, they produce the synaesthetic phenomena witnessed by the poet. The energies themselves, however, are but aspects of an immanent and all-pervasive life force that animates both mind and Nature.

The "one Life" that "meets all motion and becomes its soul" produces the "rhythm in all thought"—a significant indication, insofar as it represents the life force transcending thought itself. At the same time this elemental power also gives rise to "joyance"—a term that, as M. H. Abrams points out, must be taken to signify, not the feeling or sentiment we ordinarily associate with it, but an awareness within the individual subjective nature of its oneness with Life itself.[12] A reflection of Ishmael's in "The Grand Armada" voices a similar awareness: "But even so, amid the tornadoed Atlantic of my being, do I myself still for ever centrally disport in mute calm; and while ponderous planets of unwaning woe revolve around me, deep down and deep inland there I still bathe me in eternal mildness of joy" (*Moby-Dick*, p. 326).

Like the "joyance" of Coleridge's "Eolian Harp," such "eternal mildness of joy" proceeds from the very nature of consciousness, its relation to the Life within itself. For Ishmael as for Coleridge, such a feeling clearly transcends all transient emotions. By associating it with the procreative process (represented in the gestation and birth of

---

[12]M. H. Abrams, "Coleridge's 'A Light in Sound': Science, Metascience, and the Poetic Imagination," *Proceedings of the American Philosophical Society*, 116 (Dec., 1972), 471–72. See also Owen Barfield, *What Coleridge Thought* (Middletown, Conn.: Wesleyan Univ. Press, 1971), ch. 3, esp. pp. 37–40.

whales), Ishmael emphasizes both its involuntary character and pervasive presence throughout Nature.

Since the planetary symbolism of the passage recalls that of *Mardi*, moreover, it seems appropriate to compare its significance with that of Melville's earlier romance. There the soul was said to revolve about "the great central Truth, sun-like, fixed and luminous forever in the foundationless firmament." That central truth was equated with God. The soul, the narrative implies, revolves about a God it contains within itself. In "The Grand Armada" Ishmael observes that "amid the tornadoed Atlantic of my being" the soul remains in mute calm. Such calm can be ascribed to its pure being, which, underneath surface vicissitudes (the "tornadoed Atlantic"), remains constant and unchanging. Pursuing the analogy with *Mardi* one step further, we may identify the being of the soul with God: when Ishmael describes how "I myself still for ever *centrally* disport in mute calm," he refers, through the metaphor of centrality, to the innermost or essential principle of his being, which equates itself with "the great central Truth," or God.

The association of *Moby-Dick*'s planetary symbolism with *Mardi*'s is buttressed by Ishmael's use of another motif from the earlier work: the pursuers who are themselves pursued. At the conclusion of *Mardi* Taji, still in quest of Yillah, is himself hunted by the avenging spirits of Aleema's relatives. Similarly, in "The Grand Armada," Ahab, pursuing a group of sperm whales, finds himself chased by Malays eager to plunder the *Pequod*. The symbolic significance of the double pursuit as characterizing the human condition dawns upon him, substantiating Ishmael's later reference to the "ponderous planets of unwaning woe."

At the same time, "far beneath this wondrous world upon the surface," Ishmael writes, "another and still stranger world met our eyes as we gazed over the side. For, suspended in those watery vaults, floated the forms of the nursing mothers of the whales, and those that by their enormous girth seemed shortly to become mothers" (*Moby-Dick*, p. 325). At the center of all mortal dangers and vicissitudes there is life, the life-giving principle, birth or procreation. This principle is not merely physical but spiritual as well. In the transparent stillness of the "watery vaults" where the maternal whales lie, Ishmael anticipates symbolically the mute calm at the center of "the tornadoed Atlantic of my being." The life that dwells in these still waters is thus identified with being itself. Through his description of how newborn whales, in suckling, "while yet drawing mortal nourishment," appear as if "still spiritually feasting upon some unearthly reminiscence," Ishmael symbolizes the procession of living forms from a divine source that, like the pantheistic principle of pure energy, infuses itself in all things. With the life principle, "joyance" abides not as a transient emotion but as the natural accompaniment of the procreative impulse. Like Coleridge, Ishmael sees this feeling as issuing from the very nature of consciousness. It is the experience of vitality itself. But, unlike Coleridge, he ascribes it to the procreative (or creative) rather than sustaining or subsisting nature of life. For Ishmael, the spiritual element of being is always more closely interfused with its material and human condition.

In his letter to William Sotheby, Coleridge had stressed the need for the poet's heart and mind to be *"intimately* combined & *unified"* with the "great appearances in Nature." In "The Eolian Harp" the passage of wind through the instrument gives rise to the poet's intuition of "the one Life within us and abroad." Since the perceiving of that "one Life" depends upon the union of heart and intellect with Nature, the disruption of either faculty or their harmony with each other can produce a loss of vision. Perception of the pantheistic oneness of things depends, then, upon a subjective element. Coleridge's "Dejection" Ode carries such dependence to an even greater extreme; here, not only the perception of divine immanence but even that immanence itself becomes a function of the mind's power to infuse and pervade Nature:

> O Lady! we receive but what we give,
> And in our life alone does Nature live:
> Ours is her wedding garment, ours her shroud!
> And would we aught behold, of higher worth,
> Than that inanimate cold world allowed
> To the poor loveless ever-anxious crowd,
> Ah! from the soul itself must issue forth
> A light, a glory, a fair luminous cloud
> Enveloping the Earth—
> And from the soul itself must there be sent
> A sweet and potent voice, of its own birth,
> Of all sweet sounds the life and element! (*P.W.*, p. 365)

Strictly speaking, the Mind cannot actually enter Nature. What occurs instead is a re-creation of Nature within the Mind: through the influence of the "one intellectual breeze" depicted in "The Eolian Harp," conveying the stream of sensation and phenomena, the Mind is made to "tremble into thought." Such thought represents the creation of Nature out of the fragmentary chaos of impressions. Nature itself possesses no existence. It is solely through the Mind, which organizes such impressions into coherent forms, that we are able to affirm the existence of things: "we receive but what we give." As the following line ("And in our life alone does Nature live") makes clear, the thought that creates Nature is itself but an involuntary expression of the mind's creative energeia. The "marriage" of polarities elsewhere described by Coleridge as resulting in the mind's engendering Nature is now evoked, but only to reiterate its dependence on the self: "Ours is her wedding garment, ours her shroud!"

The imaginative engendering of Nature can assume the form of a visual radiance or effulgence ("A light, a glory, a fair luminous cloud / Enveloping the Earth—") or of sound ("A sweet and potent voice, of its own birth"). In either case, it affirms the humanizing power of imaginative thought. Just as within all "sweet sounds" we recognize the human voice as their "life and element," so within all appearances of Nature we detect some trace of the element of mind that produces them. Since the mind's creative self-assertion is involuntary, Nature must be considered a manifestation inseparable from the very datum of consciousness itself. In chapter 12 of his *Biographia Literaria* Coleridge had sought to set forth the philosophical grounding for these notions. In reading the work, Melville was bound to encounter it.

Because the treatment of the relation between mind and Nature in chapter 12 of the *Biographia* differs somewhat from Coleridge's other presentations (partly on account of his plagiarism from Schelling), and because the form of this relation—defined in terms of an identity between subjective and objective—manifests itself so strikingly in the "Mast-head" meditation of *Moby-Dick,* it seems appropriate to consider it at some length.[13]

The transcendental philosophy of Schelling had asserted a fundamental parallelism between Nature and intelligence. In adopting Schelling's transcendental idealism, Coleridge presents the unity of subjective and objective as the end and aim of all philosophy:

All knowledge rests on the coincidence of an object with a subject. . . . For we can *know* that only which is true: and the truth is universally placed in the coincidence of the thought with the thing, of the representation with the object represented.

Now the sum of all that is merely OBJECTIVE, we will henceforth call NATURE, confining the term to its passive and material sense, as comprising all the phaenomena by which its existence is made known to us. On the other hand the sum of all that is SUBJECTIVE, we may comprehend in the name of the SELF or INTELLIGENCE. Both conceptions are in necessary antithesis. Intelligence is conceived of as exclusively representative, nature as exclusively represented; the one as conscious, the other as without consciousness. Now in all acts of positive knowledge there is required a reciprocal concurrence of both, namely of the conscious being, and of that which is in itself unconscious. Our problem is to explain this concurrence, its possibility and its necessity. (*Coll. W.,* VII:1, 252–55)

[13]For commentary on the subjective and objective in Coleridge generally, see Barfield, ch. 5, esp. pp. 63–67.

Such an explanation necessitates a movement either from objective to subjective, or vice versa. The former, according to Coleridge, must consist of "the perfect spiritualization of all the laws of nature into laws of intuition and intellect" (*Coll. W.*, VII:1, 256). Beginning with the apparent chaos of natural phenomena, the mind progressively discovers the laws that govern their operation and that, as it were, express their innermost essence. In their purest and most revealing form, such laws become one with those of thought, exhibiting the nature of the mind itself (recalling the similar theme of Emerson's *Nature* and "Humanity of Science"). Concerning the opposite movement, from subjective to objective, Coleridge then asserts:

> The other position, which not only claims but necessitates the admission of its immediate certainty, equally for the scientific reason of the philosopher as for the common sense of mankind at large, namely, I AM, cannot so properly be intitled a prejudice. It is groundless indeed; but then in the very idea it precludes all ground, and separated from the immediate consciousness loses its whole sense and import. It is groundless; but only because it is itself the ground of all other certainty. Now the apparent contradiction, that the former position, namely, the existence of things without us, which from its nature cannot be immediately certain should be received as blindly and as independently of all grounds as the existence of our own being, the transcendental philosopher can solve only by the supposition, that the former is unconsciously involved in the latter; that it is not only coherent but identical, and one and the same thing with our own immediate self-consciousness. (*Coll. W.*, VII:1, 259–60)

Significantly, Coleridge defines the external world merely as the sum of "all the phaenomena by which its existence is made known to us." This is, he writes, its "passive and material sense." The material sphere, then, does not exist in itself—it constitutes simply the manifestation of something external to mind or consciousness. From other indications we know that, for Coleridge, matter consists of the concrete or physical expression of elemental spiritual energies or forces, such as light and gravitation. In themselves, these forces have no power to assume a single coherent form. Their appearance as the coherent whole we call Nature implies an act of representation. Such representation requires both a representing power and an object of representation. The representing power, or mind, we describe as internal; the object of representation, as external. Neither designation signifies anything in itself: what is external exists only by opposition to the internal, and vice versa. As merely relative designations they imply, moreover, the existence of an absolute that encompasses them both.

This absolute is knowledge. In the transcendental philosophy assimilated by Coleridge, knowledge consists, not of a correspondence between a thing and the image the mind forms of it (which affirms the distinct and independent reality of both thing and image), but rather of an identification or "coincidence" of the two, their fusion or merging into one. By means of this identification or "concurrence" (another term employed by Coleridge to describe the process) the separate reality of both representation and represented object is annulled: if the two can be combined, their combination implies the presence of an element common to both, forming their essence or ground. Knowledge thus appears as an act not of intellection (the establishment of a correspondence between an object and its representation in the mind) but of being: in knowledge, both the object represented and its representation may be said to have their existence. As a fundamental assertion of being, knowledge is, then, not merely that which is made possible by the relation of a thing to its representation, but rather that *which itself makes possible* both the thing and its representation, as the subjective and objective aspects of such knowledge.

The apparent polarity between representation and the thing represented is expressible also, according to Coleridge, as one between what is conscious and that which is without consciousness. Such a polarity suggests that in merging the two, the objective or Nature becomes endowed, as it were, with consciousness, while the subjective or mind assimilates the phenomenal or material (to use Coleridge's expression) nature of things into itself. This process suffices to explain both the animation of the "great appearances in Nature" with the "one Life" and the influx of sensory perceptions through the "one vast intellectual breeze" upon the mind.

The identity of subjective and objective also explains the assertion of the objective from the purely subjective datum of self-consciousness. This datum, which according to Coleridge "not only claims but necessitates the admission of its immediate certainty," must be described as groundless, "but only because it is itself the ground of all other certainty." The concept of a ground (borrowed from Kant) must not be confused here with the notion of a rational explanatory gesture; it refers, rather, to that which makes possible the very existence of something, the ground of the possibility of its being. In describing self-consciousness (the realization of the I AM) as groundless because it is the ground of all other certainty, Coleridge seeks to define it as that which makes all certainty possible insofar as it is itself an assertion of being, which precedes and constitutes the ground of all things.

But the assertion of the I AM, "when separated from the immediate consciousness," "loses its whole sense and import." In other words, the assertion I AM can possess significance only as the self-assertion of a particular individual. Here, both form and content of the statement merit consideration. As uttered by a particular individual, the assertion I

AM represents not merely a descriptive statement about a state of affairs external to that individual. Instead, this statement is itself the assertion of being, something that belongs inseparably to the individual's very being. In sum, the self-consciousness of which Coleridge speaks must be regarded as the individual's essence, as that which establishes its existence.

Such self-consciousness, according to Coleridge, exists simultaneously with a belief in the existence of things outside us. Their relation, he continues, can be resolved "only by the supposition, that the former [belief in the existence of things outside us] is unconsciously involved in the latter" [self-consciousness]. That such a belief can be "not only coherent but identical, and one and the same thing with our own immediate self-consciousness," is possible only because self-consciousness is itself but a part of consciousness, whose content consists in large part of impressions of external things. Thus in consciousness we have at once a consciousness of our own existence and of the world, both experienced as elements of a comprehensive subjective medium that forms the essence of our being. In this medium we experience our own existence, as a datum of consciousness. Simultaneously, that experience is an assertion of our being, containing within itself as part of its burden the external world or Nature, whose existence is thus simultaneously asserted along with that of the self.

Turning now to a celebrated passage from "The Mast-head" in *Moby-Dick,* we encounter the theme we have traced thus far in Coleridge, the identity of subjective and objective, and the birth of the objective within the subjective, expressed with all the conscious artifice of fiction:

> but lulled into such an opium-like listlessness of vacant, unconscious reverie is this absent-minded youth by the blending cadence of waves with thoughts, that at last he loses his identity; takes the mystic ocean at his feet for the visible image of that deep, blue, bottomless soul, pervading mankind and nature; and every strange, half-seen, gliding, beautiful thing that eludes him; every dimly-discovered, uprising fin of some indiscernible form, seems to him the embodiment of those elusive thoughts that only people the soul by continually flitting through it. In this enchanted mood, thy spirit ebbs away to whence it came; becomes diffused through time and space; like Wickliff's sprinkled Pantheistic ashes, forming at last a part of every shore the round globe over.
>
> There is no life in thee, now, except that rocking life imparted by a gently rolling ship; by her, borrowed from the sea; by the sea, from the inscrutable tides of God. But while this sleep, this dream is on ye, move your foot or hand an inch; slip your hold at all; and your identity comes back in horror. Over Descartian vortices you hover. And perhaps, at mid-day, in the fairest weather, with one half-throttled shriek you drop through that transparent

air into the summer sea, no more to rise for ever. Heed it well, ye Pan-theists![14] (*Moby-Dick*, p. 140)

Through comparison of this passage with a similar one from *Mardi*, the results of Melville's "Coleridgean" speculations become clear.[15] Near the beginning of the earlier work the narrator ascends the mast and beholds the following prospect:

> The entire western horizon high piled with gold and crimson clouds; airy arches, domes, and minarets; as if the yellow, Moorish sun were setting behind some vast Alhambra. Vistas seemed leading to worlds beyond. To and fro, and all over the towers of this Nineveh in the sky, flew troops of birds. Watching them long, one crossed my sight, flew through a low arch, and was lost to view. My spirit must have sailed in with it; for directly, as in a trance, came upon me the cadence of mild billows laving a beach of shells, the waving of boughs, and the voices of maidens, and the lulled beatings of my own dissolved heart, all blended together. (*Writings*, III, 7–8)

Here the impression is of a fantastic Eastern setting. Almost half a century earlier the lure of the Orient had exerted its attraction upon Euro-

[14]In his essay "The Composition of *Moby-Dick*" (*American Literature*, 47 [1975], 343–60), James Barbour attempts to furnish a chronology of the various stages in the writing of Melville's novel. According to his schema, "The Mast-head" would presumably fall in the first or second stage, i.e., from autumn 1850 to early 1851 (pp. 358–59). Even if Barbour's conjecture is correct, I see no reason to rule out the possibility of late additions—which could include the final meditative passage. This passage might then have been composed virtually anytime prior to publication in the fall of 1851. With regard to the whole question of dating stages in the composition of *Moby-Dick*, see Robert Milder's "The Composition of *Moby-Dick*: A Review and a Prospect," *ESQ*, 23 (1977), 203–16. There seems no reason to assume an overly rigid view of the compositional process (which assigns whole chapters to distinct stages). On that issue the crucial remark occurs in Melville's letter to Hawthorne (June 29, 1851): "Since you have been here, I have been building some shanties of houses (connected with the old one) and likewise some shanties of chapters and essays" (*Letters*, p. 132)—which suggests *additions* to various chapters (such as, possibly, "The Mast-head").

[15]For another perspective on how the fusion of subjective and objective in "The Mast-head" transforms Melville's earlier representation of the pantheistic consciousness, see *White-Jacket*. In "The Jacket Aloft," we encounter a feeling of oneness with all things: "And it is a very fine feeling, and one that fuses us into the universe of things, and makes us a part of the All . . ." (*Writings*, V, 76). As in *Moby-Dick*, the vigil induces an absent-minded reverie: "and still one hundred feet above even *them* I lay entranced; now dozing, now dreaming" (p. 77). From this state, the narrator is abruptly recalled: "But when, like lightning, the yard dropped under me, and instinctively I clung with both hands to the '*tie*,' then I came to myself with a rush, and felt something like a choking hand at my throat." Here, however, the feeling of oneness, in contrast to that in *Moby-Dick*, is suggested by an abstract reflection, rather than the immediate experience of consciousness: "to think that, wherever we ocean-wanderers rove, we have still the same glorious old stars to keep us company; that they still shine onward and on, forever beautiful and bright, and luring us, by every ray, to die and be glorified with them." Moreover, the narrator in his reverie thinks not of the scene before him but of "things past, and anon of the life to come." His abrupt recall to self-consciousness is brought about not by an imagined fall into the abyss, but by his shipmates' deliberate lowering of the yardarm (thinking he is a ghost).

pean Romantic authors: Byron (*The Giaour, The Corsair, The Bride of Abydos*), Southey (*The Curse of Kehama, Madoc, Thalaba the Destroyer*), Chateaubriand (*Les Aventures du dernier abencerage*). America too knows of it through Irving's *Alhambra*. For Romanticism, the East represents a new realm of possibilities for the imagination. Of these possibilities Melville is also conscious: "Vistas seemed leading to worlds beyond." The narrator's imagination identifies itself with a bird in flight, symbolizing what Keats had called "the viewless wings of poesy." Thus transported, the narrator beholds, "as in a trance," a tropical scene, the object of his desires.

Throughout the reverie Melville transports the mind progressively away from the actual scene to another produced by the imagination. By contrast, the movement of reverie in "The Mast-head" is one that immerses the individual consciousness in external Nature, until all phenomena seem but reflections of the soul itself. The remarkable similarities in language between the two passages (the "cadence of mild billows," the "blending together" of different phenomena) serve only to clarify their fundamental difference. Whereas the imagination in *Mardi* must deny external Nature to create its own ideal sphere, consciousness in "The Mast-head" attempts to immerse itself in that same Nature. The differences between the passages also point to Melville's increasing tendency toward exploration of the actual nature of consciousness as a whole, rather than of a single faculty such as the imagination.

In the "blending cadence of waves with thoughts" Melville employs an image similar to that of "The Eolian Harp": "Rhythm in all thought." That rhythm, we recall, had revealed the presence of a higher spiritual energy, one that through its polarities and their alternation of force produces such a rhythm. But the same energy also manifests itself in the material or external world. Melville's passage hints at a similar notion. The "blending cadence" of internal and external, subjective and objective, implies a higher immanent energy to which both thought and waves may trace their source. In contrast to Coleridge, however, nowhere does the narrator specify that source. For all its suggestiveness, the "blending cadence" fails to affirm the presence of a power like "the one Life within us and abroad" whose action produces the observed concurrence.

What it does depict is an identity or fusion of subjective and objective similar to that described in the *Biographia Literaria*. Like Coleridge, moreover, Melville presents this fusion as one between the conscious and that which is without consciousness. Such a fusion involves—as in Coleridge—a "reciprocal concurrence" of both. The medium in which they merge is that of "unconscious reverie." Here the term *unconscious* must be understood in a sense different from the Freudian one. For Melville, "unconscious reverie" implies a vacancy: it contains neither the I AM assertion of self-consciousness nor the experience of Nature as a world external to that of consciousness. What results from the absence of these is not pure nothingness but a dreamlike state in which what passes before the mind is neither distinctly subjective nor objective. This state is made possible by the fact that, as in Coleridge, subjective and objective are themselves endowed with only a relative significance. Each exists by opposition to the other, and with the collapse of either—as depicted by Melville in the present instance—its opposite is likewise annulled, leaving only the medium of "unconscious reverie."

Reverie, in turn, is said to produce a loss of identity. For Coleridge in the *Biographia,* such identity must be equated with self-consciousness. But self-consciousness, as we have seen, is experienced only as a datum within the larger or more comprehensive field of consciousness, which also includes as part of its content the material perception of an external or objective world. By defining identity solely as a form of consciousness, Melville can speak of a genuine loss of identity (which would not be possible were such identity simply the sum of an individual's specific features). This loss occurs when the mind ceases to be conscious of itself, when self-consciousness dissolves through a transformation of the whole field of consciousness. In that state, the external world, which had been given as an immediate datum of consciousness along with the self, becomes something more than Nature, an apparent analogue to the "World-Soul" celebrated by the later Schelling. Without losing its material or concrete aspect, it becomes pervaded or suffused by thought. The thought-element previously responsible for the assertion of self-consciousness now passes into the visible appearance of Nature.

At this point the narrative perspective undergoes a sudden alteration. With the introduction of the "mystic ocean" at the youthful dreamer's feet, we witness what must surely be subjective being presented as objective reality. Through the ocean's "mystic" aspect (suggestive of an obscure or mysterious character of significance) Melville infuses a subjective element into the depiction of external Nature: the sense of mystery that the spectacle can belong only to the mind that beholds it. In another sense, however, the subjective element belongs to Nature itself, if we think of Nature (following Coleridge) as the sum of "all the phaenomena by which its existence is made known to us." By means of the ambiguous double perspective, it becomes possible to observe a concurrence of subjective and objective. If present at the dreamer's feet as an external or objective reality, the ocean is, nevertheless, perceived subjectively (hence its "mystic" aspect); but this subjective perception remains objective in the sense of containing all the phenomena by which the ocean's existence is made known to the mind.

In the "visible image of that deep, blue, bottomless soul, pervading mankind and nature," Melville presents an analogue to the expression of the "one Life within us and abroad" in Coleridge's "Eolian Harp." But it is an analogue with a difference. The "bottomless soul" can be bottomless in two senses: as infinite fullness, or as infinite vacancy. Such a vacancy would correspond to the "vacant, unconscious reverie" described earlier. In addition, the feeling of vacancy displays the result when the self experiences a loss of self-consciousness—the vertigo of falling into an infinite abyss, in which there is no longer an external world confronting consciousness with its opposing and tangible reality, but only the soundless depths of the "World-Soul" that absorbs all self, all sense of individual being.

The continuation of Melville's narrative enacts such a process: "and every strange, half-seen, gliding, beautiful thing that eludes him; every dimly-discovered, uprising fin of some indiscernible form, seems to him the embodiment of those elusive thoughts that only people the soul by continually flitting through it." Since these "half-seen, gliding, beautiful" things appear within the shimmering waters of that "mystic ocean" whose existence is at once subjective and objective, it becomes likewise impossible to decide what kind of reality to attribute to them. Here the text increases the ambiguity with its indication that such things are only "half-seen" and finally elusive: even if one assumes the mystic ocean as objectively real, it remains questionable whether such forms do not in fact belong to the realm of the subjective or imaginary; if so, they become objectively real as phenomenal manifestations to the eye and mind of the youthful dreamer. All of which recalls naturally Coleridge's assertion in the *Biographia,* "that the former [the objective] is unconsciously involved in the latter [the subjective]; that it is not only coherent but identical, and one and the same thing with our own immediate self-consciousness."

At this point, the nature of representation itself calls for consideration. In the *Biographia* Coleridge had pointed out how intelligence or consciousness is conceived of as "exclusively representative," nature as "exclusively represented," observing the necessity in knowledge for their "reciprocal concurrence." By depicting in "The Mast-head" the tendency of consciousness to form the images it sees into representations, Melville attempts to reveal the autonomous quality of such a faculty, its involuntary impulse to image forth an external Nature. This impulse issues from the creative energy of the mind itself. On account of the merging of subjective with objective, such energy can produce the objective *within* the subjective. In at least one important respect, the process differs from that described by Coleridge, for whom the objective is always genuinely contained within the subjective. By contrast, Melville suggests that the forming of an objective world by the subjective, though involuntary, is illusory. Through its tendency to represent, to impart a coherent form to the images that pass before it, the mind ultimately embodies itself in the "great appearances in Nature."

But we have, within the passage itself, a suggestion of how the objective appears within the subjective. Through the image of every "dimly-discovered, uprising fin of some indiscernible form," the mind appears to grasp a tangible "embodiment" of its thought. That "embodiment" is only apparently concrete, since what it embodies is not objective Nature but only the subjective element of consciousness. By seeking to grasp its thought through such illusory apparitions, moreover, the mind finds itself at last without clear apprehension of either thought or image. Subjective and objective dissolve into a blended medium that lacks the reality of either consciousness or external Nature. For Romanticism, the symbol had expressed a transparent revelation of the divine essence. In *Moby-Dick* Nature as symbol becomes obscuration rather than revelation, only "seeming" to embody thoughts too elusive in themselves to define. Even within the realm of the subjective, objective appearances remain deceptive. Ultimately, the "objective Nature" produced by the subjective reveals only the illusoriness of its own assertion.

The unusual shift, at this moment, from third to second person in the text ("In this enchanted mood, thy spirit ebbs away to whence it came") both implies and proceeds from the assumption that there is no longer any difference between internal and external, subjective and objective. The subjective consciousness of the youth is also my consciousness, because the self-awareness that had given it its individual identity has not been lost. Of course, Ishmael also addresses the reader directly elsewhere in the novel, and the practice occurs in Dickens, Harriet Beecher Stowe, and other writers of the time. In the present instance, however, the shift appears unusual because the passage begins with a clearly delineated third person (the "absent-minded youth"); moreover, Melville almost emphasizes the shift by his later reference to "your identity." At the same time, the naturalness with which he effects this transition cannot but raise other questions: Is the second person whom the text addresses really the reader? Or is it not, perhaps, the voice of the dreamer speaking, as it were, to himself? Such multiple possibilities become ultimately a means of exhibiting the very concurrence of subjective and objective which the text seeks to assert, the dissolution of barriers separating internal from external, self-consciousness from consciousness of what is outside us.

The continuation of the passage takes up a theme similar to that of Coleridge's "Eolian Harp": "There is no life in thee, now, except that rocking life imparted by a gently rolling ship; by her, borrowed from the sea; by the sea, from the inscrutable tides of God." Here the "one Life within us and abroad" appears again, albeit under a somewhat different form. Likewise, the manifestation of that Life, as "rhythm in all thought," confronts its equivalent in the "rocking life imparted by a gently rolling ship." Above all, the concept of a higher spiritual energy "which meets all motion and becomes its soul" is now adumbrated by the waves of a sea whose motion derives from "the inscrutable tides of God." Like the "rhythm in all thought," such tides manifest an immanent divine energy pervading and acting through the material sphere. Nevertheless, in contrast to the lines from "The Eolian Harp," the whole passage places itself in question, since it but prolongs the imaging of an objective Nature within the subjective consciousness described earlier.

As an expression of that consciousness, the "inscrutable tides of God" would then mirror the creative overflow of the mind's own energy. But if the consciousness of the dreamer has also become *my* consciousness, those tides become the manifestation of an objective reality within all consciousness. By the fascination it exerts upon the spectator, this apparently objective reality lulls him into a trance-like state that ultimately brings about the individual's destruction. At the same time what "The Mast-head" meditation suggests is the inevitability or naturalness of the mind's arriving at the illusion of such a concurrence, as though it were but the result of some innate tendency in the mind itself which causes it to produce such an illusion.

The result of the apparent concurrence can but promote a more intensive questioning of the nature of that pantheistic essence that ordains and establishes such a relation between mind and Nature. Like the symbolic revelation of "The Whiteness of the Whale," which finally causes blindness, the loss of identity through a concurrence of subjective and objective destroys the individual consciousness through its absorption into the world-soul. The irrational aspect of such a process leads thematically to Ahab's impassioned defiance of the divine energy that governs that process, a defiance that is itself but part of Melville's larger polemic throughout the novel against the inscrutable purpose that pervades the whole relation between mind and Nature. In this polemic, in which the scriptural consciousness that "I am fearfully and wonderfully made" is neither negated nor diminished, nor the ultimate unknowability of Nature avoided, what emerges finally is the sense that there is no "parallelism of Nature and intelligence," no possible "Humanity of Science" (Emerson) that can impart a positive moral significance to this relation of self to Nature. Instead, there is only the consciousness of the inhumanity of such a relation as something that proceeds from "the inscrutable tides of God."

Of course, one misses something if one fails to notice also the rich element of humor that—as so often in Melville—lends its coloring to the whole of "The Mast-head" passage. Like an aura, or some luminous rainbow mist, one feels it somehow suspended above the passage: there may be death and destruction on the sea, the inflamed fury of the hunters amidst the wreckage of their boats left in the whale's wake, but above there remains the "serene, exasperating sunlight, that smiled on, as if at a birth or a bridal." Here, in "The Mast-head," such humor becomes irony, but one other than what we are now accustomed to as its modern form. In his *Ideen* Friedrich Schlegel had characterized irony as "clear consciousness of the eternal agility, of the infinitely abundant chaos" (*Krit. Ausgabe*, II, 263, no. 69). Elsewhere, in the *Lyceum Fragments*, he maintains: "There are ancient and modern poems [*Gedichte*] which breathe throughout and overall the divine breath of irony. There lives in these a true transcendental buffoonery. Inwardly, the mood which surveys all and which infinitely elevates itself over everything finite, including its own art, virtue, or geniality; outwardly, in the realization of the mimic manner of an ordinary good Italian *buffo*" (*Krit. Ausgabe*, II, 152). The significance of this declaration is further borne out by an utterance in the *Gespräch über die Poesie:* "Even in wholly popular genres such as, for example, the drama, we require irony; we require that the circumstances, the individuals, in short the whole play of life be truly apprehended and represented as a play" (*Krit. Ausgabe*, II, 323). For Friedrich Schlegel, then, irony is the perception of a consciousness that has become conscious of itself and hence of the whole of our phenomenal or external existence as but the content of that consciousness.[16]

This Schlegelian conception of irony undergoes certain important modifications in Kierkegaard. In his *Concept of Irony* Kierkegaard observes:

> If we consider irony as it directs itself against the whole of existence, it here again sustains the opposition between essence and phenomenon, between the internal and the external. It might seem that as absolute negativity it were identical with doubt. It must be borne in mind, however, that doubt is a conceptual determination while irony is the being-for-itself of subjectivity. . . . With doubt the subject constantly seeks to penetrate the object, and his misfortune consists in the fact that the object constantly eludes him. With irony, on the other hand, the subject is always seeking to get outside the object, and this he attains by becoming conscious at every moment that the object has no reality. (p. 274)

Here it seems important to stress the difference between irony and doubt: with the former, the opposition between internal and external, essence and phenomenon, becomes an object of *play*, which is also what imparts to irony its comic element.

In "The Mast-head" we encounter traces of something akin to both the Schlegelian and Kierkegaardian forms of irony. Like Friedrich Schlegel, Melville too displays awareness of the existence of the "great appearances of Nature" within the individual consciousness. For him,

---

[16]For more on this topic, see Raymond Immerwahr, "The Subjectivity or Objectivity of Friedrich Schlegel's Poetic Irony," *Germanic Review*, 28 (1951), 173–91.

too (even more noticeably in *The Confidence-Man*), all of life can seem but a play: the question of what, if anything, lies beyond appearances pervades the whole of his novel. Yet the delight in existence itself, the beauty and sensuousness of experience, remain as part of the ironic mood. Like Kierkegaard, Melville feels the ironic capacity to dismiss the object. Only, for him, significantly (as for Friedrich Schlegel before him), that "object" is but an appearance. Melvillean irony, like Kierkegaard's, consists of the ability to yield to a constant *play* between internal and external, to dwell in the opposition between essence and phenomenon without resolving it. Like the play of sunlight upon the waves, or the dream-vision of reverie, Melvillean irony conjures up for itself the spectacle of its own immersion in Nature without, finally, acceding to it. To be able to dismiss these "great appearances of Nature"—that is the privilege of irony. But, at the same time, what irony thereby confronts is the reality of its own subjectivity. If the dismissal of appearances can afford the pleasure of lightness and comic grace, the consequent return to consciousness itself must nevertheless come as the final moment of irony, one in which the self is neither more nor less than the measure of both the freedom and limits of its own subjectivity.

## "The Necessity of Atheism"

On March 25, 1811, the young Shelley is expelled from Oxford for his pamphlet *The Necessity of Atheism*. Two years later, in *Queen Mab*, he voices once more through the figure of Ahasuerus his defiance of the traditional God. Summoned by a fairy, Ahasuerus appears and, after rehearsing his history and the curse pronounced by God upon him, declares:

> Thus have I stood, —through a wild waste of years
> Struggling with whirlwinds of mad agony,
> Yet peaceful, and serene, and self-enshrined,
> Mocking my powerless tyrant's horrible curse
> With stubborn and unalterable will,
> Even as a giant oak, which heaven's fierce flame
> Had scathed in the wilderness, to stand
> A monument of fadeless ruin there;
> Yet peacefully and movelessly it braves
> The midnight conflict of the wintry storm,
> As in the sun-light's calm it spreads
> Its worn and withered arms on high
> To meet the quiet of a summer's noon.
>
> (Reiman and Powers, p. 57)

In *Moby-Dick* Melville makes use of a similar theme and imagery.[17] Of Ahab's first appearance after the Pequod embarks on its southward passage, Ishmael observes:

There seemed no sign of common bodily illness about him, nor of the recovery from any. He looked like a man cut away from the stake, when the fire has overrunningly wasted all the limbs without consuming them, or taking away one particle from their compacted aged robustness. His whole high, broad form, seemed made of solid bronze, and shaped in an unalterable mould, like Cellini's cast Perseus. Threading its way out from among his grey hairs, and continuing right down one side of his tawny scorched face and neck, till it disappeared in his clothing, you saw a slender rod-like mark, lividly whitish. It resembled that perpendicular seam sometimes made in the straight, lofty trunk of a great tree, when the upper lightning tearingly darts down it, and without wrenching a single twig, peels and grooves out the bark from top to bottom, ere running off into the soil, leaving the tree still greenly alive, but branded. Whether that mark was born with him, or whether it was the scar left by some desperate wound, no one could certainly say. (*Moby-Dick*, pp. 109–10)

[17]For Melville's reading of Shelley and a list of Shelley's works owned by Melville, see Sealts, *Melville's Reading*, p. 94. *Essays, Letters from Abroad, Translations and Fragments* contains the *Defence of Poetry* as well as "On Life," "Speculations on Metaphysics" and "Speculations on Morals." The present location of Melville's copy of Shelley's *Poetical Works* (ed. Mrs. Shelley) is unfortunately unknown. This edition, according to Melville's note, was acquired by him only in 1861. For evidence of his reading of Shelley's *Defence* while composing *Mardi*, however, see Davis, pp. 187–88. And, for evidence of his reading of Shelley while composing *Pierre*, cf. his remark in that novel on "Shellian dietings" (p. 299)—an apparent reference either to Shelley's long note on vegetarianism in *Queen Mab* or to his later essay "A Vindication of Natural Diet." Finally, for Melville's reading of Shelley before 1861, see also the account in John Thomas Gulick's journal of a conversation with Melville (April 20, 1859): "The ancient dignity of Homeric times afforded the only state of humanity, individual or social, to which he could turn with any complacency. What little there was of meaning in the religions of the present day has come down from Plato" (quoted from Jay Leyda's *Melville Log: A Documentary Life of Herman Melville, 1819–1891*, 2 vols. [New York: Harcourt, Brace, 1951], II, 605). Here Melville's final assertion and the general tenor of his remarks echo Shelley's *Defence* and other essays. Cf. esp. Shelley's observation in the *Defence* that "Plato, following the doctrines of Timaeus and Pythagoras, taught also a moral and intellectual system of doctrine comprehending at once the past, the present, and the future condition of man. Jesus Christ divulged the sacred and eternal truths contained in these views to mankind, and Christianity, in its abstract purity, became the exoteric expression of the esoteric doctrine of the poetry and wisdom of antiquity" (Reiman and Powers, p. 496). And, similarly, in Mary Shelley's preface to *Essays, Letters from Abroad, Translations and Fragments:* "No prose author in the history of mankind has exerted so much influence over the world as Plato. From him the Fathers and commentators of early Christianity derived many of their most abstruse notions and spiritual ideas" (cited from Shelley, *C.W.*, v, viii). Melville's remark on Plato may also derive from Emerson's *Representative Men*—a suggestion I owe to Professor Sealts. See Emerson, *C.W.*, IV, 39, 40: "Out of Plato come all things that are still written and debated among men of thought"; "Calvinism is in his Phaedo; Christianity is in it."

Like Shelley, Melville employs the image of a tree scarred by lightning to suggest defiance of God. Ahab's resemblance to "a man cut away from the stake" evokes the idea of a victim of auto-da-fé; the description of the lightning's mark upon the tree as a branding recalls Cain and hints at a divine curse. Later, the significance of Ahab's scar is taken up once more. In "The Candles," seeing the corposants ignite the masts of the Pequod, Ahab exclaims:

> "Oh! thou clear spirit of clear fire, whom on these seas I as Persian once did worship, till in the sacramental act so burned by thee, that to this hour I bear the scar; I now know thee, thou clear spirit, and I know that thy right worship is defiance. To neither love nor reverence wilt thou be kind; and e'en for hate thou canst but kill; and all are killed. No fearless fool now fronts thee. I own thy speechless, placeless power; but to the last gasp of my earthquake life will dispute its unconditional, unintegral mastery in me. In the midst of the personified impersonal, a personality stands here. Though but a point at best; whencesoe'er I came; whereso'er I go; yet while I earthly live, the queenly personality lives in me, and feels her royal rights. But war is pain, and hate is woe. Come in thy lowest form of love, and I will kneel and kiss thee; but at thy highest, come as mere supernal power; and though thou launchest navies of full-freighted worlds, there's that in here that still remains indifferent. Oh, thou clear spirit, of thy fire thou madest me, and like a true child of fire, I breathe it back at thee." (*Moby-Dick*, pp. 416–17)

In his *Prometheus Unbound* Shelley had incorporated similar themes.[18] Where Ahab declares, "I now know thee, thou clear spirit, and I now know that thy right worship is defiance," Prometheus can say to Jupiter:

> Fiend, I defy thee! with a calm, fixed mind,
> All that thou canst inflict I bid thee do;
> Foul Tyrant both of Gods and Humankind,
> One only being shalt thou not subdue.
> Rain then thy plagues upon me here,
> Ghastly disease and frenzying fear;
> And let alternate frost and fire
> Eat into me, and be thine ire
> Lightning and cutting hail and legioned forms
> Of furies, driving by upon the wounding storms.
>
>                              (Reiman and Powers, p. 143)

---

[18]For another treatment of the relation between *Moby-Dick* and Shelley's *Prometheus Unbound*, Mario d'Avanzo, "Ahab, the Grecian Pantheon and Shelley's *Prometheus Unbound*: The Dynamics of Myth in *Moby-Dick*," *Books at Brown*, 24 (1971), 19–44. D'Avanzo interprets Ahab as an inverted Shelleyan Prometheus—more awkward, surely, than simply seeing him as a direct model for Ahab. On Ahab and Prometheus (without reference to Shelley), Richard Chase, *Herman Melville: A Critical Study* (New York: Macmillan, 1949), pp. 3–4, 45–48.

With Ahab's "To neither love nor reverence wilt thou be kind" we may compare Prometheus's claim:

> I gave all
> He has, and in return he chains me here
> Years, ages, night and day. . . .
>
> (Reiman and Powers, p. 147)

Ahab owns the fire's "speechless, placeless power" but disputes its "unconditional, unintegral mastery" in him. In his speech to Jupiter, Prometheus manifests a similar attitude:

> Aye, do thy worst. Thou art Omnipotent.
> O'er all things but thyself I gave thee power,
> And my own will.
>
> (Reiman and Powers, p. 143)

This will forms the essence of the "queenly personality": it signifies what cannot be subdued by force. Byron's Manfred, who defies the authority of the spirit Arimanes, offers an analogue to it. But Manfred's defiance differs from that of Ahab or Prometheus since Arimanes is, as Manfred observes, not God but merely one of God's creations.

Of course, Ahab's defiance also resembles that of Satan in *Paradise Lost*.[19] This resemblance is reinforced by the Romantic interpretation of Milton's epic.[20] For Blake and Shelley in particular, Satan represents the true hero of the poem, symbolizing the energy of the creative imagination. Melville's marking of the following passage in his copy of Shelley's *Defence of Poetry* attests to his sympathy with such a view:

> Milton's Devil as a moral being is as far superior to his God, as one who perseveres in some purpose which he has conceived to be excellent in spite of adversity and torture, is to one who in the cold security of undoubted triumph inflicts the most horrible revenge upon his enemy, not from any mistaken notion of inducing him to repent of a perseverance in enmity, but of the alleged design of exasperating him to deserve new torments. Milton has so far violated the popular creed (if this shall be judged to be a violation) as to have alleged no superiority of moral virtue to his God over his Devil. And this bold neglect of a direct moral purpose is the most decisive proof of the supremacy of Milton's genius. (Cowen, "Melville's Marginalia," x, 113)

In one sense, of course, Shelley's *Prometheus Unbound* is itself an interpretation of Milton's epic. But certain elements in Ahab's speech that

---

[19]See Henry Pommer, *Milton and Melville* (Pittsburgh: Univ. of Pittsburgh Press, 1960), pp. 89–104, which does not, however, mention this passage from *Moby-Dick* or cite parallels from *Paradise Lost*.

[20]Ibid., p. 90.

do not bear a close analogy to anything in *Paradise Lost* make it possible to trace Melville's specific affinity to Shelley.

The "personified impersonal," which contains the individual personality within itself, exhibits the pantheistic element of Ahab's assertions. This "personified impersonal" is but another name for God, impersonal in his own nature but personified by man. By suffusing the world with his own essence, he assimilates the individual personality into himself. As Prometheus exclaims in an apostrophe to Jupiter, "But thou who art the God and Lord—O thou / Who fillest with thy soul this world of woe" (Reiman and Powers, p. 144). We have seen how Melville's attraction to Romantic pantheism had led to the "Coleridgean" explorations of "The Mast-head." For Coleridge, God as the being of the world represents the identity of subjective and objective. As a result of his decisive rejection of that identity, Melville finds himself compelled to pursue other forms of pantheistic belief. In poems such as "The Eolian Harp," Coleridge had envisioned the pantheistic presence as a higher, spiritual form of energy. The "Dejection" Ode attempts to unite the notion of God as divine energy with the subjective-objective identity taken over from Schelling. Consciousness itself is seen as a form of energy. Its element is life ("And in our life alone does Nature live"). Melville too, as we have seen, attempts to fuse the two notions in the "Mast-head" meditation. There the imagination is portrayed as a vital force, a creative *energeia*, which produces an external world for itself from phenomenal impressions. Ultimately, however, such a formulation proves unsatisfactory as a form of pantheism, on account of the imagination's tendency toward creative illusion. In contrast to Coleridge, Shelley conceives of God purely as power or energy. Since this power is distinct from intelligence or consciousness, its existence does not imply the necessity of worshiping it.[21]

To the substance or essence of God, Ahab ascribes at least two forms: power and love. Traditional Christian theology had sought to reconcile them, making God both in equal measure. Here they are opposed: love is the "lowest form," power the "highest." Of Shelley's Prometheus, who is also a god, Panthea says:

> the overpowering light
> Of that immortal shape was shadowed o'er
> By love. . . .
>
> (Reiman and Powers, p. 162)

---

[21]Cf. T. Walter Herbert, *Moby-Dick and Calvinism* (New Brunswick, N.J.: Rutgers Univ. Press, 1977), p. 84: "Melville's notion that divine powers resist the spiritual inquiries of men is analogous to Calvinistic belief in the sovereign holiness of God, but his claim to absolute self-sovereignty in the face of such transcendent opposition is uniquely Melvillean." Here we must add: also Shelleyan. Cf. further, Lawrance Thompson, *Melville's Quarrel with God* (Princeton: Princeton Univ. Press, 1952), pp. 232–33.

The tempering of an overwhelming divine effulgence for mortal eyes recalls similar instances in Dante, the Old Testament, and Homer. In the Romantic period it occurs in Keats's *Fall of Hyperion*. For Shelley, the process affects not only the appearance but also the nature of the divinity itself.

The highest form of that divinity Ahab describes as "mere supernal power"—as if implying the possibility of something higher. Earth addresses Prometheus in a similar fashion:

> Subtle thou art and good, and though the Gods
> Hear not this voice—yet thou art more than God,
> Being wise and kind.—
>
> (Reiman and Powers, p. 140)

Against the onslaught of "mere supernal power," Ahab asserts, "there's that in here that still remains indifferent." Such indifference differs from that of Byron's Manfred, which proceeds from the inner desolation of a soul obsessed with guilt; it suggests rather Shelley's Ahasuerus and Prometheus, both, in their defiance of a God, "peaceful, and serene, and self-enshrined." It is its "self-empire" (Prometheus) that permits the soul to feel "her royal rights."

Ahab's final exclamation ("Oh, thou clear spirit, of thy fire thou madest me") also recalls a similar passage in Shelley. Jupiter speaks of his authority to the assembled gods:

> All else has been subdued to me—alone
> The soul of man, like unextinguished fire,
> Yet burns towards Heaven with fierce reproach and doubt
> And lamentation and reluctant prayer,
> Hurling up insurrection, which might make
> Our antique empire insecure, though built
> On eldest faith, and Hell's coeval, fear.
>
> (Reiman and Powers, p. 180)

In addition to defying God, Ahab had also asserted His common nature with humanity ("of thy fire thou madest me"), an idea implied in, but not restricted to, pantheism.[22] A source for it occurs in Prometheus's assertion, mentioned earlier: "I gave all / He has." Here Shelley reverses the direction of divine effulgence, making it proceed from man (Prometheus) to God. By postulating such a dependence of the divine upon the human, Shelley differs from Melville. Their difference is based on a concept peculiar to Shelley: the notion that by imagining a God

[22]For more analysis, see Braswell, pp. 26–27.

man thereby creates one, whom the act of his mind endows with real substance.[23]

Since God himself is a creation of the imagination, it is at least possible in theory to imagine a higher power. Such a power would possess the characteristics of a moral rather than physical force. Its nature is revealed as Demogorgon dethrones Jupiter. Asked by Jupiter to identify himself, Demogorgon answers: "Eternity—demand no direr name" (Reiman and Powers, p. 181). Elsewhere in the poem, Panthea describes his appearance:

> I see a mighty Darkness
> Filling the seat of power; and rays of gloom
> Dart round, as light from the meridian Sun,
> Ungazed upon and shapeless—neither limb
> Nor form—nor outline; yet we feel it is
> A living Spirit.
>                                   (Reiman and Powers, p. 171)

The higher power to which I have referred is not Demogorgon himself but what may perhaps best be described as Necessity. From Asia's colloquy with Demogorgon it appears that such a power must be something other than God, "for," as Demogorgon observes, "Jove is the supreme of living things." Asked to define the nature of that power, Demogorgon can only say:

> —If the Abysm
> Could vomit forth its secrets:—but a voice
> Is wanting, the deep truth is imageless.
>                                   (Reiman and Powers, p. 175)

In Melville too its nature is merely hinted at. Following his apostrophe to God as fire in "The Candles," Ahab asserts: "There is some unsuffusing thing beyond thee, thou clear spirit, to whom all thy eternity is but time, all thy creativeness mechanical. Through thee, thy flaming self, my scorched eyes do dimly see it" (*Moby-Dick*, p. 417). Unlike the pantheistic nature of God, this power does not suffuse the world but remains in some sense beyond it. Accordingly, it participates in a different eternity from that of God. That higher eternity is not one of infinite duration but one to which even the concept of duration itself no longer applies. As the immanent energy of the universe, a pantheistic God subsists or perdures in a material sense. Its eternity consists of an infinite extension of material time, through which we measure the existence of the universe. A power outside of or beyond such a universe possesses no relation to its

[23]Cf. Blake's theory of emanations, esp. in *The Four Zoas*.

time. It is a power of this nature that Melville depicts through Ahab's assertion.

A God who represents the interfused energy of the world acts by impelling the material element directly. Such action resembles that of physical forces: hence Ahab's reproach that its creativeness is only "mechanical." A higher, purely spiritual power possessing nothing in common with matter must act upon it in a different fashion altogether.

By means of these features it becomes possible to distinguish Melville's concept of the higher power from that of Shelley. What the British poet had envisaged as a reorganization of the divine energy (displacement of Jupiter, liberation of Prometheus), Melville ascribes to a different source altogether. We have seen that it cannot be pantheistic. It does not affect the divine energy pervading and governing the world. Nevertheless, the mere fact of its existence places Ahab's defiance of God in a different light from that of Romantic Satanism. Such defiance appears no longer merely negative but rather as the aspiration toward a yet higher form of divinity. Such divinity must possess what Shelley calls a "moral superiority" to human nature. In his next novel, *Pierre*, Melville questions once more the "moral superiority" of the existing Deity, albeit from a different perspective. *Moby-Dick* had depicted that Deity as acting externally upon the individual through natural forces; *Pierre* examines the effect of the same divine providence upon the inner nature of mind or consciousness.

PART VI

## Subjectivity and Objectivity

# 17 Emerson: Toward a Natural History of Intellect

On his return from Europe in the spring of 1833 Emerson was able to read Frederic Henry Hedge's review of Coleridge's writings, which had appeared in the March issue of the *Christian Examiner*. In a letter to his brother Edward, Emerson praises Hedge's review for the new views it offers in the realm of thought.[1] For Hedge who, like Emerson, was beginning to be caught up in the intellectual ferment that would develop a few years later into New England Transcendentalism, the review of Coleridge had furnished an opportunity to survey the different systems of transcendental idealism then prevalent in Germany. In particular, Hedge devotes a detailed exposé to Fichte's *Wissenschaftslehre*. This exposé is of the utmost significance for Emerson, since from it he appears to have drawn much of his knowledge of German (especially post-Kantian) idealism at this time.[2] His first work, *Nature* (1836), attests to the influence of such thought. Hedge's exposé is also significant because it

[1]*Letters*, I, 402, 412–14. Also Joel Porte, *Representative Man: Ralph Waldo Emerson in His Time* (New York: Oxford Univ. Press, 1979), pp. 55–57.

[2]On Hedge, see Stanley Vogel, *German Literary Influences on the American Transcendentalists* (New Haven: Yale Univ. Press, 1955), pp. 114–18 and, on Hedge's review of Coleridge specifically, pp. 116–17. Vogel later asserts: "Frederic Henry Hedge . . . has never been given sufficient credit for his leadership in the Transcendental movement. One of the few Transcendentalists to be educated in Germany, he became the most important teacher of German literature and philosophy in the group. His influence at the meetings of the Transcendental Club and his personal friendships with the other Transcendentalists bolstered up the strength of the movement. Even more important were his interpretations of German philosophy, which were among the first clear and concise explanations to be published in the *Christian Examiner* and other periodicals" (p. 160). As I try to demonstrate in this chapter, however, Hedge's misinterpretation of Fichte exerts a crucial influence upon Emerson's epistemology of the self. On the personal relations of Hedge and Emerson, see Ralph R. Rusk, *The Life of Ralph Waldo Emerson* (New York: Scribner's, 1949), pp. 207–8.

transforms Fichte's system in certain crucial respects while purporting to describe it. Emerson's own speculations, in turn, assimilate and express that system in yet other ways. Such a process of transmission is not merely the "history of an error" (Nietzsche) or of progressive distortions of an original. It exhibits, rather, a creative transmutation whose content possesses historical significance.

In passing from Fichte to a figure like Emerson, transcendental idealism ceases to be philosophy. Even Emerson's first book already represents a turning away from pure philosophy. This shift is not uniquely American, but corresponds to similar European tendencies during the same period. Here one has only to think of a work like Feuerbach's *Principles of the Philosophy of the Future* (1843), in which the opposition to rationalism and to logic in the Hegelian (dialectical) sense is clearly enunciated.[3]

Rationalism assumes that the content of thought is in essence identical with its form: thought consists of determining the relation between different concepts. In the final phase of European rationalism represented by Hegel, the form of thought (dialectic) is subsumed into its content, which is itself in a process of becoming. At that stage thought is identified with the essence of things, of the world: it is being in the process of becoming idea. In so doing, it contains its creative principle and teleology within itself. On that basis it becomes possible to identify thought in its becoming with God (as creative energeia). The result is a "divinization" of thought. Feuerbach rejects this divinization: for him, thought represents an anthropological or human phenomenon. For Emerson, on the other hand, because of dominant theological influences in early nineteenth-century America, such divinization was still possible. It assumes, however, a different form from that of European rationalism. Post-Kantian German idealism before Hegel had postulated consciousness as the starting point of all philosophy. Emerson too assumes consciousness as his point of departure, but in a different sense. For Fichte and Schelling, consciousness expresses the assertion of a self. In this respect, it is formal: it exists because it posits something (itself), and being itself is nothing more nor less than such an act of self-assertion.

To Emerson, by contrast, consciousness represents an act of pure seeing. It is the absorption of the world of external phenomena into the mind (or soul), and this absorption assimilates the content of experience. Such experience of the external world (as well as of the self) is one and

---

[3]The following account of the turning away from philosophy (Feuerbach, Kierkegaard et al.) owes something to Heidegger's speculations in his *Nietzsche*. Cf. Martin Heidegger, *The End of Philosophy*, trans. Joan Stambaugh (New York: Harper & Row, 1973), esp. chs. 1–2. Heidegger's account of rationalism, however (which he sees as inseparable from the issue of an "end" to philosophy) seems to me to fail to account sufficiently for the relation of form to content in such philosophy.

the same with the being of that world.[4] For Emerson, the being of the world is the blending or merging of a seeing consciousness with the objects it perceives. Both are held inescapably in the fluid medium of experience, which is all that exists of world, or time, or substance. Experience in this sense, as the fusion of consciousness and external world, can also be seen as containing thought, which is the element of consciousness. Hence experience precludes pure thought: a phenomenological seeing has already absorbed the world into itself, and in so doing imparts a being to that world—thus thought, which as consciousness has become one with external things, "knows" the external world in a moment of immediate apprehension that transcends the limits of rational thought. It is this form of immediate apprehension in the early Emerson which precludes the need for pure philosophy.

Through its apprehension of the world the mind tastes all the sensuous appeal of the sensations of touch, fragrance, color, and sound, the impressions of afternoon sunlight or of a landscape fading into the distance. In addition, by seeing the external world, consciousness, as it were, creates that world. The experience of such creation, which becomes part of its total experience, leads to the "divinization" of the world within the medium of consciousness. In the process, thought passes imperceptibly into the life of feeling and sensation. Here Keats had anticipated Emerson: "O for a Life of Sensations rather than of Thoughts!" (to Benjamin Bailey, Nov. 22, 1817; *Letters*, I, 185). For Keats such longing forms part of his desire for an escape from self-consciousness, which he associates with thought. By contrast, consciousness in Emerson transcends thought. For him, affirmation of the primacy of consciousness over thought implies a deliberate renunciation of formal philosophy. This movement is not without its own inner tensions and contradictions: the Reason that Emerson exalts over the Understanding preserves traces of the rationalism he seeks to overcome, especially in its relation to the moral sphere. Nonetheless, one may say that in its highest moments such Reason becomes one with consciousness as a form of pure seeing.[5]

This mode of vision, unlike rationalism, possesses no defining form: in absorbing or assimilating the external world, it can only consist of a

---

[4]In his *Freedom and Fate: An Inner Life of Ralph Waldo Emerson* (Philadelphia: Univ. of Pennsylvania Press, 1953), Stephen Whicher asserts: "The enthusiastic vision of a rebirth into greatness, in the might of the God within, that would inaugurate a spiritual revolution in society also is thus the dynamic element in his early thought" (p. 70). For another account of subject and object in Emerson, see Julie Ellison, *Emerson's Romantic Style* (Princeton: Princeton Univ. Press, 1984), p. 180.

[5]On Reason and Understanding in Emerson see Sherman Paul, *Emerson's Angle of Vision* (Cambridge: Harvard Univ. Press, 1952), pp. 38–39; Joel Porte, *Emerson and Thoreau: Transcendentalists in Conflict* (Middletown: Wesleyan Univ. Press, 1966), pp. 84–89; Henry A. Pochmann, *German Culture in America* (Madison: Univ. of Wisconsin Press, 1957), pp. 179–86.

pure openness to impressions of phenomena. Its only form is that of the phenomenal world, but such a form does not appear *in* consciousness precisely because it is the form *of* consciousness itself. Rationalism, on the other hand, assumes the presence of what we may describe as a *normative form* for thought: presupposed is the idea of a *relation* between one concept or thought-determination and another. Thought then expresses itself through the nature of such relations. But the sense of the normative form of rationalism as a limitation upon the content of thought leads first to a radical transformation of the concept of "form" in thought (the Hegelian dialectic, in which rational form is subsumed into the content of thought), and subsequently, in figures like Emerson, to the rejection of form altogether, which is at the same time a renunciation of pure philosophy or rationalism.

In one respect, such a renunciation manifests that tendency toward the subjective which Emerson himself had classified as the essential characteristic of Romantic or modern literature. From another perspective, however, such a tendency must be defined not simply as affirmation of, but rather as an objectification of, the subjective. For Emerson consciousness becomes one with thought through fusion of thought with the external world. By identifying itself with thought, consciousness becomes objective to itself as thought, which is to say, as consciousness that is simultaneously self-consciousness. This self-consciousness or awareness of itself *as a consciousness* is possible only because such consciousness is apprehended by thought that "experiences" itself as that consciousness.

At the same time, the identification of thought with consciousness in Emerson must be distinguished from the transcendental idealism of a Fichte or a Schelling, which preserves the normative form of rationalism even as it adopts consciousness as a content for thought. In place of the normative rational form that Fichte or Schelling set over consciousness, Emerson yields to the moment as the phenomenological content of that consciousness. The reception of the external world into the mind or soul is thereby subsumed under an element of transience. We receive impressions of external things, of colors, sounds, fragrances, and light, but such impressions are contained within our apprehension of transience or the passage of time, which is the true content of consciousness. The awareness that allows the mind to assimilate the external world is necessarily conscious of its own perdurance, and *this* consciousness, which is the phenomenological apprehension of transience, makes possible its perception of that world as a single manifold of impressions.

The relation of thought or consciousness to the external world in the early Emerson would not, however, be possible without a transcendental idealism that first asserts the possibility of representing the external world as contained within the medium of consciousness. Only within the context of such idealism does his identification of thought with consciousness assume its full significance. Beginning with transcendental idealism, which he had assimilated through the accounts of Hedge and others, as a point of departure, he had sought to objectify consciousness. The desire to objectify what is in its essence subjective had meant, on the one hand, an immersion of that consciousness in the profoundest depths of the subjective element, in other words, those of the external world, and at the same time a raising or elevating of that world through its assimilation by consciousness to the level of a divine epiphany, a moment of pure transparence. To understand and appreciate the inner exigencies behind this desire to elevate consciousness (and in so doing to reject formal philosophy), it is necessary to turn to Emerson's own point of departure, the transcendental idealism of Fichte and its representation by Hedge.

In Fichte's *Wissenschaftslehre* (I shall consider the system in its earliest form, the *Grundlage der gesammten Wissenschaftslehre*), the relation of thought to the external world is developed in the form of a relation between the "I" and the "not-I." The being or essence of the "I" is equated with its assertion of itself: *"That whose being (essence) consists simply in positing itself as existing,* is the I, as absolute subject. As it *posits* itself, so it *is;* and as it *is,* so it *posits* itself; and the I is accordingly for the I absolute, and necessary. What does not exist for itself is not an I" (*Gesamtausgabe,* 1:2, 259–60). Similarly: *"To posit oneself* and *to be* are, as used of the I, fully identical. The proposition, 'I am, because I have posited myself,' can accordingly also be expressed, *'I am absolutely, because I am'"* (1:2, 260). Correspondingly, what does not assert or "stablish" (posit, *setzen*) itself, cannot have being in the absolute sense in which the "I" has it— hence, can have being *for* that "I" only in the subordinate sense of being opposed to the "I," as the "not-I." Because the only form of absolute being comes from self-assertion or a self-"stablishment" (self-positing), the "not-I" can have *no being in itself.* Its only being is that which it has by opposing the "I," and even this being it does not possess *in itself,* since without asserting itself it cannot actively oppose the "I"—rather, the "I" opposes *it.*

By equating being with self-assertion, Fichte ultimately identifies being with consciousness: what asserts or "stablishes" itself must in so doing be conscious of itself as a self, that is, as something that acts. The consequence of this identification of being with consciousness is to exclude the possibility of being *in* an object or substance. No longer can we say that something contains being within itself, as a property of its substance, in other words, that being inheres in something, and hence that the substance of something is not identical with its being. For Fichte, the being of something is the assertion of its substance, or, more properly, that substance is substance only insofar as it asserts itself: in effect, substance itself is nothing more or less than an act of self-assertion. Within such a context, consciousness becomes the knowledge of self-assertion. This self-assertion is being and, as such, absolute because in consciousness the self knows it is asserting itself. The object of its knowledge (the self) is at this moment one and the same with the subject of such knowledge. The "I" is absolute because it brings subject and object together. The medium of its self-identification is consciousness.

It should thus be clear that the nature of consciousness for Fichte is purely formal. It consists simply of the knowledge of self-assertion. The phenomenology of perception, memory, and experience are not subsumed by it. I have dwelt upon these points at some length in order to emphasize the genuine rupture that separates Emerson's notion of consciousness from that of transcendental idealism. This extends to the relation between consciousness or thought and the external world. In Fichte, the external world or "not-I" is produced by the "I"'s excluding from itself whatever does not assert or "stablish" itself: "Originally nothing is posited ["stablished"] except the I; and this alone is absolutely posited. . . . Hence something can be posited absolutely only against the I. But what is opposed to the I = the *not-I*" (*Gesamtausgabe*, 1:2, 266).

The exclusion of the "not-I" from the "I" is not simply logical or discursive; since the assertion of the "I" gives it its very being, the same assertion, by excluding what is not part of it from itself at the moment of its self-assertion, thereby "stablishes" the reality of that which it excludes. Of this development Fichte observes: "Insofar as the not-I is posited, the I is not posited; for through the not-I the I is fully cancelled out [nullified]. Now the not-I is posited *in the I:* for it is posited against it; but all positing-against presupposes the identity of the I, in which something is posited, and then something posited against what is posited" (*Gesamtausgabe*, 1:2, 268). Since the assertion of something imparts to it its being, an assertion of the "not-I" would cancel out or annul the being of the "I." By asserting the "not-I" *within* the assertion of the "I" (as that which the "I" excludes), Fichte's system preserves the reality of the "not-I" or the external world. But the being of that world is contained within the "I" or consciousness: by asserting itself, the "I" brings the world into existence, but only so long as it is sustained by a self-assertive act of consciousness. The "not-I" or external world is thus literally maintained in existence by its dialectical opposition to the "I"—without this, it can have no being.

In Hedge's review of Coleridge's writings, which forms the principal source of Emerson's knowledge of Fichte at this time, the radical innovation embodied in Fichte's identification of being with self-assertion and hence with consciousness is obscured and even reduced to the level of epistemology. In the history of Emerson's development, such a lacuna or misprision must be judged significant.[6] It forms a stimulus for his notion of consciousness as a form of pure seeing and, by so doing, contributes to his rejection of traditional philosophy, his quest for a higher, transcendent form of knowledge that would be at the same time a form of existence. To the immanent knowledge that comes through pure consciousness Emerson would have been impelled by his reading of Hedge's review and its representation of the Fichtean system. Of course, in the shaping of Emerson's general attitude toward philosophy, many influences converge. But in the specific form his response assumes at a given moment, certain circumstances play a crucial role. Because it represents virtually the only detailed account of post-Kantian idealism available to Emerson at the time, Hedge's misinterpretation of Fichte is of decisive significance.

A misinterpretation that is not creative but merely regressive, if it remains the only channel of transmission for a given influence, can produce a creative misinterpretation that, by essentially denying its own role as interpretation, defines the end of the mode of thought originally represented. With regard to Hedge's review, Emerson's *Nature* performs this function. It is neither a critique nor a reinterpretation of transcendental idealism. By absorbing elements of the latter, it becomes a response that through its own creative energies fails to develop a coherent representation of the original influence (in this instance, Fichte). Instead, it asserts precisely the renunciation of the rational process of the latter as something creative: pure consciousness or pure seeing, which rejects the formation of any specific thought, becomes the vitalization of thought in general in and through consciousness. The lacuna that forms through the failure of Hedge's misinterpretation of Fichte becomes the occasion for a concentration of creative energies that in Emerson's *Nature* lead to a new perspective upon rationalism itself, and ultimately, to the rejection of that rationalism.

In his review of Coleridge's writings, Hedge offers the following summary of transcendental idealism:

In the transcendental system, the *object* is to discover in every form of finite existence, an infinite and unconditioned as the ground of its existence, or

[6]For Emerson and Fichte, see Pochmann, pp. 195–96. Pochmann claims "there is not, in the published record, conclusive assurance that Emerson read Fichte either in the original or in translation" except for the portions of *The Destination of Man* (*Die Bestimmung des Menschen*) in Hedge's *Prose Writers of Germany* (1847). But Vogel notes significantly that "from Fichte he [Emerson] copied a few extracts without as yet [prior to 1836] knowing the original language" (p. 107). Pochmann characterizes the "me" and "not-me" in *Nature* as "commonplaces" which "need not be referred to any specific source" (p. 187). See also René Wellek, *Confrontations* (Princeton: Princeton Univ. Press, 1965), p. 197. It is not merely in his use of the "me" and "not-me," however, that Emerson manifests the influence of Hedge's misprision of Fichte, but in his whole mode of developing the relation between Nature and self based upon the nature of consciousness.

rather as the ground of our knowledge of its existence, to refer all phenomena to certain *noumena*, or laws of cognition. It is not a *ratio essendi*, but a
*ratio cognoscendi;* it seeks not to explain the existence of God and creation,
objectively considered, but to explain our knowledge of their existence. (p.
121)

This summary is remarkable for several reasons. It describes transcendental idealism from a Kantian perspective (see Kant, *Gesammelte
Schriften*, III, 242) but equates the *"noumena"* with "laws of cognition"—
an interpretation that corresponds most closely to Fichte's reading of
Kant. But even Fichte would have defined the *noumena* as objects rather
than laws of cognition. Yet the remainder of Hedge's description surely
applies more to Kant's system than to Fichte's: "It is not a *ratio essendi*,
but a *ratio cognoscendi*."

We have just seen how Fichte's *Wissenschaftslehre* attempts in a radically
innovative fashion to merge the two. By seeing transcendental idealism
simply as a refashioning of epistemology, Hedge is led in turn to ascribe
to the Fichtean system a purely epistemological ground or basis:

> The first proposition in the "Wissenschaftslehre" is stated thus, A = A. In
> this proposition the first term is a something, A unconditionally proposed;
> the second term is the same A reflected upon. I propose A, and then,
> reflecting upon it, find that it is A. This identity arises not from any quality
> in the thing proposed; it exists solely in my own consciousness. A = A,
> because I, the being who proposed it, am the same with I, the being who
> reflects upon it. Consequently the proposition, A = A, is equivalent to the
> proposition, I = I. (p. 122)

It would be easy to show how for Fichte the assertion *I = I* is in fact quite
different from *A = A,* and how it proceeds from the other by a not
entirely unproblematical deduction. What is most significant in Hedge's
interpretation, however, is his equating of *A* with *A* based upon their
identity in consciousness. Such an equation suggests that the truth of *A
= A* is only relative. Above all, it implies that the concept *A* possesses no
content in itself: its sole content is that which it acquires by becoming an
object of consciousness. As such, its only being is its presence in the
mind. But the presence of something in the mind or consciousness does
not guarantee it a constant being or existence. It becomes subject to the
receptivity and flux of consciousness itself. Its content depends upon its
formation and presence in consciousness (without which it has no content), whereas Fichte's "not-I" within the "I" does not depend upon the
"I" for its content: by asserting itself, the "I" at the same time asserts the
"not-I," and the only reason why we say the "not-I" is contained within
the "I" is that the former does not assert or "stablish" itself.

Hedge's summary also contains an interesting footnote that sheds further light upon the nature of his misinterpretation. He begins by apologizing that "it was found necessary to abridge the process so much, that perhaps the conclusions may not appear strictly consequential." By way of attempting to clarify his previous summary, he then says: "Let it be understood, then, that affirmation and negation stand for existence and non-existence, —the *I* and *not-I*, —which, of course, when absolute must eventually exclude each other" (p. 122). But for Fichte "I" and "not-I" are *not* synonymous with "existence and non-existence." In fact, the relation between them is of a different kind altogether. To the representing power or the "I" (*der Vorstellenden*) must be opposed an object to be represented (*ein Vorzustellendes*), or the "not-I." By equating the "I" and "not-I" with existence and nonexistence, Hedge implies in effect that the only possible form of being must be one contained *within* consciousness. This is something quite different from Fichte's identification of consciousness *with* being, in which the self-assertion of consciousness is equivalent to the being of the "I." Hedge's summary opens up the possibility of Emerson's creative misinterpretation of idealism in *Nature* by positing consciousness as the element that *contains* being, such that all things have being only by becoming objects of such a consciousness. Being is then equivalent to the formation of the object within consciousness, rather than the self-assertion of consciousness itself. Such idealism would carry Coleridge's famous exclamation one step further: "O Lady! we receive but what we give, / And in our life alone does Nature live."

Near the beginning of *Nature* Emerson observes that "Philosophically considered, the universe is composed of Nature and the Soul. Strictly speaking, therefore, all that is separate from us, all which Philosophy distinguishes as the NOT ME, that is, both nature and art, all other men and my own body, must be ranked under this name, NATURE" (*Coll. W.*, I, 8). A little later, in describing the influence of Nature upon the mind, he adds: "When we speak of nature in this manner, we have a distinct but most poetical sense in the mind. We mean the integrity of impression made by manifold natural objects" (p. 9).

This "integrity of impression" is created by containing all individual perceptions or impressions within a single mind or consciousness. In that consciousness divers phenomena converge to form a coherent whole. As with Hedge, the element of Nature in Emerson's account can be none other than consciousness itself. The existence or being of Nature is then equivalent to the formation of an integrated impression within consciousness. As purely phenomenal appearance, that impression has no being in itself. Its only mode of being is presence. In so defining it, Emerson differs somewhat from Hedge, since the "presencing" of Nature in the mind is governed by an external force rather than mind itself. Emerson appeals here to a Wordsworthian concept of

Nature as an external power, alien to the mind. This power informs all the unexplained and inexplicable phenomena: "language, sleep, madness, dreams, beasts, sex" (*Coll. W.*, 1, 8). Because of the obscurity of such phenomena, Nature's "presencing" in the mind assumes a symbolic significance. That obscurity is uncanny: it refers the mind to a power outside itself, and yet, because the only possible "situation" of an object must be within the field of consciousness, such a power remains ultimately placeless and hence in a strange sense omnipresent. Nature, then, comes into existence in the "integrity of impression" made by natural objects in consciousness, but the power behind Nature remains external to consciousness, a situation that creates the possibility of a natural symbolism.

We have seen that for Emerson, as for Hedge, Nature comes into existence through its formation in consciousness. For Emerson the formation of Nature is also attended with another sense. In speaking of the "integrity of impression" produced by natural objects, he had described the experience as "poetical." An aesthetic element thus enters into the mind's creation of Nature. This element pertains to something more fundamental than art. It is the joy the mind experiences in its own creative energy, as it produces Nature within itself. κόσμος is beauty, Emerson declares, and he could also recall that the root of αἰσθητικός is perception or seeing. In the process of seeing by which consciousness brings Nature into existence, it experiences simultaneously that coming-into-existence as a creating of consciousness itself in Nature. By so doing, it apprehends the creative assertion as a datum *within* consciousness, which is the source of the feeling Emerson describes as "joy." For him, the "morning of the world" (Shelley, *Hellas*) occurs in each act of consciousness: it is the birth of Nature in the mind, occurring in time but lifted by its creative aspect above temporality. The morning of the world becomes an eternal moment proleptically foreshadowing its own fulfillment while suspended in that same prolepsis as the highest moment because it symbolizes the creative capacity of consciousness.

By depicting the formation of the "not-I" or Nature within the mind as a creative assertion of consciousness, Emerson transcends Hedge's definition of the "I" as delimiting itself by the "not-I": in forming Nature, the mind re-creates itself, as it were, giving an infinite expansion to the field of consciousness. But the creative aspect that Emerson imparts to consciousness is not without its cost: to create implies the existence of creative energies, and these in turn must seek an equilibrium or perfect stasis in fulfillment. Creative energy in this case signifies desire, and specifically, the desire to achieve in the creative assertion of consciousness a transcendence of temporality. Creativity is creative as long as the act of creation remains incomplete, in process. From the moment it is finished, the creative force ceases to be creative. The creative nature of the Emersonian consciousness is thus impelled by its own internal tendency to seek a fulfillment that transcends the temporal character of the creative process. Such transcendence involves the immediate apprehension of pure energy itself, the source of that process. Emerson thus comes to posit stages or levels of consciousness, the highest of which represents transcendent fulfillment of its creative desire:

> To the senses and the unrenewed understanding, belongs a sort of instinctive belief in the absolute existence of nature. In their view, man and nature are indissolubly joined. They never look beyond their sphere. . . . When the eye of Reason opens, to outline and surface are at once added, grace and expression. These proceed from imagination and affection, and abate somewhat of the angular distances of objects. If the Reason be stimulated to more earnest vision, outlines and surfaces become transparent, and are no longer seen; causes and spirits are seen through them. The best, the happiest moments of life, are these delicious awakenings of the higher powers, and the reverential withdrawing of nature before its God. (*Coll. W.*, I, 30)

It is in such moments that, "Standing on the bare ground, —my head bathed by the blithe air, and uplifted into infinite space, —all mean egotism vanishes. I become a transparent eye-ball. I am nothing. I see all. The currents of the Universal Being circulate through me; I am part or particle of God."

These moments signify the annihilation of consciousness as a creative assertion of Nature. The sense of the "I" disappears, and with it, the experience of the creation of Nature within the self as a re-creation of consciousness. Hence the "reverential withdrawing of nature before its God." Its God is the pure energy that brings it into being within the mind, and which mind, freed now from its own activity, beholds as the source of its essence.

Such moments, as Emerson well knew, are precarious: they come to the mind only as privileged instances of vision. As a result, Emerson's attitude in *Nature* necessarily becomes one of prolepsis. The soul awaits the higher moments that will enable it to transcend the desires produced by its own creative energy. Correspondingly, Emerson's renunciation of Fichtean idealism with its essentially dialectical opposition between "I" and "not-I," self and Nature, becomes clear. The internal opposition between "I" and "not-I" can be dissolved in higher moments of consciousness and hence possesses no absolute validity. It is subsumed as a lower stage of consciousness in its relation to the Nature it creates within itself. This renunciation of the absolute value of the "I"—"not-I" relation occurs in favor of a prolepsis: the anticipation of transcendent moments. Historically, such a renunciation must be judged significant. It indicates above all a renunciation of rationalism in favor of a more

,nanent and immediate mode of being. For transcendental idealism ,ter Kant already postulates the possibility of an immanent or immedi-,te knowledge, through the identification of being with consciousness in Fichte, or the subjective-objective identity in Schelling. What Emerson envisions, however, is the possibility of redefining being itself as a mode of pure seeing in which what is seen is the energy that animates that seeing itself. The renunciation of rationalism is significant above all because the prolepsis (anticipation of transcendent moments) that re-places it is itself not rational. The transition from rationalism to the kind of proleptic attitude expressed by Emerson and later, in an even pro-founder sense, by Nietzsche, indicates a sort of rupture or discontinuity: one does not arrive at such an attitude through any development of rationalism, and this in turn implies that a closure of the rationalistic phase has occurred somewhere in between. One may even see Emerson's proleptic attitude as the expression of a desire to recover what was lost in the rupture: the simple affirmation of an immanent transcendence does not need to be rationalized, and for this reason is, as an attitude, all-sufficient. All-sufficient, one should perhaps say, with regard to ra-tionalism but not in relation to itself, since its nature as prolepsis implies that it must always anticipate fulfillment without ever being able to assert that fulfillment as something which belongs to it through its own nature or essence.

# 18  *Margaret Fuller:*
## Woman in the Nineteenth Century

In a letter to an unidentified correspondent, dated before her removal to Groton, Massachusetts, in 1833, Margaret Fuller writes: "Yet, as my character is, after all, still more feminine than masculine, it would some-times happen that I put more emotion into a state than I myself knew. I really was capable of attachment, though it never seemed so till the hour of separation. And if a connexion was torn up by the roots, the soil of my existence showed an unsightly wound, which long refused to clothe itself in verdure."[1] Here, significantly, ten years before the appearance of *Woman in the Nineteenth Century,* she invokes already the concept of the

---

[1]Quoted from *Margaret Fuller: American Romantic,* ed. Perry Miller (New York: Double-day, 1963), p. 30. According to a letter I have received from Robert Hudspeth, the letter fragment (printed by James Freeman Clarke in the *Memoirs of Margaret Fuller Ossoli*) has not been recovered. Professor Hudspeth conjectures that the letter is to George Davis or perhaps to Clarke himself.

self later to be expressed in that work. For her, each individual self consists not of a single nature but in effect of two natures—masculine and feminine—combined in different proportions.[2] Of their interrelation we are told, in *Woman in the Nineteenth Century:* "By Man I mean both man and woman: these are the two halves of one thought. I lay no especial stress on the welfare of either. I believe that the development of the one cannot be effected without that of the other. My highest wish is that this truth should be distinctly and rationally apprehended, and the conditions of life and freedom recognized as the same for the daughters and the sons of time; twin exponents of a divine thought" (Myerson, p. 83).

Inasmuch as the "development of the one cannot be effected without that of the other," these two natures may be said to coexist in a dialectical relationship where the condition of each nature affects that of the other. On account of such a relationship, the two natures (or "characters") can be seen to represent a transformation of the eighteenth-century schema of the faculties. For Kant and Schiller (especially *On the Aesthetic Education of Man*) these faculties are in conflict with each other: the most fruitful and productive state occurs when they are held in a tension of equilibrium.[3] From the notion of an equilibrium it is but a step to Schiller's idea of a mediating faculty (the aesthetic impulse or drive), whose function is to preserve a harmony between the others through its own creative or expressive activity (an idea later assimilated by Matthew Arnold in his "Literature and Science").[4]

With Margaret Fuller, on the other hand, the relation of the two "characters" or natures becomes at once both dialectical and creative:

[2]On masculine and feminine elements of the self, see Bell Gale Chevigny, *The Woman and the Myth: Margaret Fuller's Life and Writings* (Old Westbury, N.Y.: The Feminist Press, 1976), pp. 217–18.

[3]Cf. Schiller, *On the Aesthetic Education of Man*, p. 93: "Personality must keep the sensuous drive within its proper bounds, and receptivity, or Nature, must do the same with the formal drive."

[4]Ibid., p. 141: "Our psyche passes, then, from sensation to thought *via* a middle disposition in which sense and reason are both active *at the same time*. Precisely for this reason, however, they cancel each other out as determining forces, and bring about a negation by means of an opposition. This middle disposition, in which the psyche is subject neither to physical nor to moral constraint, and yet is active in both these ways, pre-eminently deserves to be called a free disposition; and if we are to call the condition of sensuous determination the physical, and the condition of rational determination the logical or moral, then we must call this condition of real and active determinability the *aesthetic*." On the relation of Schiller's notion to Arnold, cf. *The Complete Prose Works of Matthew Arnold*, ed. R. H. Super (Ann Arbor: Univ. of Michigan Press, 1960–1977), x, 64–65: "Interesting, indeed, these results of science are, important they are, and we should all of us be acquainted with them. But what I now wish you to mark is, that we are still, when they are propounded to us and we receive them, we are still in the sphere of conduct and knowledge. And for the generality of men there will be found, I say, to arise . . . an invincible desire to relate this proposition to the sense in us for conduct, and to the sense in us for beauty."

development of each nature within the individual acts as a stimulus to the other. Consequently, the goal envisioned in *Woman in the Nineteenth Century* is not the development of women in the ordinary sense but rather of the feminine nature, which will in turn lead to the elevation of all humanity of a higher and more spiritual stage. Through the constraints to which feminine nature has been subjected, humanity has in effect crippled its own growth, the possibility of most fully developing its faculties. If the two natures are "two halves of one thought," "twin exponents of a divine thought," they represent two aspects of a self that remains incomplete as long as either does not fulfill its innate potential. But the fulfillment of each is inseparable from that of the other. Hence the difference that separates Margaret Fuller's concept of nature or character from the faculties of Kant and Schiller. For her these natures are fluid elements, passing freely into each other, acting upon each other in the fashion of chemical reagents: "Male and female represent the two sides of the great radical dualism. But, in fact, they are perpetually passing into one another. Fluid hardens to solid, solid rushes to fluid. There is no wholly masculine man, no purely feminine woman" (Myerson, p. 161). Elsewhere in the same work, she offers a more detailed analysis of the feminine nature:

> The electrical, the magnetic element in woman has not been fairly brought out at any period. Every thing might be expected from it; she has far more of it than man. This is commonly expressed by saying that her intuitions are more rapid and more correct. (p. 152)

> The especial genius of woman I believe to be electrical in movement, intuitive in function, spiritual in tendency. (p. 161)

In woman, nature is not to be equated with the self. It forms, rather, but one of its elements. As a result, there can be no such thing as a feminine consciousness. Consciousness implies a sense of self as that to which all perceptions refer. By contrast, the feminine nature (according to Margaret Fuller) represents merely a mode through which these perceptions occur.

In its concept of the feminine genius or nature, *Woman in the Nineteenth Century* thus exemplifies a transitional stage in an ideational formation, the unifying into a concept of what earlier were merely tendencies. In Herder's *Ideen zur Philosophie der Geschichte der Menschheit*, with its emphasis upon a secular concept of mankind (*Menschengeschlechts*— Herder deliberately avoids the term *human race*), it had been necessary to consider the characteristics of the two sexes, especially in their conformity or relation to each other. Herder also speaks of the vital forces (*organische Kräfte*) both in mankind and other living things. Nevertheless, he makes no attempt to relate these forces specifically to either the masculine or feminine nature. Each possesses certain forces; none is seen as peculiar to it. In *Woman in the Nineteenth Century* such forces are equated specifically with one nature or the other (the electrical or intuitive, for instance, with woman). Even here, however, the feminine has not yet become a concept: this could occur only by defining it as the totality of consciousness in woman, a development that falls outside our present sphere.

With the description of an electrical or magnetic element in woman we enter once more the world of Romantic *Naturphilosophie,* the theory of a continuum between physical and spiritual energies, the idea that both are but manifestations of a more fundamental or elemental form of energy. Through her study of Goethe, above all, Margaret Fuller was bound to encounter it, in the *Maximen und Reflexionen* and the *Gespräche mit Eckermann.* For her, however, the continuum is based not merely upon a common element (the energy that manifests itself in different forms); rather, there exists simultaneously a progression in activity, from the electrical that is but a natural force—hence, endowed only with the mere vitality of Nature—to the intuitive, with its manifestation of conscious intelligence. In its perception of the world and in its relation to it, the self is initially purely passive; by progressing to the spiritual, that relation becomes active as a tendency or striving that seeks fulfillment by expressing itself.

In such a concept of the self all boundaries dissolve in the fluid interrelation between different natures within the self. Through her perception of a more fluid character in these natures or elements, Margaret Fuller was bound to arrive at a different concept of their interaction. Whereas Kant had described the faculties by defining their proper limits in relation to each other, for Fuller each nature may be said, in contrast, to infuse and enrich the other. In that sense the natures or characters of which she speaks are not predisposed to a single form of activity (the rational, the aesthetic, and so forth), but constitute, rather, more fundamental modes of perception and striving. Hence the possibility of a truly creative dialectic within the self, whereby each nature enriches the resources of the other: the feminine through its intuitive and emotional perception of the nature of things, allowing it to apprehend what lies beyond the compass of the rational intellect, the psychological, the inner movements of the soul, the fundamental tendencies determining the relation of one being to another; the masculine through its ordering of external Nature and thought. From their interaction and fusion arises the possibility of, on the one hand, a deeper and richer mode of thought, by which the rational approaches the suprarational or the immanent values of life, and, on the other, the giving of form to the feelings and aspirations by which we live.

But if the concept of self expounded in *Woman in the Nineteenth Century* consists of an interaction of two natures, what it ultimately embodies is not a fixed or determinate state but one perpetually in the process of formation. Because of the aspect of change or becoming implied, as well as its consequences, one may speak of a teleological aspiration in the creative dialectic of the two natures: fulfillment of the self's possibilities through the interaction of man and woman upon each other. From a teleological perspective, masculine and feminine represent the forces or energies through which the striving for fulfillment (complete development of each of these natures) manifests itself, what Margaret Fuller herself had termed the "tendencies." It is characteristic of her vision that her concept of the self should be one of striving and aspiration rather than a determinate condition or state. We know from various indications of her disposition to view her own life as the unfolding of an inner entelechy, a perspective she could also have found in Goethe's *Dichtung und Wahrheit*. Unlike Goethe, however, she sees it not as a process analogous to those of external Nature (although possessing the aspect of the "organic"), but rather as one of conscious effort. Its goal is: development of all the creative and productive capacities of the soul. The polemic for woman in the nineteenth century springs from the fact that the nature she embodies has been deprived of its chance for self-fulfillment. Hence the self (conceived as the sum of the two natures, masculine and feminine) is barred from certain all-important and unrealized possibilities. But if the self's potential is in fact infinite, in a sense it can never be complete or whole. The theme of constant aspiration toward a higher mode of existence that runs through all of Margaret Fuller's life thus corresponds to her perception of the self's innermost essence.

From the standpoint of a creative and spiritual fulfillment as the inner teleology of life, she can then ask whether, in addition to praising poets and priests: "Shall we not name with as deep a benediction those who, if not so immediately, or so consciously, in connection with the eternal truth, yet, led and fashioned by a divine instinct, serve no less to develope and interpret the open secret of love passing into life, energy creating for the purpose of happiness" (Myerson, p. 85). From this passage it becomes clear that the law of development, of spiritualization, is none other than that of life itself: the process by which physical or material energy is transmuted into spiritual expression, "energy creating for the purpose of happiness," whose ultimate source and model is sex and procreation, the "love passing into life," seen here as the type of all creative processes. As such it represents the transmission of energy from one being to another, from the mind to the works it creates as forms of self-expression, the transformation of material force into spiritual aspiration. A neoplatonic schema manifests the process of ascension through the continuum or scale of being: the invocation of an endless procession of "forms of life more highly and completely organized than are seen elsewhere."

But the ultimate teleology behind all forms of creative activity is the development of the self: "Here, as elsewhere, the gain of creation consists always in the growth of individual minds, which live and aspire, as flowers bloom and birds sing, in the midst of morasses; and in the continual development of that thought, the thought of human destiny, which is given to eternity adequately to express, and which ages of failure only seemingly impede" (Myerson, pp. 91–92). The thought of human destiny must not be equated with thought in the purely rational sense. It represents, rather, an innate principle of development contained in each individual, corresponding to the organic principle by which plants and animals assume their proper form.

We have seen earlier how the two natures, masculine and feminine, form only elements, as it were, of the self. Through their creative dialectic, in turn, they produce that self. In her description of this dialectic the author of *Woman in the Nineteenth Century* exemplifies her affinities with the whole Romantic mode of thought, especially with its concept of a fruitful opposition by which two opposing forces produce, through their action upon each other, a yet higher stage of reflection. It remains to specify what is unique in the form the concept assumes in *Woman in the Nineteenth Century:* the notion, namely, of the passing of each element into the other, which becomes the means of engendering a "more highly or completely organized form of life." Such a process is not, ultimately, rational, but one that proceeds on a deeper level. It assumes in effect the permeation of each nature by the other, which is to say, the pervading of each mode of vision by the other's susceptibilities and elements, the coloring of thought by emotion, the tendency toward form in one's innermost impulses and passions.

As with the most fruitful forms of discourse or interchange, absorption of another's nature presupposes an unconstrained receptivity, a free acceptance of the other nature that does not attempt to define it in advance by means of a given concept (as for instance with Kant's analysis of the faculties) nor to determine beforehand its effect upon oneself. Such receptiveness could proceed only from a belief in that nature itself, as a form of vitality or life, hence something possessing immanent values. For the assimilation of these values, only a voluntary yielding of oneself to others and to lived experience could suffice. Only by absorbing another nature into one's own does it become possible to apprehend its values, which cannot be understood by the rational intellect but only vitally, as it were, through experience. In the medium of the magnetic or intuitive, the self finds the possibility of such apprehension—which is to say: in the feminine nature. In this respect the plea for the feminine in

*Woman in the Nineteenth Century* becomes an apology for the source of all genuine creative impulses, for only by absorbing can the self create.

In advocating openness to experience, Margaret Fuller also anticipates the later Romantic attitude that ascribes inherent values to life itself—here one has only to think of Dostoyevsky's passionate polemics on the love of life, of the "wet, sticky leaves" and the "slanting rays of the sun," or of Hawthorne's equally profound exploration of the theme in his Elixir of Life manuscripts. To perceive the interrelation between the two fundamental natures (masculine and feminine) it had been necessary to have recourse not only to intellect but to the kind of inner experience that passes under the name of intuition. Perhaps such a perception may itself exemplify the work's dominant theme: the necessity for development of the feminine nature, of the element which imparts to the self its receptivity and its sensibility.

# 19    *Hawthorne:* The Blithedale Romance

Among the most interesting features of the eighteenth-century concerto form as it developed was the use of a cadenza: a freely improvised recapitulation of the major themes of a movement by the solo instrument, which permitted a certain amount of embellishment and elaboration. Two of Hawthorne's romances exhibit a literary analogue to it: in *The House of the Seven Gables,* the story of Alice Pyncheon, and, in *The Blithedale Romance,* the chapter entitled "Zenobia's Legend." Thematically, the latter is of the highest significance. It brings together the two principal and complementary subjects of the romance: the notion of psychological "possession" and its diametrical opposite, love, which consists of self-surrender or submission to being assimilated by an other, rather than desiring to assimilate that other. The desire to assimilate or possess is in turn bound up with the condition of Romantic subjectivity. The sense of the unknowability of the other as a private or individual self acts upon the first self as a stimulus to overcome the subjective abyss and possess the other through knowledge of its motives, the motor or spring of its activity.[1]

---

[1]One thinks here of Hawthorne's personal inclinations and tendencies. In Caroline Ticknor's *Hawthorne and His Publisher* (Boston and New York: Houghton Mifflin, 1913), Howard Ticknor relates: "He liked best to be taken to such plain, miscellaneous hotels as the Astor, or Bixby's, to be entered anonymously as 'a friend' of his companion, to carry no money, to know nothing of the details of the journey, to make only chance acquaintances whom he could anatomize, but who could have no clue to him, and to be brought back home as mutely as he had been taken away" (p. 9). Of Hawthorne's practice of silent observation at Ticknor's, we are told: "And 'Hawthorne's chair' was here in a secluded

Both the subjective abyss (that is, the other's unknowability) and the desire to bridge it through psychological possession are expressed in Zenobia's story of the Veiled Lady. The narrative begins with Theodore's wager that he will find out the Veiled Lady's identity. As has been pointed out, veil symbolism pervades the whole of the romance; one is irresistibly reminded of Hawthorne's earlier story "The Minister's Black Veil."[2] But surely—if it is possible to compare the two works in terms of veil symbolism—the shift from a black to white veil is both revealing and decisive. It indicates that the significance of the veil resides not in a sense or consciousness of sin but rather in the condition of subjective isolation that separates each individual from all others, a condition that creates—as Hawthorne had already observed in the earlier tale—a compelling dialectical relation between self and other, between the desire of the one to know the other and the other's resistance to this desire.

Nevertheless, the subjective isolation the veil imposes upon its subject is itself a torment that the self seeks in another fashion to be rid of. Thus the Veiled Lady offers Theodore the option of lifting "this mysterious veil, beneath which I am a sad and lonely prisoner, in a bondage which is worse to me than death" (Centenary, III, 112–13). But the crucial choice is not between lifting or not lifting the veil, but whether Theodore is willing to pledge himself to the being behind it before seeing her: "But, before raising it, I entreat thee, in all maiden modesty, to bend forward, and impress a kiss, where my breath stirs the veil; and my virgin lips shall come forward to meet thy lips; and from that instant, Theodore, thou shalt be mine, and I thine, with never more a veil between us! And all the felicity of earth and of the future world shall be thine and mine together" (Centenary, III, 113). The essence of such a pledge would be surrender of the self to an other, exposure of its most sacred feelings or

niche where he could see and yet be out of sight; here he could observe all without being subjected to outside observation; for he was quite invisible unless one stepped up through the little gate into the counting-room. In this one chair, it was for many years Nathaniel Hawthorne's custom to ensconce himself whenever he visited the 'Corner'; he often spent whole hours here, resting his head upon his hand apparently in happy and satisfying sympathy with his environment" (pp. 10–11). In his *Personal Recollections of Nathaniel Hawthorne* (New York, 1893; rpt. New York: Haskell House, 1968), Horatio Bridge writes: "He shrank habitually from the exhibition of his own secret opinions, and was careful to avoid infringement upon the rights of others, while thoroughly conscious of his own" (p. 57). E. P. Whipple sees the same desire to possess through knowledge of the other as exemplified in the fiction: "There is a strange fascination to a man of contemplative genius in the psychological details of a strange crime like that which forms the plot of The Scarlet Letter, and he is therefore apt to become, like Hawthorne, too painfully anatomical in his exhibition of them" (review of *The Scarlet Letter*, in *Graham's Magazine* [May, 1850], quoted from *Hawthorne: The Critical Heritage*, ed. J. Donald Crowley [London: Routledge & Kegan Paul, 1970], p. 161).

[2]Hyatt Waggoner, *Hawthorne: A Critical Study*, rev. ed. (Cambridge: Harvard Univ. Press, 1963), pp. 192–93.

affections without guarantee of a corresponding emotion in the other nor the certainty of a subjective communion. And yet, as the words of the Veiled Lady imply, only through such an act of faith is this communion possible at all: "my virgin lips shall come forward to meet thy lips; and from that instant, Theodore, thou shalt be mine, and I thine." The initiative of the one prompts a response from the other—the other's awareness of the risk involved in the act of faith inspires a return of the initial affection. The Veiled Lady's knowledge that Theodore's kiss proceeds from a voluntary surrender of self, a willingness to let himself be possessed by another, incites her to respond by a similar initiative, an equivalent surrender of self that she seals by allowing her lips to come forward and meet his.[3]

"And from that instant . . . thou shalt be mine, and I thine": what sense does this expression of possession assume here? To the extent that it depends upon the self's surrender to an other, it is not the act itself of possessing that is voluntary—rather, the voluntary nature of self-surrender precludes the possibility of violence in the act of possessing which gives the self its self-consciousness or self-awareness in appropriating the other. In assimilating or accepting the other's self-surrender, the self loses its own sense of self, replacing it by consciousness of the other—not, however, as an other, but rather as one and the same as itself. The difference between this relationship and possession lies in the mutuality of self-surrender, through which each self becomes conscious of its "displacement," so to speak, onto an other. Each self finds a new life, a new consciousness, *within* the other, having experienced a loss of self in accepting the other into itself. As a result, the sense of self as both finite and a power that seeks to dominate what is external to it disappears. In the new consciousness that emerges, there is no longer the sense of self as something opposed to an other: instead, the self is now represented in the other through the process of self-surrender and acceptance that expresses its affections.

The consciousness of the self's representation in the other is borne out in the question the Veiled Lady puts to Theodore: "Dost thou hesitate to pledge thyself to me, by meeting these lips of mine, while the veil yet hides my face? Has not thy heart recognized me?" (Centenary, III, 113). Such recognition could only imply the heart's encounter with an emotion corresponding to its own, an other answerable in its affections to the self, which makes possible the self's perception of its reflection in that other. The repetition of the pledge ("by meeting these lips of mine") serves but to emphasize its reciprocal nature: only through such reci-

[3]Here Hawthorne's description of the relation of self to other parallels Chillingworth's account in *The Scarlet Letter:* "And so, Hester, I drew thee into my heart, into its innermost chamber, and sought to warm thee by the warmth which thy presence made there!" (Centenary, I, 74).

procity can the subjective abyss separating one individual from another be overcome. It is overcome not through *knowledge* of the inner nature of the other—this would constitute psychological possession—but rather through an expression of the affections that permits a genuine communion in which the sense of self is transcended through a consciousness that both absorbs and experiences a loss of self into the other.

As the Veiled Lady explains, Theodore does have another choice: to lift the veil before giving her a kiss. To do so, however, is to subject himself henceforward to a life of unrelieved sadness, the heart-wastage of a feverish quest for the other who has now been lost. One is tempted to ask: what significance attaches to his lifting the veil before giving her a kiss? If the veil symbolizes the subjective abyss that divides them, to lift it before kissing her becomes tantamount to a violation of something sacred, the privacy of the other's inner nature.[4] After such an act, the kiss itself is meaningless: its whole significance depends upon its voluntary quality in the face of the other's unknowability, its expression of a willingness to expose the self through affection for that other. By lifting the veil Theodore destroys the impulse to an answering affection that would have secured his happiness. By profaning the sacredness of the other as a source of affection, he abolishes the possibility of experiencing the return of faith in affection that forms the ground of any subjective communion.

His wish to "know" the other before surrendering himself to her serves but to represent a desire that pervades the whole of the romance through Coverdale's narrative consciousness: the impulse to possess the other psychologically through knowledge of his or her secret motives or affections. Like a fluid medium in which the characters move and act, the Coverdalean consciousness seems impelled by some involuntary passion, analogous to yet different from that of sex, prompting it to delve into those natures. For such consciousness, knowledge of the other becomes something oddly akin to sexual possession, and there is all the eroticism of the sexual relation in the experience by which psychological possession is achieved: the sense of the other's resistance, the excitement of overcoming it through violence, the sensation of power that arises from retaining self-control while subjecting the other to oneself. At one point in the narrative Coverdale himself explicitly notices the analogy

---

[4]Cf. the parallel in Melville's *Pierre:* "She [Isabel] darted one swift glance at Pierre; and then with a single toss of her hand tumbled her unrestrained locks all over her, so that they tent-wise invested her whole kneeling form close to the floor, and yet swept the floor with their wild redundancy. Never Saya of Limeean girl, at dim mass in St. Dominic's cathedral, so completely muffled the human figure. To Pierre, the deep oaken recess of the double-casement, before which Isabel was kneeling, seemed now the immediate vestibule of some awful shrine, mystically revealed through the obscurely open window" (*Writings*, VII, 149). Melville goes on to give the scene an ironic development, but that irony does not really affect the mystery of the self, which is adumbrated elsewhere in *Pierre* as well.

between sexual and psychological possession. After the discussion of women's rights which takes place at Eliot's Pulpit, he finds himself alone with Priscilla, following Zenobia's departure with Hollingsworth. "No doubt," he confesses, "it was a kind of sacrilege in me to attempt to come within her maidenly mystery. But as she appeared to be tossed aside by her other friends, or carelessly let fall, like a flower which they had done with, I could not resist the impulse to take just one peep beneath her folded petals" (Centenary, III, 125, a passage that recalls III, 47: "Zenobia is a wife! Zenobia has lived, and loved! There is no folded petal, no latent dew-drop, in this perfectly developed rose!").

But it is Coverdale's relationship with Zenobia, above all, that most clearly manifests the force and nature of the desire for possession. Zenobia herself senses it; it expresses itself through a particular kind of look or gaze (insofar as sight is associated with knowledge, one may ascribe to Coverdale something of the psychology of the voyeur). Prompted by such awareness as she nurses him through his illness, she asks: "What are you seeking to discover in me?" "The mystery of your life," he answers, "surprised," as he says, "into the truth by the unexpectedness of her attack" (Centenary, III, 47). This mystery, as the preceding passage in the text makes clear, centers upon whether Zenobia has been married before—in other words, whether she has been (both sexually and psychologically) possessed by another. Significantly, Coverdale looks upon her question as an attack. In one sense it is clearly that, inasmuch as the attempt to violate the sanctity of another self represents an act of psychological violence or aggression. But the admission is also significant for revealing the wish of the possessive impulse to conceal itself even as it seeks to penetrate the other. Exposure of that desire is tantamount to making the self vulnerable to the other, since desire, too, is in some sense an affection that commits the self to its pursuit. Hence the other's knowledge of that desire as a controlling motive creates in turn the possibility of both resistance and/or possession—for the other can possess the self by manipulating its controlling motive.

Possession, then, differs from love in depending upon a forced penetration of the other while simultaneously preserving the sanctity of one's own self from that other. In this fashion the sense of power is retained by achieving an assimilation of the other's consciousness into one's own. Instead of identifying with that other, one treats it merely as an object (of desire). Hence the other becomes something the self appropriates or makes use of. As an object of desire it offers in possession a gratification that comes from the self's not having had to submit to its own desire in order to attain its object. In this respect, the element of desire that informs the drive for possession differs radically from that of love; the whole sensation of power that accompanies the former proceeds from the fact that here the self dominates its own desire rather than becoming subject to it. Its sense of power requires that the self somehow avoid objectification (treatment as an object), while simultaneously subjecting everything outside itself to such treatment. Thus *it* remains pure consciousness; all else becomes merely an object for that consciousness.

In order to objectify the other, the self must first grasp the motive of that other's inner nature: only then, when it has comprehended the principle behind the other's activity, can it treat that other as an object. But the other resists this attempt to penetrate to the secret of its nature, by concealing its real self behind a facade. Thus Coverdale says of Zenobia that she "bent her head towards me, and let me look into her eyes, as if challenging me to drop a plummet-line down into the depths of her consciousness." Once the other becomes aware of the self's voyeuristic gaze, that gaze loses its efficacy or force. It operates only as long as the other remains unaware of it. Consequently, the other's resistance produces a state of frustration: "A bachelor always feels himself defrauded, when he knows, or suspects, that any woman of his acquaintance has given herself away. Otherwise, the matter could have been no concern of mine. It was purely speculative; for I should not, under any circumstances, have fallen in love with Zenobia. The riddle made me so nervous, however, in my sensitive condition of mind and body, that I most ungratefully began to wish that she would let me alone" (Centenary, III, 48).

Such passages reveal the problematic quality of the narrative itself, fraught with inner tensions as well as repressions and resistances. Why should a bachelor feel defrauded when he knows or suspects a woman of his acquaintance has given herself away? In order for the self to obtain a sense of power from its voyeuristic assault, the other it seeks to possess must offer the prospect of an inner nature not already possessed by another through the affections. An individual in love surrenders his or her self to the other, assimilating simultaneously the other's consciousness. Henceforward, that individual no longer retains a consciousness of self. As a result, it no longer resists the other's desire for possession or the voyeuristic gaze through a wish to protect itself. Penetration of its defenses, the violation of its privacy, cannot yield the intruder the sense of possessing that self because of the loss of self-consciousness. Since surrender of self implies a loss of self-consciousness, the whole Romantic desire for loss of self-consciousness can be seen in this context as a desire for absorption by some other, the desire through voluntary submission to such absorption to obtain a higher form of consciousness in which the reality of the finite or individual self disappears. Thus submission to absorption by an other represents in effect an expansion of consciousness and hence, in a way, of the self. The only other possible form of self-expansion, possession of an other, demands that another con-

sciousness be assimilated into the self. In the process, it acquires a consciousness of the other as within itself, a consciousness it possesses and
treats as object rather than subject.

The difference between love and psychological possession may thus be
defined as one between voluntary self-surrender and the forced or violent absorption of the self by an other. Consciousness of the other as
one's own self through the other's voluntary surrender contrasts with
consciousness of that other as an object, resulting from the aggressive
assimilation of that other. The great similarity between the two desires
suggests that the self animated by one impulse may pass over to the
other—perhaps the danger most feared by Coverdale. Hence his reti-
cence and defensiveness: "Otherwise, the matter could have been no
concern of mine. It was purely speculative; for I should not, under any
circumstances, have fallen in love with Zenobia." In composing *Mid-
dlemarch,* George Eliot appears at one point to have thought of having
Dorothea Casaubon fall in love with Lydgate, the brilliant young physician, rather than Will Ladislaw; the union of Coverdale and Zenobia
(suggested by Zenobia herself near the end of the romance) belongs to
the same family of emotional possibilities.

The danger (as perceived by Coverdale) that the desire for possession
may actually be transformed into love or self-surrender arises from the
element common to both, a drive toward sublimation of self in some
higher form of consciousness proceeding from either possession or the
loss of self-consciousness. That the one would become the other results
from the fascination exerted by the opposite possibility: for the desire to
possess, the temptation or allure of being possessed (this is how it views
love), in which it transfers the satisfaction of its own impulse onto the
other by perceiving or imagining itself as that other, hence as possessing
the self; for love, the temptation to possess the other within the self by
treating that other not as its own self—whereby it sublimates its desire
for that self—but as an object, sublimating that other to its own desire.
The temptation is all the greater since the intensity of experiencing the
other as an object of desire fully equals the experience of that other as
one's own self. Coverdale's danger, as he perceives it, is that in his desire
to know another he will ultimately surrender himself as a means of
obtaining such knowledge: by allowing himself to fall in love with
Zenobia, he would offer her the possibility of loving him, which in turn
creates the opportunity of knowing her as an other whom one experiences as one's own self. The danger (but also the temptation) is that in so
doing one exposes oneself to possession, should she decide to exploit his
self-surrender by simply appropriating his self without offering herself
in return.

Here the prospect of being possessed exercises almost as much of an
allure as possession itself. Coverdale's ambivalence toward these two

possibilities produces the state of anxiety he represents under the form of a quest for knowledge: "The riddle made me so nervous, however, in my sensitive condition of mind and body, that I most ungratefully began to wish that she would let me alone." His need for solitude issues from an inner confusion—the inability to choose between a simple desire for possession and the more complex drive that yields to affection in the hope of obtaining a vicarious gratification, deriving from a mixture of the affection itself and the apprehension of one's self as assimilated by another.

Here, as elsewhere, the problem of choosing between the one and the other is created in part by the limits of knowledge, the subjective abyss separating one individual from another. As a result, experience itself assumes an intensely subjective coloring: what we experience belongs not so much to an external world but rather to the mind itself. In the chapter entitled "The Boarding-House," Coverdale expresses such a view through the metaphor of drama: "There now needed only Hollingsworth and old Moodie to complete the knot of characters, whom a real intricacy of events, greatly assisted by my method of insulating them from other relations, had kept so long upon my mental stage, as actors in a drama" (Centenary, III, 156). By means of this analogy, it becomes possible to represent the mind as at once both subjective and objective:

> I began to long for a catastrophe. If the noble temper of Hollingsworth's soul were doomed to be utterly corrupted by the too powerful purpose, which had grown out of what was noblest in him; if the rich and generous qualities of Zenobia's womanhood might not save her; if Priscilla must perish by her tenderness and faith, so simple and so devout; —then be it so! Let it all come! As for me, I would look on, as it seemed my part to do, understandingly, if my intellect could fathom the meaning and the moral, and, at all events, reverently and sadly. The curtain fallen, I would pass onward with my poor individual life, which was now attenuated of much of its proper substance, and diffused among many alien interests. (Centenary, III, 157)

Here Coverdale's confession that he "began to long for a catastrophe" implies that the "mental stage" on which the protagonists enact their parts is not simply a passive mirror for the representation of events occurring in an external world; rather, as the medium for his own desires and repressions, it becomes itself a determining influence upon the dramatic representation. Through the blending of subjective perspectives, Coverdale's novelistic consciousness merges with the protagonists' to create a denouement whose dramatic quality expresses the essence of novel or romance. In so doing, his proleptic desire passes imperceptibly from something like the external world into that of mind, an oneiric realm governed by desire and repression in which both character and action assume a more fluid existence, susceptible to the kinds of distortions that color the representations of our dreams.

But the "catastrophe," too, must be seen in terms of the relation between these characters and the consciousness that represents them: Coverdale's longing for that catastrophe manifests the desire to reclaim a subjectivity that has involuntarily passed over from the self to others without experiencing the gratification of knowledge, which is to say: without being able to experience the other as its own self—without, in other words, being able to replace the self that it "displaces" by another that represents in some sense its equivalent. Coverdale's longing for the destruction of the protagonists is thus a longing to be rid of a subjectivity that produces only suffering because it allows itself to be displaced and hence fails to preserve the relation of consciousness to itself that forms the essence of the Romantic self. Coverdale's subjectivity loses the sense that the content of consciousness belongs to the self rather than to what is outside it (the other), the sense that such content consists of assimilating the external world into the self, where the ability to assimilate expresses the self's potency over such a world.

In the present instance, on the contrary, the self is subjugated by that world: Coverdale's mental stage, for all its appearance of absorbing the protagonists into the mind, involves in fact the opposite process, a subordination of mind to what it observes, so that Coverdale's only sense of self is "now attenuated of much of its proper substance, and diffused among many alien interests." Such subordination is not the same as assimilation to the external world, although various rapprochements can serve to narrow the distance between them. The fundamental difference is that in being subordinated the mind does not experience the gratification of either possessing or being possessed—it neither experiences the other as itself nor as an "other," hence misses the sensation that comes from the domination of the one by the other. What occurs instead might be described as a loss of potency or power: the self creates a world (its mental stage) which though seemingly internal is in one sense actually external, inasmuch as it is not assimilated into the self but conversely—consciousness becomes one with that world, so as no longer to be able to distinguish itself from what it observes.

This loss of consciousness, of the ability to separate oneself from what one sees, makes Coverdale subject to the world of the protagonists: hence his desire to be rid of it, or, in effect, of his own dependency. Here the dilemma of consciousness is precisely its inability to stop perceiving. Once drawn into such activity, it necessarily exposes itself to the latter's inherent temptations: specifically, the desire to possess, which occurs as soon as it ceases to surrender itself to the perceiving process—in other words, as soon as it attempts to dominate that process. At that stage, the object perceived ceases to be simply part of the content of consciousness:

henceforward, the mind sees it as that which gives it a relation to itself. The perceived object is what the mind must "possess" in order to satisfy its need for power over the world it observes.

But if Coverdale experiences a loss of self when his subjectivity passes over into that world, it is equally possible—as Hawthorne elsewhere indicates—to experience a loss of self in love which is not compensated for by an assimilation of the other as a replacement for one's lost self. This loss of self without compensation occurs when an individual surrenders himself or herself without eliciting a corresponding self-surrender from the other. As Coverdale remarks of Zenobia's union with Westervelt:

> How many a woman's evil fate has yoked her with a man like this! Nature thrusts some of us into the world miserably incomplete, on the emotional side, with hardly any sensibilities except what pertain to us as animals. No passion, save of the senses; no holy tenderness, nor the delicacy that results from this. Externally, they bear a close resemblance to other men, and have perhaps all save the finest grace; but when a woman wrecks herself on such a being, she ultimately finds that the real womanhood, within her, has no corresponding part in him. Her deepest voice lacks a response; the deeper her cry, the more dead his silence. The fault may be none of his; he cannot give her what never lived within his soul. But the wretchedness, on her side, and the moral deterioration attendant on a false and shallow life, without strength enough to keep itself sweet, are among the most pitiable wrongs that mortals suffer. (Centenary, III, 103)

"Holy tenderness" and delicacy: in these are implied a sense of the other within the self which leads to mutual self-surrender and what might be described as mutual transference of subjectivity: what the self loses in such transference, its consciousness of the external world's relation to itself, is replaced by consciousness of the world's relation to the other in which it now lives. So that subjectivity, in the sense of a relation between self and world, is preserved in such transference—only its terms have changed. Yet, as the passage implies, such change is not without a difference, since the tenderness that encompasses it can be described as holy. Its sacred quality results from the fact that the consciousness of the relation of the external world to an other which replaces consciousness of self *is* in some sense really the other's own consciousness, transferred now to the self. It is the self's responsibility for the other consciousness which gives to its affection this sacred or holy quality.

# 20 *Melville:* Pierre

At the end of *Pierre* Melville has his protagonist enter a picture gallery where he discovers, among other things, a copy of Guido Reni's Beatrice Cenci. In the winter of 1857, during his sojourn in Rome, Melville would actually see the original. In 1852, while composing *Pierre,* he could have drawn upon Shelley's description of it from the preface to *The Cenci.*[1] In his own description, significantly, Melville employs the same motif as Shelley—the hood of "black crape" corresponding to Shelley's "mantle," in both instances metaphorical rather than real (although the actual painting had portrayed the face of a young girl completely enveloped in drapery). In the course of *The Cenci* this motif appears on several occasions. Hearing that the assassins of Count Cenci have confessed to their crime, attesting by implication to her own complicity, Beatrice exclaims:

> O white innocence,
> That thou shouldst wear the mask of guilt to hide
> Thine awful and serenest countenance
> From those who know thee not! (Reiman and Powers, p. 294)

Later, her final words to her brother are:

> For thine own sake be constant to the love
> Thou bearest us; and to the faith that I,
> Though wrapped in a strange cloud of crime and shame,
> Lived ever holy and unstained. (Reiman and Powers, p. 300)

In his ethics Shelley proposes a fundamental distinction between human nature, depicted as essentially innocent, and those accidental perversions through which it assumes an immoral character. Such perversions, according to Shelley, are brought about by the mind's error in acquiescing in certain suggestions that necessarily occur to it under given

---

[1]According to Stuart Curran, *Shelley's Cenci: Scorpions Ringed with Fire* (Princeton: Princeton Univ. Press, 1970), "The fame of the portrait in the English-speaking world of the nineteenth century rested on [Shelley]" (p. xi). Similarly, Henry Murray in the notes to his edition of *Pierre* (1949; rpt. New York: Hendricks House, 1957), pp. 502–3: "Shelley's *Cenci* (1819) was largely responsible for the compelling fascination exerted by Guido's head upon the intellectuals and *spirituelles* of the succeeding generation." I know of only one other account of the Cenci history from this time: Stendhal's in his *Chroniques italiennes.* But Stendhal remained unknown for almost half a century. Both he and Shelley worked from manuscript sources for their accounts of Beatrice Cenci.

circumstances.[2] On being adopted, they lead to pernicious consequences. Crime accordingly appears in tragedy as "the fatal consequence of the unfathomable agencies of nature; error is thus divested of its wilfulness; men can no longer cherish it as the creation of their choice" (from *A Defence of Poetry;* Reiman and Powers, pp. 490–91). Given the conjunction of certain circumstances, the impulse to do evil inevitably arises. To yield to such impulses represents not an act of choice but merely a surrender to psychological suggestion. Only resistance or conscious rejection qualifies as an act of choice.[3]

In *The Cenci* the thought of parricide arises naturally in the minds of Beatrice and Giacomo. For Beatrice it occurs as a result of her rape by the Count. As depicted by Shelley, it represents reaction rather than action, the desire of an innocent soul to purify itself of the evil contaminating it. Given Beatrice's belief in her moral and spiritual pollution by her father, it is, according to Shelley, only natural that she should seek to cleanse herself through some act of retribution. For Shelley her belief is erroneous but not immoral. Nor can anything prevent the thought of parricide from arising under such circumstances. Only at the critical moment at which thought becomes act can the mind exercise choice. As Orsino, speaking of the nature of self-examination, observes:

> Such self-anatomy shall teach the will
> Dangerous secrets: for it tempts our powers,
> Knowing what must be thought, and may be done,
> Into the depth of darkest purposes. (Reiman and Powers, p. 260)

Hence Beatrice controls not the thought of parricide itself (what "*must* be thought") but only the choice whether or not to execute it (what "*may* be done"). Since her crime represents a natural consequence of erroneous but not immoral beliefs, she is paradoxically right in the final act to assert her innocence.[4] Such beliefs are not voluntarily assumed but simply the product of her time and circumstances.

---

[2] For more analysis, see Earl R. Wasserman, *Shelley: A Critical Reading* (Baltimore: Johns Hopkins Univ. Press, 1971), pp. 109–22.

[3] For some interesting parallels in Charles Brockden Brown, cf. *Edgar Huntly:* "It must at least be said that his will was not concerned in this transaction. He acted in obedience to an impulse which he could not controul, nor resist. Shall we impute guilt where there is no design? Shall a man extract food for self-reproach from an action to which it is not enough to say that he was actuated by no culpable intention, but that he was swayed by no intention whatever?" (*Novels and Related Works,* IV, 91–92) and *Ormond:* "Sinister considerations flow in upon us through imperceptible channels, and modify our thoughts in numberless ways, without our being truly conscious of their presence" (II, 157).

[4] Cf. Curran, p. 95: "*If* God is to be considered wise and just, then death *must* come to Cenci, and in contrast, if death does not come to Cenci, no such God exists—only a dark and destructive chaos of values, the sound and fury and nothingness emanating from her father's spirit. On these grounds Beatrice claims her paradoxical innocence in the final act. She is not hypocritical nor untruthful, nor is there in her desire for life the taint of ruthless self-interest that has appeared to some."

With this Shelleyan view of the nature of evil, we may compare Melville's treatment of the subject in *Pierre*. Here, as in Shelley, the placing of a character in certain circumstances leads to the suggestion of immoral impulses. Like Shelley, furthermore, Melville's narrator does not condemn such impulses—offering merely an ironic acknowledgment of their inevitability. Of the underlying sexual nature of Pierre's attraction to Isabel we are told: "But Pierre, though charged with the fire of all divineness, his containing thing was made of clay" (*Writings*, VII, 107). Since the causes of his attraction are incipient in human nature itself, the resulting desire represents not merely a possible but necessary consequence.

Such reasoning suggests the Shelleyan element in Melville's analysis. To be sure, that analysis is not without significant resemblances to Hawthorne: the passion of Hester Prynne and Arthur Dimmesdale in *The Scarlet Letter* or, in a related vein, Reuben Bourne's desertion of the dying Roger Malvin in "Roger Malvin's Burial." In each instance Hawthorne contrasts natural impulse against a higher moral imperative—the love of Hester and Dimmesdale for each other against their mutual obligations to Chillingworth, Reuben Bourne's involuntary impulse for self-preservation against his duty to his dying friend. In each case the victory of natural over moral impulse gives rise to a similar theme: an exhortation to compassion and understanding of moral weakness which, although not exonerating from blame, asserts the necessity for forgiveness and humanity. Hawthorne's psychology, like that of M. G. Lewis in *The Monk*, focuses not so much upon the anatomy of the mind's surrender to impulse as its consequences in the life of the protagonist. The result is an analysis of guilt and its psychological effects, the development of the self after its surrender to sinful passion.

Since there is no way to protect the mind from the *suggestion* of immoral impulses, it cannot be held responsible for them. When Pierre decides to pass off Isabel as his wife, the narrator remarks:

> Yet so strange and complicate is the human soul; so much is confusedly evolved from out itself, and such vast and varied accessions come to it from abroad, and so impossible is it always to distinguish between these two, that the wisest man were rash, positively to assign the precise and incipient origination of his final thoughts and acts. Far as we blind moles can see, man's life seems but an acting upon mysterious hints; it is somehow hinted to us, to do thus or thus. For surely no mere mortal who has at all gone down into himself will ever pretend that his slightest thought or act solely originates in his own defined identity. (*Writings*, VII, 176)

As the boundaries between subjective and objective, internal and external dissolve, moral responsibility for one's acts becomes not only unclear but problematic. Even if conscious of its impulses before acting, must the mind accept responsibility for its acts? Or should such responsibility fall upon that which instigates such impulses? Arguably, without the impulse, there can be no occasion for moral choice. Without temptation, sin itself becomes impossible.

Here Melville differs significantly from Shelley. For Shelley, the mind is responsible for its acts, since it alone decides whether or not to execute them. To Melville, such a position seems "idealistic." In fact, the mind does not exercise complete power of choice: what occurs as suggestion is not so much an option but rather a hint that already *conduces* to action. According to this view, if immoral acts represent natural consequences of certain impulses, ultimately responsibility for such acts belongs to the power that originally causes the impulses: God, Nature, or fate.

Elsewhere in *Pierre* Melville attempts to specify the nature of such impulses. In his second interview with Isabel at the farmhouse, Pierre becomes conscious of the special character of her attraction:

> To Pierre's dilated senses Isabel seemed to swim in an electric fluid; the vivid buckler of her brow seemed as a magnetic plate. Now first this night was Pierre made aware of what, in the superstitiousness of his rapt enthusiasm, he could not help believing was an extraordinary physical magnetism in Isabel. And—as it were derived from this marvelous quality thus imputed to her—he now first became vaguely sensible of a certain still more marvelous power in the girl over himself and his most interior thoughts and motions; —a power so hovering upon the confines of the invisible world, that it seemed more inclined that way than this; —a power which not only seemed irresistibly to draw him toward Isabel, but to draw him away from another quarter—wantonly as it were, and yet quite ignorantly and unintendingly; and, besides, without respect apparently to any thing ulterior, and yet again, only under cover of drawing him to her. For over all these things, and interfusing itself with the sparkling electricity in which she seemed to swim, was an ever-creeping and condensing haze of ambiguities. (*Writings*, VII, 151)

Here Melville implies that in succumbing to Isabel's attraction, Pierre, though conscious, possesses no control over his impulses. The scene borrows a terminology derived from theories of animal magnetism. Indirectly Melville suggests that the phenomena purportedly described by such theories have no reality except in Pierre's imagination. Thus Isabel's attraction seems "an extraordinary physical magnetism" to Pierre only because of "the superstitiousness of his rapt enthusiasm." Similarly, to his "dilated senses" Isabel "*seemed* to swim in an electric fluid"; the "vivid buckler of her brow *seemed* as a magnetic plate." Beneath such illusory appearances subsists another reality: Isabel's sexual attractiveness, and its effect upon Pierre.

Her influence points to a tacit submission on Pierre's part, implying voluntary consent. If involuntary acts carry no responsibility, the mind assumes such responsibility the moment it becomes aware of the nature of its acts and persists in them. But what if it should, although conscious, find itself unable to break the spell? Melville describes the dilemma without attempting to resolve it when he says that Isabel's attraction for Pierre "had bound him to her by an extraordinary atmospheric spell— both physical and spiritual—which henceforth it had become impossible for him to break, but whose full potency he never recognized till long after he had become habituated to its sway" (*Writings*, VII, 151). Of course the reality of such a spell inheres in his own nature and impulses rather than in her. Yet to say so does nothing to lessen its force.

The necessity for self-examination, which bears upon such a dilemma, constitutes another link between Melville and Shelley. For Shelley, the mind must first become conscious of the immoral nature of certain impulses in order to resist them. This consciousness it achieves through what he describes as "self-anatomy."[5] As Cythna in *The Revolt of Islam* urges: "Reproach not thine own soul, but know thyself, / Nor hate another's crime, nor loathe thine own" (*P.W.*, p. 120). Such self-knowledge is precisely what Pierre resists in the early stages of the novel. Of his initial sympathy with Isabel the narrator remarks: "Thus, already, and ere the proposed encounter, he was assured that, in a transcendent degree, womanly beauty, and not womanly ugliness, invited him to champion the right" (*Writings*, VII, 107). Here sexual attraction, masked ironically by unconscious casuistry, constitutes the force drawing Pierre and Isabel together.

Later, Melville exhibits the process of "self-anatomy" in his protagonist. Yet, even as he strives to grasp the true nature of his relation to Isabel, she remains the symbolic embodiment of self-concealment and mystery—above all, through her long dark tresses, which conceal her face and figure at will. Similarly, many of her scenes with Pierre are shrouded in twilight or nocturnal darkness. Like her hair, such darkness symbolizes both self-concealment and sexual passion.

In this setting Melville develops Pierre's incestuous passion for her. Like the darkness accompanying it, such passion belongs to the realm of subliminal suggestion and desire surrounding the mind like a fluid atmosphere, avoiding the light of self-questioning even as it exerts its own attracting force. Like Giacomo in *The Cenci*, Isabel refuses to clarify her wishes and desires with Pierre. When he attempts to examine the motives behind his relationship with her, she instinctively diverts his attention. In response to his questions, she can only answer that she was "born in the midst of a mystery, bred in mystery, and still surviving to mystery." Through the falling of her hair around Pierre as they em-

[5]For more analysis, see Wasserman, pp. 109–22.

brace, Melville symbolizes both their immersion in, and concealment of, their incestuous passion from themselves and others. The motif appears for the last time at the novel's conclusion. Poisoning herself, Isabel falls over the already lifeless body of Pierre, "and her long hair ran over him, and arbored him in ebon vines." Her dying words are: "All's o'er, and ye know him not!" Pierre's death becomes his final act of self-concealment.

Against such self-concealment and its symbol, Melville juxtaposes Lucy. Both name and character signify her symbolic association with light. The opposition between Lucy and Isabel recalls the contrast between fair and dark heroines in Gothic romance. But Melville is not content simply to embody the contrast. Instead, he explores its psychological significance as part of Pierre's imaginative consciousness.[6] Such consciousness assimilates the romance world, through whose symbolism it then expresses its own subliminal desires. As a result the appearances of that world are made to conform to Pierre's own changing perceptions. This accounts for the interchangeability of the heroines' features: "For an instant, the fond, all-understood blue eyes of Lucy displaced the as tender, but mournful and inscrutable dark glance of Isabel. He seemed placed between them, to choose one or the other; then both seemed his; but into Lucy's eyes there stole half of the mournfulness of Isabel's, without diminishing hers" (*Writings*, vii, 129). At the beginning of the work, Lucy appears as a fragile and evanescent vision, "fleecily invested" in her white, flowing dress. The light associated with her is diffuse and diaphanous. Later, her face manifests the hard, brilliant whiteness and clarity of "a chiseled statue's head" (*Writings*, vii, 328).

By merging perception and consciousness in such fashion, Melville reveals his affinity with Shelley in epistemological terms. In his "Speculations on Metaphysics" Shelley had stated: "It is an axiom in mental philosophy, that we can think of nothing which we have not perceived. When I say we can think of nothing, I mean, we can imagine nothing, we can reason of nothing, we can remember nothing, we can foresee nothing. . . . A catalogue of all the thoughts of the mind, and of all their possible modifications, is a cyclopedic history of the Universe" (*C.W.*, vii, 59). For Shelley, the equation of perception with thought signifies the latter's objective nature, its dependence upon the external world. Melville reverses that dependence: for him, the subjectivity of *Pierre* influences all perceptions within it. Hence there can be no such thing as a purely "objective" representation of an object. Everything appears through the transforming medium of consciousness. Such consciousness not only perceives but also thinks. When Pierre meets Isabel for the second time and finds himself attracted to her, that attraction acquires

---

[6]For a view of *Pierre* as the novel Pierre himself writes, see Raymond Nelson, "The Art of Herman Melville: The Author of *Pierre*," *Yale Review*, 59 (1969), 197–214.

for him the appearance of a "spell." In perceiving it as such, he assimilates his impression to his familiarity with the theory of animal magnetism. The narrator comments: "This spell seemed one with that Pantheistic master-spell, which eternally locks in mystery and in muteness the universal subject world, and the physical electricalness of Isabel seemed reciprocal with the heat-lightnings and the ground-lightnings nigh to which it had first become revealed to Pierre" (*Writings*, VII, 151).

The "Pantheistic master-spell, which eternally locks in mystery and in muteness the universal subject world" is the medium of consciousness. In saying that Isabel's "magnetic" spell *seemed* one with it, the narrative suggests that an illusory phenomenon momentarily becomes as real as consciousness itself, filling that consciousness with the same objective vividness as natural phenomena (the ground-lightning and heat-lightning). For Melville himself, only the "Pantheistic master-spell" of consciousness truly exists. But by allowing the narrative voice to pass into Pierre's reflections, he affirms the "objective" appearance of subjective phenomena.

# PART VII

# Poetics

# 21 Poe, Cousin, and Kant: Transformation of a Neoclassical Aesthetic

In one of his early reviews, a critique of N. P. Willis's *Tortesa the Usurer,* Poe asserts that "the perfection of dramatic, as well as of plastic skill, is found not in the imitation of Nature, but in the artistical adjustment and amplification of her features" (*C.W.,* x, 28). In this statement is contained one of the germs of Poe's theory of art. Nature exists for the artist, not to be copied but perfected. From such a viewpoint it is but a short step to the elaboration of an aesthetics of landscape gardening, a subject in which English writers of the Augustan age had evinced much interest. Poe's own fascination with it furnishes another instance of his affinity with the style and thought of the eighteenth century. His personal aesthetic may be found in his story "The Landscape Garden," where it is expressed through the aspirations of the protagonist, Ellison. Here the landscape garden is said to offer "the fairest field for the display of invention, or imagination" because it contains the richest possibilities for the "endless combining of forms of novel Beauty." Its superiority to other forms of art is adduced on the grounds that its elements are "at all times, and by a vast superiority, the most glorious which the earth could afford" (*Coll. W.,* ii, 707).[1]

The description of landscape gardening as an "endless combining of forms of novel Beauty" is significant. Poe envisages all the arts as consisting of the combination of elements of one kind or another. In one of his earliest critical reviews (*Southern Literary Messenger,* Oct., 1836) he remarks: "There is no greater mistake than the supposition that a true

---

[1]In his study *Poe's Fiction: Romantic Irony in the Gothic Tales* (Madison: Univ. of Wisconsin Press, 1973), pp. 124–25, G. R. Thompson characterizes "Landor's Cottage" as one of Poe's hoaxes. By relating it to the tradition of landscape aesthetics, however, we obtain a view of its place in Poe's overall aesthetic.

originality is a mere matter of impulse or inspiration. To originate, is carefully, patiently, and understandingly to combine" (*C.W.*, XIV, 73). Poe consistently maintains this proposition to the end of his life; a famous passage from his posthumously published essay "The Poetic Principle" declares: "Inspired by an ecstatic prescience of the glories beyond the grave, we struggle, by multiform combinations among the things and thoughts of Time, to attain a portion of that Loveliness whose very elements, perhaps, appertain to eternity alone" (pp. 273–74). Art is envisaged as an effort to discover those combinations or arrangements of elements whose internal relations reflect the eternal laws of harmony which constitute the supernal Loveliness. Because of such formal harmony—and not because of its sensuous qualities—Pater will later assert that "all art aspires to the condition of music."

From the standpoint of his insight into art as a combination or arrangement of elements, Poe elsewhere takes up the question of the distinction between fancy and imagination: " 'The fancy,' says the author of the 'Ancient Mariner,' in his *Biographia Literaria*, 'the fancy combines, the imagination creates.' And this was intended, and has been received, as a distinction. If so at all, it is one without a difference; without even a difference of *degree*. The fancy as nearly creates as the imagination; and neither creates in any respect. All novel conceptions are merely unusual combinations. The mind of man can *imagine* nothing which has not really existed. . . . Thus with all which seems to be *new*—which appears to be a *creation* of intellect. It is resoluble into the old. The wildest and most vigorous effort of mind cannot stand the test of this analysis" (*C.W.*, X, 61–62).[2] Nowhere do we see more clearly what separates Poe from English (as well as German) Romanticism.[3] Here the formal is opposed to the organic concept of creation. Art is defined as being at once independent and dependent upon Nature. Whereas in Romantic aesthetic speculation art had gradually assumed the role of a second Nature,

[2]For further comment on Poe's critique of the Coleridgean distinction, Edward H. Davidson, *Poe: A Critical Study* (Cambridge: Harvard Univ. Press, 1957), pp. 57–61; also mentioned in Sidney P. Moss, *Poe's Literary Battles: The Critic in the Context of His Literary Milieu* (Durham, N.C.: Duke Univ. Press, 1963), p. 180. For the problem of "originality" in general, esp. from a Romantic perspective, Walter Jackson Bate, *The Burden of the Past and the English Poet* (Cambridge: Harvard Univ. Press, 1970), pp. 107–18, esp. 113, 116–18.

[3]In his essay on Poe in *A History of Modern Criticism, 1750–1950* (New Haven: Yale Univ. Press, 1955–), René Wellek acutely argues that Poe's affinities are with neoclassicism rather than Romanticism (the same argument advanced by Barton Levi St. Armand with reference to Poe's attack on Coleridge's fancy-imagination distinction specifically, in Richard P. Benton, ed., *Poe as Literary Cosmologer* [Hartford: Transcendental Books, 1975], pp. 4–7). But, as I attempt to show both here and elsewhere, if Poe's mode of poetic analysis is in some respects neoclassical, its ends are ultimately Romantic: the symbolic significance of beauty qua aesthetic ideal, in particular, defines him as part of the Romantic "aesthetic" tradition of Keats and Shelley and as a precursor of the Pre-Raphaelites and Baudelaire.

governed correspondingly by organic laws of creation, Poe attempts to establish the autonomy of the aesthetic realm precisely on the basis of its laws, which are no longer analogous to those of Nature but transcend it through a higher or more absolute perfection. Considered in itself, such a statement would amount to no more than a reiteration of eighteenth-century aesthetic principles, but in Poe it assumes an original aspect as a result of its visionary neoplatonic character. All aesthetic combinations are but an effort to mirror a divine harmony that remains beyond the compass of human knowledge, a harmony of whose splendor the artist receives only fleeting and partial glimpses.

For this very reason Poe considers it impossible to speak of Beauty in an absolute sense. In his "Philosophy of Composition" he observes that "when, indeed, men speak of Beauty, they mean, precisely, not a quality, as is supposed, but an effect—they refer, in short, just to that intense and pure elevation of *soul—not* of intellect, or of heart— . . . which is experienced in consequence of contemplating 'the beautiful'" (*C.W.*, XIV, 197–98).[4] To speak of Beauty in an absolute sense, as a property or quality of things, presupposes a knowledge of that divine splendor of which we possess but an "ecstatic prescience." By no other means is it possible to apprehend the true nature of Beauty itself.

As a consequence of defining beauty as an effect rather than a quality, Poe's aesthetics necessarily relates itself to the psychology of perception originating with Locke and upon which the eighteenth century had sought to construct its theory of the beautiful, and later, of the sublime. By associating his aesthetics with such a perspective, Poe ultimately adopts the threefold division of the faculties proposed by Kant: Pure Reason, Practical Reason, and Judgment.

Reference to this Kantian schema first appears in Poe's review of Bulwer-Lytton's *Critical and Miscellaneous Writings* (Nov., 1841). In it Poe merely declares that Bulwer's every word evinces the highest appreciation of "the right, the beautiful, and the true" (*C.W.*, x, 213). To find Poe's fullest discussion of the schema, we must turn to "The Poetic Principle": "Dividing the world of mind into its three most immediately obvious distinctions, we have the Pure Intellect, Taste, and the Moral Sense. I place Taste in the middle, because it is just this position which, in the mind, it occupies" (XIV, 272). An attempt has been made on the basis of such statements to demonstrate the influence of Kant upon Poe's critical speculations.[5] It would be erroneous, however, to claim direct

---

[4]An interesting combination of the aesthetics of the beautiful with that of the sublime, in a Longinian rather than Romantic sense.

[5]Glen A. Omans, "'Intellect, Taste, and the Moral Sense': Poe's Debt to Immanuel Kant," in *Studies in the American Renaissance* (1980), ed. Joel Myerson (Boston: Twayne, 1980), pp. 123–68.

influence in this case. All of Poe's references to Kant are either charged with ridicule or are merely comic. The question arises: how are we to explain the resemblance?

Here the mediating figure is clearly Victor Cousin, a disciple in his early years of Kant, a later friend of Hegel, active in the reform of the French educational system under Guizot.[6] His pervasive influence upon French Romanticism has not yet received adequate assessment. Interestingly, Nerval mentions him as one of his "anciens maîtres" [old masters] at the Sorbonne (*Oeuvres*, I, 115). Cousin's philosophical system passes under the name of Eclecticism, but it remains in fact essentially within the sphere of Kant's influence. His *Cours de philosophie* (1836), consisting of lectures on "the foundation of the absolute ideas of the true, the beautiful, and the good," is clearly Kantian, but it owes some of its most interesting features to Fichte, Schelling, and, of course, Cousin himself.

There are few references to Cousin in Poe. Perhaps the most significant is that in which he speaks of "the sentiment of the beautiful": "that divine sixth sense which is yet so faintly understood—that sense which phrenology has attempted to embody in its organ of *ideality*—that sense which is the basis of all Cousin's dreams—that sense which speaks of God through his purest, if not his *sole* attribute—which proves, and which alone proves his existence" (*C.W.*, XI, 255–56).

By comparing some passages from the *Cours* with several previously cited from Poe's criticism, we may gain some idea of the extent of Cousin's influence. Whereas Poe speaks of the necessity of perfecting Nature through art, Cousin says: "Thus the beautiful is an absolute idea and not a copy of an imperfect, finite, and contingent nature. The idea can make its appearance in the bosom of nature; but there it is invariably veiled and mutilated; it appears in a more striking manner in human productions, because the hand guided by intelligence approaches more closely the model conceived by the latter; but the idea can never realize itself there entirely" (p. 190). Here the philosophical substructure of Poe's aesthetics makes itself manifest. From this passage it will become apparent how Poe is both able to preserve the framework of eighteenth-century aesthetic speculation and simultaneously to anticipate the Aestheticism of a Mallarmé or an Oscar Wilde. Beginning with the neoclassical dictum of Nature's imperfection in relation to art, Cousin infers, in neoplatonic fashion, the existence of an absolute idea immanent within Nature but only imperfectly revealed. A comparison with earlier writers illustrates his transformation of his sources. Whereas these had sought to define the beautiful merely as a harmony in the relation of elements

---

[6]The importance of his (as-yet) unexplored influence upon Poe noted by T. O. Mabbott in *Coll. W.*, III, 1040–41 (n. 4).

to each other, Cousin ascribes to the idea of the beautiful a real and concrete existence. Just as Plato had spoken of the Idea as the "really real Reality," so for Cousin it is the idea of the beautiful—and not its manifestation—which is most real.

Thus the idea "appears" in Nature, but its appearance is necessarily imperfect, since, in expressing itself through natural elements, it cannot reveal itself in pure and unadulterated form. But since its essence as an idea can only be thought, intelligence—which participates in the same element or medium—can approximate it. The beautiful thus becomes the object of an artistic quest. Out of the search for beauty, as something capable only of transient and imperfect apprehension by the senses, develops the essence of Aestheticism. But whereas Pater and the Pre-Raphaelites had sought to achieve through refinement of the senses an apprehension of the beautiful in its purely sensuous splendor, Cousin maintains that it is above all an ideal, something evoked by sensuous appearance but not to be identified with it. Its elevation to the level of the ideal ensures its autonomy: "The feeling of the beautiful, inspired by the presence of an object, be it natural or artificial, is pure and divested of all foreign associations. It does not relate to the pleasurable, nor to the pathetic, nor to the useful, nor to imitation, nor to religion, nor to morals. Art should have no other aim than to inspire the feeling of the beautiful, it should not serve any other purpose; it belongs neither to religion nor to morals, but like these it draws us toward the infinite, of which it manifests one of the forms. God is the source of all beauty, as of all truth, all religion, all morality. The highest aim of art is then to awaken in its own manner the feeling of the infinite" (*Cours de philosophie,* p. 226).

The doctrine of the autonomy of the aesthetic realm, announced by Kant in his *Critique of Judgment,* anticipates the Aesthetic doctrine of "art for art's sake." From a similar standpoint Poe can assert: "there neither exists nor *can* exist any work more thoroughly dignified—more supremely noble than this very poem—this poem *per se*—this poem which is a poem and nothing more—this poem written solely for the poem's sake" (*C.W.,* xiv, 272). Expressed in such a fashion, the doctrine of aesthetic autonomy becomes a slogan, a rallying cry, for Aestheticism. But whereas for Aestheticism art engenders its own religion, Poe conceives of art as an end in itself only insofar as it manifests one of the forms of the infinite, or God. In his *Cours* Cousin declares: "All works of art are then nothing more than an approximation: the final term of the ideal is in the infinite, or in God" (p. 207). For Poe, similarly, art is merely the means, imperfect and ephemeral, by which we approach the infinite. But it is only one of the means. In *Eureka* he proclaims the alliance of art with science—the one in pursuit of the idea of the beautiful, the other engaged in a quest for the true. Neither affects the validity of its counterpart; both are equal in their separate spheres. Yet there is a sense in which, for Poe, all these disciplines share something in common. It explains his efforts to merge the science of probability with the imaginative and fictional in his tales of ratiocination, or his exposition of the relations governing thought, motion, and mind in "Mesmeric Revelation."

We have seen that for Poe the beautiful cannot exist in its pure form in Nature. Cousin had asserted that the source of all beauty was to be found in God. On yet another level, similarly, Poe's aesthetics embraces neoplatonism and in so doing escapes the tyranny of neoclassical rules. Plotinus had spoken of God as the One, the original source of all being. The emanation of being through various levels, however, can also be seen as an emanation of beauty. From its source in God or the One, it filters down in ever-decreasing intensity through the different degrees of being. Since it exists in its pure form only as the One, nothing less can satisfactorily reflect its divine splendor. All the rules of neoclassical art are thus rejected as inadequate: they pertain only to a lesser degree of beauty, hence carry only a relative rather than absolute validity.

Nevertheless, the mind possesses an "ecstatic prescience" of the "supernal Loveliness." Its element is none other than thought. Through the perception of earthly beauty, the mind receives the idea of an eternal beauty, to whose existence it approximates in thought. Since its earthly existence makes it impossible for the mind to achieve more than an imperfect apprehension of the eternal beauty, it necessarily seeks to sustain itself at the highest possible level of aesthetic apprehension, that of the ideal. "The highest aim of art," Cousin argues, "is thus to awaken in its own manner the feeling of the infinite." In inspiring us with the sentiment of the infinite, art raises the mind to the highest form of aesthetic experience, in which it perceives the ideality of the One.

The aesthetics of literary effect formulated by Poe is here established upon a philosophical basis. Since the work of art cannot embody the beautiful in itself, it seeks to evoke the idea of it. The intensity with which it enables us to conceive of this idea becomes the criterion of its elevation. Speaking of poetry specifically, Poe declares: "A poem must intensely excite. Excitement is its province, its essentiality. Its value is in the ratio of its (elevating) excitement" (*C.W.*, XIII, 151). The Longinian principle is thus reinterpreted. Excitement is transferred from the realm of feeling to knowledge. By being elevated through aesthetic excitement, the mind achieves an apprehension of the divine.

In "The Poetic Principle" the insight is subjected to even further refinement. Poe now attempts to distinguish between excitement considered merely as a psychological effect, and a true elevation of the soul. The result is an evaluation of the poetry of Tennyson from a new standpoint. "I regard him," Poe says, "as the noblest poet that ever lived. . . . I call him, and *think* him the noblest of poets—*not* because the impressions he produces are, at *all* times, the most profound—*not* because the poetical excitement which he induces is, at *all* times, the most intense—but because it *is*, at all times, the most ethereal—in other words, the most elevating and the most pure" (*C.W.*, xiv, 289). Such elevation permits the purest apprehension of the beautiful inasmuch as it raises the soul to a level at which the beauty of the One shines forth to a degree approaching that of its pristine essence. In such a state, beauty becomes completely ethereal, or purged of all the dross of matter. As it loses its materiality, it draws near to the rarefied state of the purely ideal.

The praise Poe lavishes upon Tennyson is significant in another respect. Even in his earliest reviews Poe had invariably accorded an enthusiastic response to the works of the British poet. But the elevation of Tennyson in the last of Poe's critical essays to the supreme pinnacle of poetry comes as the final expression of a tendency that had already begun to manifest itself in Poe's middle years: a turning away from the Romanticism of Wordsworth and Coleridge conjoined with an ever-deepening appreciation of the aesthetic tendency that originates with Keats and Shelley and culminates in the poems of Tennyson's early years and the effusions of the Pre-Raphaelite circle. Already in a review of Longfellow from the year 1842 we find Keats singled out for special praise: "Of the poets who have appeared most fully instinct with the principles now developed, we may mention *Keats* as the most remarkable. He is the sole British poet who has never erred in his themes. Beauty is always his aim" (*C.W.*, xi, 76). Elsewhere in the same review Poe says: "It is chiefly, if we are not mistaken—it is chiefly amid forms of physical loveliness (we use the word *forms* in its widest sense as embracing modifications of sound and color) that the soul seeks the realization of its dreams of BEAUTY" (*C.W.*, xi, 80). One thinks of poems like the "Ode to a Nightingale" (mentioned in an earlier review by Poe) or the "Eve of St. Agnes," in which even the modifications of sound and color are allowed to assume the dignity of forms. All such forms are, however, but transitory and fleeting phenomena from which a vision of the beautiful arises. It would be erroneous, on the whole, to infer the presence of a neoplatonic theory of beauty in Keats. To be sure, there are intimations of it—as in the famous lines of the "Ode on a Grecian Urn": " 'Beauty is truth, truth beauty,'—that is all / Ye know on earth, and all ye need to know." But such intimations remain at the level of momentary intuitions. Nor do we find anything more in Tennyson. Only in Shelley is beauty reified into a pure and eternal essence informing all things. A common theme, nevertheless, runs through all three poets: the idea of beauty as the supreme poetic objective.

Through the neoplatonism of Cousin, as we have seen, Poe was able to understand this idea in a new light. For him, beauty comes to represent something undisclosable in itself, but which we can nevertheless approach through poetic evocation. Here, as pointed out earlier, the aesthetics of literary effect is given a philosophical basis. From an aesthetic perspective, moreover, the necessity for unity of effect also becomes manifest. Through a corresponding unity in our impression of beauty, the mind is elevated to a higher or more ethereal level. Such unity is but another name for purity. Above all it stands for the purity of the image through which we achieve a sensuous apprehension of the divine.

By means of the trajectory just traced, it becomes possible to see the deeper grounds of Poe's opposition to allegory. In his second review of Hawthorne (Nov., 1847) he writes: "Under the best circumstances, it must always interfere with that unity of effect which to the artist, is worth all the allegory in the world" (*C.W.*, xiii, 148). All this, to be sure, had been implied even in his first discussion of allegory, nearly ten years before. But now such criticism is invested with a deeper meaning. The true purpose behind the "unity of effect" Poe speaks of is not merely the conveyance of aesthetic pleasure. Instead, as a result of the Romantic and neoplatonic conception of art which he adopts from Cousin—a conception at the same time permeated by the influence of eighteenth-century aesthetic speculation—Poe sees the doctrine of unity of effect as the means by which the mind is enabled to elevate itself through sensuous apprehension to a perception of the divine One that constitutes the source of the beautiful.

Thus in his last poems, such as "Ulalume" and "The Bells," Poe pursues an ideal of beauty that operates solely through those "modifications of sound and color" which he had sought to raise to the level of forms. For only through sensuous apprehension does the mind attain a true idea of the beautiful in its essence. Beauty alone, accordingly, now stands as the proper theme of all higher poetry.

We have examined the route by which Poe passes from a neoclassical aesthetics to the doctrines of Aestheticism. In the process, a concept of allegory at first indistinguishable from that of symbolism is gradually filtered out and finally rejected as a diversion from that beauty which elevates the mind to the level at which it apprehends the divine essence. There is an affinity, of course, between such a concept and the symbolism of a Coleridge or a Wordsworth. That affinity, nevertheless, must not obscure the differences. Poe consistently asserts that the beauty of art can only *evoke* the idea of the beautiful. Never in his writings does he exhibit any trace of that belief in Nature as a revelation of the divine essence so characteristic of the other authors mentioned here. For Poe, Nature itself is only transitory and ephemeral. Such a Nature can only evoke, but never reveal. It marks the difference between an aesthetics of effect and an aesthetics of revelation.

The "contemplation of the beautiful" is thus for Poe the summons to a higher ideal: the essence of the beautiful in its most etherealized form. In his final work, the "prose poem" *Eureka,* he takes up the motions of the celestial spheres, as affording the most ideal realization possible of eternal beauty within the realm of temporal things. The result: a rapturous paean on the harmony of the universe. His rhapsody combines the aesthetic with the intellective, the beautiful with the true. As such it offers an even more spiritualized form of aestheticism, in which a physical is replaced by an intellectual sensuousness. Poe thus looks beyond even the fin de siècle aestheticism of a Pater or a Wilde, to the yet subtler ruminations of a Valéry. With this development, we arrive at the notion of a poem as an intellectual rather than sensuous apprehension of the world, but one that through the autonomy of the work of art no longer refers to any world other than that which it engenders itself.

## 22    *Emerson on Classic and Romantic*

In his early essay *Racine et Shakspeare* Stendhal had offered the following definitions of Romanticism (*Romantisme*) and Classicism. Romanticism represents "the taste of the present time." Classicism is—"the taste of our grandfathers."[1] In 1829 the presentation of Hugo's *Hernani* on the French stage had led to the famous "*bataille d'Hernani*" ("the battle of Hernani"). In France—as in England—the relation of Romanticism to Classicism is a polemical one. The polemic inspires a rhetoric of exclusion, the assertion of a rigorous either-or opposition. In Germany, on the other hand, a Goethe could pass from the early Romantic or "pre-Romantic" *Sturm und Drang* phase of the *Sorrows of Young Werther* to the classicism of *Iphigenie auf Tauris* or *Torquato Tasso* and, in his last years, to the mature Romanticism of his late lyrics. The Weimar Classicism of 1795, moreover, is almost simultaneous with the Jena Romanticism (inaugurated by Schelling, the Schlegels, and their circle) of 1798.[2] Hence the impossibility of a strict chronological schema that sees the literary history of the seventeenth and eighteenth centuries as a period of Classicism followed by the Romanticism of the early nineteenth century.[3]

Seen from another perspective, however, these phenomena carry a positive, as well as negative, significance. They indicate, as it were, the

[1]Stendhal, *O.C.* xxxvii, 39.

[2]For more details, see René Wellek, "The Concept of Romanticism in Literary History," rpt. in his *Concepts of Criticism,* ed. Stephen G. Nichols, Jr. (New Haven: Yale Univ. Press, 1963), pp. 128–98.

[3]On the problems of period classification, see E. R. Curtius, *European Literature and the Latin Middle Ages,* trans. Willard Trask (New York: Bollingen, 1953), pp. 270–71.

internalization of a principle of opposition within the very nature of Romanticism. In this sense the Weimar Classicism of Schiller and Goethe must be seen as a creation of the Romantic movement itself: Romanticism engenders this form of classicism as a conscious opposite to itself.[4] What defines Romanticism in the historical sense is thus not what it says about itself, that is, its ideological or aesthetic program, but rather the whole opposition of Romantic to Classic, which is a creation of Romantic thought. Within the framework of this opposition it becomes possible for Goethe to assert at different phases of his development classicistic or Romantic attitudes—a process that occurs in Friedrich Schlegel as well. Such an opposition can also generate the energies that impel a Wordsworth to what he conceives of as the creation of a new poetic diction (the Preface to *Lyrical Ballads*), one that is—as Coleridge was to demonstrate seventeen years later in his *Biographia Literaria*—not "the natural language of real men" but a consciously poetic mode of expression, governed by anti-neoclassical norms. Similarly, for Stendhal, the assertion of the self, the will to dominance by means of love in *Le Rouge et le noir*, must be played off against all the idealistic illusions about love (which for Stendhal are neoclassical rather than Romantic).

It was characteristic of Romanticism that it should seek to internalize the principle of its opposite within itself. Contained within the Romantic mode of thought, this opposite can then act as a force that produces its own opposite (that is, the properly Romantic attitude or concept). The creation of the opposite (the Romantic) arises through apprehension of the essential nature of the classical (hence Friedrich Schlegel's early immersion in the world of classical antiquity and its expression in *Die Griechen und Römer* [1797], as well as his studies on the history of Greek poetry). We find it also in Wordsworth's assimilation of epic form in *The Prelude*. On the level of both concept and form, Romanticism must absorb what it conceives of as the essence of the classical into itself. As a result of such assimilation, it then becomes possible for the Romantic poet or author to assert the contrary. Assimilation guarantees the possibility of transcending what one assimilates: through initial identification with the assimilated material, the passing over to its opposite can then appear as a "higher stage" of development, originating from what

[4]In his essay on "The Meaning of 'Romantic' in Early German Romanticism," Arthur O. Lovejoy demonstrates that the opposition between Classic and Romantic (which Friedrich Schlegel originally terms "das Wesentlich-Moderne") exists even in the period of Schlegel's adherence to the ideals of classical antiquity. According to Lovejoy, "by 1798 Fr. Schlegel had for nearly five years been discussing Romantic poetry. And he can not have derived from *Wilhelm Meister* a conception with which he was entirely familiar before he had read that romance. What befell in 1796 was neither the discovery, nor the invention, of the Romantic doctrine of art by Fr. Schlegel, but merely his conversion to it" (in *Essays in the History of Ideas* [Baltimore: Johns Hopkins Univ. Press, 1948], p. 203).

now appears as an earlier phase of the same self.[5] Thus in the first version of Keats's *Hyperion*, the last of the Titans embodies the Satanic (and by association Miltonic) figure with which the poetic consciousness first identifies itself, until it assumes its new form as Apollo (that is, Keats himself).

With Romanticism, then, the principle of the opposite appears as internal to the nature of the Romantic mode itself. For Classicism (or its descendent, neoclassicism), on the other hand, the opposite consists precisely of what cannot be internalized into the system of classical norms. This is perhaps most clearly seen in the development of classical style in music, where in Mozart, for example, the "dissonant" passages must first be resolved into a harmony before being integrated into their respective movements (as in the slow movements of the twentieth piano concerto, in D Minor, K. 466; the last of the "Haydn" quartets, no. 19 in C Major, K. 465; or the string quintet in G Minor, K. 516).[6] Eighteenth-century classicism determines what is proper to the classical mode and distinguishes it from what is not (researches into antiquity, for example, Winckelmann). For neoclassicism, clarity is achieved only with the determination of the whole theoretical basis of the aesthetic—which is to say: not only the concepts or norms, but their relation to each other. Such clarity assimilates the equivalent of Kant's definition of the rational: the connections between "the determination of things in their existence."

For Romanticism such clarity could not be possible, depending as this clarity does upon a conception of thought and its object as two distinct things. Thus the Kantian "determination" of the object defines that object in terms of conceptual categories—a determination fundamen-

<hr>

[5]Consider Friedrich Schlegel's celebrated definition of Romantic poetry in *Athenäum* fragment 116: "Die romantische Poesie ist eine progressive Universalpoesie. Ihre Bestimmung ist nicht bloss, alle getrennte Gattungen der Poesie wieder zu vereinigen, und die Poesie mit der Philosophie und Rhetorik in Berührung zu setzen. Sie will, und soll auch Poesie und Prosa, Genialität und Kritik, Kunstpoesie und Naturpoesie bald mischen, bald verschmelzen, die Poesie lebendig und gesellig, und das Leben und die Gesellschaft poetisch machen, den Witz poetisieren, und die Formen der Kunst mit gediegnem Bildungsstoff jeder Art anfüllen und sättigen, und durch die Schwingungen des Humors beseelen. . . . Die romantische Dichtart ist noch im Werden; ja das ist ihr eigentliches Wesen, dass sie ewig nur werden, nie vollendet sein kann. Sie kann durch keine Theorie erschöpft werden, und nur eine divinatorische Kritik dürfte es wagen, ihr Ideal charakterisieren zu wollen. Sie allein ist unendlich, wie sie allein frei ist, und das als ihr erstes Gesetz anerkennt, dass die Willkür des Dichters kein Gesetz über sich leide. Die romantische Dichtart ist die einzige, die mehr als Art, und gleichsam die Dichtkunst selbst ist: denn in einem gewissen Sinn ist oder soll alle Poesie romantisch sein" (*Krit. Ausgabe*, II, 182–83). See further, Hans Eichner, "Friedrich Schlegel's Theory of Romantic Poetry," *PMLA*, 71 (1956), 1018–41.

[6]See, e.g., the discussion of K. 466 in Charles Rosen's *The Classical Style* (New York: Viking, 1971), pp. 233, 235, esp. 235 on the Romanza; also H. C. Robbins Landon and Donald Mitchell, eds., *The Mozart Companion* (New York: Norton, 1969), pp. 259–60, on the same piece.

tally distinct from the object itself. For Fichte, Schelling, and Hegel (as well as, in differing degrees, Coleridge, Wordsworth, and Shelley), on the other hand, thought or rational apprehension identifies itself with its object.[7] This object is itself in a state of becoming. In Hegel, Being exists in a condition of becoming; the principle of becoming is immanent in Being. In the *Wissenschaft der Logik* we are told that "What is the truth is neither being nor nothing, but that being—does not pass over but has passed over—into nothing, and nothing into being" (*G.W.*, xxi, 69; A. V. Miller's trans.).

This assertion is significant not only in itself but for what it reveals about the nature of Romantic dialectic. In contrast to the Socratic *elenchus*, such dialectic presupposes the basic insufficiency of both sides of an opposition. Each must then "pass over" into its opposite. Thought apprehends the necessity for the passage of one into the other. Of Being and Nothing Hegel observes, "Their truth is therefore this *movement* of the unmediated disappearance of the one into the other" (*G.W.*, xxi, 69). Such "passing over" assumes the form of an "unmediated disappearance" inasmuch as it belongs to the very nature of each side to be absorbed into its opposite. That opposite is in fact something immanent within each side, which is to say: something that belongs to the very nature of thought, in which both are contained.

The opposition of Classic and Romantic is thus one in which each engenders its opposite out of itself, where the insufficiency of each leads to an apprehension of the necessity of passing over into its opposite. Goethe's *Torquato Tasso*, written at the height of his classicistic period, exemplifies the process. In the second act, lamenting the disappearance of the Golden Age, Tasso evokes a vivid picture of that pastoral era, in language reminiscent of the bucolic poets of antiquity. To his lament the Princess replies:

> My friend, the golden age is clearly over:
> Only the Good bring it back;
> And should I confess to you what I really think,
> The golden age, with which the poet
> Seeks to flatter us, the beautiful age, it existed,
> So it seems to me, as little as it now exists,
> And if it ever existed, so did it only exist
> As it can always exist for us again. (*Werke*, v, 100)

Through the Princess's speech, Goethe envisions a transcendence of the classical (or pastoral) ideal. The concept of the "Golden Age" is not to be equated with a specific historical period. It signifies rather a state of

---

[7]Most prominently, perhaps, for Emerson in ch. 12 of Coleridge's *Biographia Literaria*, with its plagiarized material from Schelling's *System des transscendentalen Idealismus*.

mind. It is the state in which the good men of all ages ("den Trefflich-sten," as Goethe calls them in his poem "Einlass") have striven to bring about. As such, it cannot be identified with a specific mode of life (such as the pastoral). It represents an ethos, a state of mind in which all things are perceived through the moral consciousness. Such a state, which according to Goethe has never yet become universal, remains a possibility as long as the human mind can imagine it as the object of its own aspirations. Traditional Classicism, with its identification of pastoral simplicity with the Golden Age as a mode of life, is thus rejected from the standpoint of a higher moral consciousness. Such consciousness embodies itself in the perception that the true Golden Age is not to be equated with a particular mode of life but rather with a more inward element, what I have called a state of mind.

That realization could come about, however, only through initial identification of the mind with the pastoral ideal. In Tasso's speech the pastoral world is presented in all its sensuous immediacy, as the object of the heart's innermost desires, its phenomenological richness intensified by the feeling of longing which imbues the poetic consciousness. Only through such total absorption in, and identification with, this aspect of the classical ideal (the life of leisure, *otium*) can its insufficiency become manifest. Only by dwelling within this ideal world, assuming all its sensuous detail as the embodiment of its own consciousness, does the mind become conscious of what it lacks: the moral element, the aspiration toward a higher state of feeling and thought.

Thus immersion in or identification with the classical ideal becomes the basis for its ultimate rejection. It is all the more remarkable that the process should occur in a work that appears at the height of Goethe's classicistic period. Such rejection encompasses not only the classical ideal but also the imaginary world it depicts and, by implication, even its style of representation. If the classical ideal, with its equation of happiness with leisure (*otium*) is rejected in favor of moral development, that rejection must also imply the rejection of a way of life (the pastoral) that had been identified with that ideal. Hence the necessity for depicting a plurality of modes of life, each embodying some aspect of moral truth—a prospect envisioned in Goethe's unfinished epic *Die Geheimnisse*.

With this Goethean attitude toward Classicism we may compare that of Emerson.[8] Like Goethe, he recognizes that the highest beauty is that of goodness. In his lecture "Modern Aspects of Letters" he asserts that

---

[8]On Emerson and Goethe, see, *inter alia*, Stanley Vogel, *German Literary Influences on the American Transcendentalists* (New Haven: Yale Univ. Press, 1955), pp. 88–93, 97–104; Margaret Fuller's translation of *Tasso*, though unpublished till 1874, perused by Emerson in manuscript (Vogel, pp. 135–36). On Emerson and Romanticism more generally, see Lawrence Buell's recent *New England Literary Culture* (Cambridge: Cambridge Univ. Press, 1986), pp. 69–83.

there are two ends to which "all works of literature are or should be composed." The first is Truth. The second is Beauty, "which includes goodness, as the highest beauty" (*EL*, 1, 382). Such goodness is more than simply the sum of the virtues (hence the absence of any real contradiction between such an assertion and Emerson's later remark on the "dowdiness of the good"). It belongs to the nature of goodness to give constantly out of the wealth of its highest and purest resources. From its moral perspective, the concept of an ideal life, such as that incarnated by Classicism in its pastoral ideal, was bound to appear as a limitation. It assumes that certain forms (whether of life or art) have on account of their intrinsic properties attained a perfection human nature cannot surpass. Hence whoever adopts the same forms can by so doing attain to the same perfection. This attitude runs contrary to the essential tendency of Emerson's thought. For him, as for Goethe, Tasso's evocation of the Golden Age represents a mode of life that remains at the level of the senses, unilluminated by any higher moral consciousness. Out of such consciousness there arises, correspondingly, new forms of both life and art.

In a similar fashion Emerson's reaction to Goethe's *Iphigenie auf Tauris* is of the utmost significance for what it reveals about his attitude toward Classicism. In his journal for April 1, 1836, Emerson writes: "Read yesterday Goethe's Iphigenia. A pleasing, moving, even heroic work yet with the great deduction of being an imitation of the antique. How can a great genius ⟨submit⟩ ↑ endure ↓ to make paste-jewels? . . . Yet when in the evening we read Sophocles, the shadow of a like criticism fell broad over almost all that is called modern literature. The words of Electra & Orestes are like actions. So live the thoughts of Shakspear. They have a necessary being. They live like men. To such productions it is obviously necessary that they should take that form which is then alive before the poet" (*JMN*, v, 148). Such forms are those the artist encounters in his own sphere and which constitute the dominant modes of expression for his epoch: for Jeremy Taylor, Barrow, South, and Donne, the sermon; for Fielding, the novel; for Burke, the parliamentary speech. These are the forms to which the artist possesses what we may call a "life-relation"—to borrow a term from Goethe. For Emerson, such forms breathe a genuine life only at the period of their origination: a law in his theory of "the life of forms" (Henri Focillon). On account of his absorption in such forms, an artist is able to impart a corresponding life to all elements of his work. That life proceeds not simply from the artist's own inventiveness but from the vividness of his form-consciousness, which is to say: consciousness of such forms as appropriate media for a specific mode of representation.

This form-consciousness cannot be transmitted from one period to another. Hence the necessity, in each age, for creating new forms. On account of his concept of form, Emerson's attitude must be described as anticlassicistic: he does not assert the intrinsic superiority of any particular form, but rather the appropriateness of adopting whatever corresponds most closely to the form-consciousness of a given age. At the same time he maintains a reverence for classical antiquity in all its manifestations: sculpture, architecture, literature, philosophy. For Emerson it is imperative to immerse oneself in the classic—not for the purpose of imitation but rather for liberation. Such liberation constitutes a necessary consequence of the immersion, because of the inevitable disparity in form-consciousness between oneself and the classic. Such form-consciousness, as we have seen, can arise only within the individual. It belongs to that individual's vital relation to his or her own age; in some sense, it corresponds to the form of his or her consciousness itself insofar as this is determined by historical circumstances. At the same time, form-consciousness represents the individual's response to the shaping influence of those circumstances. Such form-consciousness becomes the expression of a dialectic between internal and external, subjective and objective, in which each in some measure "passes over" into the other. Thus the external world that influences the mind is already determined in part by the form of consciousness itself. Conversely, that consciousness assumes in part the form it receives from the perception of that world.

But if the relation of mind and external world in determining form-consciousness enters into the mode of a dialectic, such is not the case in the relation between a creative mind and an antecedent classicism. The assimilation of such classicism, according to Emerson, can never produce the vital form-consciousness possessed by the original creators of such forms. Similarly, the apprehension of these forms by the creative mind in a later age can never be equivalent to that of their original source. This original apprehension consists partly of vital and historical elements that cannot be reproduced. But if complete and vital apprehension of classical form represents an impossibility, if the creative mind of a later age can never arrive at an adequate concept of such a form, neither can it pass by a dialectical impulse to its opposite, as in Romanticism. For Emerson, then, assimilation of Classicism can only preclude the imitation of classical form. In itself it neither engenders nor generates a particular form. As a result, the choice of form remains open.

From another perspective, however, an element of necessity affects the form the original creative mind produces. In the same journal entry quoted from above, Emerson indicates it: "But thus it always must happen that the true work of genius should proceed out of the wants & deeds of the age as well as the writer" (*JMN*, v, 148). For this reason it becomes of the utmost importance to determine the nature of "the present age" (the title of a series of Emerson's early lectures). For Emerson, the "present age" means the nineteenth century. From the perspective of the 1830s, the essential characteristics of nineteenth-century literature become increasingly apparent. We know of the influence of Mme de Staël's seminal work *De l'Allemagne* upon Emerson during his formative years. Here he could find a clear distinction between the characteristics of "modern" literature and those of the literature of antiquity, a distinction that also expresses the difference between Classic and Romantic: "The action or event was everything in antiquity; character occupies a more prominent place in modern times; and this anxious reflection, which devours us like the vulture of Prometheus, would have seemed nothing but madness, in the midst of the clear and pronounced relations which existed in the civil and social state of the ancients" (*O.C.*, x, 262). By a dialectical impulse, an irreconcilable dissatisfaction with the existing state of things gives rise to a longing for the infinite, for that which transcends all human limits, imparting to the mind a consciousness of the divine:

> We feel ourselves as liberated, through admiration, from the shackles of human destiny, and it seems we are being vouchsafed marvelous secrets, to free the soul forever from langor and decline. When we contemplate the starry heavens, where the scintillations of light are of universes like ours, where the brilliant dust of the Milky Way traces with worlds a route in the firmament, our thought loses itself in the infinite, our heart beats for the unknown, the immense, and we sense that it is only above the realm of terrestrial experiences that our true life should begin. (*O.C.*, xi, 402–403)

Through her close personal association with the Schlegel brothers, Friedrich and August Wilhelm, Mme de Staël had been informed of these ideas and others of the German Romantic circle. In his Vienna lectures of 1812–13 (published in 1816 as *Vorlesungen über dramatische Kunst und Literatur*), August Wilhelm Schlegel incorporates many of the same ideas into his description of the classicistic attitude: "The development of the Greeks was a perfect Nature-education. . . . Their entire art and poetry is the expression of a consciousness of this harmony of all the forces. They invented the poetics of joy" (*Krit. Schriften*, v, 23). A subsequent contrast between classic and modern leads to the conclusion: "So also, then, the poetry of the ancients was one of possession, ours one of longing; the former stands firmly upon the ground of the present; the latter vacillates between recollection and presentiment" (p. 25).

From these sources Emerson could obtain the characterization of the modern that appears in his 1839 lectures on "Literature" and subsequently in his *Dial* essay "Thoughts on Modern Literature": "The poetry and speculation of the age are marked by a certain philosophic turn, which discriminates them from the works of earlier times. . . . And this is called subjectiveness, as the eye is withdrawn from the object and fixed on the subject or mind" (*C.W.*, xii, 312–13). Later in the same essay he remarks: "Another element of the modern poetry akin to this subjective tendency, or rather the direction of that same on the question of re-sources, is the Feeling of the Infinite" (p. 316). In her *De l'Allemagne* Mme de Staël had asserted: "The enthusiasm that the *beau idéal* makes us feel, this emotion full of uneasiness and of purity all together, is excited by the feeling of the infinite" (*O.C.*, XI, 402). The "Feeling of the Infinite" thus appears as a source of poetic pleasure.

At this stage of his development, significantly, Emerson can unreser-vedly affirm the expression of a "subjective tendency" in literature. In the first of his two "Literature" lectures he had boldly declared to his audience: "I readily concede that a resolute and steadfast tendency of this sort appears in the modern literature. It is the new consciousness of the One Mind (to which all have a potential access and which is the Creator) which predominates in Criticism. It is the uprise of the soul and not a decline. It is the road to good and to beauty though not to the same beauty we admire in Homer and Chaucer" (*EL*, III, 214). By means of this passage a link is established between the new tendency in literature and the aim or objective of Emerson's own Transcendental idealism. The "subjective tendency" is not to be equated with mere concern for individual personality. It proceeds, rather, from the fact that "the indi-vidual soul feels its right to be no longer confounded with numbers but itself to sit in judgment on history and literature, and to constrain all facts and parties to stand their trial before it. And in this sense the mind is subjective" (*EL*, III, 214). Consequently a rejection of the poetry of Byron is in order: "I fear we hear too clearly out of all the poems of Lord Byron this plain prose Burden: *I am Byron the noble poet who am very clever but am not popular in London*" (p. 216).

By employing poetry to reveal the relation of all things to itself, the Mind establishes its own sovereignty in the realm of Nature. Nature exists not for itself but for Mind—a relationship Emerson had already expressed, most forcefully, in *Nature*. The relationship of Nature to Mind exists within Mind itself. Because the relationship is contained within Mind or consciousness, there must be a subjective element in the very representation of Nature, by which the Mind's pervasive influence makes itself felt. The image of Nature which appears in poetry is not Nature as it is in itself but as received into the Mind, a process in which the Mind not merely accepts impressions of sensory phenomena but shapes them according to its own nature and imaginative power. In the ideal poem it should be possible to witness its influence upon what it perceives as Nature, the "shaping spirit of Imagination" exerting itself and creating the Nature it sees from within itself. It is the Mind as depicted by Wordsworth, one

> That feeds upon infinity, that broods
> Over the dark abyss, intent to hear

Its voices issuing forth to silent light
In one continuous stream; a mind sustained
By recognitions of transcendent power,
In sense conducting to ideal form,
In soul of more than mortal privilege. (*The Prelude*, pp. 461–63)

In this regard it is significant that Emerson himself should point out that "the fame of Wordsworth is one of the most instructive facts in modern literature" (*EL*, III, 217). That fame, according to Emerson, is not due to his own "feeble poetic talents." Rather: "More than any poet his success has been not his own but that of the Idea or principle which possessed him and which he has rarely succeeded in adequately expressing" (p. 217). This Idea or principle is that of the sovereign nature of the mind, and the necessity of seeing the significance of all phenomena through their relation to it.

For Wordsworth the creative power of the imagination, its shaping influence upon external impressions, enables one to speak of it as something divine. For the early Emerson, in an even more immediate sense, the individual mind is in its innermost nature part of the divine Essence. As in Wordsworth there is the consciousness of its own Godlike power, the creative energy within itself that produces the picture of the external world or Nature and, at a higher or more transcendent level, thought. But where Wordsworth employs the imagery of voices and light to form the "recognitions of transcendent power," Emerson affirms the ideal of clarity. Like Goethe, he envisions the moment "wo du klar ins holde Klare schaust" (where you gaze clearly upon sweet clarity). This moment is, for Emerson, that in which one apprehends the Divine. The mind arrives at it when the Nature it creates from within itself becomes transparent, as if illuminated in a moment of Godlike clarity. Such illumination possesses a specific significance: it consists of the moment in which the mind sees its image of the external world proceeding from itself. At that moment all images disappear in the realization of its own Godlike essence. For Emerson, in the magical moment of apprehension, the individual mind becomes one with the divine, which represents nothing other than the permanence of such an apprehension.

By following the "subjective tendency" of modern literature to its limit, then, it becomes possible to attain a "new consciousness of the One Mind." Thus the Romanticism of a Wordsworth conduces to the Transcendentalism of an Emerson. But if the apprehension of the One Mind manifests itself from one aspect as truth, it is, from another perspective, beauty as well. Hence Emerson's promise to his audience that the subjective tendency of Romanticism constitutes "the road to good and to beauty though not to the same beauty we admire in Homer and Chaucer." The new beauty of "modern" literature comes from witnessing the presence of the Mind in Nature. One observes the process of seeing itself, as it were, in which the play of sound and color, form and light is suffused by thought, which creates from it a human picture. As Emerson remarks of Wordsworth: "His inspiring genius is as he has said, the still sad music of humanity" (EL, III, 217–18). In her De l'Allemagne, similarly, Mme de Staël had written: "One must, in order to conceive the true grandeur of lyric poetry, wander through reverie in the ethereal regions, forget the noise and tumult of the earth in listening to the celestial harmony, and consider the entire universe as a symbol of the emotions of the soul" (O.C., X, 255).

For the new Romantic aesthetic, then, Nature exists to give form and color to the emotions of the soul. On various occasions Emerson cites the Greek term κόσμος, which he translates as "beauty." By itself, the world is only "earth & water, rocks & sky." The mind's perception of it, the infusion of a subjective element into external Nature, transmutes it into a vision of beauty. As August Wilhelm Schlegel expresses it: "Sensuous impressions are supposed through their mysterious alliance with the higher feelings to become sanctified, as it were; the spirit, on the other hand, wants to embody symbolically its apprehensions or inexpressible insights in sensuous appearances" (Krit. Schriften, V, 26).

In one respect, the opposition between Classic and Romantic, or ancient and "modern" literature, had been defined as one between two fundamentally differing tendencies, the objective and subjective. In his Vorlesungen über dramatische Kunst und Literatur August Wilhelm Schlegel analyzes the assimilation in Greek art of mind into its object, the subjective into external Nature. The Romantic or "modern," on the other hand, assimilates Nature into mind, becomes the expression of the mind's innermost feelings and apprehensions.

The opposition between Classic and Romantic could also be set in a historical light. From that perspective, the transition from one to the other appears as a necessary development. Initially, the mind begins with a perception of the external world. The appearance of Classic art (that is, Greek art) corresponds to this phase. It represents the poetry of the "objective," of external Nature. Only at a later stage, as the mind becomes increasingly conscious of itself, does the "subjective" or Romantic become possible. It corresponds to an inward movement of that mind or consciousness. For Emerson such a movement may be said to reflect a progressive awareness of the divine essense or nature of Mind. As pagan religion had tended toward a divinization of Nature or the external (an interpretation Emerson would have encountered in A. W. Schlegel), so the truer or higher religion ought to represent the realization that "The kingdom of God is within you." By developing the "subjective" tendency, Romantic literature, from Emerson's perspective, makes possible an apprehension of the divine within oneself. We know of Emerson's rever-

..ce, attested to on numerous occasions throughout his journals and essays, for Coleridge as a critic and thinker. His homage to Coleridge summarizes what Emerson finds most praiseworthy in "modern" literature, an embodiment of the essential qualities of the Transcendentalist vision itself: "His eye was fixed upon Man's Reason as the faculty in which the very Godhead manifested itself or the Word was anew made flesh. His reverence for the Divine Reason was truly philosophical and made him regard every man as the most sacred object in the Universe, the Temple of Deity" (*EL*, I, 378).

## 23 *Margaret Fuller:*
## *Criticism and Consciousness*

For various reasons Margaret Fuller's criticism belongs among the significant achievements of American literature of the mid-nineteenth century, and, in particular, among the fruits of the German and English influence upon New England Transcendentalism.[1] The body of her criticism, scattered throughout different journals and only partially collected by Fuller herself in *Papers on Literature and Art* (1846), constitutes something more than an expression of Transcendentalist principles in literary criticism. Both historically and in terms of its content, it participates in a later phase of thought and consciousness, in which the original Transcendental impulse is transformed to produce modifications of earlier concepts, or perhaps more accurately, the expression of those concepts in new forms or with a different content from before.[2] Such modifications become apparent in the theory of criticism developed in the "Short Essay on Critics" and exemplified in other essays such as the brief "Dialogue" between a poet and critic, or—to take one of the longer efforts—the review of "Modern British Poets," consisting, appropriately enough, largely of reflections on the theory and practice of Romantic poetry.

In her "Short Essay on Critics" Margaret Fuller defines three classes of critics. The first consists of the "subjective"—to make use, as Fuller observes, "of a convenient term, introduced by our German benefac-

---

[1]For an evaluation, see René Wellek, *A History of Modern Criticism: 1750–1950* (New Haven: Yale Univ. Press, 1955–), III, 179.

[2]See Wellek's comment in the *History*: "In spirit she comes closest not to Goethe, with his universality, not to Emerson, with his rarefied vision, but rather to Bettina and George Sand—in short, to the generous, frank, and somewhat overfervid spirit of Young Germany and liberal France" (III, 181).

tors." This class includes all those who "state their impressions as they rise, of other men's spoken, written, or acted thoughts. They never dream of going out of themselves to seek the motive, to trace the law of another nature. . . . They love, they like, or they hate; the book is detestable, immoral, absurd, or admirable, noble, of a most approved scope; —these statements they make with authority. . . . To them it seems that their present position commands the universe" (*Papers*, pt. 1, p. 2).

It would be easy enough, given the allusion to the Germans and Fuller's fervent admiration for Goethe in particular, to infer from the present passage an implicit opposition between subjective and objective, Classic and Romantic, or ancient and modern tendencies in literature. We have already encountered the development of such a contrast in Goethe's *Maximen und Reflexionen* and A. W. Schlegel's *Vorlesungen über dramatische Kunst und Literatur*. With both of these, to be sure, Margaret Fuller was undoubtedly familiar. But the nature and motive of her argument point in another direction. The inadequacy of the purely subjective attitude does not imply, as it does for Goethe, the necessity of affirming its opposite, the objective or classic. Instead, the essential element of the subjective attitude manifests itself in what represents for her the highest critical perspective: the comprehensive. This element is the subjective consciousness, or—if viewed in relation to itself—self-consciousness. For Fuller, it is an intrinsic necessity of criticism that this consciousness should be brought into relation with itself, become self-consciousness. But the act of self-relation is one it accomplishes only by assimilating the external world, the objective, through experience. It must, so to speak, go out of itself in order to return with a deeper awareness, a sense of its relation to an external world. Its motive or purpose, to relate consciousness to itself through experience, appears in Schiller's *Über naive und sentimentalische Dichtung*.[3] Here Schiller's critique of the excesses of the idealist (a development of the sentimental attitude) displays an analogue to Margaret Fuller's description of subjective criticism: "The visionary abandons Nature from mere caprice, in order to be able to submit more freely to the wilfulness of the desires and moods of the imagination. Neither in the independence from physical necessities nor the absolution from the moral does it posit its freedom. The

---

[3]Significantly, few of the secondary sources touch upon Fuller's relation to Schiller. Much emphasis, on the other hand, has been placed upon her relationship to Goethe (Vogel, Pochmann, and an early work, Frederick Braun, *Margaret Fuller and Goethe* [New York: Holt, 1910]). Fuller herself contrasts Goethe with Schiller in her essay on the former (*Writings*, p. 248). For Transcendentalist uses of Schiller's "Über naive und sentimentalische Dichtung" specifically, see Lawrence Buell, *Literary Transcendentalism: Style and Vision in the American Renaissance* (Ithaca, N.Y.: Cornell Univ. Press, 1973), p. 267. And on Schiller's essay, A. O. Lovejoy, "Schiller and the Genesis of German Romanticism," rpt. in *Essays in the History of Ideas* (Baltimore: Johns Hopkins Univ. Press, 1948), pp. 207–27.

visionary thus denies not merely the human—he denies all character, he is completely without law, he is hence indeed nothing and also good for nothing" (*Schillers Werke*, xx, 503).

But the relationship between Schiller's essay and Margaret Fuller's appears most clearly if we consider her definitions of the other two classes of critics, the apprehensive and the comprehensive.[4] Of the former she says: "These can go out of themselves and enter fully into a foreign existence. They breathe its life; they live in its law; they tell what it meant, and why it so expressed its meaning. They reproduce the work of which they speak, and make it better known to us in so far as two statements are better than one" (*Papers*, pt. i, p. 3). The "law" (a concept that carries the same significance as Emerson's "laws of Nature" or "spiritual laws") under which the foreign existence (a work, an author) subsists makes possible its apprehension by another mind or consciousness. As with Coleridge (*Biographia Literaria*, ch. 12) and Emerson, laws express both the basic operations of Nature and the fundamental structure of the mind itself. Thus, by apprehending a foreign existence, we realize the essential similarity underlying all individual minds. Moreover, that apprehension also involves knowledge of the grounds or causes behind a particular production or expression: "what it meant, and why it so expressed its meaning."

Knowledge of causes suggests that apprehension is both something less, and something more, than the consciousness that inhabits the work itself. Such consciousness need not necessarily know its own cause, the motor or spring behind all its activity. Awareness of these causes defines apprehension as something less than that consciousness. By remaining outside the other—even in identifying itself with it—consciousness perceives the force or cause motivating it. Simultaneously, through its awareness of that cause, it assimilates not only the consciousness within the work but also the impulse producing it. The relationship between its own consciousness and that of the work is thus one of identity and difference simultaneously, or—to put it more specifically—of difference *through* identification. The movement of identification that creates an awareness of cause gives rise to the sense of its own becoming that separates consciousness from the consciousness within the work itself.

The relationship between the apprehensive consciousness and the existence it seeks to apprehend possesses a fundamental affinity with the

---

[4]It is interesting to compare Fuller's description of the three classes of critics—the subjective, the apprehensive, the comprehensive—with a remark of Hegel's in *The Phenomenology of Spirit*: "The easiest thing is, to judge that which has content and solidity; more difficult, to grasp it; most difficult, that which combines these functions, to give a representation of it" (*G.W.*, ix, 11). In her essay on Goethe for *The Dial*, speaking of *Wilhelm Meister*, Fuller observes: "To see all till he knows all sufficiently to put objects into their relations, then to concentrate his powers and use his knowledge under recognized conditions—such is the progress of man from apprentice to master" (*Writings*, p. 254).

relation between the naive attitude and the object it represents in Schiller's *Über naive und sentimentalische Dichtung.* "There are moments in our life," Schiller says, "when we give a kind of love and a touching regard to Nature in plants, minerals, animals, landscapes, just as to human nature in children, in the customs of country people and of the primitive world, not because they benefit our senses, nor because they satisfy our understanding or taste (with both the opposite can often occur) but rather simply *because they are Nature*" (*Schillers Werke*, xx, 413). That we bestow upon objects of Nature "a kind of love and a touching regard" "simply *because they are Nature*" suggests we are drawn to them not through the effect such objects have upon us but rather through consciousness's active identification with them: "they are Nature." And when consciousness has reached the standpoint where it can make such a statement and find it sufficient, it will at that moment have assimilated itself to Nature, so that in expressing it, it simultaneously affirms it.

Like apprehensive criticism, this state of consciousness both identifies itself with, and in some sense transcends, its object. We give objects of Nature a type of love and a touching regard because we are conscious in identifying ourselves with them of our simultaneous difference from them, such that our identification is not a simple equation but an affirmation that inspires the affection we feel. The apprehensive critic's "naive" attitude is not therefore one of complete identification, in which consciousness simply becomes its object. Rather, the consciousness of such identification is itself part of the process, as well as the essence of the "naive" or apprehensive attitude.

Just as the "apprehensive" critic exemplifies in some respects the "naive" attitude, so is it possible to perceive in Fuller's description of the "comprehensive" critic what Schiller had called the "sentimental" perspective. Of this third class of critics Margaret Fuller writes: "Then there are the comprehensive, who must also be apprehensive. They enter into the nature of another being and judge his work by its own law. But having done so, having ascertained his design and the degree of his success in fulfilling it, thus measuring his judgment, his energy, and skill, they do also know how to put that aim in its place, and how to estimate its relations. And this the critic can only do who perceives the analogies of the universe, and how they are regulated by an absolute, invariable principle" (*Papers*, pt. i, p. 3).

Significantly the "comprehensive" class also possess the "apprehensive" quality, which forms the basis of their "comprehensive" faculty. In one respect, the comprehensive movement of consciousness is similar to that which occurs in apprehension: like the latter, it too involves identification, but having achieved this, it then proceeds to reflect upon the nature with which it identifies in relation to higher or universal principles. That relation consists of treating the nature or being with which it identifies itself as subject and object simultaneously—subject insofar as it becomes one with that being, object insofar as it then considers the being with which it identifies as merely the subject of its identification. In other words, instead of merely assimilating itself to another nature or being, the comprehensive consciousness ultimately absorbs that other being into itself, by treating it simply as an object of consciousness.

With this reflection upon consciousness and its objects, Fuller's description of the comprehensive class of critics manifests its fundamental similarity with Schiller's characterization of the "sentimental" attitude: "This individual *reflects* upon the impression the object makes on him, and solely upon this reflexion is the feeling based, in which he situates himself and in which he situates us. The object is here related to an idea, and upon that relation alone rests his poetical power. The sentimental poet therefore has invariably to do with two conflicting representations and impressions, with actuality as limit and with his idea as the infinite, and the mixed feeling which he raises is always produced from this double source" (*Schillers Werke*, xx, 441).

The reflection upon an object of consciousness (*der Gegenstand*) creates a relation between that object and an idea. All the poetical force of the sentimental, Schiller goes on to say, rests upon such a relation. As with Margaret Fuller, consciousness first identifies itself with its object, then, through its difference from it, finds itself impelled to express the relation of that object to what she calls "an absolute, invariable principle." For Schiller, there is a pathetic, moving eloquence in their relation: never can the object attain the nature of the idea, in which reposes the infinitude of the purely ideational. Consciousness here embodies, implicitly, a state of striving or aspiration: having informed or identified itself with an object, it then attempts in relating that object to an idea to pass from finite to infinite, to transcend the material element of its own content through realization of the purely ideational. The inevitable failure of its attempt engenders the feeling of the sentimental: a sense of the unbridgeable distance between finite and infinite, the material object and the idea to which consciousness seeks to raise it.

With Margaret Fuller's concept of a comprehensive criticism, the pathetic element could not exactly enter into the picture in the same fashion. In her view, the purpose of criticism can only be to establish the true nature and quality of the work of art through its relations to external objects. An element of "objectivity" thus replaces the subjective feeling that informs Schiller's definition of the sentimental: instead of the emotion that infuses or pervades consciousness from a sense of the distance between its object and an ideal, the comprehensive critical consciousness seeks only to attain a sense of that relation or distance itself. With the attainment of such a sense, its activity is complete. Like the Schillerian consciousness, it comes to rest finally in a sense of its relation to itself (insofar as it first identifies itself with an object and then determines that object's true nature through its relation to external things). But unlike Schiller, Fuller does not view the relation to oneself as the source of a particular feeling. One is tempted to ask: how could mere "objectivity," a sense of the proper relation of the object to others, become an ideal for consciousness? Perhaps, in affirming such objectivity, the Goethean element or influence, so prominent in all the rest of Margaret Fuller's literary enterprise but so conspicuously absent here, manages by this means to enter into the picture after all.

# 24    Shelley, Goethe, Adam Müller, Melville: The Concept of Tradition

In Keats's *Hyperion,* which concerns the issue of poetic succession from Milton to the Romantics, the young Apollo, appearing at the end of book III as a symbol of the new Romantic poet, is made to exclaim: "Knowledge enormous makes a God of me" (*Poems,* p. 355). His knowledge encompasses "Names, deeds, gray legends, dire events, rebellions, / Majesties, sovran voices, agonies, / Creations and destroyings" which "all at once / Pour into the wide hollows of my brain, / And deify me" (pp. 355–56). The sudden nature of this influx of knowledge is significant. It defines him as the successor to or inheritor of a tradition.[1] As such, he does not experience that tradition in its historical development. Instead, he receives it in its totality as something external to individual consciousness. By distinguishing his own consciousness from that which informs the tradition, he typifies the situation of the Romantic poet. The fusion of his consciousness with that of tradition even leads to a moment of epiphanic vision, "as if some blithe wine / Or bright elixir peerless I had drunk, / And so become immortal" (*Poems,* p. 356).

Superficially, Romanticism appears as a rebellion against tradition (Classicism or whatever). On a deeper level it attempts to apprehend that tradition in its totality, where the form assumed by tradition becomes inseparable from that of consciousness. Despite his classicizing tendencies, Keats is characteristically Romantic in regarding the relation between tradition and consciousness as problematic. The knowledge of tradition that divinizes consciousness reveals at the same time the neces-

---

[1]For further commentary, Walter Jackson Bate, *John Keats* (Cambridge: Harvard Univ. Press, 1963), pp. 403–5, and Stuart Sperry, *Keats the Poet* (Princeton: Princeton Univ. Press, 1973), pp. 194–95.

sity for creative inspiration, which must overcome such consciousness in order to appropriate its power.[2]

In one respect at least, Shelley is less radical than Keats: he does not regard the knowledge contained within tradition as external to—and hence a danger for—the individual poetic consciousness. For him, tradition exists in and through individual consciousness. We have seen how he adheres to Berkeley's idealistic dictum: "esse est percipi." This equation applies to the Shelleyan concept of tradition as well. Tradition exists through its perception by the individual mind: the ideal form that tradition assumes corresponds to the nature of the mind itself. In his *Defence of Poetry* Shelley asserts:

> But corruption must have utterly destroyed the fabric of human society before Poetry can ever cease. The sacred links of that chain have never been entirely disjoined, which descending through the minds of many men is attached to those great minds, whence as from a magnet the invisible effluence is sent forth, which at once connects, animates and sustains the life of all. . . . And let us not circumscribe the effects of the bucolic and erotic poetry within the limits of the sensibility of those to whom it was addressed. They may have perceived the beauty of those immortal compositions, simply as fragments and isolated portions: those who are more finely organized, or born in a happier age, may recognize them as episodes to that great poem, which all poets, like the co-operating thoughts of one great mind, have built up since the beginning of the world. (Reiman and Powers, p. 493)

For Shelley, the ideal totality of which tradition consists has no existence in itself.[3] The formation of such a totality, which occurs in the individual mind, represents a creative act for which only certain indi-

---

[2]Thus the situation of the young poet who receives Moneta's charge in *The Fall of Hyperion*: "If thou canst not ascend / These steps, die on that marble where thou art." The poet then feels "the tyranny / Of that fierce threat, and the hard task proposed. / Prodigious seem'd the toil . . ." (*Poems*, pp. 480–81). His anxiety, presumably, arises from the difficulty of overcoming tradition and the consequent anxiety which the knowledge of that difficulty creates—on which, see Walter Jackson Bate, *The Burden of the Past and the English Poet* (Cambridge: Harvard Univ. Press, 1970), and Harold Bloom, "Keats and the Embarrassments of Poetic Tradition," in his *Ringers in the Tower* (Chicago: Univ. of Chicago Press, 1971), pp. 131–42; more generally, Thomas McFarland, *Originality & Imagination* (Baltimore: Johns Hopkins Univ. Press, 1985), esp. chs. 1–2 and pp. 85–6, equating originality with individuality. Keats internalizes that difficulty within the poetic consciousness in such a fashion that its overcoming assumes the form of a symbolic assimilation of that tradition—when the poet ascends the steps to Moneta's shrine, he does so in a manner that deliberately recalls Dante's ascent in the *Purgatorio*.

[3]For further commentary on this and other aspects of the *Defence*, see Earl R. Wasserman, *Shelley: A Critical Reading* (Baltimore: Johns Hopkins Univ. Press, 1971), pp. 205–206, and M. H. Abrams, *The Mirror and the Lamp* (London: Oxford Univ. Press, 1953), pp. 126–31.

viduals (poets or those with a poetic sensibility) possess the capacity. Accordingly, tradition becomes a precarious possession: depending upon perception for its existence, it becomes actual only in those moments of its realization by a poetic mind. Its existence is therefore simultaneous with that of the poem or act of poetic creation itself, since the formative impulse that gives rise to the poem is the same as that which enables the mind to see disparate moments of consciousness (the content of individual poems) as forming a larger totality.[4] Elsewhere in the *Defence* Shelley avows even more explicitly the creative nature of the mind's apprehension of tradition. By unifying discrete moments of perception or consciousness, it embodies the essence of all creative processes:

All things exist as they are perceived: at least in relation to the percipient. . . . But poetry defeats the curse which binds us to be subjected to the accident of surrounding impressions. And whether it spreads its own figured curtain or withdraws life's dark veil from before the scene of things, it equally creates for us a being within our being. . . . It reproduces the common universe of which we are portions and percipients, and it purges from our inward sight the film of familiarity which obscures from us the wonder of our being. It compels us to feel that which we perceive, and to imagine that which we know. It creates anew the universe after it has been annihilated in our minds by the recurrence of impressions blunted by reiteration. It justifies that bold and true word of Tasso—*Non merita nome di creatore, se non Iddio ed il Poeta.* [None deserves the name of Creator except God and the Poet]. (Reiman and Powers, pp. 505–6)

The act of creation Shelley ascribes to poetry is synonymous with a new perception of the external universe. In poetic perception we become conscious of the act of perceiving itself, the formative power of the mind as it unifies disparate impressions into a coherent whole. The self-awareness of the perceiving faculty in the process of perception alters the very nature of our knowledge of things: "It compels us to feel that which we perceive, and to imagine that which we know."

Since all objects exist only insofar as they are perceived, to perceive them in this fashion is to impart to them a higher reality than that we ordinarily encounter. Here Shelley reintroduces the Platonic concept of degrees of reality, ascending to the level of the purely ideal. In contrast to Platonism, however, the Shelleyan scheme accords the highest degree

---

[4]In Hart Crane's great poem "The Broken Tower," the precariousness of the Shelleyan consciousness of tradition becomes fully evident: "And so it was I entered the broken world / To trace the visionary company of love, its voice / An instant in the wind (I know not whither hurled) / But not for long to hold each desperate choice" (*The Complete Poems and Selected Letters and Prose of Hart Crane*, ed. Brom Weber [New York: Liveright, 1966], p. 193).

of reality to that which is most intensely perceived, rather than that which by its nature corresponds most closely to the ideal.[5] For Shelley, the poetic *perception* of an object suffices to raise it to the ideal plane. Such perception vouchsafes to the spectator a moment of pure transparence, in which he feels the act of perception itself, the element of mind that apprehends and, in so doing, creates the object. This element is consciousness. In experiencing it the poet glimpses the presence of the divine:

> Poetry is the record of the best and happiest moments of the best and happiest minds. We are aware of evanescent visitations of thought and feeling sometimes associated with place or person, sometimes regarding our own mind alone, and always arising unforeseen and departing unbidden, but elevating and delightful beyond all expression: so that even in the desire and the regret they leave, there cannot but be pleasure, participating as it does in the nature of its object. It is as it were the interpenetration of a diviner nature through our own. (Reiman and Powers, p. 504)

The "interpenetration of a diviner nature through our own" comes about when we are liberated from the limits of our individual subjective impressions. At such moments we become aware of the nature of consciousness itself. For Shelley, then, pure consciousness transcends the subjective, which consists of a partial or imperfect awareness.

Such a concept of consciousness and its relation to poetic creation also helps to elucidate the Shelleyan idea of tradition. Like poetry, tradition must be "the record of the best and happiest moments of the best and happiest minds." In its totality such a record might be said to consist of a series of Wordsworthian "spots of time." Here the Shelleyan term *happiness* is not to be equated with the ordinary feeling of contentment. It arises from the experience of a "divine visitation," the glimpse vouchsafed to the mind of a universal consciousness.[6] At such moments the mind receives not only the vision within the poem but the totality and nature of all perception, of which the individual poem forms a part. Tradition, then, which exists only through the poetic mind's apprehension of it, is itself finally only a moment of consciousness, but—as distinguished from the individual "moments" composing it—one of universal consciousness. Hence Shelley's description of it as "that great

[5]For the relation of Shelleyan idealism to British empiricism and skeptical tradition, cf. C. E. Pulos, *The Deep Truth: A Study of Shelley's Scepticism* (Lincoln: Univ. of Nebraska Press, 1954). Pulos seems to me not to distinguish sufficiently, however, between early and later stages of Shelley's thought: see pp. 52–53, where he attempts to read *Hellas*, ll. 795–801, as a rejection of Berkeley's concept of reality as mind—here a careful examination of the text would seem to indicate precisely the opposite.

[6]On the "One Mind" and individual existence, see Wasserman, pp. 180–84.

poem, which all poets, like the co-operating thoughts of one great mind, have built up since the beginning of the world." This universal consciousness makes possible an awareness of all poems as "co-operating thoughts of one great mind." Simultaneously, it forms the element of creative perception in each of those poems. Thus, for Shelley, tradition is not simply consciousness of the totality of poetry but also of the element sustaining that totality. Through its apprehension of the poetic tradition, the mind ultimately experiences the nature of the perceiving consciousness itself.

If we compare the Shelleyan notion of tradition with that of Keats, we notice the different significance Shelley ascribes to the subjective and to the relation of the individual consciousness to tradition. For Keats in *Hyperion* the subjective had been inseparable from the nature of consciousness: it signifies a capacity to apprehend that includes feeling or passion, which in turn depend upon the individual's specific nature. For Shelley, on the other hand, the subjective represents simply a limited or imperfect form of consciousness—in its universal or pure form, consciousness ceases to be subjective. As a result, consciousness becomes for Shelley identical with tradition. For Keats it confronts and undergoes the problematic experience of tradition (an external consciousness or knowledge), which transforms it into a higher form of the same consciousness.

In both instances, tradition appears as a totality. With Keats, such a totality is endowed with a power enabling it to act upon the poetic consciousness. For Shelley, by perceiving the coherence of certain ideal moments, the mind universalizes itself. Neither appears to consider tradition in terms of individual voices or influences (the problem of Milton as a predecessor-figure for the English Romantics remains outside of these considerations). In addition, the role of consciousness in both poets is that of a passive receiving of phenomena or impressions; in Shelley's case specifically, perception conforms to the framework established by English epistemology from Locke through Hume.

From another perspective, however, it would be possible to view consciousness in terms of forces (strivings) or drives. Goethe's idea of tradition assimilates both tendencies: the notion of individual influences, and the determination of consciousness in terms of forces and aspirations. The late poem "Eins und Alles" declares:

> Sympathetically lead the good spirits,
> Gently guiding, the highest masters,
> To that which creates and created all things.
> And to create the created
> Is not thereby to arm itself with the rigid,

Effecting perpetually, the living Act.
And what was not, now wants to become
Pure suns, colorful worlds,
In no instance may it rest. (*Werke,* 1, 369)

In "Symbolum" the action of these "good spirits" is described:

Yet from above call
The voices of the spirits,
The voices of the masters:
"Neglect not to exercise
The powers of the good." (*Werke,* 1, 340)

A ceaseless activity or impulse pervades Goethe's world, imparting to all things an ascending movement. The "eternally living Act" of the World-Soul animates each and every individual or part. In such a universe there can be no being, only becoming. The activity of that world, seen in its highest aspect, is creative. From the creative source of all things, that which "creates and created all," a generative power passes into individual beings who, by responding to its influence, initiate a movement of return to their source. In this process the "good spirits" or "highest masters" participate: not only by sympathy, but by actively taking a part (*teilnehmend*).

The participation of good spirits from all ages in the creative activity of living individuals suggests that for Goethe tradition is in effect continuous with the present.[7] The concept of the chorus enters into the picture here. The conclusion to *Faust* presents different "choirs" or choruses of angels, culminating in the "chorus mysticus" that closes the drama. In certain respects, the role of the chorus in Goethe's allegorical-symbolic poem bears a resemblance to that of Mozart's *Magic Flute,* encompassing both a responsive affirmation to the soul's highest aspirations and a secret knowledge that cannot be revealed in its entirety to those dwelling in the sphere of earthly existence. Hence Goethe's predilection for depicting the influence of tradition in terms of voices—"Yet from above call / The voices of the spirits, / The voices of the masters." These voices constitute spiritual presences for the creative individuals who attend to them. The concept of the predecessor as a spiritual influence, however,

---

[7]For an overview of Goethe's relation to tradition, E. R. Curtius, "Fundamental Features of Goethe's World," in his *Essays on European Literature,* trans. Michael Kowal (Princeton: Princeton Univ. Press, 1973), pp. 73–91. Similarly, for Goethe's concept of "world literature," Fritz Strich, *Goethe and World Literature,* trans. C. A. M. Sym (1949; rpt. Port Washington, N.Y.: Kennikat Press, 1972), pp. 3–16. For Goethe's relation specifically to philosophical tradition, see Karl Viëtor, *Goethe the Thinker,* trans. Bayard Quincy Morgan (Cambridge: Harvard Univ. Press, 1950), pp. 59–76.

is overshadowed by a larger presence containing both predecessor and successor: the World-Soul that "creates and created all things."

Both tradition and the successor who feels its influence express a common creative aspiration. In fact, one may say that for Goethe influence is nothing else than the transmission of the creative impulse from one individual to another. In this respect he differs from both Keats and Shelley, each of whom, in their differing ways, associate influence with consciousness as the passive recipient of knowledge or awareness. Here one must accord a place to the German Romantic notion of the soul's animation by various "drives." This notion achieves special prominence in Schiller's *On the Aesthetic Education of Man,* which devotes particular attention to the form-drive and play-drive (*Formtrieb, Spieltrieb*) as constituents of the aesthetic process.[8] The concept of the drive or *Trieb* associates itself with that of force, which evokes the world of *Naturphilosophie* and the Goethean analogy between physical and spiritual forces. By its very nature, a force seeks equilibrium through fulfilment of its innate tendency. In human terms such a tendency assumes the form of aspiration or striving. The Goethean concept of tradition is thus in its essence anticlassicistic. What it embodies is not conformity to a norm but a ceaseless striving that influences by bestowing the creative impulse upon a successor.

For Classicism, tradition tends to be associated with form. Form represents a containing of energies: in Racine, restraint achieves a particular poignancy when the suppressed energies are those of feeling or passion. The submission of desire to sacred obligation in *Bérénice* possesses such an effect. But Goethe, despite his classicistic tendencies, cannot conceive of tradition in terms of form-restraint. According to his *Weltanschauung,* it is the nature of all things to be creative, and tradition itself is finally but the continuity of the creative process.

Before passing to Melville, it remains for us to consider one other voice (to use a Goethean term) from German Romanticism. In 1805 Adam Müller delivers his *Vorlesungen über die deutsche Wissenschaft und Literatur.* From these lectures emerges a concept of tradition differing not only from Goethe's but also from that of the Schlegels.[9] Informing the discussion throughout are a literary-historical perspective and consciousness: "The whole present world is accordingly a great tradition of all earlier situations, and when the past moreover leaves behind a letter, ruins, a genuine well-preserved sign of each of its heroes, its circum-

---

[8] See esp. the "eleventh" and "twelfth" letters, pp. 76–82, in the Wilkinson and Willoughby edition.

[9] See, for more details, Oskar Walzel, *Adam Müllers Aesthetik,* in his *Romantisches* (Bonn: L. Rohrscheid, 1934).

stances, its acts, so is this only to be grasped, by considering it within that tradition, i.e., within the countless variations which its former spirit, its senses have endured, descending down to the present time" (p. 140). More briefly: "Only in tradition does the letter live, and the letter strengthens the tradition" (p. 150).

Like Goethe, Adam Müller envisions tradition as continuous with the present. In one respect, he goes even further, calling "the whole present world" "a great tradition of all earlier situations." The statement suggests that our present consciousness is in essence coextensive with that of tradition. In fact, however, Adam Müller anticipates Matthew Arnold's later description of modernity when he speaks of the heroes, circumstances, and deeds of the past as "a letter, some ruin or other, a genuine well-preserved sign" for those who live in the present. The remnants of the past, although actually existing in the present, have become opaque, symbols whose significance, at first glance, is unclear. They are to be understood only by assimilating them into the history from which they have emerged. In the process, it becomes necessary to trace the "countless variations which [tradition's] former spirit, its senses have endured, descending down to the present time." In so doing, we arrive at their true significance, which represents the result of a historical development, of which they form a part. Such a result endows them not with a single significance but an accretion of different significances. It produces a temporal or historical totality that can be grasped only in the act of historical apprehension.

The historical totality which comes into existence through such an act of apprehension is tradition. It consists of a sense or consciousness of the process of cultural accretion itself, that process by which the life of a symbol at one phase of its development passes into the succeeding phase. This life includes its "spirit" and "sense," the totality of aspiration expressed in it, its meaning in relation to the whole of which it forms a part. The "life" of the work of art continues only within tradition— which is to say: within a consciousness of the totality that produces it. At the same time, according to Adam Müller, "the letter strengthens the tradition." How does it do this? By giving form to the apprehending consciousness. Here form suggests that consciousness endows the work with its significance. In this sense, form establishes the link between one age and another. We have spoken already of the modernity implicit in this aspect of Adam Müller's notion of tradition. To conceive of the work of art as a form within tradition implies that, at various moments, consciousness recedes from an object it had previously informed. What expresses the totality of its aspiration at a prior moment then ceases to do so, and as a result the form becomes capable of fulfilling the same role for another, later consciousness.

I have dwelt on these differing notions of tradition in order to isolate various aspects of Melville's attitude toward it. To arrive at a precise description of his view is more difficult than for the other figures discussed, if only because of the lack of any sustained or systematic pronouncements in his oeuvre. One would also have to take into account Melville's own shifting moods and emphases, as well as the difficulties created by the irony pervading so many of his later works. Nevertheless, one passage from *Pierre* merits particular attention. Late in the novel, as he gradually realizes the true nature of his attraction to Isabel, Pierre attempts to express his insights. Commenting on Pierre's book, Melville observes:

> He did not see that there is no such thing as a standard for the creative spirit; that no one great book must ever be separately regarded, and permitted to domineer with its own uniqueness upon the creative mind; but that all existing great works must be federated in the fancy; and so regarded as a miscellaneous and Pantheistic whole; and then, —without at all dictating to his own mind, or unduly biasing it any way, —thus combined, they would prove simply an exhilarative and provocative to him. He did not see, that even when thus combined, all was but one small mite, compared to the latent infiniteness and inexhaustibility in himself; that all the great books in the world are but the mutilated shadowings-forth of invisible and eternally unembodied images in the soul; so that they are but the mirrors, distortedly reflecting to us our own things; and never mind what the mirror may be, if we would see the object, we must look at the object itself, and not at its reflection. (*Writings*, VII, 284)

At first glance, the impression conveyed can easily be one of parody, specifically of Emerson. One is struck especially by the assertion that "all existing great works must be federated in the fancy; and so regarded as a miscellaneous and Pantheistic whole." The result suggests a confusing medley of themes and motifs. To clarify matters, it is necessary to consider each of the elements separately.

Despite Melville's knowledge of Coleridge, there is no reason to assume his use of *fancy* rather than *imagination* carries any negative connotation: Hawthorne, also familiar with Coleridge, often employs *fancy* for the imagination (in using the term *fancy* Melville may also, of course, have been influenced by Hawthorne). The "Pantheistic whole" must be juxtaposed against Melville's earlier description of the "Pantheistic master-spell, which eternally locks in mystery and in muteness the universal subject world." Here the "Pantheistic" element is that of consciousness. The "Pantheistic whole" consists of the totality of "existing great works" which are held together in the authorial consciousness. Its "miscellaneous" character results from the mode in which the imagination preserves such works in the memory, dissolving them into discrete elements that it recombines into new creations.

With regard to the passage as a whole, Melville's oft-quoted letter to Evert Duyckinck (March 3, 1849) is especially significant. The passage from *Pierre* had asserted simultaneously the need for both tradition and independence. The same attitudes inform Melville's remarks on Emerson in the Duyckinck letter. It seems particularly appropriate for Melville to discuss Emerson here, since in the passage from *Pierre* his relation to Emerson is precisely what is called into question. To Duyckinck, Melville points out the dependence of all authors or thinkers upon tradition: "The truth is that we are all sons, grandsons, or nephews or great-nephews of those who go before us. No one is his own sire" (*Letters*, p. 78). At the same time, he asserts his independence: "Nay, I do not oscillate in Emerson's rainbow, but prefer to hang myself in mine own halter than swing in any other man's swing."[10]

These indications suggest the attitudes in the passage from *Pierre* as Melville's own. They express a relation to tradition different from those of the Romantics discussed earlier. In diverse ways Romanticism had established a relation between the individual mind and tradition in terms of the nature of consciousness. For Keats tradition appears as the influx of knowledge into individual consciousness, for Shelley the perception of a universal consciousness. To both poets, the form of the relation is ultimately one of fusion between tradition and consciousness, a fusion that alters the nature of consciousness. For Melville, on the other hand, the individual mind *is* in a sense the universal consciousness. Hence his appeal to the "Pantheistic master-spell, which eternally locks in mystery and in muteness the universal subject world." This is not to say that solipsism is abolished—rather, the same subjective element is made omnipresent for each individual consciousness. Since the element is universal, it becomes, for precisely that reason, objective. Here, as elsewhere, Melville recurs to his favorite notion of consciousness or the self as involving various levels or degrees. In short, it possesses "depth." Just as, in *Moby-Dick*, he had sought to evoke the "deep, blue, bottomless soul, pervading mankind and nature," so now in *Pierre* he characterizes the process of self-anatomy as a "going down into oneself." For Melville, the self becomes in its deepest depths objective. Thus the subjective contains the objective within itself: to attain an objective state of consciousness is to produce or make visible the subjective essence of the self.

This is the task tradition sets itself: "all the great books in the world are but the mutilated shadowings-forth of invisible and eternally unembodied images in the soul." As a result, tradition appears as something

---

[10]For commentary on this letter, see Sealts, "Melville and Emerson's Rainbow," pp. 251–53 in his *Pursuing Melville, 1940–1980* (Madison: Univ. of Wisconsin Press, 1982).

subjective. It attempts to reveal the subjective essence of consciousness, the self's essential nature, and in so doing manifests its own one-sidedness or incompleteness. The roles Shelley ascribes to the individual mind and tradition are reversed: now the individual mind is equated with the universal consciousness, which tradition attempts to fathom and portray.

In Goethe, the omnipresence of the World-Soul, "which creates and has created all things," counteracts tradition's too-dominant influence. The chorus of "good spirits" or "highest masters" imparts to their successors a creative impulse proceeding from the source of all creation. For Melville the universal subjective consciousness fulfills a similar role: both individual mind and tradition issue from it, and its nature governs all their activity. At the same time, like Keats, Melville remains quite conscious of the possibility that tradition (in the form of a powerful predecessor-figure like Milton) may threaten to overwhelm the individual. His response is to view tradition not as consisting of discrete influences but as a totality, a "miscellaneous and Pantheistic whole." It implies the assimilation of each work into consciousness, the universal Pantheistic element. The works "federated in the fancy" or dissolved in the medium of authorial consciousness lose their proper nature to yield up elements for the imaginative faculty. In so doing, they assume the role Adam Müller had accorded to the "letter" or "form" of works in tradition, experiencing a loss of their original significance. For Melville, however, unlike Adam Müller, this loss of significance is not the prelude to renewed comprehension of the works within tradition, but rather to original creation. For him, the creative impulse originates in an awareness of their imperfection—they are "but the mutilated shadowings-forth," the "mirrors, distortedly reflecting to us our own things." As such they nevertheless serve to inspire, acting, like Goethe's chorus of spirit-voices, as "an exhilarative and provocative." The totality or "Pantheistic whole" they form must be understood, like Goethe's, as a realm of striving or aspiration. Like the subjective consciousness, with its subliminal drives, such striving seeks fulfillment, but one that is, finally, only the objectifying of that profounder universe of aspiration and desire which it represents within itself.

# PART VIII

# Epilogue: The Question
# of Representation

# 25 _Shelley_

In his essay "Über das Studium der Griechischen Poesie" Friedrich Schlegel, speaking of the intrinsic capacities and weaknesses of various literary genres, observes: "There is a type of modern drama which one may call _lyrical._ Not on account of individual lyrical parts: for each beautiful dramatic whole is combined or composed from purely lyrical elements; rather a poem in dramatic form, whose unity however is a musical mood or a lyrical analogy—the dramatic expression of a lyrical inspiration" (_Krit. Ausgabe,_ I, 240–41).

As an example he cites Shakespeare's _Romeo and Juliet,_ which is "only a romantic sigh over the fleeting brevity of youthful joy; a beautiful threnody, that this newest destiny so quickly fades away." To speak of Shakespeare's tragedy as "a poem in dramatic form"—perhaps this could occur only in an epoch in which the very concept of genre itself experiences profound transformations, by which it ceases to characterize the essence of a literary work and becomes merely one of its aspects. Out of the dissolution of genre-consciousness—a dissolution brought about, apparently, by its heightening or intensification through eighteenth-century literary theory (as though increased consciousness of form were the necessary prelude to its dissolution)—new possibilities could in turn emerge. In particular, literature can now aspire to the permanence of the fixed image or visual symbolism—in a word, to the timelessness of the pictorial arts, based upon a single, nontemporal aesthetic configuration or form. Thus drama, with its traditional development toward a peripeteia and subsequent denouement, now finds itself faced with the prospect of nondevelopmental form, either through the fixation achieved by visual symbolism within the work, or the transformation of the whole into a single lyrical expression—such as that envisaged by Friedrich Schlegel. Formally speaking, such transformations imply a diminution of the intrinsic significance of form. Form that had in classical

405

tragedy (Corneille or Racine) governed the expressive content and even the thematic significance of the work, now becomes merely an accessory to its expressive possibilities. The Romantic ideal of a fusion of form and content turns form itself into an expressive element, such as restraint upon (hence intensification of) the lyrical feeling or emotion.

In Shelley's *Cenci* this possibility achieves realization. His preface to the work attests to Shelley's awareness of its radical nature in this respect. Speaking of the relation in drama between imagery or poetry and the passions, he writes:

> I have avoided with great care in writing this play the introduction of what is commonly called mere poetry, and I imagine there will scarcely be found a detached simile or a single isolated description, unless Beatrice's description of the chasm appointed for her father's murder should be judged to be of that nature.
>
> In a dramatic composition the imagery and the passion should interpenetrate one another, the former being reserved simply for the full development and illustration of the latter. Imagination is as the immortal God which should assume flesh for the redemption of mortal passion. It is thus that the most remote and the most familiar imagery may alike be fit for dramatic purposes when employed in the illustration of strong feeling, which raises what is low, and levels to the apprehension that which is lofty, casting over all the shadow of its own greatness. (Reiman and Powers, p. 241)

By subordinating imagery to passion, poetry to the dramatic context, it becomes possible to achieve the effect envisaged by Friedrich Schlegel: drama as *lyrical* expression—not, however, as an overtly expressed lyricism, but rather as sublimated impulse or energy. Here we encounter a characteristic Romantic tendency, the desire to infuse objects with sentiment or feeling. In his description of the respective roles of imagery and passion, Shelley alludes to the doctrine of the Incarnation: "Imagination is as the immortal God which should assume flesh for the redemption of mortal passion." Even as human form, in Christ's case, is said to be the receptacle of the divine essence, so in a similar sense imagery functions as the receptacle of passion. Through the sacred office of the imagination, passion or feeling, by being expressed through imagery, is transformed or elevated to a higher level. Raised to that level, it acquires a permanence denied to it as mere passion. The "incarnation" of passion in imagery produces the highest attainable dramatic effect, the expression of human emotions in a visual or poetic symbolism.

But if the image thus possesses the power of endowing passions with permanence, it can also help to define the precise sense ascribed by Shelley to the concept of representation: a fixation in permanent form of the expressive energies of the passions, the raising to a level of stasis of what is intrinsically changing or dynamic. In this sense the portrait of Beatrice Cenci is, for Shelley, something more than a work of art. It is a "just representation of one of the loveliest specimens of the workmanship of Nature" (Reiman and Powers, p. 242). His description of the portrait both clarifies his concept of representation and defines his idea of the self's nature:

> There is a fixed and pale composure upon the features: she seems sad and stricken down in spirit, yet the despair thus expressed is lightened by the patience of gentleness. Her head is bound with folds of white drapery from which the yellow strings of her golden hair escape, and fall about her neck. The moulding of her face is exquisitely delicate; the eye brows are distinct and arched: the lips have that permanent meaning of imagination and sensibility which suffering has not repressed and which it seems as if death scarcely could extinguish. Her forehead is large and clear; her eyes, which we are told were remarkable for their vivacity, are swollen with weeping and lustreless, but beautifully tender and serene. In the whole mien there is a simplicity and dignity which united with her exquisite loveliness and deep sorrow are inexpressibly pathetic. Beatrice Cenci appears to have been one of those rare persons in whom energy and gentleness dwell together without destroying one another: her nature was simple and profound. The crimes and miseries in which she was an actor and a sufferer are as the mask and the mantle in which circumstances clothed her for her impersonation on the scene of the world. (Reiman and Powers, p. 242)

Permeating the portrait, as its overall effect, is the impression of "composure"—a composure that attests to an achieved equilibrium between the conflicting passions of its subject. Thus Beatrice Cenci appears "sad and stricken down in spirit," a feeling counterbalanced by her being "lightened by the patience of gentleness." Similarly her eyes, "swollen with weeping and lustreless," remain nevertheless "beautifully tender and serene." From this fusion of "loveliness and deep sorrow," "energy and gentleness" that "dwell together without destroying one another," there emerges the dialectic of opposites which defines the Romantic personality or self. Through the Gothic tradition in which he immersed himself during his early years (witness *Zastrozzi* and *St. Irvyne*), Shelley must have encountered those contrasts of light and darkness, clarity and turbidity, violence and serenity which constitute its defining features. By assimilating such contrasts, the self ceases to possess an autonomous nature and existence, becoming instead a medium through which conflicting energies express themselves. Hence the Romantic analogy between self and nature, each exemplifying the play of elemental forces.

With its awareness of underlying forces or drives, Romanticism abolishes the notion of a fixed character, substituting in its place the concept of self as a process by which various energies or passions achieve ascendency, undergo transformation, or disappear, a process whose operation we witness in Chillingworth, in Hester Prynne, in so many of the characters of Balzac's *Comédie humaine*, and one whose laws receive their theoretical elucidation in Schiller's *On the Aesthetic Education of Man.*

But if the self is to be defined in terms of process (the struggle for dominance between different energies), it must undergo the experience of temporality as a *rite de passage* for the subjective consciousness. By its very nature, process negates and ultimately abolishes selfhood: the self now knows only development, evolution, and decline. Its life cycle becomes comprehensible as teleology (Kant, Hegel, and others), an end or purpose that is not part of the process itself but something simultaneously transcendent yet immanent in it. For the self that refuses to be absorbed into a process and temporality, the problem becomes one of finding a means of transcending these, by achieving permanence. In literature such a quest could lead to a reflection upon the very nature of the literary medium and its intrinsically temporal character, consequently, to the search for an art that transcends temporality. Here the fundamental difference between literature and the pictorial arts emerges once more, but in a different light from before. Whereas Lessing had attempted to define the limits of each discipline or medium, Romanticism now seeks to re-create the supratemporal, the visual image, by means of literature itself, that is, a medium whose essence strives to represent the *form* of temporality. Only by so doing can it achieve its ultimate end, a genuine transcendence of time by which the self is established above and beyond the sphere of its own innate tendencies.

To achieve such transcendence it was necessary first of all to delve more deeply into the nature of pictorial art, and hence into the concept of representation. Only by means of a proper understanding of this concept could it become possible to create its equivalent in the realm of literature. Thus if representation in the visual arts signifies the creation of a timeless or ideal "moment," literature achieves a comparable result only by representing similar "moments." This it finds in the dynamic equilibrium of forces, which comprises, as it were, its moral and spiritual ideal. Through the nature of Beatrice Cenci, "in whom energy and gentleness dwell together without destroying one another," Shelley exemplifies that ideal, illustrating the consequences of a dynamic equilibrium in the moral and psychological sphere.

It remains for us to consider why the problem of fictional representation—the question whether and in what respect literature may be said to offer an adequate representation of life—which emerges already at the inception of the novel (for example, in *Don Quixote*) and which is explored with such obsessive emphasis throughout the eighteenth century, should apparently disappear in the Romantic Age, and whether that disappearance bears any relation to Romanticism's desire to transcend temporality through the visual image. Here it must be pointed out first of all that the problem does not really disappear but is, in effect, simply transformed: specifically, we now find it internalized within the represented object itself, as the question of whether that object, under the dominance of process and temporality, can ever reveal its true nature or essence. In his essay "Über das Studium der Griechischen Poesie" Friedrich Schlegel asserts: "Only through an *ideal setting* [placing] does the characteristic of an individual become a philosophical work of art. Through this arrangement must the law of the whole clearly emerge from the mass, and easily present itself to the eye; the sense, the spirit, the inner coherence of the represented essence must shine forth from itself" (*Krit. Ausgabe*, I, 245).

At this point a new question arises: by what means could the earlier problem of representation become internalized within the represented object itself? Through the subjective-objective identity first postulated by Fichte and subsequently, under a slightly different form, by Schelling, it becomes possible to see the object or world described by literature as at once both objective and subjective, through the interfusion of these two realms with each other. Desire accordingly enters into, and is expressed by, the object, whose representation is now suffused by feeling or emotion. Moreover, the postulated identity of subjective and objective opens up the possibilities of symbolism. Specifically, through the notion that consciousness achieves an epiphany in experiencing "the translucence of the Eternal in and through the Temporal," the Romantic desire for permanence transposes the object of its quest from the plane of the material image onto consciousness itself. By being reflected in this sense upon itself, consciousness transcends the temporal through a self-consciousness that is, as the awareness of its own imaginative or transforming power, a perception in the Romantic sense of the divine.

# 26   *Stendhal*

The historical novel stands as one of the literary innovations of the Romantic Age. With the *Waverley* novels of Walter Scott it emerges as a distinct genre. Balzac could draw inspiration from Scott for the first masterpiece of the *Comédie humaine*, *Les Chouans*. Elsewhere in his vast cycle he offers brief glimpses of crucial historical moments, as in *Une épisode sous la Terreur*. As with Scott, the essence of such portraits consists of a depiction of intense passions or feelings, captured at a moment of crisis. The "historical" ethos of the work emerges from the juxtaposition between the intensity of those feelings and the definite "pastness" or remoteness of their objects. As a result, the feelings themselves assume a historical character, as the creation of a distinct historical consciousness. In other words, consciousness itself is made to assimilate such objects and, in so doing, the feelings that accompany them. These feelings it recognizes as belonging to the past, but in assimilating them, it then adopts a "historical" attitude toward itself, as consciousness in a later age. Hence it carries within itself that sense of historical distance that represents the essence of the historical novel.

Through her novel *Corinne* Mme de Staël had disclosed the romantic possibilities of Italy as a literary landscape. Though not primarily historical, *Corinne* could hardly avoid introducing an element of historical consciousness in its descriptions of the Roman ruins, which affects both Corinne and Lord Nelvil. Their feelings may be summarized by Napoleon's exclamation on seeing Italy for the first time, as recounted in his memoirs: *"Italiam, Italiam!"* For both Mme de Staël and Walter Scott, the historical consciousness involves an inner relation to the past as part of the content of consciousness itself, that is, an internalized impression or sensation of historical "pastness."

From a later perspective, however, one that does not believe in the necessity of mediating one's relation to the historical past through consciousness, such impressions could seem merely a superfluous element in historical narrative, especially if considered from the viewpoint of "realism." That viewpoint we may attribute specifically to Stendhal. In the preface to his *Chroniques italiennes,* he touches upon the reasons for his special interest in the Italian Renaissance:

> I imagine my contemporaries of 1833 will be little enough touched by the naive or energetic traits one encounters here, described in a gossipy style. For me, the recital of these pieces and of these tortures furnishes me with true and unassailable facts about the human heart, upon which one loves to meditate when passing the night in a coach. . . . One must have a people in whom the force of actual sensation (feeling) (as at Naples) or of passion meditated (as at Rome) has correspondingly chased away vanity and affectation. I do not know if one can find outside Italy (and perhaps Spain before the affectation of the nineteenth century) an epoch civilized enough to be more interesting than the Riccaras and free enough from vanity to allow the human heart to be seen almost bare. One thing I am sure of, which is that today England, Germany, and France are too gangrened with affectation and with vanities of all genres to furnish, for any length of time, bright enough lights on the depths of the human heart. (*Romans et nouvelles,* II, 557)

In a sense, one might say, the claims of the "naive" and "sentimental" (Schiller) are renewed here, with the difference that Stendhal accords complete superiority to the "naive." The "modern" is equated with "affection," but—most significantly—such "affectation" does not ensue as an inevitable consequence of an earlier "naiveté." Rather, the two modes or states of feeling are juxtaposed simply as two possibilities of human development. To "actual feeling (sensation)" in the Italian Renaissance, Stendhal ascribes a certain energy or force: it requires the exertion of that energy to produce the "naive or energetic traits" displayed by the Italians of the fifteenth and sixteenth centuries. Interestingly enough, such energy has nothing to do with the underlying or elemental forces perceived by Shelley and Goethe, the energies *Naturphilosophie* locates in both the self and Nature. For Stendhal this energy is strictly human and psychological. Its manifestation is passion. Without passion, one lacks the "naive and energetic traits" of the people of the Renaissance—in other words, a personality.

From the Stendhalian perspective, then, passion is expressive in the "artistic" sense: it exhibits itself in character traits in a fashion similar to that of a painter creating a portrait on canvas. Like the portrait, moreover, these traits taken together may be said to form a "composition." Not, however, in the sense of an ideal balance of opposites such as we encountered in Shelley: Stendhal's aesthetics leads him to shun the effect of anything like formal perfection, the dynamic equilibrium achieved by the representation of contrasting elements or motifs. Instead, if one were seeking the embodiment of his aesthetics in painting, one might find an analogy with Delacroix, from whom Balzac had derived the inspiration for his *La Fille aux yeux d'or*. Like Balzac and Delacroix, Stendhal strives for the expressive rather than an aesthetic or formal ideal; just as, for Delacroix, color could assume a purely expressive significance, especially in those scenes in which it becomes dissociated from representative forms to acquire an independent existence as purely expressive gesture, so too, for Stendhal, passion becomes expressive, both in its nature and consequences. As Delacroix had introduced the color-gesture (the use of streaks of red, for instance, in his Oriental hunting scenes) to evoke a feeling, so Stendhal, similarly, employs the display of passion to excite a specific feeling different from that of the passion itself (Julien Sorel's reunion with Mme de Rênal, for instance, after he has left Verrières, performs this function).

Stendhal's rejection of "the ideal" operates not only on the aesthetic but also on the moral and spiritual plane. It accounts for his admiration of the type of the "don Juan," which he defines as "he who does not seek to conform to any ideal model, and who does not dream of the world's opinion except to outrage it" (*Romans et nouvelles*, ii, 685). Of the instances of this type in the Italian Renaissance, only two embody it in its purest form. One of these is the count François (or Francesco) Cenci.

Significantly, in his preface to the story "Les Cenci," Stendhal chooses to concentrate upon an analysis of the count rather than his daughter Béatrix (Beatrice). Of the former Stendhal remarks:

> François Cenci would have said to himself: "By what expressive actions can I, a Roman, born at Rome in 1527, precisely during the six months in which the lutheran soldiers of the Bourbon connetable committed here, on consecrated objects, the most hideous profanations; by which actions can I manifest my courage and give myself, as deeply as possible, the pleasure of braving opinion? How can I astonish my idiotic contemporaries? How can I give myself the vivid pleasure of feeling myself different from this whole vulgar mass?" (*Romans et nouvelles*, ii, 682–83)

For Stendhal, the free individual feels himself only by opposing "the masses." In this sense, consciousness (or self-consciousness) invariably assumes the form of a reflected awareness: one is conscious of the other; then, because one opposes that other, of oneself. In its essential nature, nevertheless, Stendhalian reflected consciousness differs from that of German transcendental idealism, the "I"–"not-I" system of Fichte or the reveries of Novalis. Basic to Stendhal's concept of the self is the desire to oppose the other. Such desire arises from the awareness of that other as someone external to oneself. For Stendhal, consciousness originates in that awareness, and the desire to oppose the other amounts to an assertion of the self. Since the content of consciousness is really of the other, one feels oneself only by becoming conscious of the force opposing that other.

Not only opposing, however, but dominating: in his preface Stendhal presents the "don Juan" as a type that "never thinks of others except to mark his superiority over them, make use of them in his schemes, or hate them. The don Juan never experiences pleasure by sympathy, by gentle reveries or the illusions of a tender heart. He requires, above all, pleasures which are triumphs, which can be seen by others, which *cannot be denied;* he requires the list deployed by the insolent Leporello before the eyes of the sad Elvira" (*Romans et nouvelles*, ii, 683).

In effect, the don Juan rejects the Romantic pleasure in the imaginative activity of consciousness. Instead, in a somewhat curious fashion, he depends for his gratification upon others: it is necessary for them to feel his superiority, his dominance, for him to derive any pleasure from these himself. Presumably the portrayal of his consciousness must also require depicting his triumph over another. Hence the impossibility, for Stendhal, of any direct correspondence between visual image and psychological portrait. For him, the individual is to be grasped solely by means of his acts and their effect upon others—in this case, by his triumph over them.

We have seen how for Stendhal the most significant aspects of the

Cenci narrative are embodied in the character of Francesco Cenci rather than his daughter Beatrice. In his description of Guido Reni's portrait of the latter, nevertheless, Stendhal manages to offer a glimpse of the changing canons of the new literary realism:

> The second precious portrait of the Barberini gallery is by Guido; it is the portrait of Béatrix Cenci, of which one sees so many bad engravings. This great painter has placed on Béatrix's neck a piece of insignificant drapery; he has dressed her in a turban; he would have been afraid to push the truth to the point of the *horrible,* if he had reproduced exactly the dress she made for herself, for the execution, and the dishevelled hair of a poor girl of sixteen who has just abandoned herself to despair. The head is sweet and beautiful, the expression very gentle and the eyes very large: they have the startled look of a person who has just been surprised at the moment of weeping bitterly. (*Romans et nouvelles,* ii, 684)

The description of Beatrice's look, in particular, announces the new realism: where Shelley had observed a gaze "beautifully tender and serene," Stendhal detects the "startled expression of a person who has just been surprised at the moment of weeping bitterly." But it is his speculation about Guido's use of drapery instead of Beatrice's actual garments that reveals most clearly the new tendencies. To have depicted the latter, Stendhal says, would have been "to have pushed the truth to the point of the *horrible.*" Was it not, however, precisely this aspect of the Cenci history which had been responsible for its fascination from the very beginning? Here the horrible—which is also the true—presents itself as the limit of representation. To depict it is to destroy the illusion that is representation itself—which would mean: the disclosure of what is beyond the illusion (the frame of representation), which will yield the effect of the real (for which, see Diderot, *Quatre contes,* pp. 66–67). For Stendhal, we might say, representation possesses the form and appearance of the ideal—and for that reason cannot actually "represent" the real. Only that which does not attempt to "represent" can yield the real, but what it discloses is not reality itself but the impression of that reality, as in Stendhal's celebrated account of Fabrice at the battle of Waterloo in the *Chartreuse de Parme.* Thus the aim of "realism" must be, not representation, but the transgression of its limits: what Stendhal seeks is, accordingly, not an ideal but the reality that can have no "representation."

# 27 Hawthorne

In the Gothic romance, paintings often assume a privileged role—we need think only of the very first work of that genre, Horace Walpole's *Castle of Otranto*, in which the portrait of Manfred's grandfather descends from its frame as Manfred prepares to violate Isabella. Hawthorne too makes use of the same device in *The House of the Seven Gables*, with the portrait of Colonel Pyncheon. His incorporation of Guido Reni's Beatrice Cenci into *The Marble Faun*, however, proceeds from a different aim. In the interval between *The House of the Seven Gables* and the composition of his last finished romance, Hawthorne had come to experience firsthand the splendors of the European artistic heritage in painting and sculpture. That experience, recorded at length in his French and Italian Notebooks, could then act as a shaping influence upon his conception of art in general, as well as on his sense of the relation between the visual arts and literature. At the same time, through such an influence, his idea of the role of painting in literature also assumes a new form. His description of the Beatrice Cenci in *The Marble Faun* reflects the portrait's new role:

> The picture represented simply a female head; a very youthful, girlish, perfectly beautiful face, enveloped in white drapery, from beneath which strayed a lock or two of what seemed a rich, though hidden luxuriance of auburn hair. The eyes were large and brown, and met those of the spectator, but evidently with a strange, ineffectual effort to escape. There was a little redness about the eyelids, very slightly indicated, so that you would question whether or no the girl had been weeping. The whole face was quiet; there was no distortion or disturbance of any single feature; nor was it easy to see why the expression was not cheerful, or why a single touch of the artist's pencil should not brighten it into joyousness. But, in fact, it was the very saddest picture ever painted or conceived; it involved an unfathomable depth of sorrow, the sense of which came to the observer by a sort of intuition. It was a sorrow that removed this beautiful girl out of the sphere of humanity, and set her in a far-off region, the remoteness of which—while yet her face is so close before us—makes us shiver as at a spectre. (Centenary, IV, 64)

The "sorrow that removed this beautiful girl out of the sphere of humanity" is not remorse for her crime (parricide). From the account in the French and Italian Notebooks, we know that Hawthorne's own interpretation agrees with Hilda's first impression, which comes to her through a kind of clairvoyant insight: "She is a fallen angel, fallen, and yet sinless; and it is only this depth of sorrow, with its weight and darkness, that keeps her down upon earth, and brings her within our view even while it sets her beyond our reach" (Centenary, IV, 66). With this description of Beatrice, we may compare that of Donatello—the figure who, through his sin, is humanized and assimilated into the sphere of human sympathies. If the two are compared, the role of the portrait becomes one of thematic counterposition: through its contrast with the description of Donatello, it helps to illuminate Hawthorne's theme—the idea of sin as the beginning of human consciousness, the sense of our relation to others, and the psychological bond of sympathy and guilt by which we participate in the sphere of human hopes and affections.

We have seen how Hawthorne, in his treatment of the quest for the absolute, depicts the progressive alienation of a single individual from such affections. Here, by an artifice similar to Melville's in *Pierre*, which juxtaposes the Cenci to the portrait of a stranger, Hawthorne explores another aspect of his theme. Unlike Septimius in the Elixir of Life manuscripts, Hawthorne's Beatrice does not will her alienation from the rest of humanity. That condition is, rather, forced upon her through her knowledge of sin, a knowledge she acquires as the victim of Count Cenci's incestuous passion. For insight into her state, Hawthorne could recall the lines in which Shelley describes Beatrice's experience of her rape:

> If sometimes, as a shape more like himself,
> Even the form which tortured me on earth,
> Masked in grey hairs and wrinkles, he should come
> And wind me in his hellish arms, and fix
> His eyes on mine, and drag me down, down, down!
> (Reiman and Powers, p. 298)

The sense of being dragged down to a consciousness of sin (the demonic aspect of Count Cenci being clearly evoked in the line "And wind me in his hellish arms"), which is the equivalent to "fallenness"—even without her assent to the count's sexual assault—also permeates Hawthorne's Beatrice. By becoming a living witness to Count Cenci's sin, she can, though innocent, no longer participate in the life of humanity. Her consciousness is not of herself (in which case she would still be free, sinning through choice and hence able, through remorse, to pursue a higher spiritual development). What Hawthorne suggests, rather, is that her consciousness is one of *the sin itself*, precisely because she herself did not commit it. Such awareness, according to Hawthorne, brings with it the psychological effect almost of sin itself, without its liberating influence. For the effect of committing sin is to introduce the will to a new sphere of hopes and desires, without which it remains excluded from the full range of human passions and sympathies and hence incapable of spiritualization.

In his psychological view of the nature of sin, Hawthorne differs from the standpoint expressed by Shelley. Whereas the Romantic poet had depicted sin as loss of will and hence of self (represented, in Beatrice's case, by assent to the incestuous act—something the count fails to wrest from her), Hawthorne, in contrast, sees sin in essence as a mode of consciousness. Thus his Beatrice, though innocent of the crime of incest (in the sense that she does not assent to it), does not preserve—unlike Shelley's heroine—the consciousness of self that belongs to pure innocence. Instead, through a knowledge of sin originating with another's act, she enters into a "fallen" awareness that does not bring with it (unlike Donatello's) the opening up of new hopes and desires—primarily because her will plays no part in the sinful act itself. For Hawthorne, sin is passion (hence the relation between Donatello's love for Miriam and his murder of the Capuchin who persecutes her). Without such passion, its assertion remains impossible. Thus Kenyon's suggestion that sin is necessary to spiritualize humanity—the paradox of the *felix culpa* that here receives a psychological rather than doctrinal grounding. Here, the degree of importance the self's development assumes for Hawthorne reflects the difference between the later phase of Romanticism and its earlier expression in someone like Shelley.

The role of the Beatrice portrait as a thematic counterpoise to the notion of the *felix culpa* exhibits, however, but one aspect of its significance in *The Marble Faun*: the central theme of this romance, as we have seen, is not the Fortunate Fall and man's subsequent spiritualization but the analogy between that process and the creation of art. With regard to their relationship, it seems appropriate to ask: what is Hawthorne's concept of the work of art itself, and specifically, painting?

In their conversation about Guido's portrait, Miriam at one point asks her friend how she managed to obtain permission from the owner to make her copy. "I knew," Hilda replies, "the Prince Barberini would be deaf to all entreaties; so I had no resource but to sit down before the picture, day after day, and let it sink into my heart. I do believe it is now photographed there. . . . after studying it in this way, I know not how many times, I came home, and have done my best to transfer the image to canvas" (Centenary, IV, 65). Later, as they discuss the question of Beatrice's guilt or innocence, Hilda is at one moment "startled to observe that her friend's expression had become almost exactly that of the portrait; as if her passionate wish and struggle to penetrate poor Beatrice's mystery had been successful" (p. 67). These instances are significant. They reveal that for Hawthorne the real nature of the portrait—and of painting in general—is not its material realization but rather an image in the mind, or—to speak of the Beatrice and all great art especially—the fulfillment in visual form of certain indefinable aspirations, the embodiment of otherwise inexpressible intuitions, the consciousness of some eternal truth disclosed in the expression of a face.

On account of its innate spiritual quality, such an image exists not so much on canvas as in the mind of its creator or perceiver. Hence the possibility of its transmission, as with Hilda and Miriam. Its transmissibility is also the seal of its imperishability. After seeing Raphael's Madonna della Seggiola, Hawthorne had written, in his French and Italian Notebooks: "It is my present opinion that the pictorial art is capable of something more like magic—more wonderful and inscrutable in its methods—than poetry, or any other mode of developing the beautiful." "But," he then asks, "how does this accord with what I have been saying only a minute ago? How then can the decayed picture of a great master ever be restored by the touches of an inferior hand?" The answer: "Doubtless, it never can be restored; but let some devoted worshipper do his utmost, and the whole inherent spirit of the divine picture may pervade his restorations likewise" (Centenary, xiv, 305–6).

Throughout the French and Italian Notebooks Hawthorne records the deteriorating condition of various paintings, lamenting their loss of expressiveness on account of faded hues. A random aphorism sums up his observations on this score: "But the glory of a picture fades like that of a flower" (Centenary, xiv, 189). Offsetting its material fragility and the transient quality of its medium, however, there subsists the timeless and imperishable essence of each picture (as well as each sculpture), the image by which it represents a thought to the mind and, in all great art, the form in which it embodies the heart's affections. Nowhere does this seem to have been borne in upon Hawthorne more forcefully than in his encounter with the Venus de Medici. Of this statue he observes:

> The hue of the marble is just so much mellowed by time as to do for her all that Gibson tries, or ought, to try, to do for his statues by color; softening her, warming her almost imperceptibly, making her an inmate of the heart as well as a spiritual existence. I felt a kind of tenderness for her; an affection, not as if she were one woman, but all womankind in one. (Centenary, xiv, 298)

And, later:

> The world has not grown weary of her in all these ages; and mortal man may look on her with new delight from infancy to old age, and keep the memory of her, I should imagine, as one of the treasures of spiritual existence hereafter. . . . I do not, and cannot, think of her as a senseless image, but as a being that lives to gladden the world, incapable of decay and death;

as young and fair to day as she was three thousand years ago, and still to be young and fair, as long as a beautiful thought shall require physical embodiment. (Centenary, XIV, 307–8)

Years earlier, in his story "Earth's Holocaust," Hawthorne had expressed through one of his characters the hope that the life of the soul after death might bear some resemblance to our earthly existence. Now he wishes humanity may keep the memory of the Venus de Medici "as one of the treasures of spiritual existence hereafter." For Hawthorne, then, a work of art represents something more than a source of aesthetic pleasure. It expresses, simultaneously, a type of the eternal, the clear consciousness of an existence above the realm of transience and decay. In the Romantic sense, it would be possible to speak of it as a symbol: as that which permits a "translucence of the Eternal in and through the Temporal." For Hawthorne, the Venus de Medici—like Guido's Beatrice—consists of something more than a "senseless image": its life is the life of the thought that creates it and that dwells, as it were, within it. Insofar as such thought is itself eternal, the image in which it expresses itself may claim a similar privilege.

# 28  *Melville*

Among the Romantic authors who discuss Guido Reni's portrait of Beatrice Cenci, Melville alone, significantly, refrains from offering a literal description of it. Merely designating it "that sweetest, most touching, but most awful of all feminine heads," he then observes:

> The wonderfulness of which head consists chiefly, perhaps, in a striking, suggested contrast, half-identical with, and half-analogous to, that almost supernatural one—sometimes visible in the maidens of tropical nations—namely, soft and light blue eyes, with an extremely fair complexion, vailed by funerally jetty hair. But with blue eyes and fair complexion, the Cenci's hair is golden—physically, therefore, all is in strict, natural keeping; which, nevertheless, still the more intensifies the suggested fanciful anomaly of so sweetly and seraphically *blonde* a being, being double-hooded, as it were, by the black crape of the two most horrible crimes (of one of which she is the object, and of the other the agent) possible to civilized humanity—incest and parricide. (*Writings*, VII, 351)

One may speculate on the various reasons for Melville's introduction of the picture into his narrative. The contrast between light and dark, to be sure, serves to link it with the tradition of Gothic romance, which operates as an influence upon *Pierre* in numerous places. Here, Melville adapts the tradition to his own purposes, ascribing to a blonde or fair heroine the symbolic value normally attributed to her darker counterpart. The inversion of values corresponds to a general reversal of moral values which Pierre finds deeply problematic. In the present context, the association of Beatrice Cenci with the "black crape" of "the two most horrible crimes possible to civilized humanity" only makes it more so: as a "dark" yet "seraphically *blonde*" heroine, she simultaneously suggests both Isabel and Lucy.

Interestingly enough, Melville deliberately avoids the Gothic portrait itself in *Pierre*. That is to say, he does not employ—as does Walpole—the portrait which steps down from its frame to enter into the action (*The Castle of Otranto*), or the form of a "tableau vivant," such as Hawthorne makes use of in *The House of the Seven Gables*, in which Matthew Maule, ostensibly operating through Alice Pyncheon, conjures up the vision of two of his ancestors preventing Colonel Pyncheon from revealing the secret hiding place of the Pyncheon title-deed. Hawthorne too, of course, follows the more characteristic mode for Gothic portraiture with the painting of Colonel Pyncheon, which frowns, grimaces, and clenches its fist to express its displeasure at the acts of its descendents. If the "tableau vivant" composed by Matthew Maule conveys a moral theme ("that the wrong-doing of one generation lives into the successive ones"), the use of the portrait in Gothic romance in general suggests the evocation of subliminal forces of the psyche, which often resist conscious impulses (for example, Manfred's grandfather who descends from the picture frame to prevent the rape of Isabella).

In *Pierre* Melville is not averse to having his portraits appear to "speak" to the spectator. The youthful portrait of Pierre's father "addresses" his son:

> Pierre, believe not the drawing-room painting; that is not thy father; or, at least, is not *all* of thy father. Consider in thy mind, Pierre, whether we two paintings may not make only one. . . . Look again. I am thy real father, so much the more truly, as thou thinkest thou recognizest me not, Pierre. . . . Consider this strange, ambiguous smile, Pierre; more narrowly regard this mouth. Behold, what is this too ardent and, as it were, unchastened light in these eyes, Pierre? I am thy father, boy. There was once a certain, oh, but too lovely young Frenchwoman, Pierre. Youth is hot, and temptation strong, Pierre; and in the minutest moment momentous things are irrevocably done. . . . Look again. Doth thy mother dislike me for naught? Consider. Do not all her spontaneous, loving impressions, ever strive to magnify, and spiritualize, and deify, her husband's memory, Pierre? Then why doth she cast despite upon me; and never speak to thee of me; and why dost thou thyself keep silence before her, Pierre? . . . . Look, do I not smile?—yes, and with an unchangeable smile; and thus have I unchangea-

bly smiled for many long years gone by, Pierre. Oh, it is a permanent smile! Thus I smiled to cousin Ralph; and thus in thy dear old Aunt Dorothea's parlor, Pierre; and just so, I smile here to thee, and even thus in thy father's later life, when his body may have been in grief, still . . . I thus smiled as before. . . . Consider; for a smile is the chosen vehicle for all ambiguities, Pierre. (*Writings*, VII, 83–84)

Instead of speaking to Pierre as his father, however, the portrait does so *as a portrait*: "believe not the drawing-room painting . . . consider whether we two paintings may not make only one. . . ." At one point, it even assumes a sensibility of its own: "Then why doth she cast despite upon me . . .?" In addition, it manifests awareness of its own appearance: "Consider this strange, ambiguous smile . . . more narrowly regard this mouth. Behold, what is this too ardent and, as it were, unchastened light in these eyes, Pierre?"

This consciousness of its own nature as an object is significant. It indicates that, even for Pierre, the portrait remains merely a representation rather than the individual it represents. But if so, how can it disclose facts of which Pierre himself is not yet aware? Not only to divulge, but even to reflect upon these, signalizes the presence of a distinct subjective consciousness. If not to Pierre's father, that consciousness must belong in some sense to Pierre himself. Here we may say that the portrait displaces that consciousness from the self onto an object. As representation, the portrait embodies the consciousness of the self. In other words, the self, for Melville, achieves self-consciousness only in representation. The representation *is* that consciousness itself, which as representation is then reflected back upon its source, that is, the mind or self. Hence the peculiar mode in which the portrait addresses Pierre, with the frequent repetition of his name (as if to intensify his self-consciousness). Not only the repetition of a name, but the whole tone of the discourse, mocking yet intimate, suggest that the voice addressing Pierre is not even meant for his father's but constitutes rather his own, a reflection of consciousness upon the self.

Without the embodiment of consciousness in a representation, the self possesses no means of knowing itself. In *Pierre* what both protagonist and author ultimately seek is knowledge of the self. Earlier, we have seen Melville's attitude toward that passage of Shelley's *Defence of Poetry* in which Shelley asserts the need for literature as a mirror or prism to reflect the self. Through the portrait, Melville symbolizes another means of self-reflection. For Shelley, literature furnishes a form of objectification. Such objectification is necessary for the self to perceive its own feelings and desires, by seeing these represented in relation to an object. To depict them in that relation, literature must represent not the desires themselves so much as their expression. In effect, the content of representation thus consists primarily of the expression of those desires, along with their object. For Melville, on the other hand, it is not necessary to portray desires in relation to an object. Hence his attraction to the portrait: it permits expression of the desires themselves through their embodiment in an object that is not what they seek but simply a medium for their reflection back upon the self.

Here we recall how Melville alone, among the Romantic writers who discuss Beatrice Cenci, had refrained from describing her portrait. His motive cannot be simply the fact of its being well known—almost eight years later, Hawthorne would offer a detailed account of it in *The Marble Faun*. Moreover, as we have seen, to describe or represent the portrait is in itself an act of interpretation. Even with the depictions of Pierre's father, however, what Melville emphasizes is not so much the portrait as Pierre's impression of it. In this sense his depiction of a portrait is more self-consciously subjective. It signifies the relation of consciousness to the self rather than to any external object. The subjective quality of the portrait is indicated by its appearance, which changes according to the perspective from which one views it. Thus the youthful portrait of Pierre's father asks Pierre to consider "whether we two paintings may not make only one." Fixing his gaze upon it, Pierre can finally exclaim, in Dante's famous lines:

> "Ah! how dost thou change,
> Agnello! See! thou art not double now,
> Nor only one!" (*Writings*, VII, 85)

The transformations of the face as Pierre continues to hold his imagined colloquy with it attest to the subjective nature of even the actual lineaments of the representation. For this reason Melville abstains from describing Beatrice Cenci: her importance lies not in her appearance but in what she symbolizes for Pierre and the subjective consciousness which pervades Melville's novel.

From the foregoing, one may infer that the portrait's symbolic content, from a Melvillean perspective, concerns the self and consciousness. To Pierre, the portrait illuminates the unreliability of appearances in the moral sphere. Virtue is vice; vice, virtue. Significantly, instead of meeting his gaze (as does the portrait of his father), the Beatrice dissolves immediately into the stream of his speculations upon it. Its dissolution suggests that what it fails to offer is some objectification of his own consciousness. Instead, it merges with and is absorbed into that consciousness, as expressed through the simultaneous allusion to Lucy and Isabel, the "light" and "dark" heroines who are conjoined in Beatrice's spiritual image. This dissolution into a thematic reminiscence of Lucy and Isabel is itself significant. It affirms Melville's view of the all-encompassing nature of subjectivity. Through the Beatrice Cenci, moreover, the interrelation of Isabel to Lucy is suggestively represented. Here it seems appropriate to speak of an interrelation rather than a simple relation, inasmuch as the two heroines constitute a necessary opposition within Pierre's consciousness. Like contrasting motifs, their basic unity is to be found in the thought that produces them. Correspondingly, the essential substance of the Beatrice portrait consists of its expression of those moral "ambiguities" that Pierre encounters in his desire to pursue virtue. Of these the portrait forms an "image"—which is to say: a representation of force and desire in a form that preserves them as expression.

If we survey now the course we have followed in tracing the history of the Romantic representations of Guido Reni's Beatrice Cenci, a certain pattern of development emerges. For Shelley, the portrait embodies a moral or spiritual ideal: Beatrice is one "in whom energy and gentleness dwell together without destroying one another." Her portrait exhibits a similar antithesis: "in the whole mien there is a simplicity and dignity which united with her exquisite loveliness and deep sorrow are inexpressibly pathetic." As a result, the essence or spiritual substance of the painting inheres not in its depiction of an individual personality or self but the expression from a universal perspective of a dynamic balance between opposites which possesses both moral and aesthetic significance. With Stendhal, the awareness of the implicit tendency of representation toward idealization causes a radical departure from Romantic style: instead of the permanent, Stendhal deliberately opts for the transient, the momentary impulse or expression, that which disrupts the process of idealization. Only by consciously striving not to "represent" is it possible to achieve the effect of the real, the actual personality or self.

For Stendhal, the impression of the real is, for art, equivalent to reality, since the content of that reality itself consists in essence of impressions. The implicit subjectivism of his attitude, carried one step further, develops into the Melvillean notion of the portrait as an embodiment of consciousness, which, juxtaposed against the self that perceives it, becomes self-consciousness. For Melville, then, "reality" means something different from what it signifies for Stendhal: like Stendhal, he affirms the equation of reality with consciousness, but—in contrast to Stendhal—asserts the necessity of apprehending the content of consciousness through some form of representation. The solipsistic abyss that opens up when one views the external world solely as an objectification of consciousness is transcended by appropriating the portrait as a means of thematic expression. Such is the function Hawthorne discovers for it in *The Marble Faun*. Melville too, after *Pierre*, pursues a similar course. In *Billy Budd* we encounter a complete internalization of the image: "Struck dead by an angel of God! Yet the angel must hang!" Perhaps such internalization can help to define the process of assimilation, development, and transformation which characterizes the relation of the American Renaissance to European Romanticism as a whole. As with other Romantic concepts and motifs, what occurs with the Beatrice Cenci in Melville and Hawthorne manifests both the last possible phase of development for the subject and a renewed understanding of it through creative reinterpretation.

# Primary Sources

Agassiz, Louis. *Essay on Classification.* Ed. Edward Lurie. Cambridge: Harvard Univ. Press, 1962.
——. *Methods of Study in Natural History.* Boston: Ticknor and Fields, 1864.
Alcott, A. Bronson. *Concord Days.* Boston: Roberts Brothers, 1872.
——. *The Journals of Bronson Alcott.* Ed. Odell Shepard. Boston: Little, Brown, 1938.
——. *Tablets.* Boston: Roberts Brothers, 1868.
Balzac, Honoré de. *La Comédie humaine.* Published under the direction of Pierre-Georges Castex. 12 vols. Paris: Gallimard, 1976–81. [Bibliothèque de la Pléiade]
Baudelaire, Charles. *Oeuvres complètes.* Ed. Claude Pichois. 2 vols. Paris: Gallimard, 1975–76. [Bibliothèque de la Pléiade]
Bichat, Xavier. *Anatomie générale, appliquée à la physiologie et à la médecine.* 2 vols. Paris: Brosson, 1801.
Brown, Charles Brockden. *The Novels and Related Works of Charles Brockden Brown.* Ed. Sydney J. Krause and S. W. Reid. 5 vols. to date. Kent, Ohio: Kent State Univ. Press, 1977–.
Carlyle, Thomas. *The Works of Thomas Carlyle.* Ed. H. D. Traill. 30 vols. London: Chapman and Hall, 1896–99. [Centenary Edition]
Chambers, Robert. *Vestiges of the Natural History of Creation.* London, 1844. Reprint. Leicester: Leicester Univ. Press, 1969.
Channing, William E. *The Works of William E. Channing, D.D.* 5 vols. Boston: Munroe, 1841.
Coleridge, Samuel Taylor. *Coleridge's Miscellaneous Criticism.* Ed. T. M. Raysor. Cambridge, Mass.: Harvard Univ. Press, 1936.
——. *Collected Letters of Samuel Taylor Coleridge.* Ed. Earl Leslie Griggs. 6 vols. Oxford and New York: Oxford Univ. Press, 1956–71.
——. *The Collected Works of Samuel Taylor Coleridge.* General ed., Kathleen Coburn. 9 vols. to date. Princeton: Princeton Univ. Press; London: Routledge & Kegan Paul, 1969–.
——. *The Notebooks of Samuel Taylor Coleridge.* Ed. Kathleen Coburn. 3 vols. to date. New York, Princeton, and London: Bollingen, Princeton Univ. Press, and Routledge & Kegan Paul, 1957–.
——. *Poetical Works.* Ed. E. H. Coleridge. London: Oxford Univ. Press, 1912.

Constant, Benjamin. *Oeuvres.* Ed. Alfred Roulin. Paris: Gallimard, 1957. [Bibliothèque de la Pléiade]

Cousin, Victor. *Cours de philosophie professé à la Faculté des Lettres pendant l'année 1818, par M. V. Cousin, sur le fondement des idées absolues du vrai, du beau et du bien.* Ed. Adolphe Garnier. Paris: Hachette, 1836.

Cowen, Walker. "Melville's Marginalia." Ph.D. diss., Harvard Univ., 1965.

Cuvier, Georges. *Leçons d'anatomie comparée.* 5 vols. Paris: Baudouin, 1800–1805.

——. *Le Règne animal, distribué d'après son organisation.* 4 vols. Paris: Deterville, 1817.

Davy, Humphry. *The Collected Works of Sir Humphry Davy.* Ed. John Davy. 9 vols. London: Smith, Elder, 1839–40.

De Quincey, Thomas. *The Collected Writings of Thomas De Quincey.* Ed. David Masson. 14 vols. Edinburgh: A. and C. Black, 1889–90.

Diderot, Denis. *Jaques le Fataliste et son maitre.* Ed. Simone Lecointre and Jean Le Galliot. Geneva: Droz, 1976.

—— *Oeuvres.* Ed. André Billy. Paris: Gallimard, 1951. [Bibliothèque de la Pléiade]

——. *Quatre contes.* Ed. Jacques Proust. Geneva: Droz, 1964.

Einstein, Albert. "Autobiographical Notes," in Paul Arthur Schilpp, ed., *Albert Einstein: Philosopher–Scientist,* 3d ed. La Salle, Ill.: Open Court, 1970.

Emerson, Ralph Waldo. *The Collected Works of Ralph Waldo Emerson.* General ed., Alfred R. Ferguson. 3 vols. to date. Cambridge: Harvard Univ. Press, 1971–.

——. *The Complete Works of Ralph Waldo Emerson.* Ed. Edward Waldo Emerson. 12 vols. Boston and New York: Houghton Mifflin, 1903–1904. [Centenary Edition]

——. *The Early Lectures of Ralph Waldo Emerson.* Ed. Stephen E. Whicher, Robert Spiller, and Wallace E. Williams. 3 vols. Cambridge: Harvard Univ. Press, 1959–72.

——. *The Journals and Miscellaneous Notebooks of Ralph Waldo Emerson.* Ed. William H. Gilman et al. 16 vols. Cambridge: Harvard Univ. Press, 1960–82.

——. *The Letters of Ralph Waldo Emerson.* Ed. Ralph L. Rusk. 6 vols. New York: Columbia Univ. Press, 1939.

Fichte, J. G. *J. G. Fichte–Gesamtausgabe der Bayerischen Akademie der Wissenschaften.* Ed. Reinhard Lauth and Hans Jacob. 19 vols. to date. Stuttgart–Bad Cannstatt: Frommann (Holzboog), 1964–.

Fuller, Margaret. *Margaret Fuller: Essays on American Life and Letters.* Ed. Joel Myerson. New Haven: College and Univ. Press, 1978.

——. *Papers on Literature and Art.* Pts. I and II. London: Wiley & Putnam, 1846. Reprint. New York: AMS Press, 1972.

——. *The Writings of Margaret Fuller.* Ed. Mason Wade. New York: Viking, 1941.

Geoffroy Saint-Hilaire, Étienne. "Mémoire sur les rapports naturels des MAKIS LEMUR, L. et Description d'une espèce nouvelle de Mammifère." *Magasin encyclopédique ou journal des sciences, des lettres et des arts,* vol. I (Paris, 1796), pp. 20–49.

——. *Philosophie anatomique.* 2 vols. Paris: Méquignon-Marvis, 1818–22.

Goethe, J. W. von. *Goethes Werke.* Ed. Erich Trunz. 14 vols. Hamburg: Wegner, 1948–60. Later editions published by Beck, Munich. [Hamburger Ausgabe]

Hawthorne, Nathaniel. *The Centenary Edition of the Works of Nathaniel Hawthorne.* Ed. William Charvat et al. 16 vols. to date. Columbus: Ohio State Univ. Press, 1962–.

Hedge, Frederic Henry. Review of "Coleridge's Writings." *The Christian Examiner,* 14 (March, 1833), 108–29.

Hegel, G. W. F. *Berliner Schriften, 1818–1831*. Ed. Johannes Hoffmeister. Hamburg: Felix Meiner, 1956.

——. *Gesammelte Werke*. In association with the Deutschen Forschungsgemeinschaft. Ed. by the Rheinisch-Westfälischen Akademie der Wissenschaften. 8 vols. to date. Hamburg: Felix Meiner, 1968–.

Herder, J. G. *Herders Sämmtliche Werke*. Ed. Bernhard Suphan. 33 vols. Berlin: Weidmann, 1877–1913.

Hölderlin, Friedrich. *Sämtliche Werke*. Ed. Friedrich Beissner. 7 vols. Stuttgart: Kohlhammer, 1943–77. [Grosse Stuttgarter Ausgabe]

Hugo, Victor. *Oeuvres complètes*. Chronological edition published under the direction of Jean Massin. 18 vols. Paris: Le Club Français du Livre, 1967–70.

Hume, David. *Enquiries Concerning Human Understanding and Concerning the Principles of Morals*. Ed. L. A. Selby-Bigge. 3d ed., rev. P. H. Nidditch. Oxford: Clarendon Press, 1975.

Jacobi, F. H. *Friedrich Heinrich Jacobi's Werke*. 6 vols. Leipzig: Gerhard Fleischer, 1812–25.

James, Henry. *Hawthorne*. London: Macmillan, 1879.

——. *The Novels and Tales of Henry James*. 26 vols. New York: Scribner's, 1907–1909. [The New York Edition]

——. *The Question of Our Speech / The Lesson of Balzac*. Boston: Houghton Mifflin, 1905.

Kant, Immanuel. *Kants gesammelte Schriften*. Ed. by the Preussischen Akademie der Wissenschaften. 27 vols. to date. Berlin: De Gruyter, 1902–.

Keats, John. *The Letters of John Keats, 1814–1821*. Ed. Hyder Rollins. 2 vols. Cambridge: Harvard Univ. Press, 1958.

——. *The Poems of John Keats*. Ed. Jack Stillinger. Cambridge: Harvard Univ. Press, 1978.

Kierkegaard, Søren. *The Concept of Irony*. Trans. Lee M. Capel. Reprint. Bloomington: Indiana Univ. Press, 1968.

Lamb, Charles. *The Works of Charles and Mary Lamb*. Ed. E. V. Lucas. 7 vols. London: Methuen, 1903–1905.

La Mettrie, Julien Offray de. *La Mettrie's L'Homme machine*. Ed. Aram Vartanian. Princeton, N.J.: Princeton Univ. Press, 1960.

Laplace, Pierre Simon de. *Oeuvres complètes de Laplace*. Published under the auspices of the Académie des Sciences. 14 vols. Paris: Gauthier-Villars, 1878–1912.

Leibniz, G. W. *Monadology and Other Philosophical Essays*. Trans. Paul Schrecker and Anne Martin Schrecker. Indianapolis: Bobbs-Merrill, 1965.

——. *Sämtliche Schriften und Briefe*. Ed. by the Deutschen Akademie der Wissenschaften. 19 vols. to date. Darmstadt and Leipzig: Akademie-Verlag, 1923–.

Malthus, Thomas. *An Essay on the Principle of Population*. Ed. Philip Appleman. New York: Norton, 1976. [Norton Critical Edition]

Melville, Herman. *Billy Budd, Sailor*. Ed. Harrison Hayford and Merton M. Sealts, Jr. Chicago: Univ. of Chicago Press, 1962.

——. *Herman Melville: Representative Selections*. Ed. Willard Thorp. New York: American Book, 1938.

——. *Journal of a Visit to London and the Continent, 1849–1850*. Ed. Eleanor Melville Metcalf. Cambridge: Harvard Univ. Press, 1948.

——. *The Letters of Herman Melville*. Ed. Merrell R. Davis and William H. Gilman. New Haven: Yale Univ. Press, 1960.

——. *Moby-Dick*. Ed. Harrison Hayford and Hershel Parker. New York: Norton, 1967. [Norton Critical Edition]

———. *The Writings of Herman Melville*. Ed. Harrison Hayford, Hershel Parker, and G. Thomas Tanselle. 8 vols. to date. Evanston and Chicago: Northwestern Univ. Press and the Newberry Library, 1968–.

Müller, Adam. *Vorlesungen über die deutsche Wissenschaft und Literatur*. Ed. Arthur Salz. Munich: Drei Masken, 1920.

Nerval, Gérard de. *Oeuvres*. Ed. Albert Béguin and Jean Richer. 2 vols. 5th ed. Paris: Gallimard, 1974. [Bibliothèque de la Pléiade]

Norton, Andrews. *A Discourse on the Latest Form of Infidelity*. Cambridge, Mass.: John Owen, 1839.

Novalis. *Schriften*. Ed. Paul Kluckhohn and Richard Samuel. 4 vols. to date. Stuttgart: Kohlhammer, 1960–.

Parker, Theodore. *Autobiography, Poems and Prayers*. Ed. Rufus Leighton. Boston: American Unitarian Association, n.d. [Centenary Edition]

———. *A Discourse of Matters Pertaining to Religion*. Ed. Thomas Wentworth Higginson. Boston: American Unitarian Association, 1907. [Centenary Edition]

———. *Sermons of Religion*. Ed. Samuel A. Eliot. Boston: American Unitarian Association, 1908. [Centenary Edition]

———. *The Transient and Permanent in Christianity*. Ed. George Willis Cooke. Boston: American Unitarian Association, 1908. [Centenary Edition]

Poe, Edgar Allan. *Collected Works of Edgar Allan Poe*. Ed. Thomas Ollive Mabbott. 3 vols. to date. Cambridge: Harvard Univ. Press, 1969–.

———. *Collected Writings of Edgar Allan Poe*. Ed. Burton R. Pollin. 2 vols. to date. Boston: Twayne, and New York: Gordian Press, 1981–.

———. *The Complete Works of Edgar Allan Poe*. Ed. James A. Harrison. 17 vols. New York: Crowell, 1902. Reprint. New York: AMS Press, 1965. [The Virginia Edition]

———. *The Letters of Edgar Allan Poe*. Ed. John Ward Ostrom. 2 vols. Rev. ed. New York: Gordian Press, 1966.

———. *Poetry and Tales*. Ed. Patrick F. Quinn. New York: Literary Classics of the United States, 1984. [Library of America]

Reed, Sampson. *Observations on the Growth of the Mind with Remarks on Some Other Subjects* (1838). Reprint. Gainesville, Fla.: Scholars' Facsimiles & Reprints, 1970. Introduction by Carl F. Strauch.

Schelling, F. W. J. *Schellings Werke*. After the original edition in new arrangement, ed. Manfred Schröter. 13 vols. Munich: Beck and Oldenbourg, 1927–59.

Schiller, J. C. F. *On the Aesthetic Education of Man*. Ed. Elizabeth M. Wilkinson and L. A. Willoughby. Oxford: Clarendon Press, 1967.

———. *Schillers Werke*. Ed. Julius Petersen et al. 33 vols. to date. Weimar: Böhlau, 1943–. [Nationalausgabe]

Schlegel, August Wilhelm. *Kritische Schriften und Briefe*. Ed. Edgar Lohner. 7 vols. Stuttgart: Kohlhammer, 1962–74.

Schlegel, Friedrich. *Kritische Friedrich-Schlegel-Ausgabe*. Ed. Ernst Behler et al. 22 vols. to date. Munich, Paderborn, and Vienna: Schöningh, 1958–.

Schleiermacher, F. D. E. *Der christliche Glaube nach den Grundsätzen der evangelischen Kirche im Zusammenhange dargestellt*. Ed. Martin Redeker. 2 vols. 7th ed. Berlin: De Gruyter, 1960.

———. *Monologen*. Ed. Friedrich Michael Schiele, expanded and rev. Hermann Mulert. 3d ed. Hamburg: Felix Meiner, 1978.

———. *Reden Ueber die Religion*. Ed. G. Ch. Bernhard Pünjer. Braunschweig: C. A. Schwetschke, 1879.

Scott, Sir Walter. *Waverley; or, 'Tis Sixty Years Since*. Ed. Claire Lamont. Oxford: Clarendon Press, 1981.

Shelley, Percy Bysshe. *The Complete Works of Percy Bysshe Shelley.* Ed. Roger Ingpen and Walter E. Peck. 10 vols. London: Ernest Benn, 1926–30. [Julian Edition]

——. *Poetical Works.* Ed. Thomas Hutchinson, corrected by G. M. Matthews. London: Oxford Univ. Press, 1970. [Oxford Standard Authors Edition]

——. *Shelley's Poetry and Prose.* Ed. Donald H. Reiman and Sharon B. Powers. New York: Norton, 1977. [Norton Critical Edition]

Spinoza, Benedictus de. *Opera.* On behalf of the Heidelberger Akademie der Wissenschaften. Ed. Carl Gebhardt. 4 vols. Heidelberg: Carl Winter, 1925.

Staël, Germaine de. *Oeuvres complètes de Mme la Baronne de Staël, publiées par son fils.* 17 vols. Paris: Treuttel and Würtz, 1820–21.

Stendhal. *Oeuvres complètes.* Ed. Victor del Litto and Ernest Abravanel. 50 vols. Paris: Cercle du Bibliophile, 1967–74.

——. *Romans et nouvelles.* Ed. Henri Martineau. 2 vols. Paris: Gallimard, 1932–33. [Bibliothèque de la Pléiade]

Tennyson, Alfred. *The Poems of Tennyson.* Ed. Christopher Ricks. London: Longman, 1969.

Wordsworth, William. *The Poetical Works of William Wordsworth.* Ed. E. de Selincourt and Helen Darbishire. 5 vols. Oxford: Clarendon Press, 1940–49.

——. *The Prelude: 1799, 1805, 1850.* Ed. Jonathan Wordsworth, M. H. Abrams, and Stephen Gill. New York: Norton, 1979. [Norton Critical Edition]

# Index

Library of Congress Cataloging-in-Publication Data

Chai, Leon
    The romantic foundations of the American Renaissance.
    Bibliography: p.
    Includes index.
    1. American literature—19th century—History and criticism—United States. I. Title.
PS217.R6C43    1987        87–5428
ISBN 0-8014-1929-8 (alk. paper)